Hudson

Frommer's®

New York City

Here's what the critics say about Frommer's:

"Amazingly easy to use. Very portable, very complete."
—*Booklist*

♦

"The only mainstream guide to list specific prices. The Walter Cronkite of guidebooks—with all that implies."
—*Travel & Leisure*

♦

"Complete, concise, and filled with useful information."
—*ws*

"Hotel information is"
—*...ay Register*

"The best series for travelers who want one easy-to-use guidebook."
—*U. S. Air Magazine*

800 - 833 - 3121
Broadway Show Tickets
www. radler. com

Other Great Guides for Your Trip:

Frommer's Portable New York City

Frommer's New York from $75 a Day

Frommer's New York City with Kids

Frommer's Irreverent Guide to Manhattan

The Complete Idiot's Travel Guide to New York City

The Unofficial Guide to New York City

Frommer's Memorable Walks in New York

Frommer's Wonderful Weekends from New York City

Frommer's® 99

New York City

by David Doty

with Cynthia Baker
Dining Update & Research by Scott DeSimon
Shopping Coverage by David Andrusia

MACMILLAN • USA

MACMILLAN TRAVEL

A Simon & Schuster Macmillan Company
1633 Broadway
New York, NY 10019

Find us online at www.frommers.com

Copyright © 1999 by Simon & Schuster, Inc.
Maps copyright © by Simon & Schuster, Inc.

All rights reserved. No part of this book may be reproduced or transmitted in any form or by any means, electronic or mechanical, including photocopying, recording, or by any information storage and retrieval system, without permission in writing from the Publisher.

MACMILLAN is a registered trademark of Macmillan, Inc.
FROMMER'S is a registered trademark of Arthur Frommer. Used under license.

ISBN 0-02-862313-4
ISSN 1090-7335

Editor: Ron Boudreau
Production Editor: Kristi Hart
Page Creation: Terri Sheehan
Photo Editor: Richard Fox
Design by Michele Laseau
Digital Cartography by John Decamillas and Ortelius Design

Front cover photo: The Lower Manhattan skyline as seen from under the Brooklyn Bridge
Back cover photo: Empire Diner in Chelsea

SPECIAL SALES

Bulk purchases (10+ copies) of Frommer's and selected Macmillan travel guides are available to corporations, organizations, mail-order catalogs, institutions, and charities at special discounts, and can be customized to suit individual needs. For more information write to Special Sales, Macmillan General Reference, 1633 Broadway, New York, NY 10019.

Manufactured in the United States of America

Contents

List of Maps

ABOUT THE AUTHORS

David Doty is president of Flatiron Communications, his own New York publishing company, named for one of his favorite city skyscrapers. A writer and editor for many years, he reports on travel, entertainment, dining, and other subjects for numerous national publications. He recently edited the *Zagat Guide to U.S. Hotels, Resorts & Spas* and has written the "Moneyed Interest" column for *Departures* magazine. David consults with Hearst Magazines Enterprises on magazine development, edits and produces the quarterly *France Insider's News,* and is on the faculty of the New School for Social Research, where he teaches a course on the history of Paris. His online work includes having created, with Cynthia Baker, the content for the Web site of Bordeaux wines (www.bordeaux.com). He would like to thank Feliciano Tapia for his culinary insights and selfless support. David can be reached via e-mail at ddflatiron@aol.com.

Cynthia Baker is a freelance writer and amateur bicycle racer who last year logged some 6,000 miles on her two-wheeled traveling companion, visiting nearly every corner of New York City for this book. She is an associate editor at *Mr. Food's EasyCooking* magazine and has reported on travel for *France Insider's News* and written for the *Zagat Guide to U.S. Hotels, Resorts & Spas.* Every year that her legs can carry her, she participates in the Empire State Building Run-Up, climbing on foot the 1,026 stairs to the 86th floor.

Scott DeSimon, who began his contributions to this book in its last edition, is particularly responsible for the updated coverage of the city's restaurants. Scott is an assistant editor at *ESPN: The Magazine,* but his real love is writing about, talking about, and obsessing about food and the current dining scene. Born and bred in Maine, he now lives in Brooklyn, where he cooks for and entertains friends in his unusually large city kitchen.

David Andrusia has written for *Interview, Details,* and *In Fashion* and was an editor at *Men's Guide to Fashion.* He's the author of six travel guides, including *New York Hot & Hip,* and two celebrated career books, *The Perfect Pitch* and *Branding Yourself.*

ACKNOWLEDGMENTS

The authors would like to thank New York City for being an inspiring and rewarding subject. We would also like to acknowledge the important contributions made by many individuals over the years, especially **Steve Reidman** (hotels), **Dick Kagan** (art galleries), and **Don Cushing** (theater).

The authors also realize their debt to **Ron Boudreau,** the book's editor, whose persistence, high standards, and unique insights are to a large degree responsible for whatever qualities this book may possess.

AN INVITATION TO THE READER

In researching this book, we discovered many wonderful places—hotels, restaurants, shops, and more. We're sure you'll find others. Please tell us about them so that we can share the information with your fellow travelers in upcoming editions. If you were disappointed with a recommendation, we'd love to know that, too. Please write to:

Frommer's New York City
Macmillan Travel
1633 Broadway
New York, NY 10019

AN ADDITIONAL NOTE

Please be advised that travel information is subject to change at any time—and this is especially true of prices. We therefore suggest that you write or call ahead for confirmation when making your travel plans. The authors, editors, and publisher cannot be held responsible for the experiences of readers while traveling. Your safety is important to us, however, so we encourage you to stay alert and be aware of your surroundings. Keep a close eye on cameras, purses, and wallets, all favorite targets of thieves and pickpockets.

WHAT THE SYMBOLS MEAN

✪ **Frommer's Favorites**

Our favorite places and experiences—outstanding for quality, value, or both.

The following abbreviations are used for credit cards:

AE	American Express	EURO	Eurocard
CB	Carte Blanche	JCB	Japan Credit Bank
DC	Diners Club	MC	MasterCard
DISC	Discover	V	Visa
ER	EnRoute		

FIND FROMMER'S ONLINE

Arthur Frommer's Outspoken Encyclopedia of Travel (www.frommers.com) offers more than 6,000 pages of up-to-the-minute travel information—including the latest bargains and candid, personal articles updated daily by Arthur Frommer himself. No other Web site offers such comprehensive and timely coverage of the world of travel.

New York Confidential

Demanding and rewarding, seductive and stern, New York has refired the imagination of travelers from around the world with all kinds of good news. The city is laying claim to one of its great periods as it prepares for the next millennium, and visitors, pumped with curiosity, are arriving by the millions, swarming the city's streets, sights, hotels, museums, restaurants, nightclubs, and theaters.

Now you may be daunted by the facade the city presents, at once alluring, tough, forbidding, and majestic. So you might just choose to skim its surface—that would be fun enough. But there's a deeper satisfaction you can mine here, beyond all the stony faces—on both the people and the buildings.

This book will help you do that. *Frommer's New York City '99* is a tool you can use to reveal Gotham's most coveted secrets: to get past the glass, steel, and concrete skin and try to touch the city's soul. This guide has been completely rewritten to give you an up-to-date insider's perspective on the world's most agile city.

Despite its undeniable glamour, the city can seem as hardened as a New Yorker. Either you'll be enthralled by the tempo and dazzle, or you'll be stunned by the noise, the intimate mingling of inhuman poverty and unimaginable wealth, the smog, and the callousness of the natives. Take heart: We New Yorkers have the old love-hate relationship with our town. We talk endlessly about escaping for the weekend, commiserate about subways that arrive late, bemoan the recent spate of cab drivers who don't know Lincoln Center from Grant's Tomb, and on and on. Yet still we stay.

There's a kind of mystical magnetism to the place that pulls in the intelligent, the creative, the determined, the overbearing, and the overblown from all over the world. Just about any language and any dialect is spoken here, from Mandarin to Brooklynese. And this is the nerve center of the world's finance and trade; the international hub of advertising, publishing, and fashion; and the creative core for theater, ballet, and music. The force that attracts so many different talents and so many varying idiosyncrasies spins in an orbit whose southern limit is the confluence of two great rivers, a spectacular bay, and the westernmost shore of the Atlantic Ocean.

The city is at once radiant and remote, nonchalant and frenetic, entertaining and exasperating. And those characteristics are exactly what make it both impossible and irresistible.

Impressions

New York's like a disco, but without the music.

—Elaine Stritch

It's a city where everyone mutinies but no one deserts.

—Harry Hershfield

1 Frommer's Favorite New York City Experiences

- **Watching the Curtain Rise at the Theater.** Whether it's Broadway, Off Broadway, or Off Off Broadway, live theater is the greatest gift the city gives its visitors. Chapter 9 tells you all you need to know about the vast theater scene.
- **Riding the Staten Island Ferry.** I sometimes wonder if the word *breathtaking* could have existed before the ferry first sailed from Manhattan into New York Harbor, out away from the city's glimmering high-rises, past the lit torch of the Statue of Liberty, and then through the silent, churning water all the way to Staten Island, a spit of land that holds back the ocean from Manhattan Island. For all the details, see chapter 7.
- **Glimpsing the City from Battery Park City.** At the tip of the island, walk along the grandest esplanade in New York. You'll find yourself in a calming sea of green with the jagged collection of downtown high-rises as backdrop. Behind you, the vigorous Hudson River whirls into the tidal harbor waters. See chapter 7 for more.
- **Improving Your Vision by Visiting the Museums and Galleries.** The Metropolitan Museum, MoMA, the American Museum of Natural History, the Guggenheim, and the galleries along 57th Street, in far West Chelsea, and throughout nearly all of SoHo can shake you out of the ordinary and show you a new way of perceiving the world. For the best New York has to offer, see chapter 7.
- **Wandering in Central Park.** On foot, on horseback, on skates, on a boat, on a bike. Do it the way you want—but do it. This Midtown patch of green will astound and embrace you. There are places you'll remember all your life, and Strawberry Fields, the memorial to John Lennon, with its Italian-tiled *Imagine,* is one of them. Bethesda Fountain, at the 72nd Street Transverse, is the spot for watching the passing parade. Chapter 7 has the full details.
- **Spotting Celebs.** It's best, I've learned, to keep a list. What were they wearing? How awful—or spectacular—did they look? Tall—or short? The town is crawling with the legends and the short stories of Hollywood and Broadway, the bubbly stars of the soaps, the rocks of the music world. Turn to chapter 6 to see where they dine and chapter 9 to discover where they hang out at night.
- **Strolling the Neighborhoods.** Get off the bus! The city's neighborhoods are similar at a quick glance, but they differ in character as much as a series of small towns. Wend through the historic streets of Lower Manhattan or Greenwich Village. Saunter the cast-iron canyons of SoHo. Or explore the lovely Flatiron District, Times Square, and Midtown. For more on New York's neighborhoods, see chapters 4 and 7.
- **Getting High.** Go to the top. Straight to the top. Head up the World Trade Center and the Empire State Building or to Windows on the World or the Rainbow Room for dinner. New York is made to be seen from above—in the full light of day and in the full glitter of night. See chapters 6, 7, and 9 for specifics.

- **Getting Fed.** In 20 years' time, New York has surpassed Paris as the world capital of great eating. There's cheap but sometimes dazzling ethnic food in neighborhoods like Chinatown, gourmet sandwich shops for those on the run and on a budget, kosher, Italian, fusion Japanese at Nobu, unsurpassed new French haute cuisine at Daniel, and fine fare 24 hours a day. Get the lowdown in chapter 6.

- **Stealing Quiet Moments on the Terrace at the Cloisters.** Far from the city's noise, this medieval wonder at the northern tip of Manhattan commands a spectacular perch from which you can admire the George Washington Bridge and the Palisades that streak the Hudson's banks. See chapter 7.

- **Hearing Shakespeare in the Park.** Under the stars, with trees rustling and the air fragrant with the perfumes of nature, the bard is given his due. In a setting as theatrical as anything on stage, Shakespeare in the Park allows your imagination to take hold. Certain truths surpass time, and Will knew them well. For details, see the box in chapter 9.

- **Stepping Out After Dark.** New York is the place to slip into a dry martini as you listen to chic cabaret stars like Bobby Short. Opera, dance, symphonies, and sins—you won't find them better anywhere than in New York. The club world is a hip, mysterious planet all its own. See chapter 9 for a roster of all your options.

- **Shopping for All Things All over Town.** You want it? New York's got it—from Bloomingdale's and Saks to couture on Madison Avenue, from Disney souvenirs to fine art and the best clothing and housewares discounters. And don't overlook the unusual pleasures of the East Village's boutiques or the trendy, though increasingly mall-like, emporia of SoHo. See chapter 8 for the latest.

- **Spending Holidays in the City.** As millions of my neighbors head out to the shores and the mountains, I love to stay in town over July 4. A peaceful hush comes over the city—until the fireworks spark. On Halloween, more than the usual ghouls walk among us in Greenwich Village. At Christmas, tiny elves set about their work in window displays on Fifth Avenue. On Thanksgiving, Betty Boop and friends walk the streets. And on Chinese New Year, a bright dragon promises great fortune ahead. See the Calendar of Events in chapter 2.

- **Having a Gay Old Time at Wigstock and the Pride Parade.** Outrageous and touching, these two celebrations of sexuality and gender bending—and reminders of the needs of people living with HIV—manifest that, for all the extreme costumes and towering heels, there is something extravagantly normal in it all. For full details, see the Calendar of Events in chapter 2.

2 Seeing Beyond the Icons & the Neon

It's easy to get visual overload from New York's immense physical impact. Equipped with this guide, you can explore all that's hidden beneath the city's surface—and reap a lifetime of dividends.

I'll never forget the first time I flew over Manhattan. The plane I was in glided up the Hudson and crossed over at Central Park. I had never seen New York from that perspective. It was more beautiful, more moving than a recent flight I'd made across the Rocky Mountains. Here, audacious and manmade, the peaks and valleys are sided by high stone cliffs, topped with spires and Chippendale pediments. There are mesas of concrete, dotted with blue swimming pools or shining with sculpted silver gargoyles. Slicing the air nearly to the clouds are rooftops green with copper, capped by radio towers, or weirdly crowned with pointed wooden water sheds. It's a forest of finials, pinnacles, pyramids, ziggurats, setbacks, domes, and thick green roof gardens. Nice show.

LOOK UP & LOOK OUT!

The best way to refresh your ability to perceive New York's almost too-familiar icons and get to the city's elusive heart is to look up while you walk. Now don't stop in the middle of the sidewalk and mindlessly glance around—always keep your wits about you, for both safety and style. And don't stare at just the most obvious high-rises, powerful though they are. As you walk, glance above the streetscape, even at what may seem unassuming buildings. Ground floors are misleading. Wonderful old buildings are often defaced with garish aluminum coverings and signs.

If you find yourself serendipitously wandering down Fifth Avenue, take a moment to stop at 43rd Street. At 510 Fifth, on the southwest corner of 43rd, is the **Chase Manhattan Bank,** a transparent modern sheet of glass that seems as miraculously light as a cloud. Best observed from the northeast corner, it was built in 1954 by the once seminal firm of Skidmore, Owings & Merrill. Here they created open upper floors, especially the second, that float in midair—the ceilings are ethereal vapors of white and the columns nothing more than buoyant wisps of cotton. And it's funny, too. Note the ground-floor safe facing Fifth Avenue, behind just a pane of glass. It seems to say, "Robbery? What robbery?" Nonetheless, though most of the impact of the upper floors remains intact, here too insensitive renovations of the ground floor have compromised the building's visual integrity.

Before continuing south along Fifth to the Empire State Building, you might wander on 44th Street toward Sixth Avenue. It's a high-class world: The **Harvard Club** is at 27 W. 44th St., and the wonderful **New York Yacht Club** at 37 W. 44th. Its breathtaking windows have incorporated the sterns of old ships, and below the bowed glass, waves of water drip down like liquefied stone.

Back on Fifth, at 42nd Street, the stately front of the beaux arts **New York Public Library** guards a wise oracle of innumerable pages. As you continue on this stretch of early–20th century New York, don't look only in the T-shirt shops. Look at what those stores and others like them have done to the buildings they're in. At the southwest corner of Fifth Avenue and 37th Street, let your eyes rise above the modernized ground floor of **404 Fifth** and note the graceful proportions of an unpretentious masterpiece, its monumental windows, and the intricate lacing of its terra-cotta. You won't read about it in other guides, but its whimsy and style deserve your attention.

That delicious confection sits near two buildings, just as easily overlooked, that were created by New York's greatest turn-of-the-century architects, McKim, Mead & White. At **409 Fifth** (southeast corner of 37th Street) and **390 Fifth** (southwest corner of 36th Street) are two grand piles, both finished in 1906, both in the palazzo style so popular in that period. The ground floors have been "improved." Yet stoically above them rest the handsome remains of, respectively, Tiffany's and Gorham's jewelry stores. At no. 409, the Corinthian columns impart a strong impression of great height; at no. 390, note the exquisite columns and cornice on the 36th Street side.

There is, of course, more to discovering New York's secrets than just observing its architecture while you walk. New York provides the opportunities and disadvantages of constant encounters with other pedestrians that you find in few other American cities. There is a bad side: The city's reputation for muggings comes from this intersection of strangers. But there's a good side too: It forces us to interact with one another, to confront who our seemingly exotic neighbors might be—and thereby who we might be. Transcending the facades of buildings and the faces of strangers ushers us straight to the heart of the city.

NATURE IN THE CONCRETE JUNGLE

Take your time to look for unexpected moments. Nature, for instance, has a deeper hold on the city than most people think. It pops up everywhere, no matter how much concrete we pour over it.

There are **peregrine falcons** living on the roofs of Fifth Avenue apartment buildings, the Met Life Building, the Bank of New York Building on Wall Street, bridges, and other aeries. Around the grounds of the New York Public Library at 42nd and Fifth, you can sometimes see them swoop down to get their lunch to go. In fact, 70% of New York State's breeding peregrine falcons live in the city. Other creatures—besides rats and roaches—drop by New York. In the last few years, **coyotes** have been wandering in Van Cortlandt Park in the Bronx, and **avian species** of all kinds fly into Central Park's Ramble in fall and spring.

When you wander along the rivers, keep your eyes open for fins cutting the water: **Dolphins**—and some even say sharks—frolic up the East and Hudson rivers.

One of my favorite natural lovelies is the **pear tree,** bearing plump fruit in late summer and early autumn, at the northeast corner of 11th Street and Fifth Avenue. Other **trees** around town also confirm nature's resilience: One grows seemingly right out of a wall, no soil, on Mulligan Place, a charming courtyard of antique houses on Sixth Avenue between 10th and 11th streets. Another insists on its right to life at the northwest corner of Madison Avenue and 84th Street, in front of a row of lovely houses; it grows from the basement-level sidewalk, again no visible soil, and up through and around a grate, having nonchalantly incorporated the metal into its trunk.

No matter what you've heard though, even alligators, those scaly prehistoric survivors, cannot subsist in the rigors of the city's sewers.

ON THE WATERFRONT

Do more than visit the East River's **South Street Seaport,** which I find too commercial. It didn't have to be that way. One of New York's most wonderful places to visit is also a waterfront development, but across town on the Hudson River, relatively new, and more like real New York. The **World Financial Center** and **Battery Park City** offer an intersection of commerce, shopping, history, and natural beauty that South Street Seaport only dimly imitates. The buildings and parkland here, and the unsurpassed walkways along the Hudson, are visually blocked from the "main city" by high-'rises, and they don't invite you in with the same carnival atmosphere as the Seaport.

But cross over West Street and into the **Winter Garden** (full of a grove of native American palm trees, slender and ever-so nonchalant, as if they were in the most natural setting in the world). Then head out to the **North Cove**—a real harbor right here in New York—where massive yachts moor next to tiny sailboats. Follow the southern end of the pier and walk to the river. There, just as the western end of the cove forms a barrier to the Hudson River, turn back toward the city. The tips of some of the world's earliest skyscrapers break the sky. Farther south, the Twin Towers stand straight and higher than you can imagine. Inside their barrel-vaulted glass house, the palm trees reach to the ceiling of the Winter Garden. Back along the river, in the distance, the Statue of Liberty still lights our imagination and Ellis Island still welcomes strangers. You take in more than 100 years of history in a single glance. There are people shopping, living, working, trading stocks, plying the river in sailboats and barges, and generally going about their daily lives in the spectacular waterfront city that is New York. It's a magical place to stand, and from it you'll get another glimpse into the soul of this place.

Impressions

I like to walk the streets, lost, but I recognize that New York is the world's greatest lie. New York is Senegal with machines.

—Federico García Lorca

3 New York Today

New York City just won't sit still long enough for anyone to capture its definitive portrait. It insists on displaying many contrary moods at once. Its past, present, and future tug at each other right before your eyes. The cacophony of this constant flux drowns out anyone who would claim to be able to fix the limits of New York today.

As you're coming around a corner in Chelsea, the past zooms forward on an antique sign announcing TO LET: CARRIAGES, COUPES, HANSOMS—HORSES TAKEN IN BOARD (check out 109 W. 17th St., west of Sixth Avenue, second floor). Simultaneously, a fellow traveler in Midtown passes the construction zone along the resurgent Times Square and glimpses the near future. As one group moves forward on the long-anticipated redevelopment of Manhattan's riverfronts, a clashing faction (there's always an opposition in New York) marshals its clout to quash parts of the project.

Through the dissonance a certain tenor does emerge. There have been big improvements in three areas: economics, safety, and entertainment blockbusters that'll have you wondering if you haven't landed in the movie version of Gotham.

A few years back, the city reduced its hotel taxes from an outrageous 19.25% plus $2 (for good, greedy measure) per night to a more palatable 13.25%, but still plus that annoying $2. The result has been historic hotel occupancy rates, which have led in unavoidably capitalistic turn to a rise in the average room rate to $189, the highest in the country. (You'll be happy to learn that this book's accommodations chapter details the best choices above, below, and at that average.)

The cost of dining in the city's 17,000 restaurants, which had actually dropped in the mid-1990s, has held relatively stable in the last year, just about matching what it was in the early 1980s. That's not a bargain by the standards of early-bird specialists, but it's an average that includes very expensive caviar–and–foie gras places.

And foreign visitors find that hotels and restaurants, as well as shopping and entertainment, are often dramatically cheaper here than at home.

CRIME'S DOWN, BROADWAY'S UP

Mayor Rudolph Giuliani delights in taking credit for this city's dramatic drop in crime—though lower crime rates have been a nationwide phenomenon. Homicides have come down to 1960s levels. As for the hole in the ground where people ride, overall crime has dropped more than 50% since 1990. Of course, New York hasn't suddenly become the merry old land of Oz, but you're certainly safer here than TV shows, movies, and Washington-based bashers would have you believe—in fact, you're safer here than a mile from the Capitol.

One neighborhood that has benefited from this more civilized tone is Greenwich Village, which until a few years ago the local police precinct had abandoned to beer-toting, boom box–blasting thugs. Now its charm has reemerged, so evening strolls through this particularly historic district should be on every visitor's agenda.

And there are lots of visitors. Last year, a record 32.5 million people traveled to New York City, with about 6 million from foreign countries. Foreign and domestic visitors spend well over $18 billion per year. You'll want to reserve a hotel room as far in advance as possible, for occupancy rates have gone above 80%, hitting record levels.

One of the biggest assets of New York is its restaurant scene, which remains the world's hottest and hippest, with great chefs reigning at places like Le Cirque 2000, Daniel, Nobu, Jean Georges, and other haute-cuisine contenders. At press time, the leading edge of the have-to-be-in-the-place-of-the-moment crowd was pulling every string to get a table at Moomba, one of Leonardo DiCaprio's regular hangouts. The ever-expanding spate of theme restaurants (which tend to offer more memorable memorabilia than meals) continues to amuse patrons with frights (Jekyll & Hyde Club), bikes (Harley-Davidson Cafe), strikes and balls (Official All Star Cafe), and striking looks (Fashion Cafe, where the "owners" are supermodels Claudia Schiffer, Elle Macpherson, and Naomi Campbell). They've joined the behemoths of the genre, Planet Hollywood and the Hard Rock Cafe. Also growing in popularity is let's-pretend-we're-in-Paris outdoor dining at such places as Bryant Park Grill, Luna Park, and Verbena.

Broadway theater keeps getting a good report on its financial health, and nearly all of Times Square, West 42nd Street in particular, is being transformed from Sin Central to Family Funland, a phenomenon spurred by the Walt Disney Company's $34-million (supported by lots of tax breaks) renovation of the New Amsterdam Theater into a state-of-the-art center for family entertainment. For a complete report, see "Neighborhoods of Note" in chapter 7, and the theater section of chapter 9.

EXPRESS LANES & POTHOLES ON THE ROAD TO THE MILLENNIUM

As the new Times Square barrels ahead, New York is moving forward on other fronts. Downtown buzzes with conversions of office buildings into living lofts. The Museum of Jewish Heritage is now open at the southern end of Battery Park City, not far from the new National Museum of the American Indian, which itself opened just a few years ago. But the firmly established uptown institutions aren't resting on their endowments: The American Museum of Natural History has added smashing exhibits on dinosaurs, biodiversity, and primitive vertebrates and will in the coming couple of years open a spanking new planetarium.

Galleries and auction houses from fashionable Madison Avenue to SoHo continue to boom along with record earnings. Newer galleries, once again fleeing the high rents they create by making their neighborhoods attractive, have turned far West Chelsea into a cutting-edge art frontier, joining the pioneers who had already been there for a few years.

West Chelsea is at the forefront of another movement as well: the redevelopment of the Hudson River waterfront. The waterfront—which could and should be as delightful as the quays along the Seine in Paris—has been a dumping ground for ill-kept highways, eyesore derelict buildings, and hideous civic constructions. The successful lesson of Battery Park City, where generally graceful buildings share space with acres of lush green park, has taught New Yorkers to appreciate their right to pleasant riverfront access.

Impressions

There are 2 million interesting people in New York and only 78 in Los Angeles.
                                                                    —Neil Simon

The same has been true of Chelsea Piers, where the *Titanic* was once due to arrive with great fanfare. At 23rd Street and the Hudson, the four renovated piers from the early 1900s (the original buildings were designed by Warren & Wetmore of Grand Central Terminal fame) are now home to a grand sports/health/fitness facility that's state-of-the-art. They draw bountiful, and often beautiful, crowds on weekends, all within view of the Hudson, under a great expanse of uninterrupted sky.

New York has long been known as a shopper's best friend, and worst nightmare (for shopping addicts, New York is just what the doctor didn't order). Its already top-flight stores have lately been joined by the invasion of the megaemporiums, like Kmart (there's even one in the East Village!), Filene's Basement, Bed Bath & Beyond, the Barnes & Noble Superstores, Toys 'R' Us, and Bradlee's. There will always be a Macy's, which itself is in the middle of a dynamic boom of price-light stores all along West 34th Street.

Along upper Madison Avenue you can test your credit limits on the booming strip of boutiques that now includes Moschino, Prada, Armani, Valentino, Yves Saint Laurent, and quasi fashion saint Ralph Lauren.

Fifth Avenue is in the best shape it has been in years. Most of the cheesy electronics-and-rugs stores (with misleading signs like SELLING OUT ENTIRE STOCK!!!—I mean, what else do merchants do with their stock?) have been replaced with shops more appropriate to the land of Tiffany and Cartier: Façonnable started the re-upscaling of Fifth, and now there's Liz Claiborne, Movado, A. Testoni, Versace, and the Museum Collection.

But never fear—the popular marketeers still hold a place for lower-ticket gewgaws on Fifth in the 50s. The seemingly unstoppable theme-parking juggernaut plows ahead: Disney has a store on Fifth (the House of Goofy is also now blindingly present on 42nd Street at Seventh Avenue). The Warner Bros. Studio Store still packs them in at 57th Street and Fifth Avenue (it has new digs on Times Square as well). Coca-Cola continues to sell logo sweatshirts between 56th and 55th streets, and NikeTown, next to Trump Tower, is a frenetic temple to modern consumerism with its floors of products, huge video screens, and surprisingly tasteful entryway. Banana Republic, the Gap, Emporio Armani, and the new NBA—The Store also crowd Fifth in the 50s.

Harlem hasn't been in such good shape since the Renaissance of the 1920s. Not only are large numbers of visitors heading uptown to see gospel services, but all kinds of New Yorkers themselves are finding it possible once again to feel safe enough to hang out in its jazz boîtes and nightclubs. Drew Nieporent, the developer of Downtown spots like Nobu and Tribeca Grill, is reopening the historic Minton's Playhouse, not far from the in-the-works Harlem U.S.A. entertainment complex. As the neighborhood attracts larger numbers of visitors, it's still important to know where you can go, and if you're not sure, to go with a group tour.

Celluloid heroes never die, and New York is no exception. After a few lean years, the city is enjoying renewed popularity among the film, commercial, and TV worlds. The number of movies made in 1997 hit a record 213, up substantially from 1995. The bigger rise came in TV production, with the number of shooting days up to 7,458, an increase of 16% from 1996. Over the last few years, many TV series set in Manhattan were actually shot in Manhattan, such as *Friends, Mad About You, Spin City*, and *Law & Order*. As for "tawk," as we say, not only Rosie, the reigning Queen of Nice, but also Letterman, Regis and Kathie Lee, Sally Jessy, Ricki, and a few of the daytime soaps chatter in their studios in the city. In addition, Bill Cosby's sitcom is filmed here. But, I regret to remember, Jerry Seinfeld never came home before he went into syndication land.

Wall Street's spectacular 1990s rise has had its cheery effect on the city's economy, but, as we most recently learned in the late 1980s, what goes up does come down—and sometimes go boom! There has also been a bull market in software and multimedia, especially in the lofts of the Flatiron District and Downtown—after all, that's where the "creatives" are and the new thrust in electronics is away from the technonerds and toward the "content providers."

As is true across the nation, New York City faces the battle of the reduced government budget. And there continues to be saber rattling out of Washington, with Congress threatening to eviscerate the National Endowment for the Arts and other such groups (mostly from prehistoric saber-toothed politicians who haven't understood that the arts are important to a great swath of the American public). Some would say that the Walt Disney 42nd Street deal is an example of corporate welfare, so why can't we also afford to encourage more experimental artists, help the homeless, educate inner-city youth, and keep the subways running on time? It's unclear how any national or local budget cuts would affect your experience of New York, but threats to the cultural subsidies could lead to a reduction in entertainment offerings, from opera to musical theater. Or, as budget hawks would have it, "only" a few arts administrators would lose their jobs and unprofitable venues go out of business. The logic is, if people aren't willing to pay for something by buying tickets, they shouldn't be taxed for it either. Say we apply the same standard to Congress itself . . . ?

Yet despite even more dire predictions in the past (remember "Ford to City: Drop Dead"?), New York has always managed to survive and, in the last few years, to blossom. Like every other community in America, this city is made up of people who are stumbling their way toward the 21st century—but here we trip along with a style all our own. The essential magic of New York and the dreams that drive artists and entrepreneurs to adopt this city—and millions of visitors to drop in—aren't about to fade away. The legends about New York City are potent because they're the truth about New York City.

4 Story Time: The History of the High-Rise

A confluence of factors led Manhattan to be the world capital of the high-rise—and its birthplace. Though Chicago insists that the first skyscraper was built along the lake, the truth is New York, again, comes out on top.

The title belongs to the appropriately named **Tower Building,** once at 50 Broadway, created by architect Bradford Lee Gilbert. What gave it this distinction? It was the first building with an iron skeleton, hidden behind exterior walls that were no more than a curtain of stone. That revolutionary iron-framework technique allowed the walls and floors to be supported individually at each story. The 11-story Tower Building went up in 1889, the same year the Eiffel Tower, another important engineering feat showing the promise of iron, gave Paris its jaunty pinnacle.

Before the Tower Building, New York architects dreamed about building higher. Yet a pair of factors kept them down.

Prior to the introduction of the elevator, few buildings surpassed six stories, the comfortable height for humans to climb. The elevator expanded the potential, as we've seen in our own time, to dizzying heights. The safety elevator, with a spring mechanism that could break the fall of a cab if its supporting ropes gave way, was invented in 1853 by Elisha Graves Otis. In 1857, the first passenger safety elevator—Otis's invention was already used for freight in factories—was installed in the cast-iron–fronted **Haughwout Store** (still at 488 Broadway, at Broome Street).

In 1870, the **Equitable Building** was the first office building to use elevators to lift its occupants up through its seven and a half stories. And some say this combination of factors—an office building served by an elevator—was the opening volley in the battle for tallest bragging rights. By 1875, many 10-story office buildings cast their long shadows on the Wall Street area (one you can still see, from 1882, is the twin-steepled **Temple Court,** at 119–129 Nassau St., at Beekman).

But, even though they could now use elevators to whisk people up through their buildings, architects of the 19th century were stuck at about 10 stories by another factor. The higher they built, the thicker the walls at the ground floors had to be to support themselves. In fact, according to an intriguing book on the subject, *Rise of the New York Skyscraper* (Yale University Press), by Sarah Bradford Landau and Carl W. Condit, a building 150 feet tall without an iron skeleton would have to have 3-foot-wide load-bearing walls at the bottom floor. This was impractical for many reasons, not least because it meant losing a large amount of rentable space on the commercial ground floor.

PROVING THEIR METAL

Then along came Bradford Lee Gilbert. He had been a consulting architect with the iron horse—the railroads—gaining experience in constructing iron bridges and train sheds. The lot on which he was commissioned to build was only 21½ feet wide, and the adjoining plots were unavailable. Given that an elevator had to be installed and that 6 feet had to be used for the side walls, the ground floor would be only about 8 feet wide. Gilbert claimed that the skeleton solution came to him like "a flash." He could support both the floors and the walls if he turned an iron bridge on one end.

Though Gilbert was the first to use a metal skeleton to hold up the Tower Building, there were precedents to the notion, however misty and vague. In the early and mid-19th century, in both Britain and France, well-known structures went up using a web of iron or steel arches to support glass ceilings, removing the weight from the walls and significantly reducing the number of columns needed to support the roof. The novel **Crystal Palace** in London employed this technique, permitting the ceiling to span a large open interior plane interrupted by few support columns. Many pavilions in **Les Halles,** the marketplace in Paris built by Victor Baltard, were constructed in a similar technique. Iron was also what Gustave Eiffel was all about. The engineer built not only the graceful, if impractical, iron tower that bears his name but also a great number of metal bridges, viaducts, and other structures throughout France. And even America. Eiffel designed the interior bracing that holds up the Statue of Liberty.

In 1853, for a world's fair, New York built its own glass-and-steel **Crystal Palace** in what is now Bryant Park, and it remained there until it burned down in 1858. Another import from London, cast iron, was commonly used in New York, especially in the factory lofts of SoHo (check out Greene Street), beginning in the early 19th century. In fact, by the 1820s many storefronts were adorned with cast-iron columns, made to look like more expensive hand-carved stone, but cast, less expensively, in a decorative mold. This allowed the introduction of large glass display windows, a notion imported from France. (Some say the technique of cast iron was developed not in England but in 17th-century France. The eastern colonnade of the Louvre, commissioned by Louis XIV, supposedly uses iron inside the columns. The architect was Claude Perrault, brother of Charles, who wrote *The Mother Goose Rhymes.*)

Cast iron was, in some respects, no more than a mere fanciful "curtain" covering plain stone walls. And by 1822 it was used structurally in columns to support balconies. There are claims that a building in New York predating the Tower Building used iron at every floor, but not, it would seem, to support the exterior walls.

New York is a catastrophe . . . a beautiful catastrophe.

—Le Corbusier, architect

Even given all these possible, and sometimes distant, inspirations, Gilbert alone created the first nearly full skeleton (iron ran only up to the seventh floor, whereafter he relied on traditional building methods). And he had to fight City Hall to get his plans approved. He was given the go-ahead, but people still stood outside the 11-story wonder in windstorms to see when it would collapse. In 1914 it did collapse, but only because its owner couldn't pay his taxes and sold the building, and down it came.

By then, however, the small building had made its big mark. For a variety of reasons, Manhattan saw other metal-framed skyscrapers rapidly go up. Because it is an island, Manhattan has limited ground space, and, contemporaneous with Gilbert's discovery and the development of the safety elevator, the demand for office space, high above the pollution of the street, exploded. The nature of Lower Manhattan also played a role: Right below the surface it has hard schist that supports the weight of tall structures. In a city where money is holy, it wasn't too difficult to break with the Western tradition of never daring to raise oneself higher than a church's steeple. Ego also came into play, as it always does in New York: "I want it bigger, damnit! I don't care how much it costs!"

The **American Surety Building** rose in 1896 to a height of 21 stories, looking like a gigantic column. In the late 19th and early 20th centuries, there was no preexisting design vocabulary for skyscrapers, so most of them took on a neoclassical aspect. The true early New York skyscraper is often recognizable by its tripartite design, borrowed directly from Greek columns: The bottom floors are the highly ornamented base, then comes a long less-decorated shaft, followed by the top floors' capital, a crowning achievement that can include everything from terra-cotta to sculpted stone and often terminating in an intricate, lovely cornice.

Louis Sullivan, best known for his work in Chicago, disapproved of this backward-looking aesthetic. He felt that a new idiom was necessary and expressed his talents and opinions in New York. Few people stop to note the **Bayard Building** at 65 Bleecker St., at the end of Cosby Street. But it's a Sullivan, and a graceful one, too. Follow the long piers that run up the building's sides, revealing and tracing its structure, to the angelic ornamentation coursing along the top floors.

New York didn't take much inspiration from this restrained Sullivan building, preferring the work of another architect of the time, Cass Gilbert, famous for his many superbly elaborate structures. He's best known for his 1913 Gothic "Cathedral of Commerce," the engagingly witty **Woolworth Building** at 233 Broadway; at 30 stories it remained the world's tallest until first the Chrysler Building and then, quickly rising higher, the Empire State Building split the sky.

The early action wasn't all downtown, however. The **Flatiron Building,** one of the most whimsical of its time, holds pride of place on a three-sided plot where Broadway, Fifth Avenue, and 23rd Street meet. Its softly curving lines, resembling basket weave, its triangular shape (which gave it its name—it looked like a giant flatiron), and its prowlike front defiantly plowing traffic off to either side, all combine to make a peculiar but endearing, proud building. Designed by D. H. Burnham & Company, it was finished, with a full metal skeleton, in 1903. At 21 stories, it held its regal head above all the buildings north of the Financial District for many years. Though relatively short today (and boasting its original steam-driven elevator), it still stands erect and lordly, if a touch eccentric.

As the skyscraper moved Uptown, the denizens of Downtown were beginning to miss little things like light, sky, and air. Architect Ernest Flagg created the now-demolished needlelike **Singer Building** in 1908 to prove his point with a point: He felt that skyscrapers could let the sunshine in if they limited their towers on the upper floors to only 25% of the site's area. But not everyone was paying attention. Even the great architectural firm of McKim, Mead & White continued to erect massive structures like the 1914 **Municipal Building,** at the end of Chambers Street where Park Row and Centre Street merge, which is as oppressive as it is impressive.

THE DOOR OPENS FOR DECO & THE CURTAIN RISES ON THE HIGH-RISE

The days of unregulated skyscrapers came crashing down in 1916 when the city passed a new zoning law restricting both the height and the bulk of buildings. This was good news not only for those who longed for their day in the sun but also because it led to the step-back design of the art deco period, perhaps the look most associated with Gotham. As the city's commercial center moved to what is now Midtown (where there's also schist beneath the surface), so did the tower, first in the area around the ever-shorter Grand Central Terminal.

All the deco towers are worth a visit for their fabulous exquisitely detailed interiors: the **Chanin Building** (at the southwest corner of 42nd Street and Lexington Avenue), the incomparably elegant **Chrysler Building** (at the northeast corner of 42nd and Lexington; those elevators!), the **Fred F. French Building** (at the northeast corner of Fifth Avenue and 45th Street; a Middle Eastern eye-popping mélange), **Rockefeller Center** (at Fifth Avenue and 50th Street—especially the interior of Radio City Music Hall), and the more-beautiful-than-Fay-Wray **Empire State Building** (at Fifth Avenue and 34th Street). Most of the great deco towers went up while the flappers scarfed down illegal hooch and everyone got giddy rich in the stock market.

Then *crash!* With the arrival of the Great Depression, the skyscraper hit bottom. There was no one to rent all the office space. Construction stopped until after World War II. During that period, many of Europe's most important architects came to New York to escape the ravaged Old World, bringing with them the new theories of the International Style. The **United Nations Secretariat Building,** built in 1947 at First Avenue and 42nd Street, is an elegant if uninviting slab, best appreciated from afar and from the river. Soon after it came **Lever House** (1952) and the **Seagram Building** (1958). By 1961, the Seagram, with its expansive out-front plaza, had inspired the city to change zoning laws again. All high-rises, as these ever-more-boxy steeples were now called, would be set back from the street and offer a public plaza area, and then, unlike the deco towers, go up in straight lines. The result wasn't always happy.

You have only to look at the **Pan Am Building** (1963), now the **Met Life Building,** behind, on top of, and weighing down on poor old Grand Central Terminal and splitting the city in two. Most of the blame goes to architect Walter Gropius. The building's developers got away with their hubris by "buying" the air rights above Grand Central.

In the 1960s and early 1970s, all along Sixth Avenue in the West 40s, perpendicular steel and glass formed a wall of straight lines. Time, however, has a funny way of changing our—or at least my—perceptions. This stretch that once seemed so monotonous and anonymous now looks positively classical, since the introduction of tacky 1970s "expressionism" and 1980s postmodern flimflam.

Like certain still-fabulous disco hits that can make you move again, there are a few architectural gems from the 1970s. What can be said about the you-can't-miss-it **World Trade Center** from 1973? It's probably too tall and, up close, boringly repetitive, but it looks good from afar and great when you're lying on your back in its plaza, and it has a remarkable restaurant (Windows on the World reoccupies its aerie) and grand views. The 1978 **Citicorp,** at Lexington Avenue and 53rd Street—which Andy Warhol once called his favorite New York building—provides the East Side with a frisky, sloping silhouette and a skin of smooth aluminum. And the **United Nations Plaza** (1976 and 1983), at 44th Street and First Avenue, is a bright glass sculpture that refreshes its neighbors as much as a tall drink of clear water.

THE GOOD, THE BAD & THE POSTMODERN

Among the many distressing 1980s buildings—so many of them just seem big and designed less by architects than by landlords—is the **Park Avenue Plaza** (1981). From 52nd to 53rd streets between Park and Madison, this too-big-for-its-britches monstrosity hangs like a threat over the couldn't-hurt-a-fly Racquet and Tennis Club. To make matters sadder, the Park Avenue Plaza was designed by the same firm that built, long before this group, the Lever House.

At 55th Street and Madison, the **AT&T Building,** now called the **Sony Building,** has an interesting story. It was completed in 1984 by Philip Johnson, who gave it a perhaps-too-cute Chippendale top. But at least it broke the spell of the glass curtain with its stone walls, and it did have its open-air public plaza, for which it was given substantial tax breaks by the city. Sony, after purchasing the building, decided that it owed the city and its citizens nothing and closed in the plaza (where you'll now see the self-serving Sony Wonder Technology Lab, which is fun for kids, but we want our plaza back). The **IBM Building,** at 57th Street and Madison Avenue, is quite attractive. It was finished in 1983 and still maintains its tax-beneficial interior courtyard. But there have been rumblings that the building is considering other options. The last thing Midtown needs is other options—it needs safe, clean, bathroom-equipped public spaces that the public, through its generous tax breaks, have paid for. End of discussion.

In the last few years, the West Side around Times Square has seen a spurt of growth, inspired not only by the changes in that neighborhood but also by tax incentives. None of the buildings is of particular aesthetic note, though some of their lights (especially **Morgan Stanley's** at 47th Street and Broadway) do dazzle. The buildings of Lower Manhattan's **Battery Park City,** on the other hand, designed in great part by Cesar Pelli from 1985 to 1988, are new and bold and occupy the riverfront with style.

On East 57th Street, where much of the noise of the last few years has been about the decidedly popular aesthetics of places like the stores of Levi's and Warner Bros., there are some welcome developments. **NikeTown,** as I mentioned, has an unexpectedly tasteful storefront. Across 57th, **Chanel** put up a 17-story tower, designed by Charles Platt, that's as easy for the untrained eye to mistake for "common" as a Chanel suit—but it's slim, refined architectural couture. Just next door is an even more lovely building that should be finished by the time you read this. The **Louis Vuitton Tower** was designed by Christian de Portzamparc, a Frenchman best known for the engaging sloped top of the Cité de la Musique in Paris. Here his plans project a refreshingly new glass look, cut on the bias, so to speak, and lighted with soft-palette neon tubes.

It's a happy development that New York, the home of the high-rise, can boast these two buildings that rise to and meet the challenge of great contemporary architecture. Is there anyone else out there with the money—and the vision—to keep New York at the top of the high-rise heap?

2

Planning Your Trip to New York City

Here are the basics you'll need to design your trip effectively and easily—everything from general visitor information to special travelers' interests, from a calendar of the city's best events to various transportation options for getting in and getting out.

1 General Visitor Information

The best source for general information on New York City (besides this book, of course) is the **New York Convention & Visitors Bureau,** 810 Seventh Ave. New York, NY 10019 (a high-tech public information center is scheduled to open at this address, between 52nd and 53rd streets, in January 1999; hours weren't determined at press time).

Before you arrive, call its 24-hour hot line at ☎ **800/NYC-VISIT** from anywhere in the United States and Canada (from outside North America or once you're in New York, dial ☎ **212/397-8222**).

The hot line allows you to order literature including a **Big Apple Visitors Kit,** detailing hotels, restaurants, theaters, attractions, events, and more (allow 4 to 6 weeks for delivery; you'll pay about $5 to receive the packet in the United States). To speak to a travel counselor call ☎ **212/484-1222** (Mon–Fri 9am–5pm EST). Multilingual counselors are available. The bureau has a Web site at **www.nycvisit.com.**

If you're looking to tour a specific neighborhood with an "expert" guide, contact the **Big Apple Greeter** at ☎ **212/669-8159**—at least 1 week ahead of your arrival. It's a nonprofit organization of specially trained New Yorkers who volunteer to take visitors around town for a *free* 3- to 4-hour tour of a particular neighborhood. And they say New York isn't friendly! The office is open Monday to Friday 10am to 5pm.

2 Information for Travelers with Special Needs

FOR FAMILIES

Don't leave the kids home alone. New York is just as big a playground for the younger set as it is for you.

For the last few years, as a result of the startling decrease in crime and the sudden increase in family-oriented entertainment as exemplified by the "new" Times Square, the city's sidewalks are full of pint-sized visitors who love its eye-popping delights. There are hundreds

Siteseeing: The Best New York City Web Sites

Anyone who has ever done research on the Web knows that entering a search for something like "New York" will generate tens of thousands of responses, most useless and dull. So I've gathered here some of my favorite New York Web sites.

- **www.panix.com/clay/nyc/**   Commonly referred to as New York City Reference, this handy site is a virtual hyperlink index of New York–related sites. Begun in 1995, it's regularly updated, and at press time there were 1,835 links covering every subject area from laundry to theater to "webcams: live picture of New York City."
- **www.amnh.org/**   The American Museum of Natural History's Web site not only provides the predictable information about the museum's current and upcoming exhibits but also allows you to try intriguing experiments and to hyperlink to other great sites.
- **www.nytimes.com**   You have to register to enter the *New York Times'* site, and there may be a fee to access some sections, but it's worth the trouble for the cultural coverage. At the site you'll find comprehensive listings of cultural events in New York, a collection of critics' reviews, and Sunday's Arts & Leisure section, which is posted for 7 days.
- **www.TheInsider.com/nyc/index.html**   This straightforward site presents an archive of features ranging from New York survival tips to the city's best coffee bars. Most articles link to a photo gallery, so you'll have a visual preview of your Gotham visit.

of ways to keep the kids entertained, from children-specific museums and theater to theme-park restaurants.

For details, check out the section "Especially for Kids" in chapter 7. In addition, many places cater specifically to kids—see the boxes "Family-Friendly Hotels" in chapter 5 and "Family-Friendly Restaurants" in chapter 6.

For those who want a guide devoted exclusively to travel with children, you might buy a copy of *Frommer's New York City with Kids.*

FOR TRAVELERS WITH DISABILITIES

There is, finally, general consensus on what many of us knew all along: People with special physical needs enjoy travel and deserve equal access. The Americans with Disabilities Act and state and local laws require an increasing number of buildings and other public spaces to accommodate people with disabilities. Even so, to be sure that the places you want to go to are fully accessible, it's best to call first.

Hospital Audiences, Inc., has an information hot line (☎ **888/424-4685** Mon–Fri 9am–5pm) providing details about accessibility at cultural institutions, hotels, restaurants, and transportation as well as cultural events adapted for people with disabilities. Trained staff members answer specific questions based on your particular physical needs and the dates of your trip. The nonprofit organization also publishes *Access for All,* a 210-page guidebook on accessibility at many of the city's cultural institutions, available by sending a $5 check to **Hospital Audiences, Inc.,** 220 W. 42nd St., 13th floor, New York, NY 10036 (☎ **212/575-7676;** TDD: 212/575-7673).

For a packet of information on accessible hotels, restaurants, transportation, museums, and sites, send a $5 check to the **Society for the Advancement of Travel**

for the Handicapped (SATH), 347 Fifth Ave., Suite 610, New York, NY 10016 (☎ 212/447-7284; fax 212/725-8253).

For airport transfers from JFK, La Guardia, and Newark airports, **Gray Line Air Shuttle** (☎ **800/451-0455** or 212/315-3006) operates minibuses with lifts to midtown hotels by reservation only. Taxis are required to carry people who have folding wheelchairs and seeing-eye or hearing-ear dogs.

Public buses are an inexpensive and easy way to get around New York. All buses' back doors are supposed to be equipped with wheelchair lifts (though the city has had complaints that not all are in working order). Buses also "kneel," lowering their front steps for people who have difficulty boarding. Passengers with disabilities pay half-price fares (75¢). The subway isn't yet fully wheelchair accessible, but a free brochure about subway accessibility, *Accessible Transfer Points,* is available by contacting MTA Customer Assistance, 370 J St., Room 702, Brooklyn, NY 11201 (☎ **718/330-3322;** TTY: 718/596-8273).

Other helpful organizations are **The Lighthouse, Inc.,** 111 E. 59th St., New York, NY 10022 (☎ **800/334-5497** or 212/821-9200), a vision-rehabilitation organization that stages concerts and art exhibits by people with impaired vision and sells Braille subway maps, and the **American Foundation for the Blind,** 11 Penn Plaza, Suite 300, New York, NY 10001 (☎ **800/232-5463** or 212/502-7600).

Specially trained volunteers from the **Big Apple Greeter** (☎ **212/669-8159;** TTY: 212/669-8273) take visitors with all kinds of disabilities around town. Reserve at least 1 week ahead. Active travelers can get paired up for an afternoon run or roll in Central Park with volunteers from the **Achilles Track Club,** 42 W. 38th St., New York, NY 10036 (☎ **212/354-0300**). Children with disabilities have their own specially designed playground at the **Asser Levy Park,** East 23rd Street and Asser Levy Place, 1 block from the East River (☎ **212/447-2020**).

FOR GAY & LESBIAN TRAVELERS

Lesbian and gay culture is as much a part of the city's basic identity as yellow cabs, high-rises, obnoxious but amusing characters, and fabulous theater. The lavender crowd will want to see especially "Staying 'Out'" in chapter 5 for accommodations choices, "Only in New York" in chapter 6 for restaurants that cater mostly to a gay and lesbian crowd, and "The Lesbian & Gay Scene" in chapter 9 for nightlife suggestions.

All over Manhattan, but especially in neighborhoods like the **West Village** and **Chelsea,** shops, services, real-estate agencies, restaurants, video-rental stores, bookshops—the whole gamut of commercial and social life—have a lesbian and gay flavor. Boutiques (like Don't Panic and its T-shirts, Condomania and its latex outfits, the Pleasure Chest and its accoutrements) that originally started as small businesses serving locals have grown into national or international businesses.

You'll find lesbian and gay musical events, like performances by the **Gay Men's Chorus** (☎ 212/924-7770) and by members of **OutMusic** (☎ 212/330-9197); outrageous festivals like **Wigstock** (see "New York City Calendar of Events" later in this chapter); gathering spots like the **Lesbian and Gay Community Services Center** (see below); and health programs sponsored by **Gay Men's Health Crisis (GMHC),** 119 W. 24th St. (AIDS hot line: ☎ **212/807-6655**), and many other organizations. If you're traveling with HIV, this city just might be the best place to visit. Its support and medical services are unrivaled.

Every gay person who travels to New York will want to visit the **Stonewall Bar** on Christopher Street, in nearly the same location as the famed Stonewall Inn once stood. (Neighbors have recently been threatening to have the bar closed for disturbing their peace; in response, the bar has put in soundproofing, so it might survive).

On the night of June 27, 1969, customers at the original Stonewall, tired of constant police harassment, decided to fight back. That milestone marks the beginnings of the contemporary gay liberation movement, though it was one event on a continuum that stretches back in time to Sappho's poetry and no doubt to the cave people and their ancestors. The usually celebratory, always engaging, **Lesbian and Gay Pride March** is held in late June to commemorate the Stonewall "Riots." In the preceding week, there are all kinds of events, from simple parties to major political fundraisers—see "New York City Calendar of Events" later in this chapter.

Recently, **Christopher Street,** famous the world over as the main drag of New York gay-male life, has experienced a renaissance after years of declining fortunes. It's still a touch seedy—and quite a bit "touristy." But many stores and bars line the street, mostly from Seventh Avenue South to Hudson Street. But **Chelsea**—especially Eighth Avenue from 16th to 23rd streets and West 17th to 19th streets from Fifth to Eighth avenues—has taken up where Christopher Street left off.

Meanwhile, women are discovering that more and more places are opening to cater to their desires. Lesbians are benefiting—and no doubt suffering too—from attention in the media, and their profile is rightly on the rise nationally as well as in the city.

The **Lesbian and Gay Community Services Center,** is temporarily located at 1 Little W. 12th St., at the corner of Hudson Street (☎ **212/620-7310**), until the renovation of its permanent home at 208 W. 13th St., between Seventh and Eighth avenues, is complete sometime in the year 2000. The center (☎ **212/620-7310**), is open daily 9am to 11pm and is the meeting place for more than 400 lesbian, gay, and bisexual organizations. The center also runs 26 programs of its own, including one for gays and lesbians newly relocated to New York. You can call to request the Community Calendar of Events that lists happenings like lectures, dances, concerts, readings, and films. Also at the center is the Pat Parker/Vito Russo Library, the city's largest lending library for gay and lesbian literature.

A good source for lesbian and gay events during your visit is *Homo Xtra (HX),* a weekly magazine you can pick up in appropriate bars, clubs, and stores. Lesbians now have their own version, *HX for Her,* with lots of "Lesbo Musts" and listings of clubs, bars, and other spots for socializing and finding culture, religion, sporting distractions, and so on. Another choice is *Next* magazine.

The **Organization of Lesbian and Gay Architects and Designers (OLGAD)** (☎ **212/475-7652**) publishes a map called "A Guide to Lesbian & Gay New York Historical Landmarks." It's available free by calling and leaving your name and address on the answering machine or by writing OLGAD, P.O. Box 927, Old Chelsea Station, New York, NY 10113.

FOR SENIOR TRAVELERS

One of the benefits of age is that travel often costs less. New York subway and bus fares are half price (75¢) for people 65 and older, and many museums and sites (and some theaters and performance halls) offer discounted entrance and tickets to seniors. You can also contact the **American Association of Retired Persons (AARP)**, 601 E St. NW, Washington, DC 20049 (☎ **202/434-2277**), for information on lodging, transportation, and sightseeing discounts.

Don't wait until you're paying your hotel bill to ask about special senior rates—ask when you book. Look for "early bird" specials in many coffee shops and for prix-fixe pretheater menus (see chapter 6 for more on smart ways to save money when you dine). Remember that New Yorkers are a skeptical bunch, so bring an ID card, especially if you've kept your youthful glow.

Some unscrupulous tricksters try to take advantage of seniors, so don't talk to strangers who give you a line like "I just found this envelope full of cash, and you can get part of it if you withdraw your own money from the bank." That's an obvious con, but others are more suave. Be as skeptical as a New Yorker whenever you're approached, especially by someone who has a long story that promises to give you something for nothing. For safety tips, see "Fast Facts: New York City" in chapter 4.

FOR STUDENT TRAVELERS

Many museums, sites, and theaters offer reduced admission to students, so don't forget to bring your valid student ID and valid proof of age. To save money on food, grab a sandwich at any of the ubiquitous Korean groceries or eat at no-frills diners (you might want to check out the boxes "Affordable Gourmet to Go," "Choice Choices $15 & Under," and "The New York Deli News" in chapter 6). Even better in the warmer months, head to the Union Square Greenmarket at Park Avenue South, Broadway, and 17th Street (Monday, Wednesday, Friday, and Saturday) and make your own fresh-picked picnic.

For low-cost and safe accommodations, your best bets are the various YMCAs and Hostelling International–New York (see chapter 5). By the way, don't even think about camping here. I once met some very nice French students planning to stay out overnight in the city's parks. That's not an option. It's more than uncomfortable—it's illegal, dangerous, and (heaven forbid in this town!) unsightly.

3 When to Go

If you're planning a visit with specific interests in mind, certain times of year may be better than others. Culture enthusiasts might come in fall, winter, and early spring, when the theater and performing-arts seasons predictably reach their heights. During summer, many cultural institutions, especially Lincoln Center, offer free or nearly free entertainment. Those who want to see the biggest hits on Broadway usually have the best luck in the theaters' slower months of January and February.

Gourmets might consider coming to New York in June, during Restaurant Week, when the skyscraping temples of haute scale down the cost of a fixed-price meal to match the year—this year to $19.99. Serious calorie consumers might also find it easier to get the best table at the hippest restaurants during July and August, when New Yorkers escape the city's muggy air for weekends in places like the Hamptons.

Outdoorsy types can hit the ocean beaches or join in myriad Central Park activities all summer long. And if you prefer to walk every city block to take in the sights, spring and fall prove best for the mildest and most pleasant weather and are the seasons for street festivals and parades.

NEW YORK CITY CALENDAR OF EVENTS

The following calendar is by no means exhaustive. So much happens in New York, and much of it is serendipitous or last minute. But this list does include the best annual events. For certain listings, exact days and phone numbers weren't available at press time, but you can call the appropriate venue or the New York Convention and Visitors Bureau at ☎ 212/484-1222 (Mon–Fri 9am–5pm EST) for more details closer to the date (the bureau's toll-free number is for ordering literature only).

Ongoing Events

- **The Annex Antiques Fair and Flea Market.** At this outdoor emporium of nostalgia, on Sixth Avenue at 26th Street, a keen eye will note trinkets and treasures, junk and stars, who often circulate. The truly dedicated arrive at dawn. Entry $1. Held Saturday and Sunday. Call ☎ **212/243-5343.**

- **Union Square Greenmarket.** The city's largest farmer's market is the perfect place for people-watching or shopping for picnic provisions, including home-made bread and cookies, Hudson Valley cheeses, local fruits, organic foods, fresh vegetables and salad greens, flowers, ciders, just-squeezed juices, and New York State wine. Held Monday, Wednesday, Friday, and Saturday at Union Square and 17th Street. Call ☎ **212/477-3220.**

January

- **New York National Boat Show.** Slip on your docksiders and head to the Jacob K. Javits Convention Center for the 89th edition, which promises a leviathan fleet of boats and marine products from the world's leading manufacturers. Call ☎ **212/922-1212.** January 2–10.

- ✪ **Winter Antiques Show at the Seventh Regiment Armory.** This is New York's most important, prestigious, socially acceptable, and expensive antiques show. If you can wrangle an invitation to the benefactors' opening night, you'll see high-society ladies swoop down like hungry raptors to pick up the crème before us lowly folks get through the doors. The armory is at 643 Park Ave., at 66th Street. January 15–24 (preview January 14).

- **Antiques at the Other Armory.** Younger, trendier dealers with more affordable collectibles show at the 26th Street Armory (at Lexington Avenue) during the first weekend of the Winter Antiques Show. A free shuttle runs between the two locations. Call ☎ **212/255-0020.** January 15–17.

February

- **Chinese New Year.** The celebration of the new lunar year, is marked by 2 weeks of street festivals, culminating in a nighttime parade starring a slinking dragon that winds through the tiny streets of Chinatown amid boisterous crowds and, traditionally, fireworks (though the city has banned their use in recent years). February 16.

- ✪ **Westminster Kennel Club Dog Show.** Poodles prance, spaniels strut, and pugs parade at Madison Square Garden in front of some 30,000 canine fanciers who pant for America's most important dog show. All 2,500 competing pooches are American Kennel Club Champions of Record in contention for the Best in Show trophy. Call ☎ **212/465-6741.** Mid-February.

- **Manhattan Antiques and Collectibles Triple Pier Expo.** More than 600 dealers in furniture, artwork, jewelry, textiles, and toys exhibit their treasures for 2 consecutive weekends on piers 88, 90, and 92 along the Hudson River between 48th and 51st streets. Call ☎ **212/255-0020.** February 26–28 and mid-November.

March

- **International Cat Show.** Frisky, Fluffy, Jessie, Puff, and some 800 other felines deign to compete for Best of Show at Madison Square Garden. Call ☎ **212/465-6741.** Early March.

- **Art Expo New York.** Held at the Jacob K. Javits Convention Center, this is the world's largest trade show of *popular* art, with 1,250 booths displaying everything from original oils to posters, sculpture to decorative arts, tasteful to dubious. Open to the public the last few days. Call ☎ **212/216-2000.** March 4–8.

- **St. Patrick's Day Parade.** Don something green and head to Fifth Avenue from 44th to 86th streets (celebration central: around St. Pat's, of course) for what's billed as the world's largest civilian parade with more than 150,000 marchers and untold hordes of spectators playing bagpipes, wearing shamrock-shaped eyeglasses, and generally cavorting about. March 17.

- **Ringling Bros. and Barnum & Bailey Circus.** The circus comes to town in grand style with elephants and bears and other circus animals parading from the railroad at Twelfth Avenue and 34th Street to Madison Square Garden early on the morning before the first performance. Call ☎ **212/465-6741.** March to April.

- **Greater New York Orchid Show.** The 18th annual show at the World Financial Center's Winter Garden features rare, exotic orchids from all over the world. Call ☎ **212/945-0505.** Late March.

- ✪ **New Directors/New Films.** The kleig lights are turned on up-and-coming directors at this film series sponsored in tandem by the Museum of Modern Art (MoMA) and the Film Society of Lincoln Center. Screenings are at the Museum of Modern Art, 11 W. 53rd St. Call ☎ **212/875-5610.** Late March to early April.

April

- **The Easter Parade.** If you were planning to slip on a tasteful little number—say something white with a simple flower or two that matches your gloves—you will not be the grandest lady in this springtime hike along Fifth Avenue from 44th to 57th streets. Once upon a time New York's gentry came out in discreet toppings. Today, it's do it big, do it flamboyant—and all the more fun for that, if a touch more notice-me neurotic. April 4.

- **Opening Day at Yankee Stadium.** The men in pinstripes announce that spring is in the air when the first ball is thrown out—usually by some star or politician. Let's hope by the time you read this that George Steinbrenner has stopped his bat-rattling about moving da Bronx Bombers and has instead started repairing the house that Ruth built to a state that precludes massive concrete chunks falling into the bleachers. For tickets call TicketMaster at ☎ **212/307-1212** or Yankee Stadium at ☎ **718/293-6000.**

- **Opening Day at Shea Stadium.** Diamond-loving New Yorkers continue to find the shine in the Mets' efforts—if not their performance. Opening day is a time of perennial hope. For tickets and information, call ☎ **718/507-8499.**

- **Greater New York International Auto Show.** Hot wheels from all over the world whirl into the Jacob K. Javits Convention Center for the largest auto show in the United States. Call ☎ **212/216-2000.** April 10–18.

- **Seventh on Sixth Fashion Shows.** Fashion's bigwigs show off on Sixth Avenue what they've been brooding over in their Seventh Avenue studios. The women's fashion shows are held in Bryant Park (hence the Sixth) but have been cloaked in a general brouhaha with the defection of major designers. But no matter. All the glamminess surrounding the twice-a-year event (April and November) still manages to spill out from the giant white tents under which the catwalks slink. You'll need an invitation to get in (try buying a closetful of full-price couture).

May

- ✪ **Bike New York: The Great Five Boro Bike Tour.** This free-wheeling adventure covers 42 car-free miles through the five boroughs, starting in Manhattan at Wall Street and finishing on Staten Island with a huge picnic and celebration. Some 30,000 participants make this the largest recreational bicycle ride in the United States. Call ☎ **212/932-0778** to register. Early May.

- **International Fine Arts Fair.** An upstart that began in 1994, this show at the Seventh Regiment Armory is now one of the art world's most important events, with more than 70 galleries showing a treasure trove of European and American works. Call ☎ **212/472-0590** during the show. Early May.

- **Ninth Avenue International Food Festival.** Cancel dinner reservations and spend the day sampling sizzling Italian sausages, homemade pierogi, spicy curries, and an assortment of other ethnic dishes. Street musicians, bands, and vendors add to the festive atmosphere at one of the city's best street fairs, stretching along Ninth Avenue from 37th to 57th streets. May 22–23.
- **Fleet Week.** Navy and Coast Guard ships, aircraft carriers, and 10,000 uniformed personnel invade New York for a week of exhibitions and demonstrations, especially fun for the kids. Hosted by the *Intrepid* Sea-Air-Space Museum. Call ☎ **212/245-0072.** May 26–31.
- ✪ **Bird-Watching in Central Park.** And you thought the only wildlife in Manhattan was alligators in the sewers and your fellow passengers on the subway. Central Park, along the Atlantic flyway, is an avian wonderland, with some 275 species sighted—from parrots to bald eagles. For information on spring migration bird-watching, call the Urban Park Rangers at ☎ **212/427-4040.** May to June.
- **Washington Square Outdoor Art Exhibition.** This Greenwich Village tradition, in its 68th year, features the works of 250 artists displayed on 20 blocks in and around Washington Square Park around Memorial and Labor Days. Call ☎ **212/982-6255.** May 29–31, June 5–6, and September 4–6 and 11–12.

June

- **The Belmont Stakes.** The third jewel in the Triple Crown is held at the Belmont Park Race Track in Elmont, Long Island. Call the New York Racing Association at ☎ **718/641-4700.** Early June.
- ✪ **Lesbian and Gay Pride Week and March.** A week of cheerful happenings, from simple parties to major political fund-raisers, precedes a zany parade commemorating the Stonewall Riot of June 27, 1969, which for many marks the beginning of the gay liberation movement. The parade starts at 52nd Street and goes down Fifth Avenue, passes St. Patrick's (with the inevitable controversy), and ends in the West Village, where there's a huge dance party. Call ☎ **212/807-7433.** June 19–27.
- ✪ **Restaurant Week.** Dine for only $19.99 at some of New York's finest restaurants. Participating places vary each year, so watch for the full-page ads in the *New York Times* and other publications. Reserve instantly. Some extend their offers through summer to Labor Day (see chapter 6).
- **Metropolitan Opera.** Free evening performances are given in the city parks. Past performers have included the likes of Luciano Pavarotti and Kathleen Battle. Call ☎ **212/362-6000.** June to July.
- **SummerStage.** This summer-long series of free or low-cost outdoor concerts in Central Park features famous and up-and-coming rock, world music, pop, folk, and jazz artists (some past performers: Ziggy Marley, Guided by Voices, Pharaoh Sanders, Mary Chapin Carpenter). Call ☎ **212/360-2777.** June to August.
- ✪ **Shakespeare in the Park.** First-rate actors (Michele Pfeiffer and Kevin Kline have performed) take the stage at Central Park's newly renovated Delacorte Theater for free Shakespeare under the stars. Thank you, wherever you are, Joe Papp. For more details, see "The New York Shakespeare Festival" in chapter 9. Call ☎ **212/539-8500.** June to August.
- **Classic & Cool on the Hudson.** Free outdoor concerts begin at sunset at the World Financial Center's Winter Garden, in a spectacular palm-fronded, glass-walled riverfront setting. Call ☎ **212/945-0505.** June to August.
- **Summer Street Festivals.** There are many street fairs—some with minor gambling, some with traditional Italian music, some with hairy guys in T-shirts, always lots of teddy bears to win—sponsored by neighborhoods, ethnic groups,

and Italian churches in the Village, including St. Anthony of Padua, West Houston and Sullivan streets. Call ☎ **212/777-2755.** June to August.

July

✪ **Fourth of July.** Start the day amid the upbeat crowds at the Great July Fourth Festival in Lower Manhattan, and end it oohing and aahing at the Macy's fireworks display over the East River; call ☎ **212/695-4400.** If you haven't moved on up to a dee-luxe apartment in the sky, the best vantage point (despite the crush, potholes, and oil slicks) is from the FDR Drive, which closes to traffic several hours before sunset. July 4.

✪ **Rockefeller Center Flower and Garden Show.** As nature is in full bloom around the city, colorful summertime clusters gussy up midtown. Rockefeller Plaza between 48th and 51st streets is transformed into a fabulous flowering meadow by top landscape designers and gardeners. Call ☎ **212/632-3975.** Mid-July.

• **Midsummer Night's Swing.** Dancing duos head to the Lincoln Center Fountain Plaza for romantic evenings of swing, salsa, and tango under the stars to the sounds of top-flight bands. Dance lessons are offered with the purchase of a ticket. Call ☎ **212/546-2656.** July and August.

• **Summergarden Concerts.** Diverse music from the 20th century mingles with works by Rodin, Matisse, and Picasso in the Museum of Modern Art's sculpture garden during this free weekend concert series. Along with the rest of the museum, the garden will undergo reconstruction sometime in the next couple of years as it recovers its original design created by Philip Johnson in 1954. Call ☎ **212/708-9480.** July and August.

✪ **Lincoln Center Festival '99.** This festival has it all—theater, ballet, contemporary dance, opera, music, puppets, and media-based art. Recent editions have featured performances by Ornette Coleman, the Royal Opera, the Royal Ballet, and the New York Philharmonic. Call ☎ **212/546-2656.** July and August.

• **Mostly Mozart.** World-renowned soloists and ensembles—Alicia de Larrocha and André Watts have performed in the past—are featured at this 2-week series at Avery Fisher Hall. Call ☎ **212/875-5030.** July and August.

August

• **Lincoln Center Out-of-Doors.** Free music and dance performances are held in the outdoor spaces of Lincoln Center. Call ☎ **212/546-2656.** August to September.

• **New York Fringe Festival.** Held mainly in a variety of Lower East Side venues for a mainly hipster crowd, this 2-year-old arts festival presents alternative as well as traditional theater, dance, comedy, performance art, and a do-your-own-thing ethic. It's not "fringe" to another festival, just to the concept of festivals. Call ☎ **212/307-0229.** Mid- to late August.

✪ **U.S. Open Tennis Championships.** This is one of the major events on the pro tour and one of the four grand-slam events, held at the slick new facilities at Flushing Meadows Park in Queens. Tickets go on sale in May. Call ☎ **718/760-6200.** Late August to early September.

September

✪ **West Indian–American Day Parade.** An annual Brooklyn event that's a true discovery—for those who still don't know about the extravagant costumes, pulsating rhythms (soca, calypso, reggae), bright colors, folklore, food (jerk chicken, oxtail soup, Caribbean soul food), and 2 million hip-shaking revelers. It's New York's largest street celebration, held on Eastern Parkway in Crown Heights, Brooklyn. Call ☎ **718/774-8807.** September 6.

- **Broadway on Broadway.** This 1-day free show features the songs and casts from virtually every Broadway production performing on a stage erected in the middle of Times Square. Call ☎ 212/768-1560. Early September.
- ✪ **Wigstock.** You might experience the Lady Bunny, Misstress Formika, Sherry Vine, Hedda Lettuce, Lypsinka, and even RuPaul—plus hundreds of other drag queens from fabulous to freaky. Wigstock outgrew its original East Village location, Tompkins Square Park, and has recently been held on the pier at 11th Street on the Hudson River and other Downtown venues, and another move may be in the offing. For a preview, or forewarning, rent *Wigstock: The Movie.* For information, call the Lesbian and Gay Community Services Center at ☎ 212/620-7310 or the Wigstock hotline at ☎ 212/213-2438. Labor Day weekend.
- **Feast of San Gennaro.** Little Italy revels in a crush of eating, drinking, and merrymaking into the wee hours during this week-long celebration based on Neapolitan religious tradition. It recently made headlines with charges that organized crime had been profiting. Now, who'd've believed that? Along Mulberry Street, north of Canal. Mid-September. There's also a fun Italian-inspired street festival in Greenwich Village at Carmine and Bleecker streets in late September, formerly sponsored by Our Lady of Pompeii Church.
- ✪ **New York Film Festival.** Historic hits *Pulp Fiction* and *Mean Streets* both had their U.S. premieres at the Film Society of Lincoln Center's 2-week festival, perhaps the world's most important celebration of cinema. Call ☎ 212/875-5610. Late September to early October.

October

- **Ice-Skating.** Show off your style in the limelight at the diminutive Rockefeller Center rink (☎ 212/332-7654) or in Central Park at the larger Wollman Rink (☎ 212/396-1010). October to April.
- **Feast of St. Francis of Assisi.** Animals from goldfish to elephants are blessed as thousands of Homo sapiens look on at the Cathedral of St. John the Divine. Call ☎ 212/662-2133. Early October.
- **SoHo Arts Festival.** It began as a small block party in 1993, and now this free 3-day festival attracts about 250,000 visitors to the more than 100 exhibits at SoHo galleries and museums. Early October.
- **International Fine Arts and Antiques Dealers Show.** Considered by many as the opening of the fall arts season, this show attracts dealers and collectors from all over the world to the Seventh Regiment Armory. Call ☎ 212/472-0590 during the show. Mid-October.
- ✪ **Next Wave Festival.** One of the city's most important cultural events takes place at the Brooklyn Academy of Music and showcases experimental new works by renowned or up-and-coming international artists of dance, theater, and music. Call ☎ 718/636-4100. October to December.
- ✪ **Greenwich Village Halloween Parade.** Extreme nuns, extravagant cross-dressers, walking corpses, and other things that go bump in the night come out for the Halloween Parade. The route has changed through the years, and most recently this favorite-of-the-natives sequence of sequins has started after sunset at Spring Street and marched up Sixth Avenue to 23rd Street or Union Square. Check the papers for the exact route. October 31.

November

- ✪ **New York City Marathon.** You have to see it to believe it—New Yorkers actually being *nice* to one another, cheering on strangers, and feeding runners Gatorade. Join in the enthusiastic team spirit along First Avenue north of 59th Street or on the East Drive of Central Park. Call ☎ 212/860-4455. November 7.

- **Chase Championships of the Corel WTA Tour.** The top 16 singles players and 8 doubles teams compete at Madison Square Garden in what was formerly the Virginia Slims tournament. Call ☎ **212/465-6741.** Mid-November.

✪ **Macy's Thanksgiving Day Parade.** The procession from Central Park West and 77th Street and down Broadway to Herald Square at 34th Street continues to be a national tradition. A couple of years back there were some very serious snafus with the balloons, so maybe what has always been the real fun in New York—on the chilly night before, Snoopy, Betty Boop, Rocky, Bullwinkle, and friends would inflate to life before your eyes on Central Park West at 79th Street—might no longer be open to the public or might move. Call ☎ **212/494-5432** for new details. November 25.

✪ **Big Apple Circus.** New York City's homegrown circus is a favorite with children and the young at heart. A tent is pitched in Damrosch Park at Lincoln Center. Call ☎ **212/268-2500.** November to January.

December

✪ **Lighting of the Rockefeller Center Christmas Tree.** The towering, glittering tree is lit by the mayor, accompanied by an ice-skating show, singing, entertainment, and a crush that'll make you wish for a si-i-lent night. Call ☎ **212/632-3975.** Early December.

- **Holiday Trimmings.** Stroll down festive Fifth Avenue, and you'll see doormen dressed as wooden soldiers at FAO Schwarz, a 27-foot sparkling snowflake floating over the intersection outside Tiffany's, the Cartier building ribboned in red, wreaths warming the necks of the New York Public Library's lions, and fanciful figurines in the windows of Saks and Lord & Taylor. Throughout December.

- **Christmas Traditions.** Traditional holiday events include the Rockettes in the Radio City Music Hall Christmas Spectacular (☎ **212/247-4777**), *A Christmas Carol* at The Theater at Madison Square Garden (☎ **212/465-6741**), and Tchaikovsky's *Nutcracker* performed by the New York City Ballet at Lincoln Center (☎ **212/870-5570**).

   One of the most popular Christmas concerts (even though technically it should be sung at Easter) is the sing-along, with the National Chorale, to Handel's *Messiah* at Avery Fisher Hall (☎ **212/875-5030**). Don't worry if the only words you know are "Alleluia, Alleluia!"—a lyrics sheet is given to ticket holders.

   The city's churches stage an abundance of first-rate musical performances. Look at the schedules for St. Thomas Church (Episcopal; ☎ **212/757-7013**), St. Ignatius Loyola (Roman Catholic; ☎ **212/288-3588**), the Riverside Church (interdenominational; ☎ **212/870-6700**), and the Cathedral of St. John the Divine (Episcopal; ☎ **212/662-2133**).

- **Lighting of the Hanukkah Menorah.** Everything is done on a grand scale in New York, so it's no surprise that the world's largest menorah (32 feet high) is at Manhattan's Grand Army Plaza, Fifth Avenue and 59th Street. Hanukkah celebrations begin December 4 with the lighting of the first of the giant electronic candles.

- **Kwanzaa Holiday Expo.** Music, dance, and exhibitions mark the traditional African-American holiday at the Jacob K. Javits Convention Center (☎ **212/216-2000**).

✪ **New Year's Eve.** Forget Vegas! The millennium is about to dawn, and the biggest party of them all still, and will always, happen in Times Square, where hundreds of thousands of raucous revelers count down in unison the year's final seconds until the new lighted ball drops at midnight at 1 Times Square (☎ **212/354-0003**).

Other unique events are First Night (☎ **212/922-9393**), a liquor-free gala throughout the city, often with a dance under the celestially decorated and restored ceiling of Grand Central Terminal, and a spectacular fireworks show at Tavern on the Green in Central Park (☎ **212/360-3456**), which acts as starting gun for a 5-mile midnight run sponsored by the New York Road Runner's Club (☎ **212/860-4455**). The Cathedral of St. John the Divine (☎ **212/662-2133**) is known for its New Year's Eve concert.

4 Getting There

BY PLANE

Three major airports serve the New York metropolitan area: **John F. Kennedy International Airport (JFK)** (☎ **718/244-4444**) and **La Guardia Airport** (☎ **718/533-3400**), both in Queens, and **Newark International Airport** (☎ **201/961-6000**), in just-across-the-Hudson-River New Jersey.

Almost every major domestic carrier serves the New York area. Here's a handy list of toll-free numbers and Web sites: **America West** (☎ **800/235-9292;** www.americawest.com), **American** (☎ **800/433-7300;** www.americanair.com), **Continental** (☎ **800/525-0280;** www.flycontinental.com), **Delta** (☎ **800/221-1212;** www.deltaair.com), **Midwest Express** (☎ **800/452-2022;** www.midwestexpress.com), **Northwest** (☎ **800/225-2525;** www.nwa.com), **TWA** (☎ **800/221-2000;** www2.twa.com), **US Airways** (☎ **800/428-4322;** www.usairways.com), and **United** (☎ **800/241-6522;** www.ual.com).

In recent years there has been rapid growth in the number of start-up, no-frills airlines serving New York. These smaller, sometimes struggling airlines may offer lower fares—and all that that implies. You might check out **AirTran** (☎ **800/247-8726;** www.airtran.com), **Carnival** (☎ **800/824-7386;** www.carnivalair.com), **Frontier** (☎ **800/432-1359;** www.frontierair.com), **Kiwi** (☎ **800/538-5494;** www.jetkiwi.com), **Midway** (☎ 800/446-4392; www.midwayair.com), **Tower Air** (☎ **800/34-TOWER** or 718/553-8500; www.towerair.com; caveat: there have been regular complaints about Tower Air flights taking off *hours* late with no explanations and no apologies), and **Vanguard** (☎ **800/826-4827;** www.flyvanguard.com).

Most major international carriers also serve New York—see chapter 3 for more.

TRANSPORTATION TO & FROM THE NEW YORK AREA AIRPORTS

For transportation information for all three airports (JFK, La Guardia, and Newark), call **Air-Ride** (☎ **800/247-7433**); it gives recorded details on bus and shuttle companies and private car services registered with the New York and New Jersey Port Authority. On the arrivals level at each airport, the Port Authority also has information counters where you can make reservations. Most transportation companies have courtesy phones near the baggage-claim area.

Generally travel time between the airports and midtown Manhattan by taxi or car is 1 hour for JFK, 45 minutes for La Guardia, and 50 minutes for Newark. Allow extra time during rush hour or if you're taking a bus.

You might save a few dollars, but still I'd advise that you stay out of the subway and off the city buses when you're bound for the city or the airport. Manhattan is your most likely destination, and there's just no convenient, safe city transportation from or to any of the airports—until, maybe, when they finish the long-promised link between midtown and JFK (but even then, some of the plans I've seen involve staircases, transfers, and other unnecessary hassles). The subways and buses that currently serve the airports involve multiple transfers and staircases up and down which you must drag your luggage. On some subways you'd be traveling through undesirable neighborhoods. Spare yourself the drama.

There are three transportation options between the airports and Manhattan: taxis, private car and limousine companies, and bus and shuttle services.

TAXIS   Taxis are a quick and convenient way to travel to and from the airports. They're available from uniformed dispatchers at designated taxi stands outside the terminals (follow the GROUND TRANSPORTATION or TAXI signs at all three airports). Fares, whether fixed or metered, don't include bridge and tunnel tolls ($3.50 to $4) or tip (15% to 20% is customary). Taxi fares include all passengers in the cab and luggage—never pay more than the metered or flat rate, except for tolls, as a tip, or 8pm to 6am, when a 50¢ surcharge applies on New York yellow cabs. Remember if you're traveling en masse that taxis have a limit of four passengers.

- **From JFK:** It's possible that the flat rate of $30, popular except among cab drivers, might still be in effect when you get here. Check with the dispatcher. Otherwise, to and from Manhattan, expect the fare to be metered and run $30 to $40.
- **From La Guardia:** $20 to $25, metered.
- **From Newark:** The dispatcher for New Jersey taxis gives you a slip of paper with a flat rate ranging from $30 to $43 (toll and tip extra), depending on where you're going in Manhattan, so you'll have to be precise about your destination. The yellow-cab fare from Manhattan to Newark is the meter amount plus $10 and tolls (about $40 to $45, perhaps a few dollars more with tip).

PRIVATE CAR & LIMOUSINE SERVICES   Private car and limousine companies provide 24-hour door-to-door airport transfers that are convenient and easy to use. Call at least 24 hours in advance (even earlier on holidays), and a driver will meet you near baggage claim or at your hotel. Vehicles range from sedans to vans to limousines and tend to be relatively clean and comfortable. Prices vary by company and the size of car reserved, but expect to pay around $30 for JFK and Newark and $20 for La Guardia, plus tolls and tip, for a basic sedan with one stop. There are many companies, and I've had the best luck with **Allstate** (☎ **800/453-4099** or 212/741-7440) and **Tel-Aviv** (☎ **800/222-9888** or 212/777-7777).

BUS COMPANIES & THE SHUTTLE SERVICE   Buses and shuttle services provide a comfortable and less expensive option for airport transfers. Gray Line Air Shuttle serves all three airports; Gray Line Airport Express and Carey Transportation serve JFK and La Guardia; Olympia Trails serves Newark.

Gray Line Air Shuttle (☎ **800/451-0455** or 212/315-3006) vans depart JFK, La Guardia, and Newark every 20 minutes 6am to midnight and will drop you off at most hotels between 23rd and 63rd streets in Manhattan. You must reserve at the ground-transportation desk or by using the courtesy phones in the baggage-claim area. Service from most major mid-Manhattan hotels to all three airports operates 5am to 7pm. You must reserve 1 day in advance to arrange a hotel pickup. The one-way fare for JFK is $16.50, for La Guardia $13.50, and for Newark $18.50.

An Airport Warning

Never accept a car ride from the hustlers who hang out in the terminal halls. They're illegal, don't have proper insurance, and aren't safe. You can tell who they are because they'll approach you with a suspicious conspiratorial air and ask if you need a ride. Not from them, you don't. Sanctioned city cabs and car services wait outside the terminals.

Cyber Deals for Net Surfers

It's possible to get great information as well as great deals on airfare, hotels, and car rentals via the Internet. A good place to start is Macmillan Travel's site, **Arthur Frommer's Outspoken Encyclopedia of Travel** (**www.frommers.com**), where you'll find lots of up-to-the-minute travel information—including the latest bargains and candid articles updated daily by Arthur Frommer himself.

Microsoft Expedia (**www.expedia.com**)   The best part of this multipurpose travel site is the Fare Tracker: You fill out a form on the screen indicating that you're interested in cheap flights to New York and, once a week, Expedia e-mails you the best airfare deals. The site's Travel Agent will steer you to bargains on hotels and car rentals, and you can book everything on-line.

Preview Travel (**www.reservations.com** and **www.vacations.com**)   Another useful site, Reservations.com has a Best Fare Finder that'll search the Apollo computer reservations system for the three lowest fares for any route on any days. Just fill out the form on the screen with times, dates, and destinations, and within minutes, Preview will show you the best deals. If you find an airfare you like, you can book your ticket on-line—you can even reserve hotels and car rentals. If you're in the preplanning stage, head to Preview's Vacations.com site, where you can check out the latest package deals by clicking on Hot Deals.

Travelocity (**www.travelocity.com**)   This is one of the best travel sites out there. In addition to its Personal Fare Watcher, which notifies you via e-mail of the lowest airfares for up to five destinations, Travelocity will track in minutes the three lowest fares for any routes on any dates. You can book a flight then and there, and if you need a rental car or hotel, they'll find you the best deal via the SABRE computer reservations system (a huge database used by travel agents).

E-Savers Programs   Several major airlines offer a free e-mail service known as **E-Savers,** via which they'll send you their best bargain airfares on a weekly basis. Once a week (usually Wednesday), subscribers receive a list of discounted flights to and from various destinations. Now here's the catch: These fares are available only if you leave the very next Saturday (or sometimes Friday night) and return on the following Monday or Tuesday. But the fares are cheap, so it's worth taking a look. See above for a list of airlines and their Web sites.

Epicurious Travel (**travel.epicurious.com**), another good travel site, allows you to sign up for all these airline e-mail lists at once.

—*Jeanette Foster*

Gray Line Airport Express (☎ **800/451-0455** or 212/315-3006) buses depart JFK and La Guardia every 20 minutes 6am to midnight and make two stops in Manhattan: Grand Central Terminal (41st Street between Park and Lexington avenues) and the Port Authority Terminal (42nd Street just west of Eighth Avenue). Buses to JFK and La Guardia depart every 20 minutes 5am to midnight. One-way fare for JFK is $12 and for La Guardia $10.

Severe disagreements between the Port Authority and **Carey Transportation** (☎ **800/456-1012** or 718/632-0500) a couple of years back led the Authority to terminate Carey's contracts and barred its buses from their former pick-up points, but at press time Carey continued to operate to and from the city's two airports. Buses depart JFK and La Guardia every 20 to 30 minutes 6:30am to midnight and arrive at

Carey's bus stand on Park Avenue between 41st and 42nd streets. From there, free shuttles serve many major midtown hotels (check with yours when you reserve). Buses to JFK and La Guardia depart the Grand Central Terminal location every 20 to 30 minutes 5am to midnight. To request shuttle service from your hotel to Grand Central, call the above number. One-way fare for JFK is $13 and for La Guardia $10. Children under 12 ride free with a parent.

Olympia Trails (☎ 212/964-6233) provides service between Newark and four Manhattan locations: the World Trade Center (next to the Marriott World Trade Center Hotel on West Street), Pennsylvania Station (the station is at Seventh Avenue between 31st and 33rd streets; the pickup point is the northwest corner of 34th Street and Eighth Avenue and the drop-off point the southwest corner), the Port Authority Bus Terminal (buses pickup and drop-off at gates 317 and 318 of the terminal's Airport Bus Center on 42nd Street between Eighth and Ninth avenues), and Grand Central Terminal (the station is at 42nd Street, between Vanderbilt and Lexington avenues; buses pick up and leave passengers on the south side of 42nd Street, in front of the airlines-reservations building). Buses depart from Newark to all four locations every 15 to 30 minutes 6am to midnight and to the Port Authority Bus Terminal at 12:30, 1, and 2am and every 20 minutes 3:30am to 5am. From Penn Station and Grand Central, service is every 15 to 30 minutes 5am to 11pm, from the World Trade Center Monday to Friday every 30 minutes 6:15am to 8pm and Saturday and Sunday every 30 minutes 7:30am to 7:30pm, and from the Port Authority Bus Terminal every 20 to 30 minutes 5am to midnight and at 1, 2:45, and 4:15am. Passengers to and from the Grand Central Terminal location can connect to Olympia's free Midtown shuttle vans, which service most hotels between 30th and 65th streets. The one-way fare is $10.

BY TRAIN

Amtrak (☎ 800/USA-RAIL) runs frequent service to New York City's Pennsylvania Station (Seventh Avenue between 31st and 33rd streets), where you can easily transfer to your hotel by taxi, subway, or bus. To get the best rates, book early (as much as 6 months in advance) and travel on weekends.

Here are a few sample 1998 fares and travel times: **Boston**—$43 to $64 one way (4½ to 5 hours); **Chicago**—$141 one way, $160 to $304 round-trip (18 to 20 hours); **Philadelphia**—$36 to $43 one way on regular train (1½ to 2 hours), $55 to $71 one way on Metroliner express train, reservations required (1 hour); **Washington, D.C.**—$60 to $83 one way on regular train (3½ to 4 hours), $87 to $112 one way on Metroliner express train, reservations required (3 hours).

BY BUS

Buses arrive at the Port Authority Terminal (Eighth Avenue between 40th and 42nd streets), where you can easily transfer to your hotel by taxi, subway, or bus.

Here are sample 1998 fares and travel times via **Greyhound Bus Lines** (☎ 800/231-2222 or check your local phone book): **Boston**—$60 round-trip (4 to 5 hours); **Chicago**—$174 round-trip (16 to 18 hours); **Philadelphia**—$32 round-trip (2 to 3 hours); **Washington, D.C.**—$60 round-trip (4 to 5 hours).

BY CAR

From the New Jersey Turnpike (I-95) and points west, there are three Hudson River crossings into the city's west side: the Holland Tunnel (Lower Manhattan), the Lincoln Tunnel (Midtown), and the George Washington Bridge (Upper Manhattan). The toll at each is $4 for cars heading into the city; there's no outbound toll.

From upstate New York, take the New York State Thruway (I-87), which crosses the Hudson on the Tappan Zee Bridge ($2.50 toll) and becomes the Major Deegan Expressway (I-87) through the Bronx. For the east side, continue to the Triborough Bridge ($3.50 toll) and then down the FDR Drive. For the west side, take the Cross Bronx Expressway (I-95) to the Henry Hudson Parkway or the Taconic State Parkway to the Saw Mill River Parkway to the Henry Hudson Parkway south ($1.50 toll).

From New England, the New England Thruway (I-95) connects with the Bruckner Expressway (I-278), which leads to the Triborough Bridge ($3.50 toll) and the FDR on the east side. For the west side, take the Bruckner to the Cross Bronx Expressway (I-95) to the Henry Hudson Parkway south ($1.50 toll).

Once you arrive in Manhattan, park your car in a garage (expect to pay at least $20 to $30 per day) and leave it there. Don't use your car for traveling within the city. Public transportation, taxis, and walking will easily get you where you want to go without the headache of parking, gridlock, and dodging crazy cabbies.

3 For Foreign Visitors

You've seen it all already—the high-rises, the glittering nightlife and shopping, the attitude of the natives. New York's global media profile might make it appear familiar, but Hollywood and TV, music videos, and news images all distort as they reflect. The gap between image and reality can make certain situations puzzling for the foreign—or even domestic—visitor. So here I've compiled almost everything you'll need to know.

1 Preparing for Your Trip

ENTRY REQUIREMENTS

DOCUMENT REGULATIONS   Citizens of Canada and Bermuda may enter the United States without visas, but they'll need to show proof of nationality, the most common and hassle-free form of which is a **passport.**

The U.S. State Department has a **Visa Waiver Pilot Program** allowing citizens of certain countries to enter the United States without a visa for stays of fewer than 90 days of holiday travel. At press time they were Andorra, Argentina, Australia, Austria, Belgium, Brunei, Denmark, Finland, France, Germany, Iceland, Ireland, Italy, Japan, Liechtenstein, Luxembourg, Monaco, the Netherlands, New Zealand, Norway, San Marino, Spain, Sweden, Switzerland, and the United Kingdom.

Citizens of these countries need only a valid **passport** and a **round-trip air or cruise ticket** in their possession upon arrival. If they enter the United States first, they may subsequently visit Mexico, Canada, Bermuda, and/or the Caribbean and then return to the United States still without a visa. More information is available from any U.S. embassy or consulate.

Citizens of countries other than the ones listed above, those traveling to the States for reasons or length of time outside the restrictions of the waiver program, or those who require waivers of inadmissibility must have two documents:

- A valid **passport** with an expiration date at least 6 months later than the scheduled end of their visit to the United States (some countries are exceptions to the 6-month validity rule; contact any U.S. embassy or consulate for details)
- A **tourist visa,** available from the nearest U.S. consulate

To obtain a visa, you must submit a completed application form (in person or by mail) with a 1½-inch-square photo and the required application fee. There may also be an issuance fee. Usually you can obtain a visa right away or within 24 hours, but it may take longer June to August. If you can't go in person, contact the nearest U.S. embassy or consulate for directions on applying by mail. Your travel agent or airline office may also be able to provide you with visa applications and instructions. The U.S. consulate or embassy that issues your visa will determine whether you'll receive a multiple- or single-entry visa. The Immigration and Naturalization Service officers at the port of entry in the United States will determine your length of stay.

MEDICAL REQUIREMENTS   No inoculations are needed to enter the United States unless you're coming from, or have stopped over in, areas known to be suffering from epidemics, particularly cholera or yellow fever.

If you have a disease requiring treatment with medications containing narcotics or with drugs requiring a syringe, carry a valid signed prescription from your physician to allay suspicions that you're smuggling drugs. If you do need prescription drugs, your doctor should provide you with a generic prescription, since the brands you're accustomed to buying back home may not be available in the United States.

CUSTOMS REQUIREMENTS   Every visitor 21 or over may bring in, free of duty: 1 liter of alcoholic beverages; 200 cigarettes or 100 cigars (but no cigars from Cuba), and $100 worth of gifts. These exemptions are offered to travelers who spend at least 72 hours in the United States and who haven't claimed them in the preceding 6 months. It's forbidden to bring foodstuffs (particularly cheese, fruit, meats) and plants (vegetables, seeds, tropical plants) into the country. Foreign visitors may bring in or take out up to $10,000 in U.S. or foreign currency with no formalities; larger sums must be declared to Customs on entering or leaving. For more information, call U.S. Customs at ☎ **800/697-3662.**

INSURANCE

Unlike many other countries, the United States doesn't have a national health-care system. The cost of medical care is extremely high, and I strongly advise all travelers to secure health coverage before setting out on their trip. You may want to take out a comprehensive travel policy that covers sickness or injury costs (medical, surgical, hospital); loss or theft of your baggage; trip-cancellation costs; guarantee of bail in case you're arrested; and costs of accident, repatriation, or death. Such packages (for example, Europe Assistance in Europe) are sold by automobile clubs, as well as by insurance companies and travel agencies and at some airports.

MONEY

The U.S. monetary system has a decimal base: One American **dollar** ($1) = 100 **cents** (100¢). **Bills** commonly come in $1 (a "single" or "buck"), $5, $10, $20, $50, and $100 denominations (the last two aren't welcome when you pay for small purchases and are usually not accepted in taxis or at subway token booths). There are six **coin** denominations: 1¢ (one cent or "penny"); 5¢ (five cents or "nickel"); 10¢ (ten cents or "dime"); 25¢ (twenty-five cents or "quarter"); 50¢ (fifty cents or "half-dollar"); and the $1 pieces (both the large silver dollar and the smaller Susan B. Anthony coin).

Credit cards are the most convenient and widely used method of payment at hotels, motels, restaurants, and retail stores. Commonly accepted cards in descending order are Visa (BarclayCard in Britain), MasterCard (EuroCard in Europe, Access in Britain, Diamond in Japan), American Express, Discover, Diners Club, enRoute, JCB, and Carte Blanche. Credit cards are often necessary to secure a deposit when renting a car and useful for cash advances and withdrawals.

Credit cards and **bank cards** can often be used to withdraw cash at automated teller machines (ATMs) found throughout New York City and the country. Check with your credit-card company or bank before leaving home to confirm that your card will be accepted. Also find out if service fees are charged on cash advances or money withdrawals and if there are limits on the frequency or amount of money you can withdraw.

Traveler's checks in U.S. dollars are accepted at most hotels, motels, restaurants, and large stores. Sometimes picture ID is required. American Express, Thomas Cook, and Barclay's Bank traveler's checks are readily accepted in the United States.

You can **wire money** or have it wired to you very quickly using Western Union at ☎ **800/325-6000** or American Express's MoneyGram at ☎ **800/926-9400.**

SAFETY

Tourist areas in Manhattan are generally safe, and the city has experienced a dramatic drop in its crime rate. Still, crime is a national problem, and U.S. urban areas tend to be less safe than those in Europe or Japan. You should always stay alert, use common sense, and trust your instincts. If you feel you're in an unsafe area or situation, you probably are and should leave as quickly as possible. Keep valuables at home, don't wear flashy jewelry or clothing, be discreet when reading maps so you don't look like an easy mark as a "distracted tourist," and always keep your hotel room door locked. For more, see "Safety" under "Fast Facts: New York City" in chapter 4.

DRIVING   Safety while driving is particularly important. Question your rental agency about personal security and ask for a brochure of traveler safety tips when you pick up your car. Obtain from the agency written directions or a map with the route marked in red showing how to get to your destination. And, if possible, arrive and depart during daylight hours.

Always keep your car doors locked, whether the vehicle is attended or unattended. Never leave any packages or valuables in sight because thieves will break car windows. If someone attempts to rob you or steal your car, don't resist. Report the incident to the police department immediately.

An inviolable rule of thumb for New York: Don't even think of driving within the city (especially not in neighborhoods you don't know, including parts of Harlem, the Bronx, and Brooklyn). Like many cities, New York has its own arcane rules of the road, confusing one-way streets, incomprehensible street-parking signs, and outrageously expensive parking garages. Public transport, will get you anywhere you want to go quickly and easily, and that's where you'll be most comfortable. If you do drive to New York in a rental car, return it as soon as you arrive and rent another when you're ready to leave the city. If you dare to arrive in your own car, park it in one of those garages that have monthly charges about equal to a mortgage payment, and then don't take your vehicle out again until you leave the city.

2 Getting to the United States

Travelers from overseas can take advantage of the **APEX (advance-purchase excursion) fares** offered by all major U.S. and European carriers. Aside from these, attractive values are offered by **Virgin Atlantic** (☎ **01293/747-747** in the U.K.; www.fly. virgin.com) from London's Heathrow to New York.

In addition to the domestic airlines listed in chapter 2, many international carriers serve John F. Kennedy International Airport. **British Airways** (☎ **0345/222-111** in the U.K.; www.british-airways.com) has daily service from London as well as direct flights from Manchester and Glasgow. Canadian readers might book flights on **Air Canada** (☎ **800/776-3000;** www.aircanada.ca), which offers direct service from Toronto, Montréal, Ottawa, and other cities, or on **Canadian Airlines** (☎ **800/ 426-7000;** www.cdair.ca).

Continental (☎ **01293/776-464** in the U.K.; www.flycontinental.com) flies to Newark from London, Manchester, Madrid, Paris, and Frankfurt. **Aer Lingus** flies from Dublin and Shannon to New York (☎ **01/844-4747** in Dublin or 061/415-556 in Shannon; www.aerlingus.ie). **TWA** (www2.twa.com) has nonstop service to New York from Barcelona, Madrid, Milan, Paris, and Rome. **United** (☎ **0181/990-9900** in the U.K.; www.ual.com) serves those cities and London, Amsterdam, Brussels, and Zurich. **American** (☎ **0181/572-5555** in the U.K.; www.americanair.com) flies non-stop from London, Manchester, Paris, Brussels, and Zurich. **Delta** (☎ **0800/414-764** in the U.K.; www.delta-air.com) flies to New York from most major European cities. **Qantas** (☎ **13 12 11** in Australia; www.qantas.com.au) and **Air New Zealand** (☎ **13-2476** in New Zealand; www.airnewzealand.co.nz) fly to the West Coast and will book you straight through to New York City on a partner airline.

If you're arriving by air, no matter what the port of entry, cultivate patience and res-ignation before setting foot on U.S. soil. Getting through immigration control may take as long as 2 hours on some days, especially summer weekends, so read this guide-book while you wait and continue planning your stay in New York. When you book your flight, allow 2 to 3 hours to clear Customs and Immigration between your inter-national arrival and your domestic departure.

In contrast, for the Canadian traveler arriving by car or rail from Canada, the border-crossing formalities have been streamlined to the vanishing point. And for the traveler by air from Canada, Bermuda, and some places in the Caribbean, you can sometimes go through U.S. Customs and Immigration at the point of departure, which is much quicker.

3 Getting Around the United States

The United States is a massive country and, unlike in Europe, travel by rail, bus, or car isn't the way to undertake a whirlwind cross-country tour. The fastest way to cover large distances is by airplane.

In conjunction with their transatlantic or transpacific flights, some large U.S. air-lines offer special discount tickets for any of their U.S. destinations (American Air-lines' **Visit USA** program and Delta's **Discover America** program, for example). These cut-rate tickets or coupons aren't available in the United States and must be purchased before you leave home. This system is the best, easiest, and fastest way to see the United States at low cost. You should obtain information well in advance from your travel agent or the office of the airline concerned because the conditions attached can change without advance notice.

International visitors can buy a **USA Railpass,** good for 15 or 30 days of unlimited travel on Amtrak. The pass is available through many foreign travel agents. Prices in 1998 for a 15-day pass were $260 off-peak and $375 peak; a 30-day pass cost $350 off-peak and $480 peak (off-peak is September 1 to May 31). With a foreign passport, you can buy passes at some Amtrak offices in the United States, including New York, Boston, Chicago, Los Angeles, Miami, San Francisco, and Washington, DC. Reserva-tions are generally required and should be made for each part of your trip as early as possible by calling ☎ **800/USA-RAIL.**

Train travel is relatively quick, inexpensive, and convenient along the northeast corridor between Boston, New York, and Washington, DC. You zip from city center to city center, without having to travel to and from far-flung airports. However, keep in mind the limitations of long-distance rail travel in the United States. For example, it can take up to 20 hours to travel between New York and Chicago. In addition, service is rarely up to European standards: Delays are common, routes limited and often infrequently served, and fares rarely significantly lower than discount air travel. Thus, approach a cross-country train trip in America with these caveats in mind.

Though bus travel between cities has traditionally been the most economical form of public transit, at this writing bus passes are priced slightly higher than similar train passes. Greyhound, the sole nationwide bus operator, offers an **Ameripass** for unlimited travel for 7 days ($199), 15 days ($299), 30 days ($409), and 60 days ($599). Bus travel can be both slow (New York to Chicago can take 18 hours) and uncomfortable, so it isn't for everyone. In addition, bus stations are often in undesirable neighborhoods. For more information, contact Greyhound Bus Lines at ☎ **800/231-2222.**

FAST FACTS: For the Foreign Traveler

Automobile Organizations   Auto clubs are an excellent source of travel information, including maps, guidebooks, accident and bail-bond insurance, and emergency road service. The **American Automobile Association (AAA)**, or Triple A, is the largest auto club in the United States, with offices nationwide. Some foreign auto clubs have reciprocal agreements with AAA; inquire with your auto club before leaving home to see if you can benefit from AAA's services. Otherwise, some car-rental agencies provide maps, itineraries, and other services.

Automobile Rental   To rent a car in the United States you need a valid driver's license, a passport, and often a major credit card. The minimum age is usually 25, but some companies will rent to younger people and add a surcharge. It's a good idea to buy maximum insurance coverage unless you're positive your own auto or credit-card insurance is sufficient. Car-rental companies often charge extra for one-way drop-offs, refueling, child seats (required for kids under 5), additional drivers, and returning the car early. All major car-rental agencies have branches in Manhattan; check the Yellow Pages directory under Automobile Renting for locations. Rates vary, so it pays to call around. Stick to the major companies (Avis, Alamo, Budget, Dollar, Enterprise, Hertz, National) because what you might save with smaller companies might not be worth the headache if you have mechanical troubles on the road.

As a frequent renter of cars, I find that in major cities like New York it's sometimes much less expensive to rent a car from a nearby smaller town or from an airport rather than from the city center. You might consider taking the train to a destination outside the city and then renting and returning your car there.

Business Hours   In general, **retail stores** are open Monday to Saturday 10am to 6pm, Thursday 10am to 8:30 or 9pm, and Sunday noon to 5pm (see chapter 9 for more precise schedules). **Banks** tend to be open Monday to Friday 9am to 3pm and sometimes Saturday mornings. **Post offices** are open Monday to Friday 10am to 5 or 6pm and Saturday 9am to noon; New York's main post office, on Eighth Avenue between 31st and 33rd streets, is open 24 hours. **Business offices** are generally open Monday to Friday 9am to 5pm.

Currency Exchange   Foreign exchange bureaus, common in Europe, are rare in America. You'll find some in major international airports and major tourist cities, but not in smaller cities and towns. So it's a good idea to bring travelers check in U.S. dollars and rely on credit cards for paying hotel, restaurant, and other large bills.

In New York City, the best exchange rates are usually available at **Avis Currency Exchange,** formerly Harold Reuter & Co. (☎ **212/661-0826**). You can check its daily exchange rates on the Internet at **www.avisnet.com**. At press time, there were three locations: Room 332 East in 200 Park Ave., at 45th Street; the sixth floor in Stern's department store, 899 Sixth Ave., at 33rd Street; and Times Square at 1451 Broadway, between 41st and 42nd streets.

There are two other reliable, though often slightly more costly, choices. **American Express** (☎ **800/AXP-TRIP**) has many offices throughout the city, including JFK Airport; 1185 Sixth Ave., at 47th Street; 374 Park Ave., at 53rd Street; Macy's at Herald Square, 34th Street and Broadway; and 65 Broadway, between Exchange Place and Rector Street. **Thomas Cook Currency Services** (☎ **212/753-0132**) has locations at JFK Airport; 1590 Broadway, at 48th Street; and 511 Madison Ave., at 53rd Street.

Drinking Laws　The laws governing the sale and consumption of alcoholic beverages are different in every state, but in general the minimum age is 21, as it is in New York. Liquor stores, the only outlets for wine as well as hard liquor in New York, are closed on Sundays, holidays, and election days while the polls are open. Beer can be purchased in grocery stores and delis all day Monday to Saturday and Sunday after noon.

Electric Current　Electricity in the United States runs on 110-volt, 60-cycle AC current, versus the 220-volt, 50-cycle AC current used in most of Europe. If you're bringing electrical appliances, like a hair dryer or shaver, that aren't dual-voltage, you'll need a voltage transformer and a plug adapter with two flat parallel pins. Some people find it cheaper to buy new appliances here than to buy a transformer.

Embassies/Consulates　All embassies are in Washington, D.C. Some countries have consulates general in major U.S. cities, and most have a mission to the United Nations in New York City. **Australia:** Embassy, 1601 Massachusetts Ave. NW, Washington, DC 20036 (☎ **202/797-3000**). Consulate General, 630 Fifth Ave., New York, NY 10111 (☎ **212/408-8400**). **Canada:** Embassy, 501 Pennsylvania Ave. NW, Washington, DC 20001 (☎ **202/682-1740**). Consulate General, 1251 Ave. of the Americas, New York, NY 10020 (☎ **212/596-1600**). **Ireland:** Embassy, 2234 Massachusetts Ave. NW, Washington, DC 20008 (☎ **202/462-3939**). Consulate General, 345 Park Ave., New York, NY 10154-0037 (☎ **212/319-2555**). **New Zealand:** Embassy, 37 Observatory Circle NW, Washington, DC. 20008 (☎ **202/328-4800**). Consulate General, 780 Third Ave., New York, NY 10017 (☎ **212/832-4938**). **United Kingdom:** Embassy, 3100 Massachusetts Ave. NW, Washington, DC. 20008 (☎ **202/462-1340**). Consulate General, 845 Third Ave., New York, NY 10022 (☎ **212/745-0202**).

Emergencies　Dial ☎ **911** for **fire,** police, and **ambulance.**

If you have a medical emergency that doesn't require an ambulance, you can walk into a hospital's 24-hour emergency room (usually a separate entrance). For a list of hospitals, see "Fast Facts: New York City" in chapter 4. Because emergency rooms are often crowded and waits long, one of the walk-in medical centers listed under "Doctors" in "Fast Facts: New York City" might be a better option. Otherwise, call ☎ **212/737-2333,** a referral service available 8am to midnight, for doctors who make house calls. Don't be surprised if the first question you are asked in your agony is, Do you have medical insurance?

Dental Emergency Service at ☎ **212/679-3966** makes referrals, and **Preventive Dental Associates** at ☎ **212/683-2530** has a 24-hour answering service. The **Poison Control Center** is at ☎ **212/764-7667** or 212/340-4494. The **Crime Victims Hot Line** is ☎ **212/577-7777,** and the **Sex Crimes Report Line** is ☎ **212/267-7273.** Two 24-hour pharmacies are **Duane Reade** at Broadway and 57th Street (☎ **212/541-9708**) and Third Avenue and 74th Street (☎ **212/744-2668**).

Gasoline (Petrol) One U.S. gallon equals 3.79 liters and .83 British imperial gallon. Rental cars run on unleaded gas that costs about $1.30 or less a gallon if you fill your own tank (self-serve) and about 10¢ more per gallon if the station attendant does it (full service).

Holidays On the following holidays, banks, government offices, post offices, private companies, and many stores, restaurants, and museums are closed: January 1 (New Year's Day), third Monday in January (Martin Luther King Jr. Day), third Monday in February (Presidents' Day), last Monday in May (Memorial Day), July 4 (Independence Day), first Monday in September (Labor Day), second Monday in October (Columbus Day), November 11 (Veterans Day/Armistice Day), last Thursday in November (Thanksgiving Day), and December 25 (Christmas Day). The Tuesday following the first Monday in November is Election Day.

Legal Aid If you're stopped for a minor infraction (like speeding), never attempt to pay the fine directly to a police officer. You may be arrested on the much more serious charge of attempted bribery. Pay fines by mail or directly to the clerk of the court. If you're arrested, it's best to stay calm and respectful and say nothing to the police before consulting a lawyer. Under U.S. law, an arrested person has the right to have an attorney present during any questioning and is allowed one phone call to a party of his or her choice. Call your embassy or consulate.

Mail The main post office in New York City, Eighth Avenue between 31st and 33rd streets, is open 24 hours. You may receive mail in care of general delivery at the main post office of the city or region you're visiting with prior arrangement. To receive general-delivery mail in New York City, call ☎ **212/330-3099.** The addressee must pick it up in person and show proof of identity.

Mailboxes on street corners are blue with a red-and-white logo and carry the inscription U.S. MAIL. Within the United States, it costs 32¢ to send a first-class letter weighing up to 1 ounce and 20¢ for a standard 4.25- by 6-inch postcard. To Canada, it costs 46¢ for a letter up to a half ounce and 40¢ for a postcard. Airmail to Europe, Australia, New Zealand, and elsewhere costs 60¢ for a letter up to a half ounce, 50¢ for an aerogram stationary letter (which you can buy at post offices), and 50¢ for a postcard.

Newspapers/Magazines The *New York Times*, one of the world's most respected newspapers, is renowned for its coverage of international events, but there's loads of daily local coverage as well. The Friday and Sunday issues have exhaustive sections dedicated to special events; exhibitions; openings; and theater, film, and music schedules.

The weekly newspapers the *Village Voice* and *New York Press* (both free in Manhattan) have entertainment listings with a Downtown slant. Three other magazines useful for entertainment listings are *New York* (especially its back-of-the-book "Cue" section), *The New Yorker* (front-of-the-book listings), and *Time Out New York.*

Many newsstands in New York City carry a selection of international newspapers and magazines. For nearly all major newspapers and magazines from around the world, head to **Hotalings News Agency,** 142 W. 42nd St., between Broadway and Sixth Avenue (☎ **212/840-1868**).

Taxes   In the United States there's no value-added tax (VAT). There's a $10 **Customs tax** payable on entry to the United States and a $6 **departure tax,** usually added on to the price of an international airline ticket. Sales tax is often levied on goods and services by state and local governments and varies from state to state and city to city. It's usually not included in the price tags on merchandise but is added at the cash register. These taxes aren't refundable. In New York City, the **sales tax** is 8.25%, but there has been talk of reducing or eliminating it at some point, at least on clothing purchases under $500. The **hotel tax** is 13.25% plus $2 per room per night (including sales tax). The **parking garage tax,** added to already high basic fees, is 18.25%.

Telephone/Fax   In New York, I advise caution when using **pay phones.** In fact, I use only pay phones bearing the distinctive green-and-blue Bell Atlantic logo. Many other phones belong to unscrupulous companies that provide bad service and charge unconscionably high rates. Pay phones located directly against the outside wall of a store or other commercial space might belong to fly-by-night phone companies; the store owner usually receives a commission for allowing the phone to be proximate to his or her property but will disavow any responsibility for returning your money if the phone doesn't work properly.

To confuse matters more, in the last few years it has been possible for a phone that belongs to Bell Atlantic to use a long-distance carrier that charges higher than market rates. If you're making a long-distance call, press 00 (zero, zero—not the letter *O*) and ask the operator to identify the company for whom he or she works. My advice: If the operator doesn't work for Bell Atlantic, AT&T, MCI, or Sprint, hang up and use another phone.

Recently, new multimedia phone booths that use AT&T, another reliable company (now in the business of handling local calls) as their carrier, have been popping up in Manhattan. Recognizable by their sleek, tilted stainless-steel design, the booths are as much information kiosks as phones, with video screens providing restaurant and entertainment listings. It's uncertain whether they'll fade away or become a fixture on the streets. You can help decide by using or avoiding them.

For local calls: Bell Atlantic pay phones can be found on street corners; in the lobbies of some public buildings; and at restaurants, stores, and gas stations. The Bell Atlantic charge for a local call is 25¢ for the first 5 minutes, payable in nickels, dimes, or quarters. Check for the green-and-blue Bell Atlantic logo, pick up the receiver, deposit the coins, and listen for the dial tone.

Starting in late 1998, there are three area codes in New York City: Two in Manhattan (212 and 646) and another, 718, for Brooklyn, the Bronx, Queens, and Staten Island. At press time, the rules for dialing local calls hadn't yet been determined, since Bell Atlantic and the New York State Public Service Commission had appealed a decision by the Federal Communications Commission. The battle was over how you would make local calls within the same area code. You can skip dialing the 1 and area code when dialing from within the same area code if Bell Atlantic and the state have their way. Or, if the FCC wins, you'll always have to dial 1 and the area code before the number even if you're dialing from 212 to 212 or from 718 to 718 (and of course from 212 to 646, or from 212 or 646 to 718, and vice versa). The fight wasn't over by the time we went to press, so check the instructions on a phone booth or in a phone book, ask a friendly New Yorker, or dial 0 and ask the operator. Calls between 212, 646, and 718 cost 25¢.

For long-distance calls: To make a direct domestic long-distance call, check first for the carrier in the manner I've described above. If the carrier is one on my list, then dial 1, the area code, and the seven-digit local number. To make an operator-assisted long-distance call (collect, credit card, and so on), check first for the carrier, then dial 0, the area code, and the local number. An operator will come on the line. Companies like AT&T, Sprint, and MCI have access codes (for instance, if you have an AT&T account, dial 10-ATT-0 and then follow the directions above) that should get you directly onto their lines. Phone numbers with an 800, 877, or 888 area code are toll-free calls; those with a 900 area code are billed at an extra, sometimes astounding, rate.

For direct international calls: Check for the carrier and then dial 011, the country code, the city code, and the phone number. To make an **operator-assisted call,** check for the carrier and then dial 01, the country code, the city code, and the phone number; an operator will come on the line after the call is dialed. Some country and city codes are as follows: **Australia** 61, Melbourne 3, Sydney 2; **Ireland** 353, Dublin 1; **New Zealand** 64, Auckland 9, Wellington 4; **United Kingdom** 44, Belfast 232, Birmingham 21, Glasgow 41, London 71 or 81. You can request to be connected with an overseas operator by dialing 0.

Most hotels have **fax** machines available for their guests, usually for a charge in addition to the cost of the call. Some stationary stores and copying centers also have public fax machines. Be prepared for a rate of $5 for the first page. Some hotels will even charge you for *receiving* a fax, which costs them nothing other than paper, since the caller pays for the connection. Feel free to express your deep displeasure with this minor but annoying gouging.

Telephone Directories   The local phone company provides two kinds of phone directories. The most useful one for travelers is the **Yellow Pages,** which lists local business and services by industry type. Look there for automobile-rental agencies, drugstores, places of worship, and all kinds of other information. At the front of the book, the Inside Interest Pages are a guide to Manhattan with museums and sites, transportation information, seating plans of some sports stadiums and performance centers, and much more. An address locator immediately follows.

The general directory, the **White Pages,** lists personal residences and businesses separately in alphabetical order by name. The first few pages are devoted to community-service numbers and include a guide to long-distance and international calling and a list of area and country codes. At the center of the White Pages, edged in blue, is a guide to local, state, and federal government offices.

For local directory assistance (area codes 212, 646, and 718), dial ☎ **411.** This is a free call from Bell Atlantic public pay phones and can also be used to ask addresses. For numbers in all other area codes, check the carrier, then dial **1,** the appropriate area code, and ☎ **555-1212.**

Time   The United States covers such a large area that it falls across six time zones, an important thing to keep in mind when calling and traveling long distances. From east to west, standard time zones are eastern (EST), central (CST),

A Phone Call Warning

Before calling from a hotel room, ask the hotel operator if there are any surcharges for local or long-distance calls and which company carries the calls. There are almost always unacceptably high additional charges, and they can be as much as $1 even for a local call. You can avoid these charges by using a public pay phone, calling collect (which in itself can cost more), or, the best choice, using a telephone calling card (refer to the rules of the company from which you got the card). Feel free to inform the management that you find such surcharges offensive.

---

mountain (MST), Pacific (PST), Alaska (AST), and Hawaii (HST). When it's noon in New York City, it's 11am in Chicago, 10am in Denver, 9am in Los Angeles, 8am in Anchorage, and 7am in Honolulu.

In most of the United States (except Arizona, Hawaii, and part of Indiana) daylight saving time is in effect from the first Sunday in April to the last Saturday in October. In other words, clocks are set 1 hour ahead in spring and turned 1 hour back in fall (mnemonic device: spring ahead, fall back).

For the correct local time in New York, dial ☎ 212/976-1616.

Tipping   Tips are a very important part of certain workers' salaries, so it's necessary to leave appropriate gratuities. Unlike in most of Europe, tips aren't automatically added to restaurant and hotel bills. A tip to the waitperson of 15% to 20% of the total check is customary (in New York City just double the 8.25% tax to figure the appropriate tip).

Other tipping guidelines: 10% to 15% of tab to bartenders, $1 to $2 per bag to bellhops, 15% to 20% of the fare to taxi drivers, $1 per day to hotel maids, $1 per item to checkroom attendants, $1 to valet parking attendants, and 15% to 20% to hairdressers. Tipping theater ushers, gas station attendants, and cafeteria and fast-food restaurant employees isn't expected.

Traveler's Assistance   Travelers Aid helps distressed travelers with all kinds of problems, including accident, sickness, and lost or stolen luggage. The New York City office is on the second floor at 1451 Broadway, at 41st Street (☎ 212/944-0013); there are also offices in the international arrivals buildings at JFK Airport (☎ 718/656-4870) and at Newark Airport (☎ 201/623-5052).

4

Getting to Know
New York City

Each of New York's Neighborhood's has its own identity, and the larger city is in effect a series of small towns. Even individual blocks and streets keenly safeguard their local characteristics. This chapter gives you an insider's take on Manhattan's mosᵗ distinctive neighborhoods and streets, tells you how to get around town, and serves as a handy reference to everything from personal safety to libraries and liquor.

1 Orientation

VISITOR INFORMATION

INFORMATION OFFICES   Here are convenient addresses where you can collect details about the city:

- **New York Convention & Visitors Bureau,** 870 Seventh Ave., between 52nd and 53rd streets (☎ **212/484-1222;** calls taken Mon–Fri 9am–5pm). The bureau is scheduled to open its new public information office in January 1999 (hours weren't yet determined at press time). If you didn't call the information hot line at ☎ **800/NYC-VISIT** before you left home to request literature, stop by the office to pick up subway maps, free tickets to TV tapings, discount coupons for theater tickets, and brochures on sightseeing, dining, shopping, and current happenings. The office also has a staffed information desk and computerized info kiosks.

- **Times Square Visitors Center,** in the Embassy Theater, Seventh Avenue between 46th and 47th streets (no phone at press time; open daily 8am–8pm). The city's first large-scale tourist office occupies a renovated landmark 1925 theater. Several agencies operate here: The **Times Square Business Improvement District** staffs an information desk, **Gray Line Tours** sells tickets for bus tours and Circle Line boat tours, the **League of American Theaters and Producers** sells full-price theater tickets (the TKTS booth across the street will still sell discounted tickets), and the **Metropolitan Transportation Authority (MTA)** sells subway MetroCards. In addition, there'll be public rest rooms, ATMs, computer terminals with Internet access operated by Yahoo, and a newsstand. You might want to spend the day!

  The Times Square Visitors Center also offers **free Times Square walking tours,** on Fridays at noon, rain or shine, led by an actor who explores the Theater District's architecture, history, and current trends.

- **Grand Central Partnership,** at Grand Central Terminal, East 42nd Street at the corner of Vanderbilt Avenue (☎ **212/818-1777**). There's an information window inside the newly restored Grand Central Terminal and a cart out front, open Monday to Friday 8:30am to 6:30pm and Saturday and Sunday 9am to 6pm.
- **34th Street Partnership,** in Penn Station, Seventh Avenue between 31st and 33rd streets (☎ **212/868-0521**). This window is open Monday to Friday 8:30am to 5:30pm and Saturday and Sunday 9am to 6pm. The group also maintains carts at the Empire State Building (year-round), Fifth Avenue and 34th Street; outside Madison Square Garden, Seventh Avenue at 32nd Street (except when it's colder than 30°F outside); and in Greeley Square, 32nd Street where Broadway and Sixth Avenue cross (summer only). The carts are open daily 9:15am to 4:45pm.
- **Manhattan Mall,** Sixth Avenue and 32nd Street (☎ **212/465-0500**). Travelers' tips are available on the first floor of this vertical series of shops Monday to Saturday 10am to 8pm and Sunday 11am to 6pm.
- **Big Apple Greeter** (☎ **212/669-8159**). Specially trained volunteer New Yorkers take visitors around town for a free 3- to 4-hour visit of a specific neighborhood. And I bet you'd heard New Yorkers were rotten to the core! You must call at least 1 week ahead to arrange a visit. The office is open Monday to Friday 10am to 5pm.
- **South Street Seaport Visitors' Center,** 12 Fulton St., at Front Street (☎ **212/748-8600**). Mainly a welcome center for Seaport visitors, its museum, and the surrounding neighborhood, the center nonetheless provides some general information like subway maps. It's open 10am to 5pm in winter (to 6pm in summer).
- **Heritage Trails** (☎ **888/4-TRAILS**). This company operated two information kiosks last year from mid-May to the end of October and is likely to be running them again this year during the same months. Located in front of Trinity Church (at Broadway and Wall Street) and in Pier A plaza (in Battery Park), the kiosks distribute information on major attractions and sell Heritage Trails walking tour tickets. They're staffed Monday to Saturday 9am to 3pm.

PUBLICATIONS   For comprehensive listings of films, concerts, performances, theater, operas, ballets, sporting events, museum and gallery exhibits, street fairs, and special events, there are many local publications, with world status, to choose from. Refer to the Friday and Sunday editions of the ***New York Times,*** the weekly newspapers the ***Village Voice*** and ***New York Press*** (both free in Manhattan), and the weekly magazines ***New York, The New Yorker,*** and ***Time Out New York.***

CITY LAYOUT

Open the sheet map that comes free with this book and you'll see the city comprises five boroughs: **Manhattan,** where most of the visitor action is; the **Bronx,** the only borough connected to the mainland; **Queens,** where Kennedy and La Guardia airports are located and which borders the Atlantic Ocean and occupies part of Long Island; **Brooklyn,** which is also on Long Island and is famed for its attitude, accent,

---

Impressions

I love New York. I've always loved New York. And I love it as much now as when it was New Amsterdam.

—George Burns

and Atlantic-front Coney Island; and **Staten Island,** the least populous borough, bordering Upper New York Bay on one side and the Atlantic Ocean on the other.

I'll take Manhattan as my primary focus, for all the obvious reasons. Even in New York, when people in the "outer" boroughs talk about "going into the city," they mean going to Manhattan Island, the long finger of bony high-rises pointing southwest off the mainland and surrounded by the Harlem River to the north, the Hudson River to the west, the East River (really an estuary) to the east, and the fabulous expanse of Upper New York Bay to the south. Most of what makes New York famous is on this, its smallest borough (13½ miles long, 2¼ miles wide, 22 square miles).

Nearly all of Manhattan is laid out on a grid system of numbered streets and avenues that meet at right angles. The dividing line between this orderly pattern and the chaotic older jumble of streets to the south is about at 14th Street. In the warren of neighborhoods below 14th—including Greenwich Village, the East Village, the Lower East Side, Little Italy, NoHo, SoHo, Chinatown, TriBeCa, and the South Street Seaport and Financial District (Lower Manhattan)—you'll need our sheet map and an appreciation for serendipitous discovery, if not humor. Even New Yorkers often find themselves confused when they're at the corner where West 4th Street intersects West 11th Street. Ask nearly any New Yorker if Pell Street runs parallel to Division Street, and you're likely to get a "How would I know?"

Still, north of 14th Street, the rational grid system adopted in 1811 makes finding your way easy. A New Yorker's hint: Never say "ave." for "avenue." Rushed though New Yorkers are, they always find time for this peculiarly formal appellation.

Avenues run north and south ("uptown" and "downtown"). Most are numbered. **Fifth Avenue** divides the east side from the west. **First Avenue** is all the way east and **Twelfth Avenue** is all the way west. **Broadway,** the paved tracing of an ancient Native American trail, is the exception—it runs more or less straight north-to-south from the northern end of the island until it reaches West 79th Street, where it begins to cut a diagonal from the northwest to the southeast nearly all the way to the tip of the island. Three of the more important unnumbered avenues on the East Side, most north of about 14th Street, are **Madison** (east of Fifth), **Park** (east of Madison), and **Lexington** (east of Park). Unnumbered avenues at various points on the West Side are **Avenue of the Americas** (which all New Yorkers call Sixth Avenue), **Central Park West** (Eighth Avenue north of 59th Street), **Columbus Avenue** (Ninth Avenue north of 59th), and **Amsterdam Avenue** (Tenth Avenue north of 59th).

Avenue addresses are irregular. For example, 994 Second Avenue is at East 51st Street but so is 320 Park Avenue; thus it's important to know a building's cross street to find it easily.

Streets run east and west (crosstown) and are numbered consecutively increasing to the north, beginning from 1st Street a block north of Houston Street. East 51st Street, for example, begins at Fifth Avenue and runs to the East River, and West 51st Street begins at Fifth Avenue and runs to the Hudson River. Even-numbered street addresses are on the south side and odd on the north. Street addresses increase by about 50 per block starting at Fifth Avenue. For example, in the grid north of 14th Street, nos. 1 to 50 East are just about between Fifth and Madison avenues, while nos. 1 to 50 West are just about between Fifth and Sixth avenues. Traffic generally runs east on even-numbered streets and west on odd-numbered streets, with a few exceptions, like the major thoroughfares—**14th, 23rd, 34th, 42nd, 57th, 72nd, 79th, 86th,** and so on—which have two-way traffic.

Whenever you're giving a taxi driver an address or whenever you're given an address by someone, always specify or ask for the cross streets or avenues. New Yorkers, especially most cab drivers, wouldn't know where to find 994 Second Avenue, but they do know where to find 51st and Second. Again, don't simply ask for the numbered address of the Museum of Modern Art, ask where it is and what it's between: "53rd Street between Fifth and Sixth avenues." The numbered avenue or street address is given only as a further precision. In this guide, cross streets are provided after most street addresses. If you have only the numbered address on an avenue and need to figure out the cross street, put new batteries in your calculator and refer to the address locator in the front of the Yellow Pages.

Another way New Yorkers indicate location is with the terms ***uptown*** and ***downtown.*** *Uptown* means north of where you happen to be and *downtown* south. But Uptown and Downtown also refer to vague psychographical aspects of the city and evoke the attitudes and lifestyles of the people who live there (as in Billy Joel's mind-numbingly repetitive, but useful for this example, "Uptown Girl"). The exact meaning depends on who's doing the talking and where they happen to be standing.

The same goes for ***east side*** and ***west side.*** Something can be located on the east side, meaning east of Fifth Avenue. But *the* East Side most likely refers to the Upper East Side and perhaps alludes to the neighborhood's stereotypically upscale reputation. *Downtown* can mean more artsy, more black clothing, and more wacky independence.

Some people who live below 14th Street claim they get a nosebleed once they pass north of that physical and psychological boundary; some who live on the East Side snobbishly report that they never go below 14th Street. Go figure.

NEIGHBORHOODS IN BRIEF

Manhattan neighborhoods differ as much as some cities. None has exact boundaries and all have multiple, splintered personalities. Here's my take on each, starting at the southern tip of the island and proceeding north through the most important neighborhoods—including the city's central artery, Fifth Avenue.

Lower Manhattan: South Street Seaport & the Financial District   Twisting narrow concrete canyons, tracing the city's earliest thoroughfares and Native American pathways, yield to dramatic vistas across the seaside enormity of Upper New York Bay. The area south of Chambers Street, including the Battery, Wall Street, South Street Seaport, and City Hall, is both the oldest and the newest part of Manhattan: oldest because this is where the island was first settled by the Dutch in 1625 and newest because 30% of the land is fill (the skyscrapers rest firmly on bedrock).

Hiding in the shadows of the neo-Gothic Woolworth Building, the modern highrise Twin Towers, and the postmodern World Financial Center are such historic buildings as the 1766 St. Paul's Chapel (Manhattan's oldest church) and the 1907 reconstruction of the Federal-style Fraunces Tavern (originally built in 1719 and in which Washington bade farewell to his officers). The wonderful parkland of Battery Park City, greenbelting the World Financial Center and various kinds of residential architecture, hugs the Hudson and provides seductive views of the Statue of Liberty.

During the week this neighborhood is the heart of capitalism (the Stock Exchange) and politics (City Hall), and the sidewalks are crowded with the business-suit set. But

A Map Note

Though Midtown is officially the area between the Hudson and East rivers from 34th to 59th streets, the Midtown maps in this guide have been extended to include 14th to 59th streets.

it's a nine-to-five district and empty on weekends, so urban romantics take advantage of the freedom to stroll the pedestrian-only parts of Nassau Street, visit its historic sites, or gaze up at the skyscrapers' magnificent architectural details on their way to Battery Park, where they depart for the Statue of Liberty and Ellis Island.

One fine way to wend your way through the serpentine arteries is by following the self-guided Heritage Trails tours (pick up a four-color map and guide for $1 at Federal Hall, 26 Wall St., at Nassau, or at the information kiosks in front of Trinity Church, at Broadway and Wall Street, and at Pier A in Battery Park).

The city is encouraging residential development in the area, which will mean lots of changes—such as apartments and lofts replacing office space and an increase in late-night eateries, services, and pedestrians—over the coming years.

TriBeCa   North of Chambers Street, west of Broadway, and south of Canal Street is the *Tri*angle *Be*low *Ca*nal Street, or TriBeCa. Since the 1980s, as SoHo became saturated with chic, the spillover has been quietly transforming TriBeCa into one of the hippest new residential neighborhoods, populated by stars and everyday families, which has earned it the nickname Triburbia.

Historic streets like White (especially the Federal-style building at no. 2) and Harrison (the complete stretch west from Greenwich Street) evoke a bygone, more human-scaled New York. Alongside the history is an ever-more firmly rooted arts and dining scene—cutting-edge galleries and independent filmmakers (Robert DeNiro's Tribeca Film Center) are setting up shop in former industrial buildings next door to hot new restaurants (DeNiro again, co-owner of Nobu and Tribeca Grill) frequented by the famous and their tagalongs. Recently, the *People* magazine crowd, including heart-quickener Brad Pitt and the now-unavailable John F. Kennedy Jr., has been gobbling up co-ops and condos in the area around North Moore Street.

Chinatown   New York City's most famous ethnic enclave is bursting past its traditional boundaries and encroaching on Little Italy and the Lower East Side.

The neighborhood's narrow bustling streets, south from Canal west to Broadway and east to East Broadway, are lined with fragrant—sometimes pungent—fish and vegetable markets, exotic bakeries, curiosity shops, and hundreds of inexpensive restaurants. If you're looking for a San Franciscoesque Chinatown with colorful pagodas, you may be disappointed, since old tenements and lofts prevail (though some phone booths have been tricked up with pagoda-like toppings).

But who needs faux Chinese in such a vigorous community? Questionable curiosities, like a ticktacktoe-playing chicken, crowd next to mysterious herbal medicine shops and, to Westerners, indecipherable signs and sounds. Dining is the main draw, and it's not just for mainland Chinese anymore thanks to the recent influx of Vietnamese, Thai, and Hong Kongese restaurants. On Sunday, when the rest of New York quietly sips Uptown caffè lattes while brunching over the *New York Times,* Chinatown is at its liveliest during dim sum time.

SoHo   In the early 1960s, cutting-edge artists began occupying drab and deteriorating 19th-century manufacturing lofts. This artistic outpost quickly became, and still is, the trendiest neighborhood in the city. Located *So*uth of *Ho*uston (pronounced "*House*-ton") and north of Canal Street between Lafayette Street and Sixth Avenue, SoHo is a major attraction for its historic cast-iron architecture, influential arts scene, fashionable restaurants, and stylish boutiques.

The SoHo Historic District encompasses within 26 blocks the highest concentration of cast-iron architecture in America. The landmark Haughwout Building at Broadway and Broome Street is a jewel. On weekends, the cobbled streets and narrow sidewalks, especially SoHo's main drag of West Broadway, are crowded with gallery goers and serious shoppers.

Walk along Greene Street and look up at the stunning ensemble of columns, roofs, and elaborate details—it's all in cast iron, not stone. For a quick view of a purer SoHo, back before gentrification and all the boutiques, head east of Broadway to Crosby Street between Spring and Broome, where a chimera of cobblestoned 19th-century New York survives the concrete present.

Some critics claim that SoHo is becoming a victim of its own popularity—witness the recent departure of several imaginative galleries and independent boutiques to TriBeCa and Chelsea as well as the influx of suburban mall–style stores like Eddie Bauer, Williams-Sonoma, and Smith & Hawken. Profitable commerce doesn't have to dictate that proper art galleries be replaced by poster stores or that unique shops give way to outlets found all across America. I hope.

Little Italy In the early 1900s this neighborhood, bounded by the Bowery and Broadway on the east and west and Canal and Houston streets to the south and north, was populated nearly 100% by people of Italian birth or heritage.

Today Mulberry Street, the main artery, is virtually all that recalls the authentic sights, sounds, and smells of Little Italy's heyday—groceries with homemade pasta, cheese, and sausage; shops with Italian imports like records and hand-painted bowls; garlicky aromas and boisterous laughter emanating from family restaurants; creamy cannoli and crunchy biscotti stacked high in pastry-shop windows; and the *ssssccchhh* of machines frothing milk for cappuccino. A few women still stand in the doorways speaking with the fast-disappearing peculiar accent that combines Southern Italian influences with New York street tawk. The big event, the Feast of San Gennaro festival, takes place every September.

Architectural highlights in the area are Old St. Patrick's Cathedral (1809–15), the former Police Headquarters with baroque detailing (1909, now luxury condos for the likes of Cindy Crawford), and the Romanesque Revival Puck Building (1855). Lately there has been a kind of drift from SoHo (mainly hippish restaurants and cafes) into these once-mean streets, centered on the corner of Prince and Mott.

The Lower East Side In 1894, the 4 square miles that made up the Lower East Side were the most densely populated on earth, with 986 people per acre. Of all the successive waves of immigrants and refugees who passed through here from the mid–19th century to the 1920s, it was the Eastern European Jews who left the most lasting impression on the neighborhood, which extends south of Houston to Canal Street and east of the Bowery.

This is the place in Manhattan for mouth-puckering pickles straight from the brine barrel and fresh-from-the-oven bialys. It also boasts the city's only kosher winery (Schapiro Wine Co., 126 Rivington St.) and matzoh bakery (Streit Matzoh Co., 150 Rivington St.), despite the fact that the neighborhood today is mostly Hispanic (about 40%) and Asian (about 30%). The signposted Historic Orchard Street Bargain Shopping District bustles on Sunday (many stores are closed Saturday for

Impressions

Nobody's going to come from the boondocks anymore and live in SoHo and be an artist. You can't afford to park there, let alone live there.

—Pete Hamill

Jewish Sabbath). The Lower East Side Tenement Museum offers a poignant glimpse into 19th-century immigrant life. But be careful in your wanderings—there are some desolate and crime-ridden streets. Avoid the area at night.

Greenwich Village   Tree-lined streets crisscross and wind, following ancient streams and cow paths. Each block reveals yet another row of Greek Revival town houses, a well-preserved Federal-style house, or a peaceful courtyard or square. This is "the Village," from Broadway west to the Hudson River, bordered by Houston Street to the south and 14th Street to the north. It defies Manhattan's orderly grid system with streets that predate it, and unless you live here it may be impossible to master the lay of the land. Three lovely streets for a promenade back through history are Bedford (note the extremely narrow house at no. 75½ and the rebuilt clapboard Federal at no. 77), Commerce (note the twin mansard roofs at nos. 39 and 41), and the entire crescent of St. Luke's Place.

Free love, bohemia, poetic musings, and general seductive batty behavior have been and are the nonconformist balance for the genteel feeling of many of its quiet, sometimes even family-friendly, blocks. It was 19th-century artists like Mark Twain, Edgar Allan Poe, Henry James, and Winslow Homer who first gave the Village its reputation for embracing the unconventional. Later, it was home to generations of painters, poets, writers, musicians, political radicals, and starry-eyed students.

Culture and counterculture rub shoulders in caffès, internationally renowned jazz clubs, neighborhood bars, small theaters, and an endless variety of tiny shops and restaurants. The Village was where the 1969 Stonewall Riot gave form to the modern gay-rights movement, on Christopher Street, still a center of the gay community even if it has faded from its central importance in the 1970s. On warm afternoons, Washington Square Park is a stage for street performers and a study lounge for students at New York University, whose sometimes ill-considered buildings are scattered around the neighborhood and sometimes clash in visual violence with their surroundings. The Victorian Gothic Jefferson Market Library (1874–77), at Sixth Avenue and 9th Street, is now a library but was once a prison (if you come during spring or summer note the beautiful garden behind it tended by the neighbors). And it seems that every other address marks the spot where a famous book was penned, play was previewed, speakeasy was hidden, or even spirit of the past still haunts.

Beneath the nostalgic patina, however, be wary of the shady characters in the sometimes seedy area west of Hudson Street, especially at night, when cross-dressers lease dubious charms to an odd mix of customers. On weekends, groups of boisterous teenagers commute in to hang out on Bleecker, West 4th, 8th, and surrounding streets. Washington Square Park was cleaned up a couple of years back, but there's never any telling when the pusher man will be back.

At the Hudson River end of Christopher Street, you could begin a wonderful walk along the river. A party atmosphere often reins at the foot of Christopher, but you can quickly escape the sometimes threatening feel (don't worry!) and thumping music and amble peacefully either north or south. Many local residents use the piers for sunbathing, sometimes charmingly *au naturel.* Watch for the development of Hudson River Park, which should stretch from the Battery to the tip of Manhattan all along the river, to make this area blossom in the years to come.

The East Village & NoHo   This is arguably Manhattan's most eclectic neighborhood, a fantastic, funky weave of 100-year-old Italian pastry shops, still-vibrant

Manhattan Neighborhoods

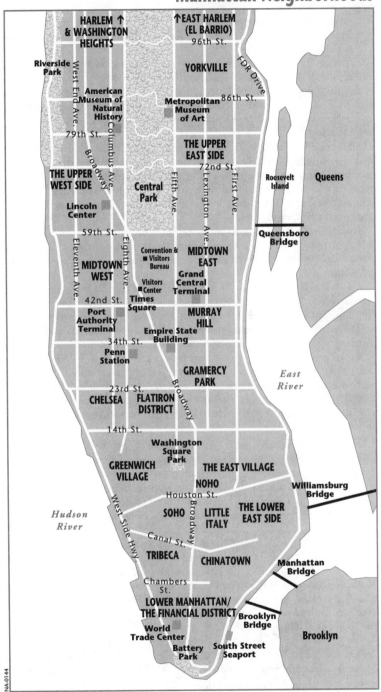

HARLEM ↑ & WASHINGTON HEIGHTS

↑EAST HARLEM (EL BARRIO)

96th St.

Riverside Park

YORKVILLE

West End Ave.

FDR Drive

American Museum of Natural History

86th St.

Metropolitan Museum of Art

79th St.

Columbus Ave.

Broadway

THE UPPER EAST SIDE

THE UPPER WEST SIDE

Central Park

72nd St.

Fifth Ave.

Lexington Ave.

First Ave.

Roosevelt Island

Queens

Lincoln Center

Queensboro Bridge

59th St.

Eighth Ave.

Eleventh Ave.

MIDTOWN WEST

Convention & Visitors Bureau

MIDTOWN EAST

Visitors Center

Grand Central Terminal

42nd St.

Times Square

Port Authority Terminal

Empire State Building

MURRAY HILL

34th St.

Penn Station

GRAMERCY PARK

East River

23rd St.

Broadway

CHELSEA

FLATIRON DISTRICT

14th St.

Washington Square Park

GREENWICH VILLAGE

THE EAST VILLAGE

NOHO

Houston St.

SOHO

Broadway

LITTLE ITALY

THE LOWER EAST SIDE

Williamsburg Bridge

Hudson River

Canal St.

West Side Hwy.

TRIBECA

CHINATOWN

Manhattan Bridge

Chambers St.

LOWER MANHATTAN/ THE FINANCIAL DISTRICT

Brooklyn Bridge

World Trade Center

Battery Park

South Street Seaport

Brooklyn

NA-0144

47

Ukrainian and Polish enclaves, cheap ethnic eateries next door to trendy restaurants, tiny kitschy boutiques, independent Off and Off Off Broadway theaters, after-hours clubs, and folk-music cafes.

East from Third Avenue and stretching from Houston to 14th streets, it's home to a constantly changing cast of characters that includes young professionals, longtime residents, young gays and lesbians, cross-dressers, squatters, drug addicts, street walkers, and a few punk rockers who don't realize—or perhaps simply can't remember—that spiked orange hair left town with Sid Vicious. St. Mark's Place is the main thoroughfare.

Until the 1960s, the East Village was considered just a part of the Lower East Side and experienced successive waves of immigrants whose presence remains. By the 1950s the Beat Generation took up residence, and by the 1960s it had received its present moniker, once the hippies tripped psychedelically through its walkups and head shops. The punks came next, and then, for a brief but shining moment in the 1980s, it was the hottest arts scene in town.

For a view of a more genteel time in the East Village's past, visit 21 Stuyvesant St., which survives with much restoration from 1804, and the Renwick Triangle's town houses, dating from 1861 (both sites are between Third and Second avenues, at about 10th Street).

Always stay alert in the East Village: The landscape changes from one block to the next, especially the farther east you go, and venture only with care beyond Avenue A into Alphabet City (avenues B, C, and D)—these streets can be dangerous.

The western section, around Broadway and Lafayette, sometimes called NoHo (for *No*rth of *Ho*uston), is experiencing a renaissance marked by stylish restaurants and funky antiques shops, and even a Kmart (with a great view south from its bad cafeteria) at Astor Place. The area is also an architectural treasure trove that includes the sadly neglected but heroically beautiful remains of the Colonnade Row mansions (1833); the Greek Revival Old Merchant's House (1832), remarkably intact inside and out; the Joseph Papp Public Theater (1849–59); Cooper Union (1859); and many lovely cast-iron buildings.

Chelsea   A low-rise, very gay-friendly composite of town houses, tenements, lofts, and factories, Chelsea comprises roughly the area west of Sixth Avenue from 14th to 30th streets. Its main artery, Eighth Avenue, is a series of eclectic shops and good, well-priced restaurants, including Italian, French, Hispanic, American, and *comidas chinas y criollas* (a curious blend of Chinese and Cuban foods brought to this country by immigrants who first tried to escape Communism by leaving Asia for Cuba and then left Cuba for North America). Gyms, late-night clubs, and thriving bars spice the mix.

The Chelsea Hotel, on 23rd Street between Seventh and Eighth avenues, is an architectural and literary landmark, fronted by delicate ironwork balconies and with a reputation for being home to all kinds of writers and artists (Mark Twain, Thomas Wolfe, and Tennessee Williams were guests; Sid Vicious killed girlfriend Nancy Spungeon here). Handsome town houses fill the blocks from 20th to 22nd streets, from Ninth to Tenth avenues, in an area that once was the farm of Clement Clarke Moore, the author of *A Visit from St. Nicholas*.

One of the most influential trends in Chelsea has been the establishment of a "gallery row" on far West 22nd Street and its vicinity (especially of note: Paula Cooper, Matthew Marks, and Feigen Contemporary). The power of art can also be seen in the Joyce Theater, now New York's principal modern-dance venue, and the Kitchen (formerly of SoHo), which cooks up an experimental stew of music, video, and performance art. This new direction—along with the burgeoning indoor/outdoor weekend flea market trade along Sixth Avenue north of 23rd Street, the development of the Chelsea Piers sports complex, and the renovation of the area's historic buildings—has led to a new morning for Chelsea.

The Flatiron District & Gramercy Park   These adjoining and at places overlapping neighborhoods are my favorites. Dotted with four small historic parks (Union Square, Gramercy, Madison Square, and Stuyvesant), their streets have been rediscovered by citizens, realtors, and visitors. The area has evolved into the city's hippest and best place to eat, spend frenzied time at late-night clubs, and shop for everything from tasteful housewares to used books and records, from Agnès B. to J. Crew, from super-stores to antiques boutiques. The commercial spaces are often large loftlike expanses with witty designs and graceful columns.

The Flatiron District, from 14th to 23rd streets, from Park Avenue South to Sixth Avenue, is dense with nearly uniformly preserved buildings from its heyday in the late 19th and early 20th centuries. Patrician cast-iron structures stand straight up against more whimsical architecture, such as the Flatiron Building, the cake slice of undulating, rusticated limestone and terra-cotta that lends the district its name.

Within the larger, more amorphous Flatiron District is the officially designated Ladies' Mile Historic District, where such venerable institutions as Tiffany & Co. and Lord & Taylor once catered to the carriage trade. Today again, many fine home furnishings stores (ABC Carpet & Home is seductively beautiful and fittingly expensive) and other classy shops occupy the elegant spaces. In Union Square, perhaps the most beautiful small park in Manhattan, don't miss the Greenmarket, where regional farmers sell fresh produce, flowers, and baked goods (Monday, Wednesday, Friday, and Saturday). On the western side of Union Square are numerous trendy restaurants and sidewalk cafes. At no. 33 Union Square West, and later at 860 Broadway, Andy Warhol had his Factory in its earliest, most psychedelic years (but by the time he was shot, he had moved the Factory uptown to the then-chicer climes of Murray Hill).

The stretch of Fifth Avenue here has undergone a shopping renaissance in the last few years. In the blocks from 14th to 23rd streets, you can now find the boutiques of Joan & David, Paul Smith, Emporio Armani, Kenneth Cole, and Otto Tootsi Plohound, as well as more popular shopping at the Body Shop, Express, the Gap, Banana Republic, and J. Crew. A block west, on Sixth Avenue, department stores that attracted the middle class in the 19th century have been recently restored to a magnificent series of large-scaled emporia offering everything from jeans to the mind-boggling housewares selections at Bed Bath & Beyond. Also on Sixth are a number of off-price bargain heavens, such as Burlington Coat Factory and Filene's Basement.

Gramercy Park is the area's eastern quarter, from about 16th to 23rd streets, from Park Avenue South to about Second Avenue. On Park Avenue South in the upper teens and 20s, where Gramercy meets Flatiron, is a lively restaurant-and-bar singles scene. Gramercy Park itself, at 21st Street and Lexington Avenue, is a 1½-acre oasis of green securely locked behind a wrought-iron fence (it's the city's only surviving private park; note the statue of actor Edwin Booth, brother of Lincoln assassin John Wilkes, in its center). Embellishing the lovely park are exclusive apartment buildings, one-time mansions including those lodging the National Arts Club and the Players, and two charming houses on the west side with New Orleans–style ironwork porches.

For a true discovery of old New York, visit the blocks around Stuyvesant Square, most notably Rutherford Place and East 15th, 16th, 17th, and 18th streets from Third to Second avenues. Graceful old row houses and large leafy trees mix with historic buildings of the Friends (or, less officially, the Quakers), who maintain places of worship and schools near Stuyvesant Park.

At the northern edge of the two neighborhoods, on 23rd Street and Fifth Avenue, is another of Manhattan's lovely little parks, Madison Square. Across from its northeastern corner once stood Stanford White's original Madison Square Garden (in whose roof garden White was murdered in 1906 by possibly deranged, but definitely jealous, millionaire Harry K. Thaw). It's now surrounded by the overly massive New York Life Insurance building, the masterful New York State Supreme Court building, and the Metropolitan Life Insurance Company, whose tower in 1909 was the tallest building in the world at 700 feet (at night the now-stripped-down colorfully lit top shimmers).

All along Park, Broadway, Fifth, and Sixth, progressive computer, publishing, and advertising companies occupy many of the upper floors of the exquisite turn-of-the-century buildings. For more on this area, see "Neighborhoods of Note" in chapter 7.

Fifth Avenue   This is Manhattan's articulating spine. Through it pulsates the city's life force and from it flows an animated élan. Your first acquaintance with this prominent axis is on the restrained stretch called Museum Mile, starting at El Museo del Barrio at 104th Street and then paralleling Central Park as it passes the Museum of the City of New York, the International Center of Photography at 94th Street, the Guggenheim, and other highlights of the city's cultural capital, until it ends at the Metropolitan Museum of Art at 82nd Street.

The rich digs of the upper crust front the eastern side of Fifth, facing the park across the street. Jacqueline Kennedy Onassis lived and died here (at no. 1040), and scandal-tainted but still brilliant New Yorker Woody Allen, various Rockefellers, uncounted well-heeled industrialists, media magnificents, and social-arbitrating poobahs still do.

Dividing the island into west and east, Fifth Avenue offers a wondrous walk starting at 60th Street, at the entrance to Central Park, and heading south through the middle of Midtown's jumbled retail offerings, from the popular to the nearly priceless—FAO Schwarz, Bergdorf Goodman, Warner Bros., Tiffany's, Walt Disney, Christian Dior, Cartier, the Gap, and the NBA Store.

World-famous landmarks line the glittering canyon: self-aggrandizing Trump Tower, imposing art deco Rockefeller Center, the neo-Gothic flamboyance of St. Patrick's Cathedral, the beaux arts New York Public Library, the steely beauty of the Empire State Building, and then, all the way downtown, to the curious wedge-shaped Flatiron Building at 23rd Street and even farther to the arch in Washington Square Park, where the avenue ends. Fifth evolves from haute couture to tchotchkes, from reputable merchants to electronics-and-rug-store rip-off artists, from staid to eccentric, from the 20th century and back through time.

Midtown West & the Garment District   This vast area from 34th to 59th streets west of Fifth Avenue encompasses several smaller neighborhoods. The most important are the Theater District and Times Square, ablaze in neon and activity and undergoing massive redevelopment.

There's no city like New York City for musicals, dramas, and comedies. Most of the great Broadway theaters light up the streets just off Times Square. The XXX theaters, 25¢ peep shows, and porn shops are nearly all gone. In their place is an ongoing renewal that has emphasized family-oriented and tourist-friendly entertainment (the Walt Disney Company is playing a major role), restored theaters, lively theme restaurants (Official All Star Cafe, Comedy Nation, Copperfield Magic Underground), and retail shops (Virgin Megastore and a branch of the Warner Bros. store). Sensory bombardment is the rule, with ever-more-daring neon signs lighting up the world's crossroads.

The renovations and repopularization of Times Square, the former capital of sleaze, have been largely successful. It's bright with lights, noise, and mobs of the overstimulated with strained necks and excited voices. Everyone who comes to New York will want to stop in Times Square to glance around at all the larger-than-life advertising billboards, gigantic neon displays, and, at 42nd street on the Times Square Building (where the New Year's Eve ball drops), the giant Panasonic video screen and the "zipper" at its waist, updating you on world events, the stock market, and sports. A newer, zippier "zipper" is on the Stanley Morgan Building at 47th Street. On the norteast corner of 42nd and Seventh stands the spanking-new headquarters of Condé Nast Publications, the take-no-prisoners publisher of chic titles like *Vanity Fair, Glamour, Vogue, GQ,* and, appropriately, *Self* (plans at press time called for a new ESPN sports-themed restaurant to open the premises). They've joined others in making Time Square both the capital of popular entertainment and a nerve center of mass communications.

West 57th Street, along with Times Square, has seen its fair share of change recently, with an explosion of theme restaurants like the Hard Rock Cafe and the Motown Cafe, which flaunt their nouveaux-riche status nearly next door to old–New York nobility like Carnegie Hall. Planet Hollywood, the restaurant, landed first on 57th Street, but it plans to lift off and set down in the new Planet Hollywood Hotel in Times Square by the end of 1999.

Midtown West is also home to the Museum of Modern Art, Restaurant Row, Radio City Music Hall, the Diamond District, and the *Intrepid* Sea-Air-Space Museum.

Very important for New York, though not necessarily for visitors unless you're profiting from the sample sales, is the Garment District, running along Seventh Avenue in the 30s. This capital of the fashion industry is housed in buildings, dour from the outside, that hide sometimes fabulous interiors where top designers set style's standards. Streets bustle with double-parked trucks, rolling carts hung with frocks and furs, and flyers announcing sample sales.

Important for both New Yorkers and visitors is the well-priced shopping district centered at Herald Square, Sixth Avenue and 34th Street. Like its Midtown cousin Times Square a few blocks north, Herald Square, and all of 34th Street, has been the focus of a renaissance, in large part inspired by the city's booming tourist business. For years the grayish pink shopping bags of the decidedly downscale but popular Conway's, which has three stores on 34th Street, have been staples of the bargain-hunting set. Now with Macy's and the Gap as anchors, at 34th and Sixth, lots of other popularly priced stores have moved in: There's Dr. Jay's with a vast selection of designs and designers (lots of hip-hop apparel, as well as Calvin Klein, Ralph Lauren, and Timberland), Payless Shoes, Foot Locker, Athlete's Foot, Banana Republic, Structure, Limited Express, HMV, and, as if to grant the big-boys' stamp of approval, even Kmart (just west of Seventh) and Disney (just west of Fifth).

The Manhattan Mall, at 33rd and Sixth, has reclaimed its pride and vibrates with life again. Nearby, at 33rd and Seventh, the Hotel Pennsylvania is undergoing—thank the stars, both kinds—an 18-month restoration that'll transform it into the sports-themed Official All Star Hotel, yet another product from the people who brought you Planet Hollywood. On Eighth Avenue between 31st and 33rd streets, 36 years after a new generation of robber barons stole from us the irreplaceable original Penn Station (by McKim, Mead & White), the beaux arts beauty of the main post office, with its two-street-long row of Corinthian columns (also by McKim, Mead & White), is being reborn as the new public area of Penn Station. Expect this burst of business and renewal to stay on a roll as long as the tourists keep coming.

Midtown East & Murray Hill   The area east of Fifth Avenue from 34th to 59th streets has more subtle, if aloof, charms than its western counterpart. It's no less engaging.

Magnificent architectural highlights include the recently repolished Chrysler Building with its stylized gargoyles glaring down on passersby. Park Avenue from 46th to 57th streets boasts some of the great masterpieces of the International Style of architecture, including the glass-clad Lever House and the superbly proportioned Seagram Building. Surviving amid these postwar beauties and serving as a visual-reference counterpoint are such landmarks from an earlier New York as the Racquet and Tennis Club and St. Bartholomew's, both of which bare the stamp of the city's great turn-of-the-century architectural geniuses, McKim, Mead & White.

The neighborhood includes many of the city's most venerated old-time hotels (the Waldorf-Astoria), high-priced world-renowned restaurants, and corporate headquarters. Midtown East also claims the beaux arts tour de force Grand Central Terminal, which has recaptured, after a massive renovation, its rightful place as a gallant and uplifting entry point to this great city.

The stretch of 57th Street between Fifth and Lexington avenues has been known for high-fashion boutiques (Chanel, Burburry, Hermès) and high-ticket galleries (Marlborough, Leonard Hutton), but change is underway since Warner Bros., Levi's, and Nike squeezed in their more popular attractions. Still, even with the arrival of these typical mall stores, Chanel is sure to stay, having put up a tasteful tower that's in the fine Manhattan tradition of alluring modern architecture.

Far east, swank Sutton and Beekman places are enclaves of beautiful town houses, luxury living, and tiny pocket parks that look out over the East River. Along this river is the United Nations, which isn't officially in New York City, or even the United States, but is on a parcel of international land belonging to member nations.

Murray Hill, which actually begins somewhere north of East 23rd Street, is most clearly recognizable in the area north of 34th Street to 42nd Street, from Third to Madison avenues. This residential quarter, lined with beautiful brownstones, evokes the quiet neighborhoods of London. Among its gems are the charming carriage house at 148 E. 40th St. and the entire block of East 38th, all between Lexington and Third avenues. Sniffen Court, at 150–160 E. 36th St., also between Lexington and Third, consists of Romanesque Revival brick houses from about 1850 set back in a picturesque mews. In 1905, Cass Gilbert, responsible for the frothy pile called the Woolworth Building, created a lovely French- and Italian-inspired town château at 37th Street and Madison Avenue (now the Consulate General of Poland). The area's visitor and cultural highlight is the Pierpont Morgan Library at 36th and Madison.

The Upper West Side & Morningside Heights   North of 59th Street and west of Fifth Avenue, the Upper West Side contains Lincoln Center, arguably the world's premier performing-arts center; the American Museum of Natural History, whose renovated Dinosaur Halls reopened a few years back to rave reviews and whose Hayden Planetarium was recently torn down so a 21st-century version can go up in its place; and, stretching all the way across to the East Side, Central Park, an 843-acre urban playground and masterpiece of landscape design.

Central Park West has a distinctive skyline marked by the towers of luxury apartment buildings like the art deco Majestic and the massive and eerie Dakota, both at 72nd Street and occupied by stars of films, TV, and CDs. Just off Central Park (76th Street) and along Riverside Drive (75th to 77th streets and around 105th Street) are enclaves of elegant brownstones, now home to the neighborhood's mainly yuppie population. A vibrant, democratic, but gentrified street life can be seen on Broadway, especially from 72nd to 86th streets, though too many ungainly high-rises have been put up in the last few years. In an undisguised attempt to imitate the broad boulevards of Paris, Broadway's backbone is a central island of green dividing the uptown from the downtown traffic. (At some spots, it's lovely to get a bench here on sunny days, though often beer-drinking types and threadbare gardening threaten the mood.)

There's good shopping and lots of sidewalk-cafe life on Columbus Avenue (especially from Lincoln Center to 86th Street) as well as on certain parts of on-again/off-again Amsterdam Avenue in the 70s and 80s. Farther north is the area called Morningside Heights—be awake and alert if you walk here near the Cathedral of St. John the Divine, which likes to bill itself as the world's largest Gothic cathedral, and Columbia University.

The Upper East Side   The main attraction of the neighborhood north of 59th Street on the East Side is Museum Mile (see "Fifth Avenue" above) fronting Central Park.

Manhattan's wealthiest families live from Lexington to Fifth avenues, from 60th to 78th streets, with Park Avenue the most sought-after address. Its reserved facades mask opulent apartments as big as houses, two to three stories high with private elevator landings, fanciful staircases, and soaring entryways. Let alone the furniture!

Within the confines of the neighborhood are wonderful one-time mansions (Henry Clay Frick's, now housing the Frick Collection, and Andrew Carnegie's, now the Cooper-Hewitt Museum), two important synagogues (the Fifth Avenue Synagogue and Temple Emanu-El), terribly private clubs (the Metropolitan at Fifth and 60th), and an elegant mélange of landmarked town houses: neo-Georgian, neo-Renaissance, and Italianate, of limestone and brownstone, bowfronted and richly detailed. East 70th Street, just beyond the Frick from Madison east to Lexington, is to my eye one of the world's most charming residential urban passages. Gracie Mansion, East 88th Street at the East River, is something you don't see every day in this city—a house set in its own green park, and it's reserved for the mayor.

Affordable restaurants and active street life, including lots of singles meeting grounds, aren't found here until you move to Third Avenue and east.

Credit-card shoppers will find paradise on Madison Avenue in the boutiques of upscale designers like Armani (in a cool, quiet modern Tuscan building that I like but has some neighbors turning up their high-profile noses), Valentino, Moschino, Prada, and Ralph Lauren (in a fanciful neo–French Renaissance landmark mansion with sculpted ornamentation, chimneys, and dormers, at 72nd Street). Calvin Klein's home items and fashions are displayed in a pristine zenlike new store. Prestigious art galleries (Knoedler and Hirschl & Adler) line the same avenue and its side streets.

Harlem & East Harlem   The area north of 110th Street to 168th Street, from the East and Harlem rivers, to Morningside Heights and St. Nicholas Avenue, has become again a visitor destination. During the glorious days of the Cotton Club and other late-night jazz centers, African-American music worked its way under the skin and into the veins of the entire planet, eventually leading to rock 'n' roll, Motown, and rap and transforming nearly every aspect of contemporary pop culture.

Though the long lines of limousines no longer stretch beside its late-night hang-outs, Harlem is the destination of choice for things like Sunday-morning gospel services (the Abyssinian Baptist Church, at 138th Street between Seventh and Lenox avenues, is popular) and soulful well-priced restaurants. Plans are that by the time you read this, there should be an entertainment-and-shopping complex at 125th Street and Frederic Douglass Boulevard. Called Harlem U.S.A., it will occupy a site that has seen its promise dissipate in the past. But if the dream this time comes true, you could find yet another Disney Store, yet another Cineplex Odeon, and yet another Old

Navy. A nearby draw (at 118th Street and Adam Clayton Powell Jr. Boulevard) is Minton's Playhouse, a revival of a legendary restaurant/jazz club, recently developed by Drew Nieporent and Robert DeNiro, partners in many TriBeCa ventures.

Within this too-often-hazardous neighborhood (certain areas, such as Frederick Douglass Boulevard from 110th to about 125th, aren't recommended for foot tourism), fabulous enclaves of brownstones, cultural centers, and, of course, churches provide an opportunity to experience a different facet of New York. On Sugar Hill (from 143rd Street to 155th Street, between St. Nicholas and Edgecombe avenues) and Striver's Row (West 139th Street between Adam Clayton Powell Jr. and Frederick Douglass boulevards) are a significant number of fine town houses. For cultural visits, there's the Morris-Jumel Mansion, the Schomburg Center, the Studio Museum, and the Apollo Theater. Farther east and south, Italian restaurants still occupy Pleasant Street, and the Spanish Harlem open-air market enlivens Park Avenue.

Don't wander thoughtlessly through Harlem, especially not at night. And if it's your first time here, you should join a group tour—day or night.

Washington Heights & Inwood   At the northern tip of Manhattan, Washington Heights encompasses the area from 155th Street to Dyckman Street, and Inwood runs north of that to the end of the island. Fort Tryon Park is the main draw for its sweeping, serene views of the towering Palisades across the Hudson River and, more important, for the Cloisters, which houses the Metropolitan Museum's medieval collections in a building that incorporates parts of medieval monasteries and churches. The Dyckman Farmhouse was built in 1783 and, now a museum, remains the only remaining Dutch Colonial structure in Manhattan. It's the historic crown jewel of this overlooked neighborhood.

Inwood Hill Park is Manhattan's only remaining stretch of "primeval" forest, meaning it has never been harvested for trees or developed for buildings, but stands as it did in the days before Europeans colonized the island. Since this northern reach of Manhattan was the last neighborhood developed for residential use, there are many fabulous art deco apartment buildings.

2 Getting Around

Between gridlock and subway delays, you often just can't get there from here, unless you're on foot—especially when you're going crosstown in Midtown at midday. Slip into something comfortable and hit the pavement.

BY SUBWAY

It screeches, it stinks, it's scary, and it's as much a part of the city as the Empire State Building. In fact, the subway is about 30 years older than the Empire State and needs even more internal maintenance. But you really can't miss the experience. Some 3.5 million people per day zip through the hole in the ground that delivers them where they're going quickly and inexpensively. The bedraggled subway, or "train" as it's called here, carries its bedraggled riders 7 days a week, 24 hours a day, to major destinations and attractions faster than buses and certainly more cheaply than taxis.

The **subway fare** is $1.50 (half price for seniors and the disabled), and children under 3 feet 8 inches tall ride free (up to three per adult). You can pay the fare with **tokens,** but why bother anymore since the **MetroCard**—a magnetically encoded "credit" card that debits the fare when swiped through the turnstile—is so much cheaper and easier. It can be used for up to four people by swiping up to four times (bring the whole family), and MetroCards, but not tokens, allow you to transfer free

On the Sidewalks of New York

Walking and (tsk! tsk!) jaywalking are the major means of self-propulsion for New Yorkers, and they stride across wide but crowded pavements with skill, dodging taxis, buses, bike messengers, in-line skaters, unscooped poop, and other pedestrians (including people huddled over maps—Yo! Pull over!) I recommend that you never take your walking cues from the natives. Wait for walk signals and always use crosswalks to avoid becoming a flattened statistic. You wouldn't want to take home a jaywalking ticket as a souvenir, now would you?

Another hint: Walk as if you're driving, staying to the right and paying attention to such things as cars and buses that don't yield the right of way and to bikers who blithely break the law—flying along sidewalks and dashing the wrong way on one-way streets.

You'll want to wander more slowly than New Yorkers take to eat a full meal—so avoid moving too many abreast. As a friend of mine says, slow-moving or stalled groups seem like rocks in a stream that force the flow around them. To me, in the game of sidewalk, large groups advance like a clumsy football line absentmindedly interrupting a nimble basketball press.

from buses to subways or vice versa within a 2-hour period (swipe just once for transfers for up to 4 people). In addition, every time you put $15 or more on a MetroCard, it's automatically credited 10%—that's one free ride for every $15.

Unlimited-use MetroCards, which can't be used for more than one person, are available as 1-day ($4), 7-day ($17), and 30-day ($63) passes. MetroCards and tokens are for sale at token booths located in the stations. Maps are available at most token booths and tourist information centers.

The subway system basically recapitulates the lay of the land above ground, with most lines in Manhattan running north and south, like the avenues, and a few lines east and west, like the streets—see the subway map on the inside back cover of this book. To go up and down the East Side and to the Bronx and Brooklyn, take the 4, 5, or 6 train. To travel up and down the West Side and also to the Bronx and Brooklyn, take the 1, 2, 3, or 9 line; the A, C, E, or F line; or the B or D line. The N and R lines first cut diagonally across town from east to west and then shake under Seventh Avenue before shooting out to Queens. The crosstown S line, the Shuttle, runs back and forth, back and forth, between Times Square and Grand Central Terminal. Downtown, across 14th Street, the L line works its own crosstown magic.

The outsides of some subway entrances are marked UPTOWN ONLY (northbound) or DOWNTOWN ONLY (southbound); read carefully, as it's common for visitors to head in the wrong direction. (If you do make a mistake, wait for a major station like 14th Street or 42nd Street so you can get off and change for the other direction without paying again.) The days of graffiti-covered cars are gone (forever, please!), and most are air-conditioned (though during the dog days of summer the platforms are about as comfortable as an auto-da-fé).

For travel directions and information, call the **New York City Transit's Travel Information Center** at ☎ **718/330-1234** (daily 6am–9pm). To request the *Token Trips Travel Guide* brochure, which gives subway and bus travel directions to more than 120 popular sites, call the Customer Service department at ☎ **718/330-3322** (weekdays 9am–5pm).

Subway Safety Tips

In general, the subways are safe, especially in Manhattan. There are panhandlers and questionable characters like anywhere else in the city, but subway crime has gone down to 1960s levels. Stay alert and trust your instincts. Don't chat up strangers, watch your personal belongings, and step lively getting off the train.

It's best to use the subway only during the day and early evening; take a bus or taxi later on. If you do travel off-hours or a station is uncomfortably empty, wait for the train in view of the token booth clerk or in off-hours waiting areas marked by yellow signs suspended from the ceiling. Always ride with the conductor, who's usually in the center, and most crowded, car (you'll see his or her head stick out when the doors open). Empty or nearly empty cars are that way for a good reason. Don't ride in the last car.

BY BUS

Less expensive than taxis and more user-friendly than subways (they provide a mobile sightseeing window on Manhattan), buses are a good transportation option. Their very big drawback: They get stuck in maddening Midtown gridlock when you might as well walk—or crawl on all fours.

Bus stops are located every 2 or 3 blocks on the right-side corner of the street (facing the direction of traffic flow). They're marked (or are supposed to be marked) by a curb painted yellow and a blue sign with a bus emblem and the route number or numbers. Guide-A-Ride boxes at most stops display route maps and hilarious schedules. Most routes operate 24 hours, but service is infrequent at night. Some say that New York buses have a herding instinct: They come only in groups. During rush hour, main routes have "Limited" buses, identifiable by the red card in the front window; they stop only at major cross streets. To make sure the bus you're boarding goes where you're going, just ask. The drivers are helpful, as long as you don't hold up the line.

Each major avenue has a bus route running uptown or downtown and connecting with crosstown bus lines at major intersections, including Madison/Chambers streets, Houston, 8th/9th, 14th, 23rd, 34th, 42nd, 49th/50th, 57th, 66th/67th, 72nd, 79th, 86th, 96th, and so on. If you pay with a MetroCard (see "By Subway"), you can transfer free to another bus or even to the subway for up to 2 hours, unless you've chosen the unlimited-rides options (see "By Subway"), which gives you nearly complete transfer freedom. If you use a token, you must request a free transfer slip that allows one change only to an intersecting bus route (legal transfer points are listed on the transfer paper) within 1 hour of issue. Transfers from tokens can't be used to enter the subway.

The **bus fare** (like the subway fare) is $1.50, payable with a **MetroCard, subway token,** or in **exact change.** Like the subway, buses honor the various discount Metro-Card plans that the MTA introduced last year. Bus drivers don't make change, and fare boxes don't accept dollar bills or pennies. The fare for seniors and for passengers with disabilities is 75¢, and children under 3 feet 8 inches tall ride free (up to three per adult). While traveling, look out the window, not only to take in the sights but also to keep track of cross streets so you know when to get off. Signal for a stop by pressing the tape strip above and beside the windows and along the metal straps. Exit through the pneumatic back doors (not the front door) by pushing on the yellow tape strip; the doors open automatically—pushing on the handles is useless unless you're as buffed as Hercules. Most city buses are equipped with wheelchair lifts. They also "kneel," lowering down to the curb to make boarding easier.

You can find bus maps at most tourist information centers and in some subway stations, but rarely on buses. For travel directions, call the **New York City Transit's Travel Information Center** at ☎ **718/330-1234** (daily 6am–9pm).

BY TAXI

Forget about hopping into the back seat and having some double-chinned, cigar-chomping, all-knowing driver slowly turn and ask nonchalantly, "Where to, Mac?" Nowadays taxi drivers speak only an approximation of English and drive in engagingly exotic ways. Things have gotten so bad that the city has provided drivers with a list of polite phrases ("It would be a pleasure to help you put your luggage in the trunk!"— yeah, sure!) and posting a TAXI RIDER'S BILL OF RIGHTS sticker in the cabs. While waiting for improvements, we can take comfort that the average fare in Manhattan— $5.75—makes a taxi ride here a bargain compared to the rates in the world's other major cities.

Official New York City taxis, licensed by the Taxi and Limousine Commission, are yellow, with the rates printed on the door and a light with a medallion number on the roof. Never accept a ride from any other "taxi" service. You can hail a taxi on any street, and drivers are required by law to take you anywhere in the five boroughs, to Nassau or Westchester counties, or to Newark Airport. A taxi is available if the center light on the roof (with the number) is illuminated.

The **base fare** on entering the cab is $2 (a surcharge of 50¢ is added 8pm–6am). The cost is 30¢ for every $^1/_5$ mile or 20¢ per minute in stopped or very slow-moving traffic. Don't let the few dishonest cabbies con you: There's no extra charge for each passenger or for luggage. However, you must pay bridge or tunnel tolls (sometimes the driver will front the toll and add it to your bill at the end; most times you pay the driver before the toll). A 15% to 20% tip is customary. Always ask for the receipt—it comes in handy if you need to make a complaint or have left something in a cab. For complaints and lost property, call ☎ **212/221-TAXI**. A taxi isn't required to take more than four people.

Putting on a seat belt in the back of a cab is good idea you can now act on—the city has finally forced taxis to provide working belts. At the same time, invasive as ever, the city decided to remind riders to buckle up and take their belongings by pumping into cabs the often-too-loud recorded voices of luminaries like Plácido Domingo, Judd Hirsch, and Joan Rivers.

BY CAR

Forget it. It's not worth the headache. You don't know the rules of the road (written or unwritten) or the arcane alternate-side-of-the-street parking regulations. You don't want to find out the monstrous price of parking violations or the Kafkaesque tragedy of liberating a vehicle from the tow pound. If you do arrive in New York City by car, park it in a garage (expect to pay at least $20 to $30 per day) and leave it there for the duration of your stay. If you drive a rental car in, return it as soon as you arrive and rent another on the day you leave.

BY TRAIN TO THE SUBURBS

New York residents love Manhattan—and long to leave it any chance they get. Four regional railroads whisk weekend travelers to unexpectedly lovely Atlantic Ocean and Long Island Sound beaches, summer houses, historic sites, and nature in the outer boroughs, suburbs, and beyond.

The **Long Island Rail Road** (☎ **718/217-5477**) runs from Pennsylvania Station, at Seventh Avenue between 31st and 33rd streets, to Queens (ocean beaches, Shea Stadium, Belmont Park) and points beyond on Long Island (even more spectacular beaches and exclusive summer hot spots like Fire Island and the Hamptons).

Metro North (☎ 800/638-7646 outside the city, or 212/532-4900) departs from Grand Central Terminal, 42nd Street and Lexington Avenue, for areas north of the city where there are historic homes (like Hyde Park), golf courses, and yacht clubs in such destinations as Westchester County, the lovely hillsides of the Hudson Valley, and the swank precincts of Connecticut.

The Port Authority Trans-Hudson **PATH** (☎ 800/234-7284 or 201/216-6557) system connects New Jersey, including Hoboken and Newark, to Manhattan by subway-style trains (stops in Manhattan are at the World Trade Center, Christopher and 9th streets, and along Sixth Avenue at 14th, 23rd, and 33rd streets). **New Jersey Transit** (☎ 800/772-2222 or 201/762-5100) operates some commuter trains directly to Pennsylvania Station and others that connect to the PATH trains.

If you're planning to investigate the areas around Manhattan, you may want to check out *Frommer's Wonderful Weekends from New York City.*

FAST FACTS: New York City

Ambulance Dial ☎ 911.

American Express Travel service offices are at many Manhattan locations, including Macy's, at Herald Square, Sixth Avenue and 34th Street (☎ 212/695-8075). For a few more addresses, see "Currency Exchange" under "Fast Facts: For the Foreign Traveler" in chapter 3.

Area Codes From late 1998, there'll be three area codes in the city: two in Manhattan, **212** and **646,** and **718** for Brooklyn, the Bronx, Queens, and Staten Island. At press time, dialing procedures for local calls hadn't been determined. Before making a call, check for instructions in a phone book or on a phone booth or dial 0 and ask the operator. It may always be necessary to dial 11 digits (1, the area code, and the number), even when making a call in the same area code.

Automobile Rental See "Fast Facts: For the Foreign Traveler" in chapter 3.

Business Hours See "Fast Facts: For the Foreign Traveler" in chapter 3.

Dentists The Dental Emergency Service at ☎ 212/679-3966 makes referrals and Preventive Dental Associates at ☎ 212/683-2530 accepts same-day appointments and has a 24-hour answering service.

Doctors For medical emergencies requiring immediate attention, head to the emergency room of the nearest hospital (see "Hospitals" below). For other health problems, and to avoid emergency-room waits, there are several walk-in medical centers, like the **New York Healthcare Immediate Care,** 55 E. 34th St., between Park and Madison avenues (☎ 212/252-6001). The clinic, affiliated with Beth Israel Medical Center, is open Monday to Friday 8am to 7pm and Saturday and Sunday 9am to 2pm. An office visit is about $100. A 24-hour referral service for doctors who make house calls can be reached by calling ☎ 212/737-2333. One excellent physician, who sees patients by appointment, is Anthony Bennardo, my own doctor, at 126 E. 19th St. (☎ 212/529-5222). Tell him I sent you.

Embassies/Consulates See "Fast Facts: For the Foreign Traveler" in chapter 3.

Emergencies Dial ☎ 911 for fire, police, and ambulance. The **Poison Control Center** is at ☎ 212/764-7667 or 212/340-4494.

Fire Dial ☎ 911.

Hospitals   Downtown: New York Downtown Hospital, 170 William St., at Beekman Street (☎ **212/312-5000**); St. Vincent's Hospital, Seventh Avenue and 11th Street (☎ **212/604-7000**); and Beth Israel Medical Center, First Avenue and 16th Street (☎ **212/420-2000**). **Midtown:** Bellevue Hospital Center, First Avenue and 27th Street (☎ **212/562-4141**); New York University Medical Center, First Avenue and 33rd Street (☎ **212/263-7300**); and Roosevelt Hospital Center, Tenth Avenue and 58th Street (☎ **212/523-4000**). **Upper West Side:** St. Luke's Hospital Center, Amsterdam Avenue and 113th Street (☎ **212/523-4000**). **Upper East Side:** New York Hospital's Emergency Pavilion, York Avenue and 70th Street (☎ **212/746-5050**), and Lenox Hill Hospital, 77th Street between Park and Lexington avenues (☎ **212/434-2000**). Don't forget your insurance card.

Hot Lines   The 24-hour Crime Victims Hot Line is ☎ **212/577-7777**; Sex Crimes Report Line ☎ **212/267-7273;** Suicide Prevention Help Line ☎ **212/532-2400;** Samaritans' Suicide Prevention Line ☎ **212/673-3000;** local police precinct numbers ☎ **212/374-5000;** Department of Consumer Affairs ☎ **212/487-4444.**

Libraries   The main research branch of the New York Public Library is on Fifth Avenue at 42nd Street (☎ **212/340-0849**). This beaux arts beauty houses more than 38 million volumes. Don't miss the special exhibits and behind-the-scenes tours. The visually stunning reading rooms should be restored to their former glory this year. More efficient and modern, if less charming, is the mid-Manhattan branch at 40th Street and Fifth Avenue, across the street from the main library. There are other branches in almost every neighborhood, including the very sleek and modern Science, Industry, and Business Library in the former B. Altman Department store on 34th Street between Fifth and Madison.

Liquor Laws   See "Drinking Laws" in "Fast Facts: For the Foreign Traveler" in chapter 3.

Newspapers/Magazines   See "Fast Facts: For the Foreign Traveler" in chapter 3.

Pharmacies   There are two 24-hour pharmacies, both Duane Reades, one at Broadway and 57th Street (☎ **212/541-9708**) and the other at Third Avenue and 74th Street (☎ **212/744-2668**).

Police   Dial ☎ **911** to reach the police in an emergency; otherwise, call ☎ **212/374-5000** for the number of the nearest precinct.

Post Office   The main New York City post office is on Eighth Avenue between 31st and 33rd streets and open 24 hours (☎ **212/967-8585**). There are branches and drop boxes throughout the city.

Rest Rooms   Public rest rooms are as hard to come by as an empty taxi in a downpour. The new Visitors Center in Times Square (the Embassy Theater, Seventh Avenue between 46th and 47th streets, open daily 8am–8pm) should have facilities. Grand Central Terminal has cleaned up its rest rooms, somewhat—great news if you're in Times Square or Grand Central. But only out of desperation should you take your chances with places like Penn Station and Port Authority, where cleanliness is not highly regarded. Your best bet is to head to hotel lobbies, museums, and department stores like Macy's, Lord & Taylor, and Bloomingdale's. Restaurants often post intimidating signs like REST ROOMS FOR CUSTOMERS ONLY, but if you look clean-cut and ask nicely (or beeline it to the john), you shouldn't have a problem. There's a program underway to install self-cleaning pay public toilets in the parks, but I wouldn't try to hold it.

The Top Safety Tip

Trust your instincts, because they're usually right. Walk with a sense of purpose and self-confidence and don't stop in the middle of the sidewalk to pull out and peruse your map. You'll rarely be hassled. If you do find yourself accosted by someone with or without a weapon, remember to keep your anger in check and that the most reasonable response (maddening though it may be) is *not* to resist.

Safety Thanks to Hollywood films, political posturing in Washington, and sensationalistic journalism, many out-of-towners believe creepy characters leer from every doorway waiting to attack every unsuspecting passerby. That's only true sometimes. There's crime in New York City, but millions of people spend their lives here without being robbed and assaulted. In fact, New York is safer than any other big American city, listed by the FBI as somewhere around 150th in the nation for total crimes. Still, you aren't in Kansas anymore (the countryside of Kansas, that is—since Kansas City itself is *not* less dangerous than New York). Visitors can make particularly easy and usually obvious targets for swindlers and thieves, so you should always follow basic precautions.

Men should carry their wallets in their front pockets and women should keep constant hold of their purse straps. Cross camera and purse straps over one shoulder, across your front, and under the other arm. Never hang a purse on the back of a chair or on a hook in a bathroom stall; keep it in your lap or between your feet with one foot through a strap and up against the purse itself. Avoid carrying large amounts of cash. You might carry your money in several pockets so if one is picked the others might escape. Skip the flashy jewelry (especially if it's fake) and keep valuables out of sight when you're on the street.

Panhandlers are seldom dangerous but should be ignored (more aggressive pleas should firmly be answered, "Not today"). New Yorkers who aren't up to no good won't walk up to you with some long sob story ("I live in the suburbs and was just attacked and don't have the money to get home"). If someone approaches you with an elaborate tale, it's most definitely a confidence game. Walk away and don't feel bad. Be wary of an individual who "accidentally" falls in front of you or causes some other commotion because he or she may be working with someone else who will take your wallet when you try to help. You will lose if you place a bet on a sidewalk card game or shell game. Never accept a ride from a limousine or gypsy cab that's not an official yellow medallion taxi. Though subways run 24 hours, it's best to take a bus or taxi after 9 or 10pm (see "Getting Around" earlier in this chapter).

The Lower East Side, the deep East Village, the western fringes of the Times Square area, much of Harlem, and the city parks are best avoided at night. If you plan on visiting the Bronx or many sections of Brooklyn at any time of day, take a taxi directly to and from your destination and don't wander the side streets. In the rest of the city, if you find yourself on a deserted street that feels unsafe, it probably is. Leave as quickly as possible.

Remember that New York has experienced a dramatic drop in crime and, especially in the neighborhoods visitors are prone to frequent, is (I'll say it again) generally safer than other American cities.

Taxes **Sales tax** is 8.25% on meals, most goods, and some services, though there has been political chatter about reducing or eliminating it, especially on clothing under $500. **Hotel tax** is 13.25% plus $2 per room per night (including sales tax). **Parking garage tax** is 18.25%.

Transit Information For information on getting to and from Kennedy, La Guardia, and Newark airports, see "Getting There" in chapter 2 or call **Air-Ride** at ☎ **800/247-7433.** For information on subways and buses, see "Getting Around" earlier in this chapter or call the **New York City Transit's Travel Information Center** at ☎ **718/330-1234** (daily 6am–9pm). To request the brochure *Token Trips Travel Guide,* which gives subway and bus travel directions to more than 120 popular sites, call ☎ **718/330-3322.**

Traveler's Assistance See "Fast Facts: For the Foreign Traveler" in chapter 3.

Useful Telephone Numbers The number for the New York Convention and Visitors Bureau once you're in the city is ☎ **212/484-1222** (Mon–Fri 9am–5pm). For the correct time, ask a friendly stranger or dial ☎ **212/976-1616.** For the current weather and next day's forecast, check the upper-right corner of the *New York Times* or call ☎ **212/976-1212.** For phone numbers and addresses, dial ☎ **411, 212/555-1212,** or 646/555-1212 (a free call from Bell Atlantic pay phones). For the latest information on movies, call ☎ **212/777-FILM.**

5

Accommodations

New York's hotels have been kept nearly full and their rates at historic highs by the seemingly endless waves of visitors who all want to have their date with one of the world's most desirable urban destinations. Occupancy rates have gone through the high-rise roofs, to the loftiest level since the 1940s. For the first qaurter of 1998, these rates will hit an average of 80.5%, compared with 76.4% for the same period in 1997. And prices have followed: Average room rates hover around $189, an increase of almost 14% over 1997's first-quarter rates making New York the country's most expensive hotel town.

What you'll need before you begin searching for a place to stay is this chapter, where you'll find the best hotels in every price range. I let you in on the famous palaces and the secret bargains: lush rooms full of fresh flowers overlooking the twinkling skyline, no-nonsense midlevel modern rooms with all the amenities, and Spartan rooms with little in the way of comforts that are still clean and safe.

THE RULES OF THE GAME　The most important rule: Whether you want a high-priced pleasure palace or a no-frills bargain property or something in between, *always ask for the lowest-priced package available.* Find several hotels that look appealing and call them all. (That's why I've included every available toll-free number.)

Reservation agents won't volunteer the information—you have to pull it out of them and have to be open-minded. Are you coming to New York on the weekend? Most hotels offer dramatically less expensive weekend packages. Are you a senior citizen? Then ask about senior discounts. Or inquire about holiday, family, or all-inclusive packages with meals, theater tickets, or sightseeing tours. Corporate rates are frequently available to individuals.

Another tip: Look in the Travel section of the Sunday *New York Times* for some of the best weekend deals. Also note that one hotel might offer a large suite with a terrace for the same price as a small but more luxurious room in another hotel. Decide which feature is more important to you.

Manhattan is a small island, but which neighborhood to stay in may figure in your considerations. If you're coming just for the weekend, decide what you want to do in that short time. If you're here to shop, Midtown East hotels offer easy access to upscale Madison Avenue shops and all the major department stores. Midtown West hotels are within walking distance of Times Square and most Broadway theaters.

Getting New York Real

Nearly anyone can find a room to fit nearly any budget in this chapter, as long as you get New York real: The rooms in lower-priced hotels are *not* as good as those in the higher-priced categories—only cheaper. There are bargain hotels, but don't expect the Plaza at motel prices. If it is a bargain you're looking for, reserve well in advance and use the strategies laid out on the following pages.

Choose a hotel on the Upper East Side if you're coming especially to see Museum Mile. If you want to concentrate on the Statue of Liberty, Ellis Island, SoHo, and Chinatown, a Downtown hotel would be your best choice.

Finally, are you most comfortable with what you know, like Hilton, Marriott, or Hyatt? Or would you prefer the personal attention you might get at a smaller hotel, like the Mansfield or Morgans?

RESERVATION SERVICES These companies buy rooms in bulk and resell them to the public at rates claimed to be discounted. I recommend you first reserve directly with the hotel and then call one of these services to see if you can find a better price. All work with a limited number of hotels. **Accommodations Express** (☎ 800/950-4685) says it offers 10% to 40% discounts off rack rates. **Express Hotel Reservations** (☎ 800/356-1123) claims to extend savings of $29 to $80 per night with room rates between $99 and $265. **Hotel Reservations Network** (☎ 800/96-HOTEL) promotes savings of 20% to 50% off rack rates. **Quickbook** (☎ 800/789-9887) asserts it can take 60% off rack rates. And **Room Exchange** (☎ 800/846-7000) says it can offer 40% to 50% off rack rates.

BED & BREAKFASTS Surprise! There are thousands of B&Bs in New York, ranging from Spartan to splendid, dirt cheap to outrageous. A B&B stay can be especially economical for several people traveling together. Credit cards are often accepted only for the deposit; you may have to pay the balance with a traveler's check, certified check, or cash. I've received complaints about what B&Bs say they offer and what they actually deliver, so be sure to get all promises in writing and an exact total up front. And try to pay by credit card so you can dispute payment if the B&B fails to live up to its promises.

Here are some suggestions: **At Home in New York Inc.,** P.O. Box 407, New York, NY 10185 (☎ 800/692-4262 or 212/956-3125; fax 212/247-3294); **City Lights Bed & Breakfast,** P.O. Box 20355, Cherokee Station, New York, NY 10021 (☎ 212/737-7049; fax 212/535-2755); **Manhattan Home Stays,** P.O. Box 20684, Cherokee Station, New York, NY 10021 (☎ 212/737-3868; fax 212/265-3561); **Manhattan Lodgings,** 70 E. 10th St., Suite 18C, New York, NY 10003 (☎ 212/475-2090; fax 212/477-0420); **New World Bed & Breakfast,** 150 Fifth Ave., Suite 711, New York, NY 10011 (☎ 800/443-3800 or 212/675-5600; fax 212/675-6366); **New York Bed and Breakfast Reservation Center,** 331 W. 57th St., Suite 221, New York, NY 10019 (☎ 800/747-0868 or 212/977-3512); **Urban Ventures,** 38 W. 32nd St., Suite 1412, New York, NY 10001 (☎ 212/594-5650; fax 212/947-9320).

1 Best Bets

- **Best New Bargain to Watch For:** Ian Schrager (known for the high-end Royalton, Paramount, and Morgans, as well as for a slew of new acquisitions in 1998) has purchased the **Henry Hudson Hotel,** 353 W. 57th St., and says he'll turn the 1929 building into 700-suite property with rates around *$75 a night.* Don't expect luxury

Rooms to Grow

The New York hotel market is so strong that the industry's adding 6,000 beds by 2000, an increase of 10%. Here are some hotels, open either in late 1998 or likely to open in 1999 or early 2000, that hold the most promise.

The biggest news in bargains is taking shape at the **Henry Hudson Hotel,** 353 W. 57th St., with rates that, the owners claim, will be around $75 per night—*for a suite.* Upscale hotelier Ian Schrager bought the place and plans to use his usual partner in design, Philippe Starck, to create about 700 suites he describes as "modern YMCA." The hotel's name may change, and it may not open until 2000, but it's worth keeping an eye out for. Schrager, who also opened the Royalton, Paramount, and Morgans, went on a buying spree in 1998 and picked up the Barbizon, the McAlpin, the Radisson, and the St. Moritz.

The Downtown hotel scene is definitely heating up. When the **SoHo Grand** opened a couple of years back, at the southern end of this generally hotel-less region, it soon filled up with an artsy crowd. The **Mercer** has recently added another option for those in search of smart Downtown digs. Other hip purveyors of contemporary chic have plans of their own too.

Brian McNally, who launched Balthazar (see chapter 6), announced his intention to build **Astor Place,** a 180-room luxury hotel. Scheduled to open this spring, it's at Astor Place, on the corner of Lafayette Street, straddling the East and West villages. On a much smaller scale, restaurateur Jean-Claude Iacovelli, tired of hearing his European friends complain about SoHo's lack of inexpensive rooms, decided to open **Velli,** 132 W. Houston St. (☎ **212/979-7614**). Their gain can be yours too. The units—most with shared baths—go for about $100, but there are only 10, so call well in advance.

There's big news for those who like a theme atmosphere for their Midtown stays. Inspired by the success of the Official All Star Cafe in Times Square (see chapter 6), its owners have plans for New York's first Vegas-style theme hotel. The **Official All Star Hotel,** Seventh Avenue and 33rd Street, is scheduled to open across from Madison Square Garden after a much-needed $40-million renovation of the Hotel Pennsylvania. Among those in the All Star group are Planet Hollywood's president, Robert Earl.

And that leads to another deal. The folks on Planet Hollywood are also planning a theme hotel, which, barring last-minute financial drama, would bring the first **Planet Hollywood Hotel** to the southwestern corner of Broadway and 47th Street, in the heart of Times Square. The company's flagship restaurant on 57th Street is expected to move into the 50-story hotel. Scheduled opening? In time for New Year's Eve 1999.

It also seems that other theme purveyors, like Hard Rock Cafe, House of Blues, Harley-Davidson Cafe, the Virgin Group, and even Opry Land, have their sights set on building new New York hotels. "Extending the brand" is here big time!

at this price, but it definitely has great promise. Note that the hotel's name may change and it may not open until 2000 (see the box "Rooms to Grow").

- **Best New Year's Eve Lookouts:** Any rooms overlooking the Times Square celebration that'll be the universe's biggest and best bring-in-the-millennium party are likely to have been reserved years ago. Even so, it's worth calling the hotels

Midtown is also the site of many new or planned moderately priced hotels. **Marriott Courtyard** (☎ 800/321-2211) is converting an office building at 53rd Street and Third Avenue into a 320-room hotel and is constructing another with 244 rooms from the ground up at 40th Street and Sixth Avenue; rates are expected to be around $175 per night. **Holiday Inn** (☎ 800/HOLIDAY) has renovated the Martinique Hotel, with 531 rooms, at Broad-way and 32nd Street.

More expensive (rooms start at $245 per night), the **Fitzpatrick Grand Central**, 141 E. 44th St. (☎ 212/818-1746), is the second New York property for this Dublin-based company (the Fitzpatrick Manhattan Hotel was first). The 156-room Irish-theme hotel opened last May in a converted office building.

New York has been waiting a long time for the unnamed-at-press-time hotel going up at 42nd Street and Eighth Avenue, across from the Port Authority Bus Terminal. Designed by Arquitectonica, the Miami far-forward architectural group, the 600-room eyepopper, complete with a bolt of lightening zapping its facade, is rising to 57 stories, along with the rest of E-Walk, a 200,000-square-foot entertainment-and-retail complex to include a Sony multiplex theater and a theme restaurant.

The luxury Midtown market will expand with two notable additions. The American Radiator Building at 40 W. 40th St., an architectural gem with Gothic overtones that overlooks Bryant Park, is being recast as the 170-room **Bryant Park Hotel.** One of the partners? Brian McNally, again, so it ought to have style and attract the stylish, especially during the fashion shows. One of my favorite French hotel groups, luxury chain **Sofitel** (☎ 800/SOFITEL), will open its first New York property in a brand-new 30-story limestone-and-glass tower on 44th Street between Fifth and Sixth avenues, neighboring the Royalton, the Algonquin, and the Iroquois. The **Iroquois,** 49 W. 44th St. (☎ 800/332-7220), has undergone its own $10-million upgrade that could place it again in the top tier of the city's hotels—in both style and price (you'll easily pay $200 and up). By the way, James Dean fans, this is the place where he lived part of his notorious, short life, from 1951 to 1953. If you're looking for Dean's ghost, ask for room 803.

The Financial District will see several new hotels in 1999 and 2000, including the first hotel built in Battery Park City itself, an **Embassy Suites** (☎ 800/EMBASSY), which will be part of an entertainment complex overlooking the Hudson River. A 325-room **Ritz-Carlton** (☎ 800/241-3333) will occupy 10 floors of 17 Battery Place, and the Cipriani restaurant/hotel family promises "the most exclusive hotel in America" in a landmark building at 55 Wall St. Lots of noise has been coming from 55 Wall, where the fashionable and the merely rich have been gathering for paparazzi-heavy parties. Mix that with a name like Cipriani, and you have a whole new world way downtown.

that have some rooms with great views of the action: the **Crowne Plaza Manhattan,** 1605 Broadway (☎ 800/243-NYNY); **Doubletree Guest Suites,** 1568 Broadway (☎ 800/222-TREE); **Hotel Edison,** 228 W. 46th St. (☎ 800/637-7070); **Millennium Broadway,** 145 W. 44th St. (☎ 800/622-5569); **New York Marriott Marquis,** 1535 Broadway (☎ 800/843-4898);

and **Novotel New York,** 226 W. 52nd St. (☎ **800/NOVOTEL**). And the planned **Planet Hollywood Hotel,** at 47th Street and Broadway, could open in time for you and the family to watch the ball drop.

- **Best Service:** For the ultimate pampering, you can't do better than the **Carlyle,** 35 E. 76th St. (☎ **800/227-5737**), where the staff-to-guest ratio is two-to-one. But such personal attention in Manhattan comes with a price tag.

- **Best for Business Travelers:** In Lower Manhattan, the **Millenium Hilton,** 55 Church St. (☎ **800/835-2220**), and **Marriott World Trade Center,** 3 World Trade Center (☎ **212/938-9100**), tie for the title with their ideal locations and first-rate amenities. In Midtown East, the **Drake Swissôtel,** 440 Park Ave. (☎ **800/ DRAKENY**), has a convenient address as well as the Swissôffice business center, with, among other advantages, complimentary use of fully equipped meeting rooms for 2 hours.

- **Best for Computer Geeks:** At the **Casablanca Hotel,** 147 W. 43rd St. (☎ **888/ 922-7225**), you can sip complimentary cappuccino while surfing the Web on computers in the lounge.

- **Best for a Romantic Getaway:** Even harried New Yorkers stow away for a love-in weekend at the **Inn at Irving Place,** 56 Irving Place (☎ **800/685-1447**). Like a page stolen from a Gilded Age novel, the Inn is historically evocative, in 19th-century surroundings. Luxury is the rule, from an antique Victorian drawing room to graciously appointed guest rooms. Its Gramercy Park address and no-children-under-12 policy make for a very adult and very peaceful setting.

- **Best Trendy Hotels:** The **SoHo Grand,** 310 West Broadway (☎ **800/637-7200**), with its cool Downtown location and even cooler bar and restaurant, competes for star power with Ian Schrager's endlessly hip, intense "design statement" the **Royalton,** 44 W. 44th St. (☎ **800/635-9013**). My crystal ball tells me that the **Mercer,** 99 Prince St. (☎ **888/918-6060**), and the **Astor Place** and **Bryant Park** (see "Rooms to Grow") will soon nip at their hip heels.

- **Best Moderately Priced Hotel:** The **Hotel Metro,** 45 W. 35th St. (☎ **800/ 356-3870**), is a Midtown West gem that gives you a surprisingly good deal, including a marble bath. On the Upper East Side, the **Franklin,** 164 E. 87th St. (☎ **800/600-8787**), a stylish boutique hotel, is near Museum Mile.

- **Best Budget Hotel:** For plain and compact rooms in Greenwich Village, your choice is the **Washington Square Hotel,** 103 Waverly Place (☎ **800/222-0418**) or, *if* you don't mind sharing a bath, the **Larchmont,** 27 W. 11th St. (☎ **212/989-9333**). In Midtown East the **Quality Hotel Fifth Avenue,** 3 E. 40th St. (☎ **800/668-4200**), and in Midtown West the **Quality Hotel & Suites Rockefeller Center,** 59 W. 46th St. (☎ **800/567-7720**), offer affordable rooms smack in the middle of all the action.

- **Best Alternative Accommodations:** For a youthful international clientele and a friendly, artsy, late-night club atmosphere, book at the **Gershwin Hotel,** 7 E. 27th St. (☎ **212/545-8000**). The cheap (maximum $27) dormitory-style beds at **Hostelling International–New York,** 891 Amsterdam Ave. (☎ **212/932-2300**), are clean, and the place is well maintained and even has a garden out back.

- **Best Health Club:** Downtown, the **Marriott World Trade Center,** 3 World Trade Center (☎ **212/938-9100**), has one of the city's largest hotel pools and a great workout space, with views to match. In Midtown, **Le Parker Méridien,** 118 W. 57th St. (☎ **800/543-4300**), is home to Club La Racquette, a comprehensive fitness center with a rooftop pool and racquetball, squash, and handball courts. And the redone Midtown **Peninsula,** 700 Fifth Ave. (☎ **800/759-3000**), has a trilevel 35,000-square-foot fitness center and spa.

- **Best Views:** For looking out over Lower Manhattan, the **Marriott World Trade Center,** 3 World Trade Center (☎ **212/938-9100**), is unrivaled. Uptown, from a perch in the **Plaza,** 768 Fifth Ave. (☎ **212/759-3000**), Central Park rolls out like a long calm sea of green.
- **Best Hotel Restaurants:** Taking top honors is Sirio Maccioni's world-famous **Le Cirque 2000,** in the New York Palace, 455 Madison Ave. (☎ **212/303-7788**). The French cuisine is *magnifique;* the setting colorfully spectacular; and the crowd thin, rich, and mostly famous. Jean-Georges Vongerichten's latest table, **Jean Georges,** in the Trump International Hotel & Tower, One Central Park West (☎ **212/ 299-3900**), is discreetly elegant with prices to match. Stay at the Surrey Hotel if you want to sample Daniel Boulud's take on French classics at **Cafe Boulud,** 20 E. 76th St. (☎ **212/288-3700**), since he'll be moving his restaurant (see the Surrey Hotel).
- **Best Amenity for A-Types:** The **Lowell,** 28 E. 63rd St. (☎ **800/221-4444**), boasts a suite with a private gym.
- **Best for Travelers with Disabilities:** Aware that not all disabilities are wheelchair related, the **Hotel Delmonico,** 502 Park Ave. (☎ **800/821-3842**), recently opened the Lighthouse Suite for people who are blind or visually impaired. The 600-square-foot suite, which costs around $275 per night, features large-print books and newspapers, an enlarged numerical clock with Braille, and rounded furniture. For travelers with wheelchairs, the **New York Marriott Marquis,** 1535 Broadway (☎ **800/843-4898**); **Crowne Plaza Manhattan,** 1605 Broadway (☎ **800/243-NYNY**); and **Sheraton New York,** 811 Seventh Ave. (☎ **800/ 325-3535**), offer showers that accommodate wheelchairs and other welcome features.
- **Best Freebies:** The **Mansfield,** 12 W. 44th St. (☎ **800/255-5167**), offers complimentary continental breakfast, cappuccino in the lobby, after-theater dessert buffet Monday to Saturday accompanied by live harp music, Monday night music recitals, and free parking. From May to October, the **Kimberly,** 145 E. 50th St. (☎ **800/ 683-0400**) gives guests a complimentary 3-hour sunset cruise.
- **Best Weekend Package:** Expect packages similar to one recently offered by the **Millennium Broadway,** 145 W. 44th St. (☎ **800/622-5569**). The Bravo Broadway Weekend in 1998 included a luxury room for two on Saturday night, two tickets to the Saturday evening and Sunday matinee performances of your choice, and Sunday brunch, all for $575 per room.

2 South Street Seaport & the Financial District

See the "Downtown Accommodations" map (p. 69) for hotels in this section.

VERY EXPENSIVE

Marriott Financial Center Hotel. 85 West St. (Albany & Carlisle sts.), New York, NY 10006. ☎ **800/242-8685** or 212/385-4900. Fax 212/385-9174. 517 units. A/C MINIBAR TV TEL. $289–$370 double; $299–$369 Concierge Level; $550–$1,500 suite. AE, CB, DC, DISC, JCB, MC, V. Valet parking $23. Subway: 1, 9 to Rector St.

As Battery Park City's World Financial Center boomed with the arrival of corporate giants like Merrill Lynch and American Express, this highly efficient Marriott opened in 1990 just across West Street to accommodate the influx of business travelers. Regular rooms have two-line phones with data port and voice mail, and Concierge Level rooms come with fax machines, coffeemakers, bathrobes, and complimentary continental breakfast. The business center buzzes with PC workstations; a conference room

A Note on Rates

The prices I quote in this chapter are "rack rates," the ones that'll be quoted if you call the hotel directly and don't ask for a discount package. But *always* ask about packages.

with a speaker phone; and photocopying, mailing, and shipping services. The health club with indoor pool and sauna is a useful antidote to the high pressures of making lots of money, as is a walk along the nearby Battery Park City esplanade.

Dining: JW's is the more formal dining room, serving continental fare. Battery Park Tavern is a casual bar with typical bar food.

Amenities: Concierge, room service (Mon–Fri 6am–1am, Sat–Sun 6am–midnight), hotel response hot line allowing you to press one number for all hotel-related problems and questions. Business center, health club.

✪ **The Millenium Hilton.** 55 Church St. (Fulton & Dey sts.), New York, NY 10017. ☎ **800/835-2220** or 212/693-2001. Fax 212/571-2316. 657 units. A/C MINIBAR TV TEL. Mon–Fri: $300 double; $350 Millenium room (junior suite); $450–$1,500 suite. Weekend: $159 double (superior room/guaranteed high floor); $209 Millenium room (junior suite); $450–$1,500 suite. Extra person $30. Children under 19 free in parents' room. AE, CB, DC, DISC, JCB, MC, V. Parking $35. Subway: 1, 9, C, E to World Trade Center.

This is the top choice in the Financial District for bulls and bears, whether they're charging on weekdays or hibernating on weekends. Facing the World Trade Center but reaching only halfway up, the 58-story tinted-glass monolith opened in 1992. In 1994 Hilton took over, quickly renaming it—obviously without running a spell check—and remaking it into Lower Manhattan's best hotel. For those on business, there are modern amenities, like in-room fax machines, two-line phones with data port, a 24-hour business center, and abundant space for working and relaxing. Pleasure travelers take advantage of the weekend-planning service (suggestions for tours, sightseeing, dining, shopping, and the like). The rooms feature teak and maple furniture, marble baths, bathrobes, and slippers; rooms on higher floors offer glorious views of Lower Manhattan and the Hudson and East rivers.

Dining: Taliesin serves contemporary American food in a Frank Lloyd Wright–inspired dining room. The Grille and Connoisseur Bar are more casual.

Amenities: Concierge, 24-hour room service, complimentary car service to Midtown. Business center, fitness center with pool.

EXPENSIVE

✪ **Marriott World Trade Center Hotel.** 3 World Trade Center (Liberty & Vesey sts.), New York, NY 10048. ☎ **800/228-9290** or 212/938-9100. Fax 212/444-3444. 821 units. A/C MINIBAR TV TEL. $250–$370 double; $259 Executive Floor; $349–$1,750 suite. AE, CB, DC, DISC, EURO, JCB, MC, V. Valet parking $23. Subway: 1, 9, C, E to World Trade Center.

When this hotel, between and connected to the Twin Towers, opened as the New York Vista in 1981, there were no other hotels in the Financial District. By the early 1990s the Millenium and Marriott Financial Center had come on the scene, attracting businesspeople with services and amenities not available at the Vista. So when the Vista closed in 1993 after the terrorist bombing of the Twin Towers, it had a lot of catching up to do. It reemerged in 1994 after $60 million in renovations and with a new name. The changes are dramatic: There's a sweeping waterfall in the three-story atrium lobby, and wood and carpeting have replaced outdated smoked glass and brass. The rooms are larger and have floor-to-ceiling windows, two-line phones, and interactive TV

Downtown Accommodations

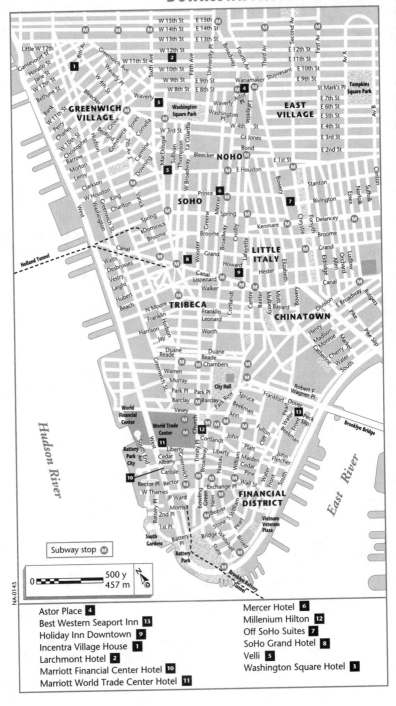

Subway stop Ⓜ

0   500 y
457 m

NA-0145

Astor Place **4**
Best Western Seaport Inn **13**
Holiday Inn Downtown **9**
Incentra Village House **1**
Larchmont Hotel **2**
Marriott Financial Center Hotel **10**
Marriott World Trade Center Hotel **11**

Mercer Hotel **6**
Millenium Hilton **12**
Off SoHo Suites **7**
SoHo Grand Hotel **8**
Velli **5**
Washington Square Hotel **3**

services; the baths are marble and come with all the amenities. Executive Floor guests receive complimentary breakfast, beverages, and hors d'oeuvres. A great health club with an indoor pool, an indoor jogging track, a racquetball court, and saunas completes this full-service hotel.

Dining: The Greenhouse Cafe, with lush foliage and a glass ceiling, offers American food. The Tall Ships Bar & Grill serves lunch, dinner, and cocktails.

Amenities: Concierge; 24-hour room service; tour, sightseeing, transportation services. Business center, health club.

MODERATE

Best Western Seaport Inn. 33 Peck Slip (Front & Water sts.), New York, NY 10038. ☎ 800/HOTEL-NY or 212/766-6600. Fax 212/766-6615. 72 units. A/C TV TEL. $144–$204 double. Rates include breakfast. Children under 18 free in parents' room using existing bedding; cribs free, rollaway $25. AE, CB, DC, DISC, MC, V. Parking $20. Subway: 2, 3 to Fulton St.

This is the only one of the few hotels in Lower Manhattan that doesn't cater to the business crowd. It's in tourist-heavy South Street Seaport, within walking distance of Chinatown, SoHo, Little Italy, and the ferries to the Statue of Liberty, Ellis Island, and Staten Island. Housed in an 1852 building with well-restored exterior, the rooms are done in what they call "Old New York Federal Style" but look more like "Old Best Western Federal Style." Each is equipped with a refrigerator, VCR, hair dryer, and safe, and some have terraces with fine views. Weekend packages, rooms with sofa beds, and complimentary breakfast make this a good value for families. There's no room service, but nearby restaurants abound (best bet: Bridge Cafe—see chapter 6).

3 Chinatown & SoHo

See the "Downtown Accommodations" map (p. 69) for hotels in this section.

VERY EXPENSIVE

✪ **Mercer Hotel.** 99 Prince St. (at Mercer St.), New York, NY 10012. ☎ **888/918-6060** or 212/966-6060. Fax 212/965-3838. 75 units. A/C MINIBAR TV TEL. $350–$430 double; $850–$1,850 suite. AE, DC, MC, V. Parking $26. Subway: N, R to Broadway/Prince St.

André Balazs, a longtime nightcrawler on the Manhattan scene and owner of L.A.'s chic Chateau Marmont, opened the Mercer in April 1997. After 11 years on the drawing board, the hotel finally gives the Grand (below) pricey competition in SoHo, which sports few other alternatives. Opened to rich hipsters (Leonardo DiCaprio, Sophia Coppola) for a 2-month dry run to work out any bugs, the Mercer had a running start in the race for celebrity credit cards. The comfortable lobby feels like a private club, and the staff scurries about in Isaac Mizrahi–designed outfits. The rooms, by *dernier cri* French designer Christian Liaigre, have high ceilings and simple furnishings. Most have full ceiling-to-floor French windows that open out to small wrought-iron balconies. The rooms are business friendly, with modem/fax hookups, two-line phones, and in-room safes.

Dining: The Kitchen is open 24 hours. At press time the hotel was negotiating with celebrated chef Jean-Georges Vongerichten (see Trump Hotel, in this chapter, and Jean Georges, Jo-Jo, and Vong in chapter 6) to lend his toque part-time.

Amenities: Concierge, 24-hour room service, free local phone calls. Nearby health club privileges, private meeting rooms.

EXPENSIVE

⊙ **SoHo Grand Hotel.** 310 W. Broadway (Grand & Canal sts.), New York, NY 10013.
☎ **800/965-3000** or 212/965-3000. Fax 212/965-3141. 371 units. A/C MINIBAR TV TEL.
$209–$349 double; $949–$1,149 penthouse suite. AE, CB, DC, DISC, EURO, JCB, MC, V. Valet
parking $30. Subway: N, R to Canal St.

This stop-off for the image conscious was, in 1996, the first new hotel to open in
SoHo in more than a century. Designer William Sofield created a chic interior, incorporating SoHo styles from the 1870s to the 1990s. The lobby is dramatic, and the
guest rooms, though small, boast custom-designed furnishings, including desks that
resemble artists' drafting tables and end tables that look like sculptors' stands. The
bath decked out in ceramic subwaylike tile have pedestal sinks. In-room conveniences
include interactive cable TVs with on-demand movies, two-line phones with voice
mail and data port, and safes. Pets are welcome. Expect the Mercer (above) to give the
Grand competition for the Downtown arts-and-model crowd.

Dining: Canal House serves New England tavern fare, and the Grand Bar, some-
time-local-hip hangout, looks over West Broadway, SoHo's main thoroughfare.

Amenities: Concierge, 24-hour room service, free local phone calls. Fitness room.

MODERATE

Holiday Inn Downtown. 138 Lafayette St. (Canal & Howard sts.), New York, NY 10013.
☎ **800/HOLIDAY** or 212/966-8898. Fax 212/966-3933. 237 units. A/C TV TEL. $165–$199
double; $229–$249 junior suite. AE, CB, DC, DISC, JCB, MC, V. Valet parking from $25.
Subway: 6 to Canal St.

Holiday Inn has decorated the hotel with Asian touches, like green marble with brass
accents in the lobby. The guest rooms are what you'd expect from the chain: Each has
a sitting area, a desk, a safe, two phones, computer/fax data ports, and voice mail; the
junior suites have in-room fax machines. The hotel's Pacifica restaurant serves mainly
Cantonese cuisine—but why eat in the hotel when there are so many better (and less
expensive) choices in nearby Chinatown, SoHo, and Little Italy (see chapter 6)?
Amenities include a concierge, room service (daily 6:30am–10pm), and privileges at a
nearby health club for a fee.

4 The Lower East Side

See the "Downtown Accommodations" map (p. 69) for the hotel in this section.

INEXPENSIVE

Off SoHo Suites. 11 Rivington St. (Chrystie St. & the Bowery), New York, NY 10002.
☎ **800/OFF-SOHO** or 212/979-9808. Fax 212/979-9801. 38 units, most with bathroom.
A/C TV TEL. $97.50 economy suite (2 people maximum); $169 deluxe suite (4 people maximum). AE, EURO, MC, V. Parking $12. Subway: F to Second Ave.; J, M to Bowery.

If only this clean, well-kept, and fairly priced hotel were anywhere else. On the Lower
East Side, along a stretch filled with warehouses, supply depots, and second-hand
restaurant equipment stores, it's not only considerably "off SoHo" but also off most
everything else. There is one point where it's right on: It offers relatively spacious suites
for significantly less than the tiny rooms in Midtown. The economy suites are really
private bedrooms that share, if the "suite" next door is occupied, a kitchen and a bath.
The deluxe suites are truly what the name implies: They have a bedroom, bath, fully
equipped kitchen, and dining area. The modern furnishings and marble baths, along
with the airy feeling of the rooms and the rates, make this a great alternative if you

don't mind a seedy neighborhood. Off-SoHo Cafe is open for all three meals and provides daily room service 6am to midnight.

5 Greenwich Village

See the "Downtown Accommodations" map (p. 69) for hotels in this section.

INEXPENSIVE

✪ **Larchmont Hotel.** 27 W. 11th St. (Fifth & Sixth aves.), New York, NY 10011. ☎ **212/989-9333.** Fax 212/989-9496. 55 units, none with bathroom. A/C TV TEL. $60–$70 single; $85–$90 double. Rates include continental breakfast. Children under 13 free in parents' room. AE, CB, DC, DISC, MC, V. Parking $17. Subway: 4, 5, 6, N, R, L to Union Square; F to 14th St.

On a landmark brownstone block in a quiet residential part of the Village is one of New York's most affordable and delightful small hotels. But if you won't share a bath, don't read further. If you don't mind communal commodes, however, many attributes recommend the place. Each guest room is tastefully done with rattan furniture, a writing desk, a wash basin, and a ceiling fan. Every floor has a bath and small kitchen. Breakfast is served in a downstairs cafe. Book well in advance; word is out about this formerly well-kept secret.

✪ **Washington Square Hotel.** 103 Waverly Place (Fifth & Sixth aves.), New York, NY 10011. ☎ **800/222-0418** or 212/777-9515. Fax 212/979-8373. 180 units. A/C TV TEL. $120 double; $130 twin; $150 quad. Extra bed $12. Rates include continental breakfast. AE, MC, JCB, V. Parking $22. Subway: A, B, C, D, E, F, Q to West 4th St.

You won't easily find a better bargain. The Washington Square has many things going for it, especially a great location and a fabulous price. Overlooking Washington Square Park in the heart of the Village, this friendly hotel is family owned and family managed. The small lobby is highlighted by a marble floor and a gate of wrought iron and brass. The rooms are plain, compact, and quiet. It's well worth paying a few extra dollars for a room facing south, on a high floor, for maximum sunshine (others can be a bit dark). And now that all the rooms have windows that can be opened, the hotel's only former drawback—a certain fustiness in some rooms—is gone.

Breakfast is served in the attached CIII restaurant (owned by daughter Judy). The small fitness room has a treadmill, a stationary bike, and the like. To keep prices down, there's no bellhop or room service, but the staff is accommodating. Ask about the walking tours and jazz packages.

6 Gramercy Park

See the "Midtown Accommodations" map (pp. 78–79) for hotels in this section.

EXPENSIVE

✪ **The Inn at Irving Place.** 56 Irving Place (17th & 18th sts.), New York, NY 10003. ☎ **800/685-1447** or 212/533-4600. Fax 212/533-4611. 12 units. A/C MINIBAR TV TEL. $275–$350 double; $375–$395 suite. Rates include continental breakfast. AE, CB, DC, JCB, MC, V. Parking $20. Subway: 4, 5, 6, N, R to Union Square.

In adjoining 1834 Greek Revival town houses, carefully restored by owner Naomi Blumenthal, this jewel is arguably New York's most intimate, romantic, and historically evocative hotel, a favorite with honeymooners, world-class travelers, and New York couples on amorous weekend retreats snuggling in four-posters between lush Frette linens. The decor is lavishly Victorian—each unique room has a fireplace (non-working) and antiques, period paintings, Oriental rugs, and fresh flowers. All rooms have VCRs and dual-line phones with data port (a fax machine and computer with

Internet hookup are available downstairs). One drawback is that some rooms have limited drawer space, but why not adjust by limiting your packing to, say, only a couple of pairs of Calvins or lacy teddys? The cozy parlor is the perfect place to loll through Edith Wharton's *Age of Innocence*. (The writer was born nearby on 23rd Street, and there's a room here named for Countess Olenska, one of the novel's characters.) Children under 12 aren't allowed.

Dining/Diversions: The tearoom serves breakfast, light lunch, and tea. The highly rated Verbena, not affiliated with the hotel but just downstairs, serves wonderful contemporary American cuisine (see chapter 6). Fine cigars, cocktails, and appetizers are available at the chic Cibar Lounge (see chapter 9).

Amenities: Concierge, 24-hour limited room service (drinks and snacks), business/secretarial services. Nearby health club privileges for $25 fee.

MODERATE

Gramercy Park Hotel. 2 Lexington Ave. (21st & 22nd sts.), New York, NY 10010. ☎ **800/221-4083** or 212/475-4320. Fax 212/505-0535. 360 units. A/C TV TEL. $160 double; $190–$230 1-bedroom suite with pullout sofa bed. Children under 12 free in parents' room. AE, CB, DC, DISC, EURO, JCB, MC, V. Parking $20. Subway: 6 to 23rd St.

The original heartbreak hotel! There are so many reasons that this should be one of New York's great spaces. Hip restaurants and shops abound on nearby streets, and it's the only large hotel in the area. It opened in 1924 as the grande dame of Gramercy Park, a neighborhood that feels like a quiet London square complete with private park—restricted to residents of the elegant town houses that surround it and to hotel guests, who can also get a key. But today the Gramercy, amid so much history and in such a fine neighborhood, is faded and frayed. The spacious rooms need renovating (one I visited had red-wine stains on the wallpaper), the furnishings need updating, and the fixtures need modernizing. The hotel is, by New York standards, moderately priced and offers monthly rates. If you do go, insist on a suite overlooking the park.

INEXPENSIVE

Carlton Arms. 160 E. 25th St. (Lexington & Third aves.), New York, NY 10010. ☎ **212/679-0680** (reservations) or 212/684-8337 (guests). 52 units, 20 with bathroom. $60–$88, 1–3 persons without bathroom; $70–$98, 1–3 persons with bathroom. MC, V. Parking $16. Subway: 6 to 23rd St.

Some of the best new art being done in New York is on the walls, ceilings, and closets of this backpacker's delight of a hostel/hotel on the outskirts of Gramercy Park. Originally a single-room-occupancy hotel, the Carlton was acquired by college students who invited artists to use every empty space as a canvas. The rooms are basic—*very* basic, the kind you'd want to sleep in only if you couldn't afford better. Each has a sink, and some have baths. Reserve in advance because the place is popular with students and foreigners, who benefit from special discounts. Take note: The construction noise in the neighboring lot has made late sleeping and afternoon naps impossible. Be sure to ask if it's still crashing along.

✪ **Gershwin Hotel.** 7 E. 27th St. (Fifth & Madison aves.), New York, NY 10016. ☎ **212/545-8000.** Fax 212/684-5546. 94 units, 31 4-person dorms. $70–$120 double; $70–$130 triple; $22 dorm bed. AE, MC, V. Parking $20. Subway: 6 to 28th St.; N, R to 28th St.

This budget-conscious hotel, operated by Interclub Hotel (specialists in youth-oriented accommodations), caters to up-and-coming writers, actors, artists, and models. The lobby of the early 20th-century Greek Revival–style building is filled with pop art by resident artist/designer Lynne Packwood, evoking, if not to say imitating, Lichtenstein and Warhol. The rooms range from dorms sleeping four to standard doubles with baths to superior doubles with baths, air-conditioning, TVs, and phones. The renovated rooms feature unique furniture, like designer nightstands hand-painted by Packwood. The funky Gallery Cafe adjacent to the lobby, the billiard room, and the rooftop garden that hosts films and barbecues give the Gershwin the ambiance of an oxymoron: an artsy fraternity or sorority house.

Hotel 17. 225 E. 17th St. (Second & Third aves.), New York, NY 10003. ☎ **212/475-2845.** Fax 212/677-8178. 150 units, 4 with bathroom. $75 double; $120 3-person suite without bathroom; $140 4-person suite without bathroom. No credit cards. Parking $25. Subway: 4, 5, 6 to 14th St.; L to First Ave.

The neighborhood is great, the block is peaceful, and Hotel 17 is in a 100-year-old landmark building. Madonna did a photo shoot in room 114, David Bowie had a por-trait done in another, and fashion spreads have been shot on the roof. But did any of the celebs spend the night? I doubt it. The rooms are small, dark, basic, and hot in summer (air-conditioning costs extra); TVs and phones are only in units with a bath. The staff seems to be on career tracks that preclude hotel management, but the ameni-ties, thankfully, include a safe. All that doesn't stop the tragically hip or merely starving from staying here. So if "I stayed in the same rundown hotel where Madonna had her picture taken" is on your life's checklist, it won't get any cheaper than this.

7 Chelsea

See the "Midtown Accommodations" map (pp. 78–79) for hotels in this section.

MODERATE

Chelsea Hotel. 222 W. 23rd St. (Seventh & Eighth aves.), New York, NY 10011. ☎ **212/243-3700.** Fax 212/243-3700. 400 units, most with bathroom. A/C TV TEL. $135–$185 double; $285–$350 suite. AE, DC, JCB, MC, V. Valet parking $18. Subway: 1, 9, C, E to 23rd St.

Lots of atmosphere, ghosts of writers and artists, and an inescapable shabbiness com-bine to create a hotel like no other in the world. If you're looking for dependable, pre-dictable comforts and cleanliness, go elsewhere. But if you want to be immersed in the past, sometimes still clinging to the furniture, reserve a room here. If this place were the kind that had a Visitor's Comments Book, you'd expect complaints, or praise, from Tennessee Williams, William Burroughs, Eugene O'Neill, Bob Dylan, Arthur Miller, and Mark Twain. Venerable owner Stanley Bard holds court at the designated land-mark, an 1884 redbrick Victorian fancy with graceful cast-iron balconies enlivening the facade. The lobby is an art gallery filled with museum-quality works by prominent current and former residents.

The hotel has 400 rooms, but with an ever-changing array of long-term residents, only 100 or so are available at any one time. The rooms and suites are individually fur-nished. Maid service is optional (!), and though some suites have kitchens, there are no amenities in the kitchens or the baths (bring your own utensils and shampoo). And there's no restaurant (unless you count El Quijote, not associated with the hotel), bar, health club, or other boringly bourgeois attributes of ho-hum hotels.

INEXPENSIVE

Chelsea Inn. 46 W. 17th St. (Fifth & Sixth aves.), New York, NY 10011. ☎ **212/640-6469.** Fax 212/645-1903. 25 units, 17 with bathroom. A/C TV TEL. $89–$109 double without bath-room; $119–$139 double with bathroom; $159–$199 suite for up to 4. AE, DISC, MC, V. Parking $20. Subway: 6, N, R to Union Square.

With a 19th-century brownstone front, the Chelsea Inn resembles a European *pensione*. The landmark building is filled with antiques, and all the rooms have kitchenettes.

Most of the suites and studios now have baths, but some rooms still share one bath for every two rooms. It's on the same block, if you care, as the restaurant Flowers (see chapter 6), and the club Splash (see chapter 9), and is within screaming distance of Cheslea nightlife and Union Square's shopping and restaurants.

✪ Chelsea Savoy Hotel. 204 W. 23rd St. (at Seventh Ave.), New York, NY 10011. ☎ **212/ 929-9353.** Fax 212/741-6309. 90 units. A/C TV TEL. $99–$175 double. Children under 13 free in parents' room. AE, MC, V. Parking $16. Subway: 1, 9 to 23rd St.

The new Chelsea Savoy is a much-needed addition to Chelsea, a neighborhood abloom with new art galleries and weekend flea markets but formerly devoid of clean, affordable hotels. While most of the city's newest hotels are carved from existing buildings, the six-story Chelsea Savoy was built from the ground up. The furnishings and decor are simple: There's a large, brightly lit sitting room off the small lobby; the rooms are painted off-white, with plain wood furniture, TVs, and minirefrigerators; the boxlike baths are tiled floor to ceiling. The rooms in back are quieter, but those overlooking Seventh Avenue have better views. A restaurant and bar opened in summer 1998.

8 Midtown West

See the "Midtown Accommodations" map (pp. 78–79) for hotels in this section.

VERY EXPENSIVE

✪ Essex House, Hotel Nikko New York. 160 Central Park South (Sixth & Seventh aves.), New York, NY 10019. ☎ **800/645-5687** or 212/247-0300. Fax 212/315-1839. 597 units. A/C MINIBAR TV TEL. $350–$380 double; $395–$2,000 suite. 2 children under 18 free in parents' room. AE, CB, DC, DISC, JCB, MC, V. Valet parking $33. Subway: 1, 9, A, B, C, D to Columbus Circle.

A few years back, Japan's Nikko Hotels, owners of the Essex House, completed a $75-million renovation, but the hotel has been up for sale, so if a new owner is found, more changes could be on the way. The lobby is an art deco masterpiece, and the larger rooms are decorated in faux Louis XVI or imitation Chippendale and equipped with TVs with VCRs, dual-line phones with data port, fax machines, and safes. The marble-and-chrome baths are fit for an emperor with double sinks, separate tubs and showers, hair dryers, and robes. The rooms overlooking Central Park are more expensive, but the view is spectacular. Service is particularly attentive.

Dining/Diversions: Les Célébrités (see chapter 6) serves fine French cuisine in an elegant room. Cafe Botanica serves new American cuisine in a greenhouselike setting. Journeys is a clublike wood-paneled bar.

Amenities: Concierge, 24-hour room service, Nikko Kids program, complimentary weekday car service to Wall Street. Business center, fitness center with trainers and spa treatments.

✪ Millennium Broad. 145 W. 44th St. (Sixth Ave. & Broadway), New York, NY 10036. ☎ **800/622-5569** or 212/768-4400. Fax 212/768-0847. 627 units. A/C MINIBAR TV TEL. $315–$335 double; $570–$2,500 suite. Children under 13 free in parents' room. AE, DC, CB, JCB, MC, V. Valet parking $32. Subway: 1, 2, 3, 9, N, R to Times Square.

The Millennium Broadway (which, unlike the unaffiliated Millenium downtown, knows how to spell) includes the five-floor Manhattan Conference Center, with 33 dedicated meeting rooms and 11,000 square feet of exhibition space. Accordingly, the hotel caters to business travelers with in-room amenities like two-line phones, modem hookups, voice mail in four languages, and ironing boards. Club rooms, on floors 46 to 52, feature larger-than-normal desks, fax machines, coffeemakers, and complimentary continental breakfast and evening cocktails at the top-floor Club Lounge. At the

---

ⓘ Family-Friendly Hotels

Once upon a time, traveling children were regarded by New York hotels as little more than a small body sleeping in an adult's room. Then New York was reborn as a family-friendly city. Many New York hotels now make it attractive for parents to take along the younger set:

At **Doubletree Guest Suites** (p. 83) you'll find a Kids Club, designed by the Please Touch Museum of Philadelphia, plus an entire floor of childproof suites. The **Essex House, Hotel Nikko New York** (p. 75) offers the Nikko Kids program, which provides toys like coloring books and Frisbees, milk and cookies at bedtime, colorful sheets, and other services. The hotel has been up for sale, so check if the program is still being offered.

The **Paramount** (p. 85) offers a stocked playroom full of stuffed animals to help supervised children get through rainy days. The **Novotel** (p. 84–85) has a children's playroom and gives the kids cute toys.

Other hotels, because of their location, price, or accommodations, can also be good family choices for those advantages alone:

The **Quality Hotel & Suites Rockefeller Center** (p. 88–89) has a great Midtown location near all the Times Square action, reasonable rates for suites ($189 to $239), and complimentary continental breakfast. Kids under 19 and under stay free with their parents. The **Helmsley Middletowne** (p. 94) offers fully equipped kitchens in large rooms of a converted apartment building within easy walking distance of Midtown attractions.

The **Hotel Beacon** (p. 97) and the **Milburn** (p. 97), while not luxurious, are on the family-oriented Upper West Side and have rooms and suites with kitchens and multiple bedding choices. The **Salisbury Hotel** (p. 85) has a good West 57th Street location, near all the theme restaurants, as well as oversize rooms and affordable suites. The **Gorham** (p. 83) offers kitchenettes and different bedding arrangements. If you can stand it, Nintendo is also provided.

---

same time, the Millennium's Times Square location and well-priced weekend packages make it a good option for leisure travelers. A 1997 refurbishment gave the guest rooms a fresh look: a new color scheme, burnished wood furniture, and polished chrome accessories evoking art deco. Sometime in 1999, watch for 125 high-tech luxury rooms to open in a new 22-story tower adjoining the existing hotel.

Dining: Restaurant Charlotte is highly regarded, the equal of any fine dining room in the Times Square neighborhood.

Amenities: Concierge, room service (daily 6am–11:30pm). Business center, fitness center, Hudson Theatre.

The Peninsula. 700 Fifth Ave. (at 55th St.), New York, NY 10019. ☎ **800/262-9467** or 212/247-2200. Fax 212/903-3949. 243 units. A/C MINIBAR TV TEL. $365–$510 double; $700–$5,200 suite. Extra bed $20. 1 child under 13 free in parents' room. AE, CB, DC, DISC, EURO, JCB, MC, V. Valet parking $36. Subway: E, F to 53rd St.

The Peninsula closed in January 1998 for a complete refurbishment of its guest rooms, which should include installation of new desks, ergonomic chairs, fax machines, data ports, and dual-line speakerphones. It reopened in late 1998 with increased prices reflecting the improved amenities (rates listed above are prerenovation). What I'm sure wouldn't change is the old-world elegance of the 23-story beaux arts landmark (1905) abundant in the public spaces (especially the grand foyer) and guest rooms.

Dining/Diversions: Adrienne (a new name might follow the renovations) serves outstanding contemporary American food in a belle-époque setting. Le Bistro is a casual restaurant, and the Gotham Lounge serves afternoon tea and cocktails. The Pen-Top Bar and Terrace (see chapter 9) offers cocktails, casual dining, and dramatic views of Midtown. (Word is that it will be brightened up during the renovations, and I hope the shockingly inattentive service will be corrected.)

Amenities: Concierge, 24-hour room service, business/secretarial services. Large rooftop health club and spa with pool (one of New York's best), which should be spiffed up during the renovations.

The Plaza Hotel. 768 Fifth Ave. (58th & 59th sts.), New York, NY 10019. ☎ **800/759-3000** or 212/759-3000. Fax 212/759-3167. 901 units. A/C MINIBAR TV TEL. $380–$655 double; $525–$15,000 suite. AE, DC, DISC, JCB, MC, V. Valet parking $35. Subway: N, R to 60th St.

Designed by Henry J. Hardenbergh (who also gave us the Dakota Apartments), this 1907 French Renaissance–style palace rightfully deserves its National Historic Landmark status and boasts the most idyllic location of any hotel in the city. Having appeared in dozens of movies and been made up glamorously in all of them (except when it was a child's playground in *Home Alone 2*), the Plaza is an internationally recognized symbol of New York. Prince Walid bin Talal of Saudi Arabia, along with CDL Hotels International of Singapore, snatched control from Donald Trump and now runs the show. The new owners have made undramatic cosmetic changes, toning down the blinding gold leaf and gaudy chandeliers in the public spaces and sprucing up the guest rooms (some feature 14-foot ceilings, crystal chandeliers, carved marble fireplaces, and mahogany doors). Rooms can be small, and if they don't afford a view of the park, feel even smaller, especially at these prices. But the amenities are always first class: Frette sheets, fluffy towels, and phones with dual-line service and data port. Make sure to inquire about special weekend packages.

Dining/Diversions: The gardenlike Palm Court is a favorite for tea or Sunday brunch. The Oak Room (see chapter 9) and the classic Edwardian Room serve American fare in a men's-club setting, though proposed plans could turn the latter into a modern urban bistro—*very scary* and lamentable if it comes true. The Oak Bar is popular for drinks, and the Oyster Bar (not to be confused with the better one at Grand Central) is a casual fish house/pub.

Amenities: Concierge, 24-hour room service. Exercise room, use of the nearby Atrium Health Club, which has a pool.

RIHGA Royal Hotel. 151 W. 54th St. (Sixth & Seventh aves.), New York, NY 10019. ☎ **800/937-5454** or 212/307-5000. Fax 212/765-6530. 500 units. A/C MINIBAR TV TEL. $425–$550 1-bedroom Royal, Imperial, or Pinnacle suite; $900–$1,000 2-bedroom Imperial or Pinnacle suite; $1,500 1-bedroom Crown Royal suite; $2,700–$3,000 Grand Royal suite. Children under 15 free in parents' suite. AE, CB, DC, DISC, EURO, JCB, MC, V. Parking $40. Subway: B, D, E to 53rd St.

Opened in 1990, this is the first U.S. venture of RIHGA (Royal International Hotel Group and Association), based in Osaka, Japan. The Japanese reputation for providing excellent service and technological innovation is upheld at the 54-story suites-only hotel in the heart of Midtown, catering to businesspeople, notably the international entertainment set. There are three grades of deluxe suites, with separate living and dining rooms, work and dining tables, three phones with two lines and dataport, VCRs, and two TVs. Imperial Suites also feature CD players and fax machines. Top-of-the-line Pinnacle Suites (above the 40th floor) include chauffeur-driven airport transfers, personalized business cards, and a free cellular phone. A full-service concierge handles business and entertainment requests.

Midtown Accommodations

NA-0146

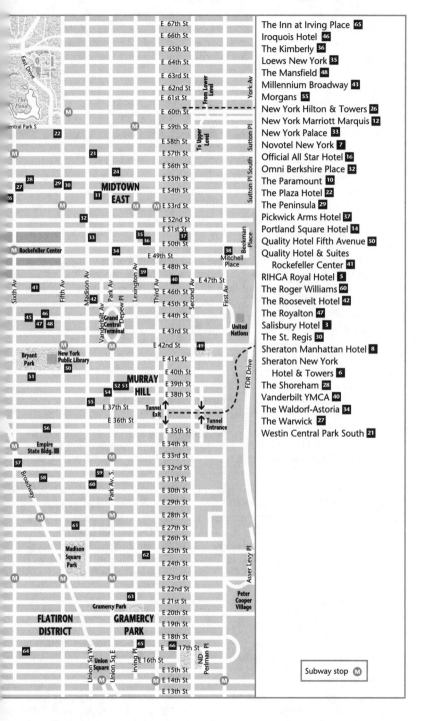

The Inn at Irving Place 65
Iroquois Hotel 46
The Kimberly 36
Loews New York 35
The Mansfield 48
Millennium Broadway 43
Morgans 55
New York Hilton & Towers 26
New York Marriott Marquis 12
New York Palace 33
Novotel New York 7
Official All Star Hotel 16
Omni Berkshire Place 32
The Paramount 10
The Plaza Hotel 22
The Peninsula 29
Pickwick Arms Hotel 37
Portland Square Hotel 14
Quality Hotel Fifth Avenue 50
Quality Hotel & Suites
   Rockefeller Center 41
RIHGA Royal Hotel 5
The Roger Williams 60
The Roosevelt Hotel 42
The Royalton 47
Salisbury Hotel 3
The St. Regis 30
Sheraton Manhattan Hotel 8
Sheraton New York
   Hotel & Towers 6
The Shoreham 28
Vanderbilt YMCA 40
The Waldorf-Astoria 34
The Warwick 27
Westin Central Park South 21

Subway stop Ⓜ

Dining/Diversions: The Halcyon serves contemporary American cuisine and has pre- and posttheater menus. The Lobby Lounge is highlighted by African mahogany.

Amenities: Concierge, 24-hour room service, complimentary weekday shuttle to Wall Street. Business center, fitness center.

✪ **The Royalton.** 44 W. 44th St. (Fifth & Sixth aves.), New York, NY 10036. ☎ **800/635-9013** or 212/869-4400. Fax 212/869-8965. 205 units. A/C MINIBAR TV TEL. $315–$380 double; $450 suite. AE, DC, EURO, MC, V. Valet parking $28. Subway: B, D, F, Q to 42nd St.

This was the second entry into the New York hotel market for Ian Schrager and the late Steve Rubell, who first tested the waters with the equally hip Morgans, after they had given up the legal entanglements of 1970s-disco-heaven Studio 54. The Royalton has been a show stopper from the start: This Theater District hotel is *designed*—lighting fixtures that look like rhinoceros horns, service people dressed in de rigueur black, furniture with attitude. Still with all the loud, futuristic noise inside, the sign out front is so subtle as to be easily missed. It's all the work of French interior designer Philippe Starck, who in his ever-present genius does sometimes make you want to whisper, "Oh, Philippe, shut up!"

Averaging 400 square feet, the guest rooms are spacious enough to have separate small areas for entertaining, working, and sleeping. All contain a queen- or king-size bed, VCR, refrigerator, and state-of-the-art telecommunications system; some have working fireplaces and baths with 5-foot-wide round tubs built into a concave slate wall. The lobby rest rooms are a must visit—you'll see why.

Dining/Diversions: The restaurant 44 (see "Best Bets" in chapter 6) serves creative American food to people from the publishing industry who can get a table because they run up big bills with regularity. The Round Bar, a cozy curved nook at the front of the lobby, has *Jetsons*-like furnishings but is patterned after the Ritz Bar in Paris. The bar at 44 serves light fare around the clock.

Amenities: Concierge, 24-hour room service, business/secretarial services. Fitness room with personal trainers and massage therapists.

Westin Central Park South. 112 Central Park South (Sixth & Seventh aves.), New York, NY 10019. ☎ **800/325-3589** or 212/757-1900. Fax 212/757-9620. 208 units. A/C MINIBAR TV TEL. $330–$545 double; $600–$3,300 suite. AE, DC, DISC, EURO, JCB, MC, V. Valet parking $35. Subway: N, R or B, Q to 57th St.

The Westin Luxury Collection took over this hotel when, in late 1997, the Ritz-Carlton chain suddenly withdrew its affiliation with the property. Several years ago, a $20-million face-lift augmented the opulence of the public spaces and the guest rooms. All accommodations have marble baths, polished wood, and lots of brocade. Only the views differ, and those overlooking Central Park are the best and most expensive. Each room is equipped with two dual-line phones with data port and nice touches like terry-cloth bathrobes. Westin plans to freshen up the decor and add another 20 rooms facing the park.

Dining/Diversions: Fantino restaurant serves continental cuisine on Gianni Versace–designed Rosenthal china. Fantino Bar has become a popular watering hole largely due to the engaging charms of bartender Norman Bukofzer.

Amenities: Concierge, 24-hour room service, complimentary weekday shuttle to Wall Street. Business center, fitness center with Central Park views.

EXPENSIVE

The Algonquin. 59 W. 44th St. (Fifth & Sixth aves.), New York, NY 10036. ☎ **800/555-3000** or 212/840-6800. Fax 212/944-1419. 165 units. A/C TV TEL. $189–$329 double; $199–$700 suite. Extra person $25. Rates include buffet breakfast. AE, CB, DC, DISC, ER, EURO, JCB, MC, V. Parking $25. Subway: B, D, F, Q to 42nd St.

Staying "Out"

Since the city has one of the world's largest, loudest, and most powerful gay and lesbian populations (and a corresponding number of similar visitors), hotels here are neutral on the question. If readers encounter prejudice, for any reason, they're encouraged to write me. Nonetheless, some gays and lesbians might wish to seek out particularly gay accommodations in New York, though these usually don't match the standards of the city's top hotels.

Colonial House Inn. 318 W. 22nd St. (Eighth and Ninth avenues), New York, NY 10011 (☎ 800/689-3779 or 212/243-9669; fax 212/633-1612). In the heart of gay-friendly Chelsea, this charming 1850 brownstone has 20 rooms decorated with original artwork; some have fireplaces and some have refrigerators, but all have TVs, air-conditioning, and phones. A free continental breakfast is served. The roof deck is great on sunny days or for relaxing over evening refreshments. The 24-hour concierge is helpful for dining and entertainment questions. Its units (eight with bath) cost $65 economy, $80 standard, and $99 deluxe. No credit cards are accepted.

Chelsea Pines Inn. 317 W. 14th St. (Eighth and Ninth avenues), New York, NY 10014 (☎ 212/929-1023; fax 212/620-5646). On the Chelsea/West Village border is the newly renovated Chelsea Pines Inn. The rooms in the 1850 row house are decorated with original Hollywood movie posters. They're clean and comfortable and have refrigerators, TVs with free HBO, air-conditioning, and phones. The staff is helpful, and continental breakfast is served. There's a year-round greenhouse, and on nice days the backyard garden is open. Its 23 units cost $75 to $89 for a double with a shared bath, $85 to $99 for a queen-size room with a private shower and shared toilet, $89 to $99 for a queen-size room with a bath, and $95 to $109 for a deluxe room with a bath. American Express, Carte Blanche, Diners Club, Discover, enRoute, EuroCard, MasterCard, and Visa are accepted.

Incentra Village House. 32 Eighth Ave. (12th and Jane streets, above Abingdon Square), New York, NY 10014 (☎ 212/206-0007). The two 1841 redbrick Greenwich Village town houses that make up the Incentra are listed with the National Trust for Historic Places. They're decorated with antiques. Twelve units have a bath, TV, and phone. Ten have working fireplaces, and most have kitchenettes. The rates are $99 single, $149 double, and $179 suite. American Express, MasterCard, and Visa are accepted.

This landmark Theater District hotel is best known for its past, when the Round Table group of writers Dorothy Parker, Robert Benchley, Alexander Woollcott, and other literati traded boozy quips here in the 1920s. Even today, ringing for afternoon tea or a pre- or posttheater cocktail from a plush sofa in the oak-paneled lobby, you'll understand the attraction this turn-of-the-century hotel holds for artistic types. The rooms, alas, have been another story. The major $5-million renovation, ongoing at press time, should not only update amenities but also bring the relatively small guest rooms in line with their posh surroundings. I hope.

Dining/Diversions: The Oak Room features continental cuisine and big-name cabaret entertainment. Drinks and pub fare are available in the Blue Bar. A couple of years back, an ambitious program of readings (by the likes of Spalding Gray and Frank McCourt) and concerts (singers from the Metropolitan and City operas) was begun here, and management promises to continue it.

Amenities: Room service (daily 6:30am–11:30pm). Nearby health club privileges for a fee.

The Ameritania. 1701 Broadway (at 54th St.), New York, NY 10019. ☎ **800/922-0330** or 212/247-5000. Fax 212/247-3316. 206 units. A/C TV TEL. $195–$225 double; $265–$450 suite. Rates include continental breakfast. Children under 17 free in parents' room. AE, DC, DISC, JCB, MC, V. Parking $20. Subway: B, D, E to Seventh Ave.; N, R to 57th St.

Fans of *The Late Show with David Letterman* already know the Ameritania, aka Hotel 54, thanks to Mujibur and Sirajul, clerks who work in a gift shop on the hotel's street level and were introduced to the nation by Letterman's prying cameras. The Top 10 reasons to stay here (which *used to* include more reasonable prices): location, comfortable guest rooms, location, marble baths, recent renovations, junior suites okay for families, kids under 17 stay free, location, and, of course, Mujibur and Sirajul.

✪ **Casablanca Hotel.** 147 W. 43rd St. (Sixth Ave. & Broadway), New York, NY 10036. ☎ **888/922-7225** or 212/869-1212. Fax 212/391-7585. 48 units. A/C MINIBAR TV TEL. $235–$265 double; $350 suite. Rates include continental breakfast. 2 children under 13 free in parents' room. AE, DC, JCB, MC, V. Parking $18. Subway: 1, 2, 3, 9, N, R to Times Square; B, D, F, Q to 42nd St.

Opened in 1997, the Casablanca is Times Square's only luxury boutique hotel and New York's—and perhaps America's—only Morrocan-theme hotel. The only thing missing is Bogart and Bergman: Vibrant Moorish-style mosaic tiles, warm wood paneling, and potted palms greet you in the lobby, and the guest rooms boast custom-designed rattan armchairs, carved headboards, and ceiling fans. In-room touches include refrigerators stocked with bottled water, iced tea, and fine chocolates and Caswell-Massey toiletries in the baths, which are embellished with iridescent tiles and gold-trimmed mirrors. The service is attentive, though many of the rooms in the former single-room-occupancy hotel are small. The rooftop garden and second-floor courtyard are perfect for summer lounging.

Dining/Diversions: Rick's Café (guests only) serves complimentary refreshments throughout the day and has a working fireplace, a piano, a 41-inch movie screen, and computers with Internet access.

Amenities: Complimentary on-line concierge, business/secretarial services, complimentary tea and cookies throughout the day, complimentary wine and cheese weekday evenings, complimentary videos for in-room viewing. Free access to nearby New York Sports Club, with pool and sauna.

Crowne Plaza Manhattan. 1605 Broadway (48th & 49th sts.), New York, NY 10019. ☎ **800/243-NYNY** or 212/977-4000. Fax 212/333-7393. 770 units. A/C MINIBAR TV TEL. $199–$429 double; $400–$950 1-bedroom suite; $600–$1,250 2-bedroom suite. 2 children under 19 free in parents' room on existing bedding. AE, CB, DC, DISC, EURO, JCB, MC, V. Valet parking $34. Subway: 1, 9 to 50th St.; N, R to 49th St.

When Holiday Inn Worldwide went upscale in 1994 with its new Crowne Plaza line, this became its international flagship. In the heart of Times Square and near most Broadway theaters, the 46-story burgundy glass tower is as good as a Holiday Inn gets. The modern guest rooms were recently redecorated with contemporary furnishings and marble baths and come with extras like hair dryers, coffeemakers, irons and ironing boards, safes, and pay-per-view movies. The top four floors are devoted to Crowne Plaza Club rooms, where you receive free continental breakfast, evening hors d'oeuvres, and amenities like terry-cloth robes, turndown service, and two-line phones with data ports.

Dining/Diversions: Samplings still has a better view than menu but serves light contemporary American fare that's improving; you might try some of the better neighborhood restaurants (see chapter 6). The Balcony Cafe serves breakfast and lunch. There's also the Lobby Bar for drinks.

Amenities: Concierge, 24-hour room service. Business center, large fitness center with 50-foot pool.

✪ **Doubletree Guest Suites.** 1568 Broadway (47th St. & Seventh Ave.), New York, NY 10036. ☎ **800/222-TREE** or 212/719-1600. Fax 212/921-5112. 460 units. A/C MINI-BAR TV TEL. $225–$245 suite; $350–$450 conference suite. Extra person $20. Children under 12 free in parents' suite. AE, DC, DISC, JCB, MC, V. Parking $30. Subway: N, R to 49th St.

For less than the cost of a normal room in many nearby Times Square hotels, you can get a suite at the Doubletree with a separate bedroom and living room with sofa bed, a dining/work table, a refrigerator, a wet bar, a microwave, a coffeemaker, two TVs, and three phones with voice mail. For businesspeople, conference suites feature work stations and are large enough for small meetings. What's more, this is a family-friendly hotel with a floor of childproof suites and special amenities for kids, such as the Kids Club, designed by Philadelphia's Please Touch Museum, featuring a playroom, an arts-and-crafts center, and computer and video games. Cribs and strollers are available, and there's a kids' room-service menu.

Dining/Diversions: Center Stage Cafe serves continental and American cuisine. The Broadway Museum Cabaret provides piano-bar entertainment.

Amenities: Concierge, 24-hour room service, children's programs, complimentary tea and coffee service. Business center, fitness center, Kids Club.

The Gorham. 136 W. 55th St. (Sixth & Seventh aves.), New York, NY 10019. ☎ **800/735-0710** or 212/245-1800. Fax 212/582-8332. 118 units. A/C TV TEL. $195–$360 double; $225–$400 junior suite; $425 penthouse suite. Children under 16 free in parents' room. AE, CB, DC, EURO, JCB, MC, V. Parking $20. Subway: B, D, E to 53rd St.; B, N, R, Q to 57th St.

A major 1993 renovation reestablished the Gorham as an affordable contemporary choice in Midtown West, and a 1997 face-lift refreshed the bright new look. The large rooms have fully equipped kitchenettes; two queen-size or one king-size bed; and baths with marble tubs, hair dryers, makeup mirrors, and phones. The suites feature a separate sitting room with a sofa bed and whirlpool bath. Large cable TVs with Nintendo and a location not far from Times Square and the theme restaurants there and on 57th Street make the Gorham a favorite with kids.

Dining: Buffet breakfast is served in a private breakfast room.

Amenities: Concierge, breakfast room service (daily 7–10am), dinner room service (daily 6–10pm) from Castellano's Italian restaurant next door, business/secretarial services. Fitness center.

✪ **The Mansfield.** 12 W. 44th St. (Fifth & Sixth aves.), New York, NY 10036. ☎ **800/255-5167** or 212/944-6050. Fax 212/764-4477. 129 units. A/C TV TEL. $229 double; $279 suite; $650 penthouse suite. Rates include continental breakfast. AE, MC, V. Free parking. Subway: 4, 5, 6 to Grand Central; B, D, F, Q to 42nd St.

In 1994, Bernard Goldberg and his Gotham Hospitality Group (they also own the Franklin, Roger Williams, Shoreham, and Wales) took over the Mansfield, transforming it from lackluster into stylish. Their renovations on this 1904 residence for well-to-do bachelors incorporated details like the lobby's 16-foot coffered ceiling, the hallways' terrazzo floors, and the oval staircase's mahogany railing. The guest rooms, all with soundproof windows, are decorated with headboards in metal mesh and white-and-beige linens; the marble baths feature chrome faucets, European hand-held showerheads, and plenty of shelf space. For the price, the free extras are unequaled: continental breakfast, cappuccino in the lobby, after-theater dessert buffet Monday to Saturday accompanied by live harp music, Monday-night music recitals, an extensive CD and video library, and parking at no extra cost (in New York?).

New York Hilton and Towers at Rockefeller Center. 1335 Sixth Ave. (53rd & 54th sts.), New York, NY 10019. ☎ **800/HILTONS** or 212/586-7000. Fax 212/315-1374. 2,136 units. A/C MINIBAR TV TEL. $227–$332 double or twin; $500–$2,750 Tower suite. Extra person $30. Children under 19 free in parents' room. AE, DC, DISC, ER, EURO, JCB, MC, V. Valet parking $35. Subway: B, D, E to 53rd St.; E, F to 53rd St./Fifth Ave.

The Hilton squeezes more than 2,100 units into 46 stories and almost always overflows with convention goers. The cubbyhole-size rooms feature wall-to-wall blue-tinted windows and conveniences like hair dryers, coffeemakers, and irons with ironing boards. Since 1990, the hotel has spent more than $150 million to renovate, with most of that sum going to create the Tower, an intimate hotel-within-a-hotel from the 38th to 44th floors; it offers larger rooms and its own reception area, a lounge with a video phone desk, and a concierge. Tower guests receive complimentary continental breakfast buffet and afternoon tea and snacks, and each room has a fax machine, two-line phone with data port, and safe.

Dining: Choices include two restaurants, Players Sports Bar, the Mirage cocktail lounge, and the International Promenade, serving breakfast, coffee, and afternoon tea. Check chapter 6 for better restaurants.

Amenities: Concierge, room service (daily 5am–1am), hotel hot line that allows guests to call one number for all hotel-related problems, children's programs (May–Sept). Business center, fitness center ($9 per day/$16 per stay).

✪ **New York Marriott Marquis.** 1535 Broadway (45th & 46th sts.), New York, NY 10036. ☎ **800/843-4898** or 212/398-1900. Fax 212/704-8930. 1,919 units. A/C MINIBAR TV TEL. $189–$360 double; $380 double Concierge room; $350–$3,500 suite. AE, CB, DISC, JCB, MC, V. Parking $30. Subway: 1, 2, 3, 9, N, R to Times Square; N, R to 49th St.

The construction of the 50-story Marriott Marquis was a milestone for Times Square in 1985. Advocates hailed it as a sign of the neighborhood's resurgence, but the Helen Hayes and Morosco theaters were destroyed to make room for it, leading theater lovers to argue that it portended the end of Broadway. Both the hotel and the Great White Way have thrived in ways no one could've predicted. Though many New Yorkers continue to love to hate the pedestrian-unfriendly John Portman–designed hotel, it's a top choice of travelers. Its centerpieces are Portman's signature atrium, rising 37 floors to be the world's tallest, and the glass-enclosed elevators that zip up the atrium's center at knee-buckling speed. The surprisingly large guest rooms have three phones, desks, coffeemakers, and hair dryers. Concierge Level amenities include a complimentary continental breakfast and evening hors d'oeuvres. In 1997, the hotel completed a $20-million redecoration, which, among many improvements, added specially designed work stations and ergonomic chairs to every room.

Dining/Diversions: On clear nights, the View, the three-story revolving rooftop restaurant (see chapter 9), offers some good views; on cloudy nights it offers only mediocre food and bad music. There are several restaurants and lounges in the atrium and many better ones just steps from the hotel (see chapter 6).

Amenities: 24-hour room service. Business center, health club with whirlpool and sauna, American Express travel desk.

Novotel New York. 226 W. 52nd St. (at Broadway), New York, NY 10019. ☎ **800/NOVOTEL** or 212/315-0100. Fax 212/765-5369. 474 units. A/C MINIBAR TV TEL. $189–$319 double; $600–$705 suite. 2 children under 17 free in parents' room. AE, CB, DC, JCB, MC, V. Parking $16. Subway: 1, 9 to 50th St.; B, D to 53rd St.

Near the Broadway theaters, the Novotel New York was built over an existing four-story building, so don't be surprised by the small street-level entrance. Once you've taken the elevator up to the seventh-floor Sky Lobby looking down Broadway to Times Square, you'll find a perfectly nice French-modern hotel with some spectacular views. The decor isn't earth-shattering, but the guest rooms are soundproof; have king-size, sofa, and/or two double beds; and come with safes, a large movie selection, and spacious baths. Two children under 17 can sleep free in their parents' room, and both receive complimentary breakfast and a bag of surprises featuring a toy Dolfi, Novotel's mascot; in the lobby, the Children's Corner has a Lego table, and Café Nicole has a kids' menu. Business travelers can make use of a computer and fax machine in the lobby's Business Corner, as well as laptop and cellular phone rental.

Dining/Diversions: Café Nicole, on the seventh floor, offers European cuisine, terrace dining, and entertainment.

Amenities: Room service (daily 6:30am–midnight). Business center, fitness room.

The Paramount. 235 W. 46th St. (Broadway & Eighth Ave.), New York, NY 10036. ☎ **800/ 225-7474** or 212/764-5500. Fax 212/354-5237. 618 units. A/C TV TEL. $220–$280 double; $425–$525 suite. Children under 13 free in parents' room. AE, DC, MC, V. Parking $16. Subway: 1, 2, 3, 9 to Times Square; A, C, E to Port Authority.

If you like your hotel room bigger in style than in square feet, designer Philippe Starck transformed the old Century Paramount into something for you. A worldly crowd that oozes money seems to have been put in place by the decorator. The lobby's neo–art deco design was inspired by the great transatlantic ocean liners, with a staircase that seems to float and leads up to the mezzanine, a popular perch for people-watching. The extremely compact rooms are unmistakably Starck: stainless-steel baths, silk-screen headboards (*The Lacemaker,* by Vermeer, might hover larger than life over your dreams), and wacky touches like a swiveling armoire staring at you like a cyclops's single eye. Amenities include two-line phones with data ports, TVs with VCRs, and fresh flowers. A well-equipped playroom is kid-friendly, but unless you get a suite be prepared to get the little ones their own room.

Dining: The Whiskey (see chapter 9) bar is eternally trendy and inexcusably haughty, Dean & DeLuca runs the gourmet cafe, and there's dining in the Mezzanine. Physically connected but not affiliated with the hotel is Coco Pazzo Teatro, a popular Italian restaurant run by Pino Luongo (see Le Madri, chapter 6).

Amenities: Concierge, 24-hour room service. Children's playroom, business center, fitness center.

Salisbury Hotel. 123 W. 57th St. (Sixth & Seventh aves.), New York, NY 10010. ☎ **800/ NYC-5757** or 212/246-1300. Fax 212/977-7752. 194 units. A/C TV TEL. $239–$279 double; $269–$429 1-bedroom suite; $399–$499 2-bedroom suite. Extra person $20. Rates include continental breakfast. Children under 16 free in parents' room. AE, CB, DC, JCB, MC, V. Parking $18. Subway: N, R or B, Q to 57th St.

This no-frills hotel across from Carnegie Hall is housed in a 1930 neo-Gothic building that has always been owned by the Calvary Baptist Church next door. Since the rooms were originally in an apartment hotel, they're significantly larger than those in most New York hotels, and most have kitchenettes with a sink and small refrigerator. All have large walk-in closets, sofas, cable TVs, and phones with data port and voice mail. In 1997, the suites were outfitted with small business centers. The location and price of the one-bedroom and two-bedroom suites make them great for families. Room service is available 24 hours from nearby restaurants (menus are in the rooms), and health-club privileges at Le Parker Méridien are available for a small fee.

✪ **Sheraton Manhattan Hotel.** 790 Seventh Ave. (at 52nd St.), New York, NY 10019. ☎ **800/325-3535** or 212/581-3300. Fax 212/541-9219. 650 units. A/C MINIBAR TV TEL. $209–$385 double; $450–$600 1-bedroom suite; $750 2-bedroom suite. Rates include continental breakfast. 2 children under 19 free in parents' room. AE, CB, DC, DISC, ER, JCB, MC, V. Parking $25. Subway: B, Q to 53rd St.

Much smaller than its sibling hotel across the street, the Sheraton Manhattan caters to business travelers. It closed for 5 weeks in 1997 to undergo a complete renovation. The result: All rooms boast Corporate Club status, meaning they have oversize desks, ergonomic rolling desk chairs, Hewlett-Packard OfficeJet printer/fax/copier machines, and dual-line phones with data ports and voice mail. New amenities include evening hors d'oeuvres in the expanded Club Lounge and in-room coffeemakers with Starbucks coffee. Service is efficient given the hotel's size.

Dining: Bistro 790 serves American and Mediterranean food.

Amenities: Concierge, 24-hour room service, free local phone calls. Business center, fitness center with pool.

Sheraton New York Hotel & Towers. 811 Seventh Ave. (at 53rd St.), New York, NY 10019. ☎ **800/325-3535** or 212/581-1000. Fax 212/262-4410. 1,801 units. A/C MINIBAR TV TEL. $189–$275 double; $209–$385 Club Level room; $450–$700 suite. 2 children under 19 free in parents' room. AE, CB, DC, DISC, ER, JCB, MC, V. Parking $30. Subway: B, D to 53rd St.

With its Midtown West location and large number of rooms, the Sheraton New York has always been convention central. Now, with the 1997 opening of the state-of-the-art Executive Conference Center with 12 meeting rooms for 10 to 75 people, the Sheraton attracts its share of the midsize business market too.

Recent renovations made the hotel more efficient, but with 1,801 rooms, don't expect the front-desk personnel to greet you smilingly by name. Set up for the business traveler, each room features an oversize desk and phone with voice mail and data port. Amenities for Club Level guests (floors 41 to 48) include work areas with a Hewlett-Packard OfficeJet printer/fax/copier, coffeemakers with Starbucks coffee, hair dryers, fully stocked minibars, and complimentary continental breakfast and evening hors d'oeuvres in the Club Level lounge.

The Towers is an upscale hotel-within-a-hotel on the 49th and 50th floors with its own registration desk. Its 54 rooms boast down comforters, Frette linen, fresh flowers, and valet stands. Complimentary breakfast, afternoon tea, cocktails, and appetizers are served in the Tower lounge.

Dining/Diversions: Streeter's New York Cafe is a casual restaurant, and Hudson's Sports Bar & Grill has 30 TVs and satellite feed.

Amenities: Concierge, 24-hour room service, free local phone calls. Business center, health club, free use of the pool across the street at the Sheraton Manhattan, Executive Conference Center.

✪ **The Shoreham.** 33 W. 55th St. (Fifth & Sixth aves.), New York, NY 10019. ☎ **800/553-3347** or 212/247-6700. Fax 212/765-9741. 84 units. A/C TV TEL. $245 double; $295 suite. Rates include continental breakfast. AE, DC, MC, V. Parking $14. Subway: E, F to 53rd St./Fifth Ave.; B, Q to 57th St.

Sleek and modern, this boutique hotel owned by the Gotham Hospitality Group (which also owns the Franklin, Mansfield, Roger Williams, and Wales) doesn't compromise on comfort. It's a good small alternative to its pricier and more convention-prone Midtown neighbors. The lounge has anodized aluminum furniture, and the guest rooms have beds with back-lit headboards (perforated steel, through which tiny beams of light tastefully shine), neutral-colored furnishings, and stainless-steel torchières. The sofas and chairs are covered in velveteen. Each room includes a refrigerator stocked with complimentary mineral water, a cedar-lined closet, and a CD player and a VCR to enjoy selections from the hotel's extensive library. You can work out at the nearby Cardio Fitness health club. The hotel has plans to add 96 more rooms in an adjacent building.

Dining: La Caravelle, a fine and very expensive French restaurant, is adjacent.

Amenities: Complimentary evening dessert buffet, coffee bar.

The Warwick 65 W. 54th St. (at Sixth Ave.), New York, NY 10019. ☎ **800/223-4099** or 212/247-2700. Fax 212/957-8915. 422 units. A/C MINIBAR TV TEL. $265–$315 double; $450–$600 1-bedroom suite; $550–$1,200 2-bedroom suite. Children under 17 free in parents' room. AE, DC, JCB, MC, V. Parking $28. Subway: B, Q to 57th St.; B, D to 53rd St.

The 36-story art deco Warwick was built in 1926 by publishing tycoon William Randolph Hearst as an apartment building for his Hollywood friends, including his mistress, Marion Davies, who had a specially designed floor. (Conveniently, Hearst's office building was, and still is, 5 blocks away.) Now the Warwick is the flagship property of Warwick International Hotels. A couple of years ago, a new manager arrived, and the hotel is all the better for it (improvements continue with renovations through 1999). The general manager is now making sure the hotel matches the high standards other properties in the chain are known for.

Because the building was originally residential, the rooms are oversize and have spacious closets and large marble baths. Some suites even have wraparound terraces (ask for the wonderful no. 2706, which was Cary Grant's residence for 12 years). Newly renovated rooms, ask for one, are decorated with traditional mahogany furniture and flowery fabrics.

Dining: Ciao Europa is a Northern Italian restaurant that serves breakfast, lunch, and dinner (see chapter 6); Randolph's bar, a great after-work/cocktails place, has a light menu of salads and sandwiches.

Amenities: Concierge, 24-hour room service. Business center, fitness center.

MODERATE

✪ **Hotel Metro.** 45 W. 35th St. (Fifth & Sixth aves.), New York, NY 10001. ☎ **800/356-3870** or 212/947-2500. Fax 212/279-1310. 175 units. A/C TV TEL. $160–$225 double; $225–$300 suite. Rates include continental breakfast. AE, DC, MC, V. Parking $18. Subway: B, D, F, N, Q, R to Herald Square.

Only recently are Americans finding out what foreign travelers have known for a long time—the Metro is as good a hotel as exists for the crowd who prefer moderately priced places with some design style. This art deco jewel near Herald Square has larger rooms than you'd expect for the price, decorated with stylish headboards, nightstands, and Man Ray photos on the walls. The rooms have phones with data port and voice mail, TVs with movie channels, and marble baths with hair dryers. The view of the Empire State Building from the rooftop terrace is a Kodak moment. Room service from the Metro Grill and the fitness room are bonuses.

INEXPENSIVE

✪ **Best Western Manhattan Hotel.** 17 W. 32nd St. (Sixth Ave. & Broadway), New York, NY 10001. ☎ **800/551-2303** or 212/736-1600. Fax 212/563-4007. 201 units. A/C TV TEL. $119–$179 double; $159–$259 suite. Children under 14 free in parents' room. AE, DC, DISC, MC, V. Subway: B, D, F, N, Q, R to Herald Square.

In the shadow of the Empire State Building and within the growing area known as Koreatown, the Best Western Manhattan occupies a beautiful beaux arts building just steps from Macy's and Madison Square Garden. The rooms have in-room coffee, Nintendo games, and hair dryers, while most suites—your best buy—have whirlpool baths. The hotel boasts two restaurants: Dae Dong, a Manhattan branch of the very good Queens Korean restaurant of the same name, and Tullio's, a 24-hour Italian place with a rooftop bar. Tullio's also provides around-the-clock room service. The hotel has a new business center and a fitness room.

Comfort Inn Midtown. 129 W. 46th St. (Sixth Ave. & Broadway), New York, NY 10036. ☎ **800/567-7720** or 212/790-2700. Fax 212/790-2760. 80 units. A/C TV TEL. $109–$199 double. Children under 14 in parents' room free. AE, DC, DISC, MC, V. Subway: 4, 5, 6, 7, S to Grand Central.

Apple Core Hotels spent $10 million refurbishing the Hotel Remington, rechristening it the Comfort Inn Midtown last year. The renovation brightened the public spaces, and the small rooms now don't seem so bad after all—especially for the price. Front rooms have more light. Additions include a fitness center, a business center, and in-room amenities like coffeemakers and hair dryers. What hasn't changed is the excellent location, steps from Times Square, Rockefeller Center, and the Theater District.

✪ **Herald Square Hotel.** 19 W. 31st St. (Fifth Ave. & Broadway), New York, NY 10001. ☎ **800/727-1888** or 212/279-4017. Fax 212/643-9208. 120 units, most with bathroom. A/C TV TEL. $75–$105 standard double; $95–$125 large double. AE, DISC, JCB, MC, V. Parking $21. Subway: N, R to 28th St.

Near the Empire State Building and Macy's, the former home of *Life* magazine has been reincarnated as a clean, comfortable budget hotel. Welcoming guests is Philip Martiny's sculpted cherub known as *Winged Life* over the entrance. Inside, tribute is paid to the former occupant with the magazine's covers everywhere. The accommodations are small but come with safes. Manager Abraham Puchall and his staff willingly dispense advice on sightseeing and shopping, and the money you save here will go a long way toward shopping splurges.

Hotel Edison. 228 W. 46th St. (Broadway & Eighth Ave.), New York, NY 10036. ☎ **800/637-7070** or 212/840-5000. Fax 212/596-6850. 869 units. A/C TV TEL. $115–$135 double; $120–$170 suite. AE, CB, DC, DISC, MC, V. Parking $20. Subway: A, C, E to 42nd St./Times Square; N, R to 49th St.

At these prices, right in the Theater District, don't expect a Broadway smash, but it'll do for a mediocre run. With rooms older than some people might like, and older than many of the people who stay in them, the Edison is in the center of the ever-friendlier, ever-safer Times Square. If you find you don't want to do time in your room, you can visit the downstairs cafe and bar, which attract a vibrant crowd of Broadway "gypsies," other theater hangers-on, and some New Yorkers who come for the old-time atmosphere. The rooms are often booked by tour groups.

✪ **Portland Square Hotel.** 132 W. 47th St. (Sixth & Seventh aves.), New York, NY 10036. ☎ **800/388-8988** or 212/382-0600. Fax 212/382-0684. 145 units, most with bathroom. A/C TV TEL. $94 double with 1 bed; $104 double with 2 beds; $109 for 3 people in 2 beds; $125 for 4 people in 2 beds. AE, JCB, MC, V. Parking $24. Subway: B, D, F, Q to Rockefeller Center.

A hotel room you'd dare to sleep in for a price cheaper than a Broadway ticket? Check out the Portland Square. Another Puchall family project (see Herald Square Hotel above), this budget place, once home to Broadway cast members like James Cagney, has kept its Theater District heritage alive. The small lobby and tiny rooms are decorated with memorabilia of the 1920s and 1930s and photos of turn-of-the century New York. The clean, simple rooms are furnished in a way that reflects the price. There's a small exercise room and a self-service business center with fax machines and computers. Don't let the signs marring the front windows scare you off.

✪ **Quality Hotel & Suites Rockefeller Center.** 59 W. 46th St. (Fifth & Sixth aves.), New York, NY 10036. ☎ **800/567-7720** or 212/719-2300. Fax 212/921-8929. 192 units. A/C TV TEL. $119–$179 double; $189–$239 suite. Rates include continental breakfast. Children under 19 free in parents' room. AE, CB, DC, MC, V. Parking $25. Subway: B, D, F, Q to 49th St./Rockefeller Center.

Reserve it right away! For a reasonable rate, you get a comfortable, tastefully furnished room, which if not plush with brocade and antiques at least has amenities you'd expect from a more expensive hotel—coffeemaker, hair dryer, iron and ironing board, and phone with voice mail and data port. The 1902 landmark building, with a beautiful beaux arts facade and lobby with mahogany and marble, has been recently renovated to include a fitness center and a business center and meeting rooms. The location, between Rockefeller Center and Times Square, is ideal for both business and pleasure, and complimentary continental breakfast and free local phone calls add to the bargain.

9 Midtown East & Murray Hill

See the "Midtown Accommodations" map (pp. 78–79) for hotels in this section.

VERY EXPENSIVE

✪ **The Four Seasons Hotel New York.** 57 E. 57th St. (Park & Madison aves.), New York, NY 10022. ☎ **800/332-3442** in the U.S., 800/268-6282 in Canada, or 212/758-5700. Fax 212/758-5711. 370 units. A/C MINIBAR TV TEL. $565–$750 double; $1,050–$5,000 1-bedroom suite; $2,300–$2,800 2-bedroom suite. Room with terrace $50 extra. 1 child under 19 free in parents' room. AE, CB, DC, ER, JCB, MC, V. Valet parking $37. Subway: 4, 5, 6, N, R to 60th St.

Hollywood wearing deconstructed Italian designer clothes meets Manhattan in the grand but frosty lobby. Aging, rich rock stars spice the brew, as can anyone with a generous expense account or a wad of cash to drop. Designed by I. M. Pei in 1993, the limestone-clad tower rises 52 stories, providing hundreds of rooms with a view. You'll immediately know this place is special, and it knows it too. The lobby has marble floors and a high back-lit onyx ceiling. The guest rooms, among New York's largest (averaging 600 square feet), have entrance foyers, sitting areas, desks with leather chairs, and sycamore-paneled dressing areas. The Florentine marble baths have separate tubs and showers. Other special touches include goose-down pillows, Frette linen, and slippers. You'd expect less? Then you haven't heard that $1 million was spent on *each* room.

Dining: Fifty-Seven, Fifty-Seven is a fine contemporary New American grill and popular power-breakfast and lunch spot. The snazzy Bar offers 14 types of martinis to wash down light meals. The Lobby Lounge features lunch, afternoon tea, cocktails, and hors d'oeuvres.

Amenities: Concierge, 24-hour room service. Business center, fitness center, spa.

Morgans. 237 Madison Ave. (at 37th St.), New York, NY 10016. ☎ **800/334-3408** or 212/686-0300. Fax 212/779-8352. 113 units. A/C MINIBAR TV TEL. $290–$310 double; $415–$650 suite. AE, DC, DISC, MC, V. Parking $32. Subway: 6 to 33rd St.; 4, 5, 6 to Grand Central.

Ian Schrager's first boutique hotel (also see the Barbizon, Paramount, Radisson Empire, Royalton, "Best Bets," and "Rooms to Grow") opened in 1984 as a low-profile "anti-hotel" without a sign or a staff experienced in hotel management. There's still little to give away its Murray Hill location—except for the limos occasionally dropping off some high-profile type. But today the staff is experienced and competent. The hotel's original designer, Andrée Putman, also renovated the stylish interior in 1995; it eschews the *épater les bourgeois* quotient of the Starck-designed Paramount and Royalton. The rooms are in a monochrome palette of taupe, camel, and ivory, with some black thrown in, and have custom maple cabinets, desks, and window seats. The small baths are Putman signature, with black-and-white-checkered walls, stainless-steel sinks, and hospital-like fixtures. An updated communications system means that the rooms have fax machines and direct two-line phones with conference and speaker capability.

Dining/Diversions: Asia de Cuba (see chapter 6) was one of 1997's most-touted restaurant openings. A private breakfast room is on the fourth floor. In the cellar, Morgans Bar is a late-night spot for musicians, artists, and models.

Amenities: Concierge, 24-hour room service. Complimentary access to nearby New York Sports Club.

✪ **New York Palace.** 455 Madison Ave. (50th & 51st sts.), New York, NY 10022. ☎ **800/ NY-PALACE** or 212/888-7000. Fax 212/303-6000. 891 units. A/C MINIBAR TV TEL. $400–$750 double; $800–$1,500 1-bedroom suite; $1,600–$1,900 2-bedroom suite; $12,000 triplex suite. 2 children under 19 free in parents' room. AE, CB, DC, DISC, ER, EURO, JCB, MC, V. Parking $46. Subway: 6 to 51st St.

The Sultan of Brunei bought this convenient Midtown palace from the Queen of Mean and restored the public rooms with an opulence befitting nouveau royalty. Facing St. Patrick's Cathedral and towering 55 stories over the landmark 1886 McKim, Mead & White–designed Villard Houses, the New York Palace has put complaints of mediocre rooms behind it. The $100-million renovation created a more open, welcoming lobby and carefully updated the aging guest rooms. And as the new home of the revered Le Cirque, the hotel stars center stage in gourmets' dreams. There's also a new high-tech fitness center, which offers aromatherapy and massage therapies. The brand-new Executive Hotel, on floors 31 to 39, offers additional amenities like a dedicated concierge and complimentary food and beverage throughout the day served in the Executive Lounge.

Dining: Le Cirque 2000 (see chapter 6) moved in with high-color panache. Istana serves Mediterranean cuisine and should not be overlooked: It transcends its hotel-restaurant class. The staff is welcoming and helpful.

Amenities: Concierge, 24-hour room service, complimentary weekday shuttle to Wall Street. Business center, fitness center.

The Roosevelt Hotel. 45 E. 45th St. (at Madison Ave.), New York, NY 10017. ☎ **800/ 223-0888,** 888/TEDDYNY, or 212/661-9600. Fax 212/885-6162. 1,040 units. AC TV TEL. $320 double; $560–$1,700 suite. AE, DC, DISC, MC, V. Parking $18. Subway: 4, 5, 6, 7 to Grand Central.

This 1924 grande dame near Grand Central Terminal had become a dingy blight on the landscape until a $65-million renovation brought it back to life in 1997. Architectural adornments, such as tall wall sconces and a brass pendant clock, which had been removed over the years were rescued from dusty storage rooms and returned to embellish the lobby, graced with 27-foot-tall fluted columns and a beautiful ceiling mural. The guest rooms, with mahogany furnishings and floral bed coverings, are outfitted for the 1990s with in-room movies and two-line phones with data port. And let us not forget that Theodore Roosevelt was a native New Yorker.

Dining: The Colonial Room and the Palm Room serve light continental fare in a classic setting. The Madison Club Lounge has extensive cognac and port listings.

Amenities: Concierge, 24-hour room service. Business center, fitness center.

✪ **The St. Regis.** 2 E. 55th St. (at Fifth Ave.), New York, NY 10022. ☎ **800/759-7550** or 212/753-4500. Fax 212/787-3447. 303 units. A/C MINIBAR TV TEL. $475–$585 double; $650–$5,000 suite. AE, CB, DC, ER, EURO, JCB, MC, V. Valet parking $36. Subway: E, F to 53rd St./Fifth Ave.

In 1991, a $150-million restoration by ITT Sheraton (which itself was subsequently bought by the Starwood Hotels group) revived the old-world elegance of this classic beaux arts hotel, and the cost was passed on to guests with some of New York's highest room rates. You do, however, get what you pay for: grand public spaces and guest rooms filled with Louis XV–style furnishings, silk wall coverings, chandeliers, and marble baths with two sinks and separate tubs and shower stalls. Your clothing (two items per person) is pressed as soon as you arrive, each floor has a 24-hour butler who delivers a fresh-fruit plate every day. Fresh flowers perfume your suite.

Dining: Lespinasse (see chapter 6) serves rightfully acclaimed French cuisine with an Asian accent in an opulent dining room. The King Cole Room (see chapter 9), where the Bloody Mary was invented, is a great setting for cocktails. The Astor Court serves afternoon tea under a vaulted ceiling.

Amenities: Concierge, 24-hour room service. Business center, health club.

✪ **The Waldorf-Astoria and Waldorf Towers.** 301 Park Ave. (49th & 50th sts.), New York, NY 10022. ☎ **800/WALDORF** or 212/355-3000. Fax 212/421-8103. 1,280 units. A/C MINIBAR TV TEL. Waldorf-Astoria: $385–$425 double; $450 minisuite; $500–$800 1-bedroom suite; $800–$1,025 2-bedroom suite. Waldorf Towers: $425–$450 double; $1,000–$6,500 suite. AE, CB, DC, DISC, EURO, JCB, MC, V. Valet parking $37. Subway: 6 to 51st St.

The legend lives on in much better shape thanks to the $200 million Hilton Hotels spent to renovate the legendary art deco lobby masterpiece. Each room has a unique decor, and all feature marble baths and the standard necessities.

The exquisite, and more exclusive, Waldorf Towers occupies floors 28 to 42 and has a separate entrance. The rooms and suites feature authentic and reproduction English and French antiques, and many have dining rooms, full kitchens, and maid's quarters. The Towers is renown for excellent butler service and respect for privacy. The Presidential Suite is aptly named, having welcomed many American and world leaders who make this their home when they're in town. It's quite a dramatic scene when the U.S. president is here—cavalcades, armed guards, and helicopters buzzing overhead.

Dining: Yes, the Waldorf Salad was invented here, and many new creations are coming out of the revived Peacock Alley, a dining room just off the central lobby; it deserves the effusive praise it has received for the creative French food of chef Laurent Gras. Bull & Bear serves traditional steaks, chops, and seafood at lunch and dinner. Oscar's serves breakfast, lunch, and dinner in its newly redone bistro setting. Ingaiku serves some of Midtown's best Japanese food, and Sir Harry's Bar serves drinks.

Amenities: Concierge, 24-hour room service. Tower services include butler service, private entrance, and two concierges. Business center, state-of-the-art fitness center run by Plus One Fitness, which provides guests with workout clothes and shoes.

EXPENSIVE

Beekman Tower Hotel. 3 Mitchell Place (First Ave. & 49th St.), New York, NY 10017. ☎ **800/ME-SUITE** or 212/355-7300. Fax 212/753-9366. 171 units. A/C TV TEL. $289 studio suite; $259–$349 1-bedroom suite; $519 2-bedroom suite. Extra person $20. Children under 13 free in parents' room. AE, CB, DC, DISC, JCB, MC, V. Valet parking $23. Subway: 6 to 51st St.

This bold art deco tower built in 1928 presides over a small enclave of historic luxury town houses. Purchased by the Manhattan East Suites Hotels way back in 1963, Beekman Tower underwent a multimillion-dollar renovation in 1990. All the handsome suites boast sitting areas; dining areas; and fully equipped kitchens with microwaves, coffeemakers, and dishwashers; some have terraces. The hotel might be out of the way for easy foot tourism, but corporate travelers, U.N. visitors, and those looking for the quiet of a residential neighborhood should appreciate its location.

Dining: The Zephyr Grill serves breakfast, lunch, and dinner in a deco setting. The Top of the Tower (see chapter 9) has an open-air terrace popular for evening cocktails and skyline views.

Amenities: Concierge, room service (daily 7am–1am), business/secretarial services, grocery shopping service, complimentary in-suite coffee and tea. Fitness center.

Crowne Plaza at the United Nations. 304 E. 42nd St. (First & Second aves.), New York, NY 10017. ☎ **800/879-8836** or 212/986-8800. Fax 212/986-1758. 314 units. A/C MINIBAR TV TEL. $265 double; $345–$595 suite. AE, CB, DC, DISC, JCB, MC, V. Valet parking $18. Subway: 4, 5, 6, 7, S to Grand Central.

At the pleasant Crowne Plaza (until 1997 the Tudor), the guest rooms are furnished with classic English reproductions and boast cable TVs with in-room movies and large marble baths with hair dryers and makeup mirrors. Some suites have Jacuzzi tubs and terraces with views of the Chrysler Building. Business travelers appreciate dual-line speaker phones with data port and voice mail as well as the business center. The Crowne Plaza is convenient for those who have East Side appointments, and though it's a bit out of the way, visitors interested in a quiet neighborhood and quick access to the U.N. should find it fits the bill.

Dining: Cecil's Restaurant features continental cuisine at breakfast, lunch, and dinner. The Regency Lounge is open for cocktails.

Amenities: Concierge, 24-hour room service. Business center, fitness center.

Doral Court. 130 E. 39th St. (Lexington & Park aves.), New York, NY 10016. ☎ **800/ 22-DORAL** or 212/685-1100. Fax 212/889-0287. 198 units. A/C MINIBAR TV TEL. $174–$279 double; $350 suite. Children under 12 free in parents' room. AE, CB, DC, DISC, ER, EURO, JCB, MC, V. Parking $25. Subway: 4, 5, 6, 7, S to Grand Central.

The three Doral properties in this chapter (see below) share a quiet Murray Hill location and are near Rockefeller Center, the United Nations, the Empire State Building, and Grand Central Terminal. The Doral Court, the largest, received a complete renovation in 1998, acquiring a more contemporary style. The rooms contain king-size beds, dressing alcoves, walk-in closets, and writing desks; suites offer living rooms, kitchenettes, and balconies. The Courtyard Cafe serves meals indoors or out in a secluded garden spot and offers room service daily 7 to 10:30am and 5 to 10pm. The Doral Court's guests have signing privileges at the Doral Tuscany and use of the Doral Fitness Center 1 block away.

In 1997, the 200-unit **Doral Park Avenue,** 70 Park Ave.. at 38th Street, New York, NY 10016, (☎ **800/22-DORAL** or 212/687-7050; fax 212/949-5924), underwent a $5-million refurbishment. It's now the most costly of the three ($195–$380 double), and though it no longer shares signing privileges with the other Dorals, guests still have use of the fitness center 1 block away. The 122-unit **Doral Tuscany,** 120 E. 39th St., between Lexington ans Park avenues, New York, NY 10016 (☎ **800/ 22-DORAL** or 212/686-1600; fax 212/779-78220, is the smallest of the three but offers the largest rooms ($194–$229 double). With 1998's renovations, the hotel got a much more modern look..

✪ **Drake Swissôtel.** 440 Park Ave. (at 56th St.), New York, NY 10022. ☎ **800/ DRAKENY** or 212/421-0900. Fax 212/688-8053. 487 units. A/C TV TEL. $235–$385 double; $345–$550 1-bedroom suite; $750 2-bedroom suite. Extra person $30. Children under 15 free in parents' room. AE, CB, DC, DISC, EURO, JCB, MC, V. Valet parking $30. Subway: 4, 5, 6, N, R to 59th/60th sts.; E, F to 53rd St./Lexington Ave.

For no-nonsense travelers who prefer efficiency to charm, the well-located Drake, part of the prestigious Swiss chain, is the answer. Since this was originally built as an apartment house, each room is large enough for a king-size or European twin beds, walk-in closet with safe, a sitting area, an oversize desk, and a refrigerator. A $35-million improvement updated the rooms and added the Swissôffice business center and a state-of-the-art fitness center.

Dining: The Drake Bar and Lounge serves European and American food and Swiss wines.

Amenities: Concierge, 24-hour room service, complimentary car service to Wall Street weekday mornings. Swissôffice business center with meeting rooms complimentary for first 2 hours, fitness center.

Hotel Elysée. 60 E. 54th St. (Madison & Park aves.), New York, NY 10022. ☎ **800/ 535-9733** or 212/753-1066. Fax 212/980-9278. 99 units. A/C TV TEL. $224–$265 double;

$295–$775 suite. Rates include continental breakfast. AE, CB, DC, JCB, MC, V. Valet parking $24. Subway: E, F to 53rd St./Park Ave.

The Elysée sets the standard for the growing trend of service-oriented boutique hotels. A 1994 renovation rendered the charming East Sider a favorite with the power elite and a discerning European clientele. The decor, and the people, in the lobby are strikingly stylish. The intimate but ample guest rooms are decorated with antique furniture, and the Italian marble baths come with Caswell-Massey toiletries. The Piano Suite boasts a Steinway that once belonged to Vladimir Horowitz. Complimentary breakfast, afternoon tea, and cocktail-hour wine and cheese are served in the attractive second-floor sitting room and library.

Dining: Monkey Bar (see chapter 6) is a gourmet restaurant and late-night gathering spot for the see-and-be-seen crowd.

Amenities: Concierge, room service from Monkey Bar during lunch and dinner hours, business/secretarial services. Complimentary privileges at nearby New York Sports Club.

The Kimberly. 145 E. 50th St. (Lexington & Third aves.), New York, NY 10022. ☎ **800/ 683-0400** or 212/755-0400. Fax 212/486-6915. 184 units. A/C TV TEL. $235–$340 double; $255–$425 1-bedroom suite; $399–$665 2-bedroom suite. Extra person $25. Children under 17 free in parents' room. AE, DC, DISC, JCB, MC, V. Valet parking $25. Subway: 6 to 51st St.

Suites, with dining areas, living rooms, fully equipped kitchens, marble baths with deep tubs, and private balconies, make up most of the hotel, but its regular rooms are handsome and comfortable too, with double beds and minirefrigerators. In-room amenities include two TVs, two-line phones with data port, fax machines, and irons and ironing boards. A unique bonus is the complimentary 3-hour sunset cruise that circles Manhattan island on the New York Health & Racquet Club yacht (May–Oct). Reasonable summer and weekend rates mean you could be standing on your private balcony overlooking Manhattan for a lot less than you'd pay for a cell-like room in many Midtown hotels.

Dining/Diversions: The Tam-Tam Bar is an American bistro. Tatou (see chapter 9) is a supper club for dinner, dancing, and cocktails.

Amenities: Clef d'Or concierge, 24-hour room service. Access to New York Health & Racquet Club, with a pool, tennis courts, indoor golf, a fitness center, and a spa.

Omni Berkshire Place. 21 E. 52nd St. (at Madison Ave.), New York, NY 10022. ☎ **800/ THE-OMNI** or 212/753-5800. Fax 212/754-5037. 366 units. A/C MINIBAR TV TEL. $229–$389 double; $450–$695 suite. Children under 17 free in parents' room. AE, DC, DISC, JCB, MC, V. Valet parking $32. Subway: E, F to 53rd St./Fifth Ave.

Reopened in 1995 after a major renovation, the Omni Berkshire is ideally located in the heart of Midtown, a block from Rockefeller Center, making it a favorite overnight respite for business travelers. The classic Regency-style lobby complements the rooms, which are decorated in soft oyster and gold and boast marble baths. The in-room business amenities include work desks, fax machines, two-line phones with data ports, voice mail, and complimentary daily *New York Times.*

Dining: Top-rated Kokachin features fresh seafood prepared with French and Asian accents. There's casual dining at the Atrium Court.

Amenities: Concierge, 24-hour room service. Business center, health club.

✪ **The Roger Williams.** 131 Madison Ave. (at 31st St.), New York, NY 10016. ☎ **888/ 448-7788** or 212/448-7000. Fax 212/448-7007. 209 units. AC TV TEL. $175–$275 double. Extra person $15. Rates include continental breakfast. 2 children under 12 stay free in parents' room. AE, DC, MC, V. Free parking. Subway: 6 to 33rd St.

In 1997, the Gotham Hospitality Group rescued the down-and-out Roger Williams and turned it into a first-rate boutique hotel not unlike the Gotham's other properties (the Franklin, Mansfield, Shoreham, and Wales). Architect Rafael Viñoly created the 1928 hotel's new $11-million minimalist look, using wood, limestone, titanium, slate, and steel. A Steinway grand piano—played during regular concerts—is the center-piece of the 20-foot-high lobby. The guest rooms are small, but custom-designed fur-niture, such as retractable work stations, makes ingenious use of the limited space. Free amenities include bottled water, gourmet coffee at the all-day cappuccino bar, and a library of CDs for guest to play in their rooms. The hotel has no restaurant, but the nearby American Place (see chapter 6) provides room service for lunch and dinner. Access to a local health club costs $15.

MODERATE

Helmsley Middletowne Hotel. 148 E. 48th St. (Third & Lexington aves.), New York, NY 10017. ☎ **800/843-2157** or 212/755-3000. Fax 212/832-0261. 194 units. A/C TV TEL. $160–$205 double; $275–$325 1-bedroom suite; $475–$600 2-bedroom suite. 2 chil-dren under 13 free in parents' room. AE, CB, DC, JCB, MC, V. Valet parking $27. Subway: 6 to 51st St.

A converted apartment building that still feels like one, the Middletowne doesn't have a lobby, restaurant, or health club. What it does have are large, relatively affordable rooms and suites. They come with refrigerators, two-line phones with fax and com-puter hookup, bath phones, makeup mirrors, and two large closets. The suites with fully equipped walk-in kitchens make this an attractive choice for families who want to save on the high cost of eating out. The Midtown East location puts many attrac-tions within walking distance.

Loews New York. 569 Lexington Ave. (at 51st St.), New York, NY 10022. ☎ **800/836-6471** or 212/752-7000. Fax 212/758-6311. 722 units. A/C TV TEL. $149–$239 double; $250–$700 suite. Extra person $20. Children under 17 free in parents' room. AE, CB, DC, DISC, JCB, MC, V. Parking $27. Subway: 6 to 51st St.

A $26-million renovation in 1991 made this hotel popular with tour groups and busi-ness travelers. The modern lobby bustles with bellmen loading and unloading luggage from tour buses. The rooms are small but contain minirefrigerators, desks, safes, and marble baths. The 17th-floor Club 51 rooms offer amenities like complimentary continental breakfast, evening cordials, and videotapes. The Lexington Avenue Grill has a typical, reasonably priced burger and pasta menu. Room service is available daily 7am to 11:30pm, and the facilities include a business center and a fitness center.

INEXPENSIVE

Hotel Grand Union. 34 E. 32nd St. (Madison & Park aves.), New York, NY 10016. ☎ **212/683-5890.** Fax 212/689-7397. 95 units. A/C TV TEL. $83 double; $95 triple; $110 quad. AE, DISC, MC, V. Parking $20. Subway: 6 to 33rd St.

This is a favorite of international travelers who don't need showy lobbies, fancy rooms, or room service. The Grand Union offers spacious, if drab, rooms for a song. Your best bet is to ask for a renovated room. The single elevator makes for long waits, but chat-ting with the helpful front desk is a good way to pass the time. A coffee shop next to the lobby serves breakfast, lunch, and dinner.

Pickwick Arms Hotel. 230 E. 51st St. (Second & Third aves.), New York, NY 10022. ☎ **800/PICKWIK** in the U.S., 800/874-0074 in Canada, or 212/355-0300. Fax 212/755-5029. 320 units, most with bathroom. A/C TV TEL. $100–$130 double. AE, CB, DC, MC, V. Parking $22. Subway: 6 to 51st St.

Though Manhattan's East Side is known for its posh residences, don't even *begin* to think you'll be ensconced in anything similar at these rates. Still, without plush ameni-ties, you'll be getting a great location. The sometimes astoundingly small rooms are spare, some might even say monk-like, but take the money you save staying here and splurge eating at nearby Lutèce (see chapter 6). Or just paying next month's mortgage. A rooftop garden with skyline views, a deli, and a cocktail lounge add appeal, and the place is basically clean, safe, and well located for Midtown jaunts.

✪ **Quality Hotel Fifth Avenue.** 3 E. 40th St. (at Fifth Ave.), New York, NY 10016. ☎ **800/228-5151** or 212/447-1500. Fax 212/213-0972. 189 units. A/C TV TEL. $115–$195 double. Extra person $10. 2 children under 19 free in parents' room. AE, CB, DC, DISC, EURO, JCB, MC, V. Parking $18. Subway: B, D, F, Q to 42nd St.

The location, price, and quality of the accommodations make this among the best deals to be had in New York. Across Fifth Avenue from the New York Public Library, near Grand Central, Rockefeller Center, and Times Square, the hotel is clean and comfortable, but don't expect frills, Frette, or fabulous-size accommodations. The rooms come with either one or two double beds or a queen-size bed, a work area, and a phone with data port (free local calls). Rooms with a queen-size bed also have a sofa bed or sitting area. For the best view, ask for a high-floor room ending with the number 5. Complimentary morning coffee and newspapers are served in the second-floor gallery. Guests have access to a nearby health club, with a pool, for $15.

Vanderbilt YMCA. 224 E. 47th St. (Second & Third aves.), New York, NY 10017. ☎ **212/ 756-9600.** Fax 212/755-7579. 421 units, 6 with bathroom. A/C TV. $66–$81 double; $81–$91 triple; $101–$121 quad; $121 suite. MC, V. Parking $20. Subway: 6 to 51st St.; E, F to Lexington/Third aves.

This coed YMCA boasts a friendly, youthful atmosphere and a good Midtown location within walking distance of the United Nations, Rockefeller Center, and Grand Central Terminal. The rooms are Spartan and tiny—I repeat, tiny—but the beds do somehow fit, as do the TVs, dressers, and desks. The more expensive rooms have sinks, and the suites have private baths. The communal baths and showers are clean, and you're provided towels and soap. The athletic facilities include two pools. The rooms are booked far in advance. The sports facilities and reasonably priced meals at the International Cafe alone make the Y a worthwhile stop.

10 The Upper West Side

See the "Uptown Accommodations" map (pp. 100–101) for hotels in this section.

VERY EXPENSIVE

Trump International Hotel & Tower. One Central Park West (at 60th St.), New York, NY 10023. ☎ **888/44-TRUMP** or 212/299-1000. Fax 212/299-1150. 167 units. A/C MINIBAR TV TEL. $395 superior suite; $475 deluxe suite; $625–$800 executive suite; $1,350 2-bedroom suite. Children free in parents' room. AE, DC, MC, V. Valet parking $42. Subway: 1, 9, A, B, C, D to Columbus Circle.

Donald Trump's "trophy property" opened in 1997 amid great fanfare. The luxury hotel took up residence in an existing 52-story former–office building that was updated with a glass-and-steel facade designed by Philip Johnson. It offers several signature services that set it apart. Each guest is assigned a personal Trump Attaché, who provides comprehensive business and personal services. With advance notice, a chef from Jean Georges will prepare a gourmet meal in your room's kitchen and serve it course by course.

The tastefully styled guest rooms are on floors 3 to 17 (the other floors are residential condominiums) and feature 10-foot ceilings and windows nearly as tall, some affording views of Central Park and the Manhattan skyline. Besides the standard two-line phones with data port, each room is equipped with a fax machine, an entertainment center (TV, VCR, CD), a full kitchen stocked with china and crystal, and a telescope for taking in the views. The 6,000-square-foot fitness center and spa features a 55-foot lap pool, personal trainers, and a full range of rejuvenating treatments. A surprisingly cultivated venture from the 1980s Bad Boy.

Dining: Jean Georges (see chapter 6) serves contemporary French cuisine by celebrated chef Jean-Georges Vongerichten.

Amenities: Trump Attaché individualized service, concierge, 24-hour room service, free local phone calls, children's programs, free tea service on arrival. Business center, health club, spa.

EXPENSIVE

Radisson Empire Hotel. 44 W. 63rd St. (at Broadway), New York, NY 10023. ☎ **800/ 333-3333** or 212/265-7400. Fax 212/315-0349. 400 units. A/C MINIBAR TV TEL. $250–$270 double; $550–$700 suite. Extra person $20. Children under 14 free in parents' room. AE, CB, DC, DISC, EURO, JCB, MC, V. Parking $25. Subway: 1, 9 to 66th St.; 1, 9, A, B, C, D to Columbus Circle.

One block from Central Park and across from Lincoln Center, the Radisson is ideally located for both daytime and nighttime activities. A $35-million renovation turned a stodgy old property into an acceptable Upper West Side option. High-tech conveniences include two-line phones with data port and voice mail and remote-controlled TVs, VCRs, and CD players in the rooms and heated towel bars, hair dryers, and makeup mirrors in the baths. At press time, Ian Schrager acquired the Radisson but hadn't yet announced if he planned to rename the hotel or have his designer, Philippe Starck, impose the Starck style of Schrager's other properties (the Paramount, Morgans, and Royalton).

Dining: The West 63rd Street Steakhouse serves breakfast, lunch, and dinner and has a bar (but be sure to try nearby Picholine, see chapter 6).

Amenities: 24-hour room service. Fitness center.

MODERATE

The Mayflower Hotel on the Park. 15 Central Park West (61st & 62nd sts.), New York, NY 10023. ☎ **800/223-4164** or 212/265-0060. Fax 212/265-5098. 365 units. A/C TV TEL. $180–$195 double; $200–$220 double with park view; $215–$245 suite; $270–$295 suite with park view; $350–$800 penthouse terrace suite. AE, CB, DC, DISC, ER, JCB, MC, V. Parking $28. Subway: 1, 9, A, B, C, D to Columbus Circle.

The Mayflower is across from Central Park and near Lincoln Center. Though the hotel underwent a 1991 renovation, some rooms are still being made over—be sure to ask for a renovated room. The rooms are generally spacious, though some baths are small, and most include a king-size or two queen-size beds, walk-in closets, a service pantry, and a refrigerator. The more expensive higher-up front rooms offer spectacular park views. Many Lincoln Center performers are housed here, and you may see them working out on the ballet barre in the exercise room. I've received vociferous complaints about inconsistent service, however, and at these prices you shouldn't have to demand a proper welcome. For dining, the Conservatory offers a park view along with breakfast, lunch, and dinner. Amenities include room service (daily 7am–10pm) and a fitness center.

INEXPENSIVE

The Guest Rooms at the West Side YMCA. 5 W. 63rd St. (Broadway & Central Park West), New York, NY 10023. ☎ **800/348-YMCA** or 212/787-4400. Fax 212/875-1334. 525 rms, 25 with bathroom. A/C TV. $69 double without bathroom, $95 double with bathroom. AE, MC, V. Parking $10–$20. Subway: 1, 9 to 66th St.; 1, 9, A, B, C, D to Columbus Circle.

Another Y with a great location (see the Vanderbilt YMCA above), this one in a National Historic Landmark building is steps from Lincoln Center and Central Park. A multimillion-dollar renovation of the public areas and guest rooms has made it more attractive and modern than the typical Y, but it is a Y. The showers and baths are down the hall, and the rooms are small, though they do have air-conditioning, TVs, and maid and even room service. The location and price keep it full almost every night, so book in advance. Overnight guests can use the athletic facilities, which include two pools, gyms, an indoor running track, handball and racquetball courts, and more.

✪ **Hostelling International–New York.** 891 Amsterdam Ave. (at 103rd St.), New York, NY 10025. ☎ **800/909-4776** or 212/932-2300. Fax 212/932-2574. 624 beds, 4 units with bathroom. A/C. $22–$24 AYH members; $3 extra nonmembers. Stays limited to 7 days. JCB, MC, V. Parking $18. Subway: 1, 9 to 103rd St.

With a top price of $27, it just doesn't get any cheaper. Luckily, cheap here doesn't mean so-bad-you-could-die. Housed in a 100-year-old neoclassical landmark building renovated at a cost of $15 million, the hostel offers 624 beds in rooms sleeping two, four, six, or eight. There's a coffee bar, a cafeteria, and a large garden out back that makes for a friendly atmosphere and encourages mingling between foreign visitors and Americans. The upper Upper West Side neighborhood has improved over the years, with many restaurants and clubs opening up, but all sightseeing attractions are a subway ride away. Unlike most hostels, this one operates 24 hours and has no curfew.

Hotel Beacon. 2130 Broadway (at 75th St.), New York, NY 10023. ☎ **800/572-4969** or 212/787-1100. Fax 212/787-8119. 210 units. A/C TV TEL. $145 double; $185–$375 suite. Extra person $15. Children under 17 free in parents' room. AE, CB, DISC, MC, V. Parking $15. Subway: 1, 2, 3, 9 to 72nd St.

A few blocks from Lincoln Center, Central Park, and the Museum of Natural History, the Beacon is one of the Upper West Side's best budget choices for families who don't mind minimal comforts and sometimes drab surroundings in a gentrified neighborhood where baby strollers battle in-line skaters for sidewalk space. Every generous-size room and suite features double beds, fully equipped kitchenettes, and cable TV. There's no room service, but with great gourmet markets like Zabar's and Fairway nearby, cooking is an attractive alternative, and there are plenty of restaurants in the neighborhood. Amenities include hair dryers, complimentary coffee, in-room movies, same-day valet/laundry service, and a coin-operated laundry.

The Milburn. 242 W. 76th St. (Broadway & West End Ave.), New York, NY 10023. ☎ **800/ 833-9622** or 212/362-1006. Fax 212/721-5476. 106 units. A/C TV TEL. $119–$145 studio; $149–$195 suite. Extra person $10. 2 children under 12 free in parents' room. AE, CB, DC, MC, V. Parking $13. Subway: 1, 9 to 72nd St.

On a quiet side street a block from the Beacon, the Milburn offers the same great neighborhood in an all-suite hotel housed in an apartment building (105 of the 120 units have been converted). The studios and suites have kitchenettes equipped with a stove, refrigerator, sink, microwave, and coffeemaker. The rooms and hallways have been renovated in the past couple of years, there's a choice of twin-, queen-, or king-size beds, and all the baths are new. Still, the decor is modern mismatch, and the comforts are limited. There's no restaurant, but some neighborhood restaurants offer discounts to guests. A pass to the nearby Equinox Fitness Club is available for $11.

11 The Upper East Side

See the "Uptown Accommodations" map (pp.100–101) for hotels in this section.

VERY EXPENSIVE

✪ **The Carlyle.** 35 E. 76th St. (at Madison Ave.), New York, NY 10021. ☎ **800/227-5737** or 212/744-1600. Fax 212/717-4682. 180 units. A/C MINIBAR TV TEL. $355–$525 double; $550–$2,400 suite. AE, DC, MC, V. Valet parking $39. Subway: 6 to 77th St.

If you've ever wondered how the rich and famous live, check into the Carlyle. Movie stars and heads of states (including JFK, supposedly once when he was visited by Marilyn) have lain their heads on the fluffy pillows. Why they choose the Carlyle is clear—its hallmark attention to detail. With a staff-to-guest ratio of two-to-one, service is simply the best. The English manor–style decor is luxurious but not excessive, creating the comfortable ambiance of a city apartment. The guest rooms range from single chambers to seven-room suites, some with terraces and pantries. All have marble baths with whirlpool tubs and amenities like Ysatis de Givenchy perfume and Givenchy aftershave. Pets are welcome.

Dining/Diversions: The formal Carlyle Restaurant features French cuisine and is famous for its Sunday brunch. The less formal but still dressy Cafe Carlyle is the supper club where living legend Bobby Short entertains and Woody Allen has played his clarinet (see chapter 9). Charming Bemelmans Bar (named after children's book illustrator Ludwig Bemelman, who created the Madeline books and painted the mural here) also offers live entertainment. The Gallery serves afternoon tea.

Amenities: Concierge, 24-hour room service, business/secretarial services. High-tech fitness center, with sauna and massage room.

✪ **The Lowell.** 28 E. 63rd St. (Park & Madison aves.), New York, NY 10021. ☎ **800/221-4444** or 212/838-1400. Fax 212/319-4230. 65 units. A/C MINIBAR TV TEL. $415 double; $615–$815 1-bedroom suite; $915–$1,015 2-bedroom suite. Extra person $30. AE, DC, DISC, ER, JCB, MC, V. Valet parking $45. Subway: B, Q to 63rd St.

The Lowell is in a historic landmark building that still sports its art deco facade of brick and glazed terra-cotta. From the moment you enter the unassuming lobby with deco and French Empire pieces and a registration desk with a signed Edgar Brandt console, you know you're in a posh place. The rooms and suites are individually appointed with fine antiques that embody old-world elegance. Scandinavian down comforters, king-size feather pillows, and Frette terry-cloth robes heighten the appeal. The marble baths with brass fixtures have hair dryers, makeup mirrors, and Gilchrist & Soames toiletries. Each suite is unique, with features like a fully equipped kitchenette, a wood-burning fireplace, a garden terrace, or even a private gym.

Dining: The Post House serves giant steaks and lobsters in a classic American setting. The Pembroke Room serves breakfast, tea, and weekend brunch.

Amenities: Concierge, room service (daily 7am–midnight). Fitness center with spa treatments available.

✪ **The Mark.** 25 E. 77th St. (Fifth & Madison aves.), New York, NY 10021. ☎ **800/THE-MARK** in the U.S., 800/223-1588 in Canada, or 212/744-4300. Fax 212/744-2749. 180 units. A/C MINIBAR TV TEL. $380–$420 double; $625–$2,800 suite. Extra person $30. Children under 16 free in parents' room. AE, CB, DC, DISC, JCB, MC, V. Valet parking $35. Subway: 6 to 77th St.

After a $35-million renovation, the Mark positioned itself as the Carlyle's Upper East Side rival. It's superbly elegant. Behind the 1929 building's art deco facade is a neoclassical decor. The lobby's custom-designed Biedermeier furniture and marble floors prepare you for the lovely guest rooms, which are large and feature king-size beds with triple sheeting, overstuffed chairs, upholstered sofas, and museum-quality art. Fresh flowers, two-line phones, in-room fax capabilities, and VCRs are standard. The baths are marble or ceramic tile and have oversize tubs, heated towel racks, and luxury toiletries. In a tony neighborhood, it's a home away from home for art lovers (near the Met and Madison Avenue galleries) and those shopping the couture boutiques.

Dining: Mark's (see chapter 6) serves sublime contemporary French food in a wood-paneled English setting. Its Sunday brunch is one of New York's best, and its afternoon tea is a new institution among Upper East Side ladies, both young and old. Mark's Bar, with a separate 77th Street entrance, serves hors d'oeuvres and cocktails.

Amenities: Award-winning concierge, 24-hour room service, complimentary weekday car service to Wall Street and Friday and Saturday evening car service to Theater District. Fitness center.

The Pierre. Fifth Ave. (at 61st St.), New York, NY 10021. ☎ **800/332-3442** or 212/838-8000. Fax 212/940-8109. 202 units. A/C MINIBAR TV TEL. $475–$675 double; $725–$3,700 suite. Rollaway bed $25. Children under 19 free in parents' room. AE, CB, DC, ER, EURO, JCB, MC, V. Valet parking $35. Subway: N, R to 60th St./Fifth Ave.

Towering over the southeast corner of Central Park and under the management of Four Seasons–Regent hotels, the 42-story Pierre epitomizes luxury with public rooms that are opulent but not ostentatious and guest rooms that are comfortable and classic. Recent renovations restored the property's grande-dame elegance and equipped it with enough high-tech efficiency to accommodate the needs of business travelers. There are 28 types of rooms and suites that vary greatly in size, configuration, and decor, and service is friendly to all. Packing and unpacking service is provided on request.

Dining: Cafe Pierre serves fine French food. The Rotunda, with its trompe-l'oeil ceiling, is the hotel's signature room and serves afternoon tea, light meals, and cocktails.

Amenities: Concierge, 24-hour room service, complimentary car service to Theater District. Business center, fitness center.

The Regency. 540 Park Ave. (at 61st St.), New York, NY 10021. ☎ **800/233-2356** or 212/759-4100. Fax 212/826-5674. 360 units. A/C TV TEL. $250–$500 double; $575–$850 1-bedroom suite; $700–$999 2-bedroom suite. Extra person $25. AE, CB, DC, DISC, EURO, JCB, MC, V. Valet parking $35. Subway: N, R to 60th St./Lexington Ave.

The Loews Hotel Group's flagship New York property is known as the temporary home to many foreign dignitaries, a very occasional rock star, corporate executives, and other well-seasoned travelers. They head here for the hotel's attentive personalized service and understated elegance. The decor is, appropriately, Regency style. A recent $5-million refurbishment added two-line phones, fax machines, cable TVs, and refrigerators to every room, and the large marble baths come with TVs and phones. A $25-million "restyling" in late 1998 brought more dazzle to the rooms, lobby, and restaurant.

Dining: The 540 Park restaurant is known for its power breakfast of bagels, coffee, and hostile takeovers, but serves lunch and dinner, too. The Library is perfect for reading or playing a game of chess while enjoying a light but sophisticated meal.

Amenities: Concierge, 24-hour room service, children's programs. Business center, fitness center.

EXPENSIVE

The Barbizon. 140 E. 63rd St. (at Lexington Ave.), New York, NY 10021. ☎ **800/223-1020** or 212/838-5700. Fax 212/888-4271. 300 units. A/C MINIBAR TV TEL. $230–$320

Uptown Accommodations

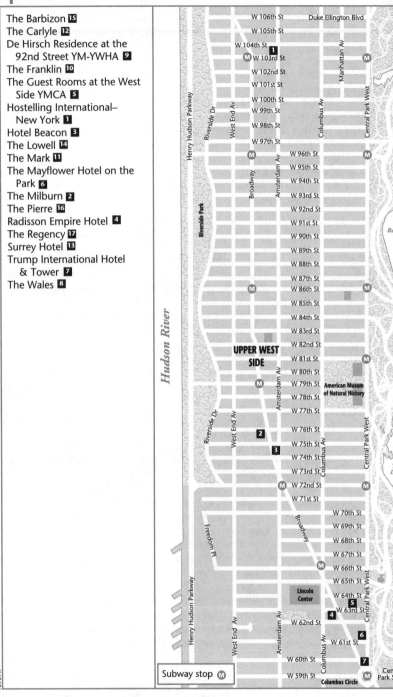

Subway stop **M**

NA-0147

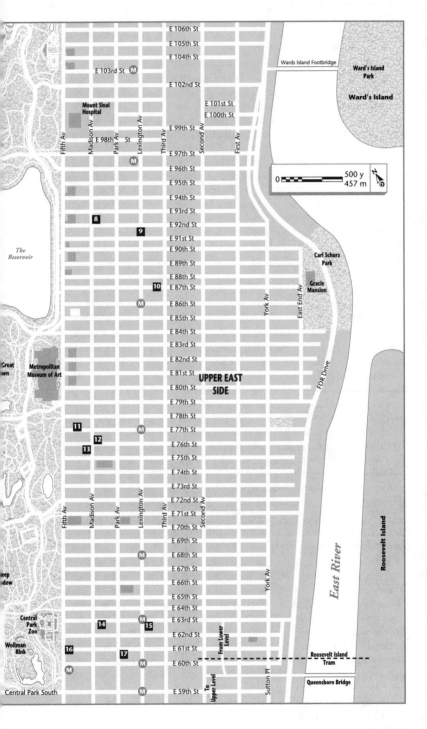

double; $400–$800 suite. Children under 12 free in parents' room on existing bedding. AE, DC, DISC, MC, V. Parking $29. Subway: B, Q to 63rd St.

This neo-Gothic building has been famous since the 1920s, when it began as a women-only hostelry where Grace Kelly, Candice Bergen, and Sylvia Plath all stayed over the years. Then, it served as a nothing-special hotel, perfect for putting up visiting parents who wanted to stay safely and conveniently in Midtown near Bloomingdale's and Central Park. Now, the Barbizon has emerged from a $40-million renovation. Tower Suites have been added, the art deco elegance of the lobby has returned, and the rooms are decorated with custom iron headboards and contemporary furniture and artwork. In-room amenities include two-line speakerphones with data ports and CD players on which to play selections from the hotel's collection. Ian Schrager, the hotelier known for developing boutique hotels like Morgans, the Paramount, and the Royalton, purchased the Barbizon in 1998 but at press time hadn't announced his plans for the hotel.

Dining: There's a breakfast room and a lobby bar and lounge.

Amenities: Concierge, 24-hour room service, business/secretarial services. Complimentary access to on-site Equinox Fitness Club, with a pool and spa.

Surrey Hotel. 20 E. 76th St. (at Madison Ave.), New York, NY 10021. ☎ **800/ME-SUITE** or 212/288-3700. Fax 212/628-1549. 130 units. A/C TV TEL. $250–$290 studio suite; $295–$345 1-bedroom suite; $545–$635 2-bedroom suite. Extra person $20. Children under 13 free in parents' room. AE, CB, DC, DISC, JCB, MC, V. Valet parking $35. Subway: 6 to 77th St.

Those who stay at the Surrey will now have to content themselves with chef Daniel Boulud's food from Café Boulud, a casual French spot he's opening in the space once occupied by Daniel, his restaurant that had seen itself listed among the top 10 in the world and changed the Surrey from a best-kept secret to a sought-after hotel. Daniel has bid adieu to the Surrey and declared bonjour to the old Le Cirque space at 610 Park Ave. (see chapter 6). This all-suite lodging is a few steps from the Carlyle, meaning it too is centrally located, near Central Park, Madison Avenue boutiques, and Museum Mile. The lobby decor is 18th-century English, and the guest rooms are accented with molded ceilings, beveled-glass mirrors, and antiques. All 130 suites have fully equipped kitchens, dining areas, cable TVs, and large baths.

Dining: Café Boulud serves relatively moderately priced French cuisine.

Amenities: Concierge, room service (daily 7–10am, noon–3pm, 6–10pm), complimentary in-suite coffee and tea service, grocery shopping service. Fitness center.

The Wales. 1295 Madison Ave. (at 92nd St.), New York, NY 10128. ☎ **800/428-5252** or 212/876-6000. Fax 212/860-7000. 86 units. A/C TV TEL. $229 double; $299–$329 suite. Rates include continental breakfast. AE, MC, V. Parking $28. Subway: 4, 5, 6 to 86th St.; 6 to 96th St.

In the exclusive Carnegie Hill neighborhood, this nine-story Victorian has been renovated by the Gotham Hospitality Group (see the Franklin, Mansfield, Roger Williams, and Shoreham). Rediscovered architectural features, including a marble staircase, oak woodwork, and numerous fireplaces, were restored. The rooms are small, but the suites are spacious and come with either a king- or queen-size bed and a sofa bed in the living room; many have fireplaces. Every guest room has a TV with VCR; videos are available at the front desk. Central Park and some museums are nearby, but most city sights are a cab ride away. Pluses besides the free breakfast and the lovely neighborhood are complimentary afternoon tea and Sunday chamber-music concerts.

Dining: Adjacent to the lobby are Busby's, which serves American food, and Sarabeth's Kitchen, a neighborhood favorite (see chapter 6).

Amenities: Room service from Busby's (daily 7am–10pm).

MODERATE

✪ **The Franklin.** 164 E. 87th St. (Lexington & Third aves.), New York, NY 10128. ☎ **800/600-8787** or 212/369-1000. Fax 212/369-8000. 53 units. A/C TV TEL. $189–$209 double. Rates include continental breakfast. AE, MC, V. Parking free. Subway: 4, 5, 6, to 86th St.; 6 to 96th St.

You *can* stay on the Upper East Side in style, without paying outrageous prices. In another renovation by the Gotham Hospitality Group (see the Mansfield, Roger Williams, Shoreham, and Wales), designer Henry Stoltzman has dressed up the small rooms with illuminated canopied beds, custom cherrywood-and-steel furniture, TVs with VCR, cedar closets, and modern baths. Breakfast is served in a stylish lounge. Good service only adds to the hotel's appeal.

INEXPENSIVE

De Hirsch Residence at the 92nd Street YM-YWHA. 1395 Lexington Ave. (at 92nd St.), New York, NY 10128. ☎ **800/858-4692** or 212/415-5650. Fax 212/415-5578. 372 units, none with bathroom. A/C. $53 per night, $715 per month single; $38 per person per night, $485–$575 per person per month shared room. AE, MC, V. Parking $20. Subway: 4, 5, 6 to 86th St.; 6 to 96th St.

As with Manhattan's other Ys, travelers on a tight budget should contact the 92nd Street Y well in advance. The de Hirsch Residence isn't a transient hotel as such, but a residence that offers safe, comfortable, and affordable rooms, each with either one or two single beds, a dresser, and bookshelves; there's a $3 surcharge for air-conditioning. Each floor has a large communal bathroom, a fully equipped kitchen/dining room, and laundry facilities. Besides the good location near Central Park and Museum Mile, the best reason to stay here is that you can take advantage of the Y's state-of-the-art fitness facility (pool, weights, racquetball, aerobics) and top-rated cultural happenings (see chapter 9). There are plans to add 200 rooms sometime in 1999.

6

Dining

Every New Yorker is a critic. We have *opinions* on restaurants like people from off our island have lawns—convictions are our turf. So just as suburbanites announce who they are by manicuring their front yards, we take the measure of one another by the ideas we keep and the restaurants we frequent. Nearly every one of us has a favorite Chinatown haunt; is convinced of the superiority of a certain Italian hideaway; knows the best place for pizza; and claims to control the superlative list of hip sidewalk cafes, cozy gardens, and late-night eateries.

If cities had traceable DNA, New York's fundamental genetic code would undoubtedly have a complex strand constructed solely of restaurants. Yet we New Yorkers can be fickle: One moment a restaurant is hot; the next it's passé. So restaurants close with a frequency we wish applied to the arrival of subway trains. Always call ahead.

The sheer variety of eating places is enough to send you shopping for "easy fit" sizes. That's due in part to our immigrant mix. Let a newcomer arrive and see that his or her native foods aren't being served and *zap!*—there's a restaurant, cafe, or grocery to fill the void.

The restaurants I've chosen for this chapter are my roster of merit. I wish there were room for more—especially those serving inexcusably bad food at unconscionably high prices.

PRICES   New York restaurants tend to be crowded, their tables closely packed, and it isn't because we long for another few minutes of intimacy with strangers (though there is one benefit: overhearing an amusing snippet worth repeating to friends). The cause? The high cost of real estate, which is also reflected in what you're charged.

Whatever your categories are, especially if you're from the reasonably priced American heartland, New York's restaurants will all seem *expensive.* Yet remember that good value abounds, and I've cited inexpensive restaurants in every neighborhood—including some of the city's best-kept secrets. Those on a tight budget will want to see the boxes "Choice Choices $15 & Under" and "Affordable Gourmet to Go." And at the end of the chapter I recommend the best ethnic eating and other good-value options.

In the last few years, many of New York's very tippity top, never-pander restaurants started offering **special summer prix-fixe lunches,** sometimes dinners, at a cost mimicking the year ($19.99 in 1999). Though participating restaurants shift and you're most likely to encounter these specials only during Restaurant Week in June, check

Impressions

Though one can dine in New York, one could not dwell there.

—Oscar Wilde

with a few of your out-of-price-range favorites, especially since some extend their discounts until Labor Day. Gotham Bar & Grill and Aureole, for instance, have offered these prix-fixe lunches throughout the year. Reserve as far in advance as possible.

DINING DETAILS   Don't take any guff from uptight **tuxed-up maître d's** in fancy restaurants who treat you like an intruder in their private paradise. Haughtiness is a relic from an era when snobbishness masqueraded as sophistication. If any of them tries to take your money while giving you a hard time, take your money elsewhere.

Chefs now go to the gym, too, and one result is that restaurants as haute as the fabulous Jo Jo and Lutèce or as lowly as a vegetarian student cafeteria offer greater numbers of **low-fat dishes** that won't disappoint the flavor-hungry.

Two simultaneously emerging trends could send the calorie conscious into a coma. Artisanal bakers like Tom Cat and Ecce Panis have popularized **specialty breads** in restaurants around town. At Aquavit, for instance, dried blueberry–and–walnut rolls are offered alongside the standard sourdough. Hip Balthazar has an adjacent bakery, and the refined Bouley Bakery has just a few tables but fabulous baked goods to go. As for desserts, **pastry chefs** are enjoying much-deserved new attention, and the city's top restaurants are showing off show-stopping masterpieces. Some of the most artistic presentations arrive at Moomba, Le Cirque 2000, Aureole, and Payard Pâtisserie and Bistro.

For more popular tastes, **theme restaurants** continue to draw huge crowds (see the box "Where the Themes Are the Message" later in this chapter). But even in finer places of the genre, like Michael Jordan's new steak house in Grand Central Terminal, don't expect to see the celebrities chowing down their burgers at the next table: This is real life, not *Entertainment Tonight,* so they're spending their profits at chic venues like Moomba, Le Cirque, and Odeon. But you could go there, too.

RESERVATIONS   Reservations are nearly always a good idea, especially if your party is more than two. Don't even think of showing up with six or more without reservations, even if the restaurant doesn't normally take them.

GRATUITIES   Tipping is easy—and necessary—in New York. The way to do it: Double the 8¼% sales tax and *voila!* Happy waitperson. In fancier venues, add another 5% for the captain. If the wine steward helps, hand him or her 10% of the bottle's price. Leave a dollar per item, for the checkroom attendant.

1 Best Bets

- **Best Place to Dine on New Year's Eve 1999:** For a glittering decor and a magical setting that make for a festive ambiance year-round, try **Tavern on the Green,** in Central Park at West 67th Street (☎ **212/873-3200**). *If* you can still get a table.
- **Best Spot for a Break-the-Bank Celebration:** The wonderfully colorful choice is **Le Cirque 2000**, 455 Madison Ave. (☎ **212/303-7788**), which matches a daring modern decor with its 19th-century town-house setting and serves masterful French food with reserved elegance.
- **Best Spot for a Romantic Dinner:** Downtown, reserve at **One If By Land, Two If By Sea,** 14 Barrow St. (☎ **212/228-0822**), where candles and lush piano music

take you back in time and put you in the mood. In Midtown, try **March,** 405 E. 58th St. (☎ **212/754-6272**), for a sublime meal in a cozy town house.

- **Best View:** At press time, the **Rainbow Room,** 30 Rockefeller Plaza (☎ **212/ 632-5000**), changed hands and reduced its public dining hours. Still, it has no Midtown competition for its elegant style and vista, rendering the city a sparkling jewel of art deco towers, twinkling bridges, and gleaming modern high-rises. At One World Trade Center, **Windows on the World** (☎ 212/524-7011) has made a triumphant return to its lofty position as the highest fine dining in the world.

- **Best Spot for a Business Lunch: The Four Seasons Grill Room,** 99 E. 52nd St. (☎ **212/754-9494**), is the top choice of New York's power elite.

- **Best Spot for Breakfast:** In the Four Seasons Hotel, 57 E. 57th St., **Fifty-Seven, Fifty-Seven** (☎ 212/758-5757) is noted for its Hollywood mogul munchers.

- **Best Spot for Brunch:** For Uptown elegant, try **Café des Artistes,** 1 W. 67th St. (☎ **212/877-3500**). For Uptown casual, head to **Sarabeth's Kitchen,** 423 Amsterdam Ave. (☎ **212/496-6280**). And for Downtown casual, the choice is **Danal,** 90 E. 10th St. (☎ **212/982-6930**).

- **Best Stop Before the Theater:** There's **Chez Josephine,** 414 W. 42nd St. (☎ **212/ 594-1925**), for nostalgia *à la française,* or **Orso,** 322 W. 46th St. (☎ **212/489-7212**), if you can get in, for Italian. Since I like light Japanese before the theater, I also suggest you head early to **Sushisay,** 38 E. 51st St. (☎ **212/755-1780**), and then get a cab crosstown.

- **Best Pastry and Dessert:** The star-studded showstopper **Moomba,** 133 Seventh Ave. South (☎ **212/989-1414**), offers a dessert named Cookie Jar, created by Wendy Israel—it's so good that chocoholics will forget about the famous faces around them. Close to Upper East Side museums and shopping, **Payard Pâtisserie and Bistrio,** 1032 Lexington Ave. (☎ **212/717-5252**), has a $15 sampler that'll revive any flagging energy.

- **Best Wine Lists:** At 455 Madison Ave., **Le Cirque 2000** (☎ **212/303-7788**) boasts a superb collection of French, Italian, and American vintages picked out by two in-house sommeliers. And **Montrachet,** 239 W. Broadway (☎ **212/219-2777**), has many well-priced bottles. If you don't know how to choose, the staff at both is happy to help.

- **Best Martini:** Taste the French martini (Absolut, Chambord, and pineapple juice) at **Fifty-Seven, Fifty-Seven,** in the Four Seasons Hotel at 57 E. 57th St. (☎ **212/ 758-5757**), or the refreshing summertime watermelon version at the trendy and friendly **Cub Room,** 131 Sullivan St. (☎ **212/677-4100**).

- **Best American Cuisine:** Over many years **Gotham Bar & Grill,** 12 E. 12th St. (☎ **212/620-4020**), and **Aureole,** 34 E. 61st St. (☎ **212/319-1660**), have delivered consistent quality. **Gramercy Tavern,** 42 E. 20th St. (☎ **212/477-0777**), is still the hot new kid even with all the recent competition.

- **Best Chinese Cuisine:** At **New York Noodletown,** 28½ Bowery (☎ **212/349-0923**), the decor is no-star but the food is celestial and well priced. For a more sophisticated ambiance with a touch of French panache, you can't do better than **Tse Yang,** 34 E. 51st St. (☎ **212/688-5447**). For dim sum, go to **Jing Fong,** 20 Elizabeth St. (☎ **212/964-5256**), where crowds don't mean that quality suffers.

- **Best French Cuisine:** Every night, **Chanterelle,** 2 Harrison St. (☎ **212/966-6960**), proves that a New York French restaurant can serve excellent food and still make you feel at home. And **Daniel,** 620 Park Ave. (☎ **212/288-0033** for info), will offer a marvelous contemporary take on the classics when it opens in its new space in early 1999.

- **Best Italian Cuisine:** In Greenwich Village, **Il Mulino,** 86 W. 3rd St. (☎ **212/673-3783**), remains a stalwart of brick walls, low lighting, and wondrous pastas. And in Midtown West, **San Domenico,** 240 Central Park South (☎ **212/265-5959**), gets high marks for owner Tony May's consistently correct versions of Northern Italian.
- **Best Japanese Cuisine:** In Midtown, **Sushisay,** 38 E. 51st St. (☎ **212/755-1780**) serves delectable raw fish. In a category of its own is the inventive **Nobu,** 105 Hudson St. (☎ **212/219-0500**), with Peruvian and Californian influences, serving Japanese like you've never had it.
- **Best Mexican Cuisine:** Leading the trio is **Zarela,** 953 Second Ave. (☎ **212/644-6740**), which also boasts the best margarita; two others close behind are **Mi Cocina,** 57 Jane St. (☎ **212/627-8273**), and **Rosa Mexicano,** 1063 First Ave. (☎ **212/753-7407**).
- **Best Seafood:** The black bass ceviche alone keeps **Le Bernardin,** 155 W. 51st St. (☎ **212/489-1515**), at the top of the world's great fish restaurants.
- **Best Thai Cuisine:** For friendly prices, the top choice is **Thailand Restaurant,** 106 Bayard St. (☎ **212/349-3132**). **Vong,** 200 E. 54th St. (☎ **212/486-9592**), offers gourmet Thai with a French accent.
- **Best Vegetarian Cuisine:** Who knew tempeh and tofu could taste as good as at **Angelica Kitchen,** 300 E. 12th St. (☎ **212/228-2909**)?
- **Best Steak House:** In Brooklyn, **Peter Luger's Steakhouse,** 178 Broadway (☎ **718/387-7400**), offers an old-fashioned take on steak, which doesn't get better than how it's served here. In Manhattan, **Sparks Steak House,** 210 E. 46th St. (☎ **212/687-4855**), serves up first-rate steaks in a classy "masculine" atmosphere.
- **Best Costumes:** At **Lucky Cheng's,** 24 First Ave. (☎ **212/473-0516**), the waitresses are waiters but the food's a bit of a drag, too.
- **Best Uptown People-Watching:** In the New York Palace Hotel, **Le Cirque 2000,** 455 Madison Ave. (☎ **212/794-9292**), draws a prestigious crowd of celebrities, socialites, politicians, ladies who lunch, media types, and business moguls.
- **Best Downtown People-Watching:** Each week, **Moomba,** 133 Seventh Ave. South (☎ **212/989-1414**), attracts more famous faces than grace the pages of *People* magazine. Relatively longtime survivors in the cool wars are **Balthazar,** 80 Spring St. (☎ **212/965-1414**), **Odeon,** 145 W. Broadway (☎ **212/233-0507**); and **Nobu,** 105 Hudson St. (☎ **212/219-0500**).
- **Best New Hip Scene:** Once again, as in the entry above, the award goes to **Moomba,** 133 Seventh Ave. South (☎ **212/989-1414**). You didn't know? Just ask Leo-nardo DiCaprio, Madonna, Denzel Washington, and . . .
- **Best Old Hip Scene:** Finally back on the New York A- list is the **"21" Club,** 21 W. 52nd St. (☎ **212/582-7200**). While the cream of American society, like the Kennedys and Kissingers, have always had regular tables up front and kept their vintage wines in the cellar, the former speakeasy had worn a bit. Now, like a welcome ace coming down on a jack, 21 is the place to be again.
- **Best Singles Scene Straight:** Nobody minds waiting for a table at **Lemon,** 230 Park Ave. South (☎ **212/614-1200**), where the bar hosts a stylish partner-hungry mob.
- **Best Singles Scene Gay:** Men seeking men with Chelsea physiques can't beat **Che 2020,** 149 Eighth Ave. (☎ **212/243-2020**), though for the food they'd do better at **Viceroy,** 160 Eighth Ave. (☎ **212/633-8484**).
- **Best Bathrooms:** For their Philippe Starck–crafted humor, check out **"44"** in the Royalton, 44 W. 44th St. (☎ **212/944-8844**). For example, in the men's room,

Top Toques Set New Trends

New Yorkers idolize the star chefs. This fervid dedication, along with the city's improved economic fortunes, means the market is prime for the new ventures of the best talents.

Way back in 1991, **Jean-Georges Vongerichten,** who had nearly single-handedly created light fine dining at Lafayette, opened the first of his own acclaimed restaurants, **Jo Jo** (p. 158). By 1994, he had opened **Vong** (p. 149), where he pioneered fusion cuisine, blending Thai flavors with French technique. And in 1997, Donald Trump convinced Vongerichten to open **Jean Georges** (p. 152), which was showered with four bright stars from the very first reviews. The latest? Rumors are Vongerichten intends to head up **Mercer Kitchen,** 99 Prince St. (☎ 212/918-6060), in SoHo's brand-new Mercer Hotel.

David Bouley set the critics' and foodies' knees to trembling when in 1996 he closed his beloved eponymous TriBeCa restaurant to join Warner LeRoy, the P. T. Barnum of dining who owns Tavern on the Green, in reopening the venerable **Russian Tea Room,** 150 W. 57th St. (no phone at press time). Their partnership has since been dissolved, leaving Bouly more time to focus on his other ventures. He's building an international cuisine cultural center in TriBeCa, starting with **Bouley Bakery,** 120 W. Broadway (☎ 212/964-2525), where you can savor sautéed skate on a bed of fennel and figs or grilled guinea hen and foie gras. There are only 12 tables, but you could always settle for a delicious loaf of bread from the adjacent bakery. The center should soon include the rebirth of the upscale **Bouley** restaurant, a training kitchen for budding geniuses, and a retail store. Bouley also expects to open an Austrian restaurant, tentatively named **Danube,** nearby.

Daniel Boulud built his reputation at Le Cirque, where he spent 6 years as executive chef before opening **Daniel** (p. 158) in 1993. An instant success, Daniel could attain even higher heights when, in a move scheduled for early 1999, it takes over the space vacated by Le Cirque several years ago at 620 Park Ave. Joining the multiple-restaurant game, Boulud opened **Café Boulud,** 20 E. 76th St. (☎ 212/288-0033), in Daniel's original space late in 1998; it serves French fare in a less-formal setting. Boulud recently teamed up with his former pastry chef, François Payard, to open **Payard Pâtisserie and Bistro** (p.159).

Perhaps the biggest news in 1998 was the expansion of the Cipriani family's empire. Arrigo Cipriani and his son, Giuseppe, (who also owns Harry's Bar in Venice and Harry Capriani restaurant in New York's Sherry-Netherland hotel), first branched out with their **Downtown Retaurant** in SoHo. Last year, in quick order, they announced they'd open **55 Wall Street** as well as **Cipriani Midtown** and **Cipriani Dolci Café,** the last two in Grand Central Terminal. Then, for a whopping $4-million a year, they got hold of the lease for the **Rainbow Room,** and disappointed diners from all over by announcing it would be open to the public only for Sunday brunch, Friday dinner, and one Monday evening a month. Can it be true?

there's a useful waterfall that flows when you, er, pass an electronic eye, mirrors are everywhere (guess what's behind them), and amusing confusion reigns at every turn.

2 Restaurants by Cuisine

AFGHANISTANI
Pamir (p. 160)

AFRICAN
Meskerem (p. 143)

AMERICAN
Aggie's (p. 126)
Alley's End (p. 133)
America (p. 131)
Bridge Cafe (p. 111)
Brooklyn Diner USA
  (p. 140)
Che 2020 (p. 133)
Coffee Shop (p. 131)
Comedy Nation (p. 140)
EJ's Luncheonette (p. 160)
Empire Diner (p. 133)
Ess-A-Bagel (p. 151)
Fanelli (p. 121)
Fashion Cafe (p. 140)
Hamburger Harry's (p. 142)
Hard Rock Cafe (p. 140)
Harley-Davidson Cafe
  (p. 140)
Jackson Hole (p. 160)
Jekyll & Hyde Club (p. 141)
Josie's Restaurant and Juice
  Bar (p. 155)
Motown Cafe (p. 141)
The Odeon (p. 117)
Official All Star Cafe (p. 141)
Park View at the Boathouse
  (p. 159)
Planet Hollywood (p. 141)
Prime Burger (p. 151)
The Saloon (p. 155)
Sarabeth's Kitchen (p. 154)
Serendipity 3 (p. 161)
SoHo Kitchen and Bar (p. 121)
"21" Club (p. 135)
Walker's (p. 118)

ASIAN FUSION
Asia de Cuba (p. 146)
Lemon (p. 131)
Lucky Cheng's (p. 123)
Republic (p. 132)

BBQ
Tennessee Mountain (p.144)

BRAZILIAN
Churrascaria Plataforma (p. 140)
Coffee Shop (p. 131)

CHINESE
Jing Fong (p. 118)
Joe's Shanghai (p. 118)
La Caridad 78 Restaurant (p. 155)
New York Noodletown (p. 119)
Pig Heaven (p. 161)
Shun Lee West (p. 153)
Tse Yang (p. 148)
Wu Liang Ye (p. 142)

CONTEMPORARY AMERICAN
An American Place (p. 146)
Aureole (p. 155)
Bryant Park Grill (p. 138)
Cub Room (p. 120)
Flowers (p. 129)
Gotham Bar & Grill (p. 124)
Gramercy Tavern (p. 128)
March (p. 145)
Mark's (p. 158)
Monkey Bar (p. 146)
Moomba (p. 125)
One If By Land, Two If By Sea
  (p. 124)
The River Café (p. 162)
Savoy (p. 120)
Tavern on the Green (p. 153)
Time Cafe (p. 122)
Tribeca Grill (p. 115)
Union Square Cafe (p. 129)
Verbena (p. 130)
The Viceroy (p. 133)
Water's Edge (p. 163)
Windows on the World (p. 111)

CONTINENTAL
Café des Artistes (p. 152)
The Four Seasons (p. 144)
Madison Bistro (p. 150)
Petrossian (p. 152)
Rainbow Room (p. 134)
Tavern on the Green (p. 153)

CUBAN

La Caridad 78 Restaurant (p. 155)

ETHIOPIAN

Meskerem (p. 143)

FRENCH

Balthazar (p. 120)
Bar 6 (p. 125)
Café des Artistes (p. 152)
Cafe Luxembourg (p. 154)
Chanterelle (p. 115)
Chez Josephine (p. 139)
Danal (p. 121)
Daniel (p. 158)
Destinée (p. 159)
Florent (p. 127)
14 Wall Street (p. 114)
French Roast Cafe (p. 127)
Jean Georges (p. 152)
Jo Jo (p. 158)
L' Express (p. 132)
La Boîte en Bois (p. 154)
La Bonne Soupe (p. 143)
La Côte Basque (p. 135)
La Goulue (p. 158)
La Nouvelle Justine (p. 141)
Le Bernardin (p. 134)
Le Cirque 2000 (p. 144)
Le Périgord (p. 145)
Lespinasse (p. 145)
Lutèce (p. 145)
Madison Bistro (p. 150)
Montrachet (p. 114)
The Odeon (p. 117)
Payard Pâtisserie and Bistro
    (p. 159)
Picholine (p. 152)
Steak Frites (p. 131)
Vong (p. 149)

GREEK

Estiatorio Milos (p. 138)

HISPANIC

La Caridad 78 Restaurant
    (p. 155)
La Taza de Oro (p. 133)

INDIAN

Bombay Dining (p. 123)
Dawat (p. 149)

ITALIAN

Barolo (p. 119)
Caffè Bondí (p. 131)
Caffè Grazie (p. 160)
Carmine's (p. 139)
Ciao Europa (p. 141)
Cinque Terre (p. 149)
Da Umberto (p. 128)
Il Bagatto (p. 123)
Il Cortile (p. 121)
Il Mulino (p. 124)
Le Madri (p. 132)
Osteria del Circo (p. 142)
Rao's (p. 161)
San Domenico (p. 135)

JAPANESE

Nobu (p. 115)
Sushisay (p. 146)

JEWISH

Sammy's Roumanian (p. 122)

KOREAN

Won Jo (p. 144)

MEDITERRANEAN

Luna Park (p. 132)
Picholine (p. 152)

MEXICAN

Mi Cocina (p. 126)
Rosa Mexicano (p. 150)
Zarela (p. 151)

MOROCCAN

Bar 6 (p. 125)

PIZZA

John's Pizzeria (p. 128)
Patsy's Pizzeria (p. 161)

ROUMANIAN

Sammy's Roumanian (p. 122)

RUSSIAN

Petrossian (p. 134)

SCANDINAVIAN

Aquavit (p. 135)

SEAFOOD

Blue Water Grill (p. 130)
Gage & Tollner (p. 163)

Le Bernardin (p. 134)
Oyster Bar (p. 150)

SOUP
La Bonne Soupe (p. 143)
Soup Kitchen International (p. 143)

SOUTH AMERICAN
Coffee Shop (p. 131)
Patria (p. 129)

SOUTHEAST ASIAN
Café Asean (p. 126)

SOUTHERN & SOUL FOOD
Sylvia's Restaurant (p. 162)
Tennessee Mountain (p. 144)
Wilson's Bakery and Restaurant
   (p. 162)

SOUTHWESTERN
Citrus (p. 154)
Mesa Grill (p. 129)
Miracle Grill (p. 122)
Tapika (p. 142)

SPANISH
Solera (p. 147)

STEAK HOUSE
Peter Luger's Steakhouse
   (p. 162)
Sparks Steak House (p. 148)

TEX-MEX
Burritoville (p. 114)

THAI
Pongsri Thai Restaurant
   (p. 143)
Thailand Restaurant (p. 119)
Vong (p. 149)

UKRANIAN
Veselka (p. 124)

VEGETARIAN
Angelica Kitchen (p. 123)

VIETNAMESE
Nha Trang (p. 119)

3 South Street Seaport & the Financial District

See the "Downtown Dining" map (pp. 112–113) for restaurants in this section.

VERY EXPENSIVE

✪ **Windows on the World.** One World Trade Center, 107th Floor (on West St., between Liberty & Vesey sts.). ☎ **212/524-7000.** Reservations recommended well in advance. Jacket required. Main courses $25–$35; pretheater prix fixe $35; prix-fixe brunch $32.50. AE, CB, DC, DISC, MC, V. Mon–Fri noon–2pm; Mon–Thurs 5–10:30pm, Fri–Sat 5–11:30pm, Sun 5–10pm; brunch Sun 11am–3pm. Subway: E to World Trade Center; 1, 9, R to Cortlandt St. CONTEMPORARY AMERICAN.

The interior design leaves me cold, but that's just fine: Who needs to look at the inside when all New York's out the window? The new American food menu got a recent boost with the arrival of culinary director Michael Lomonaco, formerly executive chef at the "21" Club. Windows is a membership dining room at weekday lunch, and while anyone can get a table, nonmembers are charged a $15 per-person fee (there's no extra charge for Saturday lunch or Sunday brunch). In addition to Windows, the main dining room, there's the **Greatest Bar on Earth** for drinks, à la carte dining, and dancing, and the **Skybox,** a smoking lounge where cigars are definitely permitted. **Cellar in the Sky,** which had served four-course prix-fixe dinners with specially chosen wines, was due to reopen soon after press time. Expect a new name, dining à la carte, and a continued emphasis on fine wine.

I can't imagine a trip to New York without a stop for dinner or at least drinks at this most Manhattan experience.

MODERATE

✪ **Bridge Cafe.** 279 Water St. (at Dover St.). ☎ **212/227-3344.** Reservations recommended. Main courses $12–$22; prix-fixe lunch $30; prix-fixe dinner $40; prix-fixe brunch

Downtown Dining

 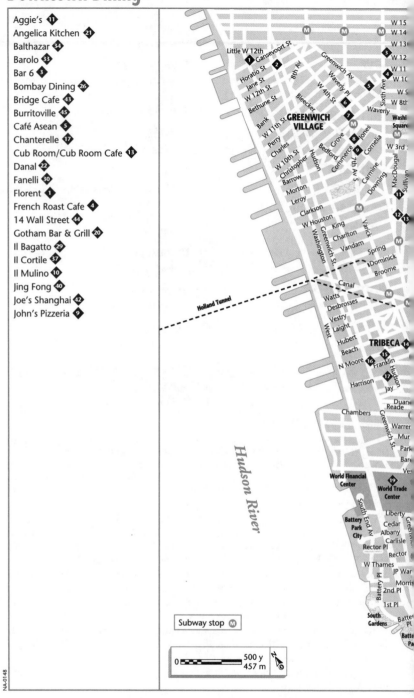
Subway stop Ⓜ

0 ⸺ 500 y
457 m

Hudson River

GREENWICH VILLAGE

TRIBECA

Holland Tunnel

World Financial Center

World Trade Center

Battery Park City

South Gardens

NA-0148

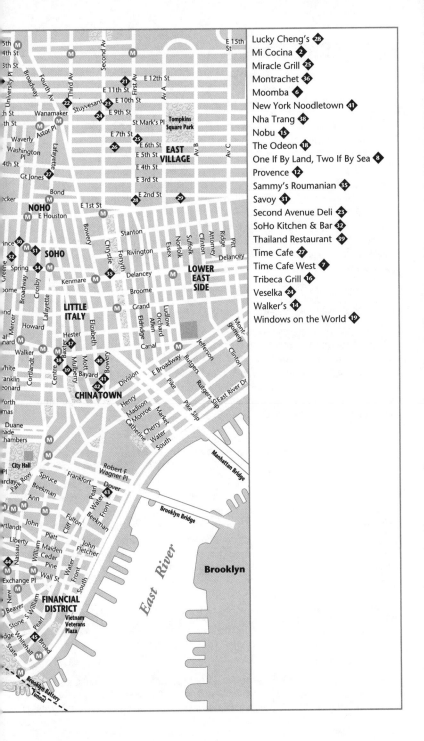

Lucky Cheng's 🔶28
Mi Cocina 🔶2
Miracle Grill 🔶25
Montrachet 🔶36
Moomba 🔶6
New York Noodletown 🔶41
Nha Trang 🔶38
Nobu 🔶15
The Odeon 🔶18
One If By Land, Two If By Sea 🔶8
Provence 🔶12
Sammy's Roumanian 🔶35
Savoy 🔶31
Second Avenue Deli 🔶23
SoHo Kitchen & Bar 🔶32
Thailand Restaurant 🔶39
Time Cafe 🔶27
Time Cafe West 🔶7
Tribeca Grill 🔶16
Veselka 🔶24
Walker's 🔶14
Windows on the World 🔶19

Thank You for Not Smoking

The city's strict no-smoking laws have meant a near eradication of nicotine clouds in restaurants, and you don't even have to ask for the "no smoking" section anymore. Those who wish to smoke will want to call ahead to see if it's even possible.

$14.95. AE, CB, DC, MC, V. Sun–Mon 11:45am–10pm, Tues–Fri 11:45am–midnight, Sat 5pm–midnight; brunch Sun 11:45am–4pm. Subway: 4, 5, 6 to Brooklyn Bridge/City Hall. AMERICAN.

The trick in the area directly around South Street Seaport is to find a good restaurant, and Bridge Cafe is the place. It's on a block that hasn't been "renovated" into cute boutiques, a few blocks north of the Seaport but definitely worth the couple of minutes' walk. The menu changes every 2 months, but you might start with chilled lemon broth with shrimp. The pasta main course makes for a good and inexpensive meal. For a dollar or two more, there's pan-roasted chicken, marinated red trout, roast duck, or buffalo steak. In a part of town where quality is often second to turnover, Bridge Cafe is a pleasant exception.

14 Wall Street. 14 Wall St., 31st floor (Broadway & Broad St.). ☎ **212/233-2780.** Reservations recommended. Main courses $20–$24; prix-fixe breakfast $10. AE, DC, MC, V. Mon–Fri 7:30am–9:30pm. Subway: 4, 5 to Wall St. FRENCH.

Here's an ideal spot for a refined meal during a Downtown tour. Located in what was J. P. Morgan's penthouse when he kept offices and a discreet apartment here early in this century, the mahogany-trimmed dining rooms offer extraordinary views of New York harbor and classic food by chef Frédéric Feufeu. The warm goat cheese salad and two terrines (one vegetarian, one rabbit) are reassuringly familiar appetizers, and for entrees, there's roasted chicken, scallops with crabmeat and spinach, and grilled lamb chops coated in garlic, bread crumbs, and parsley.

INEXPENSIVE

Burritoville. 36 Water St. (at Broad St.). ☎ **212/747-1100.** Main courses $3.95–$9.95. AE, MC, V. Mon–Sun 11:30am–11pm. Subway: 2, 3 to Wall St.; 1, 9 to South Ferry. TEX-MEX.

For a quick, healthy, and inexpensive lunch to go in the Wall Street area, Burritoville fits the bill. The straightforward Border Burrito, a 12-inch flour tortilla bursting with spiced beans, brown rice, cheese, sour cream, and pico de gallo (heavy on the cilantro) costs just $3.95. More embellished versions incorporate spiced ground beef, spicy grilled chicken, fresh spinach and mushrooms, and grilled turkey sausage. There's also nachos, quesadillas, tacos, and fajitas. This may be fast food, but the emphasis is on freshness—all the ingredients are prepared daily without preservatives, lard, or other questionable comestibles. For six more locations in Manhattan, see the box "Choice Choices $15 & Under."

4 TriBeCa

See the "Downtown Dining" map (pp. 112–113) for restaurants in this section.

VERY EXPENSIVE

✪ **Montrachet.** 239 W. Broadway (White & Walker sts.). ☎ **212/219-2777.** Reservations recommended. Main courses $22–$30; prix-fixe dinners $35 and $42; tasting menu $75. AE, MC, V. Fri noon–2:30pm; Mon–Thurs 6–10:30pm, Fri–Sat 6–11pm. Subway: 1, 9 to Franklin St. FRENCH BISTRO.

Opened in 1985, this TriBeCa pioneer is the baby of restaurateur Drew Nieporent—who's gone on to partnership with Robert DeNiro in Tribeca Grill and Nobu—and instantly earned critical raves. After more than a decade of excellence it has evolved into one of Manhattan's "new classics." The prix-fixe lunches and dinners allow you to enjoy some of the city's best contemporary yet classic French cuisine at wonderful prices: The lunch ($19.99 on Friday only) might start with fresh pea soup, continue with braised duck legs with barley in port-wine sauce, and end with a warm chocolate soufflé with rosemary and orange. For dinner, there's an unforgettable grilled quail salad with balsamic vinegar; truffle-crusted salmon; and one of Manhattan's best roasted chickens with potato purée and garlic sauce. The vanilla-bean Savarin with warmed berries and the banana-and-chocolate gratin on linzer crust are two of the superb desserts.

Montrachet is famous for its judicious list of French and California vintages, winning a *Wine Spectator* award of excellence. You can find great bottles at good prices if you know how to select (if you don't, ask the staff to help).

✪ **Nobu.** 105 Hudson St. (at Franklin St.). ☎ **212/219-0500.** Reservations required (accepted 10am–5pm) far in advance. Main courses $20–$32. AE, DC, MC, V. Mon–Fri 11:45am–2:15pm; daily 5:45–10:30pm. Subway: 1, 9 to Franklin St. NEW JAPANESE.

You'd never think so much could be done to humble raw fish. But with the complex spices and impetuous presentations of chef Nobu Matsuhisa, traditional Japanese crosses extravagantly with Latin American and nouvelle Californian influences. Mixed textures, splashes of hot olive oil, crunchy cucumbers wrapped impulsively around sushi—it all adds up to flavors you've never encountered. You won't forget the new-style sashimi, soft-shell crab rolls, or sublime broiled black cod in slightly sweet miso sauce. The cold sake arrives in a fun green bamboo pitcher. The chef's art culminates in an uncommonly good ginger crème brûlée. Co-owned with the chef by the same team who created Montrachet and Tribeca Grill (among them, Robert DeNiro and one of New York's best restaurateurs, Drew Nieporent), this import from Los Angeles is as hip as TriBeCa. The excitement is heightened by the droll decor (check out the chopsticks-inspired chairs at the sushi bar) and the crowd.

EXPENSIVE

✪ **Chanterelle.** 2 Harrison St. (Hudson & Greenwich sts.). ☎ **212/966-6960.** Reservations recommended well in advance. Main courses $18.50–24; prix-fixe lunch $35; prix-fixe dinner $75; tasting menu $89. AE, CB, DC, DISC, MC, V. Mon–Sat noon–2:30pm and 5:30–11pm. Subway: 1, 9 to Franklin St. CONTEMPORARY FRENCH.

Chanterelle is the kind of restaurant you leave saying not only "The food was wonderful" or "The wine was sublime" but also "Thank you for a superb time." Husband/wife co-owners David and Karen Waltuch and unsurpassed maître d'/sommelier Roger Dagorn make sure of it. You're ushered through the small foyer into the stark, sophisticated dining room with a pressed-tin ceiling and widely spaced large tables. The central focus is an enormous flower arrangement created by Karen. The wait staff describes every dish, suggests complementary combinations, and makes you feel at ease. David's cooking is based on traditional French technique, but Japanese, Moroccan, and Swedish notes sneak into his culinary melodies. One signature dish appears on almost every menu—a magnificent grilled seafood sausage.

When ordering wine, it's best to depend on Dagorn, the first master sommelier in the United States. Justly proud of his outstanding wine list, he happily characterizes each one and recommends the perfect bottle in all price ranges.

✪ **Tribeca Grill.** 375 Greenwich St. (at Franklin St.). ☎ **212/941-3900.** Reservations recommended. Main courses $18–$28; prix-fixe lunch $19.99. AE, DC, MC, V. Mon–Fri 11:30am–3pm; Sun–Thurs 5:30–11pm, Fri–Sat 5:30–11:30pm; brunch Sun 11:30am–3pm. Subway: 1, 9 to Franklin St. CONTEMPORARY AMERICAN.

Choice Choices $15 & Under

Great Meal Deals

In addition to the other special lists in this chapter (see "Affordable Gourmet to Go") and the most tempting bargain ethnic eateries and pizza parlors (see "Only in New York"), there are surprising inexpensive gems you shouldn't overlook: the $8.50 Szechuan Chinese lunch menu at **Wu Liang Ye** (p. 142), the $12.95 soup-and-salad lunch at **La Bonne Soupe** (p. 143), and the $13.95 Indian prix-fixe lunch at **Dawat** (p. 149). And the "theme" restaurants, like **Planet Hollywood** and **Hard Rock Cafe** (see "Where the Themes Are the Message"), offer lots of options well within the $15 range.

It doesn't get cheaper than the $1.95 for two hot dogs and a papaya drink, available 24 hours, at **Gray's Papaya,** 2090 Broadway, at 72nd Street (☎ 212/ 799-0243), and 402 Sixth Ave., at 8th Street (☎ 212/260-3532). On the Upper East Side, **Papaya King,** 179 E. 86th St., at Third Avenue (☎ 212/ 369-0648), sells one hot dog and tropical fruit drink for $2.75.

You can get a fabulous deal at **Blockheads Burritos,** 499 Third Ave., at 34th Street (☎ 212/213-3332), and 954 Second Ave., between 50th and 51st streets (☎ 212/750-2020). The early-bird special, offered 4 to 7pm daily, includes a beer or a frozen margarita, soup or salad, and a designer burrito ($8.95) or a fancy fajita ($11.95).

The famous *Seinfeld* soup episode spawned imitators of Al Yeganeh's original **Soup Kitchen International** (p. 143) all around town. Two of the best, which serve soup with bread and fruit, are **Daily Soup,** 21 E. 41st St., at Madison Avenue (☎ 212/953-7687), as well as six other locations, and **Soup Nutsy,** 148 E. 46th St., at Lexington Avenue (☎ 212/927-8800).

A dependable diner with two Midtown locations is **Broadway Diner,** 1726 Broadway, at 55th Street (☎ 212/765-0909), and 590 Lexington Ave., at 52nd Street (☎ 212/486-8838). Downtown, **La Boulangère,** 49 E. 21st St., at Park Avenue South (☎ 212/475-8582), and 495 Broadway, between Broome and Spring streets (☎ 212/334-4600), is a good choice for salads, soups, and sandwiches on homemade bread. **Dojo,** 14 W. 4th St., at Mercer Street (☎ 212/505-8934), and 24 St. Mark's Place, between Second and Third avenues (☎ 212/674-9821), is a favorite for Japanese-influenced health food.

Willing to spend a little more for great food? No item on the tavern menu in the bar area of **Gramercy Tavern** (p. 128) tops $18, and you can lunch at these seven top restaurants for $19.99: **Aureole** (p. 155; after 2pm), **Cafe Luxembourg** (p. 154), **Gotham Bar & Grill** (p. 124), **Montrachet** (p. 114; Fridays only), **Picholine** (p. 152), **Tapika** (p. 142), and **Tribeca Grill** (p. 115).

Whether it's co-owner Robert DeNiro, or Bruce Springsteen, or any of untold numbers of business powerhouses you want to see, Tribeca Grill is the place to do it. The restaurant is part of the Tribeca Film Center, where many premieres are held. Yet this place takes its kitchen and integrity seriously, no doubt due in part to partner Drew Nieporent and chef Don Pintabona. The place boasts an old mahogany bar, and a feeling of historic charm, though the restaurant has been around only since 1990. The food is American with an international touch. For starters, there's a shrimp-and-vegetable spring roll with persimmon sweet-and-sour sauce, rare seared tuna with sesame noodles, and crisp fried oysters with garlic-anchovy aïoli. The sparkling main

The Best of the Chains

You'll see many low-priced chains around town, including **T.G.I. Friday's, Houlihan's, Pizzeria Uno,** and **McDonald's.** In this chapter I describe several New York chains, like **Burritoville** (p. 114), **EJ's Luncheonette** (p. 160), and **Jackson Hole** (p. 160). Among the best of the other chains are **Dallas BBQ,** for heaping portions and especially good early dinner deals; **Burger Heaven,** for burgers and other diner fare; and **Lemongrass Grill,** for flavorful Thai. Here's a listing by location:

DOWNTOWN Burritoville, 36 Water St., at Broad Street (☎ 212/747-1100); 144 Chambers St., between Greenwich Street and West Broadway (☎ 212/571-1144); 141 Second Ave., at 8th Street (☎ 212/260-3300). **Dallas BBQ,** 132 Second Ave., at St. Mark's Place (☎ 212/777-5574); 21 University Place, at 8th Street (☎ 212/674-4450). **EJ's Luncheonette,** 432 Sixth Ave., between 9th and 10th streets (☎ 212/473-5555). **Lemongrass Grill,** 80 University Place, at 11th Street (☎ 212/604-9870); 37 Barrow St., at Seventh Avenue South (☎ 212/242-0606).

MIDTOWN Burritoville, 264 W. 23rd St., between Seventh and Eighth avenues (☎ 212/367-9844). **Jackson Hole,** 521 Third Ave., at 35th Street (☎ 212/679-3264). **Burger Heaven,** 536 Madison Ave., between 54th and 55th streets (☎ 212/753-4214); 9 E. 53rd St., between Fifth and Madison avenues (☎ 212/752-0340); 20 E. 49th St., between Fifth and Madison avenues (☎ 212/755-2166); 291 Madison Ave., between 40th and 41st streets (☎ 212/685-6250).

UPTOWN Burritoville, 451 Amsterdam Ave., between 81st and 82nd streets (☎ 212/787-8181); 166 W. 72nd St., at Amsterdam Avenue (☎ 212/580-7700); 1606 Third Ave., between 90th and 91st streets (☎ 212/410-2255); 1489 First Ave., between 77th and 78th streets (☎ 212/472-8800). **EJ's Luncheonette,** 447 Amsterdam Ave., between 81st and 82nd streets (☎ 212/873-3444); 1271 Third Ave., at 73rd Street (☎ 212/472-0600). **Jackson Hole,** 517 Columbus Ave., at 85th Street (☎ 212/362-5177); 1270 Madison Ave., at 91st Street (☎ 212/427-2820); 1611 Second Ave., between 83rd and 84th streets (☎ 212/737-8788); 232 E. 64th St., between Second and Third avenues (☎ 212/371-7187). **Dallas BBQ,** 27 W. 72nd St., be-tween Central Park West and Columbus Avenue (☎ 212/873-2044); 1265 Third Ave., between 72nd and 73rd streets (☎ 212/772-9393). **Lemongrass Grill,** 2534 Broadway, between 94th and 95th streets (☎ 212/666-0888); 494 Amsterdam Ave., at 84th Street (☎ 212/579-0344).

courses include crisp baby chicken with whipped potatoes, barbecued breast of duck, and braised lamb shank with sweet-potato agnolotti and braised Swiss chard. A standout dessert is warm lemon mascarpone cake with clementines and port-wine sauce.

MODERATE

✪ **The Odeon.** 145 W. Broadway (at Thomas St.). ☎ **212/233-0507.** Reservations recommended. Main courses $15–$25; prix-fixe lunch $25; prix-fixe dinner $40. AE, DC, DISC, MC, V. Mon–Thurs noon–2am, Fri–Sat noon–3am, Sun 11:30am–2am. Subway: 1, 9 to Franklin St. FRENCH/AMERICAN.

Sure, John Kennedy Jr. might be a couple of tables away, but you really come here for the great steak frites or even the burger. Rounding out the choices are seared tuna steak with grilled squash, barbecued duck with wild rice pilaf, spinach ravioli, pizza with baby artichokes, a grilled chicken sandwich, a steamed vegetable plate, and crab-and-potato fritters. This art deco cafeteria, with a soulful wooden bar and leather banquettes, is emphatically back on, after a few lean years off, the celebs/artists/designers/models/journalists circuit.

INEXPENSIVE

Walker's. 16 N. Moore St. (at Varick St.). ☎ **212/941-0142.** Main courses $9–$15. AE, DC, DISC, MC, V. Daily 11:45am–1am; brunch Sat–Sun noon–4pm. Subway: 1, 9 to Franklin St. AMERICAN.

An 1890 pub that's still a neighborhood institution despite the influx of famous residents to TriBeCa, Walker's serves updated comfort food at reasonable prices. You can't go wrong with a hamburger, but the grilled organic chicken and seared tuna served on a bed of mesclun greens are good bets, too. The Sunday jazz brunch is popular.

5 Chinatown

See the "Downtown Dining" map (pp. 112–113) for restaurants in this section. For other choices in Chinatown, see "Only in New York" at the end of this chapter.

INEXPENSIVE

✪ **Jing Fong.** 20 Elizabeth St. (Bayard & Canal sts.). ☎ **212/964-5256.** Reservations recommended. Main courses $8.95–$19.95. AE, MC, V. Daily 9am–11pm; dim sum 9am–3pm. Subway: N, R, 6 to Canal St. CHINESE.

Don't panic when, on a Sunday around noon, you turn south off Canal and see the scores of anxious gourmets (and gourmands) who know this place's reputation for great dim sum. Brush your way through to the reception desk, and the person there will give you a number. After your number is called, an amusingly charmless escalator ride deposits you in an immense hall that resembles an industrial conference center dining room in Hong Kong. Always a fortuitous sign in Chinatown, it's filled with Chinese at countless round tables, each seating at least 10. If your group doesn't fill a table, you might be seated with others—if you're lucky enough to have Chinese neighbors, you can follow their lead in ordering. Service from the dim sum cart drivers tends toward the distracted—but, hey, you want nice or you want good food?

The dumplings are particularly memorable, and the best are the vegetable variety. Garlicky periwinkles come in their slippery shells, and you lift them gingerly with your chopsticks and suck out the meaty little insides. The crunchy spring rolls are served with Worcestershire sauce. In the center of all the hubbub is a fish counter where you can order fresh seafood.

Joe's Shanghai. 9 Pell St. (Bowery & Mott sts.). ☎ **212/233-8888.** Reservations recommended for six or more. Main courses $4.25–$12.95. No credit cards. Daily 11:30am–midnight. Subway: N, R, 6 to Canal St. CHINESE.

If your waiter insists you order the signature soup dumplings—quivering pockets filled with hot "soup" and your choice of pork or crab—don't resist. They never disappoint, and neither do the authentic Shanghai-inspired main courses, like the whole yellowfish bathed in spicy sauce or the pork, squid, and dry bean curd cooked with chile peppers. The line is usually long, but you can skip to the front if you're willing to share a table.

In case you want to see the world.

At American Express, we're here to make your journey a smooth one. So we have over 1,700 travel service locations in over 120 countries ready to help. What else would you expect from the world's largest travel agency?

do more

Travel

http://www.americanexpress.com/travel

In case you want to be welcomed there.

We're here to see that you're always welcomed at establishments everywhere. That's why millions of people carry the American Express® Card — for peace of mind, confidence, and security, around the world or just around the corner.

do more®

Cards

BISTRO

In case you're running low.

We're here to help with more than 118,000 Express Cash locations around the world. In order to enroll, just call American Express before you start your vacation.

do more

Express Cash

And just in case.

We're here with American Express® Travelers Cheques and Cheques *for Two*.® They're the safest way to carry money on your vacation and the surest way to get a refund, practically anywhere, anytime.

Another way we help you…

do more

Travelers Cheques

©1996 American Express Travel Related Services Company, Inc.

⭘ **New York Noodletown.** 28½ Bowery (at Bayard St.). ☎ **212/349-0923.** Main courses $3.25–$9.95. No credit cards. Daily 9am–4am. Subway: N, R, 6 to Canal St. CHINESE.

Its devoted following knows this is two-star food served in no-star ambiance. Grab a table, alone or with others, as soon as you walk in—no one stands on ceremony, so don't wait to be greeted and escorted. The mushroom soup is a lunch in itself, thick with earthy chunks of shiitakes, vegetables, and thin noodles. Another appetizer that can serve as a meal is the hacked roast duck in noodle soup. The salt-baked squid arrives looking like a snow-dusted plate of meaty fish. On the side, order the quick-woked Chinese broccoli or the crisp sautéed baby bok choy. Other special dishes are various sandy pot casseroles, often hearty affairs slow-simmered in clay vessels that impart inimitable flavor.

Nha Trang. 87 Baxter St. (Bayard & Canal sts.). ☎ **212/233-5948.** Reservations recommended for large parties. Main courses $6.50–$9. No credit cards. Daily 10:30am–9:30pm. Subway: N, R, 6 to Canal St. VIETNAMESE.

Vying with its neighbor New Pasteur for best Vietnamese in Chinatown, Nha Trang serves up similarly spicy food in a simple setting. It's hard to go wrong starting with refreshingly light shrimp-and-rice vermicelli rolls with sweet peanut dipping sauce or a paste of shrimp and spices rolled around real sugarcane. If you like food so hot you break a sweat, opt for chicken in chile-and-lemongrass sauce or curried squid with white rice. Sensitive palates appreciate huge bowls of coriander-scented soup overflowing with tender sliced beef, noodles, and vegetables. There's almost always a line, especially at lunch.

⭘ **Thailand Restaurant.** 106 Bayard St. (at Baxter St.). ☎ **212/349-3132.** Reservations recommended. Main courses $4.95–$12.95. AE. Daily 11:30am–11pm. Subway: N, R, 6 to Canal St. THAI.

Thai has also been added to the expanding menu in Chinatown, and this kitchen turns out first-rate dishes—aromatic, searing, full of zest and colors. When you say spicy, you'd better mean it because your tongue will sizzle like a Midtown sidewalk in August. The sliced charcoal steak with onions, hot pepper, lemon juice, and mint is a fabulously fiery, flavorful appetizer. The tasty green curry with coconut milk, eggplant, bamboo shoots, and green chiles comes with your choice of chicken, beef, pork, lamb, or shrimp. Sautéed rice noodles are a good choice to offset the tangier dishes. The whole fish, especially sea bass, are delicately crispy outside, moist and flaky inside. The coconut milk dessert, with tiny slices of ice cubes, is the perfect finish.

6 SoHo

See the "Downtown Dining" map (pp. 112–113) for restaurants in this section.

EXPENSIVE

Barolo. 398 W. Broadway (Broome & Spring sts.). ☎ **212/226-1102.** Reservations recommended. Main courses $19–$27.50. AE, CB, DC, DISC, MC, V. Sun–Thurs noon–midnight, Fri–Sat noon–1am. Subway: 6 to Spring St. NORTHERN ITALIAN.

The wonderful courtyard garden is the top draw at this Northern Italian restaurant in the center of SoHo action. Appetizers include spinach flan with creamed fontina-and-truffle paste, beef carpaccio with arugula and Parmesan, and grilled tuna salad with marinated eggplant, string beans, and boiled eggs. Many pastas are handmade, and for the Piedmont-inspired main courses there's sliced sirloin, grilled chicken breast, and grilled salmon steak with mustard-honey sauce.

Savoy. 70 Prince St. (at Crosby St.). ☎ **212/219-8570.** Reservations recommended. Main courses $19–$24; prix-fixe dinner $48. AE, DISC, MC, V. Mon–Sat noon–3pm; Mon–Thurs 6–10:30pm, Fri–Sat 6–11pm, Sun 6–10pm. Subway: R to Prince St. CONTEMPORARY AMERICAN.

Behind a silver diner-style facade hides a SoHo treasure. Despite the cozy dining room's small size, it's easy to have an intimate conversation since the noise level is controlled by an ingenious screened ceiling with sound-absorbing panels. Upstairs, a second dining room contains a bar and a fireplace used for cooking the prix-fixe dinner. Chef/owner Peter Hoffmann's creative American cuisine, accented with Mediterranean flavors, changes constantly, but a signature dish is salt-crusted baked duck—stuffed with lemons, oranges, and onions and coated with coarse kosher salt. The tender, savory meat is served with seasonal vegetables like runner beans, preserved lemons, artichokes, and grilled radicchio. Other innovative dishes are bright crimson beet soup topped with jasmine rice and tarragon roasted peppers and an entree of roasted monkfish with curry sauce and a stew of fiddlehead ferns, carrots, and chickpeas. The desserts are delectable. The wine list offers unusual Californian, French, and Italian wines at reasonable prices.

MODERATE

✪ **Balthazar.** 80 Spring St. (at Crosby St.). ☎ **212/965-1414.** Reservations recommended well in advance. Main courses $16–$25. AE, MC, V. Daily noon–12:30am; oyster bar Sun–Thurs noon–2am, Fri–Sat noon–4am; brunch Sat–Sun 11am–4pm. Subway: C, E to Spring St. FRENCH BISTRO.

It came on the scene already a legend. And while Balthazar has evolved, it seems destined for perpetual Odeon-like hipness. Red leather banquettes, a long pewter bar, and huge mirrors give the lofty space an authentic Parisian brasserie ambiance. Appropriate, since the menu offers classic French bistro fare like steak frites and seared salmon. The cold seafood platter ($56 or $96 for two) is a pricey but favorite late-night meal. For more land-locked treats, the whole roast chicken for two ($44) never fails to satisfy. Next door, Balthazar's *boulangerie* sells a variety of fresh-baked breads, desserts, salads, and sandwiches to go.

✪ **Cub Room.** 131 Sullivan St. (at Prince St.). ☎ **212/677-4100.** Reservations recommended. Main courses $16–$28; tasting menu from $65. AE. Tues–Fri noon–3pm; Mon–Sat 6pm–midnight, Sun 5:30–10:30pm; brunch Sun noon–3:30pm. Subway: C, E to Spring St.; R to Prince St. CONTEMPORARY AMERICAN.

The Cub Room hosts an up-front bar scene that's young and hot, so the surprise is the attractive, friendly back dining room, where the food is excellent, prepared by personable chef Henry Meer. Not afraid to spice up American or even French classics with a touch of Asia or anywhere else, Meer offers inventive appetizers like seared salmon on baby organic greens with bacon and tangy Caesar dressing (available as a main dish too); a salad of candy-cane beets with organic baby greens and New York State goat cheese; and lobster salad with mango, duck confit, baby beets, grilled onions, and frisée. Main courses encompass sesame-crusted yellowfin on sautéed Asian greens and house-smoked Muscovy duck breast with wild mushrooms. The wine list features a selection of independent French and American growers. Meer's creativity extends to the bar—in summer he offers mouthwateringly refreshing watermelon martinis. Could anything be better on a steamy afternoon?

Around the corner is the entrance to the more casual **Cub Room Cafe,** 183 Prince St. (☎ 212/777-0030), which serves similarly bold contemporary American fare at much softer prices (entrees $10–$16).

INEXPENSIVE

Fanelli. 94 Prince St. (at Mercer St.). ☎ **212/226-9412.** Main courses $5–$12. AE, MC, V. Daily 10:30am–midnight. Subway: N, R to Prince St. AMERICAN.

For a burger and beer in SoHo, Fanelli is the spot. The pasta and sandwiches are also filling options at one of the few places to survive the neighborhood's transformation from manufacturing outpost to urban chic. The long bar is propped up by regulars, and its corner door and pressed-tin ceiling lock in the 1872 atmosphere.

SoHo Kitchen and Bar. 103 Greene St. (Spring & Prince sts.). ☎ **212/925-1866.** Main courses $5.75–$15.75. AE, MC, V. Mon–Thurs 11:30am–2am, Fri–Sat 11:30am–4am, Sun 12:30–11pm. Subway: R to Prince St. AMERICAN.

This large, lofty SoHo space attracts an animated after-work and late-night crowd to its central bar dispensing 14 ice-cold draft beers and more than 100 wines by the glass, either individually or in "flights" for comparative tastings. The menu offers trendy and typical bar fare: barbecued chicken wings, grilled portobellos, oversize salads, and a variety of sandwiches, pastas, burgers, and thin-crust pizzas. There are also more substantial meals like sirloin steak with baked potato and vegetable.

7 Little Italy

See the "Downtown Dining" map (pp. 112–113) for the restaurant in this section. For other choices in Little Italy, see "Only in New York" at the end of the chapter.

MODERATE

✪ **Il Cortile.** 125 Mulberry St. (Canal & Hester sts.). ☎ **212/226-6060.** Reservations recommended for four and more. Main courses $12.50–$30. AE, DC, DISC, JCB, MC, V. Sun–Thurs noon–midnight, Fri–Sat noon–1am. Subway: 6, N, R to Canal St. NORTHERN ITALIAN.

Expect to wait and to see a mix of New Yorkers and visitors who know this is a quality find, fringed by lesser Little Italy *fratelli* who plop too much tomato sauce on overdone pasta. The interior has a dramatic skylit area; I prefer the cozier front room. There's a certain elegance to the menu: Like a *billet doux* from the chef, it's folded and sealed with gold foil. The second sign that you're out of the Little Italy ordinary arrives with the warm basket of focaccia, crusty small loaves, and crunchy breadsticks. You can choose an irresistible seafood salad or a caprese salad with tomatoes that taste like they should and buffalo mozzarella soft as velvet. Among the best pastas is linguettine with shrimp, lobster, and scallops in white sauce.

8 The East Village & Lower East Side

See the "Downtown Dining" map (pp. 112–113) for restaurants in this section.

MODERATE

✪ **Danal.** 90 E. 10th St. (Third & Fourth aves.). ☎ **212/982-6930.** Reservations not accepted. Main courses $12–$20. AE, MC, V. Sun–Thurs 6–10pm, Fri–Sat 6–10:30pm; brunch Sat–Sun 11:30am–3pm. Subway: 6 to Astor Place. FRENCH COUNTRY.

This charming restaurant resembles a Vermont farmhouse kitchen transplanted to New York. Weekend brunch is a favorite: aromatic coffee in bistro press pots, smoked salmon with dill pancakes, scrambled eggs with chicken-apple sausage, and grilled chicken salad with pears and blue cheese. Dinner might include a tart with spinach and goat cheese and steamed artichokes with roasted garlic mayonnaise as starters and main dishes like marinated venison tenderloin with sweet-potato purée, grilled monkfish with roasted mushrooms and shallot vinaigrette, and magret of duck with wild rice and tangerine-cranberry relish. Try not to miss the crème brûlée tart, Kahlúa cheesecake, blueberry bread pudding, and chocolate-raspberry tart.

Miracle Grill. 112 First Ave. (at 7th St.). ☎ **212/254-2353.** Reservations accepted for 6 or more in winter. Main courses $9.95–$17.95. AE, MC, V. Sun–Thurs 5:30–11:30pm, Fri–Sat 5:30pm–midnight; brunch Sat–Sun 11:30am–3pm. Subway: 6 to Astor Place. SOUTHWESTERN.

For fiery-hot food at prices that won't burn a hole in your pocket, Downtowners and Wall Streeters on their way back uptown come comfortably together in this minimally decorated dining room. In summer they sip cool margaritas in the rambling garden. The efficient wait staff keeps the water glasses full to extinguish spicy appetizers like the southwestern spring roll, a tortilla bursting with julienne carrots, cabbage, and red onion drizzled with hot peanut vinaigrette and cilantro oil. Well-prepared main courses include grilled New York strip with smoky chipotle butter and garlic-stuffed potato. The fajitas don't come out sizzling, but they're hot, especially the portobello one with spicy black beans, chunky pico de gallo, and red-cabbage salsa. Brunch serves up similarly tasty fare: eggs poached with ancho chiles and sun-dried tomato hollandaise or blue-corn pancakes with honey butter and fruit. In the Village, **Miracle Grill West** serves similar fare at 415 Bleecker St. (☎ 212/924-1900).

Sammy's Roumanian. 157 Chrystie St. (at Delancey St.). ☎ **212/673-0330.** Reservations recommended, required on weekends. Main courses $11.95–$28.95. AE, MC, V. Sun–Thurs 3–10pm, Fri–Sat 3pm–midnight. Subway: F to Delancey St. JEWISH/ROUMANIAN.

Do *not* squirt one another with the seltzer bottles! But nearly everything else goes at this dated but zany spot where you'll feel that you've walked into an audience-participation performance piece called "Cousin Murray Gets Bar Mitzvahed." Nearly before your derrière hits the chair, the seltzer and huge bowls of sour pickles, sour tomatoes, roasted peppers, and challah bread land on the table. You know all that stuff you've been reading for years is so bad for you—and so satisfying? You can't avoid it here: The favorite appetizers are chopped liver, broiled chicken livers, and grated radish and chopped onions—with schmaltz (liquid chicken fat). Garlic lovers favor a sausage called karnatzlack, and the broiled veal chops are quite good. For dessert you can make your own egg creams (the seltzer has a culinary *and* a medicinal function).

Time Cafe. 380 Lafayette St. (at Great Jones St.). ☎ **212/533-7000.** Reservations recommended on weekends. Main courses $8.50–$19.75; prix-fixe brunch $13.50. AE, MC, V. Sun–Thurs noon–midnight, Fri–Sat noon–1am; brunch Sat–Sun 10:30am–4pm. Subway: 6 to Astor Place. CONTEMPORARY AMERICAN.

This laid-back spot can provide a night's entertainment or the perfect sidewalk brunch. At street level is the cafe, in an airy modern space with a good-size bar and excellent people-watching potential. Fez, a relaxing lounge/bar with an *Arabian Nights* ambiance, is in the back. Fez Under Time Cafe is a performance space downstairs, famous for the Thursday Mingus Big Band workshop (see chapter 9). The Time Cafe features a large selection of contemporary American fare like grilled free-range chicken dressed with ancho oil and served with spicy potato salad and thin-crust pizza topped with asparagus, sun-dried tomatoes, Vidalia onions, pesto, and goat cheese. Finger food and light meals are served in the lounge and downstairs. **Time Cafe West,** in the Village at 87 Seventh Ave. (☎ 212/220-9100), offers similar fare and warm-weather rooftop dining.

INEXPENSIVE

✪ **Angelica Kitchen.** 300 E. 12th St. (First & Second aves.). ☎ **212/228-2909.** Reservations accepted for six or more Mon–Thurs. Main courses $5–$14.25; lunch deal (Mon–Fri 11:30am–5pm) $6.75. No credit cards. Daily 11:30am–10:30pm. Subway: L, N, R, 4, 5, 6, to 14th St./Union Sq. ORGANIC VEGETARIAN.

Even the most hardcore carnivore may reconsider after sampling from this vegan organic menu known for flavorful cuisine showcased in the "daily seasonal creation." One called "put on your party shoes" is a Spanish paella featuring saffron basmati rice tossed with carrots, broccoli, cauliflower, porcinis, seitan, tofu, and tempeh, served with a watercress, onion, and pear salad topped by orange-cumin dressing. For something less festive, try a "dragon bowl," a hearty blend of rice, beans, sea vegetables, steamed vegetables, and tahini-scallion dressing. The weekday lunch deal includes soup, a slice of cornbread or sourdough bread with miso-tahini spread, a salad, and kukicha tea.

✪ **Bombay Dining.** 320 E. 6th St. (First & Second aves.). ☎ **212/260-8229.** Main courses $4.75–$10.50. AE, MC, V. Daily noon–3:30pm and 5pm–midnight. Subway: F to Second Ave. INDIAN.

Some people speculate that there's one big kitchen in the alley behind the dozens of nondescript Indian restaurants lining this block. But Bombay Dining is a standout. Start with the assorted appetizers for a sampling of *samosa* (crisp vegetable-and-meat patties), *pakora* (banana fritters), *shami kebab* (spiced meat-and-bean patties), and *papadum* (crispy bean wafers with coarse peppercorns). Favorite Indian breads are *poori*, butter-fried puffed balls that resemble small balloons, and *alu paratha*, a flat bread stuffed with mildly spiced potatoes. Main courses include meats, seafood, and vegetables seasoned with exotic spices. Bring your own beer or wine and linger to enjoy the live sitar music.

Il Bagatto. 192 E. 2nd St. (Aves. A & B). ☎ **212/228-0977.** Reservations recommended. Main courses $6–$16. Tues–Thurs 7pm–midnight, Fri–Sat 7pm–1am; brunch Sat–Sun noon–4pm. No credit cards. Subway: F to Second Ave. ITALIAN.

After opening in late 1995, this small trattoria fast became a neighborhood favorite for high-end Italian at next-to-nothing prices. It's out-of-the-way location in Alphabet City kept Uptown gourmets away, until *New York* magazine voted its lasagna, offered only on Sunday, the best in town. Now the place is perpetually packed. Fortunately, the cozy bar downstairs provides the perfect parking space for a few premeal cocktails. Daily specials are always a good bet: Thursday is the traditional day for gnocchi in Rome and here, and Friday (of course) is fish day.

✪ **Lucky Cheng's.** 24 First Ave. (1st & 2nd sts.). ☎ **212/473-0516.** Reservations recommended. Main courses $10.95–$17.95. AE, DC, DISC, MC, V. Sun–Thurs 6pm–midnight, Fri–Sat 6pm–1am; brunch Sun noon–4pm. Subway: F to Second Ave. ASIAN FUSION.

You gotta have a gimmick if you want to get ahead, according to the ecdysiasts in *Gypsy,* and here the diverting twist is waiters dressed like waitresses. From this diner's diary: A waitperson—tall, dark, with almond-curved eyes—approaches. Obviously Asian and obviously male. "Hi, my name is Gretchen, and I'm German." *Ach du lieber!*

This fun place has a mixed crowd, suits and jeans, yuppies and gays. Bemused out-of-towners spice the brew. You can't shake the feeling of a New Orleans bordello miscast in *The King and I.* The food is Asian fusion, with dishes from across the continent. The chicken satay was good and the calamari crisp—but, girlfriend!, that frisée had fizzled. The huge paella was pronounced "absolute heaven." The rest of dinner was food purgatory, but who cared? We had Gretchen.

Veselka. 144 Second Ave. (at 9th St.). ☎ **212/228-9682.** Sandwiches $1.95–$5.95; main courses $5–$9. AE, DISC, MC, V. Daily 24 hours. Subway: 6 to Astor Place. UKRAINIAN DINER.

Whenever the craving hits for authentic and substantial Eastern European fare at old-world prices, Veselka fits the bill with *pierogi* (small doughy envelopes filled with potatoes, cheese, or sauerkraut), *kasha varnishkes* (cracked buckwheat and noodles with mushroom sauce), and classic soups like a sublime scarlet borscht, voted best in the city by the *New York Times* and *New York* magazine. Try the buckwheat pancakes for a perfect breakfast or brunch. This is a favorite late-night/early-morning eatery with club kids and other night demons.

9 Greenwich Village

See the "Downtown Dining" map (pp. 112–113) for restaurants in this section.

VERY EXPENSIVE

✪ **Gotham Bar & Grill.** 12 E. 12th St. (Fifth Ave. & University Place). ☎ **212/620-4020.** Reservations recommended. Main courses $29–$35; prix-fixe lunch $19.99. AE, DC, MC, V. Mon–Fri noon–2:30pm; Sun–Thurs 5:30–10:30pm, Fri–Sat 5:30–11pm. Subway: L, N, R, 4, 5, 6 to 14th St./Union Sq. CONTEMPORARY AMERICAN.

Holy survivor, Batman! Gotham continues, now a teenager, to be one of New York's best restaurants and one of the best American-food restaurants anywhere. On entering the multitiered space, you'll realize you're on stage. Players from all walks of life strut about, proud of their parts in this show with "legs." The mix is the message. Chef Alfred Portale is such a stylish original that much of what we take for "new American" came from his kitchen. Among his best appetizers: the seafood salad stacked with squid, scallops, Japanese octopus, lobster, and avocado and dressed in lemon and extra-virgin olive oil and the sautéed skate wings with eggplant caviar, mint, and cold-pressed olive oil. Main-course choices include rack of lamb with blissful garlic mashed potatoes and squab and grilled foie gras with sweet corn, polenta, and cranberry beans. Pastry chef Joseph Murphy's cheesecake surrounded by Michigan sour cherries is stylish and seductive. Solo diners feel comfortable at the long bar, and the $19.99 lunch menu is a steal.

✪ **Il Mulino.** 86 W. 3rd St. (Thompson & Sullivan sts.). ☎ **212/673-3783.** Reservations required. Jacket required/tie suggested. Main courses $23–$55. AE, MC, V. Mon–Fri noon–2:30pm; Mon–Sat 5–11:30pm. Closed July. Subway: A, B, C, D, E, F, Q to W. 4th St./Washington Sq. ITALIAN.

Once at a party I asked former mayor Ed Koch, a lifelong Village resident, to name his favorite Italian place in the neighborhood. "Il Mulino, of course," came the instant reply. He's not alone in that opinion, as the long wait at the bar (annoying because you cool your heels even with reservations) attests. From the street-side quiet-curtained windows, you wouldn't know that inside is a restaurant with a reputation as large as the facade is unassuming. When you're finally seated, a plate of wonderfully crisp zucchini arrives (an apology?). You're then ready to order any of the paramount pastas, inspired by many regions of Italy. Among them are spicy capellini all'arrabiata, spaghettini with lush clams, and a much-better-than-usual fettuccine Alfredo. The seafood, especially the salmon with porcinis special, and the veal are divine. The room is crowded but charming, with exposed brick walls, bentwood chairs, and subdued lights. It's easier to get a reservation—and a punctual table—at lunch.

✪ **One If By Land, Two If By Sea.** 17 Barrow St. (W. 4th St. & Seventh Ave. South). ☎ **212/228-0822.** Reservations strongly recommended. Jacket recommended/tie optional.

> ### 🕐 Family-Friendly Restaurants
>
> The unflagging vitality of children requires a place that not only welcomes but also distracts them. While you should always call to see if special accommodations are made for kids, certain restaurants are especially appropriate.
>
> **Serendipity 3** (p. 161) is a whimsical curiosity shop with colossal ice-cream treats. **Jekyll & Hyde Club** (p. 141) is great for a friendly little fright, and magicians and balloon sculptors populate **Comedy Nation** (p. 140). During weekend brunch, **America** (p. 131) caters to kids with crayons, books, magicians, and balloon twisters.
>
> Parents with teens should bring good humor—and ear plugs—to the **theme restaurants** around West 57th Street and in Times Square (see the box "Where the Themes Are the Message").
>
> Family-style dining takes on a fuller meaning at cavernous **Carmine's** (p. 139), where gargantuan portions of Southern Italian food feed a large brood for little damage.

Main courses $29–$41. AE, DC, DISC, MC, V. Mon–Sat 5:30pm–midnight. Subway: 1, 9 to Christopher St. CONTEMPORARY AMERICAN.

As you enter this plush space, you step back in time to when the Village was country mansions and gentlemen's farms. The fireplace crackles and a piano fills the room with melody. Flowers abound and candles flicker everywhere. Among the best appetizers are a steak tartare with crispy leeks and foie gras terrine with brioche and a citrus-scented duck gelée. The beef Wellington with bordelaise sauce is outstanding. The fish choices include farm-raised Maine salmon, flown in fresh, served with a crispy skin, creamy cabbage, lentils, and a sherry wine vinegar sauce.

EXPENSIVE

✪ **Moomba.** 133 Seventh Ave. South (Charles & 10th sts.). ☎ **212/989-1414.** Reservations required on weekends. Main courses $21–$32. AE, DC, MC, V. Daily 6pm–4am. Subway: 1, 9 to Christopher St. CONTEMPORARY AMERICAN.

Gossip-page readers know this is *the* celebrity hangout of the moment, especially late at night, when the likes of Harrison Ford, Ellen DeGeneres, Ben Affleck, and Gwyneth Paltrow fill the third-floor lounge. With persistence, you can get an early reservation, and even if you don't bump into a superstar, you'll be rewarded with a wonderful meal. Chef Frank Falcinelli and his talented team turn out an ambitious menu. Start with tuna tatare spiked with wasabi and scallions or Caesar salad with house-cured anchovies. Main courses include honey-maple–smoked squab with chanterelles and sweet-potato spaetzle and perfectly roasted chicken rubbed with foie gras and served with mashed yukon gold potatoes. For dessert, try any of pastry chef Wendy Israel's headline-grabbing creations.

MODERATE

Bar 6. 502 Sixth Ave. (12th & 13th sts.). ☎ **212/691-1363.** Reservations recommended. Main courses $7.50–$18.50; prix-fixe brunch $13.50. AE, MC, V. Mon–Thurs noon–2am, Fri noon–3am, Sat noon–3am, Sun 11am–2am. Subway: F to 14th St. FRENCH/MOROCCAN.

On weekend evenings the place, especially the front bar area, looks like a casting call for a documentary on Manhattan fast-lane, black-clad, gym-body set. At lunch, brunch, and other less glamorous moments, Bar 6 is a welcoming neighborhood French bistro with a Moroccan flair and a local crowd. Start with mussels Provençal or hummus and white-bean brandade on pita bread. Then select nicely spiced grilled merguez sausage, roasted monkfish, tangine of chicken, or *bisteeya* (a chicken pot pie with an exotic Moroccan accent). At brunch there are some Moroccan choices, pâté, eggs, grilled chicken, and pastas.

✪ **Mi Cocina.** 57 Jane St. (at Hudson St.). ☎ **212/627-8273.** Reservations recommended. Main courses $11–$19; prix-fixe dinners (Mon–Fri 5:30–6:30pm) $20 and $25. AE, CB, DC, MC, V. Thurs 11:30am–3pm; Mon–Thurs 5:30–10:30pm, Fri 5:30–11:30pm, Sat 5–11:30pm, Sun 4:30–10pm; brunch Sun 11:30am–3:30pm. Subway: A, C, E, L to 14th St. MEXICAN.

In just a few years, this unassuming but truly gourmet restaurant has shot ahead of nearly all its competition. It serves inspired, spirited dishes from many regions of Mexico, pleasing its *norteño* fans without compromising authenticity. The *pollo en mixiote* is a marvel: moist bits of chicken coated with a sublime chile sauce, wrapped in parchment and steamed in beer. The ceviche of calamari is a spicy mix of fish, red onions, tomatoes, and cilantro in garlic-lime marinade. Sautéed shrimp come with adobo chile sauce and steamed spinach. Forget whatever you think an enchilada is because here it's made with fresh tomatillo and poblano chile sauce, stuffed with vegetables and covered with a roasted tomato-and-chipotle sauce or filled with chicken and topped with mole poblano, rings of onions, and sesame seeds. Main-course shrimp are cooked in a roasted tomato, chipotle, and white-wine sauce and accompanied by spinach and white rice. Chef/owner José Hurtado Prud'homme proves that, even in such a small restaurant, if you cook it right, they will come.

INEXPENSIVE

Aggie's. 146 W. Houston St. (at MacDougal St.). ☎ **212/673-8994.** Main courses $7.95–$13.75. No credit cards. Mon–Wed 7:30am–10pm, Thurs–Fri 7:30am–11pm, Sat 10am–4pm and 6–11pm, Sun 10am–4pm. Subway: 1, 9 to Houston St. AMERICAN DINER.

Aggie describes her cooking at this diner to the arts crowd as "American fare educated in New York." That means no-fuss food with funky and unexpected twists. Breakfasts and brunches are popular for what might be the best omelets in Manhattan, but be sure to try other don't-miss dishes: the grilled chicken breast sandwich at lunch and roast duck on a nest of black-pepper pasta at dinner. Put your name in at the door because there's often a line of dressed down but highly cool people.

Café Asean. 117 W. 10th St. (Sixth & Greenwich aves.). ☎ **212/633-0348.** Reservations recommended. Main courses $9–$13; prix-fixe dinners $13 and $15. No credit cards. Sun–Thurs noon–10:30pm, Fri–Sat noon–11pm. Subway: A, B, C, D, E, F, Q to W. 4th St. SOUTHEAST ASIAN.

Dining Zone: Cornelia Street

Running between Bleecker and West 4th streets in the Village, Cornelia Street is a charming lane with seven small restaurants. One of my favorites is **Home,** no. 20 (☎ 212/243-9579), where chef David Page and co-owner Barbara Shinn keep things fresh, popularly priced, and welcoming. Contemporary dishes like a satisfying roasted lamb sandwich and perfectly prepared quail are best enjoyed in the year-round garden. Next door at no. 18 are **Le Gigot** (☎ 212/627-3737), a cozy French bistro, and **Pearl Oyster Bar** (☎ 212/691-8211), serving steamed clams, lobster rolls, and other fresh seafood in a lobster shack ambiance. The zesty Italian food at **Pó,** no. 31 (☎ 212/645-2189), has attracted a lot of attention since chef Mario Batali began appearing on the Food Network; reserve in advance. You'll also find Cuban, Moroccan, and American cuisines on this block.

Alfresco, Anyone?

Over the last few years, the city's parks have blossomed with restaurants and cafes. Of course, there's **Tavern on the Green** (p. 153) in Central Park, and on the east side of the park, along the edge of a restful lake, is **Park View at the Boathouse** (p. 159). Bryant Park, which seems like Paris on 42nd Street, has three popular choices: **Bryant Park Grill,** the **Terrace,** and the more informal **Cafe** (p. 138). Across the street from the sidewalk chic at the Coffee Shop is **Luna Park,** an easygoing spot in Union Square Park (p. 132).

Le Cirque 2000 (p. 144) features a garden cafe in the courtyard of the Villard Houses. This tony space is surrounded by private town houses from 1882 (and just behind St. Patrick's Cathedral). What with Sirio's food and following and the superb Midtown backdrop, it's *the* place for a sophisticated bite *en plein air.*

The list of restaurants with quiet gardens or other outdoor seating is long, but a few of my favorites are **Jean Georges** (p. 152), **Aureole** (p. 155), **Barolo** (p. 119), **Miracle Grill** (p. 122), **Time Cafe** (p. 122), **Home** (p. 126), **Verbena** (p. 130), **Le Madri** (p. 132), and **March** (p. 145).

In a city of skyscrapers and crowded sidewalks, rooftop dining is inevitable. **Flowers** (p. 129) and **Time Cafe West** (p. 122) are two Downtown favorites. On the Upper East Side, **Sofia Fabulous Pizza,** 1022 Madison Ave., at 79th Street (☎ **212/734-2676**), serves pricey pizza three stories up under a canopy and rotating fans.

The Terrace, at the Stanhope hotel, 995 Fifth Ave. (☎ **212/288-5800**), is the only outdoor cafe on upper Fifth Avenue, an excellent destination after a stroll in Central Park or a visit to the Metropolitan Museum.

If you're looking for old-fashioned enchantment and inventive Asian cooking, this Village spot has the best Vietnamese, Thai, Malaysian, and Indonesian cooking served in an attractively simple rustic dining room or a lovely small garden. The place is tiny but exudes charm, the service is friendly, and the prices are a real bargain. The beef-and-vermicelli appetizer salad, topped with crushed peanuts and surrounded by basil, is nearly as big as a dinner salad. The curried squid (*gaeng kheow*) is plentiful and blessed with the right texture and powerful taste. The shrimp is also worth trying.

✪ **Florent.** 69 Gansevoort St. (Greenwich & Washington sts.). ☎ **212/989-5779.** Reservations recommended. Main courses $7.95–$17.95; prix-fixe dinner (before 7:30pm) $16.50 or (7:30pm–midnight) $18.50. No credit cards. Mon–Fri 9am–5am, Sat–Sun 24 hours. Subway: A, C, E, L to 14th St. FRENCH BISTRO/DINER.

So you get that craving at 3am for boudin noir or steak frites and can't decide whether you'd like to eat with club kids, partying celebrities, cross-dressed revelers, truckers from Jersey, or the odd stockbroker? Get down to Florent, the nearly 24-hour diner *avec* bistro where you can have it all. The steak au poivre is a favorite, but you could also get a burger or grilled chicken breast sandwich or meat loaf.

French Roast Cafe. 456 Sixth Ave. (at 11th St.). ☎ **212/533-2233.** Reservations recommended. Main courses $8–$13.95. AE, DC, MC, V. Daily 24 hours. Subway: A, B, C, D, E, F, Q to W. 4th St./Washington Sq. FRENCH CAFE.

Overwhelmingly popular with college students, writers working on their novels, and assorted others, this 24-hour Village corner spot went from zero to Mach speed before most of us could say, "Have you heard about . . . ?" The food has taken critical knocks, but the crowds still keep hanging out. You'll have lots of salads to choose from (arugula and fennel, baby mixed greens, grilled leeks vinaigrette) and some hot appetizers, like wild mushroom timbale and mussels Provençal. Entrees include roasted herb chicken, vegetable plates, beef pot au feu, and trout, as well as steak, pastas, and burgers. But I like this best for a slow breakfast or brunch or as a late coffee-and-dessert place.

✪ **John's Pizzeria.** 278 Bleecker St. (Sixth & Seventh aves.). ☎ **212/243-1680.** Reservations accepted for six or more. Main courses $6–$15.75. No credit cards. Mon–Thurs 11:30am–12:30am, Fri–Sat 11:30am–1am, Sun noon–12:30am. Subway: A, B, C, D, E, F, Q to W. 4th St./Washington Sq. PIZZA.

Thin-crusted, properly sauced, and fresh, the pizza at John's has long been one of New York's best. Unlike at most pizzerias, here you order a whole pie and not by the slice, so come with friends or family. This place is *popular,* and there's often a wait. But with your first bite you'll forget any minor inconveniences.

The original Bleecker Street location still gets my nod, but at the new Theater District restaurant, 260 W. 44th St., at Eighth Avenue (☎ 212/391-7560), you dine under the stained-glass ceiling of the century-old Gospel Tabernacle Church. The locations near Lincoln Center, 48 W. 65th St. (☎ **212/721-7001**), and on the Upper East Side, 408 E. 64th St. (☎ **212/935-2895**), are also worth checking out.

10 The Flatiron District & Gramercy Park

See the "Midtown Dining" map (pp. 136–137) for restaurants in this section.

VERY EXPENSIVE   *wonderful linen-cloth!!*

✪ **Gramercy Tavern.** 42 E. 20th St. (Broadway & Park Ave. South). ☎ **212/477-0777.** Reservations required well in advance. Prix-fixe lunch $33; prix-fixe dinner $58; tavern menu $6–$18. AE, DC, MC, V. Dining room, Mon–Thurs noon–2pm and 5:30–10pm, Fri noon–2pm and 5:30–11pm, Sat 5:30–11pm, Sun 5:30–10pm. Tavern, Mon–Thurs noon–11pm, Fri–Sat noon–midnight, Sun 5–11pm. Subway: 6, R to 23rd St. CONTEMPORARY AMERICAN.

Owner Danny Meyer (whose Union Square Cafe is also one of New York's best) and chef Tom Colicchio assure that Gramercy Tavern exceeds expectations—and expectations right from the start have been high. The dining room is comfortable and luxurious without being formal, and the tavern room around the bar is even more relaxed.

The foie gras appetizer exquisitely juxtaposes tender liver with a crunchy, acidic rhubarb relish. The seared pepper-crusted tuna entree is fanned out on a bed of wilted arugula, white beans, and squash with lemon confit. Game lovers aim for rabbit sautéed with rosemary and olives. The cheese tray, an alternative to dessert or worth $12 as an extra course, features a selection from New York State, France, Spain, Italy, and England. Desserts worth the calories include warm lemon tart soufflé complemented by homemade coconut and ginger ice creams or, more decadent, warm chocolate ganache cake with vanilla bay-leaf sauce and tiny scoops of vanilla and chocolate ice cream. The tavern room serves excellent light meals, like a lamb sandwich with grilled vegetables and quail with polenta, black olives, and greens.

EXPENSIVE

Da Umberto. 107 W. 17th St. (Sixth & Seventh aves.). ☎ **212/989-0303.** Reservations required. Main courses $15–$32. AE. Mon–Fri noon–3pm; Mon–Thurs 5:30–11pm, Fri–Sat 5:30–11:30pm. Subway: 1, 9 to 18th St.; F to 14th St. ITALIAN TUSCAN.

Da Umberto doesn't look like much from the outside, but the Tuscan cooking is first rate. Specials are the right things to order, and they're likely to include an antipasto of fresh vegetables or, one of my favorites, Tuscan white-bean soup.

Flowers. 21 W. 17th St. (Fifth & Sixth aves.). ☎ **212/691-8888.** Reservations recommended. Main courses $18–$23; prix-fixe brunch $15.95. AE, DC, MC, V. Mon–Fri noon–3pm; Sun–Wed 6–11pm, Thurs–Sat 6pm–midnight; brunch Sun noon–4pm. Subway: L, N, R, 4, 5, 6 to 14th St./Union Sq.; F to 14th St. CONTEMPORARY AMERICAN.

The limos and cabs are lined up here because someone on the move is always spilling out. Come to dinner around 10pm, and you'll be in a crowd of celebrities (the Pacino/DeNiro type), sports stars (lots of Knicks), models (only the most leggy), and local artistic types. You might have to pay for this—the staff can be rude and the tables near the bar might leave you feeling you're at a club that doesn't have you on its membership list. Chef Antonio Maroto (former executive chef at the "21" Club) keeps things changing often, but you should look for grilled sea scallops with mâche salad and margarita sauce, grilled marinated quail with toasted polenta and dried apricots with Amontillado sherry sauce, and pan-roasted Chilean sea bass with warm shaved-fennel salad. In warm weather, up on the roof is a great fun place with the same pleasing cuisine.

— ✪ **Mesa Grill.** 102 Fifth Ave. (15th & 16th sts.). ☎ **212/807-7400.** Reservations recommended. Main courses $18–$28. AE, DC, DISC, MC, V. Mon–Fri noon–2:30pm; Sun–Thurs 5:30–10:30pm, Fri–Sat 5:30–11pm; brunch Sat–Sun 11:30am–3pm. Subway: L, N, R, 4, 5, 6 to 14th St./Union Sq. SOUTHWESTERN.

A must-stop destination for those interested in new American cooking, this spicy-hot restaurant has been made into a new classic by chef/owner Bobby Flay. The regular menu doesn't change much, but maybe that's the point. The dishes are almost all thrillingly inventive: The tuna is invariably perfectly cooked, with bracing spices. The pastas are innovative and quirky. And the grilled pork chops adobo have a sparky side dish of apple chutney. Other favorites: grilled salmon with red-chile honey glaze, barbecued baby chicken, and grilled loin of lamb chops.

✪ **Patria.** 250 Park Ave. South (at 20th St.). ☎ **212/777-6211.** Reservations necessary. Main courses $19–$29. AE, DC, MC, V. Mon–Fri noon–2:45pm; Mon–Thurs 6–11pm, Fri–Sat 5:30pm–midnight, Sun 5:30–10:30pm. Subway: 6, R to 23rd St. CONTEMPORARY SOUTH AMERICAN.

Its menu is a Latin lover's dream, created by chef Douglas Rodriguez, who takes a bite from Ecuador, a taste from Colombia, a dash of Dominican, and a pinch of Peruvian to create a "New Latin" cuisine. Appetizers include chilled crab-and-potato terrine with scallop-and-calamari escabeche and an empanada filled with black beans, roasted corn, and tomato salsa. Terrific entrees are plantain-coated mahi mahi with lily salad, coconut-glazed tuna loin with chayote and dried shrimp salsa, and crispy whole red snapper with coconut rice and coleslaw. ¡Ay! For those who want a little of a lot, there's a well-selected tasting menu.

✪ **Union Square Cafe.** 21 E. 16th St. (Fifth Ave. & Union Sq. West). ☎ **212/243-4020.** Reservations required weeks in advance. Main courses $18.50–$29. AE, DC, MC, V. Mon–Sat noon–2:15pm; Sun–Thurs 5:30–10:15pm, Fri–Sat 6–11:15pm; soup and oysters at the bar between lunch and dinner. Subway: L, N, R, 4, 5, 6 to 14th St./Union Sq. CONTEMPORARY AMERICAN.

In this simple yet sophisticated restaurant, owner Danny Meyer and chef Michael Romano have been turning out acclaimed food for 13 years. And Meyer has since joined other partners to launch the nearby Gramercy Tavern (above) and two new restaurants (see "Dining Zone: 11 Madison Avenue"). Professionals from the neighborhood's advertising agencies and publishing houses crowd Union Square Cafe at lunch and dinner. You'll need to reserve weeks in advance. Among the most popular appetizers is the fried calamari with spicy anchovy mayonnaise. Main courses include crisp roasted lemon-pepper duck with quinoa-basmati pilaf and spicy pear-apple chutney, and a filet mignon of tuna, marinated and grilled, and served with sautéed eggplant and rice and beans. On the side, be sure to get some hot garlic potato chips.

Verbena. 54 Irving Place (17th & 18th sts.). ☎ **212/260-5454.** Reservations recommended. Main courses $18–$29; prix-fixe dinner $58. AE, DC, MC, V. Mon–Sat noon–2:45pm; daily 5:30–10:30pm; brunch Sun 11:30am–2:45pm. Subway: L, N, R, 4, 5, 6 to 14th St./Union Sq. CONTEMPORARY AMERICAN.

This place on the ground floor of a brownstone attracts New Yorkers looking for a fine seasonal menu, quiet elegance, knowledgeable service, and a comfortable setting. Chef/owner Diane Forley often appears in the dining room to watch over the proceedings. She has cooked at the Gotham Bar & Grill, Petrossian, and others of New York's and France's very best. The warm salad of shrimp on an artichoke griddlecake is superb. Wild mushrooms float in a dusky sauce beside lightly toasted pasta. The butternut-squash ravioli, with a touch of cheese and cinnamon, will make you realize what an inventive chef can do with Italian cooking. The crème brûlée is infused, appropriately, with verbena. You might ask for a table on the peaceful garden terrace, and you'll pass through the spotless kitchen on the way.

MODERATE

Blue Water Grill. 31 Union Sq. West (at 16th St.). ☎ **212/675-9500.** Reservations recommended. Main courses $10.50–$19.95. AE, MC, V. Mon–Thurs 11:30am–12:30am, Fri–Sat 11:30am–1am, Sun 5:30pm–midnight; brunch Sun 11am–4pm. Subway: L, N, R, 4, 5, 6 to 14th St./Union Sq. SEAFOOD.

At this destination for hip daters and after-work drinkers, the eclectic menu incorporates both the Asian and the Mediterranean influences that have hypnotized New York's restaurant scene. Atlantic salmon is steamed and served with Shanghai sauce and Asian vegetables, mussels come in red curry sauce, and Moroccan-spiced red snapper is paired with warm eggplant salad and herbed couscous. Traditional palates enjoy the straightforward wood-grilled fish, chicken, and steak and fresh oysters from the raw bar. French windows open onto a row of tables on a narrow terrace.

Dining Zone: 11 Madison Avenue

By the time you read this, the striking art-deco tower at 11 Madison Ave., between 24th and 25th streets, will have on its ground floor three top-flight restaurants with plenty of seating space (you'll have to check for phone numbers).

Danny Meyer, co-owner of Union Square Cafe and Gramercy Tavern nearby, is opening two places: **Eleven Madison Park** will serve French-accented American cuisine in a majestic dining room with 35-foot windows overlooking Madison Square Park. Plans also call for a wine bar offering up to three dozen varieties by the glass. At **Tabla,** the menu will mix Indian spices with Western culinary traditions and offer Tandoori-baked breads served with microbrewed beers and carefully chosen wines.

Domus at Sign of the Dove is the renamed and remade version of Sign of the Dove, a favorite restaurant for romantics forced from its nest last year after 37 years on the Upper East Side. The new 22,000-square-foot roost is to include a formal dining room and a grand cafe with 24-foot ceilings and a 70-foot bar. It's scheduled to open in April 1999 with chef Andrew d'Amico pre-paring the same magically alluring contemporary cuisine. We'll have to wait and see if the decor is as love-inducing as it was for so many years at the Uptown spot.

Caffè Bondí. 7 W. 20th St. (Fifth & Sixth aves.). ☎ 212/691-8136. Reservations recommended. Main courses $16–$24; prix-fixe dinner $29. AE, DC, JCB, MC, V. Mon–Thurs 11am–11pm, Fri–Sat 11am–midnight. Subway: F, R to 23rd St. SICILIAN.

Bondí serves Sicilian delicacies with skill and care. The Settepani brothers who own and run the place are always ready to tell you about the food or wines. You might start with the conca d'oro, a lively salad of oranges, fennel, black olives, and red onions in an oil-and-vinegar dressing. The *insalata di fagiolini* is string beans, potatoes, and tomatoes mixed with oregano, olive oil, and vinegar. The fish soup is from an 11th-century Saracen recipe: sole, grouper, mussels, clams, and shrimp in a sauce of capers, saffron, garlic, pine nuts, and laurel leaves. Among the notable entrees are braised rabbit with white wine and sautéed shrimp in wine and béchamel sauce served with carrot-almond purée. The garden is a delight.

Coffee Shop. 29 Union Sq. West (at 16th St.). ☎ **212/243-7969.** Reservations accepted for six or more. Main courses $9–$23. AE, DC, MC, V. Tues–Sat 7am–6am, Sun–Mon 7am–2am. Subway: L, N, R, 4, 5, 6 to 14th St./Union Sq. AMERICAN/BRAZILIAN/SOUTH AMERICAN.

The crowd is pretty, so you'll ogle and drool or, if you're up to it, pose and gloat. In the bustling center of Union Square, with its greenmarket and recent veneer of chic, the scene here, despite its trendiness, maintains a friendly face and serves some good food. The service is a roll of the dice, though: Well-meaning waitpersons from Mars mix with an otherwise competent staff. During warmer months, arrive early for a sidewalk table, one of Manhattan's most-sought-after roosts. Insist on the park side, where you'll be happy under the umbrellas (the side street has too many unwelcome odors).

The superb barbecued chicken sandwich with nonfat cilantro-lime mayonnaise will keep you trim and satisfied. Brunch, with the jazz band blowing its trumpet right into your culinarily correct noncholesterol/nonfat omelet with wild mushrooms and tomatoes, is for the young at ears.

Lemon. 230 Park Ave. South (18th & 19th sts.). ☎ **212/614-1200.** Main courses $15–$24. AE, MC, V. Sun–Fri 11:30am–4pm; daily 6pm–midnight. Subway: L, N, R, 4, 5, 6 to 14th St./Union Sq. ASIAN FUSION.

Youthful singles and couples stampede to this casual bar and restaurant. Start with the duck confit spring rolls with lettuce wraps or tuna tartar with taro crisps. Entrees include Chinese braised lamb shank with eggplant fries and whole Chilean sea bass flavored with Szechuan peppercorns, cinnamon, star anise, clove, and fennel and drizzled with a Port-balsamic reduction.

Steak Frites. 9 E. 16th St. (Fifth Ave. & Union Sq. West). ☎ **212/463-7101.** Reservations recommended. Main courses $12.50–$28. AE, DC, MC, V. Mon–Thurs noon–11:30pm, Fri–Sat noon–12:30am, Sun noon–10pm. Subway: L, N, R, 4, 5, 6 to 14th St./Union Sq. FRENCH BISTRO.

Meat lovers, arm yourselves. The menu offers other choices (pasta, chicken, salads), but the thing to ask for is the steak frites for two—certified black Angus steak is perfectly, pink inside, blackened outside. The fries are nearly as good as in St-Germain.

INEXPENSIVE

✪ **America.** 9 E. 18th St. (Fifth Ave. & Broadway). ☎ **212/505-2110.** Reservations recommended. Main courses $9.95–$19.95. AE, DC, DISC, MC, V. Sun–Thurs 11:30am–midnight, Fri–Sat 11:30am–1am. Subway: L, N, R, 4, 5, 6 to 14th St./Union Sq. AMERICAN.

America is nearly as large as a continent, with a seemingly mile-high ceiling. The menu is eclectic (soups, omelets, pancakes, pastas, sandwiches, poultry, salads, meats, fish, burgers, pizza, and vegetables) with prices you're more likely to see in the heartland than in New York. Each dish has a state or city listed next to it, as the inspiration source. There's five-way chili, Long Island duck pot pie, Mississippi fried catfish, and New England clam chowder.

L'Express. 249 Park Ave. South (at 20th St.). ☎ **212/254-5858.** Reservations recommended for six or more. Main courses $7.95–$17.95. AE, MC, V. Daily 24 hours. Subway: L, N, R, 4, 5, 6 to 14th St./Union Sq. FRENCH BISTRO.

L'Express pays homage to the convivial bistros of Lyon, called *bouchons*, by offering often underrated French country cuisine, like braised tripe in tomato sauce and boudin noir with mashed potatoes. The less adventurous seeking a typical Lyonnaise specialty might opt for *quenelles de brochet* (poached pike mousse dumplings in nantua sauce). The menu is filled out with onion soup gratinée, croque monsieur, a wonderful frisée salad topped with lardons and celery galette, and steak au poivre with french fries. There's a nice selection of French and Californian wines.

Luna Park. 27 Union Sq. West (in Union Square Park, at 16th St.). ☎ **212/475-8464.** Reservations not accepted. Main courses $9–$23. AE, DC, MC, V. Mon–Tues 11am–1am, Wed–Sat 11am–2am, Sun noon–1am; brunch Sat–Sun noon–4pm. Closed winter. Subway: L, N, R, 4, 5, 6 to 14th St./Union Sq. MEDITERRANEAN.

This refreshing open-air cafe/restaurant, run by the folks from Coffee Shop (above), sits unobtrusively in the park, with tables under white umbrellas, a long bar, and even a pool table for games alfresco. The menu offers light fare like grilled tomatoes, mozzarella, and mixed greens on focaccia as well as more substantive entrees, some with imaginative flair but most ho-hum in the flavor department. The grilled boneless half chicken is marinated in yogurt and Moroccan spices and served with grilled vegetables and basmati rice. Fish includes brook trout, Atlantic salmon, and tuna steak. It's a lovely spot for a drink under the stars when the staff isn't too surly.

Republic. 37 Union Sq. West (16th & 17th sts.). ☎ **212/627-7172.** Reservations not accepted. Main courses $4–$9. AE, DC, MC, V. Sun–Wed noon–11pm, Thurs–Sat noon–midnight. Subway: L, N, R, 4, 5, 6 to 14th St./Union Sq. ASIAN NOODLES.

Cushionless, backless benches pulled up to pine-and-steel refectory tables don't encourage lingering. However, the Chinese-, Vietnamese-, and Thai-inspired menu, with an emphasis on noodles, attracts a steady stream of on-the-go customers. For a one-bowl meal, try the spicy coconut chicken (chicken slices in coconut milk, lime juice, lemongrass, and galangal) or spicy beef (rare beef with wheat noodles in spiced with chiles, garlic, and lemongrass).

11 Chelsea

See the "Midtown Dining" map (pp. 136–137) for restaurants in this section.

EXPENSIVE

✪ **Le Madri.** 168 W. 18th St. (at Seventh Ave.). ☎ **212/727-8022.** Reservations recommended. Main courses $18–$34. AE, DC, MC, V. Mon–Fri noon–2:45pm and 5:30–11pm, Sat 5:30pm–midnight, Sun 5–10:30pm. Subway: 1, 9 to 18th St. ITALIAN.

An elegant spot in a former stable redone to resemble a lovely country home in Tuscany, Le Madri is one of many Pino Luongo success stories. It remains as impressive today as it did when it opened to lavish praise in 1989. Striving to provide the best Italian home cooking (the restaurant's name means "the mothers"), Le Madri changes menus seasonally, but one thing is consistent—the thin-crust pizzas, prepared in wood-burning ovens, are excellent. Tasty appetizers might include a salad of herbed goat cheese, beets, and baby greens in walnut vinaigrette or braised rabbit with mushrooms, herbed polenta, and truffle oil. Among never-fail pastas are saffron cavatelli with broccoli rape and sausage and half-moon-shaped ravioli stuffed with spinach and ricotta and tossed with a mix of mushrooms. Grilled tuna, osso buco, and seared veal chop are superb entrees. The tiramisù is meltingly marvelous.

MODERATE

Alley's End. 311 W. 17th St. (Eighth & Ninth aves.). ☎ **212/627-8899.** Reservations recommended. Main courses $9.75–$19. DISC, MC, V. Daily 6–11pm. Closed last week in Aug. Subway: A, C, E, L to 14th St. AMERICAN.

You'll have a sense of adventure when you walk through its nearly secret entryway (just west of Eighth Avenue). You'll get another surprise when you see how large and airy the space is. This is a top pick of neighborhood types, who feel safely cosseted from the hustle outside. The grilled asparagus-and-cucumber salad with a purée of yogurt and herbed sheep's-milk cheese or the oven-roasted portobellos with a black vegetarian vinaigrette make for smart starters. Two good entrees are the bacon-wrapped pork tenderloin in barbecue sauce and tuna steak with black pepper.

INEXPENSIVE

Che 2020. 149 Eighth Ave. (17th & 18th sts.). ☎ **212/243-2020.** Reservations recommended. Main courses $9.95–$14; prix-fixe brunch $9.95. AE, MC, V. Mon–Fri 11:30am–4:30pm; daily 5pm–midnight; brunch Sat–Sun 11am–4:30pm. Subway: A, C, E, L to Eighth Ave. AMERICAN.

Che 2020 attracts sculpted-pec Chelsea Boys to its frenzied feedings. Pale green banquettes and bark-covered sconces lend a mellow, almost Far Eastern air to the space, while the serviceable menu focuses on comfort food like pork chops, meat loaf, and roasted chicken.

Empire Diner. 210 Tenth Ave. (at 22nd St.). ☎ **212/243-2736.** Reservations not accepted. Main courses $9.95–$16.95. AE, DC, DISC, MC, V. Daily 24 hours, except Tues 4–8am. Subway: C, E to 23rd St. AMERICAN DINER.

With New York's own silver stream of Chelsea characters passing through, the Empire is a sleek and stylish 24-hour diner (see the back cover of this guide), with a constantly changing cast decked out in leather, jeans, suits, stuffed T-shirts, loose knee-length shorts, and extravagant platforms. The food is basic and good: eggs, omelets, overstuffed sandwiches, vegetable plates, and a very nice turkey platter. If you want quiet, go early. If you want an eyeful, wait for the after-hours crowd.

✪ **La Taza de Oro.** 96 Eighth Ave. (14th & 15th sts.). ☎ **212/243-9946.** Reservations not accepted. Main courses $6–$9.50. No credit cards. Mon–Sat 6am–11:30pm. Subway: A, C, E to 14th St. HISPANIC.

Okay, so this place looks like a dump, with Formica, harsh lighting, and cheap paneling. But it's clean and serves some of the best Cuban, Puerto Rican, and Dominican food in Manhattan. Area Hispanics, tuned-in neighbors, cops, and other smart New Yorkers know you won't find better, or better-priced, *chutelas fritas* (fried pork chops, and say yes to the garlic). *Mondongo* might sound like a 1950s Tarzan movie, but it's actually a delicious rendering of traditional tripe soup. The beef stew (*carne guisada*) is slow-cooked until meltingly tender. The squid and shrimp dishes are always supple, never rubbery. No matter what you order, also get a plate of *negro y blanco* (black beans and white rice), then dash some vinegar and hot sauce on top. *¡Que bien!* Though the desserts are limited and there's no beer, just soda, the simple *cafe con leche* is sublime.

The Viceroy. 160 Eighth Ave. (at 18th St.). ☎ **212/633-8484.** Reservations accepted to 7:30pm. Main courses $7.50–$18.50. AE, CB, DC, DISC, MC, V. Mon–Sat 11:30am–3pm;

Mon–Wed 5:30pm–midnight, Thurs–Sat 5:30pm–1am; brunch Sun 11:30am–4pm. Subway: 1, 9 to 18th St. CONTEMPORARY AMERICAN.

You're in Chelsea, so you know this attractive place is gay-friendly. Well, gay-mobbed. Viceroy isn't as boisterous as some of the surrounding spots but does take its food seriously. Rightly popular are the barbecue quail salad; seared peppered tuna with stir-fry Asian vegetables; and roast chicken with rosemary, haricots verts, sweet corn, and garlic whipped potatoes. The wines are well chosen and fairly priced. The crowds especially line up for the $12.95 brunch, so come early.

12 Midtown West

See the "Midtown Dining" map (pp. 136–137) for restaurants in this section.

VERY EXPENSIVE

✪ **Le Bernardin.** 155 W. 51st St. (Sixth & Seventh aves.). ☎ **212/489-1515.** Reservations required 1 month in advance. Jacket required/tie optional. Prix-fixe lunches $32 and $42; prix-fixe dinner $70. AE, DC, DISC, JCB, MC, V. Mon–Fri noon–2:30pm; Mon–Thurs 5:30–10:30pm, Fri–Sat 5:30–11pm. Subway: 1, 9 to 50th St.; N, R to 49th St. FRENCH/SEAFOOD.

Food doesn't get better than Le Bernardin's flash-marinated black bass ceviche, the freshest fish awash in cilantro, mint, jalapeños, and diced tomatoes. The seafood here is the best in New York, if not the world. The prix-fixe lunches are a bargain, given the master in the kitchen. Eric Ripert's tuna tartare always exhilarates, its Asian seasoning a welcome exotic touch. Among lightly cooked dishes that shine are herbed crabmeat in saffron ravioli and shellfish-tarragon reduction; roast baby lobster tail on asparagus-and-cèpe risotto ($15 extra); and an extravagant mix of sea scallops, foie gras, and truffles from the Périgord, wrapped and steamed in a cabbage leaf and splashed with truffle vinaigrette ($15 extra). The cod, crusted, on a bed of haricots verts with potatoes and diced tomatoes, is one of my favorites. The desserts—especially the frozen rum-scented chestnut soufflé or chocolate dome with crème brûlée on a macaroon—end the meal with a flourish.

Petrossian. 182 W. 58th St. (at Seventh Ave.). ☎ **212/245-2214.** Reservations recommended. Jacket required. Main courses $24–$34; prix-fixe lunch $22; prix-fixe dinner $35. AE, CB, DC, MC, V. Mon–Sat 11:30am–3pm and 5:30–11pm, Sun 11:30am–3pm and 5:30–10:30pm. Subway: B, D, E to Seventh Ave.; N, R to 57th St. RUSSIAN/CONTINENTAL.

The unassuming sturgeon provides the great delicacy of caviar, and nowhere is it more carefully served. The prix-fixe lunch and dinner allow you to taste a bit of heaven without tithing your salary for the year. If you come here only once, I suggest you begin with the sevruga caviar. Then segue to the Large Petrossian Teaser, a gourmet's delight of caviars and salmon roe with blini and crème fraîche.

✪ **Rainbow Room.** 30 Rockefeller Plaza, 65th Floor (49th & 50th sts.). ☎ **212/632-5000.** Subway: B, D, F, Q to 47th–50th sts./Rockefeller Center. CONTINENTAL.

High atop the Rockefeller Center building that houses the NBC Studios, the Rainbow Room has 24 floor-to-ceiling windows allowing you to gaze out over glistening towers, bridges, and streetlights. From here New York is a dreamy film set, full of possibilities and pinnacles. On a clear evening you can see 50 miles in all directions. Years ago rehabilitated to its original art deco splendor, the Rainbow Room was purchased last year by the Cipriani family (see the box "Top Toques Set New Trends"), and plans were vague at press time. There was even gossip that Alain Ducasse, the only chef with six Michelin stars, might join the team. One thing's for sure: If you do get in, with or without Ducasse in the kitchen, expect to pay very large sums.

☺ San Domenico. 240 Central Park South (Broadway & Seventh Ave.). ☎ **212/ 265-5959.** Reservations required. Jacket requested at dinner. Main courses $18.95– $32.50; pretheater prix fixe $29.50. AE, CB, MC, V. Mon–Fri noon–2:30pm; Mon–Sat 5:30–11pm, Sun 5:30–10pm. Subway: N, R to 57th St. NORTHERN ITALIAN.

This is one of the few restaurants successful in preserving the best traditions of Italian food—and that's due mostly to owner Tony May. Inspired by the cuisine of Bologna, San Domenico's menu changes seasonally. Splendid appetizers may include grilled Mediterranean baby octopus with cucumbers and cherry tomatoes, chilled fava-bean soup with goat cheese and truffle oil, or a rich mix of lobster, shrimp, king crab, and baby vegetables. Favorite pasta choices: ricotta ravioli with marinated tomatoes and black olives and the extravagant handmade pasta with chives, caviar, and asparagus. Black sea bass filet in tomato-herb broth and grilled Norwegian salmon with caviar and sour cream are among the fish offerings. For meat lovers there's a roasted veal loin with braised radicchio, pearl onions, and creamy bacon sauce.

"21" Club. 21 W. 52nd St. (Fifth & Sixth aves.). ☎ **212/582-7200.** Reservations required. Jacket/tie required. Main courses $24–$39; prix-fixe lunch $25; pretheater prix fixe $29; tasting menu $85. AE, CB, DC, DISC, JCB, MC, V. Mon–Fri noon–2:30pm; Mon–Thurs 5:30–10:30pm, Fri–Sat 5:30–11:30pm. Closed Aug. Subway: B, D, F, Q to 47th–50th sts./Rockefeller Center. AMERICAN.

This is a landmark of New York business/celebrity power—and it has recently zoomed its way back onto the list of New York's most interesting dining rooms. After years of being more Ed McMahon than David Letterman, it has an updated electricity. And that's due to new owners Orient Express, who have made subtle changes in the decor and the menu, while keeping traditional favorites like the chicken hash and the famed (and terribly expensive) burger. If you long for the atmosphere of Prohibition, the downstairs bar/dining room fills the bill.

EXPENSIVE

Aquavit. 13 W. 54th St. (Fifth & Sixth aves.). ☎ **212/307-7311.** Reservations recommended. Dining room, prix-fixe dinner $62; pretheater prix fixe $39. Cafe, main courses $13–$18; pretheater prix fixe $25. AE, DC, MC, V. Mon–Fri noon–3pm and 5:30–10:30pm, Sat 5:30–10:30pm; brunch Sun noon–3pm, except summer. Subway: E, F to Fifth Ave./53rd St. SCANDINAVIAN.

When Aquavit opened its doors, it opened the eyes of New Yorkers to what fine Scandinavian food could be: Its delicate elegance is reminiscent of Japanese refinement. The space is dramatic—a soaring glass atrium, birch trees, an indoor waterfall—yet it's serene and sleek. To help you get serene and sleek, the bar offers a broad selection of aquavits, distilled liquors not unlike vodka flavored with fruit and spices and served Arctic cold. The upstairs cafe is one of New York's better bargains. It isn't cheap, but for the price you'd be hard pressed to beat the quality. In the more formal dining room, gravlax with dill flat bread, pickled fennel, and mustard sauce is a traditional opener. Main-course options include baked salmon, grilled lobster or red snapper, and loin of Arctic venison. Fortified with aquavit, you might opt for the ossetra caviar with buckwheat blini and crème fraîche ($45 extra). The $35 brunch is a Swedish smorgasbord.

☺ La Côte Basque. 60 W. 55th St. (Fifth & Sixth aves.). ☎ **212/688-6525.** Reservations required well in advance. Jacket/tie required. Prix-fixe lunch $34; prix-fixe dinner $62. AE, DC, MC, V. Mon–Sat noon–2:30pm; Mon–Thurs 5:30–10:30pm, Fri–Sat 5:30–11:30pm, Sun 5:30–10pm. Closed Sun in summer. Subway: E, F to Fifth Ave./53rd St. CLASSIC FRENCH.

La Côte Basque surrendered its original location on the east side of Fifth Avenue to New York's first Disney Store. Traditionalists were aghast because for many years serious diners went to the original to bask in its sublime food, crisp service, wonderful

Midtown Dining

NA-0149

Lespinasse 39
L'Express 67
Luna Park 77
Lutèce 50
Madison Bistro 62
March 32
Mars 11
Mesa Grill 78
Meskerem 16
Monkey Bar 40
Motown Cafe 29
Official All Star Cafe 17
Osteria del Circo 8
Oyster Bar 59
Patria 68
Petrossian 2
Planet Hollywood 28
Pongsri Thai Restaurant 15
Prime Burger 49
Rainbow Room 53
Republic 76
Rosa Mexicano 31
San Domenico 1
Solera 42
Soup Kitchen International 6
Sparks Steak House 58
Stage Deli 9
Steak Frites 74
Sushisay 47
Tapika 5
Tennessee Mountain 57
Tse Yang 46
"21" Club 43
Union Square Cafe 75
Verbena 73
The Viceroy 24
Vong 41
Won Jo 63
Wu Liang Ye 55
Zarela 51

Subway stop Ⓜ

137

Dining Zone: Ninth Avenue

Ninth Avenue from 46th to 56th streets has become a well-priced gourmet paradise with dozens of restaurants perfect for pre- and posttheater dining.

Chez Suzette, no. 675-B, between 46th and 47th streets (☎ 212/581-9717) offers fine French food and several prix-fixe dinners priced under $25. Even uninitiated palates will appreciate the Asian-nouvelle vegetarian cuisine at stylish **Zen Palate**, no. 663, at 46th Street (☎ 212/582-1669). **Chanpen,** no. 761, at 51st Street (☎ 212/586-6808), serves bold Thai food at Chinatown prices. **Island Burgers & Shakes,** no. 766, between 51st and 52nd streets (☎ 212/307-7934), is a small burger joint with a Caribbean flair that specializes in *churrascos* (flattened, grilled chicken breasts). Puerto Rican and Argentinian cuisine doesn't get much better or cheaper than at **Old San Juan,** no. 765, at 52nd Street (☎ 212/262-7013). **Vynl Diner,** no. 824, at 54th Street (☎ 212/974-2003), serves Asian-inspired fare in a funky setting. And **Bello,** no. 863, at 56th Street (☎ 212/246-6773), has food so good that men raised on their Italian mother's pasta recommend it.

---

murals depicting scenes from the Basque area of France—and, most important, to be seen. It was the site of the famed "red plush" room where Truman Capote set a chapter in his scandalous unfinished novel *Answered Prayers* (the book in which his tongue-wagging about upper-crust pals got him ejected from New York society).

Now on the west side of Fifth, with the wonderful murals intact, La Côte Basque serves food as glorious as ever. Owner Jean-Jacques Rachou mixes equal parts talent and charm. Whenever he offers the special cold seafood appetizer, order it. In such a superb restaurant, it's difficult to select the best main dishes, but I often order the rack of lamb with Provençal vegetables, the pan-seared salmon steak with sorrel sauce, or the filet of beef with foie gras and wine sauce. Do order the frozen raspberry soufflé before the meal begins (it has always been one of New York's best desserts). Drop any fears about attitude—every time I've eaten here *all* diners were treated with respect.

✪ **Estiatorio Milos.** 125 W. 55th St. (Sixth & Seventh aves.). ☎ **212/245-7400.** Reservations recommended. Main courses $18–$32; prix-fixe lunch $29.50. AE, DC, MC, V. Mon–Fri noon–3pm; Mon–Sat 5:30pm–midnight. Subway: N, R to 57th St. GREEK.

The sea stars center stage, and you'll select from the day's catch, sold by the pound and seductively displayed on ice. Appetizers like grilled fresh sardines and charred octopus with onions, capers, and peppers transport you to white-washed villages overlooking the Mediterranean. Grilled whole fish, whether Arctic char, red snapper, loup de mer, or Dover sole, is the best main-course choice: It's brushed with olive oil and herbs, perfectly and simply grilled, and then deboned tableside by the wait staff. For dessert, try the tangy homemade yogurt drizzled with honey.

MODERATE

Bryant Park Grill. 25 W. 40th St. (in Bryant Park, Fifth & Sixth aves.). ☎ **212/840-6500.** Reservations recommended. Main courses $13.95–$19.95; pretheater prix fixe $20. AE, DC, DISC, MC, V. Mon–Sat 11:30am–11:30pm, Sun 11:30am–10:30pm. Subway: B, D, F, Q to 42nd St. CONTEMPORARY AMERICAN.

This parkside place hit the restaurant scene like a tsunami a few years back when it opened as the crowning jewel in the redesign of Bryant Park (adjacent to the rear of the main public library on 42nd Street). In a solarium-like space amid majestic trees, the restaurant fills a gap in Midtown—a lovely place that's both sophisticated and casual. With about 1,000 seats, the Grill has tables inside, where the decor is domi-nated by a colorful aviary wall mural, as well as on a large terrace. Appetizers include confit of duck burritos with goat cheese, salsa, guacamole, and crème fraîche; mush-room stew with toast points, peas, sea asparagus, and tomatoes; and cold Maine crab-meat salad. Main courses range from morel mushroom pasta to pork loin.

Two other restaurants are in the park: the **Terrace** and the **Cafe.** The Terrace, on the Grill's roof, serves a cold seafood menu (main courses $12–$15). The less expen-sive Cafe (main courses $5.95–$12.95) has small tables beneath a canopy of trees for outdoor meals like salads, sandwiches, roast chicken, and vegetable couscous.

✪ **Carmine's.** 200 W. 44th St. (Broadway & Eighth Ave.). ☎ **212/221-3800.** Reservations recommended before 6pm, after 6pm accepted only for six or more. Main courses $14.50–$46. AE, DC, MC, V. Tues–Sat 11:30am–midnight, Sun–Mon 11:30am–11pm. Subway: N, R, S, 1, 2, 3, 7, 9 to 42nd St./Times Sq. SOUTHERN ITALIAN.

Everything is done B-I-G at Carmine's. The dining room is extensive enough to deserve a map, massive platters of pasta hold Brady Bunch–size portions, and large groups wait (and wait) to join in the rambunctious atmosphere at this Midtown sib-ling of the original Upper West Side restaurant. Caesar salad and a mound of fried calamari are a perfect beginning, followed by heaping portions of pasta topped with red or white clam sauce, mixed seafood, zesty marinara, and meatballs. The meat entrees include veal parmigiana, broiled porterhouse steak, chicken marsala, and shrimp scampi. The tiramisù is pie-size, thick and creamy, bathed in 'Kahlúa and marsala. Order half of what you think you'll need. The original Carmine's at 2450 Broadway (☎ **212/362-2200**) is the same—but even B-I-G-ger.

✪ **Chez Josephine.** 414 W. 42nd St. (Ninth & Tenth aves.). ☎ **212/594-1925.** Reserva-tions recommended. Main courses $17.50–$26.50. AE, DC, JCB, MC, V. Mon–Sat 5pm–1am. Subway: A, C, E to 42nd St. FRENCH BISTRO.

Jean-Claude Baker, one of the sons of the legendary Josephine, who scandalized Amer-icans and seduced the French in the 1920s, is a true New York character. He has made the city his own, and New York would be a touch more *pauvre* without him. He's a warm host who indulges guests with just the right mix of discreet savoir faire and down-to-earth friendliness. The atmosphere somehow combines a pleasing tinge of deca-dence with respectability, making this perfect for pre- or posttheater dinner or cock-tails. A jazz piano keeps things festive, and the wall posters evoke a bygone Paris. For starters, try the terrine of duck, fried oysters, or lobster bisque. A main-course favorite is cassoulet of lobster, shrimp, scallops, seafood sausage, and black beans in a light

---

Dining Zone: Restaurant Row

Just a little to the west of most of the theaters in Times Square, on 46th Street between Eighth and Ninth avenues, is a lively block of 24 restaurants, great for pre- and posttheater dining. A few best bets are **Becco,** 355 W. 46th St. (☎ **212/397-7597**), for popular two-star Italian and a good-value prix fixe; ✪ **Joe Allen,** 326 W. 46th St. (☎ **212/581-6464**), for great burgers in a pub atmosphere, with chances for celebrity-spotting; **Le Rivage,** 340 W. 46th St. (☎ **212/765-7374**), a rare old-fashioned French restaurant where the service is sweet and the portions are large; ✪ **Lotfi's Moroccan,** 358 W. 46th St. (☎ **212/582-5850**), with fabulous cous-cous and remarkable prices; and ✪ **Orso,** 322 W. 46th St. (☎ **212/489-7212**), for wonderful contemporary Italian served in a sophisticated rustic setting—after the shows, many stars nip in here.

Where the Themes Are the Message

The trend began when the Hard Rock Cafe opened in the early 1980s. Planet Hollywood soon followed, and West 57th Street became the site of most theme restaurants. In the 1990s, an avalanche of copycats opened in and around Times Square. By the time you read this, David Copperfield's **Copperfield Magic Underground** should magically appear at Broadway and 49th Street, **ESPN** sport a new cafe in the Condé Nast Building at 42nd Street, the **Rainforest Cafe** put down roots in the neighborhood, and **Mars** land at Broadway between 50th and 51st streets. And this year Planet Hollywood should move to its new hotel in Times Square at 47th Street.

Brooklyn Diner USA. 212 W. 57th St., Broadway and Seventh Avenue (☎ **212/581-8900**). It looks like an old-fashioned diner on the outside, but inside there are linen tablecloths and fresh flowers instead of coffee-stained Formica tabletops. The food includes better-than-you'd-expect lump crabcakes, tenderloin steak, and Valrhona chocolate fudge sundae. To justify the name, there's a 15-bite Brooklyn hot dog and an Avenue U roast beef sandwich.

Comedy Nation. 1626 Broadway, at 50th Street (☎ **212/265-5555**). Caroline Hirsch, the grande dame of comedy clubs, has jumped onto the bandwagon. Adjacent to her comedy club, Comedy Nation serves up standards like steak, chicken, and meat loaf in an atmosphere where "talking lobsters" beg not to be eaten, oversize murals celebrate America's great comedy teams, and the Late Bar mimics the set of David Letterman's *Late Show.*

Fashion Cafe. 51 Rockefeller Plaza, at 51st Street (☎ **212/765-3131**). Claudia Schiffer, Elle Macpherson, and Naomi Campbell joined up with entrepreneur Tommaso Buti to take a page right out of the actors-as-restaurateurs script, and here, too, it's mostly marketing.

Hard Rock Cafe. 221 W. 57th St., between Broadway and Seventh Avenue (☎ **212/459-9320**). You'll find a surprisingly good burger and the guitar of your favorite rock star. You won't find rock's royalty, however.

Harley-Davidson Cafe. 1370 Sixth Ave., at 56th Street (☎ **212/245-6000**). Relieve your munchies with not-as-bad-as-you-might-fear food while you take the world in a love embrace, roaring back to the high hairy days of towering handlebars. Memorabilia documents 90 years of Hog history.

---

shellfish broth. On the way out you can buy Jean-Claude's well-received biography of his mother, *Josephine: The Hungry Heart,* which you can ask him to sign.

Churrascaria Plataforma. 316 W. 49th St. (Eighth & Ninth aves.). ☎ **212/245-0505.** Reservations recommended. Prix-fixe lunch $25; prix-fixe dinner $29. AE, DC, MC, V. Daily noon–midnight. Subway: C, E to 50th St. BRAZILIAN.

It's a carnival for carnivores at this upscale all-you-can-eat Brazilian rotisserie. Salad bar teasers like octopus stew, paella, and carpaccio tempt diners to fill up too quickly, but hold out for the never-ending parade of meat. Roving servers deliver beef (too many cuts to mention), ham, chicken (try the hearts, they snap when you bite 'em), lamb, sausage—more than 15 delectable varieties—right to your table until you cannot eat another bite.

Jekyll & Hyde Club. 1409 Sixth Ave., between 57th and 58th streets (☎ 212/541-9505). Something new to scare you with, my dear? You enter through a small dark room with a sinking ceiling, and a corpse warns you of the oddities to come. There are five floors—grand salon, library, laboratory, mausoleum, observatory—of bizarre artifacts, wall hangings that come to life, and other interactive bone chillers. Kids love it.

La Nouvelle Justine. 206 W. 23rd St., between Seventh and Eighth avenues (☎ 212/727-8623). Not all theme restaurants are suitable for families. Have you been a bad boy? Here dominatrix waitresses serve French-American fare you can choose to eat doggie-style (from a dog bowl) in a high chair or a cage. House specialties (about $20) include spankings from the waitstaff.

Motown Cafe. 104 W. 57th St., between Sixth and Seventh avenues (☎ 212/581-8030). During lunch and dinner, a proto-Motown group slides and harmonizes its choreographed way through the best thing to come out of Detroit. The food isn't bad, but it's beside the point.

Official All Star Cafe. 1540 Broadway, at 45th Street (☎ 212/840-8326). Superstar athletes Andre Agassi, Wayne Gretzky, Ken Griffey Jr., Joe Montana, Shaquille O'Neal, Monica Seles, and Tiger Woods team up with restaurateur Robert Earl (of Hard Rock Cafe and Planet Hollywood) to bring you this tribute to sports. At center court is a full-size scoreboard, on the sidelines are booths shaped like baseball mitts, and video monitors guarantee that the great plays in sports history live forever. The food is straight from the ballpark—hot dogs and hamburgers, St. Louis ribs, and the like.

Planet Hollywood. 140 W. 57th St., between Sixth and Seventh avenues (☎ 212/333-7827). Arnold Schwarzenegger, Bruce Willis, Sylvester Stallone, and John Hughes joined to garner their share of theme restaurant profits. Planet Hollywood has *Star Wars*'s R2D2 and C3PO robots, Judy Garland's outfit from *The Wizard of Oz,* and James Dean's cycle from *Rebel Without a Cause,* to name a few items. The menu hasn't reached for the stars, but it offers a decent mix of American fare. Watch for a 1999 move to Times Square.

Ciao Europa. 63 W. 54th St. (in the Warwick hotel, at Sixth Ave.). ☎ **212/247-1200.** Reservations recommended. Jacket/tie recommended. Main courses $13.50–$22.75; pretheater prix fixe $24.95. AE, DC, DISC, JCB, MC, V. Daily 6:30am–11:30pm. Subway: E, F to Fifth Ave./53rd St. NORTHERN ITALIAN.

Rare in Midtown is a white-tablecloth Italian restaurant with very good food at decent prices. This is a great place to linger, with comfortable chairs, well-spaced large tables, and two walls of lovely (if inappropriate for an Italian restaurant) American history murals from the 1930s. The antipasto fantasia is a rich mix of roasted sweet peppers, asparagus, sun-dried tomatoes, portobellos, and mozzarella. To keep your check within reason, try the pastas—like linguine alle vongole (sweet small clams), rich in virgin olive oil, and half-moons filled with broccoli rape and shrimp, then spiced with garlic and rosemary.

Osteria del Circo. 120 W. 55th St. (Sixth & Seventh aves.). ☎ **212/265-3636.** Reservations required. Jacket requested. Main courses $18–$28; tasting menus $60 and $75. AE, DC, MC, V. Mon–Thurs 11:30am–2:30pm and 5:30–11pm, Fri–Sat 5:30–11:30pm, Sun 5:30–10:30pm. Subway: N, R to 57th St. ITALIAN.

In a bright airy space, this winningly upbeat place is run by the three attractive sons and wife of the legendary Sirio Maccioni, of Le Cirque 2000 fame. As befits such a family, the first review in the *New York Times* awarded Circo a well-deserved two stars. You might begin with the cacciucco soup overflowing with lobster, prawns, calamari, monkfish, clams, and mussels or the ravioli stuffed with spinach, bitter greens, and sheep's milk ricotta. The main courses include rotisserie-roasted duck breast with apricot purée, grilled fennel, and sour cherries; seared red snapper with braised artichokes, capers, and sweet onions in Vernaccia wine sauce; and a tripe stew with Parmesan gratin that recalls a family meal in northern Italy. One of the best ways to mine the nuggets of gold is to order anything named with Egidiana or Egi (Mamma Maccioni's surname).

✪ **Tapika.** 950 Eighth Ave. (at 56th St.). ☎ **212/397-3737.** Reservations recommended. Main courses $17–$26; prix-fixe lunch $19.99; pretheater menu (5:30–6:45pm) $26. AE, CB, DC, MC, V. Mon–Fri noon–2:30pm and 5–10:30pm, Sat 5–11pm, Sun 5–10pm. Subway: A, B, C, D, 1, 9 to Columbus Circle/59th St. SOUTHWESTERN.

Chef David Walzog delights diners with a sassy Southwestern menu. For starters, fresh corn tamales shine with a mouthwatering filling of barbecued baby back ribs, the meat stripped off the bone. The chipolte marinated squid is set off nicely by a brisk grilled pineapple, arugula, and tomatillo salsa. Main courses like grilled rabbit loin with habañero sauce and chile-rubbed New York strip steak rank this restaurant among New York's best. Just 8 blocks from Lincoln Center, Tapika offers a three-course pretheater menu, and if you choose, you can eat two courses before the curtain, then return for coffee and dessert after the show for no extra charge.

Wu Liang Ye. 36 W. 48th St. (Fifth & Sixth aves.). ☎ **212/398-2308.** Reservations recommended. Main courses $6.95–$26.95; prix-fixe lunch $8.50. AE, MC, V. Daily 11:30am–10pm. Subway: B, D, F, Q to 47th–50th sts./Rockefeller Center. SZECHUAN CHINESE.

The high molded ceilings, crystal chandeliers, and white tablecloths suggest French bistro more than good-value Chinese. But this relaxed restaurant serves up authentic Szechuan in Midtown at affordable prices. The hurried suit-and-tie set descend from Rockefeller Center's towers for the good-deal prix-fixe lunch, which might start with a hot-and-sour soup thick with mushrooms, bamboo shoots, and egg drop followed by a large portion of sautéed chicken with roasted chile-peanut sauce and rice. Standout specialties from the 100-plus–item menu are the thinly sliced beef tendon with roasted chile vinaigrette and the braised whole fish with Szechuan chile miso sauce. Both come spicy enough that the fortune cookie should promise, "You will quickly find relief for all that ails you."

INEXPENSIVE

✪ **Hamburger Harry's.** 145 W. 45th St. (Sixth & Seventh aves.). ☎ **212/840-0566.** Reservations recommended for large groups. Burgers $6.95–$8.95. AE, DC, DISC, JCB, MC, V. Mon–Thurs 11:30am–11pm, Fri–Sat 11:30am–11:30pm. Subway: N, R, S, 1, 2, 3, 7, 9 to 42nd St./Times Sq. AMERICAN/BURGERS.

Hamburger Harry's is the perfect stop for everyday refueling at the right price. The casual restaurant has distinguished itself by turning out delicious 7-ounce mesquite-grilled burgers that "may well be the best hamburger in New York City," according to the *New York Times.* Burger platters are a belly-busting bargain that start at $6.95

and are served with curlicue fries, homemade potato salad, or Harry's coleslaw. The bur-gers come in a variety of flavors, from plain and simple to the Ha Ha Burger—topped with Texas chili, cheddar cheese, onion, guacamole, and pico de gallo. There are also chicken breast sandwiches, vegetable burgers, burritos, Cajun catfish, and New York sirloin.

La Bonne Soupe. 48 W. 55th St. (Fifth & Sixth aves.). ☎ **212/586-7650.** Reservations recommended. Main courses $8–$18; prix-fixe lunch and dinner $18.95. AE, MC, V. Mon–Fri 11:30am–midnight, Sun 11:30am–11pm. Subway: E, F to Fifth Ave./53rd St. FRENCH BISTRO/SOUP.

For gourmet at good prices, it's hard to best this French *endroit* in Midtown, where you'll even see natives of the land of cuisine seated elbow-to-elbow at red-checked tablecloths. "*Les bonnes soupes*," are satisfying noontime meals of salad, bread, a big bowl of soup (mushroom and barley with lamb is a favorite), dessert (chocolate mousse, crème caramel, or ice cream), and wine or coffee for $12.95. Rounding out the menu are omelets, hamburgers, steaks, and very French fondues.

Meskerem. 468 W. 47th St. (Ninth & Tenth aves.). ☎ **212/664-0520.** Reservations recommended. Main courses $7–$11. DISC, MC, V. Daily 11:30am–midnight. Subway: C, E to 50th St. AFRICAN/ETHIOPIAN.

Ignore the surroundings, get over the lack of silverware, and you'll enjoy a great dining experience. Ethiopian stews of beef, lamb, chicken, and vegetables are served on communal platters and sopped up with spongy *injera* bread, made from fermented *tef,* an Ethiopian grain. Tastes range from the mild *doro alecha,* chicken seasoned with onions, garlic, and ginger in a butter sauce, to the spicy ribs dishes, simmered in a spicy berber sauce. The house specialty, *kitfo,* is Ethiopian-style steak tartare—the squeamish can ask for the beef rare instead of raw. For a little bit of everything, order a combination plate. Two combos will easily feed three.

✪ **Pongsri Thai Restaurant.** 244 W. 48th St. (Broadway & Eighth Ave.). ☎ **212/582-3392.** Main courses $6.95–$14.95. AE, CB, DC, DISC, MC, V. Daily 11:30am–11:30pm. Subway: N, R to 49th St.; E, 1, 9 to 50th St. THAI.

The warm welcome from the hostess is the first indication of good things to come. Lovingly cooked dishes, courteous service, and small touches like rice kept warm in a large silver tureen make up for the less-than-stylish decor. Start with savory *tom yum goong* (loads of shrimp and straw mushrooms in a broth seasoned with lemongrass, lime juice, coriander, and exotic herbs, served in an earthen pot). For a main course, the whole red snapper, a house specialty, is perfectly prepared, fried to a crisp outside, tender inside. It's served with a choice of five sauces—a favorite is *pla lad prik,* spiced with chiles and overflowing with fresh peppers. Other dependables are pad Thai (stir-fried rice noodles with shrimp, egg, chopped peanut, dried bean cake, and bean sprouts) and any of the curries. A Downtown branch is at 311 Second Ave., at 18th Street (☎ **212/477-4100**).

Soup Kitchen International. 259A W. 55th St. (at Eighth Ave.). ☎ **212/757-7730.** Soup $6–$16. Mon–Fri 11am–7pm. Closed summer. Subway: C, E to 50th St. SOUP.

This is it—the soup man from *Seinfeld.* And when it comes to Al Yeganeh's undeniably delicious offerings, New Yorkers take on the traits of U.S. Postal Service workers. Neither rain nor sleet nor snow stops them from lining up around the block to sample the famous potages. The 12 or so offered change daily, but don't call because he'll hang up on you. "Whatever soup you want, I have!" he snaps. He insists that no sale takes more than 7 seconds—know what you want, talk fast, or he won't serve you. Welcome to New York, bub.

Tennessee Mountain. 121 W. 45th St. (Sixth Ave. & Broadway). ☎ **212/869-4545.** Main courses $8.95–$17.95; all-you-can-eat Sun–Mon $18.95. AE, DC, MC, V. Mon–Thurs 11am–11pm, Fri–Sat 11am– midnight, Sun 11am–10pm. Subway: N, R, S, 1, 2, 3, 7, 9 to 42nd St./Times Sq. SOUTHERN BARBECUE.

New York is hardly the destination for pulled pork sandwiches, barbecued chicken, and smoked ribs, but if you're hankering for an authentic taste of the South, Tennessee Mountain satisfies with enormous rib sampler platters so lip-smacking good they put other nearby BBQ places to shame. Entrees come with your choice of two sides (collard greens, corn muffins, biscuits, fries, and the like). Nontraditionalists can nibble on vegetarian chili and crab cakes. The original Tennessee Mountain is in SoHo at 143 Spring St. (☎ **212/431-3993**).

✪ **Won Jo.** 23 W. 32nd St. (Fifth & Sixth aves.). ☎ **212/695-5815.** Reservations recommended. Main courses $9.95–$19.95. AE, MC, V. Daily 24 hours. Subway: B, D, F, N, Q, R to 34th St. KOREAN.

Though this is a popular place among cognoscenti, you won't find it in the phone book and information has no listing. I don't know why that's true, but this is a favorite for its barbecue, which you cook yourself (each table has a small grill). The barbecues are a full meal, with vegetables, kimchee, and noodles. You can choose tender sirloin, pork, chicken, or mushroom. Large wooden tables accommodate groups, and because you do the cooking yourself it's fun to come en masse. If barbecue isn't for you, *bi bim neang myun* is a filling bowl of buckwheat noodles, sliced beef, and vegetables with a three-alarm spicy sauce you mix in. *Hwe dup bap* is an assortment of raw fish over mixed vegetables and rice. The broiled fish (salmon, yellow fish, mackerel, and king fish) is delicate. Downstairs is a Japanese sushi bar, but head for the Korean upstairs. (Don't worry that they answer the phone in Korean; they do speak English.)

13　Midtown East & Murray Hill

See the "Midtown Dining" map (pp. 136–137) for restaurants in this section.

VERY EXPENSIVE

✪ **The Four Seasons.** 99 E. 52nd St. (Park & Lexington aves.). ☎ **212/754-9494.** Reservations recommended. Jacket required/tie optional. Main courses $26.50–$45; pretheater prix fixe (5–6:15pm) $43.50. AE, CB, DC, DISC, JCB, MC, V. Mon–Fri noon–2pm and 5–9:30pm, Sat 5–10:30pm. Subway: 6 to 51st St.; E, F to Lexington/Third aves. and 53rd St. CONTINENTAL.

On the ground floor of the Seagram Building, this restaurant's stunning classic modern decor interior, created by Philip Johnson, has been awarded landmark status by the city of New York. The **Grill Room** is the power place for authors, agents, and CEOs to lunch in a spectacular rosewood-clad space. The more formal **Pool Room,** where tables are widely spaced for maximum privacy, is designed around a marble reflecting pool. The Four Seasons changes its menu during the year, and there are various menus throughout the week (there's the popular light Spa Cuisine menu, pretheater prix-fixe specials, and a lunchtime bar menu with entrees like seared salmon at around $18). One of the most appreciated main dishes is steak tartare, prepared tableside. Others are roast duck au poivre and rack of lamb. The extensive wine list has long been famous.

✪ **Le Cirque 2000.** 455 Madison Ave. (in the New York Palace hotel, at 50th St.). ☎ **212/303-7788.** Reservations essential far in advance. Jacket/tie required. Main courses $26–$33; prix-fixe lunch $40; tasting menu $90. AE, CB, DC, MC, V. Mon–Sat 11:45am–2:45pm and

5:45–11pm, Sun 11:30am–2:30pm and 5:30–10:30pm. Subway: 4, 5, 6 to 51st; 1, 2, 9 to Fifth Ave./53rd St. FRENCH.

Counting the years he spent at Le Cirque's original location and his 2 years in this stunning new space, restaurateur and Manhattan icon Sirio Maccioni has been serving the dining elite for 26 years. Le Cirque 2000 envelops the traditional decor of its gilded-age mansion with new-age circus colors. And it works. It's a surreal yet still elegant big-top tent.

The food is as good as ever. Designed by Sirio and executive chef Sottha Khunn, the menu is classic Le Cirque, from the lobster salad appetizer and the paupiette of black sea bass in crispy potatoes with braised leeks and Barolo sauce to the salmon broiled with lemongrass crust, fennel meunière, and tomato *concassée*. The legendary crème brûlée Le Cirque is joined by a cake served inside a whimsical stove made of chocolate—pastry chef Jacques Torres's signature dessert is a showstopping sculpture. In season, the courtyard allows you can dine under as well as with the stars.

Le Périgord. 405 E. 52nd St. (at First Ave.). ☎ **212/755-6244.** Reservations required. Jacket/tie required. Prix-fixe lunch $32; prix-fixe dinner $52. AE, DC, MC, V. Mon–Fri noon–3pm; daily 5:30–10:30pm. Subway: 6 to 51st St.; E, F to Lexington/Third aves. and 53rd St. SOUTHWEST FRENCH.

For more than 30 years, Le Périgord has been a perennial favorite among New York bon vivants. Owner Georges Briguet greets diners at the door, and the low ceiling, warm colors, flowers, and cozy banquettes make for a romantic atmosphere. Last things first: I suggest at the beginning of the meal you order an Armagnac or a Grand Marnier soufflé for a perfect finish. Chef Pascal Coudouille is a native of France's Périgord region, and his specialty is a delectable confit de canard that melts off the bone. The wine list includes mostly grands châteaux, but there are bargains from lesser regions.

Lespinasse. 2 E. 55th St. (in the St. Regis hotel, at Fifth Ave.). ☎ **212/339-6719.** Reservations required. Jacket/tie required. Main courses $35–$43; prix-fixe lunch $44, prix-fixe dinner $120; prix-fixe vegetarian dinner $78. AE, CB, DC, DISC, JCB, MC, V. Mon–Sat noon–2pm and 5:30–10pm. Subway: E, F to Fifth Ave./53rd St. FRENCH WITH ASIAN ACCENTS.

Chef Christian Delouvrier succeeded Grey Kunz when he resigned in July 1998. The verdict wasn't yet out on the new menu, but given Delouvrier's French cuisine at Les Célébrités earned a three-star review in the *New York Times*, I expect nothing less than success.

Lutèce. 249 E. 50th St. (Second & Third aves.). ☎ **212/752-2225.** Reservations required. Jacket recommended/tie optional. Prix-fixe lunch $38; prix-fixe dinner $65. AE, DC, DISC, MC, V. Tues–Fri noon–2pm; Mon–Thurs 6–10pm, Fri–Sat 6–10:30pm. Subway: 6 to 51st St.; E, F to Lexington/Third aves. and 53rd St. MODERN FRENCH.

In just a short while new chef Eberhard Müller not only put his personal stamp on Lutèce but even put it in the running against Le Bernardin for best fish restaurant. In late 1994, after 34 years, founder/chef André Soltner and his wife, Simone, who had greeted guests, sold the restaurant amid great trepidation from New York foodies, who always considered Lutèce one of the greatest restaurants. The good news came fast from Müller: Warm oysters in champagne sauce are crowned with caviar; grilled squab is light, full of flavor, and accompanied by a ragout of morels and asparagus tips; guinea hen is baked in cabbage leaves. No one need ever have worried.

✪ March. 405 E. 58th St. (First Ave. & Sutton Place). ☎ **212/754-6272.** Reservations required. Jacket/tie requested. Tasting menus $68 and $90, with wines $93 and $125. AE, DC, JCB, MC, V. Daily 6–10:30pm. Subway: 4, 5, 6 to 59th St.; N, R to Lexington Ave. CONTEMPORARY AMERICAN.

Co-owner/host Joseph Scalice and partner/chef Wayne Nish do things right. Here's romantic Manhattan luxury as it was meant to be: a finely restored town house and a crowd of well-heeled Upper East Siders who fit the set as if they were from central casting. The usual small appetizers and large entrees have been replaced with a new menu approach: four- or seven-course prix-fixe meals that partner smaller portions of all dishes so diners can now tailor their own menu from the vegetarian, seafood, poultry, and meat selections. You can either choose your own series of dishes or leave yourself in the hands of Nish and he'll create a special chef's menu.

Steamed cod gets an earthy touch with sweet Chinese sausage. North Atlantic salmon marries five Chinese spices and is served with chicken stock highlighted by sherry vinegar. There's also a remarkable jumbo shrimp tempura with pomegranate and spicy carrot sauces. A great dessert: the grapefruit sorbet with gin syrup and coriander seed.

✪ **Sushisay.** 38 E. 51st St. (Madison & Park aves.). ☎ **212/755-1780.** Reservations required. Jacket/tie requested. Main courses $23–$45; prix-fixe dinner $50 and up. AE, DC, EURO, MC, V. Mon–Fri noon–2:15pm and 5:30–10:15pm, Sat 5–9:15pm. Subway: 6 to 51st St.; E, F to Lexington/Third aves. and 53rd St. JAPANESE.

Though New York has no dearth of fine Japanese restaurants, this import from Tokyo has incomparable sushi. Squeeze in at the very popular bar and order sushi or sashimi there (you can mostly skip the other choices; not that they're bad, they're just not at the same level). The decor is spare, the service is friendly, and the prices are steep, but you'll never say "simple raw fish" again.

EXPENSIVE

An American Place. 2 Park Ave. (at 32nd St.). ☎ **212/684-2122.** Reservations recommended. Main courses $25–$32. AE, DC, MC, V. Mon–Fri 11:45am–3pm and 5:30–9:30pm, Sat 5:30–9:30pm. Subway: 6 to 33rd St. CONTEMPORARY AMERICAN.

Long before every new U.S. restaurant billed itself as "new American with fresh local ingredients," chef/proprietor Larry Forgione forged the way with his now-classic handsome restaurant. Appetizers often include a crisp potato pancake with Wisconsin gorgonzola, grilled sweet onions, field greens, and herbs, as well as two salads—one of romaine hearts, frisée, and endive tossed with Caesar dressing and given texture by chunks of bacon and dry Jack cheese, another of warm roasted Vidalia onions with New York State prosciutto in citrus-honey vinaigrette. Forgione has always done fabulous things with American game, so try venison or rabbit or the like when they're available.

✪ **Asia de Cuba.** 237 Madison Ave. (at 37th St.). ☎ **212/726-7755.** Reservations recommended. Main courses $16–$42. AE, MC, V. Mon–Fri noon–3pm; Mon–Wed 5–11:30pm, Thurs–Sat 5pm–midnight, Sun 5–10:30pm. Subway: 4, 5, 6, 7, S to 42nd St./Grand Central. ASIAN FUSION.

The center of attention (and fun) in this Philippe Starck–designed space, one of 1997's most talked-about openings, is the long communal table where up to 35 strangers sit elbow to elbow. Ask to be seated there, not at the "real" tables scattered around. The Chino-Latino menu is innovative, too. Foie gras is seasoned with Chinese five-spice powder and served with French toast, cashews, and fruit salsa. Tamarind and rum is slathered on pork and served with mashed plantains. The servings are big enough for sharing, and don't expect traditional courses—plates are delivered to the table when ready. The balcony bar boasts an impressive selection of high-end rums and an impressive clientele.

Monkey Bar. 60 E. 54th St. (in the Hotel Elysée, Madison & Park aves.). ☎ **212/838-2600.** Reservations required. Jacket required/tie optional. Main courses $20–$34. AE, DC, MC, V.

Affordable Gourmet to Go

When it comes to getting a quick and inexpensive meal, a host of gourmet sandwich shops that disdain the humdrum will have you singing hosannah. Some are open for lunch only, and most offer innovative sandwiches from $5 to $9.

Mangia's three Midtown locations—16 E. 48th St. (☎ **212/754-0637**), in Macy's at 34th Street and Broadway (☎ **212/494-5654**), and 50 W. 57th St. (☎ **212/582-3061**)—are famous for their salad bars but also offer sandwiches like albacore tuna seasoned with dill and carrots with watercress on whole-wheat sourdough. The line moves fast at **Cosí,** 60 E. 56th St. (☎ **212/588-0888**), 165 E. 52nd St. (☎ **212/758-7800**), 38 E. 45th St. (☎ **212/949-7400**), and 11 W. 42nd St. (☎ **212/398-6660**), where flatbread baked in a brick oven is over-stuffed with such delicacies as smoked salmon, prosciutto, and blue-cheese spread, then drizzled with olive oil, vinaigrette, and the like. On a long bun, **Pret à Porter,** 245 W. 38th St. (☎ **212/719-0665**), makes the tastiest chicken and turkey sausages in town, laced with ingredients like mango chutney and tandoori paste.

E.A.T., 1064 Madison Ave. (☎ **212/772-0022**), not far from the Metropolitan Museum of Art, is the place for sandwiches made on Eli's famous bread. A few blocks from the Museum of Natural History, you can make your own at **Zabar's,** 2245 Broadway (☎ **212/787-2000**), from the overwhelming selection of meats, cheeses, breads, and prepared foods.

Barocco Kitchen, 42 Union Square East (☎ **212/254-6777**), prepares spruced-up sandwiches like grilled chicken breast with avocado mayonnaise and arugula. In the West and East Village, **Taylor's,** 523 Hudson St. (☎ **212/645-8200**) and 175 Second Ave. (☎ **212/674-9501**), is famous for huge muffins and thick brownies, but the meals between two slices are also first rate. In SoHo, **Once Upon A Tart,** 135 Sullivan St. (☎ **212/387-8869**), puts enticing flavors, like pork loin with rosemary aïoli, between the bread.

OK, so it isn't gourmet, but a burger from Wall Street's famous **McDonald's,** 160 Broadway (☎ **212/385-2063**), takes on a sophisticated air. A doorman in tails opens the door, then a host or hostess finds you a table and brings you a place mat. All the while, a tux-clad pianist, whose baby grand is topped by a candelabra, serenades you.

Mon–Fri noon–2:30pm and 6–11pm, Sat 5:30–11:30pm, Sun 6–10pm. Subway: E, F to Fifth Ave./53rd St. CONTEMPORARY AMERICAN.

Once a hangout for Tallulah Bankhead, Tennessee Williams, and company, Monkey Bar reopened a few years ago and regained its proper place in the front ranks of Midtown glamour rooms. Kurt Gutenbrunner, the most recent chef, worked for several years with David Bouley and has created a tantalizing new menu: chestnut soup with generous slices of black truffle, linguine sauced with creamy blue cheese and basil, and red snapper perked up by a sauce of blood oranges and ginger.

Solera. 216 E. 53rd St. (Second & Third aves.). ☎ **212/644-1166.** Reservations recommended. Main courses $26–$35; prix-fixe lunch $32. AE, CB, DC, DISC, JCB, MC, V. Mon–Fri noon–2:30pm and 6–10:30pm, Sat 6–10pm. Subway: 4, 5, 6 to 59th St.; N, R to Lexington Ave. SPANISH.

Solera is one of a few Manhattan restaurants that serve fine Spanish food in proper surroundings. It's the right place for tapas, those neat bite-size affairs, and options include tortilla española, with potato, eggs, and onions, and empanada gallega, filled with meats. You can make a meal from a series of these (about $3–$10). Among the best starters is wonderfully tender octopus seasoned with olive oil and paprika. Recommended main courses: grilled lamb chops with cheese-laced polenta and pan-seared trout on a bed of spinach. For dessert, try crema catalana—the Spanish version of crème brûlée—or a selection of Spanish cheeses.

✪ Sparks Steak House. 210 E. 46th St. (Second & Third aves.). ☎ **212/687-4855.** Reservations required. Jacket requested. Main courses $19.95–$29.95. AE, CB, DC, DISC, MC, V. Mon–Fri noon–3pm and 5–11pm, Sat 5–11:30pm. Subway: 4, 5, 6, 7, S to 42nd St./Grand Central. STEAK HOUSE.

When the primal urge strikes, this is where red bloods sharpen their incisors. Lobster and other shellfish are prime players, but Sparks gives its clientele what it really wants: massive, voluptuous, high-quality steaks. The wine list is one of the city's best. The service is as friendly as in a hardware store, but that just adds to the atmosphere. Expect to leave a wad of cash as thick as a steak. A recent meaty expansion gave diners 14,000 more square feet of space.

✪ Tse Yang. 34 E. 51st St. (Madison & Park aves.). ☎ **212/688-5447.** Reservations recommended. Jacket preferred. Main courses $18–$52; prix-fixe dinners $45 and $55. AE, CB, DC, JCB, MC, V. Daily noon–3pm and 6–11pm. Subway: 6 to 51st St.; E, F to Lexington/Third aves. and 53rd St. CHINESE.

A few steps from St. Patrick's Cathedral, this is a sophisticated refuge, the place to choose if you're looking for haute Chinese on the East Side. The urban rush fades as you enter the dining room with soft spot lighting, fabulous walls of pounded copper sculptures, and serene fish tanks. Tse Yang offers a heavenly Peking duck, and the sole is a well-spiced medley of tender but firm fish and mixed vegetables. The shark's-fin soup and delicate frogs' legs are rare specialties. The top-notch sommelier will guide your selection from a wine list that has won *Wine Spectator*'s Award of Excellence for many years in a row. You may be greeted at the door by young owners Annie and Larry Lo, who keep the restaurant's chic quotient high. The bar, presided over by Lou, is a

Dining Zone: Grand Central Terminal

As Grand Central Terminal emerged from its renovations, four high-end restaurants located on the balconies overlooking the Main Concourse were preparing to join the venerable subterranean **Oyster Bar** (p. 150).

Michael Jordan's The Steakhouse NYC (☎ 212/655-2300) was the first to open. The elegant ambiance, excellent steaks, and richly appointed cigar lounge are a welcome relief from the city's uninspired "theme" restaurants with star names attached. Harry Cipriani, owner of Venice's world-famous Harry's Bar, plans on offering Italian dining at **Midtown** (no phone at press time). **Matthew Kenny** (no phone at press time) serves a Mediterranean menu with entrees from $18 to $26. A wine bar/lounge tentatively named the **Campbell Apartment** (no phone at press time) should be in place in the Campbell Apartment, an ornate Florentine palazzo that served as an office until the renovation.

For lower-priced fare, head to the food court on the lower level, where you'll find **Junior's** (fabulous cheesecake), **Two Boots** (excellent pizza), **Republic** (good Asian noodle dishes), and **Mendy's Restaurant** (yes, the one from *Seinfeld*).

While you're here, you can also sample the choices in the adjacent **Met Life Building** (see opposite page).

smart choice for a cocktail or a comfortable place to enjoy a meal for one. Don't miss the special prix-fixe menu during Chinese New Year.

✪ **Vong.** 200 E. 54th St. (at Third Ave.). ☎ **212/486-9592.** Reservations recommended. Jacket/tie requested. Main courses $19–$32; prix-fixe lunch $25, pretheater prix fixe $35. AE, DC, MC, V. Mon–Fri noon–2:30pm, Mon–Thurs 6–11pm, Fri–Sat 5:30–11:30pm, Sun 5:30–10pm. Subway: 6 to 51st St.; E, F to Lexington/Third aves. and 53rd St. FRENCH/ THAI.

Chef/owner Jean-Georges Vongerichten (also of Jo Jo and Jean Georges) didn't play it safe when he let his vibrant imagination loose on his cooking and decor here. A Southeast Asian feel is created by salmon and burnt-orange tones, teak wall treatments, and a pagoda. The cuisine is an exotic fusion of French technique and Thai spices that woos a polished crowd. The salmon appetizer is marinated in lime juice and green peppercorns and served with scallion pancakes. The foie gras is flavored with ginger and mango. Main courses include black bass basking in lotus-root broth with black trumpet mushrooms and crunchy chestnuts. Don't miss the exotic desserts, like the salad of banana and passion fruit with white-pepper ice cream.

MODERATE

Cinque Terre. 22 E. 38th St. (at Madison Ave.). ☎ **212/213-0910.** Reservations recommended. Main courses $12–$26. AE, DC, MC, V. Daily 7–10am and noon–3pm; Sun–Thurs 5:30–10:30pm, Fri–Sat 5:30–11pm. Subway: 4, 5, 6, 7, S to 42nd St./Grand Central. NORTHERN ITALIAN.

At this small neighborhood eatery, chef Rick White and a full-time pasta maker celebrate the traditional cuisine of Liguria, the region known as the Italian Riviera. The appetizer of potato–and–salt cod galettes with cauliflower and caviar sounds fussy but works magically, as does the squid stew. Red sauce isn't an option on the pasta menu, where you'll find dishes like *pansotti con salsa di noci* (pasta stuffed with ricotta and herbs in walnut sauce) and fettuccine *al pesto*. Main courses are straightforward and may include roasted baby chicken and grilled marinated shrimp. The quirky wine list features reasonably priced bottles from smaller Italian vineyards, all heartily endorsed by the cheerful staff. Top off your meal with a lemon poppy seed tiramisú for a regional spin on the classic dessert.

✪ **Dawat.** 210 E. 58th St. (Third & Second aves.). ☎ **212/355-7555.** Reservations recommended. Main courses $12.95–$16.95; prix-fixe lunch $13.95; prix-fixe dinner $23.95. AE,

---

Dining Zone: The Met Life Building

Well before Grand Central Terminal emerged like a polished pearl from its dingy gray shell, surprisingly good restaurants opened in the Met Life Building, which towers over the north side of the terminal at 45th Street.

Tropica (☎ **212/867-6767**) was first, and its breezy Caribbean atmosphere and dishes with a focus on fresh seafood still draw a crowd. Commuters and New Yorkers alike gather at **Beer Bar** (☎ **212/818-1333**) for after-work "pick-me-up" cocktails and beers (the selection is extensive) and well-priced reassuring American cooking like roast chicken and chicken pot pie. Adjoining Beer Bar and managed by the same team is **Cafe Centro** (☎ **212/818-1222**), a more expensive restaurant serving French specialties with a Moroccan tinge. Rounding out the options, big and bustling **Naples 45** (☎ **212/972-7001**) offers authentic and delicious Neapolitan pizza and other Southern Italian specialties.

CB, DC, MC, V. Mon–Sat 11:30am–3pm; Sun–Thurs 5:30–11pm, Fri–Sat 5:30–11:30pm. Subway: 4, 5, 6 to 59th St.; N, R to Lexington Ave. INDIAN.

This ranks as the city's best Indian restaurant, and actress/cookbook author Madhur Jaffrey advises the kitchen on authenticity. The perfectly seasoned vegetable samosas start off the meal in the right direction, as does the *bhel poori* (rice, bits of wheat, assorted chutneys, coriander, and mango powder). The main-course lamb stew with turnips and onions is a nice break from the ubiquitous lamb vindaloo, and the salmon is brushed with a coriander chutney and rolled in a banana leaf for steaming. The room is pleasant and modern, the welcome warm. You'll pay less here than for food of equal caliber from any European kitchen in New York.

Madison Bistro. 238 Madison Ave. (at 37th St.). ☎ **212/447-1919.** Reservations recommended. Main courses $16–$26; prix-fixe dinner $29. AE, CB, DC, MC, V. Mon–Sat noon–3:30pm and 5–10:30pm, Sun 5–10pm. Subway: 4, 5, 6, 7, S to 42nd St./Grand Central. CONTINENTAL/FRENCH.

New Yorkers are a funny lot. If there isn't a good restaurant within 2 minutes' walking distance, they kvetch that they've been abandoned in a culinary desert. The neighborhood around the Madison Bistro, a block from the Pierpont Morgan Li-brary and not far from the Empire State Building, is one such area, and thankfully this charming place exists. Owner Jean-Claude Coutable, smart, suave, and friendly, guarantees the right touch of good food and elegance. Recommended pastas are pappardelle with braised rabbit, mustard, and mushrooms and cappellini with shrimp, garlic, lemon basil, and olive oil. Entrees run from grilled tuna with eggplant caviar, tomatoes, and Niçoise olives to grilled veal loin chop with wild-mushroom risotto.

✪ Oyster Bar. In Grand Central Terminal, lower level (Vanderbilt & Lexington aves.). ☎ **212/490-6650.** Reservations recommended. Main courses $10–$30. AE, CB, DC, DISC, JCB, MC, V. Mon–Fri 11:30am–9:30pm. Subway: 4, 5, 6, 7, S to 42nd St./Grand Central. SEAFOOD.

This is a New York institution located right where it should be: in the world's greatest train station, the newly renovated Grand Central Terminal. A fire in 1997 is now only a bad memory, thanks to an aggressive rebuilding. The main dining room sits under an impressive curved and tiled ceiling. A completely new menu is prepared every day, since only the freshest fish gets served. The oysters are irresistible: Kumomoto, belon, bluepoint, and on and on. You choose your live lobster from a tank or order shark, tuna, turbot, snapper, clams, squid, bass, and sturgeon. The prices can be steep, so to save money, sit at the counter for a filling lunch of, say, the unbeatable New England or Manhattan clam chowder (about $4), then indulge in the smoked rainbow trout appetizer (around $8). Look for a possible change in ownership.

Rosa Mexicano. 1063 First Ave. (at 58th St.). ☎ **212/753-7407.** Reservations recommended. Main courses $16–$28. AE, CB, DC, MC, V. Daily 5pm–midnight. Subway: 4, 5, 6, to 59th St.; N, R to Lexington Ave. MEXICAN.

Nachos, burritos, and quesadillas are what most people think are Mexican food. But no such *norteño* fare is on the menu at Rosa Mexicano, one of a trio of Manhattan's authentic Mexican restaurants—others are Zarela and Mi Cocina. Thanks to chef/owner Josefina Howard (a scholar and teacher of Mexican cookery), *real* Mexican foods like *rajas* (chile strips usually of poblano peppers), *mole poblano* (sauce made with chiles, almonds, sesame seeds, and chocolate), *pozole* (pork, chicken, and hominy stew), and ceviche (raw fish marinated in lemon juice with onions, tomatoes, green chiles, and coriander) have made their way into our vocabularies and mouths.

To start, order the trademark duo: a crimson pomegranate margarita and chunky guacamole made tableside to taste with lemon, coriander, and spice. Another appetizer worth splitting is the cold seafood platter with fish-and-scallop ceviche, shrimp, lump crabmeat, sweetwater prawns, and jalapeños filled with sardines, garnished with chile poblano mousse. Meats and seafood from the open grill are a fine bet for a main course. The grilled pork chops with ground chiles and spices have a nice afterbite.

INEXPENSIVE

✪ **Ess-A-Bagel.** 831 Third Ave. (at 51st St.). ☎ **212/980-1010.** Sandwiches $1.35–$8.35. AE, DISC, MC, V. Mon–Fri 6:30am–9pm, Sat–Sun 8am–5pm. Subway: 6 to 51st St.; E, F to Lexington/Third aves. and 53rd St. AMERICAN BAGEL SANDWICHES.

Ess-A-Bagel turns out the city's best bagel. The hand-rolled delicacies come in 12 flavors—plain, sesame, poppy, onion, garlic, salt, whole wheat, pumpernickel, pumpernickel raisin, cinnamon raisin, oat bran, and everything—and are so plump, chewy, and satisfying it's hard to believe they contain no fat, cholesterol, or preservatives. Head to the back counter for a baker's dozen or line up for a sandwich overstuffed with a scrumptious salads and spreads. Fillings can be a generous schmear of cream cheese, baked salmon or chopped herring salad (both have received national acclaim), and sun-dried tomato tofu spread. The cheerful dining room has plenty of bistro tables. There's a Downtown location at 359 First Ave. (☎ **212/260-2252**).

✪ **Prime Burger.** 5 E. 51st St. (Fifth & Madison aves.). ☎ **212/759-4729.** Reservations not accepted. Main courses $3.10–$6. No credit cards. Mon–Fri 5am–7pm, Sat 6am–5pm. Subway: 6 to 51st St.; E, F to Lexington/Third aves. and 53rd St. AMERICAN/HAMBURGERS.

This is a heavenly find, across from St. Patrick's Cathedral. The burgers and sandwiches are tasty, the fries generous and not too oily—all for a reasonable price. The front seats, which might remind you (if you're old enough) of wooden grammar-school desks that slid closed in front of you, are great fun—especially when ever-so-serious suited-up New Yorkers quietly take their places at these oddities.

✪ **Zarela.** 953 Second Ave. (50th & 51st sts.). ☎ **212/644-6740.** Reservations recommended. Main courses $12.95–$16.95; tasting menu $39. AE, DC. Mon–Fri noon–3pm; Mon–Thurs 5–11pm, Fri–Sat 5–11:30pm, Sun 5–10pm. Subway: 6 to 51st St.; E, F to Lexington/Third aves. and 53rd St. MEXICAN.

Owner Zarela Martínez has her finger on the pulse of her customers and her cuisine—and the price is just right. The restaurant crowds with a friendly assortment of connoisseurs who come for the unsurpassed authentic Mexican food, margarita lovers (this place serves Manhattan's best), high-profile publishing and business types, and a well-to-do international set who appreciate that Zarela herself moves in sophisticated circles, writes her own cookbooks (like *Food from My Heart* and, her latest, *The Food and Life of Oaxaca*), and greets customers.

While your margarita cools you down, order the *salpicón de pescado,* a snapper hash with tomatoes, scallions, jalapeños, and aromatic spices. For a main course, try shrimp braised with poblanos, onions, and queso blanco or roasted half duck with a tomato–red chile sauce with dried apricots, prunes, raisins, and pineapple. The fajitas, grilled marinated skirt steak in flour tortillas, melt in your mouth. Order the rice baked with sour cream, white cheddar cheese, poblanos, and corn to complete the eye-opening entrees. Here you'll understand that Mexican food is so much more than you ever thought. Zarela is one Mexican restaurant that prides itself on great desserts, so check out the day's specials.

14 The Upper West Side

See the "Uptown Dining" map (pp. 156–157) for restaurants in this section.

VERY EXPENSIVE

✪ **Café des Artistes.** 1 W. 67th St. (Central Park West & Columbus Ave.). ☎ **212/877-3500.** Reservations required. Jacket required for dinner. Main courses $24–$30; prix-fixe dinner $37.50. AE, DC, DISC, MC, V. Mon–Fri noon–3pm; Mon–Sat 5:30pm–midnight, Sun 5–11pm; brunch Sat noon–3pm, Sun 10am–3pm. Subway: 1, 9 to 66th St./Lincoln Center. FRENCH/CONTINENTAL.

Café des Artistes is an ebullient place where playful murals of frolicking nude nymphs set the tone. As a result of its high level of service, the restaurant is both a celebrity hangout and a favorite of locals and visitors. The menu is wide ranging, inspired mostly by France but with an occasional nod to Vienna (zwiebel rostbraten, or rib-eye paillard), Scandinavia (salmon four ways, gravlax), Italy (lush prosciutto di Parma with melon in season), the Mideast (vegetable buffet platter), and America (Louisiana bluepoint oysters). Spicy herb-crusted tuna steak and red snapper Niçoise are on the fish menu, with duck, chicken, lamb, steak, and pot au feu for meat lovers. But what brings many back is the dessert cart, offering a slice of every pie, cake, and pastry— unfailingly fabulous. Sunday brunch is popular, with a nice cold buffet and egg dishes.

For a light meal or coffee and pastries, head across the vestibule to the baby sibling, **Parlor at Café des Artistes.** This reasonably priced hideaway (open 8am–midnight) is reminiscent of Vienna with a zinc-and-mahogany bar and marble-topped tables.

✪ **Jean Georges.** One Central Park West (in the Trump International Hotel & Tower, at 60th St.). ☎ **212/299-3900.** Reservations required. Jacket required/tie optional. Main courses $28–$35; lunch tasting menu $45; dinner tasting menu $105. AE, DC, MC, V. Mon–Fri noon–2:30pm; Mon–Sat 5:30–11pm. Subway: A, B, C, D, 1, 9 to Columbus Circle/59th St. FRENCH.

That Donald Trump can be a very smart, and not just smarmy, guy. When he announced he had secured the services of Jean-Georges Vongerichten (see Vong and Jo Jo) to oversee the restaurant in his new hotel, everyone knew the rave reviews wouldn't be far behind. In the elegantly restrained Adam Tihany–designed dining room, the menu is the best of Vongerichten's past successes taken one step further.

French and Asian touches mingle with a new passion for offbeat harvests, like lamb's quarters, sorrel, yarrow, nettles, and chicory. Spring garlic soup with thyme accompanied by a plate of sautéed frogs' legs with parsley makes a great beginning. The Muscovy duck steak with Asian spices and sweet-and-sour jus is carved tableside, while the lobster tartine with pumpkin seed, pea shoots, and a broth of fenugreek (one of Jean-Georges's signature aromatic plants) receives a final dash of spices seconds before you dig in. Dinner or lunch reservations are tough to get. The best deal in the house is the lunch tasting menu. In summer, **Mistral Terrace** serves entrees from $15 to $20.

✪ **Picholine.** 35 W. 64th St. (Central Park West & Broadway). ☎ **212/724-8585.** Reservations required. Main courses $25.50–$34; prix-fixe lunches $19.99 and $28; dinner tasting menus $65 and $85. AE, DC, MC, V. Tues–Sat 11:45am–2pm; Mon–Sat 5:30–11:45pm. Subway: 1, 9 to 66th St./Lincoln Center. FRENCH/MEDITERRANEAN.

This place, which garnered three deserved stars from the *New York Times*, just keeps getting better. Chef Terrance Brennan has made it a resounding success, and around Lincoln Center few restaurants are as talked about. It's calm and welcoming, but

Brennan's inventive take on French Mediterranean classics is what packs them in. Start with the tasty ceviche of Spanish mackerel, full-flavored gnocchi with sheep's milk ricotta, or wonderful grilled octopus with fennel and potato, doused in lemon-pepper dressing. The loin of lamb is spiced with a Moroccan touch and served with a vegetable couscous and minted yogurt. The halibut comes with eggplant pancakes, tomato confit, balsamic vinegar, and basil oil, and the risotto is topped with wild mushrooms and duck with asparagus, fava beans, and white-truffle oil. If you can, insist that someone at your table order the outstanding duck risotto and filch a taste. Cheese whiz Max McCalman presides over the city's only cheese aging room, in which gourmet *fromages* from small producers mature to perfection.

EXPENSIVE

Shun Lee West. 43 W. 65th St. (Central Park West & Broadway). ☎ **212/595-8895.** Reservations recommended, especially pretheater. Main courses $14.95–$22.95. AE, DC, MC, V. Daily noon–midnight. Subway: 1, 9 to 66th St./Lincoln Center. CHINESE.

Shun Lee's passionate advocates come here for such specialties as rack of lamb Szechuan style, crabmeat with beans and mushrooms, and the singularly named Ants Climb on Tree (a stir-fry covered with cellophane noodles and garnished with greens). Call 24 hours in advance for the luscious beggar's chicken—spiced with herbs and pepper and stuffed with vegetables and pork, wrapped in lotus leaves, placed in clay soil, and baked for 4 hours; rose-petal liqueur is sprinkled on top every hour. The decor is Bruce Lee meets big-budget George Lucas, with a touch of 1930s Hollywood glamour. Kids love the monkeys and dragons in the bar area. You can choose tables in the sunken central area or the tall booths along the walls. The place is guarded by a benign white dragon that slithers the entire length of the walls.

Next to the main dining area, with another entrance, is **Shun Lee Cafe,** the West Side place for dim sum (Mon–Fri 5:30–midnight, Sat–Sun noon–2:30pm). The original **Shun Lee Palace** is at 155 E. 55th St. (☎ 212/371-8844).

✪ **Tavern on the Green.** In Central Park at W. 67th St. ☎ **212/873-3200.** Reservations recommended, necessary on holidays. Main courses $13.25–$33; prix-fixe lunch (Mon–Fri) $25; pretheater prix fixe (Mon–Fri) $23 and $28.50. AE, CB, DC, DISC, MC, V. Mon–Fri 11:30am–3:30pm; Mon–Sat 5–11:30pm, Sun 5:30pm–10:30pm; brunch Sat–Sun 10am–3:30pm. Subway: 1, 9 to 66th St./Lincoln Center. CONTEMPORARY AMERICAN/CONTINENTAL.

Warner LeRoy's Central Park fantasy palace has one of New York's best settings. Tiny twinkling lights glimmer on nearby trees, and the views over the park are wonderful. Antiques like Tiffany glass fill the space. Crystal chandeliers cast a romantic light. A festive spirit, especially at Christmas, enlivens the Crystal Room, where you should ask to be seated. Since the passing of beloved executive chef Patrick Clark last year, acting-chef Michael Schenk has overseen the kitchen. His seasonal menus have continued Clark's tradition. The seared duck foie gras, tasting deeply from the dark woods, is served with a pear-and-pecan sticky bun and a balsamic-port syrup. Other good starters: roasted lobster on lobster polenta, warm house-smoked salmon, and white bean–and–spring vegetable soup. The superb al dente pasta is made by pasta chef Renzo Barcatta. The grilled pork porterhouse is delicious and thick. Salmon is barbecued with Moroccan spices and served with a couscous cake.

Tavern is known for its down-to-earth manner. The crowd (which can be extensive, especially at holidays) includes anyone from Clint Eastwood being fêted by Lincoln Center's New York Film Festival to seniors from Des Moines on their big night out. In warm weather, some high spirits head to the magical little garden, which has introduced a cookout menu.

MODERATE

Cafe Luxembourg. 200 W. 70th St. (Amsterdam & West End aves.). ☎ **212/873-7411.** Reservations recommended. Main courses $17–$27; prix-fixe lunch $19.99; prix-fixe dinner $34; prix-fixe brunch $19.99. AE, CB, DC, MC, V. Mon–Sat noon–3pm, Sun 11am–3pm; daily 5:30pm–midnight. Subway: 1, 2, 3, 9 to 72nd St. FRENCH BISTRO.

This has been a great favorite not far from Lincoln Center ever since it opened. Some might not have predicted this longevity from the feeding frenzy at the time, but it has survived. The clean white-tiled walls, the arch faux art deco touches, and the people scene at the bar make for an attractive and distracting evening. The food is basic French brasserie: good steak frites; remarkable grilled lamb chops with ratatouille, potato gratin, and herb-lamb juice; and rabbit pot pie with black trumpet mushrooms, baby onions, carrots, and thyme. The prix-fixe lunch and dinner are smart buys, and brunch is popular. After 10pm, prices for a smoked Scottish Salmon Sandwich ($12) and good burger with fries ($11.50) encourage late-night noshing.

Citrus. 320 Amsterdam Ave. (at 75th St.). ☎ **212/595-0500.** Reservations recommended. Main courses $10.75–$19.50. AE, DC, MC, V. Mon 5:30–11pm, Tues–Fri 5:30pm–midnight, Sat 5pm–1am, Sun noon–11pm. Subway: 1, 2, 3, 9 to 72nd St. SOUTHWESTERN.

Boasting more than 100 tequilas and designer margaritas, this place could let the food become an afterthought. But chef Martin Mendoza makes creative combinations of American and Mexican ingredients. The skirt steak with cayenne-flavored onion rings and coffee-infused barbecue sauce succeeds, as does the yellowfin tuna filet on cumin-orange rice. Some dishes reach too far: The pork chops were tough and the ancho chile–rubbed chicken breast was surprisingly flavorless. The desserts, however, are the highlight of the meal. Don't miss the mammoth flan.

La Boîte en Bois. 75 W. 68th St. (at Columbus Ave.). ☎ **212/874-2705.** Reservations recommended. Main courses $16.50–$21; pretheater prix fixe $29. No credit cards. Mon–Sat noon–2:30pm, pretheater 5:30–6:30pm, à la carte 7:30–11:30pm; Sun 4–10pm; brunch Sun 11:30am–2:30pm. Subway: 1, 9 to 66th St./Lincoln Center. FRENCH.

True to its name, the tiny dining room with 15 tables has rustic wood-bedecked walls. The French country bibelots give it a comfortable feeling reminiscent of a bistro in Burgundy. After tasting the homemade pâté or warm sausage with lentils, you might think you really are in France. The house specialty, not on the menu, is a succulent roasted rack of lamb worth asking for. Other popular entrees are roasted salmon with honey-mustard glaze, sauteed medaillons of monkfish in saffron sauce served over couscous, and pepper steak. Finish with the exceptional frozen praline mousse. The $29 three-course pretheater menu is popular with the Lincoln Center crowd.

✪ Sarabeth's Kitchen. 423 Amsterdam Ave. (80th & 81st sts.). ☎ **212/496-6280.** Reservations accepted for dinner only. Main courses $14–$20. AE, CB, DC, DISC, JCB, MC, V. Mon–Thurs 8am–10:30pm, Fri 8am–11pm, Sat 9am–11pm, Sun 9am–9:30pm. Subway: 1, 9 to 79th St. AMERICAN.

Its 200-year-old family recipe for orange-apricot marmalade rooted Sarabeth's Kitchen into New York's consciousness. And now its fresh-baked goods, award-winning preserves, and creative American cooking with a European touch keep a loyal following. Sarabeth's is best known for its breakfast and weekend brunch featuring such treats as papa bear porridge with bananas, fresh cream, raisins, and honey; farmer's omelet filled with ham, leeks, potato chunks, and Gruyère; and pumpkin waffle topped with sour cream, raisins, pumpkin seeds, and honey. But lunch and dinner are just as good and a lot less crowded.

There are also two East Side locations: 1295 Madison Ave. (☎ 212/410-7335) and inside the Whitney Museum at 945 Madison Ave. (☎ 212/570-3670).

INEXPENSIVE

Josie's Restaurant and Juice Bar. 300 Amsterdam Ave. (at 74th St.). ☎ **212/769-1212.** Reservations recommended. Main courses $8–$13.75. AE, DC, MC, V. Mon–Sat 5:30pm– midnight, Sun 5:30–11pm. Subway: 1, 2, 3, 9 to 72nd St. ORGANIC/HEALTHY AMERICAN.

You have to admire the sincerity of an organic restaurant that uses chemical-free milk paint on its walls. Chef/owner Louis Lanza doesn't stop there: His adventurous menu shuns dairy, preservatives, and concentrated fats. Free-range meats and poultry augment vegetarian choices like marinated udon noodles with spicy grilled tofu and three-grain vegetable burger with homemade ketchup and caramelized onions. If wheat grass isn't your thing, the wines feature organic choices.

La Caridad 78 Restaurant. 2199 Broadway (at 78th St.). ☎ **212/874-2780.** Reservations not accepted. Main courses $2.95–$11.95. No credit cards. Mon–Sat 11:30am–1am, Sun 11:30am–10:30pm. Subway: 1, 9 to 79th St. CUBAN/CHINESE/HISPANIC.

Atmosphere is not the point here. The crowds line up for the selection of cheap and good Cuban and Chinese dishes. Huge portions of lemon pork chops, shrimp in tomato sauce, and stir-fried chicken keep this neighborhood institution packed.

The Saloon. 1920 Broadway (at 64th St.). ☎ **212/874-1500.** Reservations recommended. Main courses $8.50– $17.95. AE, DC, DISC, MC, V. Mon–Thurs 11:30am–midnight, Fri–Sat 11am–1am, Sun 11am–midnight; brunch Sat–Sun 11am–3pm. Subway: 1, 9 to 66th St./Lincoln Center. AMERICAN.

This friendly space is one of the best buys around Lincoln Center. Its varied menu offers a popular hamburger as well as salads (top choice: country with Anjou pears and goat cheese), pastas (penne with grilled salmon), pizzas, quesadillas, and vegetarian dishes. One of the best entrees is pan-roasted organic chicken breast with fricassee of wild mushrooms, roasted potatoes, pearl onions, and smoked bacon. The light and airy interior has a skates-optional policy for the wait staff, so sometimes your food whisks over on wheels. In nice weather, grab a sidewalk cafe table to watch the Broadway promenade.

15 The Upper East Side

See the "Uptown Dining" map (pp. 156–157) for restaurants in this section.

VERY EXPENSIVE

✪ **Aureole.** 34 E. 61st St. (Madison & Park aves.). ☎ **212/319-1660.** Reservations required 1 month in advance. Jacket/tie required. Prix-fixe dinners $65 and $85; prix-fixe lunches $19.99 (after 2pm) and $32. AE, DC, MC, V. Mon–Fri noon–2:30pm; Mon–Sat 5:30– 11pm. Subway: 4, 5, 6 to 59th St.; N, R to Fifth Ave. CONTEMPORARY AMERICAN.

When chef/owner Charlie Palmer opened Aureole in 1988, it quickly became one of the first contemporary American restaurants to enjoy the prestige of European legends like Lutèce and La Côte Basque. Dining here is dazzling. Set in a town house where Orson Welles once lived, the romantic 90-seat duplex room is filled with large flower arrangements and sandstone relief sculptures. In warm weather tables are set in a courtyard garden. Bring your appetite because Palmer's striking presentations and bold flavor combinations don't come in small portions.

The sea scallop sandwich—a signature starter—substitutes crispy potato pancakes for the bread. Tender filet mignon is charcoal grilled and served with red-wine sauce and morels decadently stuffed with foie gras. A potato crust envelops wild striped bass, served with broccoli rabe and black trumpet mushrooms. Aureole's artful chocolate desserts, designed by pastry chef Michael Gabriel, are justly famous. The topflight

Uptown Dining

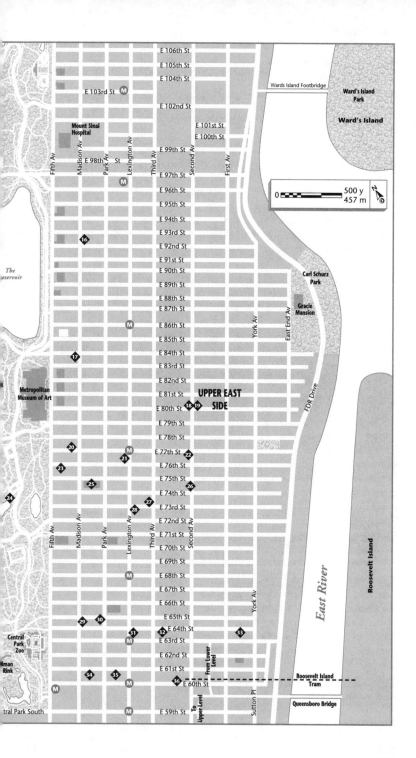

wine list includes an extensive American selection, and the professional service is always pampering. The $19.99 lunch is one of New York's best bargains.

✪ **Daniel.** 620 Park Ave. (at 65th St.). ☎ **212/288-0033** for information. Reservations required 1 month in advance. Jacket/tie required. Main courses $32–$42; prix-fixe dinners $69, $85, and $120. AE, DC, MC, V. Hours not determined at press time. Subway: 6 to 68th St. FRENCH.

In late 1997, chef/owner Daniel Boulud purchased one of the city's most coveted restaurant sites—the space once occupied by Le Cirque. He plans to move Daniel here in early 1999. In late 1998, **Café Boulud** opened in the restaurant's original space in the Surrey Hotel, at 20 E. 76th St., between Fifth and Madison avenues; it serves a moderately priced French menu.

When Boulud first opened Daniel in 1993, Patricia Wells named it one of the *world's* top 10 restaurants. The naturally elegant decor alone proved Boulud's unerring taste, and I predict the menu of the new restaurant will follow suit.

EXPENSIVE

✪ **Jo Jo.** 160 E. 64th St. (Lexington & Third aves.). ☎ **212/223-5656.** Reservations required. Main courses $19–$30; prix-fixe lunch $25; tasting menus $45 and $65. AE, DC, MC, V. Mon–Fri noon–2:30pm and 6–11pm, Sat 5:30–11:30pm. Subway: 6 to 68th St. FRENCH.

Chef/owner Jean-Georges Vongerichten garnered his first praise at Lafayette, where he nearly singlehandedly revolutionized French cooking by replacing butter- and cream-laden sauces with low-fat flavored oils and fresh vegetable juices. Imitators followed everywhere. Jo Jo, as only his friends call him, has continued to draw crowds at his breezy, relaxing, yet elegant East Side town house. Downstairs, the banquettes are red, the walls a warm yellow; upstairs, parlor-floor windows illuminate the room softly.

The menu may offer a terrine of goat cheese and potatoes with arugula juice or a foie gras terrine spiced up with green peppercorns and served with haricots verts. His shrimp with flavored carrot juice and Thai lime leaves was a precursor to many such dishes at "fusion" restaurants around town (he also owns Vong and Jean Georges). His lasagna alternates lobster with truffles and vegetables, and his salmon with citrus vinaigrette is enveloped in rice paper. To make matters better, the prices, even for wine, are lower than at any of his true competitors' restaurants.

La Goulue. 746 Madison Ave. (64th & 65th sts.). ☎ **212/988-8169.** Reservations recommended. Jacket/tie requested. Main courses $21–$28; prix-fixe brunch $23. AE, DC, MC, V. Mon–Thurs noon–3:30pm, Fri–Sat noon–4pm; Mon–Sat 6–11:30pm, Sun 6–10:30pm; brunch Sun noon–4pm. Cafe open all day. Subway: 6 to 68th St. FRENCH BISTRO.

When you want to bask in the sunshine and mingle with models, showbiz types, European *crème*, and poodles with more expensive pedicures than yours, reserve a table on the sidewalk cafe of La Goulue. Inside, the crowd can study itself in the large mirrors of the dining room. Outside, you observe your fellow lingerers as well as the swank crowd on Madison Avenue flitting from gallery to designer shop, from hair stylist to gourmet food boutique. It's a special world, all in microcosm, for the price of a salad and glass of wine.

✪ **Mark's.** 25 E. 77th St. (in the Mark hotel, Fifth & Madison aves.). ☎ **212/879-1864.** Reservations recommended. Main courses $18–$34; pretheater prix fixe $32; prix-fixe dinner $65. AE, CB, DC, JCB, MC, V. Daily 7am–10:30pm. Subway: 6 to 77th St. CONTEMPORARY AMERICAN.

Consistently rated one of New York's best restaurants, Mark's deserves its special status. Chef David Paulstich's appetizers include Maine bay scallops complemented by a surprisingly appropriate grapefruit salad and a mesa dried-tomato emulsion, fresh linguini bathed in creamy porcini sauce and accented by bits of sautéed chicken loin, and sautéed Louisiana prawns accompanied by celery-and-turnip purée and vanilla sauce. Among the main courses are superb fish dishes like pan-roasted Maine lobster with chive whipped potatoes and Armagnac juice and tender squab with bitter-chocolate sauce and artichokes, barley, and wheat berries. The roasted rack of lamb is enlivened by a fricassee of three kinds of peas, then sweetened by figs and dates and dressed in tangine sauce. The three-course pretheater dinner is an excellent value, as is the lower-priced lunch menu. After a Sunday-morning Central Park stroll, come here for brunch.

Park View at the Boathouse. On the lake in Central Park (East Park Dr. & 73rd St.). ☎ **212/ 988-0575.** Reservations recommended. Main courses $17–$24. AE, MC, V. Mon–Sat 11:30am–4pm; Sun–Thurs 5pm–midnight, Fri–Sat 5pm–1am; brunch Sun 11am–4pm. Closed winter. Subway: 6 to 77th St. AMERICAN.

On the edge of the lake and surrounded by the great green park, Park View at the Boathouse is a one-of-a-kind experience. This is the perfect respite, since it's *so* New York and *so* seemingly far away. Last year, new owners remade the place and hired acclaimed chef John Villa. Your meal might start with Indian-spiced salmon tartare with pappadam and plantain crisps. Coriander-seasoned pork loin and shrimp salad with papaya and curry vinaigrette are tasty entrees. It's easiest to walk right in during the week when the poor natives are slaving at their desks; the weekend brunch is *very* crowded, especially when the sun is shining. You've no doubt heard about the dangers of wandering in Central Park at night, but after 7pm a shuttle runs from Fifth Avenue and 72nd Street to the restaurant. There's something magical about being in Central Park after sunset, when Park View is like a tiny island from which you watch the skyline twinkle.

MODERATE

✪ **Destinée.** 134 E. 61st St. (Park & Lexington aves.). ☎ **212/888-1220.** Reservations required. Jacket requested. Main courses $14–$23; prix-fixe lunch $28; prix-fixe dinner $42; tasting menu $65. AE, DC, MC, V. Mon–Sat noon–2:30pm; Mon–Fri 5:30–10:30pm, Sat 5:30–11:30pm. Subway: 4, 5, 6 to 59th St.; N, R to Lexington Ave. FRENCH.

Chef Jean-Yves Schillinger opened this celestial place in 1997 following a tragic fire that destroyed his family's restaurant in Alsace, France, and killed his father. Destinée's tony setting and crowd is an appropriate backdrop for Schillinger's refined cuisine (he had two Michelin stars in Alsace). The excellent salmon tartar appetizer is topped with a quail egg and caviar and ringed by cucumbers cut into the shape of diamonds; the seared venison entree served with pumpkin purée, mushrooms, and fresh spaetzle attest to Schillinger's Alsatian background. For dessert, the apricot tatin is a delicious twist on the traditional upside-down apple tart.

✪ **Payard Pâtisserie and Bistro.** 1032 Lexington Ave. (at 73rd St.). ☎ **212/717-5252.** Reservations recommended. Main courses $10–$25. AE, DC, MC, V. Mon–Sat noon–2:30pm and 6–11pm; tea Mon–Sat 2:30–5pm. Subway: 6 to 77th St. FRENCH BISTRO.

This venture of Daniel Boulud, chef and owner of the highly acclaimed Daniel, and his former pastry chef, François Payard, offers the ultimate gastronomic union: Elegant cakes, pastries, and handmade chocolates fill glass cases in the pastry shop up front, while mirrors, mahogany, and bistro fare entice patrons to the cafe in back. The menu is unabashedly classic, with homemade duck confit, thick slabs of foie gras terrine, sublime steak frites, and fragrant bouillabaisse. The beautifully presented desserts rank among the city's best, and $15 buys a grand tasting.

INEXPENSIVE

Caffè Grazie. 26 E. 84th St. (at Madison Ave.). ☎ **212/717-4407.** Reservations recommended. Main courses $12.50–$19.50; Mon prix-fixe dinner $18.50; Sun brunch $12.95. AE. Mon–Sat 11:30am–11pm, Sun 11:30am–10pm. Subway: 4, 5, 6 to 86th St. ITALIAN.

This cheery, unpretentious Italian cafe is a hidden treasure on the Upper East Side, near the Metropolitan Museum of Art. It's perfect for sipping espresso or lingering over an elegant three-course meal. Appetizers like the bruschetta assortment served with a small salad and the warm white-bean salad served over prosciutto are generous enough to be a light meal. The pasta selection mixes staples (satisfying penne pomodoro and linguini pesto) with standouts (lasagna layered with grilled chicken, fresh tomatoes, cheese, and pesto). The entrees are fresh and flavorful, like veal stuffed with prosciutto and spinach and jumbo shrimp with lemon-caper sauce.

EJ's Luncheonette. 1271 Third Ave. (at 73rd St.). ☎ **212/472-0600.** Reservations not accepted. Main courses $3.50–$10.75. No credit cards. Mon–Thurs 8am–11pm, Fri–Sat 8am–midnight, Sun 8am–10:30pm. Subway: 6 to 77th St. AMERICAN.

This retro diner is popular with Uptown yups who come for hearty American fare in a 1950s setting—blue vinyl booths, Formica tabletops, a soda fountain, and a lunch counter with round stools that spin. The menu features a large selection of waffles, pancakes, and egg dishes so good you shouldn't be ashamed of indulging in a stack of banana-pecan pancakes for dinner. It also offers burgers, sandwiches, salads, and main dishes like meat loaf with mashed potatoes and black bean–and–sirloin chili topped with sour cream, cheddar, and onions. All three locations (see the box "Choice Choices $15 & Under") are kid-friendly.

✪ **Jackson Hole.** 232 E. 64th St. (Second & Third aves.). ☎ **212/371-7187.** Main courses and sandwiches $4.45–$11. AE. Daily 10:30am–1am. Subway: 6 to 68th St. AMERICAN.

Jackson Hole is a chain (for more locations see the box "Choice Choices $15 & Under") serving satisfying fast food, a couple of giant steps above McDonald's. The more than 30 topping combos are piled high on hefty 7-ounce beef or turkey burgers or grilled marinated chicken breast. Two trademarked combinations are the Eastsider, a bacon cheeseburger topped with ham, mushrooms, tomatoes, and fried onions, and the Eastsider Bronco, grilled chicken topped with the same. Other menu items: salads, omelets, and blue-plate specials. This location has garden dining.

Pamir. 1437 Second Ave. (74th & 75th sts.). ☎ **212/734-3791.** Reservations recommended. Main courses $11.95–$16.95. MC, V. Tues–Sun 5–11pm. Subway: 6 to 77th St. AFGHANISTANI.

Afghanistan's position astride the main western land route to India through the famed Khyber Pass has resulted in a culinary tradition marked by Middle Eastern and Indian influences. This unique cuisine is centered on chicken and lamb, with vegetables like eggplant and pumpkin seasoned with Indian spices.

Peruse the menu while sipping *doodh,* a refreshing mix of yogurt, club soda, mint, and a touch of salt. You might start with the combination appetizer, one of which should be *bulanee kachalou,* a tasty turnover stuffed with mildly spiced potatoes and onions, with a tangy yogurt sauce. A favorite main course is *kormae-murgh,* a hearty stew of delicately seasoned diced chicken with tomatoes, onions, garlic, and Afghan spices. Or try *quabilli palaw,* aromatic pieces of lamb under a mound of brown rice topped with almonds, pistachios, carrot strips, and raisins. Though traditional dishes go well beyond kebabs, the ones served here are particularly tasty, with juicy meats marinated in a savory blend of spices. Afghan pudding with almonds and pistachios is the perfect finish. A second location is at 1065 First Ave. (☎ **212/644-9258**).

Pig Heaven. 1540 Second Ave. (80th & 81st sts.). ☎ **212/744-4333.** Reservations recommended. Main courses $10.95–$16.95. AE, DC, MC, V. Sun–Thurs 11:30am–11:15pm, Fri–Sat 11:30am–midnight. Subway: 6 to 77th St. CHINESE.

Here an oink, there an oink. Everywhere an oink oink! Piglets and pink dominate the decor of this witty and delicious Szechuan and Cantonese restaurant—fun for adults and kids and very popular among its neighbors. Of course, there's more to the menu than pork. The cold noodles are drenched in tasty sesame sauce, which I like to order extra spicy. Among other fine appetizers are scallion pancakes and plump seafood dumplings. In deference to the barnyard friends around you, you might order the Cantonese suckling pig or shredded pork. Two other fine main courses: shrimp that have been sliced and are served in their shells and shredded beef with a well-spiced barbecue sauce.

✪ **Serendipity 3.** 225 E. 60th St. (Second & Third aves.). ☎ **212/838-3531.** Reservations recommended. Main courses $5–$15.95. AE, DC, DISC, MC, V. Sun–Thurs 11:30am–midnight, Fri 11:30am–1am, Sat 11:30am–2am. Subway: 4, 5, 6 to 59th St.; N, R to Lexington Ave. AMERICAN.

A whimsical boutique, home-style restaurant, and extravagant sweet shop, Serendipity 3 is sure to delight. Tucked into a cozy brownstone a few steps from Bloomingdale's, Serendipity's small curiosity shop overflows with odd objects, like eye charts, jigsaw puzzles, Tiffany-style lampshades, and frivolous jewelry. Downstairs, behind the boutique, are marble-topped ice-cream parlor tables where stylish shoppers enjoy tea from 3 to 6pm. Upstairs, happy people dine on foot-long hot dogs, country meat loaf with mashed potatoes and gravy, healthy Zen hash, caviar burgers, and salads and sandwiches. Serendipity's signature sweet is "frrrozen hot chocolate," but don't miss the dark double devil mousse, celestial carrot cake, or lemon ice-box pie.

16 Harlem & East Harlem

See the "Upper Manhattan Attractions" map (p. 215) for restaurants in this section.

VERY EXPENSIVE

Rao's. 455 E. 114th St. (at Pleasant Ave.). ☎ **212/722-6709.** Reservations required months in advance. Jacket required/tie requested. Prix fixe $55. No credit cards. Mon–Fri one seating at 7pm. Subway: 6 to 116th St. ITALIAN.

Politicians, movie stars, business bosses, and a host of other influentials have been coming here for years to eat home-style Italian, way out of their usual spheres of authority. It has 10 tables, a waiting list about 3 months long, and a client list any fund-raiser would sell his or her soul to possess. Some snipe that the food isn't memorable—I dare them to tell that to owner Frankie. What's interesting about the neighborhood, at the edge of East Harlem, or Spanish Harlem (El Barrio), is that it was once called Italian Harlem, though few remnants of that population remain—except Rao's and Patsy's.

INEXPENSIVE

✪ **Patsy's Pizzeria.** 2287 First Ave. (117th & 118th sts.). ☎ **212/534-9783.** Pizza $9–$10. No credit cards. Mon–Thurs 11am–midnight, Fri–Sat 11am–1am, Sun 1–11pm. Subway: 6 to 116th St. PIZZA.

The decor isn't much and the neighborhood is a trifle . . . distant. But for pizza, by the slice or pie, that has thin crust, luscious cheese, and well-balanced toppings, Patsy's Pizzeria has long had the cognoscenti willing to go out of their way for the city's best. Patsy's boasts a brick oven that has been working continuously for 66 years.

An After-Dark Tip

As is true whenever you're outside Manhattan's usual visitor paths, at night take a cab to and from your destination, keep your wits about you, and don't wander around aimlessly.

✪ **Sylvia's Restaurant.** 328 Lenox Ave. (126th & 127th sts.). ☎ **212/996-0660.** Reservations accepted for 10 or more. Main courses $8–$16. AE, DISC, MC, V. Mon–Sat 7:30am–10:30pm, Sun 12:30–7pm. Subway: 2, 3 to 125th St. SOUL FOOD.

Sylvia's has billed itself as the Queen of Soul Food since 1962. It should also bill itself as Queen of the Bargain, for here is true down-home cooking at a friendly price. Fried chicken, baked ham, and smothered pork chops will put you in mind of swinging slowly on a large wooden porch. The specials include the barbecued ribs that only Sylvia's makes—your fingers will taste better than they ever did—and such other temptations as roast beef, meat loaf, smothered steak, and turkey wings with "that down-home dressing." Stick around Sunday night for open-mike gospel (7–11pm).

Wilson's Bakery and Restaurant. 1980 Amsterdam Ave. (at 158th St.). ☎ **212/923-9821.** Main courses $6–$24. No credit cards. Daily 6am–9pm. Subway: 1 to 157th St.; A, B to 155th St. SOUL FOOD.

Wilson's goes back to 1947 and has been drawing celebrities, neighbors, and Downtowners ever since. You might catch Melba Moore, Sugar Ray Leonard, or Wesley Snipes in this cozy place. They come for the fresh ham with applesauce, fried chicken, roast pork, and leg of lamb—all served with two vegetables (everything from collard greens to mashed sweet potatoes) and hot rolls for less than $8! There's also seafood, steaks, and chops.

17 Beyond Manhattan

VERY EXPENSIVE

✪ **Peter Luger's Steakhouse.** 178 Broadway (at Driggs Ave.), Brooklyn. ☎ **718/387-7400.** Reservations highly recommended. Main courses $7.95–$28.95. No credit cards. Sun–Fri 11:45am–10pm, Sat 11:45am–11pm. Subway: J, M to Marcy Ave. STEAK HOUSE.

Porterhouse heaven! This isn't a place for "contemporary," "new," or "inventive." It isn't a place for baby vegetables. But it is the place for New York's best steak, dry-aged on the premises, served charred and pink in a beer-hall atmosphere. The German fried potatoes are crisp and delicious; the creamed spinach is for those who like such things (not me). Nonbelievers can order sole or lamb chops. But steak is why you come here.

The River Café. 1 Water St. (at the East River), Brooklyn. ☎ **718/522-5200.** Reservations required. Jacket required/tie preferred. Prix-fixe dinner $68. AE, CB, DC, MC, V. Mon–Fri noon–3pm; daily 6–11:30pm; brunch Sat–Sun noon–3pm. Subway: A to High St./Brooklyn Bridge; 2, 3 to Clark St. CONTEMPORARY AMERICAN.

The view of Lower Manhattan and New York Harbor is spectacular, at night lit up like a starry sky and during the day colored by slow river traffic. With touches evoking a stylish 1930s dining room as well as a modern pale twist, the restaurant is glamorous and the food fresh and seasonal. Prix-fixe appetizers may include sashimi-quality tuna and salmon tartares, salmon smoked over fruitwood, or green bean, goat cheese, and frisée salad. Entrees comprise crisp red snapper, roast loin of lamb, or grilled prime sirloin of beef, among many tempting others. Desserts like a Brooklyn Bridge sculpted from Valrhona marquise chocolate and praline–and–bittersweet chocolate torte provide delightful finales.

Water's Edge. The East River at 44th Dr., Long Island City, Queens. ☎ **718/482-0033.** Reservations required. Jacket required. Main courses $22–$32; tasting menu $65; vegetarian tasting menu $45. AE, CB, DC, JCB, MC, V. Mon–Fri noon–3pm; Mon–Sat 6–11pm. Subway: E, F to 23rd St./Eli. Complimentary evening ferry from Manhattan (34th St. & East River, at the heliport). CONTEMPORARY AMERICAN.

This sophisticated dining room is warmed by a fireplace—but all eyes are on the view of Midtown Manhattan. The food is just as splendid. Among the appetizing starters are Louisiana shrimp poached in orange-Sauternes infusion, ravioli of Maryland crab and roasted peppers, and sautéed foie gras with roasted artichokes. Main courses include seafood, meat, and poultry. The Maine lobster is poached in saffron broth and comes with perfect asparagus risotto and currant tomatoes. A roast Chilean seabass is served with currant tomatoes, saffron potatoes, calamata olives, and artichoke broth. The grilled breast of duck, loin of veal, steak, and baby chicken are all excellent.

EXPENSIVE

Gage & Tollner. 372 Fulton St. (near Jay St.), Brooklyn. ☎ **718/875-5181.** Reservations required. Main courses $14.95–$26.95; prix-fixe lunch $18.80; prix-fixe dinner $19.99. AE, DC, DISC, MC, V. Mon–Fri 11:30am–3:30pm and 5–11pm, Sat 3:30–11pm. Subway: A, C, F to Jay St./Borough Hall. SEAFOOD.

The first of the city's landmarked restaurant interiors (there's still only one other: the Four Seasons) is 118 years old. Gaslights flicker, shining in polished mahogany tables. Seafood is the preferred option—try the silky lobster bisque or she-crab soup to start, followed by seared sea scallops, crabmeat Virginia, or shrimp Newburg.

18 Only in New York

ETHNIC EATING ENCLAVES

CHINATOWN   There are so many good, and cheap, options that you could have dinner here for years and never tip the same waiter twice. Most travelers stay west of the Bowery, but East Broadway is booming. Wander there if only to get a look at markets with mouthwatering vegetables you've never seen before.

Besides the favorites I've listed under this neighborhood earlier in the chapter, I'd suggest **Golden Unicorn,** 18 E. Broadway (☎ 212/941-0911), especially for dim sum; **H.S.F.,** 46 Bowery St. (☎ 212/374-1319); and **The Nice Restaurant,** 35 E. Broadway (☎ 212/406-9510), an upbeat place, Hong Kong style, with great roast duck. For the perfect dessert, go to the ✪ **Chinatown Ice Cream Factory,** 65 Bayard St. (☎ 212/608-4170), where the lush, full-flavored, created-on-the-premises ice creams include green tea, mango, red bean, taro, and ginger.

LITTLE ITALY   Mulberry Street, the main thoroughfare, is strung year-round with Christmas-like lights, making for a bazaar atmosphere. The best, most consistent restaurant is **Il Cortile** (p. 121), but many others are immensely popular, with lots of waiting, noise, and usually sauce-drenched pastas. **Angelo's of Mulberry Street,** 146 Mulberry St. (☎ 212/966-1277), is more upscale than its neighbors. At **Grotta Azzurra,** 387 Broome St. (☎ 212/925-8775), there are long lines and good fun; and at **Puglia,** 189 Hester St. (☎ 212/226-8912), you find live entertainment, often by graduates of the Totie Fields (remember her?) humor school.

KOREATOWN   West 32nd Street between Fifth and Sixth avenues is lit in neon like a block in Seoul, with reliable eateries serving exquisite food. **Won Jo** (p. 144) is favored by many Koreans. Other top selections are ✪ **Hangawi,** 12 E. 32 St. (☎ 212/ 213-0077), for a serene escape on the other side of Fifth (try the tempting pumpkin porridge and Korean vermicelli at this no meat, no fish, no dairy, Asian winner); and

The New York Deli News

So this is good for you? Heaping mounds of meat, slices of cheese (not kosher!), and toppers like Russian dressing can add up to coronary crisis. But if you're like many New Yorkers, you need your daily deli.

For nonkosher fare, head to the ✪ **Stage Deli,** 834 Seventh Ave., between 53rd and 54th streets (☎ **212/245-7850**). In 1937, legendary Max Asnas opened what may be New York's oldest continuously run deli. Connoisseurs line up to sample the 36 famous specialty sandwiches named after many of the stars whose photos adorn the walls and whose bottoms fill the chairs. The celebrity sandwiches, created by the personalities themselves, are jaw-distending mountains of fixings. The Tom Hanks is roast beef, chopped liver, onion, and chicken fat, and the Dolly Parton is twin rolls of corned beef and pastrami.

Another great nonkosher choice is the **Carnegie Delicatessen & Restaurant,** 854 Seventh Ave., at 55th Street (☎ **212/757-2245**). For the quintessential New York experience, subject yourself to the surly service so you can savor the best pastrami and corned beef in town. Even big eaters may be challenged by mammoth sandwiches with names like "fifty ways to love your liver" (chopped liver, hard-boiled egg, lettuce, tomato, onion). Main courses range from goulash to roasted chicken, and blintzes come stuffed with cheese or all kinds of fruit. For dessert, the chocolate cheesecake is the only way to go.

The best kosher choice is the ✪ **Second Avenue Deli,** 156 Second Ave., at 10th Street (☎ **212/677-0606**). The service is brusque, the decor is nondescript, and the sandwiches don't have cute names, but this East Village institution is always packed thanks to generous portions of delicious kosher meat. This is the kind of food mother used to make, with high marks going to the chopped liver, pastrami, potato knishes, and a matzoh-ball soup so good you crave it even when you don't have a cold. New York still misses late founding deli man, Abe Lebewohl.

Outstanding others are **Kaplan's,** 59 E. 59th St. (☎ **212/755-5959**), for East Side class and good sandwiches, and **Katz's,** 205 E. Houston St. (☎ **212/254-2246**), for Lower East Side outings and its beloved all-beef hot dogs.

Woo Chon, farther uptown at 8 W. 36th St. (☎ **212/695-0676**), is open 24 hours and a good bet for first-timers.

LITTLE INDIA The stretch of East Sixth Street between First and Second avenues in the East Village isn't high style, but it does have good food at great prices. My favorite is **Bombay Dining** (p. 123). Also satisfying are **Gandhi,** 344 E. 6th St. (☎ **212/614-9718**), for a touch of low-light romance; **Mitali East,** 336 E. 6th St. (☎ **212/533-2508**), the king of curry; **Passage to India,** 308 E. 6th St. (☎ **212/529-5770**), for North Indian tandoori; and **Rose of India,** 308 E. 6th St. (☎ **212/533-5011**), where you ignore the decor and eat.

BAGELS

No one should visit Manhattan without tasting an authentic bagel. They come in all flavors, from plain to "everything" with a mixture of sesame and poppy seeds, garlic, onion, and salt. And just about anything comes on them now. **Ess-A-Bagel** (p. 151) is my favorite, though that could start a small riot among those who prefer **H&H Bagels,** 2239 Broadway (☎ **212/595-8003**), the Upper West Sider's weekend morning manna, open 24 hours (they'll ship anywhere); it also has locations at 639 W. 46th St. (☎ **212/595-8000**) and 1551 Second Ave. (☎ **212/734-7441**). Kosher **Pick-A-Bagel** is popular on the Upper East Side, 1475 Second Ave. (☎ **212/717-4662**) and 1083 Lexington Ave. (☎ **212/517-6590**), and in Midtown, at 200 W. 57th St. (☎ **212/957-5151**).

PIZZA

It's fast, it's fatty, and it's fun. In Italy they sell it by the meter; here we sell it mostly by the slice, and it's one of the city's great bargains. A good cheap lunch (or dinner) of a slice or two with a soda won't run more than $5 in most places. Among my favorite spots for a full pie are **John's Pizzeria,** with four locations (p. 128), and **Patsy's Pizzeria** (p. 161).

Other top choices, most for just a slice: **Freddie & Pepper's,** 303 Amsterdam Ave. (☎ **212/799-2378**), has unusual toppings—goat cheese, spinach, and asparagus, for example. ✪ **Lombardi's,** 32 Spring St. (☎ **212/941-7994**), is a reincarnation of a 1905 historic favorite, with a great coal oven; try the fresh clam pie. **St. Mark's Pizza,** 23 Third Ave. (☎ **212/420-9531**), is for thick-crust fans. **Stromboli Pizza,** 83 St. Mark's Place (☎ **212/673-3691**), satisfies East Village late-night munchies. **Two Boots to Go-Go,** 74 Bleecker St. (☎ **212/777-1033**), is perfectly located for a slice on the run during a shopping spree on lower Broadway (a sit-down location is at 37 Avenue A and the newest is in the Food Court at Grand Central Terminal). And **Vinnie's Pizza,** 285 Amsterdam Ave. (☎ **212/874-4382**), is great for an Upper West Side traditional slice.

ON THE WATERFRONT

Many restaurants take advantage of New York's privileged location by offering dramatic river views. My first choice for on-board dining is ✪ **World Yacht Cruises,** departing from Pier 81, West 41st Street at the Hudson River (☎ **212/630-8100**), with a 3-hour ever-changing view of Manhattan. My landlocked favorites are **Windows on the World** (p. 111), **The River Café** (p. 162), and **Water's Edge** (p. 163).

Other choices are **Edward Moran Bar and Grill,** 250 Vesey St. (☎ **212/945-2255**), for a lively outdoor terrace, good prices, and a panoramic view of the Hudson River; and **The Water Club,** 500 E. 30th St. (☎ **212/683-3333**), on an East River barge, where you get extraordinary views and good food.

SKY-HIGH DINING

It's good to get above it all and look down. For true Downtown drama, I'm highly happy that **Windows on the World** (p. 111) has returned to its aerie. **The Rainbow Room** (p. 134) and the **Terrace,** 400 W. 119th St. (☎ **212/666-9490**), are high-end romantic rooms with expansive views.

GAY & LESBIAN RESTAURANTS

New York restaurants are indifferent to the orientations of their customers. Still, some places specifically attract that certain crowd. Besides just about any Village restaurant, some of the places where your co-diners are likely to be gay are **Lucky Cheng's** (p. 123), **Florent** (p. 127), **The Viceroy** (p. 133), and **Che 2020** (p. 133).

Uptown, **The Townhouse,** 236 E. 58th St. (☎ **212/826-6241**), is the gathering spot for older professional gays, many in suits. The lesbian-owned **Rubyfruit Bar and Grill,** 531 Hudson St. (☎ **212/929-3343**), is a women's Village favorite. Better than most in its genre is **Manats,** 340 Bleecker St., just off Christopher (☎ **212/989-7042**), a coffee shop where gays and lesbians feel at home; it even has candlelight to go with wee-hour tête-à-têtes.

STOP WHERE YOU SHOP

On the eighth floor of **Saks Fifth Avenue,** 611 Fifth Ave., is **Cafe S.F.A.** (☎ 212/940-4080), serving yuppiefied salads and sandwiches in a stylish dining room with a fabulous view over St. Patrick's Cathedral. Escape bustling **Bloomingdale's,** 1000 Third Ave., on the sixth floor at ✪ **Le Train Bleu** (☎ 212/705-2100), a favorite for afternoon tea served Monday to Friday 3 to 5pm. The coffee shop at **Old Navy,** 610 Sixth Ave. (☎ 212/645-0663), is all the rage for its sandwich menu signed by chef Geoffrey Zakarian. **ABC Carpet & Home,** 38 E. 19th St., has added the **Parlour Cafe** (☎ 212/677-2233), whose praises were sung by Barbra Streisand who sampled 11 desserts in one sitting. The ✪ **Cafe at Sotheby's,** 1334 York Ave. (☎ 212/606-7070), where Jean-Georges Vongerichten consults, offers the least-expensive items at the auction house: soups, sandwiches, salads, and pastries from $5 to $17.75. Sold!

BREW PUBS

At last count, there were some 15 microbreweries, with more on the way. Here the brew pub image has been remade, so you'll sometimes find innovative cuisine rather than typical pub grub. ✪ **Heartland Brewery,** 35 Union Square West (☎ 212/645-3400), was voted best brew pub by *New York* magazine and has a new location at 1285 Sixth Ave. (☎ 212/582-8244). ✪ **Typhoon Brewery,** 22 E. 54th St. (☎ 212/754-9006) serves unexpectedly good Thai-inspired cuisine. A more family-oriented place is the **Times Square Brewery,** 160 W. 42nd St. (☎ 212/398-1234), which combines brewing with a pretzel bakery and restaurant. It boasts as-real-as-you-can-get-in-America German beers. The city's largest microbrewery is the **Chelsea Brewing Company,** on Pier 59 at 18th Street (☎ 212/336-6440), which has a wonderful terrace seating 100 that overlooks the Hudson River.

TWENTY-FOUR HOURS

New Yorkers live in a 24-hour-a-day town, and somebody is always there to satisfy their appetites. Between moonrise and sunup, the lifesavers include **Florent** (p. 127; closed weekdays 5–9am), where you'll find an eclectic mix of hip, drag, truckers, and daytime sleepers who'd think they were in Paris; **French Roast Cafe** (p. 127), for casual light meals or coffee and pastries; **H&H Bagels,** 2239 Broadway (☎ 212/595-8003), for kosher noshes; and **Won Jo** (p. 144), for kinky do-it-yourself Korean barbecue. **L'Express** (p. 132), on Park Avenue South in the middle of the latest singles scene, has better-than-you'd-expect French food at all hours.

THE JAMES BEARD HOUSE

The ✪ **James Beard House,** 167 W. 12th St. (☎ 212/675-4984 or 800/36-BEARD), is a New York original, serving as a focal point for all kinds of food-related activities. Professionals and passionate amateurs gather here for everything from feasts by the likes of David Bouley to Texas chuck-wagon dinners. Five-course lunches can run as high as $50, and sumptuous dinners can go up to $85—still, these are relative bargains not only because of the food, the conversation, and the unique ambiance but also because they often include wine. You can become a member of the Beard Foundation for $125 and save about $10 per lunch and $20 per dinner. This place is truly only in New York.

Exploring New York City

Like its mobile inhabitants, who shed their fashion skins with every passing season, New York constantly shifts its appearance. However, one truth never changes: Even type A Manhattanites can't experience every attraction and distraction—not only because of the city's vacillating nature but also because of its boundless diversions, packed as tight as New Yorkers in a rush-hour train. Whether you're a refined connoisseur of its museums, an awed observer of its architecture, or a bon vivant consumer of its street life, even a full lifetime isn't enough to fathom everything Gotham has to offer.

If you're in New York for the first time and for only a few days, see "The Top Attractions by Neighborhood" box. The places mentioned there, indicated later in the chapter with a star, mix my personal favorites with a few others meriting a visit by any traveler.

The outer-borough sites I list are mainly for those who already know Manhattan, but I highly recommend strolling Brooklyn Heights and visiting the American Museum of the Moving Image in Queens.

For particular neighborhoods you might want to wander, see "Neighborhoods in Brief" in chapter 4. And for more highlights on high-rises, read "Seeing Beyond the Icons & the Neon" in chapter 1.

1 In New York Harbor: Lady Liberty, Ellis Island & the Staten Island Ferry

✪ **Statue of Liberty.** On Liberty Island in New York Harbor. ☎ **212/363-7620** (general info), 212/269-5755 (ticket/ferry info). Ferry ticket/admission to Statue of Liberty and Ellis Island, $7 adults, $6 seniors, $3 children 3–17. Daily 9:30am–5pm; extended hours in summer. Subway: 4, 5 to Bowling Green; 1, 9 to South Ferry (the platform onto which you exit is shorter than the train, so ride in the first 5 cars).

No monument so embodies the nation's, and the world's, notion of political freedom and economic potential. Yet because this mighty anchor of New York Harbor is such a familiar icon—on buttons, postcards, book jackets, you name it—Lady Liberty's power to instill a shudder as you contemplate her meaning has been compromised. Reciting its dramatic proportions (index finger: 8 ft. long) has become a favorite pastime of guidebooks. But those measurements miss the point: The whole is more than the sum of its parts. I prefer to avoid

The Top Attractions by Neighborhood

Since I've classified the following top attractions by location, you could easily plan a day of hopping around Downtown, for instance, from sea level at the Statue of Liberty to bird's-eye views on the observation deck of the World Trade Center, followed by dinner in Chinatown or Greenwich Village. But if it's museums you prefer, select the top ones from this box and then turn to the "Museums & Art Galleries" section to see which others pique your interest. Or if you prefer monuments and architecture, start with the Statue of Liberty, the Empire State Building, and the others mentioned here; then opt for other choices under "New York Architectural Icons." If the weather is glorious, see the city from the Empire State Building, find a moment to walk the riverfront, or take an hour to laze on the Staten Island Ferry.

In the rest of this chapter the attractions are separated by type, and the top attractions listed here are highlighted with stars and precede the secondary sights in each category.

Downtown

- Statue of Liberty, New York Harbor (p. 167)
- Ellis Island, New York Harbor (p. 169)
- Staten Island Ferry, New York Harbor (p. 170)
- Brooklyn Bridge, Lower Manhattan (p. 171)
- New York Stock Exchange, the Financial District (p. 171)
- Battery Park City, Lower Manhattan (p. 198)
- World Trade Center, Lower Manhattan (p. 194)
- Chinatown (p.198)
- SoHo (p. 199)
- Greenwich Village (p. 199)

Midtown

- Flatiron District (p. 199)
- Empire State Building, Midtown West (p. 191)
- Times Square, Midtown West (p. 197)
- Rockefeller Center, Midtown West (p. 193)
- Museum of Modern Art, Midtown West (p. 175)
- Grand Central Terminal, Midtown East (p. 192)
- Chrysler Building, Midtown East (p. 192)
- United Nations, Midtown East (p. 195)
- Central Park (p. 200)

Uptown & Beyond

- American Museum of Natural History, Upper West Side (p. 177)
- Metropolitan Museum of Art, Upper East Side (p. 174)
- Bronx Zoo, the Bronx (p. 202)

going to the statue itself, liking better the vantage point from the Staten Island Ferry, at night, as you cross the harbor's open waters. From a peaceful spot on the deck, imagine yourself a hopeful immigrant who has just survived a journey across the Atlantic. Then you see her: Rising to a phenomenal height, her torch dramatically lit, unbent by wind or time, the Statue of Liberty reclaims her birthright. She moves your heart.

Tasting the True New York

The true New York is, as Mies van der Rohe would have said, in the details. As you dash from sight to site, take time to admire a lovely doorway or sculpted cornice, linger over a glass of wine or cup of coffee on a terrace, idle away a few minutes on a bench watching New Yorkers parade through their daily lives, or prize serene moments on the waterfronts.

On October 28, 1886, more than a million people watched as the French tricolor veil concealing the statue's face was pulled away, thus revealing the strong feminine countenance sculpted by Frédéric-Auguste Bartholdi (the interior iron framework was designed by Alexandre-Gustave Eiffel of Paris tower fame). This gift to the United States from France—which received a resoundingly successful $70-million face-lift (including the replacement of the torch's flame) in time for its centennial celebration on July 4, 1986—was meant to commemorate the two countries' friendship dating back to the American Revolution. The statue soon became a symbol of much more.

After you've seen the statue from the Staten Island Ferry and have had a moment to consider it in relative solitude, you can return to Manhattan to take the ferry directly to Liberty Island. Now you're much too close to appreciate it's the statue's height or majesty and, since more than 2 million people per year swarm the island, lines and crowds will accompany you. I recommend getting on the first ferry of the day; otherwise expect a 3-hour wait in line.

A stroll around the statue's base will give you an idea of its grandeur: 151 feet tall (305 feet including the foundation and pedestal) and weighing nearly 225 tons. Then come the real reasons for surviving the crowds: the **observation decks.** The first, a bit of a disappointment, is only at the top of the pedestal, to which you can take an elevator. Better yet, if you're in shape, climb the 354 steps (the equivalent of a 22-story building) to the crown. From there, just after you've caught your breath from the climb, you'll lose it again as you look out across the harbor and to the tip of Manhattan. And from there, the famed index finger measurement will have its impact.

Getting There: Ferries depart from Battery Park every 30 to 45 minutes 9:15am to 4:30pm. Tickets are for sale inside Castle Clinton, in Battery Park, and include transportation and entrance to both the Statue of Liberty and Ellis Island.

✪ **Ellis Island.** Located in New York Harbor. ☎ 212/363-7620 (general info), 212/269-5755 (ticket/ferry info). Ferry ticket/admission to Statue of Liberty and Ellis Island, $7 adults, $6 seniors, $3 children 3–17. Daily 9:30am–5pm; extended hours in summer. Subway to ticket booth: 4, 5 to Bowling Green; 1, 9 to South Ferry (the platform onto which you exit is shorter than the train, so ride in the first 5 cars).

More than 4 out of 10 Americans trace their ancestry to this spot. They would seem a forgetful lot, given the cries of outrage that today greet new immigrants. But back before political concerns blocked their way, 12 million newcomers sailed onto Ellis Island between 1892 and 1954. The statistics and their meaning are overwhelming, but the Immigration Museum skillfully relates the story of Ellis Island and immigration in America by putting the emphasis on personal experience.

Today you enter the Main Building's baggage room, just as the immigrants did, and then climb the stairs to the **Registry Room,** with its dramatic vaulted tiled ceiling, where millions waited anxiously for medical and legal processing. A step-by-step account of the immigrants' voyage is detailed in the **"Through America's Gate"** exhibit with haunting photos and touching oral histories. What might be the most poignant exhibit is **"Treasures from Home,"** 1,000 objects and photos donated by

Impressions

If you're bored in New York, it's your own fault.

—Myrna Loy

descendants of immigrants, including family heirlooms, religious articles, and rare clothing and jewelry. Outside, the **American Immigrant Wall of Honor** commemorates the names of more than 500,000 individuals and families, including George Washington's great-grandfather John Washington, John F. Kennedy's great-grandparents, Rudolph Valentino, Harry Houdini, and Marlene Dietrich.

Preservationists are hard at work repairing the southern end of the island, where immigrants too ill to enter the United States spent time on the hospital campus. This is where the country's public health services began.

In the last few years, New York and New Jersey engaged in petty skirmishes over who owns the island. It has been decided that New Jersey has sovereignty over most of it, though New York maintains ownership of the island's important sites. On the Jersey side, there's talk of building a hotel, a convention center, and a pedestrian bridge to the mainland. Isn't the point that Ellis Island is an island, that it's preserved so we can evince the same feelings the immigrants experienced, and we should leave it and its memories intact?

✪ **Staten Island Ferry.** Departs from the Staten Island Ferry Terminal at the southern tip of Manhattan. ☎ **212/487-8403.** Free. Hours vary seasonally, but it runs 24 hours daily every 20–30 min (less frequently late at night). Subway: 1, 9, N, R to South Ferry.

As this magical ride begins, the ferry loudly churns the foamy waters and tosses out from its old wood-piling–lined slip into New York Harbor. The spectacular city skyline rises and then recedes behind you. As the ferry passes the Statue of Liberty, you're rewarded with the same view immigrants early in this century and early in their American experience once had. It must have been an awesome sight; it still is.

You spot the expanse of the Verrazano Narrows Bridge as it spans its way from Brooklyn to Staten Island (remember the bridge from *Saturday Night Fever?* the bridge where the New York Marathon starts?), historic Governors Island, and the riverbanks of New Jersey (remember *On the Waterfront?*). In summer, it's a cool escape from the city's concrete. In more turbulent seasons, it's a moody venture onto a body of water that reminds you New York is an oceanside city. This wonderful alternative to sightseeing cruises is a commuter ship transporting residents of Staten Island to and from Manhattan Island, and the half-hour ride in each direction is free.

Two quibbles: I love the ferry so much, and have been taking it for so long, that I resented a recent ride on a new boat that was plastic, white, and all-enclosed, without decks. The only true Staten Island Ferry is made of wood and steel, is painted a yellowy orange, and has open decks all around for romantic snuggling or quiet contemplating on benches. And when will the city finally replace the scandalously dilapidated terminal on the Manhattan side? At least the Staten Island side has begun an innovative $100-million expansion of the St. George Ferry Terminal, which in 2000 will open a new home for the Institute of Art and Sciences alongside ferry operations.

2 Lower Manhattan's Stars: The Brooklyn Bridge, the Stock Exchange & the Seaport

For other area attractions, such as **Fraunces Tavern** and **Trinity Church,** see the other sections in this chapter.

✪ **Brooklyn Bridge.** Sidewalk entrance on Park Row. Subway: 4, 5, 6 to Brooklyn Bridge/City Hall.

This great span of Gothic-inspired stone pylons and intricate steel-cable webs has moved poets like Walt Whitman and Hart Crane to sing its body impressive. You can view it from afar and then, on the wood-plank pedestrian walkway elevated above the traffic, take a relatively peaceful walk. It provides a great vantage point from which to contemplate the New York skyline and the East River and a grand entry for a tour of Brooklyn Heights (see "Attractions in the Outer Boroughs" later in this chapter). You'll be surprised at the number of walkers and bikers who regularly cross the bridge, but it's best to promenade with a friend.

This massive engineering feat, designed by John Roebling, began to articulate its way across the East River in 1867. But the lovely structure, which would inspire so much affection, was plagued by death and disaster at its birth. Roebling was fatally injured in 1869 when a ferry rammed a waterfront piling on which he stood. His son, Washington, who was subsequently put in charge, contracted the bends in 1872 while working underwater to construct the bridge's towers. He oversaw the rest of the construction with a telescope from his bed at the edge of the East River in Brooklyn Heights. The final phase of construction was completed only as Washington's wife, Emily Warren Roebling, relayed his instructions to the workers. Washington refused to attend the 1883 opening ceremonies, having had a bitter disagreement with the company that financed the construction. On the day the bridge opened to the public, twelve pedestrians were killed in a stampede as a false rumor spread that it was about to collapse. Things are usually calmer now.

✪ **New York Stock Exchange.** 20 Broad St. (at Wall St.). ☎ **212/656-5165.** Free admission. Mon–Fri 9am–4:30pm. Subway: 2, 3, 4, 5 to Wall St.

Wall Street is a canyon from which the high-rises reach as far skyward as the dreams and greed of investors. But all the 9-to-5 activity in the Financial District won't seem like much unless you visit one awesome sight: the New York Stock Exchange, the world's largest securities trader, housed in a neoclassical building completed in 1903.

Surprisingly this symbol of the capital of capitalism has its main entry not on Wall Street, the main metaphor for the stock market, but on Broad Street. There, starting at 9am, you line up for free tickets (despite the number of visitors, things move pretty quickly). The highlight of the self-guided visit is the **observation gallery,** overlooking the deceptively calm trading floor where fortunes are fashioned or ravished with the flash of a hand signal. Try to be there for the ceremonial opening or closing bell. And also try to be there when the market goes into free fall—it won't seem so dull, especially if you're an investor. You can skip the video and the other exhibits along the way to the observation gallery, now lined in glass to prevent shenanigans like the yippies' tossing down dollar bills more than 20 years ago. There has been talk that the Stock Exchange would move, so get here soon.

South Street Seaport and Museum. Water St. to the East River between John St. and Peck Slip. ☎ **212/748-8600** (general info). Museum admission $6 adults, $5 seniors, $3 children. Museum, Apr–Sept daily 10am–6pm, Thurs to 8pm; Oct–Mar Wed–Sun 10am–5pm. Subway: 2, 3, 4, 5 to Fulton St.

South Street Seaport is a landmark district on the East River, encompassing 11 square blocks of historic buildings, a maritime museum, several piers, and restaurants and stores. You can explore most of the seaport on your own, but you'll need a ticket for the museum, whose galleries recount the district's history and whose holdings include the ships berthed at the pier (the 1911 four-masted *Peking* and the 1893 Gloucester fishing schooner *Lettie G. Howard,* among others). There are opportunities to cruise

Downtown Attractions

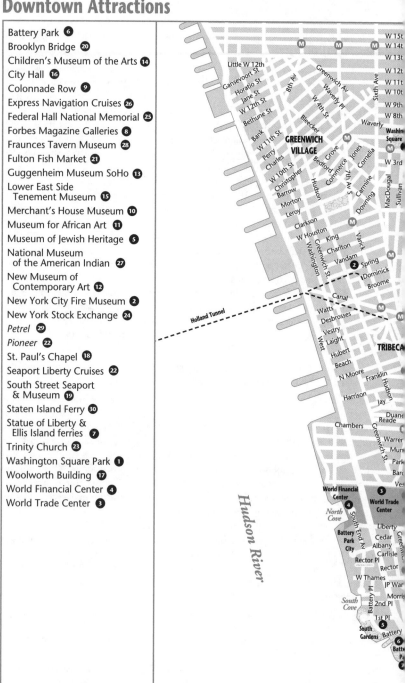

Battery Park ⑥
Brooklyn Bridge ⑳
Children's Museum of the Arts ⑭
City Hall ⑯
Colonnade Row ⑨
Express Navigation Cruises ㉖
Federal Hall National Memorial ㉕
Forbes Magazine Galleries ⑧
Fraunces Tavern Museum ㉘
Fulton Fish Market ㉑
Guggenheim Museum SoHo ⑬
Lower East Side
  Tenement Museum ⑮
Merchant's House Museum ⑩
Museum for African Art ⑪
Museum of Jewish Heritage ⑤
National Museum
  of the American Indian ㉗
New Museum of
  Contemporary Art ⑫
New York City Fire Museum ②
New York Stock Exchange ㉔
Petrel ㉙
Pioneer ㉒
St. Paul's Chapel ⑱
Seaport Liberty Cruises ㉒
South Street Seaport
  & Museum ⑲
Staten Island Ferry ㉚
Statue of Liberty &
  Ellis Island ferries ⑦
Trinity Church ㉓
Washington Square Park ①
Woolworth Building ⑰
World Financial Center ④
World Trade Center ③

NA-0151

172

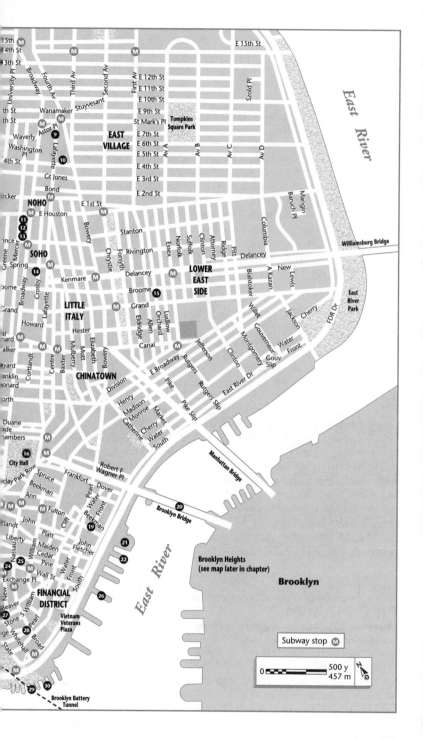

Impressions

All modern New York, heroic New York, started with the Brooklyn Bridge.
—Kenneth Clark

the river for an extra charge (see "Sightseeing Tours" later in this chapter) and a variety of events ranging from street performers and concerts to fireworks displays and outdoor ice-skating in winter (see "Staying Active" later in this chapter).

As you approach the **South Street Seaport Visitors' Center** at 12 Fulton St. to pick up a free map and guide, pause for a moment on the north side of the street. If you look back across the street, you'll note an intact row of early 19th-century buildings called **Schermerhorn Row.** These served as the counting houses for cargo unloaded on the docks at the foot of Fulton. Their upper floors are the loveliest part of the seaport. I wish that other buildings in the vicinity had been renovated with such care. However, most of the seaport is just mindlessly commercial; the stores on the ground floor of Schermerhorn Row are mostly what you'd find anywhere else. There's a relentless feeling that this is a place only to consume, not to encounter history. Of course, it would be fine to scatter stores and decent restaurants around, but they shouldn't prevent one from experiencing a unique place and moment in history. What a lost opportunity! Sure, the kids will be happy with a souvenir or another pair of baggy jeans or a cheap T-shirt, but wouldn't they have been better off with more? If you're interested in more, you might wander north of Fulton Street, along what look like rubble-strewn streets—there at least, though the buildings are mostly in ruin, you can imagine what should have been made of this place.

The one store that deserves a visit is the **Strand bookstore,** 95 Fulton St., a New York institution. As it does in its main location (Broadway and 12th Street), the Strand sells every kind of book, secondhand or review copies, for much less than the cover price (art tomes are an especially good buy).

Continue on Fulton and then cross South Street and head to the third level of **Pier 17**—bypassing all the suburban mall–style stores and bad fast-food restaurants—and go directly onto the deck overlooking the East River. You're finally out of some developer's consumerist nightmare and back in New York. The long wooden chairs will have you thinking about what it was like to cross the Atlantic on the *Normandie*. From this level you can see south to the Statue of Liberty and north to the Gothic majesty of the Brooklyn Bridge. Across the river is Brooklyn Heights, and just to the north of Pier 17 is the famous and infamous **Fulton Fish Market** (see "Only in New York" in chapter 9), the nation's largest wholesale fish market.

3 Museums & Art Galleries

THE TOP MUSEOMS

⭐ **Metropolitan Museum of Art.** Fifth Ave. at 82nd St. ☎ **212/535-7710.** Suggested admission (includes same-day entrance to the Cloisters) $8 adults, $4 seniors, children under 13 free. Tues–Thurs and Sun 9:30am–5:15pm, Fri–Sat 9:30am–8:45pm. No strollers allowed Sun. Subway: 4, 5, 6 to 86th St.

The Metropolitan Museum of Art, home of blockbuster after blockbuster exhibition, attracts more visitors than any other site in New York City. Some 5 million people a year pass through its collections—which range from deeply resonating Assyrian sculpture and the museum's justly famous Egyptian art and artifacts to classical Greek and Roman statuary; medieval treasures; Chinese vases; South and Southeast Asian and Pacific art; African art; works by the native peoples of North and South America; and

European paintings, sculpture, and decorative arts. Nearly the whole world's cultures are on display. And masterpieces from each of them are the rule.

Unless you plan on spending your entire vacation in its precincts, you cannot see all the museum. One good way to get an overview is to take advantage of the little-known **Highlights Tour.** Call ☎ **212/570-3791** to get a schedule of this and other tours (which visit specific aspects of the museum, such as the French impressionists). The least overwhelming way to see the Met on your own is to pick up a map at the round desk in the entry hall and choose specific areas you want to visit, since you certainly won't be able to see it all. You might choose 17th-century paintings, American furniture, or Egyptian mummies—there are all kinds of art and all kinds of interesting display spaces that include everything from parts of historic New York buildings to reconstructed Pompeii-era bedrooms.

The **American Wing** is bright and green, emerging so much like the New World from the fussy confines of the older European traditions surrounding it. It's a nice place to relax, especially in the peaceful **Garden Court** with its 19th-century sculpture (venture just off the court to see one of my favorites, the **Frank Lloyd Wright room**). The setting of the **Temple of Dendur** is dramatic, in a specially built glass-walled gallery with Central Park views. A newly renovated and expanded exhibit space opened in 1997 to house the museum's extensive collection of later **Chinese art.** The **Roman and Greek galleries** have also undergone changes, so if you, like I, are always dropping by to see Caligula, he has moved. If you prefer French impressionists, arms and armor, 18th-century American furniture, or African wood carvings, you can see them too. For reconstructed medieval architecture, head to the **Cloisters,** a branch of the Met in Uptown Manhattan (see "Other Museums" below).

Special exhibits and programs abound. For information on concerts and lectures, call ☎ **212/570-3949.** The museum contains several dining facilities, including the **20th-Century Sculpture Roof Garden** (where an espresso-and-wine bar is open May–Oct) and a **full-service restaurant** serving continental cuisine (☎ **212/570-3964** for reservations). The roof garden is worth visiting if you're here from spring to autumn—you'll have wide and peaceful views over Central Park and the city.

On Friday and Saturday the museum remains open late, not only for art viewing but also for dinner, socializing over cocktails, and music (see "Only in New York" in chapter 9).

✪ **Museum of Modern Art.** 11 W. 53rd St. (Fifth & Sixth aves.). ☎ **212/708-9400.** Admission $9.50 adults, $6.50 seniors/students, children under 16 free; Fri 4:30–8:30pm pay as you wish. Sat–Tues and Thurs 10:30am–6pm, Fri 10:30am–8:30pm. Subway: E, F to Fifth Ave./43rd St.

The Museum of Modern Art (MoMA, or "the Modern" as it's known to New Yorkers) boasts the world's greatest collection of 20th-century art, including everything from van Gogh (*The Starry Night*) and early Picasso (*Les Demoiselles d'Avignon*) to contemporary design. One of my favorite rooms contains the often-overlooked German expressionists. The crowd-pleasing galleries are dedicated to Matisse (*Dance* and *Goldfish*) and Monet (*Water Lilies*).

Setting course for the 21st century, the Modern has embarked on a major expansion that will attract worldwide attention and comparison to other recent museum projects, like Richard Meier's stunning Getty Center in Los Angeles and Frank Gehry's addition to the Guggenheim in Bilbao, Spain. Work isn't expected to begin for at least another year.

Japanese architect Yoshio Taniguchi will nearly double the exhibition space by adding a new eight-story building faced with glass, aluminum, and black slate. The existing building will be dramatically reconfigured—for example, the 53rd Street

On the Waterfront: Hudson River Rising

Pete Seeger, the ancient folk singer, has long been an ancient mariner on his sloop, the *Clearwater*. He has sailed the Hudson for years attempting to garner support for cleaning up one of New York's most vibrant waterways. He, and others like him, made great strides toward raising public consciousness. And now, there's even been public action.

The river is so clean that some intrepid volunteers at the **River Project,** a non-profit group that studies the Hudson and lobbies to make it safer for recreation, have been spotted swimming off Pier 26 at North Moore Street. Of course, the Hudson has a way to go before it's safe for in-water amusements (there are plans for a beach—a beach!—at the end of Ganesvoort Street).

In the meantime, an increasing number of activities are becoming available beside, on, and over the river. Wagner Park, at the southern end of Battery Park City, sponsors a **family fishing day** once a month and provides free equipment (call ☎ 212/267-9700 for information). **Sea kayaks** are available to the public at the Downtown Boathouse (no phone) on Pier 26 at the foot of North Moore Street. And Parasail New York (☎ 212/691-0055; $55 weekends, $45 week-days) tethers thrill seekers to a speedboat for a 10-minute, 400-foot-high **para-sailing** ascent with views of the Statue of Liberty, Ellis Island, and the rooftops of Wall Street. The company, operating out of the North Cove behind the World Financial Center, also rents **jetboats** and **sailboats.** Also operating at the North Cove is the Manhattan Sailing School, which is affiliated with the Manhattan Yacht Club and provides **sailing lessons** (☎ 212/786-0400 for information).

Over the coming years, as the river is cleaned up and the riverfront itself regains its rightful place as a stage for public recreation, you can expect to see many changes. For a hint of what's to come, head to **Chelsea Piers** (see p. 000). Soon that sports-and-entertainment facility will be within the ambitious **Hudson River Park** project. Plans call for parks, playgrounds, ball fields, and commercial spaces to stretch from the north end of Battery Park City, and thereby continue the wonderful greenbelting already paralleling the river is the way to West 59th Street. Off the drawing board and along the river is the first segment of a 3,300-foot **esplanade** between Clarkson and Horatio streets in Greenwich Village.

entrance will be restored but will no longer serve as main entry. Instead, visitors will arrive in a 110-foot-high **atrium** by way of 54th Street, passing through the **Sculpture Garden.** That natural oasis of sunlight, trees, fountains, and art will be central to the new design and restyled to conform to its original appearance as created by Philip Johnson (founding curator of the architecture department). The last renovation, in the 1980s, which added an escalator and large glass windows, led humorist Fran Lebowitz to quip that the Modern had evolved into a "kind of Bloomingdale's."

In the meantime, you can visit the Modern most effectively by taking the **self-guided tour** stopping at the collection's highlights, chosen by the different departments' curators. Hour-long family-oriented **gallery talks,** take place Saturdays at 10am.

The Modern is widely known for showing classic and foreign movies in the after-noon and evenings (free with admission). Every Friday night there's free jazz in the **Garden Café,** and in July and August sounds of the Summergarden concert series fill the Sculpture Garden (see "Only in New York" in chapter 9). There's also an Italian restaurant, **Sette MoMA** (☎ **212/708-9710**).

✪ American Museum of Natural History. Central Park West at 79th St. ☎ **212/ 769-5100.** Suggested admission $8 adults, $6 seniors, $4.50 children. Sun–Thurs 10am–5:45pm, Fri–Sat 10am–8:45pm. Subway: B, C to 81st St.; 1, 9 to 79th St.

Occupying a 4-block area, the American Museum of Natural History houses the world's greatest natural science collection in a group of buildings made in a mishmash of architectural styles: towers and turrets, pink granite and red brick. The diversity of the holdings is astounding: some 36 million specimens ranging from microscopic organisms to the world's largest cut gem, the Brazilian Princess Topaz (21,005 carats). If you don't have a lot of time, you can see the best of the best on daily **highlights tours** departing from the second-floor Hall of African Mammals at 10:15 and 11:15am and 1:15, 2:15, and 3:15pm.

The museum's fourth-floor dinosaur displays are the most popular exhibits, especially since recent restorations and redesign put new life in the old bones. Start in the **Orientation Room,** where an 11-minute video gives an overview of the 500 million years of evolutionary history that led to you. Continue to the **Vertebrate Origins Room,** where huge models of ancient fish and turtles hang overhead. Next come the great **dinosaur halls,** a favorite with kids not only for the mammoth and scary skeletons (my! what big teeth you have!) but also for the videos that suggest how the animals moved, the thought-provoking signs set at a kid's perspective 2 feet off the ground, and the motorized skulls simulating the way the creatures might have chewed their food. Two galleries showing **Mammals and Their Extinct Relatives** round out the fourth floor. The museum likes to boast that 85% of the exhibited fossils are the real thing, not reproductions.

Other favorites are the **animal habitat dioramas** (especially the African mammals), the **halls of minerals and gems,** and the **children's discovery room** with hands-on exhibits and experiments. A new exhibit, the **Hall of Biodiversity,** opened in 1998 to great acclaim. The museum has an **IMAX Theater** (☎ 212/769-5034; admission $12 adults, $8.50 seniors, $6.50 children, includes museum admission) showing such films as *Cosmic Voyage* on a four-story screen that gives you the impression you're taking part in the action. The museum's **Hayden Planetarium** closed in 1997 for demolition and reconstruction that should be completed in 2000.

One of my favorite family programs at the museum was under reconsideration as we went to press. So you'll need to call to find out if, on Friday and Saturday evenings, there's still a package deal that includes museum entrance, two films IMAX theater, and dinner in the museum restaurant at a great price (see "Only in New York" in chapter 9).

MUSEUM MILE

In 1978 ten of New York's finest cultural institutions located on Fifth Avenue from 82nd to 104th streets formed a consortium called **Museum Mile.** Today there are nine members (the YIVO Institute for Jewish Research moved first to 57th Street and is now part of the brand-new Center for Jewish History on 16th Street—see "Other Museums" below). One of the city's most popular cultural events is the **Museum Mile Festival,** a 1-day event every June when traffic halts and people wander down this part of Fifth unfettered by honking horns or slaloming taxis.

The "mile" begins at the **Metropolitan Museum of Art** (see "Top Museums" above) and moves north to **El Museo del Barrio.** Below is a list of the museums, which, for reasons of limited space, excludes two fine places: **Goethe House New York,** 1014 Fifth Ave., between 82nd and 83rd streets (☎ 212/439-8700), a German cultural center housed in a beaux arts town house, with changing exhibits, lectures, concerts, and the like; and the **National Academy Museum and School of Fine Arts** (formerly the National Academy of Design), 1083 Fifth Ave., at 89th Street (☎ 212/ 369-4880), which holds regular exhibits drawn from its collection, including 2,200 works by such artists as Mary Cassatt, Winslow Homer, and John Singer Sargent.

Cooper-Hewitt National Design Museum. 2 E. 91st St. (at Fifth Ave.). ☎ **212/849-8300.** Admission $5 adults, $3 seniors, children under 12 free; free Tues 5–9pm. Tues 10am–9pm, Wed–Sat 10am–5pm, Sun noon–5pm. Subway: 4, 5, 6 to 86th St.

The Cooper-Hewitt, part of the Smithsonian Institution, underwent an ambitious $20-million renovation and expansion in 1996 that gave the building a new entrance and a long-overdue refreshening. Some 11,000 square feet of gallery space is devoted to changing exhibits that are invariably well conceived, engaging, and educational. Many installations are drawn from its vast collection of industrial design, drawings, textiles, wall coverings, books, and prints.

The Cooper-Hewitt is housed in the Carnegie Mansion (1901), an unassuming little place of 64 rooms built by millionaire steel magnate Andrew Carnegie. This trifle was the first home in the city with an Otis elevator and central heating. On your way in, note the fabulous art nouveau–style copper-and-glass canopy above the entrance. Once inside be sure to visit the garden ringed with Central Park benches from various time periods.

El Museo del Barrio. 1230 Fifth Ave. (at 104th St.). ☎ **212/831-7272.** Suggested admission $4 adults, $2 seniors, children under 12 free. Wed–Sun 11am–5pm. Subway: 6 to 103rd St.

What started in 1969 with a small display in a local school classroom in East Harlem is today the only museum in America dedicated to Puerto Rican and Latin American art. The northernmost Museum Mile institution has a permanent exhibit ranging from pre-Columbian artifacts to historic photographs and handicrafts to a variety of paintings and sculpture. The display of *santos de palo*, wood-carved religious figurines, is especially worth noting. The National Latino Film and Video Festival opens the museum's fully renovated **Heckscher Theater** in early 1999.

International Center of Photography. 1130 Fifth Ave. (at 94th St.). ☎ **212/860-1777.** Admission $5.50 adults, $4 seniors, $1 children under 13; Tues 6–8pm pay what you wish. Tues 11am–8pm, Wed–Sun 11am–6pm. Subway: 6 to 96th St.

The International Center of Photography (ICP) is one of the world's premier collectors and exhibitors of this art form. Like its Midtown branch (see "Other Museums" below), ICP mounts changing exhibits that range from single-artist retrospectives to theme-oriented explorations and experimental contemporary installations.

The Jewish Museum. 1109 Fifth Ave. (at 92nd St.). ☎ **212/423-3230.** Admission $7 adults, $5 seniors, children under 12 free; Tues 5–8pm pay what you wish. Sun, Mon, Wed, Thurs 11am–5:45pm, Tues 11am–8pm. Subway: 4, 5, 6 to 86th St.

A recent major renovation and expansion of this Gothic-style mansion gave the Jewish Museum the world-class space it deserves to showcase its collections' remarkable scope of Jewish art, history, and culture. The excellent permanent installation **"Culture and Continuity: The Jewish Journey"** occupies two floors and traces the development of 4,000 years of Jewish experience. There are artifacts dating back so far you see the actual daily objects that might have served, in more quotidian moments, the authors of the books of Genesis and Psalms and Job. There's also a great collection of intricate Torahs and TV programs (as any fan of television's Golden Age knows, its finest comic moments were Jewish comedy). In addition, a variety of changing exhibits features works of art, antiquities, and ceremonial objects. The Design Shop sells works by contemporary Jewish artists and designers.

Museum of the City of New York. 1220 Fifth Ave. (at 103rd St.). ☎ **212/534-1672.** Suggested admission $5 adults, $4 seniors/children, $10 families. Wed–Sat 10am–5pm, Sun 1–5pm. Subway: 6 to 103rd St.

A wide variety of objects—including costumes, photographs, prints, maps, dioramas, and memorabilia—traces the history of New York City from its beginnings as a humble Dutch colony in the 16th century to its present-day prominence. Two outstanding permanent exhibits are the re-creation of John D. Rockefeller's master bedroom and dressing room and the space devoted to the history of New York theater. The permanent **"Furniture of Distinction, 1790–1890"** displays 33 elegant pieces representing New York's central role in American cabinetmaking that will have you eyeing your IKEA with new contempt. Kids will love **"New York Toy Stories,"** a recently inaugurated permanent exhibit showcasing toys and dolls owned and adored by centuries of New York children.

Solomon R. Guggenheim Museum. 1071 Fifth Ave. (at 88th St.). ☎ **212/423-3500.** Admission $12 adults, $7 seniors, children under 12 free; Fri 6–8pm pay what you wish. Two-museum pass, which includes one admission to the SoHo branch valid for 1 month, $16 adults, $10 seniors. Sun–Wed 10am–6pm, Fri–Sat 10am–8pm. Subway: 4, 5, 6 to 86th St.

It has been called a bun, a snail, a concrete tornado, and even a gigantic wedding cake tilted to one side, though I'm not quite sure what that last one means. Whatever descriptive you choose, Frank Lloyd Wright's only New York building, completed in 1959, is perhaps best summed up as assertively undeniable. It's a brilliant work of architecture, so consistently brilliant it competes with the art for your attention.

Inside, a spiraling rotunda circles over a slowly inclined ramp that leads you down and around from the sixth floor past changing exhibits. Permanent exhibits of 19th- and 20th-century art, including strong holdings of Kandinsky, Klee, Picasso, and French impressionists, occupy an annex called the **Tower Galleries** (a new addition that some wags claimed made the original look like a toilet bowl backed by a water tank—New Yorkers can be so kind).

The Guggenheim runs some interesting nighttime concerts and tours—see "Only in New York" in chapter 9. There's a **Downtown branch** in SoHo (see below).

OTHER MUSEUMS
LOWER MANHATTAN

Federal Hall National Memorial. 26 Wall St. (at Nassau St.). ☎ **212/825-6888.** Free admission. Oct to mid-June Mon–Fri 9am–5pm; mid-June to Sept daily 9am–5pm. Subway: 2, 3, 4, 5 to Wall St.

I find this building, while nicely historic, cold as a wintry Inauguration Day. In fact, this isn't really Federal Hall at all. That building, torn down more than a 100 years ago to be replaced by what you see, was the site of George Washington's inauguration as first president of the United States on April 30, 1789. On the steps outside the current memorial stands a stately bronze statue of perhaps the only president who could not tell a lie. The original Federal Hall served as the Capitol of the United States for just over a year, and it was there that Congress first met.

The present building is an odd amalgam: Greek Revival, with Doric columns of white Westchester marble on the outside, and Roman Revival with a rotunda on the inside. You want consistency, go to Levittown. It was constructed in 1842, after Federal Hall was destroyed, to serve as the U.S. Customs House. There are exhibits on

New York in 1789, Washington's inauguration ceremony, and the history of the site.

Fraunces Tavern Museum. 54 Pearl St. (at Broad St.). ☎ **212/425-1778.** Admission $2.50 adults, $1 seniors, children under 7 free. Mon–Fri 10am–4:45pm, Sat–Sun noon–4pm. Subway: 1, 9 to South Ferry; 4, 5 to Bowling Green.

Sure it's pretty, but it's fake. As with Federal Hall (above), the original building was torn down. This time, however, the replacement is an attempt to replicate the type of building that was here before, a Georgian house once home to one of New York's most cherished early hangouts, Fraunces Tavern. It's where George Washington gave his famous farewell speech to his officers on December 4, 1783. Before entering this 1907 not entirely faithful re-creation of James DeLancey's 1719 structure, stop to note the tall chimneys, slate-hipped roof, redbrick walls with stone trim, and doorway. They'll give you an idea of what fine American architecture from the period looked like. Inside, the ground floor has a **restaurant** (☎ 212/269-0144) high on atmospherics, and the second and third floors have a **museum** with two furnished period rooms, including an imitation Long Room (the space where Washington bid adieu).

Museum of Jewish Heritage—A Living Memorial to the Holocaust. 18 First Place (in Battery Park City). ☎ **212/968-1800.** Admission $7 adults, $5 seniors/students, children under 5 free. Sun–Wed 9am–5pm, Thurs 9am–8pm, Fri and evenings of Jewish holidays 9am–2pm. Subway: 1, 9 to Rector St.

The Museum of Jewish Heritage was dedicated in fall 1997, more than 50 years after the idea of such a museum was first proposed. Located in the south end of Battery Park City, it occupies a strikingly spare six-sided building, with a six-tier roof, that alludes to the Star of David and to the 6 million murdered in the Holocaust. The permanent exhibits—**"Early 20th-Century Jewish Life," "War Against the Jews,"** and **"Jewish Renewal"**—recount the daily lives, the unforgettable horror, and the tenacious renewal experienced by European and immigrant Jews in the years from the late 19th century to the present. Its power derives from the way it tells that story: through the objects, photographs, documents, and especially videotapes of individuals, including Holocaust victims, survivors, and their families. Perhaps the most important part of the collection is Steven Spielberg's **Survivors of the Shoah Visual History Foundation,** which provides many of the poignant first-person video narratives.

National Museum of the American Indian, George Gustav Heye Center. 1 Bowling Green (State & Whitehall sts.). ☎ **212/668-6624.** Free admission. Daily 10am–5pm (to 8pm Thurs). Subway: 1, 9 to South Ferry; 4, 5 to Bowling Green.

Under the aegis of the Smithsonian Institution, the National Museum of the American Indian opened in 1994 as new home to the collection of the former Museum of the American Indian. On display is a small yet fascinating selection of the 1 million objects and 86,000 photos assembled by George Gustav Heye over 54 years starting in 1903. The two on-premises stores have great and inexpensive gifts.

The museum is housed, incongruously, on two floors of the Alexander Hamilton U.S. Customs House, a National Historic Landmark and New York's finest example of beaux arts architecture. The 1907 building designed by Cass Gilbert is ringed with Corinthian columns, and the splendid facade flaunts monumental sculptures by Daniel Chester French representing Asia, America, Europe, and Africa.

The art and artifacts are splendid, dazzling in their colors, shapes, and materials. Seeing this museum's collection is reason enough to come to New York; it is *that* good. Yet there's something unfulfilling here. The art has been placed in "context," and my suspicions are that it's playing a secondary role to "political correctness." There are distracting video screens with voice-overs at every turn, no doubt to have Native Americans tell their own story. But you hear too many of them at once. And the logic of the layout is indecipherable. The paradox is that what has been drowned out in all this posturing is the poignant and joyful voice of the very individuals who created the art objects, which are often not even given the respect of an accompanying placard detailing the materials from which they were made. The art, and the people who created it, deserve better.

SoHo, Greenwich Village & the Flatiron District

Center for Jewish History. 17 W. 16th St. (Fifth & Sixth aves.). Phone, admission, and hours not determined at press time. Subway: L, N, R, 4, 5, 6 to 14th St./Union Sq.

Due to open this year, the Center for Jewish History will occupy a new $40-million four-building complex, part of which was once the Helen Keller Institute. The Center brings together four leading institutions of Jewish history: the **American Jewish Historical Society** (40 million documents and 30,000 books on Jewish Americana), the **Leo Baeck Institute** (documents, memoirs, and photos documenting German-speaking Jews), the **Yeshiva University Museum** (general-interest exhibits, plus a renowned collection of Judaica objects confiscated by the Nazis), and the **YIVO Institute for Jewish Research** (an academic institution concentrating on the civilization of Eastern European Jewry before the Holocaust). Besides offering a variety of public exhibits, the Center will feature a 250-seat auditorium and a kosher eatery.

Forbes Magazine Galleries. 62 Fifth Ave. (at 12th St.). ☎ **212/206-5548.** Free admission. Tues, Wed, Fri, Sat 10am–4pm. Subway: L, N, R, 4, 5, 6 to 14th St./Union Sq.

Though it has its charms, this strikes me as a museum-as-tax-writeoff. It was the private fiefdom of late publishing magnate Malcom Forbes and has objects of interest for the entire family, yours and his: Forbes's eccentric collection of hundreds of rare toy boats, rank upon rank of thousands of toy soldiers, Monopoly game boards, presidential papers and memorabilia, and Fabergé eggs and other *objets de luxe.* Personal anecdotes explain why certain objects attracted Forbes's attention and turn the collection into an oddly interesting biographical portrait.

Guggenheim Museum SoHo. 575 Broadway (at Prince St.). ☎ **212/423-3500.** Admission (includes entrance to the main Uptown branch) $15 adults, $10 seniors, children under 12 free. Wed–Fri and Sun 11am–6pm, Sat 11am–8pm. Subway: N, R to Prince St.

The Guggenheim SoHo reopened in 1996 after renovations that transformed this Downtown branch of the Solomon R. Guggenheim Museum into a futuresque space showcasing temporary installations of high-tech multimedia works. Expect to see trendy technology-inspired shows like one early exhibit, "Mediascape," an extravaganza of video and other electronic artworks by the genre's leaders: Nam June Paik (fascinating), Bill Viola (interesting), and Jenny Holzer (enough already!). In what might become an art-world trend, this was the first major New York museum to open corporately sponsored galleries. With the backing of Deutsche Telekom (a German telecommunications company) and ENEL (an Italian power company and computer developer), the new ground-floor rooms feature CD-ROM stations and interactive virtual-reality experiences. The museum as brand-extension space?

Museum for African Art. 593 Broadway (Prince & Houston sts.). ☎ **212/966-1313.** Admission $5 adults, $2.50 seniors/children. Tues–Fri 10:30am–5:30pm, Sat–Sun noon–6pm. Subway: N, R to Prince St.

This captivating museum has no permanent collection but is a leading organizer of temporary exhibits dedicated to traditional and contemporary African Art. One recent installation, "African Faces, African Figures: The Arman Collection," displayed masks

Midtown Attractions

NA-0152

182

and sculptures made by groups including the Mende, Fang, Kota, and Konga. The museum's interior was designed by Maya Lin, the architect best known for her Vietnam Veterans Memorial in Washington, D.C.

MIDTOWN

International Center of Photography Midtown. 1133 Sixth Ave. (at 43rd St.). ☎ **212/ 768-4680.** Admission $5.50 adults, $4 seniors, $1 children under 13; Tues 6–8pm pay what you wish. Tues 11am–8pm and Wed–Sun 11am–6pm. Subway: B, D, F, Q to 42nd St.

The Midtown branch of the International Center of Photography (see "Museum Mile" above for the main space) mounts some of the most interesting changing art exhibits in the city. The emphasis is on contemporary photographic works, but historically important photographers aren't ignored. Located so conveniently close to Times Square, it should be on the must-see list of any visitor.

Intrepid **Sea-Air-Space Museum.** Pier 86 (W. 46th St. at Twelfth Ave.). ☎ **212/245-0072.** Admission $10 adults; $7.50 veterans/seniors/students; $5 children 6–11; first child under 6 free, each extra child $1. May–Sept Mon–Sat 10am–5pm (last admission 4pm), Sun 10am–6pm (last admission 5pm); Oct–Apr Wed–Sun 10am–5pm (last admission 4pm). Subway: A, C, E to 42nd St. Bus: M42 crosstown.

Have you ever wondered how jet planes thunder onto ship decks without plunging off the other end? The answer is here at the U.S.S. *Intrepid*, a decommissioned aircraft carrier that proudly sports its World War II battle wounds. The world's largest naval museum is dedicated to the history of the U.S. Navy, aviation, and space and undersea exploration. Onboard are more than 40 aircraft, seemingly endless displays of memorabilia, and lots of skinny halls and winding staircases for kids and adults to wander. There are also daily guided tours of the destroyer *Edison,* the submarine *Growler,* and the lightship *Nantucket,* and exhibits like 1998's tribute to 200 years of naval service by African-Americans. The annual **Fleet Week** celebration in May brings an invasion of active ships and thousands of service personnel here. I love getting hold of the (unloaded) guns onboard and pretending to shoot down enemy aircraft as they careen overhead and strafe my position. I then return to my real life and my real enemies.

Japan Society. 333 E. 47th St. (First & Second aves.). ☎ **212/832-1155** (general info) or 212/752-0824 (recorded info). Suggested admission $3. Tues–Sun 11am–5pm. Subway: 6 to 51st St.; E, F to Lexington/Third aves. & 53rd St.

Housed in a striking modern building by Junzo Yoshimuro (1971), the U.S. headquarters of the Japan Society offers both art shows and courses that can teach you about the intricacies of an island culture that has had an impact on the world well beyond what its size would suggest. Years ago I had a friend who studied tea ceremony here. There's also a gallery where highly regarded exhibits of Japanese art are presented, renovated exhibition space, and a new show area that features changing displays whose subjects have included "Japanese Theater in the World." The Japan Society hosts a wide variety of lectures, films, concerts, and classes throughout the year.

Museum of Television and Radio. 25 W. 52nd St. (Fifth & Sixth aves.). ☎ **212/621-6800.** Admission $6 adults, $4 seniors, $3 children under 13. Tues–Sun noon–6pm (to 8pm Thurs). Subway: 1, 9 to 50th St.; N, R to 49th St.

With the TV industry's perpetual search for validation, this endlessly entertaining museum seems like destiny and a PR stunt rolled into one. Founded in 1975 by William S. Paley, former chairman of CBS, the space is a repository for more than 75,000 TV and radio programs and commercials spanning more than 7 decades. When you enter the Philip Johnson–designed limestone tower (1991), head to the **fourth-floor library,** where you can do a computer search for the program or com-

Did You Know?

You can find five sections of the **Berlin Wall,** graffiti intact, in a small park, behind 520 Madison Ave., on the north side of 53rd Street, between Madison and Fifth avenues.

mercial you want to watch on the individual consoles at which you control the playback. You can see virtually every famous TV moment—the Beatles' first appearance on *The Ed Sullivan Show,* Buzz Aldrin alighting on the moon, interviews with serial killer Ted Bundy, the falling of the Berlin Wall, and much more (from "Plop, plop, fizz, fizz" to Ed Murrow interviews). There are theaters for special screenings and several galleries with changing exhibits of art and artifacts relating to TV and radio.

Pierpont Morgan Library. 29 E. 36th St. (at Madison Ave.). ☎ **212/685-0610.** Suggested admission $6 adults, $4 seniors, children under 12 free. Tues–Fri 10:30am–5pm, Sat 10:30am–6pm, Sun noon–6pm. Subway: 6 to 33rd St.

This is an undiscovered New York treasure. The Morgan Library is a museum boasting one of the world's most important collections of medieval and Renaissance manuscripts, rare books and bindings, and master drawings rivaling any found in Europe. I could spend hours studying the intricate paintings that adorn early manuscripts, daydreaming about distracted monks sitting hour after hour at their desks. What *were* they thinking? This rich repository of Western civilization originated as the private collection of turn-of-the-century financier J. P. Morgan and is housed in the landmark Renaissance-style palazzo building (1906) he commissioned from McKim, Mead & White to hold his masterpieces.

THE UPPER EAST SIDE

Asia Society. 725 Park Ave. (at 70th St.). ☎ **212/517-ASIA.** Gallery admission $4 adults, $2 seniors, children under 13 free; free Thurs 6–8pm. Tues–Sat 11am–6pm (to 8pm Thurs), Sun noon–5pm. Subway: 6 to 68th St./Hunter College.

The Asia Society was founded in 1956 by John D. Rockefeller III with the goal of increasing understanding between Americans and Asians through art exhibits, lectures, films, performances, publications, and international conferences. The exhibits draw on a permanent collection of 285 masterpieces from throughout Asia donated by Rockefeller. The society is also a leader in presenting contemporary Asian and Asian-American art.

The Frick Collection. E. 70th St. (at Fifth Ave.). ☎ **212/288-0700.** Admission $5 adults, $3 seniors; children under 10 not admitted. Tues–Sat 10am–6pm, Sun 1–6pm. Subway: 6 to 68th St./Hunter College.

Henry Clay Frick could afford to be an avid collector of European art after amassing a fortune as a pioneer in the coke and steel industries at the turn of the century. To house his treasures and himself, he hired architects Carrère & Hastings to build this 18th-century-French–style mansion (1914), one of the most beautiful remaining on Fifth Avenue.

Most appealing about the Frick is its intimate size and setting. The interior still resembles a private home, not a museum. As you stroll from the **living hall** to the **library,** surrounded by masterpieces by Boucher, Titian, Bellini, Rembrandt, Vermeer, El Greco, and Goya, to mention only a few, it's easy to imagine what life on Millionaire's Row, as this stretch of Fifth was once known, must have been like. A highlight of the collection is the **Fragonard Room,** graced with the sensual rococo series

The Progress of Love. The portrait of Montesquiou by Whistler is stunning (an interesting story: Whistler gave his good friend this portrait, and Montesquiou in return gave the painter a lovely bed; a few years later Whistler was shocked to learn that his subject sold the painting for a tidy sum and never thought to offer the often-struggling artist *un sou*). Sculpture, furniture, Chinese vases, and French enamels complement the paintings and round out the collection.

Whitney Museum of American Art. 945 Madison Ave. (at 75th St.). ☎ **212/570-3676.** Admission $8 adults, $7 seniors, children under 12 free; free Thurs 6–8pm. Wed and Fri–Sun 11am–6pm, Thurs 11am–8pm. Subway: 6 to 77th St.

What is arguably the finest collection of 20th-century American art in the world belongs to the Whitney thanks to the efforts of Gertrude Vanderbilt Whitney. A sculptor herself, she organized exhibitions by American artists shunned by traditional academies, assembled a sizable personal collection, and founded the museum in 1930 in Greenwich Village.

Today's museum is an imposing presence on Madison Avenue—an inverted three-tiered pyramid of concrete and gray granite with seven seemingly random windows designed by Marcel Breuer (1966), a leading member of the Bauhaus group. The permanent collection consists of an intelligent selection of major works by Edward Hopper, George Bellows, Georgia O'Keeffe, Roy Lichtenstein, Jasper Johns, and other significant artists. A brand-new fifth-floor exhibit space, the museum's first devoted exclusively to works from its permanent collection, opened in 1998. There are usually several simultaneous shows, ranging from historical surveys to in-depth retrospectives. The Whitney's most important exhibit, the **Biennial,** is an invitational show of work produced in America during the preceding 2 years. It can cause a ruckus, especially among the more conservative members of the art-critique brigade, but even when the Biennial is bad or boring (and I've seen many cases of both) it still manages to be provocative in some sense. The next Biennial is this Spring.

A Midtown branch, the **Whitney Museum of American Art at Philip Morris,** 120 Park Ave., opposite Grand Central Terminal (☎ 212/878-2550; admission free), features an airy sculpture court, a small gallery for changing exhibits of 20th-century American art, and free hour-long gallery talks Wednesdays and Fridays at 1pm.

THE UPPER WEST SIDE & WASHINGTON HEIGHTS

The Cloisters. At the north end of Fort Tryon Park. ☎ **212/923-3700.** Suggested admission (includes entrance to the Metropolitan Museum of Art) $8 adults, $4 seniors, children under 13 free. Nov–Feb Tues–Sun 9:30am–4:45pm; Mar–Oct Tues–Sun 9:30am–5:15pm. Subway: A to 190th St. Bus: Madison Ave. no. 4.

I come here ven I vant to be alone. Nearly at the very northern tip of Manhattan, the Cloisters is the Metropolitan Museum's branch for medieval art. If its extraordinary collection of tapestries (the famed Unicorn series), sculpture, illuminated manuscripts, stained glass, ivory, and precious metalwork doesn't entice you, the setting will. The building incorporates actual 12th- to 15th-century cloisters from five medieval monasteries, a Romanesque chapel, and a 12th-century Spanish apse. Fort Tryon Park offers landscaped terraces, footpaths, flower gardens, and superb views of the towering Palisades across the Hudson River.

Museum of American Folk Art. 2 Lincoln Sq. (Columbus Ave. between 65th & 66th sts.). ☎ **212/595-9533.** Free admission. Tues–Sun 11:30am–7:30pm. Subway: 1, 9 to 66th St.

This museum, founded in 1961, has a wide range of works from the 18th century to the present reflecting the breadth and vitality of the folk-art field. The textiles collection is the museum's most popular, highlighted by a splendid variety of quilts. Also on

A Celluloid Moment

There are so many streets and sites that recall **movie scenes** in this town, you couldn't get them all in unless you were writing an encyclopedia. For the best celluloid overview, try Woody Allen's *Hannah and Her Sisters,* in which he gives us, via Sam Waterston, a wonderful tour of city highlights (leaving out the Empire State Building; even Woody, as Mia Farrow would no doubt agree, can make a mistake).

One unforgettable Manhattan movie moment, an icon in modern times, took place at the northwest corner of 52nd Street and Lexington Avenue: Above a subway grating—there's still one there—a great white dress billowed up on the fine young form of Marilyn Monroe. Isn't New York delicious?

---

display are whimsical whirligigs, cigar-store Indians, engaging paintings, and a variety of decorative arts. The gift shop is filled with one-of-a-kind objects and has a second location at 62 W. 50th St.

In 1998, the museum started construction on its new larger home on West 53rd Street, just down the block from the Museum of Modern Art. The new building, four times larger than the current space and promising to be nearly as significant an addition to the Midtown skyline as the redesign of the Modern, is scheduled to open in spring 2000.

New-York Historical Society. 2 W. 77th St. (at Central Park West). ☎ **212/873-3400.** Admission $5 adults, $3 seniors/children. Tues–Sun noon–5pm. Subway: B, C to 81st St.; 1, 9 to 79th St.

Woe is this poor museum! Important and a necessary part of the city's cultural landscape, it has been rocked by scandal, threats of permanent closure, and financial difficulties. But it seems to have found its footing and its funding.

The New-York Historical Society, launched in 1804, is a major repository of American history, material culture, and art with a special focus on the New York region. The grand neoclassical edifice is finally undergoing major renovations, expected to be complete in early 2000, that will transform the fourth floor into a state-of-the-art study facility and gallery displaying highlights from the fine- and decorative-arts collections.

In the meantime, you can see an ambitious schedule of temporary exhibits, such as "The History of the New York City Police" (through March 1999). On the second floor, a small selection of Tiffany lamps is on display, and paintings from Hudson River School artists Thomas Cole, Asher Durand, and Frederic Church, and others hang in the Luman Reed Gallery. Free tours are given daily at 1 and 3pm.

ART GALLERIES

The biggest news in the art gallery world has been the decreasing importance of SoHo as the capital of contemporary art. Major showrooms have moved either Uptown or to far West Chelsea. Mary Boone left SoHo and took space several years back Uptown on Fifth Avenue, and though she wasn't the first to decamp, her reputation as a dealer in some of America's most important contemporary success stories (Ross Bleckner, Eric Fischl, Malcolm Morley) made the move particularly noteworthy. SoHo, once nearly exclusively home to the most adventurous galleries, has seen its cutting-edge reputation increasingly dulled by the arrival of mall-like chain stores and galleries that are more properly called poster shops. Even before Boone made her move, other gallery owners, escaping not only the neighborhood's decreasing claim to be Trend Central but also its rising rents, began an exodus to Manhattan's newest art spot: West 21st to 26th streets, between 10th and 11th avenues, in Chelsea.

Uptown Attractions

NA-0153

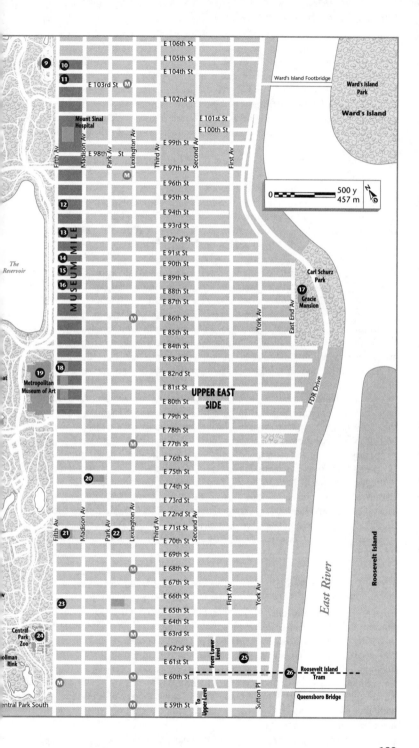

All this motion and commotion only serves to underline that Manhattan is the undisputed capital of art—and art sales. The island has more than 500 private art galleries, selling everything from old masters to contemporary flashes-in-the-pan. Galleries are open free to the public, so gallery-hopping, particularly on Saturday afternoons, is a favorite pastime. The best way to winnow down your choices is by perusing the Friday and Sunday *New York Times, New York* magazine, or *The New Yorker.* Then decide between doing the Uptown or Downtown galleries.

Uptown galleries are clustered in and around the glamorous crossroads of Fifth Avenue and 57th Street as well as on and off stylish Madison Avenue in the 60s, 70s, and 80s. Despite the dust-up over Chelsea as a new art center, the Uptown galleries maintain their quiet white-glove demeanor. Sharing those streets with neighbors who are the most affluent collectors are all kinds of blue-chip galleries, including not only old-time residents like Knoedler but also some new dealers. These include **Mitchell-Innes & Nash,** 1018 Madison Ave. (☎ **212/744-7400**); **Richard Gray,** 1018 Madison Ave. (☎ **212/472-8787**); **Winston Wachter Fine Art,** 39 E. 78th St. (☎ **212/327-2526**); and **James Danziger,** 851 Madison Ave. (☎ **212/734-5300**), a dealer in fine photographs who left SoHo after 8 years. There was talk at press time of a new **"art mall,"** at 1016 Madison Ave., where dealers would rent showrooms when they had nowhere else to exhibit.

Downtown, SoHo does remain colorful, if less edgy than it used to be, just south of Houston Street, north of Chinatown, and centered on West Broadway. In far West Chelsea, north and south of West 23rd Street and mostly between Tenth and Eleventh avenues, are a number of galleries (most well-known: Paula Cooper, Morris Healy, Matthew Marks, Barbara Gladstone, Bonin Alexander), often in the large open spaces of former garages and abandoned warehouses.

Although Uptown tends to be more traditional and Downtown more contemporary, there are constant surprises in both neighborhoods (and while I include below the names of artists or art periods in which these dealers usually trade, that can change with the whims of the creators or the market). Several important dealers showing contemporary painting and sculpture have galleries in more than one location: **Gagosian** (works by Francesco Clemente, Howard Hodgkin, David Salle, Mark di Suvero) is at 980 Madison Ave. (☎ **212/744-2313**) and 136 Wooster St. (☎ **212/228-2828**); **PaceWildenstein** (Jim Dine, Lucas Samaras, Julian Schnabel, Kiki Smith, as well as Picasso and Henry Moore) is at 32 E. 57th St. (☎ **212/421-3292**) and 142 Greene St. (☎ **212/431-9224**); and **Leo Castelli** (Jasper Johns, Roy Lichtenstein, James Rosenquist) is at 420 W. Broadway (☎ **212/431-5160**) and 578 Broadway (☎ **212/941-9855**).

Here are other major galleries:

UPTOWN **Mary Boone,** 745 Fifth Ave. (☎ **212/752-2929**); **Hirschl & Adler,** 21 E. 70th St. (☎ **212/535-8810**), 18th- to 20th-century European and American painting; **Leonard Hutton,** 41 E. 57th St. (☎ **212/751-7373**), German expressionism, Italian futurism, Russian constructivism; **Kennedy,** 730 Fifth Ave. (☎ **212/541-9600**), 18th- to 20th-century American painting; **Knoedler,** 19 E. 70th St. (☎ **212/794-0550**), Helen Frankenthaler, Nancy Graves, David Smith, Frank Stella; **Marlborough,** 40 W. 57th St. (☎ **212/541-4900**), Fernando Botero, Red Grooms, Alex Katz; **Spanierman,** 45 E. 58th St. (☎ **212/832-0208**), 19th- to early 20th-century American, Mary Cassatt, Childe Hassam, Winslow Homer; **Wildenstein,** affiliated with PaceWildenstein, 19 E. 64th St. (☎ **212/879-0500**), old master and Renaissance paintings and drawings.

DOWNTOWN **O. K. Harris,** 383 W. Broadway (☎ **212/431-3600**), a wide and fascinating variety of contemporary painting, sculpture, and photography, including a while back offerings from one of my contemporary favorites, subtle and refined works by Joanne Mattera; **Louis K. Meisel,** 141 Prince St. (☎ 212/677-1340), photo-realism and other contemporary works; **Holly Solomon,** 172 Mercer St. (☎ 212/941-5777), video art by Nam June Paik, mixed-media pieces, works by emerging artists; **Paula Cooper,** 534 W. 21st St. (☎ 212/255-1105), diverse contemporary works; **Morris Healey,** 530 W. 22nd St. (☎ 212/243-3753), diverse contemporary works; and other dealers in contemporary art, like **Matthew Marks,** 522 W. 22nd St. (☎ 212/243-1650), **Barbara Gladstone,** 515 W. 24th St. (☎ 212/206-9300), and **Alexander & Bonin,** 132 Tenth Ave. (☎ 212/367-7474).

AUCTION HOUSES

Don't overlook the two great auction houses, especially in May and November, when the impressionist and modern art sales, preceded by a week of free public exhibitions, take place. Both **Christie's,** 502 Park Ave. (☎ 212/546-1000), and **Sotheby's,** 1334 York Ave. (☎ 212/606-7000), have talked about moving, and Christie's even purchased space at 20 Rockefeller Center to which, word was, it would relocate but then had second thoughts; call ahead.

4 New York Architectural Icons

For more highlights on high-rises, see "Seeing Beyond the Icons & the Neon" and "Story Time: The History of the High-Rise" in chapter 1.

THE TOP BUILDINGS

✪ **Empire State Building.** Fifth Ave. at 34th St. ☎ 212/736-3100. Observatory admission $6 adults, $3 seniors/children under 12, children under 5 free. Daily 9:30am–midnight (tickets sold until 11:30pm). Subway: B, D, F, Q, N, R to 34th St.; 6 to 33rd St.

The Empire State Building (1931) is the Manhattan skyscraper par excellence with its graceful proportions, fabulous setbacks, and distinctive pinnacle, a glinting beacon in the night. It's an elegantly elongated ziggurat. Original plans had the building topping out at 86 floors, but one of its developers insisted on adding a mast for mooring dirigibles, making for 102 floors. One such airship successfully moored for 3 minutes, but this use of the skyscraper's tip stopped after the second attempt resulted in ballast water from an airship drenching pedestrians several stories down and several blocks away. The mast, now topped by a radio tower, was where airplanes buzzed and murdered King Kong as he, a modern Quasimodo, professed his love for his Esmeralda, played by the writhing and wide-eyed Fay Wray.

Today, the colorful antics atop the structure continue with a lighting scheme that marks the changing seasons or various events. Sometimes the Empire State Building's upper floors are bathed in red, white, and blue (on the Fourth of July or Memorial Day, for instance); sometimes in orange (Halloween); sometimes in lavender (Gay Pride Day); other times in blue (once in a commercial celebration of the release of the new blue M&M), white, or yellow.

An interesting aside about the efficiency of the good old days: The iron framework and exterior walls of limestone and polished steel were completed in only 410 days.

There are two **observation decks** where 2.5 million visitors a year gaze awestruck down on Manhattan spread at their feet. The 86th-floor observatory, at 1,050 feet, has

Impressions

It's the nearest thing to heaven we have in New York.
—Deborah Kerr to Cary Grant in *An Affair to Remember*
(about the Empire State Building)

a glass-enclosed area, but you should head outside into the bracing wind on the terrace (take a pocketful of quarters for the high-power binoculars). The 102nd-floor observatory, at 1,250 feet, is entirely glass-enclosed.

Vertigo sufferers should visit the Empire State Building for its beautiful three-story-high **lobby** lined with imported marble. Two virtual-reality movie attractions Disney-up the place. The high-tech seats at **Transporter** (☎ **212/947-4299;** daily 9am–11pm; admission $8.50 adults, $6.50 children) simulate bumps and turns as thrill-seekers explore the world of aliens or dinosaurs. The **JVC New York Skyride** (☎ **888/SKYRIDE;** daily 10am–10pm; admission $11.50 adults, $9.50 children) provides a fake, but safe, helicopter tour of Manhattan.

✪ **Chrysler Building.** 405 Lexington Ave. (at 42nd St.). Subway: 4, 5, 6, 7, S to 42nd St./Grand Central.

The Chrysler Building (1930) is perhaps the 20th century's most romantic architectural achievement, especially at night, when the lights in its triangular openings play off its steely crown. A recent cleaning added new sparkle.

There's a fascinating tale behind this building. While it was under construction, its architect, William Van Alen, hid his final plans for the spire that now tops it. Working at a furious pace in the last days of construction, the workers assembled in secrecy the elegant pointy top—and then they raised it right through what people had assumed was going to be the roof, and for one brief moment it was the world's tallest tower (a distinction stolen by the Empire State Building only a few months later). Its exterior chrome sculptures are magnificent and spooky. Its lavish ground-floor interior is art deco to the max. The ceiling mural depicting airplanes and other early marvels of the first decades of the 20th century evince the bright promise of technology at the time, before World War II, the Holocaust, the atomic bomb, ozone-layer depletion, and other perversions cast a shadow of doubt on our notion of "advancement." The elevators are works of art, masterfully covered in exotic woods (especially note the lotus-shaped marquetry on the doors). Although the observation deck closed long ago, developers have tossed around plans to turn the upper floors into a luxury hotel.

✪ **Grand Central Terminal.** 42nd St. at Park Ave. Subway: 4, 5, 6, 7, S to 42nd St./Grand Central.

After more than 2 years and $175 million, Grand Central Terminal, designed by Warren and Wetmore as well as Reed and Stem (1903–13), has emerged from its bravura renovation. Grand Central is reborn as one of the most magnificent spaces in the country. The work has reanimated the genius of the station's original intent: to inspire those who pass through this urban meeting point with lofty feelings of civic pride and appreciation for Western architectural traditions.

The greatest visual impact comes when you enter the vast **main concourse.** Cleaned of all the intrusive signs and advertisements, it boasts renewed majesty. The high windows again allow shafts of light to penetrate the space. The masterful **vaulted ceiling,** again a brilliant greenish blue, depicts the constellations of the winter sky above New York. They're lit with 59 stars, surrounded by dazzling 24-karat-gold and emitting light fed through fiber-optic cables, their differing intensities roughly replicating the magnitude of the actual stars as seen from Earth. A tiny patch near the northwest corner was left unrestored as a useful reminder of the neglect once visited on this masterpiece.

Under this firmament pass nearly 500,000 souls a day, 30,000 of them commuters dashing after their trains. So the grandeur elevates what is in essence nothing more than a transportation hub, providing a splendid stage scrim that hides miles of tracks humming with trains, electric power facilities, and endless support systems for water and sewers—a city within a city. Now that only commuters use Grand Central (it serves Metro North, Amtrak having moved to Penn Station), you have to imagine the role once played by trains in this country. Pause to hear the ghosts of the resounding voices that would call out all the stops of the 20th Century Limited and the Empire State Express and remind passengers "All aboard!"

Yet even as the commuters rush off to Connecticut and upstate communities, this dramatic beaux arts splendor serves as a hub of social activity as well. New retail and dining attractions that respect the integrity of the building's design abound—for examples of the latter, see "Dining Zone: Grand Central Terminal" in chapter 6. The **lower concourse** houses several stores, newsstands, and a food court offering everything from designer pizza to costly caviar. Retailers include Banana Republic, Kenneth Cole, and a Rite Aid drugstore.

On the east end of the main concourse, a grand **marble staircase** has been constructed, as the original plans had intended. The long-isolated **balcony** now boasts restaurants and shops.

Grand Central refuses to be intimated by the massive towers that have gone up all around it. To see its superb facade, you must descend Park Avenue to 40th Street. Then glance up at the restrained elegance of its frontal elevation: Mercury, attended by Minerva and Hercules, announces his presence by spreading his arms over the city, triumphant nearly 100 years after he first alighted here.

✪ **Rockefeller Center.** In the area bounded by 48th and 51st sts. from Fifth Ave. to Sixth Ave. ☎ **212/632-3975.** Subway: B, D, F, Q to 47th–50th sts./Rockefeller Center.

An art deco masterpiece of architecture and sculpture, Rockefeller Center boasts foyers, facades, and gardens showcasing works by more than 40 artists. It's one of the central gathering spots for visitors and New Yorkers alike. Note especially the wonderful reliefs and mosaics adorning nearly every door. There are also bronze sculptures (many by Paul Manship) and famous murals like *American Progress* and *Time,* by José Marie Sert, in the black marble lobby of the **GE Building,** 30 Rockefeller Plaza, a towering 70-story showpiece (the **Rainbow Room**—see chapter 6—is ensconced on high). A walking tour brochure highlighting the center's art and architecture is available at the main information desk in the GE Building.

The most dazzling work of art at Rockefeller Center is the interior of **Radio City Music Hall,** 1260 Sixth Ave., at 50th Street. Designed by Donald Deskey, it's one of the largest indoor theaters, with 6,200 seats. But its true grandeur derives from the stage's great proscenium arch, which from the distant seats evokes a faraway sun setting on the horizon of the sea (this is in keeping with deco aesthetics that were often inspired by the grand ocean liners of the time). The men's and women's lounges are splendid. I advise you to take the illuminating 1-hour **backstage tour** (☎ **212/632-4041;** Mon–Sat 10am–5pm and Sun 11am–5pm; $13.75 adults, $9 children under 13), which includes a delightful encounter with a Rockette as she limbers up at the barre. For information about **performances**—everything from the Easter and Christmas extravaganzas to pop-music superstars—call ☎ **212/247-4777** and see "Major Concert Halls & Landmark Venues" in chapter 9.

For a dramatic approach to the entire complex, start at Fifth Avenue between 49th and 50th streets. The builders purposely created the gentle slope of the **Promenade**—known here as the **Channel Gardens** because it's flanked to the south by La Maison Française and to the north by the British Building (the Channel, get it?)—to draw pedestrians into its embrace. The granite pools and seasonal garden display on the ground are just a hint of something as rare in Midtown as emeralds: On nearly every one of the center's setbacks, on rooftops you can't see from the street, are lovely landscaped gardens. The Promenade leads to the Lower Plaza, where there's an ice-skating rink in winter or outdoor dining in warm weather in the shadow of the gilded bronze statue of *Prometheus* (again by Paul Manship and more attractive for its setting than for its taste). All around the flags of the United Nations' member countries flap in the breeze. Just behind *Prometheus,* in December and early January, towers the city's official and majestic Christmas tree.

Underground on the **Concourse** levels are more than 2 miles of public passageways, flanked in beautiful white marble and lined with stores and restaurants. If you're a fan of NBC's *Today Show,* the glass-enclosed studio from which the show is broadcast live 7 to 9am is on the southwest corner of 49th Street and Rockefeller Plaza (bring your HI MOM! signs). **NBC Studio tours** (☎ 212/664-4000) leave every 30 minutes 9:30am to 4:30pm, Monday to Saturday (Sunday in summer), from the GE Building lobby and cost $10 (no children under 6).

Rockefeller Center, designated a National Historic Landmark in 1988, is the world's largest privately owned business-and-entertainment center, with 18 buildings on 21 acres; it was originally planned as a civic center with a new theater for the Metropolitan Opera Company on the central portion of the plot, where Prometheus now bears his flaming plunder from the gods. But soon after John D. Rockefeller Jr. agreed to lease the land from Columbia University in October 1928, the Great Depression and legal difficulties forced the city's main opera company to pull out of its commitment, leaving Rockefeller with a long-term annual lease of $3.8 million. In a sign of madness or dogged persistence, Rockefeller elected to build anyway as the nation's economy collapsed around him. More than 60 years later, this architectural wonder stands as a reminder that the city's developers can create triumphant buildings even in times of woe. So few have the vision—the guts?—anymore. Proposals last year to renovate Rockefeller Center, which include changes to the Fifth Avenue facades, were met with substantial resistance by preservationists. Look for less radical changes to spiff up this high-end real estate.

✪ **World Trade Center.** Bounded by Church, Vesey, Liberty, and West sts. ☎ **212/ 435-4170.** Subway: C, E to World Trade Center; 1, 9, N, R to Cortlandt St.

The World Trade Center, opened in 1970, is an immense complex of seven buildings on 16 acres that comprise offices, restaurants, a Marriott, an underground shopping mall, and an outdoor plaza with fountains, sculpture, and summer concerts and performances.

But the most famous tenants of all are the **Twin Towers,** each 1,350 feet high at 110 floors, with the **observation deck** atop Two World Trade Center, the southernmost of the gigantic geometric boxes. Privatized and refurbished in 1997, the observation deck now sports the name **Top of the World** (☎ 212/323-2340; open daily 9:30am– 9:30pm, to 11:30pm in summer; admission $12 adults, $9 seniors, $6 children). On the 107th floor, it's like a mini theme park, offering (besides the views and on days where clouds block the views) a 6-minute simulated helicopter tour over Manhattan, high-tech kiosks, a food court modeled after a subway car, and a nighttime light show.

I love to go right up to the windows that reach down to the floor. *Scaaary.* If that view isn't enough, head up and outside to the **rooftop promenade,** the world's highest open-air observation deck. While you're there, look straight down and wonder what Frenchman Philippe Petit could've been thinking when in August 1974 he shot a rope across to tower no. 1, grabbed his balancing pole, and walked gingerly across, stopping to lie down for a moment in the center.

For a pampered experience, make dinner reservations well in advance at **Windows on the World** (☎ 212/524-7000) or stop for a cocktail at the **Greatest Bar on Earth,** on the 107th floor of One World Trade Center (see chapter 6 for details).

The Twin Towers are significant not only for their size but also for their revolutionary design, which substituted older traditions for the techniques of high-rise building. The outside walls of conventional skyscrapers are virtually hung off structural steel supports, but the Twin Towers' exterior walls, made of closely spaced vertical columns, are load bearing. The only interior columns hold the elevators.

✪ **United Nations.** At First Ave. and 46th St. ☎ **212/963-7713.** Guided tours $7.50 adults, $5.50 seniors, $4.50 students, $3.50 children (under 5 not permitted). Daily tours every 30 min. 9:15am–4:45pm, except weekends Jan–Feb. Subway: 4, 5, 6, 7, S to 42nd St./Grand Central.

U.N. headquarters occupies 18 acres of international territory—neither New York City nor the United States has jurisdiction here—along the East River from 42nd to 48th streets. The complex, completed in 1952, was designed by an international team of architects led by American Wallace K. Harrison; among them was Frenchman Le Corbusier (note the great glass slab of the Secretariat Building, an early high-rise in New York, and the General Assembly building's quirky curved roof punctuated by a jaunty dome). **Guided 1-hour tours** take you to the General Assembly Hall and the Security Council Chamber and introduce the history and activities of the United Nations and its related organizations. Along the tour you'll see donated objects and artwork, including charred artifacts that survived the atomic bombs at Hiroshima and Nagasaki, stained-glass windows by Chagall, a replica of the first *Sputnik,* and a colorful mosaic called *The Golden Rule* based on a Norman Rockwell drawing, which was a gift from the United States in 1985.

If you take the time to wander the beautifully landscaped **grounds,** you'll be rewarded with lovely views and some surprises. The mammoth monument *Good Defeats Evil,* donated by the Soviet Union in 1990, fashioned a contemporary St. George slaying a dragon from parts of a Russian ballistic missile and an American Pershing missile.

The **Delegates' Dining Room** (☎ 212/963-7625), which affords great views of the East River, is open to the public on weekdays for lunch 11:30am to 2:30pm (reserve in advance). The **gift shop** sells flags and unusual handcrafted items from all over the world, and the **post office** sells unique United Nations stamps that can be purchased and posted only here.

OTHER BUILDINGS
LOWER MANHATTAN

City Hall. In City Hall Park, between Broadway and Park Row. Subway: 4, 5, 6 to Brooklyn Bridge/City Hall.

The small but important nerve center for the world's greatest city is appropriately housed in a great architectural treasure, designed by Joseph Mangin and John McComb Jr. (1802–11), an elegant French Renaissance and Georgian-style building set in a park. Its facade lined with rows of long windows is Alabama veined limestone that replaced the original marble and brownstone in a 1954 restoration. The cupola has the first illuminated public clock, installed in 1831, and is topped with a sculpture of Justice. Interior features include the colonnaded rotunda with a beautiful circular staircase; the Governor's Room, displaying historic paintings by John Trumbull and memorabilia such as the writing table used by George Washington; and the ornate meeting room for the city council, which is open to the public even when the council is in session.

Woolworth Building. 233 Broadway (at Park Place). Subway: 4, 5, 6 to Brooklyn Bridge/ City Hall.

When the Woolworth Building, designed by Cass Gilbert, was dedicated in 1913, President Wilson pushed a button in Washington to illuminate the structure's 80,000 bulbs. It was for 17 years the world's tallest (729 feet), until the Chrysler and Empire State buildings came along. Dubbed the "Cathedral of Commerce," the neo-Gothic Woolworth Building has a gilded crown surrounded by flying buttresses and pinnacles, all best viewed from New York Harbor. The opulent interior has blue, green, and gold mosaic vaulted ceilings sparkling over golden marble walls, polished terrazzo floors, and an elaborate marble staircase. An amusing series of sculptures atop the interior columns represents people involved in the building's construction and includes a portrait of the architect as well as a caricature of Mr. Woolworth clutching his nickels and dimes, an appropriate image of the man who paid $15.5 million in cash for its construction. It was sold last year by Venator, the oddly named successor company to Woolworth, for $155 million.

MIDTOWN

Flatiron Building. 175 Fifth Ave. (at 23rd St.). Subway: R to 23rd St.

A triangular masterpiece, fronted with limestone and terra-cotta, the Flatiron Building was one of the city's first skyscrapers and remains one of its best. It has such visual power that nearly every great photographer, from Alfred Stieglitz, Edward Steichen, and Berenice Abbott to Ernst Haas and Joel Meyerowitz, has captured its moods and contours. For more, see the entry on the Flatiron District under "Neighborhoods of Note" below and "Story Time: The History of the High-Rise" in chapter 1.

Ford Foundation Building. 320 E. 43rd St. (at Second Ave.). Subway: 4, 5, 6, 7, S to 42nd St./Grand Central.

On your way to or from the United Nations, stop in the Ford Foundation Building's magnificent interior garden. The ⅓-acre landscape thrives with a small pond, shrubbery and greenery, and full-grown trees rising up under the 12-story glass-enclosed greenhouse. This is a fine example of what modern public spaces should be like.

New York Public Library. Fifth Ave. and 42nd St. ☎ **212/869-8089** (exhibits/events) or 212/661-7220 (library hours). Main Reading Room, Mon and Thurs–Sat 10am–6pm, Tues–Wed 11am–6pm. Subway: B, D, F, Q to 42nd St.; 4, 5, 6, 7, S to Grand Central/42nd St.

The New York Public Library, designed by Carrère & Hastings (1911), is one of the country's finest examples of beaux arts architecture, a majestic structure of white Vermont marble with Corinthian columns and allegorical statues. Before climbing the broad flight of steps to the Fifth Avenue entrance, take note of the famous lion sculptures, Fortitude on the right, Patience on the left—so dubbed by former mayor Fiorello La Guardia (in a political joke?). In winter they don natty wreaths to keep warm. The interior is one of the finest in the city and features **Astor Hall,** with high arched marble ceilings and grand staircases. The stupendous **Main Reading Rooms** should reopen by or in 1999 following a restoration to bring back their stately glory.

The **Center for Humanities** (housed in this building) together with the three other major research libraries (**Performing Arts** at Lincoln Center, **Schomburg Center for Research in Black Culture** in Harlem, and the brand-new high-tech **Science, Industry, and Business Library** at 34th Street and Madison Avenue) and 82 branches form the world's most comprehensive library system. Free guided tours run Monday to Saturday at 11am and 2pm. The main branch of the library hosts a variety of exhibits that often feature rare books and prints from its holdings.

Park Avenue Modern

In the glass-and-steel ravines of Midtown East is a series of postwar masterpieces, alongside more classic New York buildings, that deserve special mention.

The **Seagram Building** (1958), on the east side of Park Avenue from 52nd to 53rd streets, is renowned for its sedate, nearly classical proportions. Stand across the Park and compare this quiet wonder, by Bauhaus guru Ludwig Mies van der Rohe, to its neighbors to the north and south. You'll see that not all high-rises are equal.

Directly across from the Seagram, on the west side of the Park, is a superb work by McKim, Mead & White, the **Raquet and Tennis Club** (1918). In the firm's telltale palazzo style, it's one more elegant reminder that above the modern intrusions of the ground-floor renovations are antique wonders.

On the West side of Park on the corner of 53rd and 54th streets, is **Lever House** (1952), an outstandingly graceful modern work of art. It was the first Park Avenue "glass-box"—but it's a glass box with grace and distinction.

Imagine how Park Avenue and all the city once looked by studying again the Raquet and Tennis Club. An earlier New York was closed in, austere, the streetscape fronted by stern stone facades, Then, suddenly what must've seemed out of nowhere, Skidmore, Owings and Merrill, dropped Lever house, a prism of light, a reflective jewel, right in the middle of all the masonry. What a breath of fresh air! Especially for those who've come to regret the boxy, uninspired modern descendants of Lever House and the Seagram Building, these two show that architecture in our time can be as exalted and invigorating as that from any period.

5 Neighborhoods of Note

For more on the areas below and on other neighborhoods you might like to stroll, see "Neighborhoods in Brief" in chapter 4 and "Seeing Beyond the Icons & the Neon" in chapter 1. For the highlights of Harlem and its environs, see "Attractions in Upper Manhattan: Harlem & Its Neighbors" later in this chapter.

TIMES SQUARE

Dazzlingly lit and pulsating with endless energy, ✪ **Times Square,** at the juncture of Broadway and Seventh Avenue, north of 42nd Street, is a triangular madhouse that draws nearly every visitor who sets foot on this island.

When people call Times Square the "crossroads of the world," they don't underestimate the power of its colossally tacky but somehow energizing neon lights, rushing crowds, souvenir shops, bars, restaurants, and hotels. What anchors it and makes it more than just an unreal and surreal destination is the huge collection of theaters that sit mostly on the side streets and stage some of the world's best drama, musical theater, and other performances.

As nearly everyone in America knows by now, Times Square has become the focus of a redevelopment project in the last few years, with everything from the latest Disney theater (the New Amsterdam) to a Disney Store, a Virgin Megastore, a Warner Bros. store, theme restaurants, and other crowd-grabbing spots (like ABC TV studios at 43rd Street and a glass-walled MTV studio between 44th and 45th Streets). It's changing so quickly that even in a daily newspaper you couldn't capture its transformations.

Impressions

On the new Times Square: I'm opposed to the redevelopment. I think there should be one neighborhood in New York where tourists are afraid to walk.

—Fran Lebowitz

I like it here in New York. I like the idea of having to keep eyes in the back of your head all the time.

—John Cale

Where else but New York could you have the simulated tourist version of a city within the urban core itself? Once this area was the lap of venal New York, where we gave vent to certain secret passions, and now it's the den of family New York, where children, their parents, local theatergoers, and most especially corporate sponsors feel safely at home. Recently, at nearly midnight, a friend and I found ourselves stopped and watching the huge TV screen at One Times Square as if we were cozily ensconced in our own private castle. We wouldn't have done that 10 years ago!

For more on the ever-changing Times Square, see the box "The Themes Are the Message" and the Midtown West section in chapter 6.

BATTERY PARK CITY

Who would've thought that landfill, especially in a time of so much mediocre building in New York, would result in one of the great contemporary treasures and best riverfront neighborhoods? ✪ **Battery Park City's** wonderful acres of green front the Hudson River. Though some feel uneasy about its well-groomed mien, I love the grassy esplanades; the World Financial Center's Winter Garden (where native American palms stripe the air in a bold geometry); the North Cove, where yachts and small sailboats bob side by side; and the garden near the southern end, one of New York's best landscape designs. Its latest features are Wagner Park, which completes the link of Battery Park City to Battery Park itself, and the Holocaust museum (see "Museums & Art Galleries" earlier in this chapter). The well-planned nature, interspersed with good architecture and sculpture, adds to the bargain of great views of the Hudson River, the Statue of Liberty, Ellis Island, and New York Harbor.

CHINATOWN

South of Canal Street, from Broadway to East Broadway, ✪ **Chinatown** is New York's most famous ethnic enclave. Chinatown has been squeezed so tightly by its traditional boundaries that for years its lovely and, to most people, indecipherable signs have been invading Little Italy and the Lower East Side. Good, sometimes great, inexpensive restaurants are the main draw, and they're concentrated between the Bowery and Baxter Street (see "Only in New York" in chapter 6). Take time to explore the narrow, bustling streets lined with fish and vegetable markets, Buddhist shrines, curiosity shops, and stores with exotic teas, sometimes as expensive as an emperor's ransom.

SOHO

Once a lovely but abandoned mass of 19th-century manufacturing lofts, ✪ **SoHo,** *so*uth of *Ho*uston and north of Canal Street between Lafayette Street and Sixth Avenue, was colonized by artists who moved into the well-lit large spaces in the 1960s and early 1970s. The buildings, especially along Greene Street, are fabulously preserved cast-iron works of art, an unsurpassed collection of a high point in American architecture. Full now of boutiques, galleries, restaurants, and an ever-increasing number of mall-like stores, SoHo is a major destination in Manhattan, though much of what made it special, what gave it its arty edge, is threatened by its very popularity. For more on SoHo, see "Neighborhoods in Brief" in chapter 4. For a look at its better art galleries, see "Art Galleries" earlier in this chapter. And for its shopping scene, see "What's New & Hot in SoHo" in chapter 8.

GREENWICH VILLAGE

From Broadway west to the Hudson River and from Houston Street to 14th Street, ✪ **Greenwich Village** is a crooked patch of land and low-rises that seems a world apart from the rest of Manhattan. Reputed for its motley mix of artists, writers, students, gays and lesbians, and all kinds of nonconformists, the historic neighborhood is supremely charming and bourgeois, too, especially Washington Mews, MacDougal Alley, and the quiet winding streets west of Seventh Avenue (in particular, Bedford and Commerce streets and St. Luke's Place—no. 10 served as the fictional exterior for the Huxtables' town house on *The Cosby Show* and the whole row was the fictional address of Audrey Hepburn in the marvelous shocker *Wait Until Dark*). Throughout the Village, there's an endless variety of small restaurants and shops, neighborhood bars, sidewalk cafes, world-famous jazz clubs, and Off Broadway theaters.

FLATIRON DISTRICT

A historic gem of a nearly intact 19th-century neighborhood, the ✪ **Flatiron District**—from 14th to 23rd streets and Park Avenue South to Sixth Avenue, named for the triangular early skyscraper that holds pride of place at 23rd and Fifth—survives because it was abandoned. Since no corporate desire to build contemporary high-rises ever threatened the area, the lovely, often cast-iron, and frequently heroic buildings along Broadway, Fifth, and Sixth maintain their integrity. The Flatiron District, along with its neighbor to the east, Gramercy Park, has become one of the city's top neighborhoods for boutiques (Armani, Paul Smith, agnès b.—see chapter 8), restaurants (especially along Union Square Park and Park Avenue South—see chapter 6), nightclubs (see chapter 9), large stores (especially along Broadway and Sixth—see chapter 8), and its wonderful Greenmarket, where regional farmers sell fresh produce, flowers, and baked goods (Mon, Wed, Fri, and Sat at Union Square Park East and 16th Street).

The ground floors have often been mutilated, so to see the true nature of the architecture, keep your eyes at and above the second floor. In what was once Ladies' Mile along Broadway, where well-to-do ladies would shop under parasols and plumed hats, is the perfect example: the former Arnold Constable Dry Goods Store at 19th Street, stretching from Broadway to Fifth. On the ground floor, callous glazed bricks destroy what is above—a fabulous fantasy of cast-iron and marble, with a dauntless mansard roof. Across Broadway is a picturesque brick daydream, where Gorham Silver once sold its wares. To admire another fine building, stand at the northeast corner of Broadway and 20th and look to the southwest corner. Recently renovated (admirably on the upper floors, garishly on the ground floor), this effervescent cast-iron knockout was once the site of Lord & Taylor. On the other side of Broadway, on the southeast corner of 20th, note the rounded front (inspired by the Flatiron's curves?) of McKim, Mead & White's Goelet Building, a polychromatic checkerboard of brickwork.

Many other fine works of architecture, along Broadway and Fifth and west to Sixth Avenue, provide a civilized home to shops and restaurants. I highly recommend an attentive and acquisitive walk in the neighborhood. For more, see "Neighborhoods in Brief" in chapter 4. For details on the Flatiron Building itself, see "Story Time: The History of the High-Rise" in chapter 1 and "New York Architectural Icons" earlier in this chapter.

6 Central Park & the Bronx Zoo

✪ **Central Park.** 59th to 110th sts. from Fifth Ave. to Central Park West. ☎ **212/794-6564** (Dairy Visitor & Information Center) or 212/360-3444 (recorded events info). Subway to main southern entrances: N, R to Fifth Ave.; A, B, C, D, 1, 9 to Columbus Circle/59th St.

No, this isn't what New York looked like before all the buildings went up. It's about as natural as a beehive hairdo—coiffed from nature's strands but positively a product of human intervention. Except for some of the 450-million-year-old schist jutting to the surface, people planted the trees, dug the lakes, and cultivated the gardens that seem so successfully natural. Central Park is as much architecture as the rest of the city, the difference being that frazzled New Yorkers come to the park's greener constructions to escape that other architecture. Indeed, on weekends the park explodes with energy as New Yorkers heed the urban-generated obsession for getting back to nature—or at least as close to nature as we can get.

What I like about Central Park is that it allows you to choose from its two aspects. There are peaceful havens for bucolic retreat or frenetic meeting grounds with as much theater as any Midtown street. Most visitors are amazed, if not run down, by the cyclists and in-line skaters who zoom through the park's drives on weekends, when they're closed to traffic. Throughout you find impromptu concerts, storytelling for kids; families of many species in the zoo; and odd groupings of folk dancers, dog walkers, berry hunters, sun worshipers, bird-watchers, bongo bangers, and other sometimes incomprehensible fraternities and sororities.

This 843-acre public playground was begun in 1858, after Frederick Law Olmsted and Calvert Vaux's Greenward Plan won the competition to create a park out of the tract of land purchased by the city in 1856 for $5 million. Various communities, including one of African Americans, lived here back when it was the countryside.

The best way to see Central Park is to wander aimlessly along the 58 miles of winding pedestrian paths, keeping in mind the following highlights. (Even though the park has the lowest crime rate of any of the city's precincts, be wary, especially in the more remote northern end, and avoid most of the park after sunset.) If you prefer to have a guide, the **urban park rangers** (☎ **888-NYPARKS** or 212/988-4952) offer free walking tours, as do companies listed in "Sightseeing Tours" later in this chapter.

Before starting your stroll, stop by the **Information Center** in the **Dairy,** midpark at about 65th Street, for more information on sights and events and an exhibit on park history and design. The events and activities in Central Park are endless. For information on theater, opera, and the like, see chapter 9. For details on sports, see "Staying Active" later in this chapter.

The southern part of Central Park is more formally designed and heavily visited than the relatively rugged and remote northern end. Not far from the Dairy is the **carousel** with 58 hand-carved horses, the **zoo** (see the separate entry below), and the **Wollman Rink** for roller- or ice-skating (☎ **212/396-1010**). The **Mall,** a long formal walkway lined with elms shading benches and sculptures of sometimes forgotten writers, leads to the focal point of Central Park, **Bethesda Fountain** (along the 72nd Street Transverse). The fountain's terrace and grandly sculpted entryway border a large **lake** where dogs fetch sticks, rowboaters romantically glide by, and dedicated early-morning anglers try their luck at catching carp, perch, catfish, and bass (large-mouthed, of course, this is New York). You can rent a rowboat at or take a gondola ride from **Loeb Boathouse** (☎ **212/517-2233**), on the eastern end of the lake. Boats of another kind are at **Conservatory Water** (on the east side at 73rd Street), a stone water basin where on Saturdays at 10am die-hard yachtsmen race remote-controlled sailboats in fierce competitions following Olympic regulations. (Model boats aren't for rent.)

If the action there is too intense, **Sheep Meadow** on the southwestern side of the park is a designated quiet zone, where Frisbee throwing and kite flying are as energetic as things get. Another respite is **Strawberry Fields,** at 72nd Street on the West Side. This is a memorial to John Lennon, who wrote "Strawberry Fields Forever" and was murdered across the street at the Dakota apartment building (72nd Street and Central Park West, northwest corner). In keeping with its goal of promoting world peace, the garden has 161 varieties of plants, donated by each of the 161 nations in existence when it was designed in 1985, and a lovely mosaic made in Italy with the word *Imagine* in its center.

Bow Bridge, a graceful lacework of cast-iron designed by Calvert Vaux, crosses over the lake and leads to the most bucolic area of Central Park, the **Ramble.** This dense 38-acre woodland with spiraling paths, rocky outcroppings, and a stream is the best spot for bird-watching and feeling as if you've discovered an unimaginably leafy forest right in the middle of the city (but because it's so isolated, don't wander there alone; at or after dusk, there tends to be much shaking of the bushes caused by members of your own species).

North of the Ramble, **Belvedere Castle** is home to the Henry Luce Nature Observatory (☎ **212/772-0210**), worth a visit if you're with children. From the Castle set on Vista Rock, the park's highest point at 135 feet, you can look down on the **Great Lawn,** which has emerged lush and green from renovations, and the **Delacorte Theater,** home to Shakespeare in the Park (see "The New York Shakespeare Festival" in chapter 9). The small **Shakespeare Garden** south of the theater is scruffy, but it does have plants, herbs, trees, and other bits of greenery mentioned by the playwright.

At the northeast end, **Conservatory Garden** (at 105th Street and Fifth Avenue), Central Park's only formal garden, is a magnificent display of flowers and trees reflected in calm pools of water. (The garden's gates once fronted the Fifth Avenue mansion of Cornelius Vanderbilt II.) **Harlem Meer** and its boathouse were recently renovated and now berths the **Dana Discovery Center** (☎ **212/860-1370**), where children learn about the environment and borrow fishing poles at no charge.

There are two main restaurants in the park, **Tavern on the Green** and **Park View at the Boathouse** (see chapter 6). Throughout its acres of green, you'll also find food carts selling hot dogs, pretzels, and other such snacks.

At the entrance to the park at 59th Street and Central Park South, you'll see a line of forlorn **horse-drawn carriages** waiting to take passengers on a ride, and often for a ride, through the park or along certain of the city's streets. Horses belong on city streets as much as chamber pots belong in our homes. I receive regular complaints from readers on this method of tourism. If you insist, a ride is at least $35 for two people and will likely last less than the quoted half hour (often only 15 minutes, and some of that time the horse may actually stop to feed from a bucket). Instead, I suggest you ride a horse from the Claremont Riding Academy (see "Staying Active" later in this chapter).

✪ **Bronx Zoo/Wildlife Conservation Park.** Fordham Rd. and Bronx River Pkwy., the Bronx. ☎ **718/367-1010**. Admission Nov–Mar $3 adults, $1.50 seniors/children under 12, under 2 free; Apr–Oct $6.75 adults, $3 seniors/children under 12, under 2 free; free Wed year-round. Nov–Mar daily 10am–4:30pm; Apr–Oct Mon–Fri 10am–5pm, Sat–Sun 10am–5:30pm. Transportation: See below.

While there are all kinds of nice things to see here, get me to the **House of Darkness**—where bats career their creepy little ways through the air. You'll be so glad there's a glass wall.

Founded in 1899, the Bronx Zoo is the largest metropolitan animal park in the United States, with more than 4,000 nonhumans living on 265 acres. Most of the old-fashioned cages have been replaced by more natural settings. One of the most impressive is the **Wild Asia Complex.** This zoo-within-a-zoo comprises the **Wild Asia Plaza** education center; **Jungle World,** an indoor re-creation of Asian forests with birds, lizards, gibbons, and leopards; and the **Bengali Express Monorail** (open Apr–Oct; $2 admission), which takes you on a narrated ride high above free-roaming Siberian tigers, Asian elephants, Indian rhinoceroses, and other non–native New Yorkers (keep your eyes peeled—the animals aren't as interested in seeing you).

You don't have to undertake a Peter Matthiessen–style journey to catch a glimpse of the beautiful and extremely rare (estimates indicate fewer than 1,000 in nature) snow leopard. The Bronx Zoo, where 74 cubs have been born, has re-created a **Himalayan Highlands Habitat** that's home to some 17 snow leopards, as well as red pandas and white-naped cranes.

The **Children's Zoo** (open Apr–Oct; $2 admission, children under 2 free) allows young humans to learn about their wildlife counterparts. Kids can compare their leaps to those of a bullfrog, slide into a turtle shell, climb into a heron's nest, see with the eyes of an owl, and hear with the acute ears of a fennec fox. There's also a farmlike area were children feed domestic animals.

A popular recent exhibit, open from spring to September, has been the **Butterfly Zone,** aflutter with 1,000 colorful specimens flying all around you inside a 170-foot-long tent—amusingly resembling a caterpillar. Call ahead to check if it will be around when you get to the zoo.

If the natural settings and breeding programs aren't enough to keep zoo residents entertained, they can always choose to ogle the 2 million annual visitors.

Getting There: The easiest way to get to the Bronx Zoo is by Liberty Line's B11 express bus running from various stops on Madison Avenue to the park entrance. The one-way fare is $4 (exact change required, bills accepted). Call ☎ **718/652-8400** for a schedule. By subway, take the no. 2 train to Pelham Parkway and walk 2 blocks west.

Central Park Zoo/Wildlife Conservation Center. Near the park entrance at Fifth Ave. and E. 64th St. ☎ **212/861-6030.** Admission $3.50 adults, $1.25 seniors, 50¢ children 3–12, under 3 free. Mon–Fri 10am–5pm, Sat–Sun 10:30am–5:30pm. Subway: N, R to Fifth Ave.

It has been nearly a decade since the zoo in Central Park was renovated, making it in the process both more human and more humane. Lithe sea lions frolic in the central pool area with beguiling style. The gigantic but graceful polar bears (one of whom, by the way, made himself a true New Yorker when he began regular visits with a shrink) glide back and forth across a watery pool that has glass walls through which you can observe very large paws doing very smooth strokes. The outdoor monkeys seem to regard those on the other side of the fence with great, and sometimes rude, disdain. In the hot and humid Tropical Zone, large colorful birds swoop around in freedom, sometimes landing next to nonplussed visitors.

In fall 1997, the $6-million **Tisch Children's Zoo** opened, delighting toddlers and preschoolers, even if some of their parents bemoaned the removal of Jonah the Whale, Noah's Ark, and other beloved structures they remembered from the original 1961 children's zoo. In their new playground, children gambol among frogs, turtles, sheep, and Vietnamese potbellied pigs.

Central Park Attractions

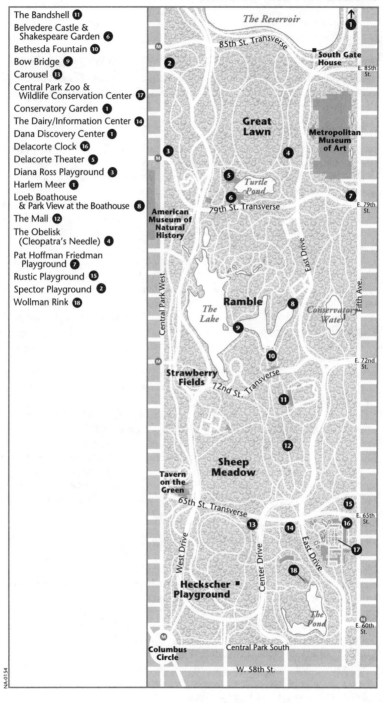

The Bandshell **11**

Belvedere Castle & Shakespeare Garden **6**

Bethesda Fountain **10**

Bow Bridge **9**

Carousel **13**

Central Park Zoo & Wildlife Conservation Center **17**

Conservatory Garden **1**

The Dairy/Information Center **14**

Dana Discovery Center **1**

Delacorte Clock **16**

Delacorte Theater **5**

Diana Ross Playground **3**

Harlem Meer **1**

Loeb Boathouse & Park View at the Boathouse **8**

The Mall **12**

The Obelisk (Cleopatra's Needle) **4**

Pat Hoffman Friedman Playground **7**

Rustic Playground **15**

Spector Playground **2**

Wollman Rink **18**

NA-0154

Though not as massive as the Bronx Zoo, nor as distant, the Central Park Zoo is, as Paul Simon once had it, "a gas."

7 Other Parks

For parks in Brooklyn and Queens, see "Attractions in the Outer Boroughs" later in this chapter.

BATTERY PARK

From State Street to New York Harbor, **Battery Park** is the departure point for ferries heading to the Statue of Liberty and Ellis Island.

I love this park because it sits so grandly adjacent to the incredibly high skyline of Lower Manhattan. The promenade, often fragrant with breezes blowing in from the sea, provides a grand vista across the harbor and out to Governors Island, Staten Island, the Statue of Liberty, Ellis Island, and beyond to the rhythmic span of the Verrazano Narrows Bridge, just near where the Atlantic Ocean begins. Much of the park is landfill, since Manhattan used to stop at about State Street. Nonetheless, Battery Park, named for the nearby guns that once protected the harbor, provides a perfect place to contemplate history.

Hundreds of years ago, the confluence of great bodies of water—the Atlantic Ocean on the other side of the New York Bay, the Hudson River leading upstate and inland, and the East River skirting around Long Island and back out to sea—led to one of the great confluences of cultures. The first European to spot this pleasant bay was Giovanni da Verrazano, an Italian sailing for France's François I in 1524 (he named the area Angoulême, after François's hometown). Though others might have come after him, it wasn't until Henry Hudson turned his *Half Moon* into the harbor in 1609 that any white man ventured for long here. Hudson sailed up the Hudson, to where Albany now mars the banks.

I like to stand at Battery Park and imagine what the Native Americans were thinking as they watched Hudson sail what must have seemed a gigantic, billowing vision into their homeland, where they had lived, archaeologists say, since at least 8,000 B.C. By 1625, the purpose of these pale-skinned invaders became clear when the Dutch established the first permanent settlement just beyond Battery Park. The Dutch and then English town eventually stretched up to Wall Street (there was a wall to keep out the Indians), and its influence and descendants spread all the way to California.

BRYANT PARK

Bryant Park is behind the New York Public Library, at Sixth Avenue between 40th and 42nd streets. This site has had a varied history, serving as hunting grounds for Native Americans before and during colonial times, the location of the city's fresh water supply from 1842 to 1911 behind 50-foot-high stone walls (the Croton Reservoir), and home to the Crystal Palace Exhibition in 1853. In 1894 it was named Bryant Park in honor of William Cullen Bryant; an imposing statue of the editor of the *New York Evening Post* is at the east end, right behind the back wall of the New York Public Library. Another statue is notable: a squat and evocative stone portrait of Gertrude Stein, one of the few outdoor sculptures of women in the city.

A recent major renovation of the park has made it one of the most tasteful green spaces in the city (it resembles nothing so much as a Parisian park), with summertime concerts and movies. Underneath the great lawn a two-story structure houses some 85 miles of shelves holding books from the New York Public Library. Midtown's haven of green is a favorite fair-weather lunch spot, whether you brown-bag it or charge it at the Bryant Park Grill (see chapter 6 for restaurant details).

UNION SQUARE PARK

Proving that there is some civility left in the city, **Union Square Park**—from 14th to 17th streets, between Park Avenue South and Union Square West—was taken back from drug dealers and derelicts years ago and turned into a superb urban asset as home to Manhattan's largest farmers' market on Monday, Wednesday, Friday, and Saturday. The seemingly endless subway work should no longer be disturbing the park's aesthetics when you get here, and this patch of green remains, with or without the construction, the focal point of the newly fashionable Flatiron and Gramercy Park neighborhoods. There are plans to extend the park's green boundaries out onto some of the surrounding concrete. Don't miss the grand equestrian statue of George Washington (Henry Kirke Brown and John Quincy Adams Ward) at the south end or, my favorite outdoor sculpture in New York, the bronze statue (by Bartholdi, the sculptor of the Statue of Liberty) of the marquis de Lafayette at the eastern end, gracefully glancing toward France. For a quick walking tour of the Flatiron District, see "Neighborhoods of Note" earlier in the chapter.

WASHINGTON SQUARE PARK

On warm summer days and early evenings, **Washington Square Park,** at the southern end of Fifth Avenue, becomes the central activity hub of Greenwich Village (see "Neighborhoods of Note" earlier in this chapter), animated by street musicians, acrobats, New York University students, people-watchers, and masters of chess and of the ancient and complex Chinese game of Go (don't take any of them up on their offers of a friendly contest; you'll lose money). The lively scene belies a macabre past. Once marshland traversed by Minetta Brook, it became in 1797 a potter's field (most green and fertile Downtown parks were originally graveyards), and the remains of some 10,000 bodies are buried here. In the early 1800s the square, or more specifically the infamous Hanging Elm in the northwest corner where MacDougal Street meets the park, was used for public executions. It wasn't until the 1830s that the elegant Greek Revival town houses on Washington Square North known as "The Row" (note especially nos. 21–26) attracted the elite. Stanford White designed Washington Arch (1891–92) to commemorate the centenary of George Washington's inauguration as first president. While in the neighborhood, peek down charming MacDougal Alley and Washington Mews, both lined with former carriage houses.

8 Historic Houses

New York's voracious appetite for change often means that older residential architecture is torn down so that money-earning high-rises can go up in its place. Surprisingly, however, this city maintains a truly fine collection of often overlooked historic houses that are more than a tale of architecture—they're the stories of the people who passed their lives in buildings that range from humble to overreaching.

The **Historic House Trust of New York City** preserves 18 houses, located in all five boroughs, and the Little Red Lighthouse (under the George Washington Bridge and famous from Hildegarde Swift's children's tale). A brochure listing their locations is available by calling ☎ **212/360-8282,** and recorded information on the houses and special events is available at ☎ **212/360-3448.** You can visit the buildings in the list below, interiors often true to the period.

Literary Landmarks

Since its earliest days, New York has been a magnet for writers. Perhaps no other city contributed as much to literary freedom as did New York when its courts ruled in 1753 that **John Peter Zenger** had not libeled then–colonial governor William Cosby, establishing the basis for the Constitution's First Amendment. (One wonders if those who today so often cite the Founding Fathers as exemplars of wisdom would grant the same freedom of the press in our own time.) By the early 19th century, the **Knickerbocker Club** was formed by a group of writers, including **James Fennimore Cooper** and **William Cullen Bryant** (his statue is behind the New York Public Library, at Sixth Avenue and 42nd Street). Their goal was to shift the literary capital of the country from New England to New York.

They obviously succeeded. Nearly every writer of note, has passed through the city. **Oscar Wilde,** stopping by on a tour, found New York a nice place to eat but unlivable. **Walt Whitman,** that great genius of brawny American verse, lived for many years in Brooklyn Heights (note at 28 Cadman Plaza the brick building; it's now condominiums but once was the headquarters of the *Brooklyn Eagle,* which Whitman edited for a while) and in Manhattan, inventing here his freely based style that would later influence so much American literature and art. **Herman Melville** lived at 104 E. 26th St., between Park and Lexington avenues, while writing and working unhappily as a clerk at the New York Customs House. An office building is there now, next to which is the 26th Street Armory, where the famed 1913 Armory Exhibit took place.

While Greenwich Village is well-known and often cited as a "bohemian" draw for creative types, all of Manhattan has literary roots. The Campanile apartment house, 450 E. 52nd St., at the East River, was once home to **Alexander Woollcott,** who invited his Round Table friends, including **Dorothy Parker,** to skewer whomever and whatever in his third-floor apartment. **Noël Coward** also lived in the building. At 444 E. 57th St., **Arthur Miller** made a new home with his new bride, Marilyn Monroe, in 1956 (after their divorce he moved out to the Chelsea Hotel in 1961, but this was her New York home when she died in 1962). **Truman Capote** was an East Side type, living for a while in his mother's pied-à-terre at 1060 Park Ave., at 87th Street, where he finished *Other Voices, Other Rooms.* **Tennessee Williams** died in a room at the Hotel Elysée (see chapter 5), where **Lillian Hellmann** and **Dashiel Hammett,** who would later live and drink all over the city, also set up housekeeping. Another Uptown hotel, the Plaza, has been a transient home for many writers, including **F. Scott Fitzgerald** and his wife, Zelda (who were soon removed on account of their loud, drunken get-togethers), and **John Dos Passos.** The Barbizon Hotel, at Lexington and 63rd Street, was home to **Sylvia Plath** in 1953 when she worked at *Mademoiselle* magazine. She later fictionalized the hotel as the Amazon (it was a women-only hotel back then) in *The Bell Jar.*

In Midtown West, the **Algonquin Hotel,** on 44th Street just east of Sixth Avenue, became the home of the Round Table, where wit and wine washed down woes and whining. The members of this group—Dorothy Parker (who said her Manhattan apartment was spare because all she needed was a place "to lay my hat and a few friends"), Alexander Woollcott, **Edna Ferber,** and founding editor of *The New Yorker,* **Harold Ross**—met here for lunch. The hotel is no longer what it once was, but the present renovations could reclaim its standing. Across the street from the Algonquin is a very modern, very pale imitation of lunchtime publishing drollery at the Royalton, where the Condé Nast editors of *Vogue, Vanity Fair,* and *The New Yorker* do their best to lay claim to a tradition that predates and precludes them.

Chelsea is the site of the **Chelsea Hotel.** Cast-iron balconies cover rooms where many writers lived and worked: Tennessee Williams, **William S. Burroughs** (he wrote *Naked Lunch* here), **Eugene O'Neill, Arthur Clarke, Bob Dylan** (he composed "Sad-Eyed Lady of the Lowlands" here), Arthur Miller (after he had divorced Marilyn Monroe and left their East 57th Street pad), **Brendan Behan,** and **Mark Twain,** who lived in many places in Manhattan. **Dylan Thomas,** who inspired Bob Zimmerman to change his name, died here after once again drinking too much at the nearby White Horse Tavern (see chapter 9). Chelsea was in fact developed by a writer. **Clement Clarke Moore,** born on West 23rd Street, owned the land and began to build on it. While living in the neighborhood, he penned *A Visit from St. Nicholas.*

Downtown, wherever you turn you'll find traces of a grand literary past. The row of incomparably beautiful Greek Revival houses on **Washington Square North** was the home of John Schuyler Moore, the fictional turn-of-the-century crime reporter in **Caleb Carr**'s fascinating best-seller, *The Alienist.* This Gilded Age setting was also the inspiration for **Henry James**'s *Washington Square* (his real grandmother lived at no. 18, now destroyed, and just next door to Carr's Moore, who lived with his fictional grandmother at no. 19). **Edith Wharton,** a good friend of James's and a fellow traveler in Manhattan's highest social circles, lived at no. 1, as did James himself. Wharton's *Age of Innocence* recounted the city as she knew it and was made into a film by a New Yorker, Martin Scorsese. Wharton was the descendant of some of Manhattan's most prominent families and in 1862 was born in the city's most fashionable neighborhood at the time, at 14 W. 23rd St. (the building is still there, near the Flatiron Building, between Fifth and Sixth avenues, though much and badly renovated).

Farther downtown, poet **Edna St. Vincent Millay** lived at 75½ Bedford St., a house that's often (and accurately) called, "the narrowest house in the Village." Millay also acted at the Provincetown Playhouse, 133 MacDougal St. (founded 1918), where Eugene O'Neill was the most famous playwright being produced. Not far away, **Richard Wright,** author of *Native Son,* used his royalties to break the color barrier and bought the house at 13 Charles St., at Waverly Place. In the small jumble of houses in Patchin Place, off West 10th Street near Sixth Avenue, lived **e.e. cummings, Djuna Barnes,** and **Theodore Dreiser.** Dreiser wrote most of *An American Tragedy,* one of the first and greatest true-crime tales, at 118 W. 11th St. (now a school).

The East Village, overrun with hipsters and junkies, was the longtime home of **W. H. Auden,** at 77 St. Mark's Place, just off First Avenue. (Funny story: His friends and supporters insisted he leave this funky neighborhood and move back to England once he got old; soon after he arrived in Oxford, he was mugged.) The spirit of the Beats—the late and lamented **Allen Ginsberg, Jack Kerouac, William Burroughs, Gregory Corso**—haunts the East Village, though they first espoused their freewheeling and druggy poetics at Columbia University Uptown. **Frank O'Hara,** who often ran with the Beats though he wasn't one himself, died when he was run over as he slept on a beach on Fire Island. Descended from the Beats, were the hippies, the yippies, the punks, Bob Dylan, the Beatles, James Dean, Maynard G. Krebs, and so much more in popular culture. After all, who dares be seen without shades anymore, daddyo?

There are many others not preserved in a museumlike state that nonetheless tell a story about a particular place and time in the past. The former **John Watson House** (early 1800s), in Lower Manhattan at 7 State St., just across from Battery Park, is the lone survivor of a magnificent row of homes. Today it's the Shrine of St. Elizabeth Ann Seton, and blessed are those who kept this marvel intact, from its slender Ionic columns to its Georgian details. It rounds the corner it occupies with singular style. Other early New York survivors are the houses, by John McComb (co-architect of City Hall), at nos. 25, 37, 39, and 41 **Harrison Street** (1796–1828) in TriBeCa. They originally stood on Washington Street.

Among the former mansions of the incalculably rich that now serve other functions are the **Cartier** boutique, Fifth Avenue and 52nd Street; the **Villard Houses,** Madison Avenue between 50th and 51st streets, by McKim, Mead & White (1886), part of the New York Palace Hotel and new home to Le Cirque 2000 restaurant; the **Pierpont Morgan Library,** Madison Avenue between 36th and 37th streets (see "Museums & Art Galleries" above); the **Cooper-Hewitt,** Fifth Avenue at 91st Street, a Carnegie mansion (see "Museums & Art Galleries"); and the **Frick Collection,** Fifth Avenue at 70th Street (see "Museums & Art Galleries").

Abigail Adams Smith Museum and Gardens. 421 E. 61st St. (First & York aves.). ☎ **212/838-6878.** Admission $3 adults, $2 seniors, children under 12 free. Tues–Sun 11am–4pm (to 9pm Tues, June–July). Closed Aug. Subway: 4, 5, 6 to 59th St.; N, R to Lexington Ave.

This is a rare survivor from the early American republic, built as a carriage house for Abigail Adams Smith, daughter of President John Adams, and her husband, William Stephens Smith. Painstakingly restored by the Colonial Dames of America, nine period rooms display predominantly Federal-style furnishings from 1800 to 1830. It's a shock, a very pleasant one, to find this jewel in its rough modern setting.

Dyckman Farmhouse Museum. 4881 Broadway (at 204th St.). ☎ **212/304-9422.** Donation suggested. Tues–Sun 11am–4pm. Subway: A to 207th St.

This fabulous find at the upper reaches of the island is the only Dutch Colonial farmhouse remaining in Manhattan, stoically and stylishly surviving amid modern apartment buildings and garish stores. Built in 1783, the brick-and-stone homestead with a gambrel roof was once the center of a 300-acre farm that was active for some 200 years. It's filled with family furniture and artifacts (toys, clothing, kitchen utensils) from the period.

Gracie Mansion. In Carl Schurz Park (89th St. & East End Ave.). ☎ **212/570-4751.** Admission $4 adults, $3 seniors. Guided tours, mid-Mar to mid-Nov Wed 10 and 11am and 1 and 2pm, by reservation only. Subway: 4, 5, 6 to 86th St.

The official residence of the mayor of New York City was built in 1799 as the country home of wealthy merchant Archibald Gracie. The elegant Federal mansion with its large front porch is reminiscent of a southern plantation house. Fiorello La Guardia made Gracie Mansion the mayor's humble abode in 1942. Only the first floor is open to the public. There are great views across the lawn and down to the East River and some of its Uptown bridges.

Lower East Side Tenement Museum. Visitors' Center at 90 Orchard St. (at Broome St.). ☎ **212/431-0233.** Tenement tour, $8 adults, $6 seniors/students. Tenement tours depart Tues–Fri at 1, 2, and 3pm; Sat–Sun every 45 min from 11am–4:15pm. Subway: F to Delancey St.; B, D, Q to Grand St.

When most people think about historic houses, they envision mansions. But New York's history was made as much on the backs of the poor as from the vast funds of the wealthy. The tenement at 97 Orchard St. (1863) provides a fascinating and poignant look into the personal histories of some of the millions of immigrants who lived on the Lower East Side. And in a country where the log cabin myth is so powerful, it's good to remember that more of our predecessors lived in tenements than in lonely homesteads out on the Great Plains.

Knowledgeable guides (the only way to visit is with the group tour) lead you into a dark and dingy urban time capsule. Several apartments have been faithfully restored to what they looked like when they were occupied by particular families whose real-life stories are recounted by the guides. Tours are limited in number, so it pays to reserve ahead. The Visitors' Center has several small exhibits of photos, videos, and a model tenement, and it offers neighborhood walking tours.

Merchant's House Museum. 29 E. 4th St. (Lafayette St. & the Bowery). ☎ **212/777-1089.** Admission $3 adults, $2 seniors. Sun–Thurs 1–4pm. Subway: 6 to Astor Place; N, R to 8th St.

Greenwich Village's only historic house museum is an 1832 Greek Revival row house that was home to prosperous merchant Seabury Treadwell. Because the home stayed in his family for nearly 100 years, it's a rare intact jewel. While the exterior dates from the early 19th century, the interior furnishings are late 19th century. Both are remarkable. The outside is as elegant as any home anywhere. The inside is filled with original furniture, carpets, draperies, paintings, decorative arts, china, and a collection of dresses, shawls, and bonnets. The best time to visit is on Sunday, when there are unscheduled tours throughout the afternoon. The last member of the family to live in the house died there in 1934 without having been married and is supposed by many to have been the inspiration for Catherine Sloper, the maiden daughter in Henry James's *Washington Square,* which itself later inspired the play and the film *The Heiress.*

Morris-Jumel Mansion. 65 Jumel Terrace (160th St. & Edgecomb Ave.). ☎ **212/923-8008.** Admission $3 adults, $2 seniors. Wed–Sun 10am–4pm. Subway: B, C to 163rd St.

This elegant Georgian mansion was built as a summer villa in 1765 by Roger Morris and is one of the few pre-Revolutionary buildings in Manhattan, though it was much altered in the 19th century. It has had a colorful history, serving as General George Washington's headquarters for a time during the Revolution and later as a tavern. In the 19th century Stephen Jumel bought it as a present for his wife, Eliza, née Brown, a woman reputed for her beauty—and her reputation. The couple altered the house (adding the portico in 1810), and Eliza furnished it in grand French Empire style. They soon decamped, though, for Jumel's native France once their purchase of the house didn't buy them a place in New York society. Eliza eventually returned to America and found a way to transfer to herself all her still-living husband's stateside assets (made mostly in the wine business) and by midcentury became one of America's wealthiest women. After Jumel's death, she married Aaron Burr, from whom she sought a divorce in 1834 but received it only in 1836 on the day he died. Today the rooms are decorated to represent different periods in the mansion's history.

Theodore Roosevelt Birthplace. 28 E. 20th St. (Broadway & Park Ave. South). ☎ **212/ 260-1616.** Admission $2 adults, children under 17 free. Wed–Sun 9am–5pm. Subway: 6 to 23rd St.; N, R to Broadway/23rd St.

New Yorkers, it would seem, are always tearing things down just to put up replicas. The present building is a faithful reconstruction on the same site of the brownstone where Theodore Roosevelt was born on October 27, 1858. Period rooms appear as they did in Teddy's youth. The parlor is in the rococo revival style popular at the time, the stately green dining room boasts horsehair-covered chairs, and the children's nursery has a window that leads to a small gymnasium built to help the frail young Teddy become more "bully." About 40% of the furniture is original. Tours are given every hour, and there's a chamber music concert on Saturdays at 2pm (included in admission). There's also a collection of Roosevelt memorabilia.

9　Over the East River

Roosevelt Island Aerial Tramway. Departing Second Ave. at 60th St. ☎ **212/832-4543.** Subway: 4, 5, 6 to 59th St.; N, R to Lexington Ave.

Gliding 250 feet over the East River, alongside the 59th Street Bridge, you have a unique view of Midtown Manhattan. On the other side is Roosevelt Island, a small strip of land 2 miles in length and at most 800 feet wide where lunatics, criminals, and the like were exiled during the 19th and early 20th centuries. The eerie ruins of a hospital haunt the south end. Today the island is a planned community with spacious parks, city views, and a few historic buildings, like a 1796 farmhouse and an 1872 lighthouse. The tram departs every 15 minutes (6am–2am Sun–Thurs, 6am–3:30am Fri–Sat) and costs $1.50 each way. Subway tokens are accepted but, as of press time, MetroCards were not.

10　Churches & Synagogues

Here's a list of places of worship you can view as tourist sites. It's by no means exhaustive, excluding such wonderful spaces as the historic **St. Mark's-in-the-Bowery,** Second Avenue and 10th Street; the charming **"Little Church Around the Corner"** (the Church of the Transfiguration) at Fifth Avenue and 29th Street; and the prestigious **St. Ignatius Loyola** (where the funeral mass for Jackie Kennedy Onassis was held) at Park Avenue and 84th Street.

Cathedral of St. John the Divine. 1047 Amsterdam Ave. (at 112th St.). ☎ **212/316-7540.** Suggested admission $1 adults, 50¢ seniors/children under 18. Tour $3; tower tour $10. Mon–Sat 7am–6pm, Sun 7am–7:30pm. Tours Tues–Sat 11am, Sun 1pm; tower tours 1st and 3rd Sat of the month. Services Mon–Sat 7:15am and 12:15 and 5:30pm; Sun 8, 9, and 11am and 7pm. Subway: 1, 9, B, C to Cathedral Pkwy.

It'll probably take a miracle to finish this quirky, colossal cathedral. Construction on the world's largest neo-Gothic church began in 1892, and it's now about two-thirds finished. They need only another $400 million, give or take a few mill, to complete the front tower, transept, and central tower.

Perhaps the most amazing aspect of the church is that it's being constructed using traditional Gothic engineering (no steel supports allowed). Master masons from Europe train apprentice stonecutters, many of them youth from Harlem.

Though the seat of the Episcopal Diocese of New York, St. John's embraces an interfaith tradition. Internationalism is a theme found throughout the cathedral's iconography; each chapel is dedicated to a different national or ethnic group. The church is known for a full calendar of high-quality concerts, speakers, and nonreligious celebrations (like the summer and winter solstice performances, often by Paul Winter). Call ☎ **212/662-2133** for event information.

Central Synagogue. 123 E. 55th St. (at Lexington Ave.). ☎ **212/838-5122.** Free admission. Mon–Thurs noon–2pm. Reform Jewish services Fri 5:45pm and Sat 10:30am. Subway: 6 to 51st St.; E, F to Lexington/Third aves. & 53rd St.

Onion-shaped green copper domes distinguish the Central Synagogue, considered the best example of Moorish Revival architecture in the city. The building (1872) was designed by Henry Fernbach, better known for his cast-iron work in SoHo. The interior is colorful stencils in blue, red, and ochre. It's the oldest continually used synagogue in the city.

Riverside Church. 490 Riverside Dr. (120th & 122nd sts.). ☎ **212/870-6700.** Admission $2 to the carillon observation platform. Daily 9am–5pm; carillon Tues–Sat 11am–4pm, Sun 12:30–4pm. Services Sun 10:45am. Subway: 1, 9 to 116th St.

This Gothic-style church is notable for its stained glass, stone carvings, and woodwork inspired by France's Chartres Cathedral. Topping the south tower is the Laura Spelman Rockefeller Memorial Carillon, a gift of John D. Rockefeller in memory of his mother, and an observation platform for excellent panoramic views. The carillon has 74 bells and was the first to exceed a range of five octaves. Originally Baptist, today the church is basically nondenominational.

St. Patrick's Cathedral. Fifth Ave. between 50th and 51st sts. ☎ **212/753-2261.** Free admission. Mon–Fri and Sun 7am–8:30pm, Sat 8am–8:30pm. Mass Mon–Fri 7, 7:30, 8, and 8:30am, noon, and 12:30, 1, and 5:30pm; Sat 8 and 8:30am, noon, and 12:30 and 5:30pm; Sun 7, 8, 9, and 10:15am, noon, and 1, 4, and 5:30pm. Subway: B, D, F, Q to 47th–50th sts./Rockefeller Center.

Large and impressive, if cold as stone, this home of the cardinal is the largest Catholic cathedral in the United States and the seat of the Roman Catholic Archdiocese of New York. The landmark has a white marble facade and spiky spires and was designed by James Renwick, dedicated in 1879, and consecrated in 1910. (Roman Catholics looking for more fitting places to pray with fewer tourists, visit St. Vincent Ferrer at Lexington Avenue and 66th Street or Our Lady of Pompeii at Carmine and Bleecker streets).

St. Paul's Chapel. Broadway between Fulton and Vesey sts. ☎ **212/602-0800.** Free admission. Mon–Fri 9am–3pm, Sun 7am–3pm. Services Sun 8am. Subway: 4, 5 to Fulton St.; N, R to Cortlandt St.

This is Manhattan's only existing pre-Revolutionary building (excluding such places as the Dyckman Farmhouse, which weren't really part of the city in their time), and it still serves its original function. As such it's Manhattan's oldest church. Completed in 1766, St. Paul's Chapel, and its **graveyard,** is steeped in history and is where George Washington regularly worshiped. (His pew is in the north aisle with the original seal of the United States on the wall behind.) The interior has 14 Waterford chandeliers and a beautiful pulpit. The exterior, influenced by London's St. Martin's-in-the-Fields, is made of Manhattan schist quarried from the graveyard where members of prominent 18th-century New York families are buried. The cemetery is one of the city's most historic preservations, and the names and carvings on the tombstones are a reminder that all the money being made in this commercial neighborhood isn't the most important aspect of our lives.

Spanish and Portuguese Synagogue (Congregation Shearith Israel). 2 W. 70th St. (at Central Park West). ☎ **212/873-0300.** Free admission. Open by appointment or for services, Fri 6:45pm, Sat 8:30am and 8pm, Sun 8am and 6:45pm, Mon 7:15am and 6:45pm. Subway: 1, 2, 3, 9, B, C to 72nd St.

Congregation Shearith Israel is the oldest Jewish congregation in the United States, dating back to 1654, when the first refugees fleeing the Spanish Inquisition arrived in New Amsterdam. The interior of the 1897 classic revival building is impressive, especially for the Tiffany windows. The congregation follows Sephardic tradition.

Temple Emanu-El. 1 E. 65th St. (at Fifth Ave.). ☎ **212/744-1400.** Free admission. Daily 10am–5pm. Services Sun–Thurs 5:30pm, Fri 5:15pm, Sat 10:30am. Subway: 6 to 86th St.; B, Q to Lexington Ave.

Many of New York's most prominent and wealthy families are members of this congregation, which helps make Temple Emanu-El the city's most famous synagogue. The largest Reform synagogue in the world is a blend of Moorish and Romanesque styles,

Talk of the Town: Getting Tickets to Rosie & the Rest

There's no place like New York for wild TV audiences. I'd wager that the majority of people who sit in these audiences are from out of the city (after all, we're working during most taping times). Something about being here, something maybe about being on camera, gets otherwise mild-mannered visitors to act like raving lunatics.

For additional information on getting tickets to tapings, call ☎ **212/ 484-1222,** the New York Convention and Visitors Bureau's 24-hour hot line. Sometimes tickets are available at the Times Square Business Improvement District booth in Times Square. Remember that standby tickets—even if you can get them—don't guarantee admission.

"Cosby"   Tapings are Thursdays at 4 and 7:30pm. You must be 16 or older. Send a postcard requesting tickets to Cosby Tickets, c/o Kaufman Astoria Studios, 34–12 36th St., Astoria, NY 11106 (☎ **718/706-5389**).

"Late Night with Conan O'Brien"   Tapings are Tuesday to Friday at 5:30pm. You must be 16 or older. Some tickets are distributed at 9am at the main lobby desk of 30 Rockefeller Plaza; 50 standby tickets (one per person) are available after regular tickets have been distributed. Write to Late Night Tickets, NBC, 30 Rockefeller Plaza, New York, NY 10112 (☎ **212/664-3056,** or 212/664-3057 for groups of up to 20).

"The Late Show with David Letterman"   Tapings are Monday to Thursday at 5:30pm. You must be 16 or older. A hundred—and the lines have a lot more people than that—standby tickets (one per person) are available at noon on taping days at the box office. Arrive early. Write 6 months in advance on a postcard, stating the number of tickets you want, to Late Show Tickets, Ed Sullivan Theater, 1697 Broadway, New York, NY 10019 (☎ **212/975-5853**).

"Live with Regis and Kathie Lee"   Tapings of this popular couple are Monday to Friday at 9am. You must be 18 or older. Standby tickets are sometimes available at the taping studio, 7 Lincoln Square, 67th Street and Columbus Avenue. Send a postcard requesting tickets (limit four) 1 year in advanceto Live

symbolizing the mingling of Eastern and Western cultures. The **Bernard Museum,** which opened in 1997 and charges no entrance fee, has three galleries of Judaic art.

Trinity Church. Broadway at Wall St. ☎ **212/602-0800.** Free admission. Mon–Fri 7am–6pm, Sat 8am–4pm, Sun 7am–4pm. Services Mon–Fri 8am and 12:05 and 5:15pm, Sat 9am, Sun 9 and 11:15am. Subway: 4, 5 to Wall St.; 1, 9, N, R to Rector St.

This landmark Episcopal church, designed by Richard Upjohn, turned 150 years old in 1996, and the parish itself turned 300 in 1997. During most of the 19th century, Trinity Church's 281-foot-high steeple was New York's tallest structure and as recognizable a symbol of the city as the Empire State Building is today. Some lament how Downtown's skyscrapers dwarf the Gothic Revival church, but, interestingly, it was the church itself that prospered as Downtown developed because it owned and sold off much of the land it owned in Lower Manhattan. Free guided tours are offered daily at 2pm and Sundays after the 11:15am service.

Surrounding the church is a **cemetery** with monuments that read like an American history book: a tribute to Martyrs of the American Revolution, Alexander Hamilton, Robert Fulton, and many more. Another reminder that mammon—this church, after all, is at the end of Wall Street—is not eternal.

Tickets, Ansonia Station, P.O. Box 777, New York, NY 10023-0777 (☎ **212/456-3054**).

"The Montel Williams Show"   Tapings are Monday to Wednesday at 10am and 1 and 3pm. You must be 17 or older. Standby tickets are available by calling the studio. Order tickets by sending a postcard to Montel Williams Show Tickets, 433 W. 53rd St., New York, NY 10019 (☎ **212/989-8101** for tickets, or 212/830-0300 for information).

"The Ricki Lake Show"   Tapings are Wednesday to Friday at 3:30 and 5:30pm. You must be 18 or older. Standby tickets are available an hour before taping at the studio, 2 E. 37th St. Order tickets by sending a postcard 3 to 4 months in advance to Ricki Lake Show, 401 Fifth Ave., New York, NY 10016 (☎ **212/889-6767,** ext. 758).

"The Rosie O'Donnell Show"   The schedule varies, but in general Rosie tapings are Monday to Thursday at 11am. No children under 5. Standby tickets (one per person), if available, are distributed at 8am at the main lobby desk of 30 Rockefeller Plaza. To order tickets (two per request, specific dates not accommodated), write 1 year in advance to Rosie O'Donnell Tickets, NBC, 30 Rockefeller Plaza, New York, NY 10112 (☎ **212/506-3288,** or 212/664-3057 for groups of up to 20).

"Sally Jessy Raphaël"   Tapings are Monday and Thursday at 8:30am. You must be 17 or older. Standby tickets are available by calling the studio. To order, send a postcard 1 month in advance to Sally Jessy Raphaël Tickets, 515 W. 57th St., New York, NY 10019 (☎ **212/582-1722**).

"Saturday Night Live"   Tapings are Saturdays 11:30pm to 1am. You must be 16 or older. Standby tickets are available at 9:15am at NBC on the mezzanine level (enter at 49th Street side of Rockefeller Plaza). To order, send a postcard to arrive in the month of August, during which time, once a year, a lottery is held to select ticket holders. That's quite an attitude for a show that hasn't been a hit, let alone good, in many years.

11 Attractions in Upper Manhattan: Harlem & Its Neighbors

Harlem, the country's most famous and fabled African-American community, and its northern neighbors, **Washington Heights** and **Inwood,** are drawing vast crowds of visitors who once trod only the usual Midtown precincts.

An expansive area north of 110th street, the three neighborhoods boast enclaves of beautiful brownstones, soul-electrifying gospel churches, historic houses open to the public, choice museums and cultural centers, parks nearly untouched since before Henry Hudson, and a reenergized jazz scene (see the box "Strangers in the Night" in chapter 9).

IN HARLEM

Over the past several years, the press has heralded the **Second Harlem Renaissance.** With all kinds of new projects in the works or on the boards, the neighborhood (from about 110th Street to 155th Street, from about St. Nicholas Avenue to the East River) has begun to dispel its reputation as a symbol of declining urban America. Those who've lived in Harlem for many years no doubt find this talk a little suspect and remember that much of what's being "discovered" has been there all along. Nonetheless, there's truth in the notion that the neighborhood has become a kind of "sleeper" hit—rediscovered first by visitors (especially Europeans and Japanese) and now by New Yorkers who head up on weekends to its music clubs, something few would've even thought of just 5 years ago.

Two new developments are causing the most stir. Last summer saw the rebirth of **Minton's Playhouse** (☎ 212/683-1212), the historic jazz club at 118th Street and Adam Clayton Powell Jr. Boulevard, made famous in the 1940s when Charlie Parker, Dizzy Gillespie, Thelonius Monk, and friends made it into the birthplace of bebop. Also on the agenda is **Harlem U.S.A.,** a shopping-and-entertainment complex at 125th Street and Frederick Douglass Boulevard. It's due to open in late 1999 and house tenants like the Disney Store, HMV, and Old Navy.

There's also talk of a **Harlem Arts Corridor** that would take shape along Central Park North (110th Street) to Fifth Avenue and as far east as Lexington Avenue. It would connect Harlem to Museum Mile (see "Museums & Art Galleries") and include a proposed Frederick Douglass Cultural Museum, a techno-cultural museum, and a mix of art and music schools, jazz clubs, and artist housing.

No matter what the newest scoop is, Harlem has always had more than its share of historic treasures too. It was settled centuries ago by Dutch farmers who named it Nieuw Haarlem. Before the American Revolution many gentleman English farmers, including Founding Father Alexander Hamilton, had country estates there. By the mid-19th century, the soil was exhausted, so the farmers, rich and poor, decamped, and early Irish immigrants squatted on the land.

Hasty developers predicted a migration of Manhattan's middle and moneyed classes into the neighborhood once the elevated railroads and subways made their way this far north. The developers had good reason for their hopes: Manhattan's best residential neighborhoods had always moved Uptown as the lower areas became more crowded, from the once-elegant Bowery to Washington Square, Union Square, Midtown East, and then finally the Upper East Side. But this time, the dollar didn't follow. Manhattan's Gold Coast, along Fifth and Park avenues, resolutely remained below 110th Street. Eastern Europeans, mainly Jews and often from the Lower East Side, occupied some of the apartments and town houses, and African Americans, some from the city and some migrants from the South, moved into the area around 135th Street.

By the early 1900s, Harlem had become the powerful center of an influential community of blacks. Mighty fraternal organizations formed, and churches, such as Abyssinian Baptist, provided a hub for social interaction. From 1925 to 1929, Harlem reigned as one of the most vibrant communities in the world. It was the time of the **Harlem Renaissance,** mainly a literary and an artistic movement that explored and appreciated the African-American experience and spread the word about its achievements and pains. Among the participants were writers Langston Hughes, Countee Cullen, and Zora Neale Hurston; painters like Romare Bearden; and photographers like James VanDerZee. Other arts flourished, among them, of course, music. Fats

---

A Note of Caution

You can find in these pages much of what you need to know about Upper Manhattan's sights. Still, since distances between the attractions are long—and there are certain unsafe areas between them—I recommend that all visitors, most especially first-timers, join a group tour.

Upper Manhattan Attractions

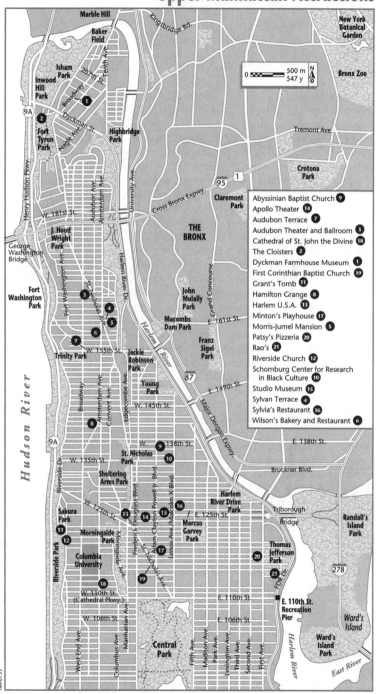

Abyssinian Baptist Church **9**
Apollo Theater **14**
Audubon Terrace **7**
Audubon Theater and Ballroom **3**
Cathedral of St. John the Divine **18**
The Cloisters **2**
Dyckman Farmhouse Museum **1**
First Corinthian Baptist Church **19**
Grant's Tomb **11**
Hamilton Grange **8**
Harlem U.S.A. **13**
Minton's Playhouse **17**
Morris-Jumel Mansion **5**
Patsy's Pizzeria **20**
Rao's **21**
Riverside Church **12**
Schomburg Center for Research in Black Culture **10**
Studio Museum **15**
Sylvan Terrace **4**
Sylvia's Restaurant **16**
Wilson's Bakery and Restaurant **6**

Waller, Duke Ellington, Louis Armstrong, Bessie Smith, Ethel Waters, and Bill "Bojangles" Robinson regularly performed.

But even in Renaissance Harlem, there was segregation to match the abominations in more-distant places like the Waldorf: The famed Cotton Club remained for whites only far longer than the Apollo Theater and the Savoy Ballroom. Still, important newspapers thrived (a survivor is *The Amsterdam News*), and banks owned by African Americans opened. Political activists like W.E.B. Du Bois and even separatists like Marcus Garvey, originally from Jamaica, spoke and wrote eloquently about their vision for a more just world. Adam Clayton Powell Sr., of Abyssinian Baptist Church, preached Christian values to a population who saw few of them evinced by the general American society. It was an explosion of art, intellect, promise, and faith.

At the end of the boom of the 1920s and with the arrival of the Great Depression, change hit Harlem hard. Its speakeasies, where liquor had flowed freely during Prohibition, lost their hold when hooch became legal again. By that time also, the jazz, the swing, and the boogie that were once the nearly exclusive province of Harlem could be heard Downtown, in clubs again awash in martinis, Manhattans, and music. Harlem's decline continued with the strife of the 1960s, 1970s, and 1980s. By 1990, *The New England Journal of Medicine* reported that men in Harlem had a shorter life expectancy than their counterparts in Bangladesh. The character of its residents as well as its rediscovery by visitors should continue to keep Harlem back on track toward the much-heralded Second Renaissance.

To find the treasures that still grace Harlem, pay a call on the **Astor Row Houses,** 130th Street between Fifth and Lenox avenues, a fabulous series of 28 redbrick town houses built in the 1880s and graced with wooden porches, generous yards, and ornamental ironwork. Equally impressive is **Strivers' Row,** West 138th to 139th street, between Adam Clayton Powell Jr. and Frederick Douglass boulevards, a group of 130 houses built in 1891 by a man named David King, who'd already developed the base of the Statue of Liberty and the original Madison Square Garden. On the north side of 139th Street are neo–Italian Renaissance residences by McKim, Mead & White. Across the street are Georgian-inspired homes. Once the original white owners had moved out, these lovely houses attracted the cream of the Harlem population, "strivers" (hence the name) like Eubie Blake and W.C. Handy.

Handsome brownstones, limestone town houses, and row houses are sprinkled atop **Sugar Hill,** 143rd to 155th streets, between St. Nicholas and Edgecombe avenues, named for the "sweet life" enjoyed by its residents. At 409 Edgecombe Ave. lived such prominent people as W.E.B. Du Bois.

Besides its bounty of architectural wealth, Harlem has several important cultural institutions. The **Schomburg Center for Research in Black Culture,** 515 Malcolm X Blvd., between 135th and 136th streets (☎ 212/491-2200; open Mon–Wed noon–8pm, Thurs–Sat 10am–6pm, and Sun 1–5pm; admission free), was originally a branch of the New York Public Library that played a central role in the Harlem Renaissance. Arthur Schomburg, a Puerto Rican black, set himself to accumulating materials about blacks in America, and his collection is now housed and preserved here. The center hosts changing exhibits related to black culture. Make an appointment—it'll be worth your while—to see the 1930s murals by Harlem Renaissance artist Aaron Douglas. The **Studio Museum,** 144 W. 125th St. (☎ 212/864-4500; open Wed–Fri 10am–5pm and Sat–Sun 1–6pm; admission $5 adults, $3 seniors, $1 children under 12), exhibits the work of black artists and historic photographs of Harlem and has in its permanent collection fascinating works by James VanDerZee of the Harlem Renaissance. Both places offer concerts, readings, and the like.

The **Dance Theatre of Harlem,** founded by Arthur Mitchell in 1969, is one of the most prestigious cultural institutions of modern-day Harlem (though most of its performances take place elsewhere in the city). You can visit the dance troupe's school, 466 W. 152nd St. (☎ **212/690-2800**), one Sunday a month, from November to May, when the students perform at an open house (tickets $5).

The legendary **Apollo Theater,** 253 W. 125th St. (☎ **212/749-5838**), which launched or abetted the careers of so many musical icons (Bessie Smith, Billie Holiday, Dinah Washington, Duke Ellington, Count Basie, Aretha Franklin) and is in large part responsible for the development and worldwide popularization of African-American music, was reserved for whites only until relatively late in Harlem history. It wasn't until 1934 that blacks were allowed into the audience. Since the 1980s, after years of deterioration, it has been revived, especially its famous Wednesday Amateur Night show. For more, see the entry under "Popular Music & Comedy" in chapter 9.

In a mixed blessing for the congregations, **Sunday-morning gospel services** at Harlem's many churches have become so popular that bus tour groups sometimes outnumber parishioners. At **Abyssinian Baptist Church,** 132 W. 138th St., between Seventh and Lenox avenues (☎ **212/862-7474**), services are at 9 and 11am. Another resounding service takes place at the **First Corinthian Baptist Church,** 1912 Seventh Ave., at West 116th Street (☎ **212/864-5976**), at 11am. Remember these are religious services, not "shows."

The highlight of the **Hamilton Heights Historic District** (roughly bordered by West 140th and 145th streets, from Hamilton Terrace to Amsterdam Avenue and mainly along Convent Avenue) is **Hamilton Grange,** 287 Convent Ave. between 141st and 142nd streets (☎ **212/283-5154**), an 1802 Federal-style frame house that was the summer home of Alexander Hamilton (it was moved to this site in 1889 and is in need of some serious attention). There are many rows of attractive houses in the enclave. Also check out 147th Street west of Broadway, a dramatic setting on a steep hill.

Another essential aspect of Harlem is its food, and it doesn't get any better than what drifts out of the soulful kitchens of **Sylvia's Restaurant** and **Wilson's Bakery and Restaurant** (see chapter 6 for details).

IN MORNINGSIDE HEIGHTS

Often included on Harlem tours are three sights actually in **Morningside Heights. Riverside Church** (see "Churches & Synagogues") took its decorative inspiration from Chartres Cathedral but was built using completely modern methods in 1930. The bell tower, really an office tower handsomely disguised, holds the world's largest carillon and bell. You can ride an elevator to the observation deck or just admire the Christ Chapel. The **Cathedral of St. John the Divine** (also see "Churches & Synagogues") sits at the border of Morningside Heights, just a few blocks from Columbia University. **Grant's Tomb,** Riverside Drive at 122nd Street (☎ **212/666-1640; daily 9am–5pm; admission free**)—yes, Ulysses Simpson and his wife, Julia, really are here—is a somewhat bombastic, partial copy of the Mausoleus tomb (in what is today Turkey) from 350 B.C., one of the Seven Wonders of the Ancient World. After years of scandalous neglect, it was reinaugurated in 1997 with a $1.8-million face-lift.

IN WASHINGTON HEIGHTS

North of Harlem is Washington Heights, 155th Street to Dyckman Street, a neighborhood whose westernmost fringe, past Broadway and to the Hudson, is a quiet residential district with many attractive art deco and faux Tudor apartment houses. (East of Broadway, the neighborhood is often inappropriate for foot tourism.) For most travelers, the main attraction here is the **Cloisters** (see "Other Museums"), the Metropolitan Museum of Art's Uptown branch housing a magnificent medieval art collection in a complex that incorporates authentic medieval architecture. It's in **Fort Tryon Park,** from West 192nd to Dyckman streets, Broadway to Riverside Drive, where local families energize the woods on the weekends.

Once the site of country estates, Washington Heights is still home to spectacular views across the river and to the world-renowned **Columbia-Presbyterian Medical Center.** Just across from the massive hospital, at Broadway and 165th Street, is its new complex, built over and around the **Audubon Theater and Ballroom,** where Malcolm X was shot dead in 1965; parts of original structure have been incorporated into the new building. The Audubon was built in 1912 by William Fox, whose name is familiar from the theater chain he built in many American cities. The theater was once completely surrounded by a lovely polychrome terra-cotta facade that included, naturally enough, three-dimensional fox heads.

Audubon Terrace, Broadway between 155th and 156th streets, is a seldom-visited cultural center that boasts several worthwhile destinations. The massive Classical Renaissance complex is austere, off-putting because it departs from the successful Manhattan tradition of using ground floors for shops, restaurants, and other pedestrian-attracting commerce. Among the places that would attract more attention if not for their Uptown location and maladroit court are the **American Numismatic Society,** the **Museum of the National Institute of Arts and Letters/American Academy of Arts and Letters,** and the true jewel, the **Hispanic Society of America** (☎ **212/690-0743**). There's a rich and little-known collection of fine arts in its free museum, including works by Goya, El Greco, Vélasquez, and de Zurbarán—a real discovery marred, alas, by its unpleasant situation.

The **Jumel Terrace Historic District,** west of St. Nicholas Avenue, between 160th and 162nd streets, is centered on the **Morris-Jumel Mansion** (see "Historic Houses"). Its former carriage drive, **Sylvan Terrace,** was lined in 1882 with relatively modest yet picturesque pale-yellow wooden houses trimmed in green and brown. Today it's given a sweetly mundane charm by children playing in front of their houses.

IN INWOOD

Inwood, north of Washington Heights and running to the tip of Manhattan Island, is another residential area, largely unknown to visitors and even New Yorkers, and now being rediscovered by young artists and others who appreciate its relatively inexpensive rents and good housing stock. Inwood remains geographically much as Manhattan Island once was—hilly, not leveled for development—and for this we have a second reason to thank Frederick Law Olmsted, the creator of Central Park. Peaceful **Inwood Hill Park** overlooking the Hudson River and the towering Palisades of New Jersey is Manhattan's only primeval forest, left more or less untouched since the arrival of the Europeans. Once the Native Americans were pushed back by the invaders, they lived in the still-existing caves here. Go on weekends, when it's more pleasantly peopled by locals. The most interesting manmade structure in the neighborhood is the Dutch Colonial **Dyckman Farmhouse Museum** (see "Historic Houses").

A fascinating aside: **Marble Hill,** on a dramatic and rocky outcropping at the southern tip of the Bronx, was once at the end of Manhattan Island—before the Harlem River Ship Canal was dug. When the canal was filled in, Marble Hill, ingloriously to some, found itself attached to the Bronx. It is today administratively part of Manhattan, a beachhead of that strange and wonderful island colonizing the mainland, across Spuyten Duyvil Creek, and adding a touch of urbane greatness to the expanse of the rest of North America.

12 Attractions in the Outer Boroughs

IN THE BRONX

Note that the **Bronx Zoo** is covered earlier in this chapter.

Museum of Bronx History. 3266 Bainbridge Ave. (at E. 208th St.), the Bronx. ☎ **718/881-8900.** Admission $2 adults, children under 12 free. Sat 10am–4pm, Sun 1–5pm, Mon–Fri by appointment. Subway: D to 205th St.; 4 to Mosholu Pkwy.

The Museum of Bronx History is located in the Valentine-Varian House, a 1758 field-stone farmhouse used for a brief time during the Revolution by British and Hessian soldiers. Operated by the Bronx County Historical Society, it relates area history with artifacts from everyday life, prints, paintings, and photographs.

   Also administered by the Historical Society is the **Edgar Allan Poe Cottage,** at the Grand Concourse and East Kingsbridge Road (☎ 718/881-8900), a simple wood-framed farmhouse built around 1812 where the poet took his wife, Virginia, in the futile hope of saving her from tuberculosis.

New York Botanical Garden. 200th St. and Southern Blvd., the Bronx. ☎ **718/817-8700.** Admission $3 adults, $1 seniors/children 6–16, under 6 free; free admission all day Wed and Sat 10am–noon. Apr–Oct Tues–Sun 10am–6pm; Nov–Mar Tues–Sun 10am–4pm. Transportation: See below.

A National Historic Landmark, the 250-acre New York Botanical Garden was founded in 1891 and today is one of America's foremost public gardens. The setting is spectacular—a natural terrain of rock outcroppings, a river with cascading waterfall, hills, ponds, and wetlands.

   Highlights of the Botanical Garden are the 27 **specialty gardens** (the formal rose garden and restored rock garden are my favorites), an exceptional **orchid collection,** and 40 acres of **uncut forest** as close as New York gets to its virgin state before the arrival of Europeans. Natural exhibits are augmented by year-round educational programs, musical events, bird-watching excursions, lectures, special family programs, and many more activities. Snuff Mill, once used to grind tobacco, has a charming cafe on the banks of the Bronx River.

   Some of the first results of a multimillion-dollar program of capital improvements bore fruit in 1997. The most important was the reopening of the **Enid A. Haupt Conservatory** (admission $3.50 adults, $2.50 seniors/children 6 to 16), a stunning series of Victorian glass pavilions that recall London's former Crystal Palace, sheltering a rich collection of tropical, subtropical, and desert plants as well as seasonal flower shows. In 1998, a brand-new **Children's Adventure Garden** debuted.

   There are so many ways to see the garden—tram, golf cart, walking tours—that it's best to call for more information.

   Getting There: The easiest way is by minibus shuttle that operates weekends, March to November, between the American Museum of Natural History, the

Impressions

New York is seen at its best in the distance . . . when the clusters of shining, metallic buildings . . . seem to rise like ascending fountains of beauty.

—Cecil Beaton

Metropolitan Museum of Art, and the Botanical Garden. Call ☎ **718/817-8700** for reservations and information. By train, take Metro North (☎ **212/532-4900**) from Grand Central Terminal to the New York Botanical Garden station. By subway, take the D or 4 train to Bedford Park Boulevard and walk east 8 long blocks.

Woodlawn Cemetery. Main gate is at Webster Ave. and 233rd St. the Bronx. ☎ **718/ 920-0500.** Daily 9am–4:30pm. Subway: 2, 5 to 233rd St. Take Metro North to Woodlawn.

This 313-acre cemetery is the final earthly mansion of F. W. Woolworth, the dime-store millionaire; Jay Gould, of the Erie and Union Pacific railroads; Fiorello La Guardia, beloved mayor of New York City who charmed and distracted its residents by reading the comic strips over the radio during a newspaper strike; suffragist Elizabeth Cady Stanton; and jazz great Duke Ellington, to name only a few. Pick up a map at the main entrance to steer you through the extravagant mausoleums, including the one of horse lover Oliver Hazard Perry Belmont modeled after the chapel at France's Château d'Amboise.

IN BROOKLYN

Brooklyn Botanic Garden. 1000 Washington Ave. (at Eastern Pkwy.), Brooklyn. ☎ **718/ 622-4433.** Admission $3 adults, $1.50 seniors, 50¢ children 6–16; free on Tues. Free tours Sat–Sun 1pm. Apr–Sept Tues–Fri 8am–6pm, Sat–Sun 10am–6pm; Oct–Mar Tues–Fri 8am–4:30pm, Sat–Sun 10am–4:30pm. Subway: 2, 3 to Eastern Pkwy./Brooklyn Museum, D & Q to Prospect Park.

Just down the street from the Brooklyn Museum (below) is the Brooklyn Botanic Garden, the most popular in the city, with some 900,000 visitors a year. The garden is most spectacular in May, when thousands of deep-pink blossoms of Kwanzan cherry trees bloom. In addition to the obligatory **rose garden,** there are more unusual exhibits, such as a **Japanese Tea Garden,** the **Shakespeare Garden** with plants mentioned in his writings, a **Children's Discovery Garden,** and the **Fragrance Garden** designed for the blind but appreciated by all noses. Inside the Steinhardt Conservatory is the world-renowned **Bonsai Museum.** Altogether, there are 52 meticulously groomed acres providing a peaceful green sanctuary.

On weekends and holidays noon to 5pm, a **free trolley** runs among the Brooklyn Botanic Garden, the Brooklyn Museum of Art, and Prospect Park and Wildlife Center. It makes the loop once an hour. For information, call ☎ **718/965-8967.**

Brooklyn Heights Historic District. Bounded by the East River, Fulton St., Court St., and Atlantic Ave., Brooklyn. Subway: A, C, F to Jay St.; 2, 3, 4, 5 to Borough Hall; N, R to Court St.

The Brooklyn Heights Historic District is one of the most outstanding and easily accessible sights outside Manhattan. Just across the Brooklyn Bridge is a peaceful neighborhood of tree-lined streets, more than 600 historic houses built before 1860, landmark churches, and restaurants. Even with its magnificent **Esplanade** that gives a sweeping perspective on Lower Manhattan's ragged skyline, it feels more like a village than part of the larger urban expanse.

This is where Walt Whitman lived and wrote *Leaves of Grass,* one of the great accomplishments in American literature. And in the 19th century, fiery abolitionist Henry Ward Beecher railed against slavery at **Plymouth Church of the Pilgrims** on Orange Street between Henry and Hicks streets (his sister wrote *Uncle Tom's Cabin*). Brooklyn Heights is so rich in architectural treasures that they would require their own book. But if you walk down **Willow Street** between Clark and Pierrepont, you'll see three houses (nos. 108–112) in the Queen Anne style that was fashionable in the late

Brooklyn Heights Attractions

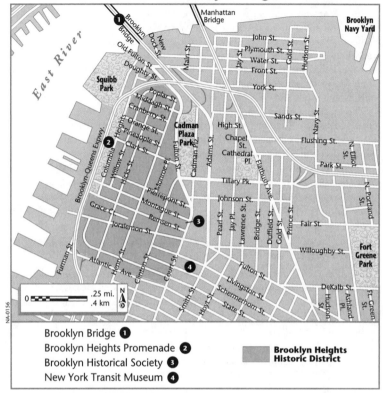

Brooklyn Bridge ❶
Brooklyn Heights Promenade ❷
Brooklyn Historical Society ❸
New York Transit Museum ❹

Brooklyn Heights
Historic District

19th century, as well as an attractive trio of Federal-style houses (nos. 155–159) built before 1829. Also visit lively **Montague Street,** full of cafes and shops.

Brooklyn Historical Society. 128 Pierrepont St. (at Clinton St.), Brooklyn. ☎ **718/624-0890.** Museum $2.50 adults, $1 children under 12; free on Mon. Mon, Thurs, Fri, and Sat noon–5pm. Subway: A, C, F to Jay St.; 2, 3, 4, 5 to Borough Hall; N, R to Court St.

A museum, a library, and an education center, the Brooklyn Historical Society is a treasure trove of information on the heritage of the borough. Permanent exhibits in the **History Museum** are organized around the community's icons: the Brooklyn Bridge, the Brooklyn Navy Yard, Coney Island, the Brooklyn Dodgers, and diverse Brooklynites. Don't miss the *Honeymooners* stage set and the Dodgers' championship flag from the 1955 World Series. It's also worth visiting the **research library** for its late 19th-century interior of black-ash paneling, brass hardware, and stained-glass windows. Call for information on walking tours, lectures, and concerts.

The Brooklyn Museum of Art. 200 Eastern Pkwy. (at Washington Ave.), Brooklyn. ☎ **718/638-5000.** Suggested admission $4 adults, $1.50 seniors, children under 12 free. Wed–Fri 10am–5pm, Sat 11am–9pm, Sun 11am–6pm. Subway: 2, 3 to Eastern Pkwy./Brooklyn Museum.

One of the nation's premier art institutions, the Brooklyn Museum of Art (simply the Brooklyn Museum until its more precise renaming in 1997) rocketed back into the public consciousness with a blockbuster exhibit a couple of years ago: "Monet and the Mediterranean" attracted 225,000 visitors.

For a long while the museum, which boasts collections representing virtually the entire history of art from across the globe, was a sleepy outpost, in danger of losing its audience. Then along came the new director, Arnold Lehman, who has undertaken an ambitious—and sometimes strange—program of Saturday-evening events (think karaoke, lesbian poetry, silent film, and disco dancing), as well as new exhibits, that aspire to create an all-important buzz. And the museum keeps getting better physically, with a major renovation that includes 30,000 square feet of gallery space.

The museum's grand beaux arts building designed by McKim, Mead & White (1897) befits its outstanding holdings, most notably the Egyptian collection of sculpture, wall reliefs, and sarcophagi rivaling any in Egypt's own museums. The distinguished decorative arts collection includes 28 American period rooms from 1675 to 1928 (the extravagant Moorish-style smoking room from John D. Rockefeller's 54th Street mansion is a favorite). Other highlights are the recently reinstalled African arts gallery, art from nearly every corner of Asia, 58 works by Rodin, American painting and sculpture (Winslow Homer, Georgia O'Keeffe), and a diverse collection of European painting and sculpture (Courbet, Monet, Cézanne, Degas).

Green-Wood Cemetery. The main gate is at Fifth Ave. and 25th St., Brooklyn. ☎ **718/ 788-7850.** Daily 8am–4pm. Subway: N, R to 25th St.

Opened in 1840, Green-Wood Cemetery soon became a popular destination for strolling Victorians who likely came as much for the funereal atmosphere as for the views afforded by being at Brooklyn's highest natural elevation. Among the half-million buried here are Samuel F. B. Morse, Lola Montez, Horace Greely, Peter Cooper, and Leonard Bernstein. A map is available at the office inside the main gate.

New York's Aquarium for Wildlife Conservation. W. Eighth St. and Surf Ave., Brooklyn. ☎ **718/265-fish.** Admission $7.75 adults, $3.50 seniors/children 2–12. Daily 10am–5pm (summer weekends to 7pm). Subway: D, F to W. 8th St./N.Y. Aquarium.

Right on the beach at Coney Island, an hour's subway ride from Manhattan, the New York Aquarium is home to hundreds of creatures plucked from the sea. Taking center stage are Atlantic bottlenose dolphins and California sea lions that perform daily during summer at the **Aquatheater.** Also basking in the spotlight are seven beluga whales, gangly Pacific octopuses, and Bertha the sand tiger shark. Black-footed penguins, California sea otters, and a variety of seals live at the **Sea Cliffs exhibit,** a re-creation of a Pacific coastal habitat. Children love the hands-on exhibits at **Discovery Cove.** Tours are also available by calling ☎ **718/265-3448.**

After seeing these ferocious-looking denizens of the deep, you might reconsider that dip into the Atlantic. But don't miss a walk on **Coney Island**'s 2.7-mile-long boardwalk and the taste of a few Nathan's Famous hot dogs (at Surf and Stillwell avenues), followed by a ride on the classic wood-frame Cyclone roller coaster, if you can stomach the mix of wieners and hurtling.

New York City Transit Museum. Boerum Place and Schermerhorn St., Brooklyn. ☎ **718/ 243-8601.** Admission $3 adults, $1.50 seniors/children under 18. Tues–Fri 10am–4pm, Sat–Sun noon–5pm. Subway: 2, 3, 4, 5 to Borough Hall; C, F to Jay St.; N, R to Court St.

I don't know, but I spend enough time in the real subway not to be seduced by this idea. I think it's strictly for those interested in the history of subways—and how many of you are there? Still, if that is your thing, you'll be happy here. Housed in a decommissioned subway station from the 1930s, the museum explores the history of mass transit from the first shovelful of dirt scooped up at groundbreaking (March 24, 1900) to the present. The subterranean exhibit includes 19 vintage cars, old turnstiles, and mosaics that were as much decoration as visual aids for those who couldn't read English-language signs.

Prospect Park & Wildlife Conservation Center. South of Grand Army Plaza bound by Prospect Park West, Parkside Ave., and Flatbush Ave., Brooklyn. ☎ **718/965-8999.** Subway: 2, 3 to Eastern Pkwy./Brooklyn Museum.

Envious of the success of Central Park across the river, Brooklyn civic leaders in 1859 embarked on planning their own 562 acres of woodland, meadows, bluffs, and ponds. Designed by Central Park's Olmsted and Vaux, Prospect Park is considered by many to be their masterpiece and the pièce de résistance of Brooklyn. The best approach is from Grand Army Plaza, presided over by the monumental **Soldiers' and Sailors' Memorial Arch** (1892) honoring Union veterans. Highlights inside the park—besides the lush landscape—are an 1857 Italianate mansion called **Litchfield Villa,** the **Friends' Cemetery** Quaker burial ground (where Montgomery Clift is eternally prone), the sadly neglected **boat house** with a white terra-cotta facade (there's talk of a restoration), the **carousel** with white wooden horses salvaged from a famous Coney Island merry-go-round, and **Lefferts Homestead** (☎ **718/965-6505**), a 1783 Dutch farmhouse with a museum of period furniture and exhibits geared toward children.

On the east side of the park is the **Prospect Park Wildlife Conservation Center** (☎ **718/399-7339;** admission $2.50 adults, $1.25 seniors, 50¢ children under 12, under 3 free). Major renovations completed in 1993 have made it a thoroughly modern children's zoo where kids can walk among wallabies, explore a prairie-dog town, and much more.

IN QUEENS

✪ **American Museum of the Moving Image.** 35th Ave. at 36th St., Astoria, Queens. ☎ **718/784-0077.** Admission $8 adults, $5 seniors, $4 children 5–18. Tues–Fri noon–5pm, Sat–Sun 11am–6pm. Subway: R to Steinway St.

If you truly love movies, go here instead of Planet Hollywood.

Unlike Manhattan's Museum of Television and Radio (see "Museums & Art Galleries"), which is more a library that promotes the industries it preserves, this is a thought-provoking museum examining how moving images—film, video, and digital—are made, marketed, and shown; it encourages you to consider their impact on society as well. It's housed in part of the Kaufman Astoria Studios, which once were host to W. C. Fields and the Marx Brothers, and more recently have been used by Martin Scorsese (*The Age of Innocence*), Woody Allen (*Radio Days*), and Bill Cosby (his "Cosby" TV series). For information on the last two, see the box "Talk of the Town: Getting Tickets to Rosie & the Rest" earlier in this chapter.

The museum's core exhibit, **"Behind the Scenes,"** is a thoroughly engaging installation spotlighting the work and methods of industry professionals with artifacts, technological gadgetry, and the requisite interactive computers where you can put words into Patrick Swayze's mouth in *Ghost* and create your own animated shorts. A Kem Flatbed film-editing table where film used to be cut and spliced sits opposite a modern Lightworks Nonlinear Editing System where segments are digitally manipulated. Special-effects benchmarks from the mechanical mouth of *Jaws* to the blending of past and present in *Forrest Gump* are explored and explained. And in a nod to Hollywood nostalgia, memorabilia that wasn't swept up by the Planet Hollywood chain is displayed, including a Hopalong Cassidy lunch box, an E.T. doll, celebrity coloring books, and Dean Martin and Jerry Lewis hand puppets.

The museum hosts film and video screenings, usually accompanied by artist appearances, lectures, or panel discussions. Silent films are presented with live music (free with museum admission). Call for a schedule.

Flushing Meadows–Corona Park. At Flushing Meadow. ☎ **718/760-6600** for special events. Subway: 7 to 111th St. or Willets Point/Shea Stadium.

Earlier in this century this area of salt marshes and mounds of smoldering trash was called in *The Great Gatsby*, by F. Scott Fitzgerald, the "valley of ashes." But then two world's fairs came, in 1939–40 and 1964–65. Alas, much of what remains from those celebrations of U.S. technological advancement is crumbling. The most dominant remnant, the **Unisphere** steel globe, was only recently granted landmark status.

The 1,200-plus-acre park is a popular fair-weather destination for its large expanses of green, playgrounds, ball fields, rowboat lake, bike rentals, and ice-skating. There are a number of cultural institutions, including the **Queens Museum of Art** (below), the **New York Hall of Science** (see "Especially for Kids" later in this chapter), and the **Queens Wildlife Center** (☎ 718/271-7761). Sports fans come for baseball in **Shea Stadium** (see "In the Grandstand" at the end of this chapter) and the **U.S. Open Tennis Championships** at the National Tennis Center (see "In the Grandstand").

P.S. 1 Contemporary Art Center. 22–25 Jackson Ave., at 46th Ave., Long Island City, Queens. ☎ **718/784-2084.** Suggested admission $4 adults, $2 seniors/students. Wed–Sun noon–6pm. Subway: E, F to 23rd St./Ely Ave.; 7 to 45th Rd./Court House Sq.

If you're interested in contemporary art too cutting edge for most museums, don't miss P.S. 1. Reinaugurated in 1997 after a 3-year, $8.5-million renovation of the Renaissance Revival building that was originally a public school, this is New York's oldest (founded in 1976) and the world's largest institution exhibiting contemporary art from America and abroad. You can expect to see a kaleidoscopic array of works. The inaugural exhibit, for example, included three larger shows by Jack Smith, John Coplans, and Jackie Winsor, as well as smaller installations by more than 50 artists, such as Vito Acconci, Susan Cianciolo, Julian Schnabel, and Richard Serra.

Queens Museum of Art. New York City Building, in Flushing Meadows–Corona Park, Queens. ☎ **718/592-9700.** Suggested admission $4 adults, $2 seniors/children, under 5 free. Wed–Fri 10am–5pm, Sat–Sun noon–5pm. Subway: 7 to Willets Point/Shea Stadium.

One way to see New York in the shortest time (albeit without the street life) is to visit the Panorama, an enormous architectural model of New York City complete with an airplane that takes off from La Guardia Airport. The 9,335-square-foot Gotham City is the largest of its kind in the world, with 895,000 individual structures built on a scale of 1 inch=100 feet. Constructed for the 1964–65 world's fair, today it mirrors most of the current cityscape thanks to a 2-year refurbishing in 1994.

ON STATEN ISLAND

This borough probably won't be high on most visitors' lists of must-see sights, but there are some wonderful houses, leafy neighborhoods, and two important destinations. **Historic Richmond Town,** 441 Clarke Ave. (☎ 718/351-1611; admission $4 adults, $2.50 seniors/children 6–18), is a sort of Williamsburg of the northeast, with costumed interpreters demonstrating traditional American crafts like printing, carpentry, and baking. Amid 27 historic buildings on the 100-acre complex is the 1695 Voorlezer's House. The **Snug Harbor Cultural Center,** 1000 Richmond Terrace (☎ 718/448-2500; free admission, various charges for special events), is an 83-acre property, once part of a 19th-century farm, that boasts beautiful grounds sloping down toward the water and 28 historic buildings, including a pristine Greek Revival row dating from between 1831 and 1880.

13 Especially for Kids

Hollywood wouldn't say it if it weren't true: New York is a great kid city. Believe Disney, which has turned nearly all of Times Square into a pint-sized person's paradise.

It isn't by accident that the adventures of cunning Macaulay Culkin in *Home Alone 2,* boyish Tom Hanks in *Big,* and skeptical Mara Wilson in *Miracle on 34th Street* take place here. From accommodations (see "Family-Friendly Hotels" in chapter 5) to mealtimes (see "Family-Friendly Restaurants" in chapter 6) and toy stores like FAO Schwarz (see chapter 8), New York is a playground for the younger set.

There are hundreds of museums, sites, and happenings especially for children that you'll love, too. For a listing of activities during your time in New York, including theater, film, storytelling, puppetry, and magic shows, consult *New York* magazine and the Friday edition of the *New York Times.* Two other helpful resources are the monthly newspapers *New York Family* and *Parentguide,* both available free at many clothing and toy stores and children's museums.

BEST BETS FOR THE UNDER-5-FOOT SET

Keeping the kids distracted is key to making sure your stay doesn't turn into a Calvin and Hobbes cartoon. Following is a list of the top 10 cool things to do. If your family has the stamina of the Energizer bunny, more suggestions follow. If an entry isn't fully detailed below, you'll find descriptions earlier in this chapter.

1. The giant dinosaurs, touchable dinosaur egg and teeth fossils, and a 94-foot blue whale "swimming" suspended from the ceiling at the **Museum of Natural History** never disappoint.
2. Kids are fascinated with the **Metropolitan Museum of Art**'s Egyptian mummies, Temple of Dendur, and large collection of arms and armor.
3. The **Children's Museum of Manhattan** has everything from storytelling and puppetry to a professional TV studio for hours of educational entertainment.
4. Kids love to monkey around at the **Bronx Zoo,** where the Skyfari Tramway gives treetop views of exotic animals. There's also a **children's zoo** (open Apr–Oct) with a pint-sized prairie dog tunnel, a spider's web for climbing, and a petting zoo. Adjacent to the zoo is the 250-acre **New York Botanical Garden** with its children's activity center, 3-foot-high hedge maze, and trolley ride.
5. Besides 19 playgrounds (the Diana Ross Playground at Central Park West and 81st Street was named the "best" by *New York* magazine), **Central Park** has hands-on nature exhibits and workshops at the **Henry Luce Nature Observatory** in Belvedere Castle (☎ 212/772-0210); an old-fashioned **carousel** (☎ 212/879-0244) with hand-carved wood horses; model boats setting sail on **Conservatory Water;** professional **storytelling** on summer Saturdays at 11am at the Hans Christian Andersen statue; and puppet shows at the Swedish Cottage **Marionette Theatre** (☎ 212/988-9093). At the $6-million **Tisch Children's Zoo** (☎ 212/861-6030) kids can hear the world through a bunny's ears, try on a tortoise shell, and cuddle up to dozens of domesticated animals.
6. Children's eyes grow wide at the year-long march of **parades** (especially Macy's Thanksgiving Day), **circuses** (Big Apple and Ringling Bros. Barnum & Bailey), and **holiday shows** (the Rockettes' Christmas and Easter performances).
7. **Broadway theater** has become an entertainment center for the whole family (which in turn has meant fewer worthwhile productions that could and should interest only thoughtful adults). The under-18 brigade has doubled its numbers in theater audiences just since the beginning of the 1990s. *Rent* attracted a young adult audience so dedicated that tickets in the first two rows have been sold for $20 in a lotto that replaced an older system of first-come, first-served. Producers have seen the future, and it is the younger theatergoer, so they offer substantially discounted student tickets (one show recently sold seats at half off for those under 18), educational tie-ins, and other promotions (a select group of theaters

Virtually New York

In a time when kids are raised on an intellectual diet of computers, video games, and TV, reality sometimes isn't engaging enough to keep them entertained. For children—and their curious caregivers—who crave computerized glitz, virtual-reality attractions are popping up all over town.

JVC New York Skyride (see the "Empire State Building" above) and the theater at **Top of the World** (see the "World Trade Center" above) simulate stomach-churning flying tours over New York. A 100-year history of New York comes alive in the 3-D IMAX film **Across the Sea of Time** showing at the Sony Theaters Lincoln Square, 1998 Broadway, at 68th Street (☎ **212/336-5000;** $9.50 adults, $6.50 children).

Transporter (see the "Empire State Building") transports participants into a world of aliens and dinosaurs on motion-simulating seats. Laser tag, virtual-reality fighter planes, and interactive arcade games lure cyberjocks to **Lazer Park,** 163 W. 46th St, at Broadway (☎ **212/398-3060;** open Sun–Thurs 10am–11pm, Fri–Sat 10am–1am; priced per game). **XS New York,** 1457 Broadway, at 42nd Street (☎ **212/398-5467;** open Sun–Thurs 11am–midnight, Fri–Sat 10am–2am; priced per game), is geared to young adults with its combination of the Cyber Café, dance music, 100 beers, laser tag, video golf, and a full galaxy of video games.

has experimented with prices as low as $5 for students). Boys and girls are amazed by the special effects in *Beauty and the Beast* and adore the felines in *Cats.* Call the **Broadway Line** at ☎ 212/302-4111 for the latest listings. The **New Victory Theater** (☎ 212/382-4020), on revived 42nd Street, is dedicated to family entertainment, and Disney's **New Amsterdam Theater** (☎ 212/307-4100), across from the New Victory, cops honors as the most kid-friendly theater if only because it's where *The Lion King* opened.

8. Kids of all ages, from curious kindergartners to apathetic high schoolers, can't help but turn dizzy with delight at Manhattan's unique **sky-high views** from atop the Empire State Building and the World Trade Center.

9. **FAO Schwarz.** Need I say more? With miles of aisles of toys, it's every child's heaven. And every parent's dread.

10. The **Sony Wonder Technology Lab,** 550 Madison Ave. (☎ 212/833-8100), is a high-tech interactive science center aimed at kids from age 8 to 18 —but adults love it too. Each visitor, or media trainee as you're dubbed, logs in with a personalized card encoded with name, picture, and voice recording. Swipe the card to enter each exhibit where, for example, you electronically "paint" your portrait in the Image Lab, mix guitar riffs with drum rolls in the Recording Studio, save New York Harbor from an oil spill, and design your own video game (the kids' favorite). You'll probably care more than your kids that Ed Schlossberg, the husband of former first child Caroline Kennedy, designed Sony Wonder.

MUSEUMS

Some of New York's museums are designed specifically for kids and nearly all the others have something that'll keep their attention, at least for a while. For the details on each, head to the main listings earlier in this chapter.

There are legions of toy soldiers and flotillas of toy boats at the **Forbes Magazine Gallery** and real and model planes on the *Intrepid's* **Sea-Air-Space Museum.** Boats of an earlier era—a fishing schooner, wooden tugboat, and four-masted sailing ship— bob at **South Street Seaport,** where there's also a children's center.

Real firefighters lead tours at the **New York City Fire Museum,** 278 Spring St. (☎ 212/691-1303), and New York's finest show off their uniforms and badges at the **Police Academy Museum,** 235 E. 20th St. (☎ 212/477-9753). At the **New York City Transit Museum,** conductors-in-training are encouraged to climb aboard classic subway cars. Kids can see old cowboy movies, cartoons, in fact become Nickelodeon producers themselves by choosing from the array of offerings at the **Museum of Television and Radio.** Every child looks with wonder on the Native American art and artifacts at the **National Museum of the American Indian.** And dollhouses and antique toys are found at the **Museum of the City of New York.**

Many museums have special children's programs, including the **Lower East Side Tenement Museum,** the **Museum for African Art,** the **Museum of Modern Art,** and the **Jewish Museum.**

Among the museums specifically dedicated to the younger set is the **Children's Museum of Manhattan,** 212 W. 83rd St. (☎ 212/721-1234; admission $5 children/adults, $2.50 seniors; open Wed–Sun 10am–5pm). It's a magical place for those 2 to 10, who can entertain themselves for hours in well-conceived activities like the Time Warner Media Center, where blossoming media moguls produce their own shows using professional-quality equipment. Temporary exhibits are also a hit: Seuss!, which runs through February 1999, allows kids to step into the pages of their favorite Dr. Seuss books—they steer the boat in *Green Eggs and Ham,* take a seat on a seven-hump Wump of Gump, and make up their own inventive word combinations with a 9-foot-long rhyme-making contraption.

Interactive programs for children 18 months to 10 years are the attraction at the **Children's Museum of the Arts,** 182 Lafayette St. (☎ 212/941-9198; admission $4 weekdays and $5 weekends adults under 65 and children over 18 months; call for hours). Right in the heart of the often childish SoHo arts scene, kids dabble in puppet making and computer drawing or join in sing-alongs and live performances.

ELEVATED & FLOATING VIEWS

The top of a **double-decker bus** can seem like the top of the world. To see the city from dizzying heights you can climb, if your child is old enough and you're young enough, the 354 steps to **Lady Liberty's** crown, take the elevator up to the **Empire State Building's** 86th-floor observation deck, or see forever from the **World Trade Center's** 107th floor. Kids also enjoy crossing the **Brooklyn Bridge** on the wood-plank walkway and rides on the **Roosevelt Island Aerial Tramway.**

The most interesting on-water sightseeing can be had aboard the 100-year-old schooner *Pioneer* from the South Street Seaport, the 70-foot yawl *Petrel* from Battery Park, and **Circle Line's** 2-hour family cruise. The **Staten Island Ferry,** which departs South Ferry and crosses New York Harbor, passing by the Statue of Liberty, is free as well as fun.

THEATER FOR KIDS

As we mention above, the theater scene for kids is flourishing. There's so much going on it's best to check *New York* magazine or the Friday *New York Times* for current listings. Besides larger-than-life Broadway shows, the following are some dependable entertainment options.

The **New Amsterdam Theatre,** 214 W. 42nd St. (☎ **212/307-4100**), brought to you by the folks who brought you Mickey Mouse, opened in 1997 to much acclaim and was the site where the innovative stage version of *The Lion King* opened. It's such a roaring success that more than likely it will still be playing when you get here, and last-minute tickets will still be next to impossible to come by. Conveniently located— for the kids—next door to the Disney Store, this newest Disney theater promises to mean that the avenue the kids'll be taking you to is 42nd Street.

The **New Victory Theater,** 209 W. 42nd St. (☎ **212/382-4020**), reopened a few years back as the city's first full-time family-oriented performing-arts center and has offered such events as a colorful performance by the Fred Garbo Inflatable Theater Co. that incorporated gymnastics, dance, juggling, and magic into one amusing show. The **Paper Bag Players,** called "the best children's theater in the country" by *Newsweek,* perform funny tales for children 4 to 9 in a set made from bags and boxes, in winter only, at Hunter College's Danny Kaye Playhouse, 68th Street between Park and Lexington avenues (☎ **212/362-0431**). Then there's the **Little Orchestra Society** (☎ **212/704-2100**) for the enjoyment of 3- to 12-year-olds, combining classical music with dance, theater, mime, puppetry, fairy tales, and stories at Lincoln Center's Avery Fischer Hall. **TADA!,** 120 W. 28th St. (☎ **212/627-1732**), is a youth ensemble that performs musicals and plays with a multiethnic perspective for family audiences.

FARTHER AFIELD

IN QUEENS   Kids can easily find a full day's entertainment at **Flushing Meadows– Corona Park.** Not only are there more than 1,200 acres of park and playgrounds, but there's also Shea Stadium, a zoo, a carousel, an indoor ice-skating rink, an outdoor pool, and bike and boat rentals. Cultural institutions in the park include the Queens Museums of Art, Theater in the Park, and the **New York Hall of Science** (☎ **718/ 699-0005; admission $6 adults, $4 children 4–15/seniors; free Thurs–Fri 2–5pm; open Tues–Fri 9:30am–2pm, Sat–Sun 11am–5pm**). The last is one of the country's top-10 science museums, and the biggest draw for children is the more than 160 hands-on exhibits.

IN BROOKLYN   Since its glory days, **Coney Island** may have declined, but the famous Cyclone roller coaster still rumbles on wooden rails, thrilling kids big and small. The boardwalk also remains and Nathan's Famous hot dogs taste as good as ever. At the **New York Aquarium** at Coney Island kids can touch starfish and sea urchins and watch bottlenose dolphins and California sea lions stunt-swim.

Brooklyn also has a small animal zoo in **Prospect Park** and a nearby **Botanical Garden.** Favorite museums are the **Brooklyn Museum of Art,** with Egyptian artifacts and special children's programming, and the **New York Transit Museum,** where kids climb aboard vintage subway cars and buses.

14 Sightseeing Tours

Taking a narrated sightseeing tour by bus or boat should be one of the best ways to see and learn quickly about New York's major sights—but keep in mind that the commentary tends to be shallow and only as good as the guide. I've taken those double-decker bus tours and haven't understood one word the guide said in any of the languages I speak. When we got to SoHo, there was total silence from the guide as we passed marvels of cast-iron architecture. There's no doubt these vehicles are fun for zipping through the city streets, but if you don't known New York before you get on, you won't know it after you get off. I've had better luck on the water tours.

My advice is to carry this book and see the sites it recommends when you hop on and off one of the double-deckers. If you prefer a more profound look at a particular aspect of the city, try one of the tours in "Mostly Walking Tours," especially any with the Municipal Art Society. Some require reservations, but it's always best to call ahead to confirm prices, times, and meeting places.

BY BUS

Gray Line New York Tours. Eighth Ave. and 42nd St. (in the Port Authority Bus Terminal). ☎ **212/397-2600.** 2-day hop-on, hop-off bus tours start at $20 adults, $20 children under 12. Operates daily. Subway: A, C, E to 42nd St.

Gray Line offers just about every sightseeing tour option and combination. There are double-decker bus tours by day and by night that run uptown, downtown, and all around the town; walking tours of Lower Manhattan and Harlem; bus tours combined with boat cruises, helicopter flights, museum entrances, and guided visits of sights. Gray Line's combination tours can save money: The bus plus Radio City Music Hall tour, for example, is $3 less than if purchased separately. Most of the offerings won't, as Mick Jagger used to pine, fire your imagination. There's also a sales office in the Times Square Visitors Center.

Kramer's Reality Tour for Seinfeld Fans. Departs from the Pulse Theater, 432 W. 42nd St. (Ninth & Tenth aves.). ☎ **800/KRAMERS** in the U.S., or 212/268-5525. Fare $37.50 (includes lunch). Reservations required. Sat–Sun at noon. Subway: A, C, E to 42nd St. Bus: M42 westbound on 42nd St.

Now that *Seinfeld* lives only in syndication, Kenny Kramer, the self-proclaimed inspiration for the wacky character Kramer, hopes his 3-hour tour can fill the void for grieving fans. Some of the famous sites you'll see: the coffee shop where the gang used to meet, the office building where Elaine worked and Kramer had his coffee-table book published, and the storefront where the Soup Nazi still dispenses his soups and verbal onslaughts. The trivia-laden tour ends with pizza, soda, and a candy bar while you live through video outtakes from the show. If it makes you feel better about the not-inconsiderable sum you're paying, Kenny Kramer says he's an official guide licensed by the City of New York.

New York Apple Tours. Eighth Ave. at 50th St. and Seventh Ave. at 41st St. ☎ **800/876-9868** (information) or 212/944-9200 (reservations). 2-day hop-on, hop-off bus tours start at $21 adults, $12 children under 12. Operates daily. Subway: C, E to 50th St.; N, R, S, 1, 2, 3, 7, 9 to 42nd St./Times Sq.

This company operates double-decker buses on a Full City tour with 46 stops from Wall Street to Harlem and a shorter Downtown tour that runs day and night. The Statue of Liberty Express ($39 adults, $23 children) offers direct bus service from Times Square to the Liberty Ferry and includes the Full City tour and entry to the Statue of Liberty and Ellis Island. The company also runs tours to Brooklyn's major attractions. Don't count on accurate information from the guides because their English (or is it Spanish? maybe French?) is hard to understand and their facts are on occasion dubious. But you can count on a 10% discount if you call the reservations number above and book ahead.

New York Double-Decker Tours. 350 Fifth Ave., Suite 6104 (at 34th St.). ☎ **212/967-6008.** 2-day hop-on, hop-off bus tours start at $19 adults, $12 children 12 and under. Operates daily. Subway: B, D, F, N, Q, R to 34th St.

The Top Sightseeing Tours

On the Water

- Circle Line Sightseeing Cruises
- New York Waterways
- *Petrel*
- World Yacht

On Foot

- Municipal Art Society
- Museum of the City of New York
- Big Onion Walking Tours
- Joyce Gold History Tours of New York

Both the Uptown/Harlem and Downtown routes stop at major sights in the most important neighborhoods, offering a fair orientation to the city. As far as the commentary goes, remember what your mother told you, don't believe everything you hear—and don't expect to hear anything at all. You can buy tickets to sights, including the Statue of Liberty and the World Trade Center observation deck, in the office before you board the bus so you won't have to wait on line later.

BY BOAT

✪ **Circle Line Sightseeing Cruises.** Departing from Pier 83, at W. 42nd St. and Twelfth Ave. ☎ **212/563-3200.** $18–$22 adults, $14–16 children under 13. Operates daily 9:30am–1pm. Subway: A, C, E to 42nd St.

I love this ride for the masses. Circle Line is the only tour company that circumnavigates the entire 35 miles around Manhattan. It takes 3 hours and passes by the World Trade Center, the Statue of Liberty, Ellis Island, the Brooklyn Bridge, the United Na-tions, Yankee Stadium, the George Washington Bridge, and more. The panoramic perspective is riveting, but the narration is only as interesting as the guide who delivers it.

Because 3 hours can be long for small children, families might opt for the new express 2-hour version ($17 adults, $9 children) or the 2-hour Family Cruise, offered Saturday and Sunday ($15 adults, $5 children).

Circle Line also runs a 2-hour Harbor Lights Cruise ($20 adults, $10 children) on weekends in April and October and daily May to October. The commented evening tour sails around the southern tip of Manhattan and to the Statue of Liberty as the sun sets and the city lights up. The DJ Cruise is a floating nightclub that makes waves from 10pm to midnight Friday and Saturday May to October ($20), and the Highlights in Jazz Cruise with live musical entertainment is offered several times in summer. There's also a sales office in the new Times Square Visitors Center.

Express Navigation Cruises. Departing from Pier 11, several blocks south of South Street Seaport at Gouverneur Lane. ☎ **800/262-8743.** $15 adults, $13 seniors, $8 children under 13. Operates Mon–Sat Apr–Sept. Subway: 2, 3 to Wall St.

To see half the city from the water in half the time of a Circle Line trip, you can take Express Navigation's high-speed commuter hydroliners on 75-minute afternoon tours from the Statue of Liberty up the East River to Gracie Mansion, the home of the mayor. There's also an all-day cruise to New Jersey's Monmouth Park horse-racing track Thursday, Saturday, and Sunday from Memorial Day to Labor Day for $25, including park admission. From December to mid-March, Express Navigation runs 4- to 5-hour whale-watching excursions every Saturday (reservations required); I haven't taken one so I can't guarantee any Moby Dick sightings.

✪ **New York Waterways.** Departing from Pier 78 at W. 38th St. and Twelfth Ave. ☎ **800/533-3779.** Harbor cruises: $16 adults, $8 children under 13; Sleepy Hollow Cruise: $35; Kykuit Cruise: $60. Operates daily Mar–Nov. Subway: A, C, E to 42nd St.

In addition to a typical 90-minute New York Harbor cruise daily from March to December, New York Waterways runs two exceptional guided day trips to historic sights in the Hudson River Valley. On the Sleepy Hollow Cruise, you sail up the Hudson to Tarrytown, where you're transferred by bus to Philipsburg Manor, a working 17th-century Dutch-Colonial farm and grist mill, and then to Sunnyside, the riverside home of Washington Irving, author of *The Legend of Sleepy Hollow.* The Kykuit Cruise includes a visit to Philipsburg Manor and a tour of Kykuit, one of the Rockefeller family homes and one of the most spectacular estates in America, particularly for its commanding view of the Hudson and renowned collections of paintings, sculpture, and antique autos. The Kykuit Cruise is immensely popular and must be reserved well in advance. Both the Sleepy Hollow and Kykuit tours last 7 hours and are offered Thursday to Sunday from Memorial Day to October.

✪ *Petrel.* Departing from the southeast end of Battery Park, near the Staten Island Ferry Terminal. ☎ **212/825-1976.** $9–$30 adults, $12 seniors/children (Sun at 1 and 2:30pm only). Operates daily May–Sept. Subway: 1, 9 to South Ferry.

By far the most exhilarating way to tour New York Harbor is aboard the *Petrel*, a 70-foot sailing yacht. There's no misinformation blasted on loud speakers, no rumbling of engines, no children running on deck—only the sound of the wind and waves and the civilized clinking of wineglasses. Named after the seabird that flies the farthest out to sea, the *Petrel* carries up to 35 passengers as fast as and wherever the wind blows. The beautiful wood yacht, a favorite of JFK (who sailed and raced her often), was built in New York in 1938. Daily sails last 2 hours and are offered in the afternoon and evening, and at night under the moonlight on weekends. Cruise times vary because the *Petrel* is a favorite for private parties, so be sure to call ahead to reserve.

Pioneer. Departing from Pier 16, at South Street Seaport. ☎ **212/748-8786.** $20 adults, $15 seniors/students, $12 children under 13. Operates daily May–Sept. Subway: 2, 3, 4, 5 to Fulton St.

As you'd expect of any boat sailing from South Street Seaport, *Pioneer* is a touch more touristy than the *Petrel*, but no less exciting. Skimming the waters of New York Harbor, you can take your turn at the wheel or help hoist the mainsail of this historic 110-foot iron-hulled schooner, built in 1885. Afternoon and evening sails last about 2 hours, and you're encouraged to pack a picnic (beer and wine permitted) to enjoy on deck. Cruises aren't narrated and reservations are highly recommended.

Seaport Liberty Cruises. Departing from Pier 16, at South Street Seaport. ☎ **212/630-8888.** $12 adults, $10 seniors, $6 children under 13. Operates daily Apr–Nov, weekends only Dec and Mar. Subway: 2, 3, 4, 5 to Fulton St.

For a harbor cruise that's short and sweet, Seaport Liberty offers 1-hour commented tours around the southern end of Manhattan past the Statue of Liberty and Ellis Island. At night there's a variety of 2-hour music cruises: Blues Cruises boogie Wednesdays June to September, Jazz Cruises jive Thursdays May to September, and DJ Cruises rock Fridays and Saturdays May to September (call for prices).

Spirit Cruises. Departing from Pier 62, at Chelsea Piers, W. 23rd St. ☎ **212/727-2789.** Lunch cruise: $36.50–$43; brunch Sun $46.50; dinner $66–$80; cocktail from $24.95; moonlight $19.95. Operates daily. Subway: C, E to 23rd St.

Spirits Cruises' three modern ships are floating cabarets that combine sightseeing in New York Harbor with freshly prepared meals, musical revues performed by the wait staff, and dancing to live bands. There's a variety of 2- and 3-hour cruises where the atmosphere is festive and fun, and a touch more relaxed than aboard World Yacht.

✪ **World Yacht.** Departing from Pier 81, at W. 41st St. and Twelfth Ave. ☎ **212/ 630-8100.** Cruise only: $20–$25 adults, $14 children under 13; cruise with meal: $39–$79 adults, $19 children under 13. Operates daily. Subway: A, C, E to 42nd St.

If you want something elegant, World Yacht is a dressy, high-quality, continental-cuisine cruise. There's a 2-hour Sunday brunch cruise with live music and a 3-hour dinner cruise featuring a 4-course meal, live music, dancing, and spectacular views. A jacket is required at dinner. Sneakers and jeans aren't permitted at any time.

MOSTLY WALKING TOURS

MUSEUMS & CULTURAL ORGANIZATIONS   The ✪ **Municipal Art Society** (☎ 212/935-3960) is a membership organization that, in its own words, "champions excellence in urban design, sanity in planning, and the preservation of the best of the city's past." It offers excellent historical and architectural tours aimed at intelligent, individualistic travelers, not the mass market. Each is led by a highly qualified guide who gives insights into the significance of buildings, neighborhoods, and history. Topics range from the urban history of Greenwich Village to the architectural history of the Flatiron District, from culture and kitsch on 57th Street to urban gardens. On Wednesdays at 12:30pm, the society sponsors a free tour of Grand Central Terminal (call for meeting place; donations accepted). On weekends, a variety of tours to the outer boroughs and beyond, including to the formal gardens of Rockefeller's Kykuit estate upstate in Pocantico Hills, is offered. Weekday walking tours are $10, weekend walking tours $15, and weekend excursions $15 to $100. The society's gallery and bookstore at 457 Madison Ave., between 50th and 51st streets, merits a visit.

If you prefer to walk off the beaten track, the **92nd Street Y** (☎ 212/996-1100) offers many unusual tours, like behind-the-scenes visits to the Brooklyn Navy Yard, artists' studios in the Meat Packing District (the far West Village), the night court system, and private clubs like the Player's Club and the Women's National Republican Club. Other themes like "Women of the Lower East Side," "Hell's Kitchen: A Polit-ical History," and "Inside Wall Street" are also offered. Bus trips include excursions to the Apollo Theater and the Bronx's Little Italy. Prices range from $15 to $60.

The ✪ **Museum of the City of New York** (☎ 212/534-1672) offers weekend walking tours, sometimes in conjunction with Big Onion Walking Tours. Past themes: "Urban Archaeology" and "East Harlem." Priced from $9.

The **Lower East Side Tenement Museum** (☎ 212/431-0233) offers weekend walking tours that explore how different immigrant groups, from original Dutch and African settlers to Chinatown's and Little Italy's most recent arrivals, have shaped the Lower East Side. Priced from $7 to $12.

INDEPENDENT OPERATORS   One of the most highly praised sightseeing orga-nizations in New York is ✪ **Big Onion Walking Tours** (☎ 212/439-1090). Enthu-siastic Big Onion guides (all hold an advanced degree in American history from Columbia University) peel back the layers of history to reveal the city's inner secrets. One of the most popular programs is the "Multiethnic Eating Tour" of the Lower East Side, where you munch on everything from dim sum and dill pickles to fresh moz-zarella. Other tours are the "East Village," "The Bowery," "Irish New York," "Historic Harlem," and numerous historic takes on Lower Manhattan. Big Onion also conducts exclusive visits to Ellis Island. Priced from $9 to $15.

✪ **Joyce Gold History Tours of New York** (☎ 212/242-5762) cut to the core of this town with fascinating stories about Manhattan and its people. Joyce Gold, an instructor of Manhattan history at New York University and the New School for Social Research, has been conducting history walks around New York since 1975. Tours are offered most weekends March to December and are arranged around themes like "The Colonial Settlers of Wall Street," "Fifth Avenue Gold Coast," and "Glitter and Fame on Central Park West." Priced at $12. Private tours are available.

Alfred Pommer has conducted **New York City Cultural Walking Tours** (☎ 212/ 979-2388) in nearly every Manhattan neighborhood for more than 10 years. He focuses on history and architecture, illustrating the past alive in the present via photographs and stories. Public tours take place Sundays at 2pm for $10. Private tours are available at $15 per hour for one to three people or $25 per hour for four or more.

Adventure on a Shoestring (☎ 212/265-2663) is a membership organization that offers public walking tours on weekends. But if you plan to spend a lot of time in New York, it may be worth paying the $40 membership fee to attend unique tours that might take you backstage at a Broadway show or to the *New York Times* newsroom. Public tours are $5.

Patricia Olmstead is a landscape designer by trade, but her summer weekends are dedicated to **Urban Explorations** (☎ 718/721-5254). One of her best tours is of the city's "Secret Gardens," but her knowledge of architecture, history, and trivia makes every tour engaging. Favorites include "Gay and Lesbian Greenwich Village," "Harlem from Colonial Times to the Present," and "SoHo Arts and Architecture." Priced at $12. Private tours are available.

Self-proclaimed "radical historian" Bruce Kayton leads unconventional **Radical Walking Tours** (☎ 718/492-0069) to conventional tourist sights. A tour of Harlem covers the Black Panthers, the Communist Party, and Malcom X in addition to the Apollo Theater and the Schomburg Center. A Greenwich Village tour focuses on riots, murder, and prohibition, and a visit to the Lower East Side is incomplete without mention of radical Jews such as Abraham Cahan (founder of the influential newspaper *Forward* in 1897). Priced at $6.

If you want to know the difference between *Morus rubra* and *Morus alba,* then **Wild Food Tours** (☎ 718/291-6825) is for you. Self-nicknamed "Wildman" Steve Brill, a naturalist, ecologist, author, and artist, takes the intrepid through city parks in search of edible wild plants. On a recent tour of Central Park, I ate cattail plucked from the lake (tastes like zucchini) and dug up burdock root in the Ramble. Wild-man Brill has a following of loyal New Yorkers. Priced at $10 or whatever you can afford.

Harlem Spirituals (☎ 212/391-0900) specializes in gospel and jazz tours of Harlem that can be combined with a meal of traditional southern soul food. A variety of options is available, including a weekday walking tour, nighttime jazz clubs, and amateur night at the Apollo Theater. Priced from $33 to $75.

For more than 10 years Larcelia Kebe, owner of **Harlem Your Way! Tours Unlimited** (☎ 212/690-1687), has been leading visitors to Harlem beyond the snapshot stops at major sights (though they're all included). She shares its distinct culture— peppered with her own social commentary—on spirited tours of brownstones, churches, jazz clubs, and soul-food restaurants. Regularly scheduled tours include the "Sights and Sounds Tour" Monday to Saturday and the "Gospel Tour" Sunday. Priced from $32. Private tours are available.

FREE NEIGHBORHOOD TOURS   The **East 42nd Street Tour,** sponsored by the Grand Central Partnership Business Improvement District (☎ 212/818-1777), focuses on the architecture and social history of this famous crosstown thoroughfare. Historian Justin Ferate shares his knowledge of area highlights, including Grand Central Terminal and the Chrysler and Chanin buildings. Tours are Fridays (weather permitting) at 12:30pm; meet at the Whitney Museum at Philip Morris, 42nd Street and Park Avenue.

The **34th Street Tour,** sponsored by the 34th Street Partnership (☎ 212/868-0521), reveals the stories behind the buildings under the guidance of architectural historian

Francis Morron and architect Alan Neumann. Tours are Thursdays at 12:30pm; meet at the Fifth Avenue entrance to the Empire State Building.

The **Times Square Tour,** sponsored by the new Times Square Visitors Center (no phone), lifts the curtain on the Theater District's history, architecture, and current trends. Led by an actor, the tours are animated and given on Fridays at noon (rain or shine); meet at the Times Square Visitors Center, in the Embassy Theater, Seventh Avenue between 46th and 47th streets.

The **Orchard Street Bargain District Tour,** sponsored by the Lower East Side Business Improvement District (☎ **888/VALUES-4-U** or 212/226-9010), explores the famous Old World shops and newer outlet stores in this discount-shopping destination. There are also stops for ethnic eats. April to December, tours are Sundays at 11am; meet at Katz's Deli at Ludlow and East Houston streets.

SELF-GUIDED TOURS If you prefer to walk the city streets on your own, check out "Neighborhoods of Note" in this chapter, "Neighborhoods in Brief" (chapter 4), and "Seeing Beyond the Icons & the Neon" and "Story Time: The History of the High-Rise" (chapter 1). In addition, look for informative plaques on buildings and signs in historic districts throughout the city.

Heritage Trails New York (☎ **888/4-TRAILS** or 212/269-1500 ext. 207) has established four well-conceived walking itineraries in Lower Manhattan. The different trails, totaling 4½ miles, are clearly marked with colored dots on the sidewalks and connect some 55 landmarks. To get the most out of the tour, purchase the four-color map and guidebook for $1 at the start, in front of Federal Hall at Broad and Wall streets, or at the informative kiosks at Trinity Church, at Broadway and Wall Street, or at Pier A in Battery Park. Several guided tours are available too, including "Highlights of Downtown," which departs daily, May to October, at 11am from the Trinity Church kiosk ($11 adults, $9 seniors, $7 children 7–12).

15 Staying Active

New York is a sports enthusiast's heaven. Whatever your pursuit, from bird-watching to rock climbing, you'll find it and a dedicated group of participants here.

ALL-IN-ONE SPORTS COMPLEX

If you're looking for everything under the same roof, head to the **Chelsea Piers Sports and Entertainment Complex** (☎ 212/336-6666). Jutting out into the Hudson River on four huge piers between 17th and 23rd streets, it's a unique experience that's as much tourist destination as recreational facility.

The Chelsea Piers are best known as a 30-acre state-of-the-art athletic complex that attracts more than 3 million people a year with two outdoor **roller rinks** (☎ 212/336-6200); two indoor **ice-skating rinks** (☎ 212/336-6100); a **golf club** (☎ 212/336-6400) with a Japanese-style four-tiered, year-round driving range; a 90,000-square-foot **field house** (☎ 212/336-6500) with basketball and volleyball courts, soccer fields, batting cages, and gymnastics facilities; and a brand-new 40-lane **bowling alley** (☎ 212/835-2695). The **Sports Center** (☎ 212/336-6000), a three-football-fields-long megafacility, does health clubs one better. It offers not only the usual cardiovascular training, weights, and aerobics but also a four-lane, quarter-mile indoor running track, a boxing ring, basketball courts, a sand volleyball court, a 25-yard indoor pool with a whirlpool and sundeck, the Northeast's largest indoor rock-climbing wall, and the **Origins Feel-Good Spa** (☎ 212/336-6780), which offers massage, reflexology, facials, and the like.

The Sports Center offers day passes from $30 to $50 to nonmembers; other facilities are pay as you go. Chelsea Piers is accessible by taxi and the M23 crosstown bus. The nearest subway is the C and E at 23rd Street and Eighth Avenue, 4 very long blocks east.

Hitters, Hackers, & Hoops, 123 W. 18th St. (☎ 212/929-7482), lets you play just about every sport under one roof. There are batting cages, a full basketball court and a smaller court for slam dunk practice, a miniature golf range, a golf drive simulator, pool tables, Ping-Pong tables, and air hockey. It's open Sunday and Monday to 7pm, Tuesday to Thursday to midnight, and Friday and Saturday to 2am.

BEACHES

In the summer swelter, New Yorkers head helter-skelter to the beach. From Manhattan, the Atlantic is a subway ride away. It takes an hour to get to **Coney Island** (go to the end of the B, F, D, or N line), home of the boardwalk and Astroland amusement park. Its huge crowds can include threatening subsets. For bigger surf and less worry, try **Rockaway Beach** in Queens (take the Far Rockaway A train to Broad Channel and then change to the A or S shuttle to Rockaway Park).

Out of the city on Long Island, the most popular (read: crowded with high schoolers) stretch of sand is at **Jones Beach,** where bikini babes bronze on 5½ miles of man-made beach. Gay men pass through the main gate and bathhouse, turn left at the ocean, and walk and walk and walk until the crowd looks familiar. **Long Beach** is a better choice for families, and **Robert Moses Beach,** the farthest east of the three, has the nicest sand and biggest waves. All three are easily reached by Long Island Rail Road (☎ 718/217-5477) from Penn Station (trains are packed by 8am). Round-trip train plus bus transportation costs $11 for Jones Beach and $12 for Long and Robert Moses beaches.

Though neither is a day trip, you can also head out to the **Hamptons,** where Hollywood and New York society play high-style getaway, and to **Fire Island,** a spit of sand with no cars but lots of different communities of singles, families, gays and lesbians, and regular folk. For the Hamptons, call the **Hamptons Jitney** at ☎ 212/936-0440 or the Long Island Rail Road (see number above), and remember to reserve a room before you leave. For Fire Island, call the Long Island Rail Road, from which you take a cab to the ferries, or **Tommy's Taxi** at ☎ 516/665-4800, a van service from various Manhattan pickup points to the ferries. For more, see *Frommer's Wonderful Weekends from New York City.*

BICYCLING

Visitors to New York shouldn't try cycling the city streets, but a slow spin around Central Park is a singular experience. The 6-mile rolling road circling the park, **Central Park Drive,** has a lane set aside for bikers, joggers, and in-line skaters. The best time to ride is when the park is closed to traffic: Monday to Friday 10am to 3pm (except Thanksgiving to New Year's) and 7 to 10pm. The drive is also closed 7pm Friday to 6am Monday, but when the weather is nice, the motley mix of strollers, joggers, skaters, and cyclists makes any movement on the pavement, including walking, hazardous. Off-road mountain biking isn't permitted. **Bite of the Big Apple Tours** (☎ 212/603-9750) conducts 2-hour guided bicycle tours of the southern half of Central Park at $30 adults and $20 children, including bicycle rental.

If you're a more serious cyclist, the **New York Cycle Club** (☎ 212/242-3900) has group rides on weekend mornings of about 50 miles that go out of the city. The **Century Road Club Association** (☎ 212/222-8062), the second oldest and largest road-racing club in America, holds races March to November on Saturday mornings at dawn. Most are open to club members only, but they're fun to watch at the start/finish line, just north of the Loeb Boathouse in Central Park.

You can rent bikes in Central Park at the **Loeb Boathouse,** midpark near East 74th Street (☎ 212/517-2233); at **Metro Bicycles,** 1311 Lexington Ave., at 88th Street (☎ 212/427-4450); at **Pedal Pushers,** 1306 Second Ave., between 68th and 69th streets (☎ 212/288-5592); and at **Toga Bike Shop,** 110 West End Ave., at 64th Street (☎ 212/799-9625). Rentals are $4 to $20 per hour and $17 to $35 per day.

BIRD WATCHING

Because New York is on the Atlantic flyway, not to mention its ample rodent food supply and relative concrete-based heat, **Central Park** is one of the top birding places in the country. Of the 800 North American species, 275 have been spotted here. The park's most famous aviary visitors have had a posh Fifth Avenue address. A pair of peregrine falcons nested and raised their young at no. 927 (at 74th Street) on the top floor, above the middle window—the best viewing point has been from the Hans Christian Andersen statue at Conservatory Water. Bring your binoculars to the wooded **Ramble** for the best birding (but don't ramble there at or after dusk, when another sort of sport, as boys will be boys, shakes the bushes). Bird-watching walks are organized by the **urban park rangers** (☎ 888/NYPARKS or 212/988-4952) and the **New York City Audubon Society** (☎ 212/691-7483). For recorded information on what has been seen where, call the **Rare Bird Alert** at ☎ 212/979-3070.

BOWLING

Bowling never rolled into Manhattan's mainstream culture—there are only three alleys on the island. The venerable **Bowlmor Lanes,** 110 University Place (☎ 212/255-8188; $4.50 per person per game), recently went high tech, and the 44 lanes set in a Greenwich Village industrial building attract a hip crowd rocking and rolling balls to the sounds of DJ and jukebox music. It's open Sunday, Tuesday, and Wednesday to 1am and Friday, Saturday, and Monday to 4am. **Chelsea Piers** (☎ 212/835-2695; $6 per person per game) has the newest alley, a $5-million facility (see "All-in-One Sports Complex" above). Serious bowlers head to **Leisure Time Bowling** on the second floor of the Port Authority Bus Terminal, 625 Eighth Ave. (☎ 212/268-6909; $4.25 per person per game), which has 30 lanes with automatic scoring.

GOLF

The best 18-hole municipal courses, both in the Bronx, are **Van Cortlandt Park,** Van Cortlandt Avenue South and Bailey Avenue (☎ 718/543-4595), and **Pelham Bay/Split Rock,** 870 Shore Rd. (☎ 718/885-1258). Though their greens aren't particularly well kept, their proximity to Manhattan keeps them crowded. You can reserve a tee-off time by calling American Golf Reservation at ☎ 718/225-4653; non–New York City resident greens fees are $24 weekdays and $26 weekends.

The **Golf Club at Chelsea Piers,** 23rd Street and the Hudson River (☎ 212/336-6400; $15 for 75 balls, club rental $2 each), has 52 all-weather, fully automated hitting stalls on four levels with a 200-yard fairway, in addition to a 1,000-square-foot practice putting green. **Randall's Island Sport Center,** on Randall's Island under the Triborough Bridge (☎ 212/427-5689; $10 for 102 balls, club rental $1 each), has a 107-tee, lighted driving range and miniature golf.

HEALTH CLUBS

For sweating with the yuppies and their personal trainers in state-of-the-art facilities, head to the **Equinox Fitness Club,** 897 Broadway (☎ 212/780-9300), or 344 Amsterdam Ave. (☎ 212/721-4200), for a $26 drop-in fee. A more iron-pumping crowd can be found at **Crunch Fitness,** 404 Lafayette (☎ 212/614-0120; $20 drop-in fee), open 24 hours. Two favorites of Midtown office workers are the **Midtown YWCA,** 610 Lexington Ave. (☎ 212/755-4500; $15 drop-in fee), and **Vanderbilt YMCA,** 224 E. 47th St. (☎ 212/756-9600; $15 drop-in fee), both with pools.

HORSEBACK RIDING

Equestrians saddle up at the **Claremont Riding Academy,** 175 W. 89th St. (☎ 212/724-5100), for a walk, trot, or canter on Central Park's bridle path. Experienced English riders can rent horses for $33 per hour; private lessons are available for beginner through advanced levels for $40 per half hour; group lessons are $35 per hour.

ICE-SKATING

New York boasts two of the most spectacular settings for ice skating in the country. The **Rink at Rockefeller Plaza,** 601 Fifth Ave. (☎ 212/332-7654; adults $7.50 to $9, children $6 to $6.75 per session, skate rental $4), is tiny, but positively romantic, especially during the holidays, when the giant Christmas tree's multicolored lights twinkle from above. Central Park's **Wollman Rink** (☎ 212/396-1010; adults $6, children $3, skate rental $3.25) is an oasis of calm when it's not overrun by school groups and rap music. The **Sky Rink** at Chelsea Piers, 23rd Street and the Hudson River (☎ 212/336-6100; adults $10, seniors/children $8, skate rental $4), the city's latest ice spot, has twin indoor rinks for recreational skating and pickup hockey games with Hudson River views. Historic ships provide the backdrop at South Street Seaport's outdoor **Ice Rink** (☎ 212/732-7678; adults $7, children $5, skate rental $4).

IN-LINE SKATING

New Yorkers in search of speed trade in their wing tips and pumps for eight wheels. **Central Park** is the most popular place for blading (see "Bicycling" for the best times), and you can rent skates for $15 a day weekdays and $25 a day weekends from **Blades East,** 160 E. 86th St. (☎ 212/996-1644), and **Blades West,** 120 W. 72nd St. (☎ 212/787-3911). Beginning skaters should attend Blades' free stopping clinics at both the East and West 72nd Street park entrances on Saturdays and Sundays 12:30 to 5:30pm, April to October. In summer, Central Park's **Wollman Rink** (☎ 212/396-1010; adults $4, children $3, skate rental $6.50) converts to a roller rink. Wollman also rents in-line skates for park use at $15 for 2 hours and $25 for the day, weekends only.

On weekends Central Park is a hotbed of skating subcultures. Head to the drive behind Tavern on the Green, where you'll find trick skaters—on one foot going backwards!—weaving through a slalom course at full speed. Or for a trip to disco purgatory, a circle of 1970s throwbacks swirls to funky tunes at the Mall.

Downtown skaters do it outdoors at **Chelsea Piers,** 23rd Street and the Hudson River (☎ 212/336-6200; adults $4, children $3, skate rental $10 per day), and in Battery Park City. For Downtown rentals, try **Blades TriBeCa,** 128 Chambers St. (☎ 212/964-1944; $16 to $27 per day).

POOL

Chelsea Billiards, 54 W. 21st St. (☎ 212/989-0096), is open 24 hours and is one of the cleanest, hippest, and largest, with 54 tables. **Corner Billiards,** 85 Fourth Ave. (☎ 212/995-1314), has 28 nicely spaced tables and waiters who bring microbrewed beer right to players; it's open to 2am Sunday to Thursday and to 3am Friday and Saturday. **Mammoth Billiards,** 220 E. 86th St. (☎ 212/535-0331), is a good Uptown hall with 12 tables; it's open 24 hours. The laws on alcohol at pool halls are complicated; many can't serve any, some might let you brown-bag your own—call ahead.

ROCK CLIMBING

Because the East Coast's premier rock-climbing center, "the Gunks," or Shawangunk Mountains, is just a few hours' drive away, there's a dedicated group of rock climbers in Manhattan. If you just want to practice bouldering, chalk up and climb on to Central Park's **Rat Rock,** midpark at 63rd Street just south of the softball fields, or **Chess Rock,** just north of Wollman Rink. To simulate the real thing, try the indoor climbing walls at **Chelsea Piers,** 23rd Street and the Hudson River (☎ **212/336-6000;** $30 to $50 day pass, $10 equipment rental), or the **City Climbing Club,** 533 W. 59th St. (☎ **212/974-2250;** $10 drop-in fee).

RUNNING

Marathoners and wannabes regularly run in Central Park on the 6-mile **Central Park Drive,** which circles the park (run toward traffic to avoid being mowed down by wayward cyclists and in-line skaters). For a shorter loop, try the midpark 1.58-mile track around the **Reservoir,** recently renamed for Jacqueline Kennedy Onassis, who often enjoyed a jog here (keep your eyes ready for spotting Madonna and other famous bodies). Unless you run as fast as Carl Lewis or Florence Griffith Joyner, it's safest to jog only during daylight hours and where everybody else does. Avoid the small walks in the Ramble and at the north end of the park. Other popular running places are Riverside Park, around the outside of Washington Square Park, and the Hudson River and Battery Park City esplanades.

The **New York Road Runners Club,** 9 E. 89th St. (☎ **212/860-4455**), the world's largest running organization, sponsors group safety runs for all levels Monday to Friday at 6:30 and 7:15pm starting at club headquarters and Saturday at 10am from just inside Central Park at Fifth Avenue and 90th Street. Throughout the year the group also sponsors races attracting enthusiastic runners of all levels. Some of the best are the December 31 Midnight Run, the Bagel Run in late February, the April Fool's Day Backwards Mile, the women-only Avon Mini Marathon in early June, the Race for the Cure in early September, and the Fifth Avenue Mile in late September.

SWIMMING

Serious swimmers count laps at **Asphalt Green AquaCenter,** 1750 York Ave., at 91st Street (☎ **212/369-8890;** $15 drop-in fee). This state-of-the-art $24-million facility boasts the city's first Olympic-standard (50 meters long and at least 7 feet deep) pool. **Chelsea Piers,** 23rd Street and the Hudson River (☎ **212/336-6000;** $30 to $50 day pass), has a brand-new 25-yard, six-lane indoor pool. A more no-frills natatorium is the 75-foot, six-lane pool at the **Midtown YWCA,** 610 Lexington Ave. (☎ **212/ 755-4500;** $15 drop-in fee). Be forewarned that a dip with the after-work crowd here can be like swimming with sharks. Certain hotels have great pools or access to nearby ones. Ask when you reserve.

TENNIS

Of the 50 or so municipal tennis courts maintained by the **New York City Parks Department** (☎ **800/201-PARK**), Central Park's 30 Har-Tru outdoor courts are the best. The verdant setting is beautiful and the atmosphere friendly, making it easy to find a partner. A season ($50) or single-play ($5 per hour) permit is required and can be obtained at the **Central Park Tennis Courts** (☎ **212/280-0201**). Courts are assigned on a first-come, first-served basis by sign-up sheets put out every half an hour for the next hour's play. When the U.S. Open is in town, stop by to try to catch the athletes warming up already hot backhands.

A good alternative to Central Park is the eight clay courts at **Riverside Park,** 96th Street and Riverside Drive (☎ **212/496-2006**), popular for scenic view overlooking the Hudson River. They tend to be less crowded and require the same city pass.

Some of the best public courts are **Crosstown Tennis Club,** 14 W. 31st St. (☎ **212/947-5780;** $38 to $88 per hour; often open to 1 or 2am daily), with four hard Deco-Turf indoor courts; **Midtown Tennis Club,** 341 Eighth Ave. (☎ **212/989-8572;** $28 to $70 per hour), with four Har-Tru indoor courts and four rooftop courts; and **HRC Tennis,** Pier 13 and 14, at Wall and South streets (☎ **212/422-9300;** $40 to $88 per hour), with eight indoor Har-Tru courts in a scenic spot.

16 In the Grandstand

New York has its fair share of professional sports teams and events. But fans aren't the only ones who enjoy a moment in the bleachers. Half the fun is watching the spectators, who range from regular Joes in the nosebleed section to first-row celebrities intentionally unsuccessfully hiding behind their Ray Bans.

BASEBALL

The **New York Mets** play at Shea Stadium, 126th Street and Roosevelt Avenue, in Flushing, Queens (☎ **718/507-8499;** Subway: 7 to Willets Point/Shea Stadium). It's a good thing for their diehard fans that the baseball season lasts a long 7 months because there always seems to be more time for the Mets to stop wallowing in or near the cellar of the National League East and take a swing at a wild-card berth.

You can catch the **New York Yankees** at Yankee Stadium, 161st Street and River Avenue, in the Bronx (☎ **718/293-6000** for the box office, or 212/307-1212 for TicketMaster; Subway: C, D or 4 to 161st St./Yankee Stadium). The "House That Ruth Built" is one of the last great ballparks in the United States, and it could be the next to go if George Steinbrenner's threats to move his team materialize. George, I cannot tell a lie: We'd love *you* to move and leave the Yankees behind!

BASKETBALL

The **New York Knicks** play at Madison Square Garden, Seventh Avenue between 31st and 33rd streets (☎ **212/465-JUMP** for the Knicks hot line, or 212/307-7171 for TicketMaster; Subway: 1, 2, 3, 9, A, C, E to 34th St.). For the past several years, the city's celebrated dysfunctional basketball family has reawakened New Yorkers' passion for hoops. The Knick's playing style—pummeling opponents more like offensive football linemen than lithe hoop masters—makes for a rousing show that keeps fans on the edge of their seats, even if Patrick Ewing can't deliver on his championship promises. Tickets are hard to come by, so plan ahead if you want a front-row seat near first fan Spike Lee.

Ever since the WNBA's inaugural season, the **New York Liberty** has electrified stands full of teenage-groupies and other dedicated fans of women's basketball with their tough-playing defense and star players Rebecca Lobo and Teresa Weatherspoon. They play at Madison Square Garden, Seventh Avenue between 31st and 33rd streets (☎ **212/465-6741** for information, or 212/307-7171 for TicketMaster; Subway: 1, 2, 3, 9, A, C, E to 34th St.).

BOXING

When marquee-name prize fights take place at **Madison Square Garden,** Seventh Avenue between 31st and 33rd streets (☎ **212/465-6741**), it doesn't so much matter who's getting knocked around inside the red velvet ropes—although a nationally televised fight here featured Evander Holyfield, Tim Witherspoon, and Lennox Lewis—as who's sitting around it. Stealing the spotlight have been such heavyweight celebs as Mel Gibson, John F. Kennedy Jr., and Rosie Perez.

FOOTBALL

Even though the city's two professional football teams play in New Jersey, they still trade on the name of the city where they should be playing. You can see the **New York Giants** and **New York Jets** at Giants Stadium, in the Meadowlands Sports Complex, East Rutherford, NJ (☎ 201/935-3900 for the box office, or 212/307-7171 for TicketMaster). Take the bus from Manhattan's Port Authority Bus Terminal, Eighth Avenue between 40th and 42nd streets (☎ 212/564-8484). Tickets are virtually impossible to get for both teams because almost every one of the 77,716 seats is sold to season ticket holders. What's more, season tickets are a prized possession—they're willed to children and fought over in divorce court—so it's rare that you can buy one from a fan on game day at the stadium. Any scattered single seats are swooped up by fans as soon as they go on sale in August. Your best bet: Head to a TV sports bar.

HORSE RACING

THOROUGHBRED You can watch thoroughbreds race at **Belmont Park Racetrack,** Hempstead Turnpike, Elmont, Long Island (☎ 718/641-4700; take the Long Island Rail Road's Belmont Special from Penn Station), or at **Aqueduct Racetrack,** Rockaway Boulevard and 110th Street, Ozone Park, Queens (☎ 718/641-4700; Subway: Far Rockaway A to Aqueduct). The famous Belmont Stakes, the third jewel in the Triple Crown, takes place in early June at the Belmont Racetrack, North America's largest racing facility. Thoroughbred racing runs from May to July and September to mid-October at Belmont and then at Aqueduct from mid-October to May. In July and August thoroughbreds head upstate to the very social (oh, hello, Governor; nice to see you, Mrs. Whitney) Saratoga Springs.

STANDARDBRED There's harness racing year-round on Monday, Tuesday, Friday, and Saturday at **Yonkers Raceway,** Central Avenue, Yonkers (☎ 718/562-9500). Take the Bee Line no. BXM4C bus from Madison Avenue and 39th Street (☎ 914/682-2020).

ICE HOCKEY

The **New York Rangers** play at Madison Square Garden, Seventh Avenue between 31st and 33rd streets (☎ 212/308-NYRS for the Rangers' hot line, or 212/307-7171 for TicketMaster; Subway: 1, 2, 3, 9, A, C, E to 34th St.). The memories of the Mark Messier–led 1994 Stanley Cup team linger on—much to the chagrin of the present underachieving team. Go to see Gretzky, and if the ice action isn't fierce enough, the brawls between fans in the blue seats are notorious.

MARATHONS

The most famous running event is, of course, the **New York City Marathon,** which takes place in 1999 on November 7. The best place to see the 25,000 participants— or at least those who've made it that far—is along First Avenue north of 59th Street or on the East Drive of Central Park. Another race that attracts elite athletes, 8,000 female runners, and lots of spectators, is the **Avon Mini Marathon** in early June (running in recent years, when the event was sponsored by Advil, have been legendary Grete Waitz, two-time NYC Marathon champion Tegla Laroupe, and 1996 Olympian Anne Marie Lauck). For information, call the New York Road Runner's Club at ☎ 212/860-4455.

SOCCER

The **New York/New Jersey MetroStars** play at Giants Stadium, in the Meadowlands Sports Complex, East Rutherford, NJ (☎ **201/935-3900** for the box office, or 212/307-7171 for TicketMaster). Take the bus from Manhattan's Port Authority Bus Terminal, Eighth Avenue between 40th and 42nd streets (☎ **212/564-8484**).

TENNIS

From late August to early September, the hottest ticket in town is to the **U.S. Open Tennis Championships** at the National Tennis Center in Flushing Meadows–Corona Park (☎ **718/760-6200,** or 212/239-6250 for Tele-Charge; Subway: 7 to Willets Point/Shea Stadium). Tickets go on sale in June. While it's next to impossible to cop final-round tickets, early-round seats are relatively abundant and just as entertaining. Wear dark glasses so the crowd of celebrities and socialites won't recognize you.

The **Chase Championships of the Corel WTA Tour** at Madison Square Garden, Seventh Avenue between 31st and 33rd streets (☎ **212/465-6741**), in mid-November, attracts the top 16 singles players and eight doubles team.

8 | Shopping

by David Andrusia

New York offers a more daring, dashing, and dizzying array of shopping choices than any other city. Whether you're looking for haute couture, cool club-land clothes, or the cheapest computer known to man, you've hit the big time, baby!

What makes shopping in Gotham such an adventure? Of course, there's the range of possibilities—options so vast they could keep even the most serious shopaholic busy for weeks. But the real fun isn't in where you go and what you buy—it's in the nonstop allure of pounding the pavement, darting in and out of cozy cafes, and rubbing shoulders with locals as you shop New York.

1 The Shopping Scene

Whether you're an Uptown diva or a Downtown duke, you'll find a shopping scene to call your own. The Big Apple beckons with everything from the fanciest European designers to the best down-and-dirty discounters; but it's the homegrown one-of-a-kind shops that are the most interesting and fun.

This past year has seen the invasion of the Italian kings of fashion, who have just about taken over Madison Avenue; the ever-growing acceptance of the East Village, which now has its own Kmart; and a flood of new stores in SoHo (see the box "What's New & Hot in SoHo"). But the really big news is the emerging neighborhood of NoLita (*No*rth of *Li*ttle *It*aly—east of SoHo and south of the East Village), whose European ambiance is the perfect backdrop to an ever-growing number of daring new stores.

THE LOWDOWN

Time was, only the very rich could make the sacred corner of Fifth Avenue and 57th Street their ground zero shopping site. At one of the most famous—and breathtaking—spots in Manhattan, where **Tiffany & Co.** has long reigned supreme, there's now a **Levi's** store at 3 E. 57th St. (☎ 212/838-2125), and a **NikeTown** across the street at 4 E. 57th St. (☎ 212/891-6453). Moreover, for better or worse, the **Warner Bros. Studio Store,** 1 E. 57th St. (☎ 212/754-0300), has expanded its existing store, directly across from Tiffany's formerly hallowed ground. And just a few blocks away is the new **NBA Store,** 666 Fifth Ave., at 52nd Street.

Should your shopping daydreams be more upscale—and look toward Europe, not Anaheim for inspiration—note that **Chanel** is now at 15 E. 57th St. (☎ **212/355-5050**); upstairs in the same building is **Frédéric Fekkai** (☎ **212/753-9500**), hair snipper to the stars, who has five floors of beauty and spa, with a cafe and a boutique to sell his products, made by Chanel in France. Not to be outdone, **Louis Vuitton** has moved into its own building on the same block— 49 E. 57th St. (☎ **212/371-6111**), a high-rise architectural masterpiece meant to dwarf Chanel.

Discount is always a New York priority. Make no mistake: Manhattan merchants cut prices deeper than anywhere else. **Daffy's,** which advertises clothes for millionaires at bargain prices (a stretch, for sure) now has a branch on East 57th Street, while **Loehmann's** has opened an enormous new facility occupying a major chunk of the original Barneys in Chelsea on Seventh Avenue at 17th Street. Unlike its progenitors, this Loehmann's is so fancy it even has its own personal shopper.

Yes, even if you don't have megabucks, you can have major fun doing the New York shopping scene. Here, we "can get it for you wholesale," to quote the classic Broadway show. Many moderately priced, mass-oriented chains have their flagships in Manhattan, so even if you think you've seen everything from **Saks Fifth Avenue** to **Limited's Express** at home, you ain't seen nothin' yet! Peek into some of your favorite chains just to see how they do it in the Big Apple.

Stores like **Crate & Barrel** have made the formerly untouchably high-priced Madison Avenue seem approachable and affordable now. Forget the concept of Madison (and the entire Upper East Side) being too rich or too European for a good time; the fact is, now that real estate on Madison is in such demand, many really good stores have gone elsewhere.

SoHo, the area *So*uth of *Ho*uston Street, is glitzier than ever, attracting more rich suburbanites than artsy locals. Much more interesting are the adjoining neighborhoods, like **NoHo** and **NoLita,** which retain the funky, avant-garde feel that SoHo had many a moon ago.

And every place you go, there's a coffee bar or a branch of **Starbucks** to help you revitalize for more shopping. The latest trend is that every store has it's own coffee bar—just a few are **Old Navy; ABC Carpet & Home; Wolfman-Gold and Good,** 117 Mercer St. (☎ **212/431-1888**), which sells tabletop pieces and country charm; and **MacKenzie-Childs,** 824 Madison Ave. (☎ **212/570-6050**), offering hand-painted whimsical ceramics, to-die-for paper plates, and home furnishings.

SHOPPING HOURS

New York is filled with businesses open 24 hours. Retail hours usually depend on the neighborhood: Business areas (like Wall Street) tend to have stores that open early— often 8am—to serve people on their way to work. Stores in funky, artistic neighborhoods (like SoHo, the Upper West Side, and the Village) tend to open around 11am or noon but stay open to at least 7pm.

Traditional retail hours (by which most department stores abide) are Monday to Saturday 10am to 6pm. Sunday hours are usually noon to 5pm. Not all stores in New York are open Sunday, but many of the larger ones and all department stores are. Some stores even open as early as 11am on Sunday. The late shopping night is usually Thursday, though some department stores stay open late on Monday, too. What's late? Usually 8:30 or 9pm.

2 Shopping Neighborhoods

One of the beauties of shopping in this city is that there are stores everywhere you turn—and that each of New York's distinct neighborhoods has in own retail identity.

Only in New York

While the city is filled with special stores and imports from all over the world, below are a few of the most unique "only in New York" experiences.

First, know that not even "icon stores" carry only outrageously expensive goods. Remember *Breakfast at Tiffany's?* Maybe all Holly Golightly could afford was engraving on a Cracker Jack ring, but you'll be pleased to know that mere mortals can shop at **Tiffany & Co.,** with quite a few lovely gifts and souvenirs in the $25 to $50 range. Conversely, you may only want to press your nose to the glass at places like **La Vieille Russie,** 781 Fifth Ave. (☎ 212/752-1727), a jewelry dealer specializing in the resale of Fabergé and assorted castoffs from the czars and their friends.

ABC Carpet & Home is more than a place for a carpet: It's a vision, a lifestyle, a dream, a mirage. Go for inspiration—to see not only beautiful things for the house and home but to feel an ambiance and way of selling things not found in many other stores. Go to be dazzled. ABC is expensive on some items and below regular retail on others. Go figure.

If you love delicious clutter, you may have trouble with all the organized tiny boxes lined up at **Tender Buttons,** 143 E. 62nd St. (☎ 212/758-7004), where there are tons of buttons from old to new, and then some. A few have been made into cufflinks; there are some Chanel-inspired styles but no Chanel fakes.

Another aspect of New York style you won't find elsewhere is the handful of specialty shops selling expensive copies of ultra-expensive accessories. **Saurez,** 450 Park Ave. (☎ 212/753-3758), carries copies of the big-name designer handbags. **René Collections,** 1007 Madison Ave. (☎ 212/327-3912), has a few handbags but specializes in copies of evening bags and faux designer jewels like Bulgari, Van Cleef & Arpels, and even Chanel make. Prices here are a fraction of the cost of the real thing.

If you want the real thing but want it the New York way, so that few at home have what you've got, perhaps a trip to **Mark Cross,** 645 Fifth Ave. (☎ 212/421-3000), will do the trick. This major leather goods maker has been the U.S. version of Hermès for over 150 years.

What makes New York shopping so exhilarating are the stores that have cropped up to meet the needs and attitudes of a neighborhood's residents, thus defining the lifestyle and flavor of their respective part of town.

SOUTH STREET SEAPORT

South Street Seaport actually comprises two main properties: the rehab of the old fish market that's been turned into a "festival marketplace;" and a block away, right on the water, **Pier 17,** a mall with more branches of more of your favorite chains—or dreaded symbols of corporate America, depending on your point of view.

THE FINANCIAL DISTRICT

Well, sure, it's got some of the oldest buildings in Manhattan. But when I think of Wall Street, I think of Gaultier at 70% off in the fashion temple known as **Century 21.** (I pay full tribute in the discount section below.) You'll also find **Sym's,** a major discounter of name-brand clothing (and, yes, schlock) for a fraction of regular retail. And, after several years with no bookstore representation anywhere in the nabe, there's finally **Borders Books & Music** at 5 World Trade Center (☎ 212/839-8049).

Zabar's is a foodie's dream, with goodies from around the world, fresh and in packages (if more than slightly overpriced). You'll also find cooking and kitchen gadgets and a never-ending flow of Woody Allen film stock characters who shop here. A few blocks away is another New York gastronomic shrine, **H&H Bagels.** If you suffer from a sweet tooth, New York has one of the few chocolatiers still making its morsels by hand, the hypercharming **Li-Lac Chocolates,** 120 Christopher St., in the Village (☎ 212/242-7374).

Several of the city's regular outdoor flea markets have small greenmarkets, but the city's best by far is the **Union Square Greenmarket,** a totally New York creation that buzzes with color and energy each Monday, Wednesday, Friday, and Saturday. The market gets sparse in the dead of winter, but from spring to fall you'll find a festival of fresh fruit, homemade sausages, cheeses, apple cider, and even wine. Vendors from the states surrounding New York drive to town and set up tables laden with the colors of the season. It's right at Union Square, where Park Avenue meets Broadway at 16th Street.

No respectable GenXer would have less than one orifice pierced. The good news is that piercing has come out of unsavory skid-row closets and onto the streets of New York. If you're looking for a hole new you, the most reputable of the piercing palaces is **Andromeda,** 33 St. Mark's Place, between First Avenue and Avenue A (☎ 212/505-9408). The surroundings are hygienic, but it's the accoutrements and adornments that make this place unique. Tattoos, too!

Nothing—and I mean nothing—is more quintessentially New York than its **outdoor flea markets.** On the most sweltering summer day or the most bracing afternoon in fall, New Yorkers of all ages come out in force, looking for bargains, books, and sometimes love. The one at 26th Street and Sixth Avenue is by far the hippest, and I've not been there once when I didn't see a supermodel, celebrity, or both.

And since this is New York, you can get a manicure while sipping a martini or stinger: Check out **Beauty Bar,** 231 E. 14th St. (☎ 212/539-1389), where a manicure is only $5 when you order a cocktail.

There are also excellent business and formal wear standbys all over the neighborhood—from **Brooks Brothers** to **Zeller's,** 204 Broadway (☎ 212/531-0417), specializing in tuxedo rental and sales. For those on a real tear, there's a small mall inside the **World Financial Center,** next door to the World Trade Center.

SOHO

In the early 1980s, SoHo really was an artists' quarter, chock-full of bohemia and home to such legendary night haunts as the Mudd Club and Paradise Garage. It then metamorphosed into a Euro-style neighborhood of studied chic. Alas, within the past several years, all varieties of mall stores have moved in, some replacing truly interesting small shops; they've done so quasi tastefully. No matter how mainstream, most stores in SoHo don't open until 11am or noon, but they do stay open until later at night. Aside from the American chain stores, there are international designer shops like **Tehen** (French), 122 Greene St. (☎ 212/431-5045), and **Country Road** (Australian), 411 W. Broadway (☎ 212/343-9544), plus a few hotshot American designers—like **Anna Sui,** 113 Greene St. (☎ 212/941-8406), and **Todd Oldham,** 123 Wooster St. (☎ 212/226-4668).

What's New & Hot in SoHo

SoHo has seen hot and is now steaming to a new level—not yet classified as middle-class boring, but bordering on the big yawn as mall stores move on down. Thankfully, plenty of hotshots are still coming on board, so you have **Marc Jacobs** in his new store at 163 Mercer St. (☎ 212/343-1490), and **Keiko New York,** 62 Greene St. (☎ 212/226-6051), offering kicky swimwear. Prada's **MiuMiu,** 100 Prince St. (☎ 212/334-5156), competes with New York's **Nicole Miller,** 134 Prince St. (☎ 212/343-1362). The simple yet chic handbags from **Kate Spade,** 59 Thompson St. (☎ 212/965-0301), have been copied so much that she recently sued a big-name American chain store.

Anthropologie, 375 W. Broadway (☎ 212/343-7070), sums up all the contradictions in SoHo style—the store is both funky and chic and offers lifestyle shopping, clothes for everyone, plus gifts and home decorating items. If it's too mainstream for you, high tail it over to **Sloopy D's,** 51 Bleecker St. (☎ 212/598-4415), which is actually in NoHo (*No*rth of *Ho*uston, where SoHo is going), for vintage finds mixed with current lines and cutting-edge chic.

Happily, you can still find some freestanding treasures. Check out **Zona,** 97 Greene St. (☎ 212/925-6750), for home furnishings and the SoHo dream. Or try **Portico Bed & Bath,** 139 Spring St. (☎ 212/941-7722), for fresh and fancy linens, soaps, and bath gels. **Caesar,** 487 Broadway (☎ 212/941-6672), has hot fashions at affordable prices, so you can have SoHo style without going broke, while **Ricky's,** 590 Broadway (☎ 212/226-5552), is a branch of a small but serious beauty-supply firm that sells every imaginable beauty trick at discounted prices.

Chains that have maintained a noncorporate identity include **Origins,** 402 W. Broadway (☎ 212/219-9764), the natural cosmetics and aromatherapy branch of Estée Lauder, and **Smith & Hawken,** the original upscale garden catalog source, with a store at 394 W. Broadway (☎ 212/925-1190). Just on the edge of SoHo is the **Aveda Institute,** 233 Spring St. (☎ 212/807-1492), not to be confused with any of the small—but fabulous—Aveda shops dotting Manhattan. Here you have a bigger selection of the body and scent line, the clothing made from recycled fabric, as well as the opportunity to sign up for massage therapy, day spa treatments, or workshops. The SoHo **Aveda** shop is at 456 W. Broadway (☎ 212/473-0280); two other locations are 140 Fifth Ave. (☎ 212/645-4797) and 509 Madison Ave. (☎ 212/832-2416).

THE LOWER EAST SIDE

Years ago, before Sunday retail was the rage, the Lower East Side became popular because it was filled with discount stores open on Sunday. In the light of the 1990s, when almost every discounter is open on Sunday, these stores aren't quite as appealing (and they discount an average of only 20%). What's more, the hard-sell on Orchard Street's shops can be pretty hard to take—and, when it comes to fashion, those ghastly Versace jeans are emblematic of these shops' stock-in-trade. Still, if you want some good pickles or pumpernickel, the Lower East Side is a nice place to eat, munch, and discover a part of New York that's disappearing. The fabric discounters and upholsterers in this district make it a good source for Martha Stewart types; you can start at **Beckenstein Home Fabrics,** 130 Orchard St. (☎ 212/475-4887).

GREENWICH VILLAGE

Nothing could be finer than a stroll through the historic West Village, and combining brownstone examinations with shopping can be major fun. Greenwich Village has several distinct personalities and shopping areas. Eighth Street—from Sixth Avenue on the west side to St. Mark's Place on the east—is the main drag for every New York teenager who likes to shop for bargain shoes and repro-retro fashions. Deeper into the Village you get serious antiques shops on Bleecker Street and serious coffee and chocolates on Christopher Street.

Condomania, 351 Bleecker St. (☎ **212/691-9442**), isn't the country's only condom shop, but it's a fine tribute to safe sex with a sense of humor, providing not only the necessities of life but plenty of party favors, souvenirs of New York (honest!), and gifts for the person who has just about everything.

THE EAST VILLAGE

East of Washington Square and New York University, the East Village remains the international standard of bohemian hip, and a major draw of young 'uns from around the world who want to go home and say they've seen it, done it, clubbed it, shopped it. Note that this neighborhood is a night owl's nest: Stores don't open until noon or 1pm and stay open until 8pm or later. **Kmart,** Astor Place at 770 Broadway (☎ **212/ 673-1540**), between 8th and 9th streets, is so out of place it's marvelous camp: Japanese kids stare and marvel at gargantuan boxes of laundry detergent as if they were Warhol designed, and the sale prices on trash food like chips and cookies are rock-bottom. (There's another Kmart, near Penn Station at 33rd Street and Seventh Avenue, for those who just can't get enough.)

Hands down, the most happening street here is East 9th. Here you'll find such shops as **Candlelande,** 305 E. 9th St. (☎ **212/260-8386**), for handmade candles and vintage candleholders, and **Geomancy,** 337 E. 9th St. (☎ **212/777-2733**), for earthenware pottery, lacquered boxes, ceramics, and so on. And you have to laugh when you pass (or shop) **Cha Cha Tchatchka,** 437 E. 9th St. (☎ **212/674-9242**). **It's a Mod, Mod World,** 85 First Ave. (☎ **212/460-8004**), made nationally famous by the lawsuit it initiated against drag diva Hedda Lettuce on Ed Koch's *People's Court* (Hedda won), carries many gift and kitsch items.

The action runs from 2 blocks north of First Avenue and ends at Avenue A. Seventh Street also has a fair number of stores, as does St. Mark's Place. While rents aren't as cheap as they once were, the East Village still plays home to antiques shops and new designers, plus an assortment of eclectic stores like the wacky and wonderful **Howdy Do,** 72 E. 7th St. (☎ **212/979-1618**), where you can find the best in kitsch sold by Brandywine and Brenda A. GoGo.

St. Mark's Place, 1 block over from East 9th Street, is the place to score hot vacuum cleaners, bicycles, Walkmen, and more from druggies on the lam; and **Lafayette Street** stretches from here to SoHo, giving you a new reason for being and for shopping—or simply for staring.

LADIES' MILE

When 23rd Street was the epitome of New York Uptown fashion (over a 100 years ago), the major department stores stretched along Sixth Avenue for about a mile from 14th Street up, and elegant women arrived in horse-drawn carriages to do their shopping. These stores stood in huge cast-iron buildings that were long ago abandoned.

In the last few years, the area has been rezoned and turned into the discount center of New York, with superstores and off-pricers filling up the dinosaur departos. Among the frogs who've turned into princes are **Filene's Basement, TJMaxx,** and **Bed Bath & Beyond,** all at 620 Sixth Ave., which has been lovingly restored on the outside. **Old Navy,** the Gap's version of an outlet store, is next door, while a **Barnes & Noble Superstore** (with coffee bar) is just 2 blocks away at 675 Sixth Ave. (☎ **212/727-1227**). Of course, **Old Navy** and **Bed Bath & Beyond** have their own coffee bars.

CHELSEA

West and south of Ladies' Mile, Chelsea was never known as a big-time shopping neighborhood, except for playing host to the original **Barneys.** Now Barneys has given up its Seventh Avenue store to none other than **Loehmann's,** at 161 W. 16th St., a fact that should make all of us who loved their campy Christmas window dressings more than a little sad.

Chelsea is also the voguish neighborhood for gay men (and, to a lesser extent, lesbians), so look for gay-interest stores along Seventh and Eighth avenues, like **Re:vision** at 192 Eighth Ave. (☎ 212/691-6067) and **Raymond Dragon** on Seventh Avenue between 17th and 18th streets (☎ 212/727-0368). (The latter is for anyone who ever dreamed of dressing like a porn star—or actually is one.)

In recent years, galleries have been moving to West Chelsea to escape the higher rents along Madison Avenue and the suburban crowds who have infiltrated SoHo. Now you can check out a great selection in the far West 20s—see "Museums & Art Galleries" in chapter 7.

34TH STREET

The shopping corridor from Fifth Avenue to Macy's, leading west on 34th Street, used to be a rather predictable march of lower-priced chain stores and cheapie shoe shops. They've all been replaced by the kings of retail, including **Disney** and **the Gap.** The retail theme of each new story is moderately priced all-American family style, culminating with a **Toys 'R' Us** on the corner of 34th Street and Broadway. A block away, near Penn Station at 33rd Street and Seventh Avenue, is a fabulous new **Kmart** (☎ 212/760-1188)—don't miss the cheap, grungy shoes or Martha Stewart's lovely linens."

THE THEATER DISTRICT & TIMES SQUARE

It's called "the biggest comeback in New York history"—yep, porn and sleaze are moving out and the neighborhood is movin' on up. At least, that's what the press releases say; many of us die-hard New Yorkers rue the passing of the local color of the old 42nd Street. Disney is a major player—it's intent on re-creating Times Square with plenty of family fun (and mass retail outlets) with a constant commitment to deweeding the area of scuzz. Richard Branson's **Virgin Megastore** has moved in. You won't be able to miss **The Disney Store** at 210 W. 42nd St. (☎ 212/221-0430)—there's enough neon and floodlit billboards to light a small town. And now the **Warner Bros. Studio Store** is across the street at 1 Times Square and **Old Navy** (a division of the Gap) is moving into 4 Times Square.

The **Times Square Visitors Center** will show you what the entire renovation project will look like when it's finished (see "Visitor Information" in chapter 4).

The Theater District is directly north and west of Times Square, along Broadway from 50th Street to 45th Street, and houses many of the Broadway theaters (the rest are on side streets) as well as a zillion touristy shops for souvenirs and postcards and things that blink in the night. Any show worth its multimillion-dollar mounting fees now has a boutique in the lobby to sell show-related merchandise.

FIFTH AVENUE

The heart of Manhattan retail is the corner of Fifth Avenue and 57th Street, but the avenue changes personality many times as it runs from uptown to downtown.

Uptown (from the 60s to the 90s) is a museum scene; Midtown (59th to 23rd streets) is a designer and big-name shopping scene; and Downtown, starting at the famous Flatiron Building on the corner of Fifth Avenue and 23rd Street, is hip and funky. Some call it SoFi (as in *So*uth *Fi*fth)—it's where you'll find everything from

Emporio Armani, 110 Fifth Ave. (☎ **212/727-3240**), to **Daffy's,** a major discounter of clothing for men, women, and children. And they're almost across the street from each other. **J. Crew** now has three stores in Manhattan as it works its way up from South Street Seaport and SoHo to SoFi at 91 Fifth Ave. (☎ **212/255-4848**).

Working your way uptown, don't overlook Fifth Avenue in the 50s, where several new stores have been opening up like Christmas packages—including the **NBA Store,** 666 Fifth Ave. **Gianni Versace,** 647 Fifth Ave., will, I hope, remain as glittering a destination as when the big guy was alive. Also note that **Rockefeller Center** is much more than a skating rink, a Christmas tree, and the location of the window-surrounded *Today* show studio—it's a promenade lined with stores, everything from a branch of the **Metropolitan Museum of Art Gift Shop,** 15 W. 49th St. (☎ **212/332-1360**); to **Teuscher Chocolates,** 620 Fifth Ave. (☎ **212/246-4416**); to a branch of the catalog store **Brookstone,** 16 W. 50th St. (☎ **212/262-3237**); to a fabulous French bookstore replete with galling Gallic sales help, **Librairie de France,** 610 Fifth Ave. (☎ **212/581-8810**).

57TH STREET

Once upon a time, nothing could be more chic than a 57th Street retail address. While the street still hosts some pretty swanky shops, it has fallen victim to the theme park fantasies of out-of-town developers—though, thankfully, much of the truly objectionable theme restaurants remain west of Fifth Avenue.

From Fifth Avenue east to Lexington Avenue, 57th Street has a dense selection of designer boutiques, galleries, antiques shops, and now discounters. The first block west of Fifth houses many designer shops and unusual specialty stores like **Wathne,** 4 W. 57th St. (☎ **212/262-7100**), where well-heeled adventurers go for riding, fishing, and safari gear; but it gets more real as you head farther west, with discounters, off-pricers, and even a McDonald's. However, after you pass 250 W. 57th St. at Broadway (**Pottery Barn, the Gap**) and you've popped into **Coliseum Books,** 1771 Broadway (☎ **212/757-8381**), your shopping options dwindle.

MADISON AVENUE

Two years ago, Madison Avenue was defined as the home of staid European designers like Ungaro, Givenchy, and Saint Laurent. Now that **Crate & Barrel** has moved in, nearly anything goes and Madison is alive once again, with affordable choices along with the exorbitant. Shoe freaks should check out **Unisa,** 701 Madison Ave. (☎ **212/753-7474**), and **Nine West,** 711 Madison Ave. (☎ **212/752-8030**), chains selling reasonably priced but good-quality shoes.

Barneys is a mecca of magnificent merchandise: You'd be hard-pressed to find another store anywhere with so impressive an array of designers duds, and Barneys private label stuff can be affordable. (Insider tip: If you're an especially fetching member of either sex, this is a great place to find a rich date—or even mate. Good luck!)

THE UPPER WEST SIDE

There's shopping on Columbus Avenue, Amsterdam Avenue, and Broadway west of Central Park all through the 60s, 70s, and 80s, but the best portrait of the Upper West Side is found in the high 70s and low 80s on Columbus. Here hipsters of all ages discover how to be chic and comfortable at the same time. Just look in at **Eileen Fisher** to get the drift, or try **Aerosoles,** 2649 Broadway (☎ **212/865-4934**), where comfortable shoes for men and women are hip, hot, and cheap.

The Sunday **P.S. 44 flea market** (see below) gives you a good look at the neighborhood's lifestyle. Teens can find tons of "finds" from small boutiques like **Lord of**

the Fleas, 2142 Broadway (☎ **212/875-8815**), which sells clothing, gifts, and accessories and even offers free condoms. If imports are your style, rush to **April Cornell,** 487 Columbus Ave. (☎ **212/799-4342**), which has not only some ethnic Indian-style clothing but also duvets and tablecloths and napkins and table settings that combine the prints of India with the colors of the Mediterranean.

3 Shopping A to Z

ANTIQUES & AUCTIONS

The beauty of the New York antiques scene is that you can find everything from museum-quality pieces with astronomical prices to rumble-tumble flea-market fun with plenty of $10 bargains.

While European dealers are forever shopping New York's most exclusive antiques stores to send back across the Atlantic things brought over on the *Mayflower* or shortly thereafter, most people are content with the pockets of pleasure to be found everywhere from Brooklyn's Atlantic Avenue to Manhattan's East 60th Street, between Second and Third avenues, to the area around Broadway and East 12th Street. If you really like funky, don't miss East 9th Street, from First Avenue on north until Avenue A, where there are a number of thrift shops for "vintage" (used and castoff) clothing and junk-filled "antiques" shops with quite fair prices. There are also a number of famous weekend flea markets and flea buildings around town.

Auctions offer antiques, of course, but they also specialize in anything collectible, from animation cells to wines. The major auction houses are **Christie's Fine Art Auctioneers,** 502 Park Ave., at 59th Street (☎ **212/546-1000**), and **Sotheby's,** 1334 York Ave., at 72nd Street (☎ **212/606-7000**). (Note, however, that one or both may be moving soon.) Every now and then a celebrity estate (Jackie O, JFK) goes up for auction; the viewing (free and open to the public) becomes the talk of the town, if only for a day.

Chelsea Antiques Building. 112 W. 25th St. (Sixth & Seventh aves.). ☎ **212/929-3939.** Subway: F to 23rd St.

Catercorner from New York's best flea market (below), this building filled with dealers is open not only during the weekend to coincide with the flea market but also during the week. Goods are priced more reasonably than at Uptown addresses, and shoppers are the type who love to prowl, touch everything, and sniff out a deal—and sometimes a date.

Manhattan Art & Antiques Center. 1050 Second Ave. (at 56th St.). ☎ **212/355-4400.** Subway: 4, 5, 6 to 59th St.; N, R to Lexington Ave.

Twenty years ago, much of the antiques business in New York was centered around the East Side in the mid-60s, with the fanciest stores on Madison Avenue and the funkier ones farther east. This antiques center was part of the area's exclusive shopping scene and has remained so, despite changing times for the rest of the storefronts. Once you've toured the over 100 stalls selling high-end to midprice goods in this enclosed center, stroll along 60th Street, where about two dozen dealers line the street.

Newel Art Galleries. 426 E. 53rd St. (First Ave. & Sutton Place). ☎ **212/758-1970.** Subway: 6 to 51st St.

Even if you don't buy a thing here, this is the perfect place if you love marveling at the truly offbeat and wonderful. There are six floors of the best furniture from ages past—be it a throne that would make King Arthur proud or an art deco dream that belongs on a movie set. Just let your jaw hang open.

BATH PRODUCTS

The bath is hot—perhaps the need for a fancy soak in the tub defines the stress of our times. In Manhattan, every place you look there's a new chain or boutique selling specialty and exclusive bath and body products. For the best selection of established European drugstore brands (nondesigner names), try either of Madison Avenue's two fancy "drugstores": **Boyd's,** 655 Madison, at 60th Street (☎ **212/838-6558**), or **Zitomer,** 969 Madison, at 76th Street (☎ **212/737-2037**).

Crabtree & Evelyn may look like an old-time British firm, but it's as American as peach kernel bath oil, with several shops all over town—try 520 Madison Ave. (☎ **212/758-6419**). **Floris,** the London fragrance house, is at 703 Madison Ave. (☎ **212/935-9100**). **Origins** is sold at department stores and has a complete store-within-a-store at Bloomingdale's (see "Department Stores"). It has a separate store at 402 W. Broadway (☎ **212/219-9764**).

Bath Island. 469 Amsterdam Ave. (at 83rd St.). ☎ **212/787-9415.** Subway: 1, 9 to 86th St.

This shop feels like a trip to California crossed with a New Age version of The Body Shop. It's an important stop for the teens who shop the West Side on weekends but also serves anyone in need of a good soak with soaps, bath items, and numerous ecologically correct potions and gift baskets. All this, plus its very own Web site at www.citysearch.com/NYC/bathisland.

Caswell-Massey Co. 518 Lexington Ave. (at 48th St.). ☎ **212/755-2254.** Subway: 4, 5, 6 to 59th St.; N, R to Lexington Ave.

I know it's a mall store, but this outpost is so veddy English and so sweet-smelling, it's worth a special trip. The aura of patchouli scent is a sexy fragrance for both women and men, and the almond soap sings.

H2O Plus. 650 Madison Ave. (at 60th St.). ☎ **212/750-8119.** Subway: 4, 5, 6 to 59th St.; N, R, to Lexington Ave.

This Chicago-based chain still seems fresh and bubbly, if a bit teeny-bopperish in its marketing stance. A variety of bath and beauty products, mostly with a natural slant and in pretty colors, is sold at moderate prices. There are great items for children: Check out the Bath Confetti for $7, a great gift for yourself or the kids.

BED LINENS

Bed Bath & Beyond is a superstore with a good selection of linens; the prices are slightly discounted, and the range of styles covers a variety of tastes (see "Housewares"). **ABC Carpet & Home** has a floor devoted to bed linen; the choices are more sophisticated than just about anyone else's, and the merchandise is slightly discounted as well (see "Housewares").

If you're willing to pay top dollar for top quality and like the ecologically friendly back-to-basics look, **Portico Bed & Bath,** 139 Spring St. (☎ **212/941-7722**), is the place to indulge in linens, towels, duvet covers, and bath accessories. If you're not willing to pay top dollar, try **Laytner's,** 512 Broadway, between Spring and Broome streets (☎ **212/965-9382**), for slightly discounted big-name American linens in a Pottery Barn–style setting; other locations are 2270 Broadway, at 81st Street (☎ **212/724-0180**), and 237 E. 86th St., between Second and Third avenues (☎ **212/996-4439**).

✪ **Porthault.** 18 E. 69th St. (Fifth & Madison aves.). ☎ **212/688-1660.** Subway: 6 to 68th St.

The most famous maker of bed linen in the world is the French luxe house of Porthault, specializing in bed sheets strewn with floral prints across white cotton or organdy costing about $4,000 per set. If that's over your budget, you can afford a shower cap or a *gant toilette*—a French glove-style washcloth. Depending on the dollar and the time of year, prices can be better here than in Paris.

Pratesi. 829 Madison Ave. (at 69th St.). ☎ **212/288-2315.** Subway: 6 to 68th St.

The Italian equivalent of Porthault is also more affordable, especially if you luck into one of the twice-a-year sales. The firm explains that most of the crowned heads of Europe were conceived on Pratesi linens, so it's bound to be good enough for you.

SoHo Mill Factory Outlet. 490 Broadway (at Broome St.). ☎ **212/226-8040.** Subway: N, R to Prince St.

It's hit or miss at this store, a de facto dumping ground for linens other stores don't want (either because they're second-quality, irregular, or downright hideous). For the latter reason, I suggest shopping here only for cheap bedcovers to throw on sleeper sofas or to use as picnic table covers; the call, of course, is yours.

Trouvaille Française. By appointment only. ☎ **212/737-6015.**

Private dealer Muriel Clark sells from her home, so you must call for an appointment. She specializes in European white work—Victorian linen from France, Belgium, England, and so on. The basis of her collection is bed linen, table linen, and Victorian white linen clothing from old-fashioned nightgowns to lacy baby gowns.

BOOKSTORES

The preeminence of national book chains is a raging issue of intellectuals and merchants alike. Until just 5 years ago, New York's range of booksellers—new, used, academic, foreign, antiquarian—was unparalleled in the Western world. In the last few years, **Barnes & Noble's Superstores** have blown into town; offering huge choices of every genre imaginable, plus reading, coffee bars, and cruising options.

A Different Light Bookstore and Cafe. 151 W. 19th St. (Sixth & Seventh 7th aves.). ☎ **212/989-4850.** Subway: 1 to 18th St.

The city's only gay and lesbian bookstore stocks just about every category—fiction, nonfiction, biography, travel, gay/lesbian studies, and more—plus cassettes, calendars, you name it. There's also a cafe, though it seems to be on its last legs. Readings and video nights are featured.

✪ **Applause Books.** 211 W. 71st St. (at Broadway). ☎ **212/496-7511.** Subway: 1, 2, 3, 9 to 72nd St.

This is the ultimate source of books on theater, cinema, and the performing arts. Biographies, screenplays, screenwriting manuals, and much more line the shelves of Applause, among the best stores of its type in the world. I applaud the salespeople, who couldn't be nicer and who know the stock like the backs of their hands.

Archivia. 944 Madison Ave. (74th & 75th sts.). ☎ **212/439-914.** Subway: 4, 5, 6, N, R to Union Square.

Here you'll find new, imported, and rare books on architecture, the decorative arts, gardening, and interior design in English and other languages. A book lover's dream!

Books of Wonder. 16 W. 18th St. (Fifth & Sixth aves.). ☎ **212/989-3270.** Subway: 6 to 77th St.

You don't have to be a kid to fall in love with this bookstore, but kids will fall in love with BOW's story readings; they take place every Sunday at 11:45am. Say hello to Pooh, Madeline, and the rest of the gang!

The Top Spas & Salons

Sure, you could wait to get home for that color or trim—but wouldn't it be much more fun to get purty in New York? From the cheapest haircut to the most luxurious spa, here's my hit list of Gotham's best.

In the early 1980s, **Astor Place Hair Designers,** 2 Astor Place, between Broadway and Fourth Avenue (☎ **212/475-9854**), was a three-man shop where $8 would buy you the punk haircut of your dreams. Today, you can get clipped for just a few bucks more, but at your own risk—nearly 100 cutters and colorists work in this trilevel factory. Best bet: Alexander (trust me).

An afternoon—or even an hour—at **Caraban Urban Spa,** 5 W. 16th St., between Fifth and Sixth avenues (☎ **212/633-6220**), is the ultimate relaxation. This cavernous candlelit place transports you immediately to Santa Fe; a massage will take you to the moon. At **D. Esse,** 56 University Place, at 10th Street (☎ **212/ 420-1576**), owner Daphne Selig is the ultimate *Parisienne,* with saucerlike eyes and a degree in chemistry. The facials here are divine, and the products are fancy, French, and unavailable anywhere else. Superstylist Gwen LeMoine Sabahi holds court at **Parlor,** 443 E. 9th St., between First Avenue and Avenue A (☎ **212/ 673-5520**), where a 1940s-era beauty shop look meets East Village kitsch. Be you a he or a she, beautiful you will be.

At **Paul Labrecque Salon and Spa,** 160 Columbus Ave., at 67th Street (☎ **212/595-0099**), you can get the best facial in the city, as proclaimed by *New York* magazine. The staff members at this wonderful spa/salon are kind and attentive and know their stuff. Heavenly massages and great haircuts, too. And at **Vidal Sassoon,** 767 Fifth Ave., at 59th Street (☎ **212/535-9200**), the stylists all undergo superstringent schooling, so a bad haircut is virtually impossible here—and great ones are likely, especially when your stylist is Gretchen or Nick. Sobeia's the color connoisseur, and Irene gives the most heavenly manicures in town.

Complete Traveler. 199 Madison Ave. (at 35th St.). ☎ **212/685-9007.** Subway: 6 to 33rd St.

Whether your destination is Texas or Tibet, you'll find what you need in this, possibly the world's best travel bookstore. In addition, there are fun and useful travel accessories, plus many rare and first-edition travel books whose facts may be outdated but whose writers' perceptions continue to shine.

Forbidden Planet. 840 Broadway (at 13th St.). ☎ **212/473-1576.** Subway: 4, 5, 6, N, R to Union Sq.

Masters of the universe, teenagers, and arrested development types congregate here for the comics and high-tech interior decor. The prices aren't low, but the range of products can't be beat, and the staff really knows what's what.

Hagstrom Map & Travel Center. 57 W. 43rd St. (Fifth & Sixth aves.). ☎ **212/398-1222.** Subway: F to 42nd St.

This bookstore with travel guides actually sells maps as well—incredible selections of cartography to meet just about any need.

Murder Ink. 2486 Broadway (at 91st St.). ☎ **212/362-8905.** Subway: 1, 9 to 86th St.

Murder, she wrote, he wrote, they wrote. This is the ultimate specialist bookstore—as much fun as a good mystery. It sells hard-to-find first editions as well as imported

English titles. Those truly in the know wait eagerly for the catalog and order by mail. If you're a mystery or true-crime fan, ask to be placed on the mailing list. **Another location:** 1467 Second Ave., between 76th and 77th streets (☎ 212/517-3222).

New York Bound. 50 Rockefeller Plaza (Fifth & Sixth aves.). ☎ **212/245-8503.**

All the editions are about New York, but I'm not talking just guidebooks—books about everything from architecture to art to transportation, plus reports from the Commission of Central Park dating back to 1861.

Oscar Wilde Book Shop. 15 Christopher St. (Sixth & 7th aves.) ☎ **212/255-8097.** Subway: 6 to Christopher St.

The first gay bookstore in the United States is still growin', still crowin', and still goin' strong: Its recent renovation allows for more titles and ancillary merchandise than ever before. The old owners were on the downtrodden side, but the nice new staff makes this landmark once again a pleasure.

Rizzoli. 31 W. 57th St. (Fifth & Sixth aves.). ☎ **212/759-2424.** Subway: N, R to Fifth Ave.

This woodsy super-Italian store keeps a soft spot in the hearts of book buyers from around the world, and with good reason: it's the ne plus ultra of an elegant Continental literary salon. You won't find career books, how-to's, and the like, but for quality fiction, cookbooks, art tomes, and other upscale reading, this is the place. And the staff actually knows Collins from Camus.

۞ The Strand. 828 Broadway (at 12th St.). ☎ **212/473-1452.** Subway: 4, 5, 6, N, R to Union Sq.

This is *the* place to buy review copies of best-sellers, art books, and paperbacks of all kinds—all at a fraction of their original price. There are scads of other choices too, especially in out-of-print selections, including—yes!—last year's Frommer's guides. The down side: The cashiers are the rudest "sales help" (as if) in town. **Another location:** 95 Fulton St., at the corner of William Street (☎ 212/732-6070), near South Street Seaport.

Traveller's Bookstore. 22 W. 52nd St. (Fifth & Sixth aves.). ☎ **212/664-0995.** Subway: B, D to Rockefeller Center.

Don't get this tiny shop mixed up with the news kiosk next door. This is the ultimate bookstore for the traveler—armchair or otherwise—with an extensive selection of guides and a small but relatively well-selected collection of travel literature. This shop will even order what it doesn't have.

Urban Center Books. 457 Madison Ave. (at 51st St.). ☎ **212/935-3592.** Subway: 6 to 51st St.

Even if you have no interest in buying a book about architecture or city planning, you owe it to your soul to browse in this store set into the side wing of the New York Palace Hotel. The architecture of the space alone is worthy of an admission fee. That there's a fine selection of books crammed into every nook is an extra.

CHOCOLATES

Manhattan is filled with chocolate specialists. The fanciest (most expensive) European brands are usually sold through department stores and flown in from Europe once a week. To get your paws on **Bernachon** chocolates from Lyon, France, head straight to **Takashimaya; Manon** chocolates are sold at **Bergdorf Goodman.** Note that I mention **Li-Lac Chocolates** in the box "Only in New York."

The Rise of NoLita

Just 3 years ago, Elizabeth Street was a nondescript adjunct to the core of Little Italy; today, it's the grooviest strip in town, star of the neighborhood known as NoLita (east of SoHo and south of the East Village). Restaurants like Rialto and the M&R attract hipsters from around the globe, and they're more than met by the emerging shopping scene. (Prince Street, just south of Houston, is NoLita's other big retail road.)

A stone's throw from NoLita proper, **Mary Adams the Dress,** 159 Ludlow St., at Houston Street (☎ **212/473-0237**), features thoughtful updates on kitschy girly-girl dresses (the kind comic-strip heroine Li'l Dot wore). Fabulous French-woman Christiane Celle has joined the NoLita revolution with a winner, **Calypso,** 280 Mott St., between Houston and Prince streets (☎ **212/965-0990**). Her ladies' shop spotlights emerging designers from here and abroad and some of the hottest accessories in town. Best of all, Christiane shares insider tips that'll have you looking like a *Parisienne* fast.

At **Elizabeth 260,** 260 Elizabeth St., between Houston and Prince streets (☎ **212/941-6158**), Brazilian owner Ignez throws light on the subject of lamps, the only focus of this stuffed little shop. You'll find everything from modern to medieval. *Note:* The hours, in typical Brazilian fashion, are quixotic; call before making a special trip.

At **Kelly Christie,** 235 Elizabeth St., between Houston and Prince streets (☎ **212/965-0686**), the eponymous Des Moines transplant is a doll, and her handmade hats are dreamy, too. You'll also giggle at her fluffy Las Vegas slut slippers, silver-toned kiddie pins, and (best of all) cuff links by "Miss Rita of L.A." For office, street, or club, **Daryl K.,** 21 Bond St., at Broadway (☎ **212/777-0713**), is sleek, sexy sportswear at its best: body-conscious drapings in fabrics like silk and chiffon. Caveat emptor: The bottle blondes who work here couldn't be snottier if they tried.

Godiva Chocolatier. 701 Fifth Ave. (54th & 55th sts.). ☎ **212/593-2845.** Subway: E, F to Fifth Ave.

Godiva opened its first U.S. store on Fifth Avenue in the early 1970s and impressed the marketplace with its fine Belgian chocolates. In the intervening years, the chocolates have remained good but Godiva is now owned by Campbell's Soup; as a result, the chocolates are made in America from the Belgian recipe and shops are popping up everywhere.

La Maison du Chocolat. 25 E. 73rd St. (Fifth & Madison aves.). ☎ **212/744-7117.** Subway: 6 to 77th St.

The most famous chocolatier in Paris has a small shop in New York, where it's hard to decide which is more fabulous—the product or the fact that your chocolates come wrapped in a box with ribbon imprinted exactly like the ones made for Hermès, only brown, of course. The little gems are flown in from Paris.

COSMETICS, FRAGRANCES & BEAUTY AIDS

Every New York department store has a mind-boggling assortment of cosmetics, makeups, fragrances, bath goodies, and health and beauty aids, but several sources have become famous for their selection. **Barneys** and **Saks Fifth Avenue,** as department-store choices, are working to deliver the unusual, the unheard of, and the newest in foreign flavors. If you find that too pat and would rather have a manicure while sipping a martini or Manhattan, not to worry—this is New York, where the impossible is done with ease. Check out **Beauty Bar,** 231 E. 14th St. (☎ **212/539-1389**); it doesn't open until 5pm but a manicure is only $5 when you order a cocktail.

Since there's some crossover in merchandise between here and the section on bath products, see above for where to buy more items with which to pamper yourself.

Aveda. 509 Madison Ave. (at 53rd St.). ☎ **212/832-2416.** Subway: 6 to 51st St.

This small shop is packed with aromatherapy and hair and skin products made using natural ingredients and scents. The quality of these products has become so internationally known and trusted among a select group that the brand name has reached almost cult status. See "The Financial District" under "Shopping Neighborhoods" for the Aveda Institute and other store listings.

Cosmetics Plus. 666 Fifth Ave. (at 54th St.). ☎ **212/757-2895.** B Subway: E, F to Fifth Ave.

This chain of discount stores sells a wide range of perfumes as well as health and beauty aids, some hard-to-find foreign brands of hair-care goods, and some makeup. The basic discount is 12% to 15%, though sometimes scents are priced cheaper still. While the store has a Fifth Avenue address, it's in the arcade to this office building with the door on West 54th Street. Other branches are scattered around the city.

Face Stockholm. 110 Prince St. (Greene & Wooster sts.). ☎ **212/334-3900.** Subway: N, R to Prince St.

The only Scandinavian makeup center in town (the world?), Face Stockholm attracts models, fashionistas, and just plain Janes alike. Why? Because this dandy shop boasts all the latest colors at a fraction of the price of some of the more hoity-toity shops. Plus, it has a lovely and unpretentious staff.

✪ **Kiehl's.** 109 Third Ave. (at 13th St.). ☎ **212/475-3400.** Subway: 4, 5, 6, N, R to Union Sq.

Kiehl's is more than a store: It's a virtual cult. Models, stockbrokers, foreign visitors, and just about everyone else stop by this always-packed old-time apothecary for simply packaged, wonderfully formulated products for women and men. Lip Balm #1 is the perfect antidote to the biting winds of city or slope.

DEPARTMENT STORES

✪ **Barneys.** 660 Madison Ave. (at 61st St.). ☎ **212/826-8900.** Subway: N, R to Fifth Ave.

Barneys boasts eight floors of menswear and eight floors of womenswear and accessories. Chelsea Passage, the gift/tabletop department, is one of the world's best such spaces. While the store prides itself on the cutting-edge style of its womenswear and accessories, its menswear ranges from the classic to the outré. The fragrance department has worked hard to be the place to find offbeat and unusual scents as well as the classics. Barneys began life in Chelsea at 142 W. 17th St., but that branch has closed. The chicer-than-thou Uptown store has already become a legend. Wear black and don't smile if you shop on the women's side. The atmosphere on the men's side is different—it's a major pickup scene for gays and straights alike. The new eatery, Fred's, in the basement is chic but so-so.

✪ **Bendel's.** 712 Fifth Ave. (at 56th St.). ☎ **212/247-1100.** Subway: N, R to Fifth Ave.

Bendel's is the last word in style and the New York look. The goods range from expensive high-ticket clothes from big-name designers, to moderately priced fashions from just-breaking-out designers, to the truly affordable. The small tabletop department will leave you breathless, and the nice tearoom is positioned so you look out on Fifth Avenue through Lalique windows. The decor is so divine you must remember to look up, down, and around and to catch the drapings of the chandeliers. The brown-and-white-striped plastic-covered cosmetic and travel accessories are a status symbol; the makeup department is small but includes brands like MAC.

✪ **Bergdorf Goodman.** 754 Fifth Ave. (at 57th St.). ☎ **212/753-7300.** Subway: E, F to Fifth Ave.

Once the fanciest specialty store in New York, Bergdorf's is now under a lot of pressure from Barneys as they compete for the high-end market. **Bergdorf Goodman Man,** 745 Fifth Ave., at 58th Street (☎ 212/753-7300), is a palace built to reflect the glory of the boom 1980s. The women's side of the street is more accessible—there's a terrific gift and tabletop floor, as well as some finely tuned designer salons. The small scale of the shop makes it feel intimate, and it lacks the nouveaux-riche feel of the Bendel's crowd. Not only the ladies who lunch but also the businesswomen who have gobs of money but no time for nonsense shop here.

Bloomingdale's. 1000 Third Ave. (at 59th St.). ☎ **212/355-5900.** Subway: 4, 5, 6 to 59th St.; N, R to Lexington Ave.

Taking up the space of a city block, this department store made its name by selling a lifestyle image to coming-of-age yuppies in the 1960s. The size of the store can be overwhelming; it pays to make a reconnaissance trip to get the overview, then move in for the kill. The store sells everything from clothing and housewares to furniture and fragrance. This is one of the few full-service department stores left in the city. Bloomie's logo merchandise lovers note: There's tons of this stuff available for souvenirs.

Lord & Taylor. 424 Fifth Ave. (at 39th St.). ☎ **212/391-3344.** Subway: B, D, F, Q to 42nd St.

As a youth, I waited for hours in the car while my mother shopped at L&T's Chevy Chase branch. ("Oh, I'll just be a minute." Yeah, right.) Now, as a big boy, I can actually go *in* the store, and do so often. Now that Altman's is gone, Lord & Taylor is the remaining paean to upper-middle-class American taste; the clothes here aren't cutting edge, but for seersucker suits, high-quality sweaters, and other staples, the store (and its trained, courteous staff) can't be beat.

Macy's. At Herald Square, West 34th St. and Broadway. ☎ **212/695-4400.** Subway: 1, 2, 3, 9, B, D, F, N, Q to 34th St.

If you've ever watched the Macy's Thanksgiving Day parade on TV—or any of Macy's other special events, like the fireworks on July 4—you owe it to the store and your conscience to buy something here. One of the largest stores in the world, Macy's takes up a city block and sells just about everything. The Cellar is one of New York's best places for housewares and tabletop items; Macy's has not only a great kids' department but also a place for kids to get their hair cut, and it sponsors various promotions and activities throughout the year.

Saks Fifth Avenue. 611 Fifth Ave. (at 50th St.). ☎ **212/753-4000.** Subway: E, F to Fifth Ave.; 6 to 51st St.

There are branches of Saks all over the country and all go so far as to call themselves Saks *Fifth Avenue.* Truth is, there's only one Fifth Avenue and one flagship store, and you haven't lived till you've spent an hour here. The reason shopping here is so good is simple—the store isn't as large as most of the other Manhattan department stores but is larger than a specialty store. The first-floor fragrance department is one of the most famous in America for its selection of products in a fragrance line and for new European brands that debut here before they make it to other U.S. counters. Note the first-floor customer information booth, where free guides to the city are given away.

Takashimaya. 693 Fifth Ave. (at 54th St.). ☎ **212/350-0100.** Subway: E, F to Fifth Ave.; 6 to 51st St.

This isn't a Japanese department store. Yes, it does have a Japanese name and is owned by a Japanese department store of icon stature, but the store itself sells sort of French country Japanese Oriental eclectic yet fashionable charm. Paris's most famous florist, Christian Tortu, has a main-floor boutique that's a work of art in its own right. You'll be just as artful after your treatment in one of the store's new private facial rooms.

DISCOUNT SHOPPING

✪ **Century 21 Department Store.** 22 Cortlandt St. (Dey & Cortlandt sts.). ☎ **212/227-9092.** Subway: J, M, Z, 2, 3, 4, 5, 6, A, C to Broadway/Nassau St.

In the Financial District, you'll find three floors of bargains for men, women, children, and households, including European designer clothes sold at a fraction of their original price. I'm talking the biggest and the best names in town. The perfume department doesn't offer large discounts but does give a store credit toward your next purchase as a thank you.

Daffy's. 335 Madison Ave. (at 44th St.). ☎ **212/557-4422.** Subway: 4, 5, 6 to 42nd St.

Daffy's on lower Fifth Avenue is bigger than its Madison Avenue counterpart, but the Madison Avenue store is so convenient you can't afford to ignore this discounter of men's, women's, and children's clothing as well as a few handbags, some lingerie, and a hat or two. Few of the brand names are well known, but bargains on mid-range merchandise can be worthwhile. Name-brand luggage is sold at the Fifth Avenue shop, while the 57th Street store is very fancy and offers the most selection in terms of designer names. **Other locations:** 111 Fifth Ave., at 18th Street (☎ 212/529-4477), 1311 Broadway, at 34th Street (☎ 212/736-4477); and 135 E. 57th St., between Park and Lexington avenues (☎ 212/376-4477).

Dollar Bill. 32 E. 42nd St. (Fifth & Madison aves.). ☎ **212/867-0212.** Subway: 4, 5, 6 to 42nd St.

Regulars note: They've moved. This discounter sells fine American and Italian designer clothing, such as men's suits from the likes of Armani and Ferré. Dollar Bill also carries designer ties and Ray Bans at 30% off. In the small women's department you'll find a strong selection of suits and separates, including some fine Italian designer names.

Filene's Basement. 620 Sixth Ave. (at 18th St.). ☎ **212/620-3100.** Subway: F to 14th St.

This Boston institution and home of the "bah-gain" has two branch stores in Manhattan; they pale when compared to the mother store but offer some discounts on men's and women's clothing, handbags, accessories, shoes, and a few brands of perfume. Every now and then a big-time European label pops up, though don't count on finding the current season's goods, especially in the downstairs men's store. And no, Filene's doesn't offer its famous bridal sales in the New York stores. Because of limits placed on this off-pricer by its vendors, the store offers more "retail stock" in other branches, so don't judge the chain on the quality of the hit-or-miss situation in New York. **Another location:** 2222 Broadway, at 79th Street (☎ **212/873-8000**).

Syms. 400 Park Ave. (at 54th St.). ☎ **212/317-8200.** Subway: 6 to 51st St.

Though Syms sells some women's clothing, it's primarily a source for mid-price men's suits and casual clothing, shoes, ties, and even luggage. (Avoid the hideous polyester-laden shirts and shockingly ugly sportswear. Frontwoman Marcy Syms had it right: An educated customer is her best customer.) Syms has a wide range of sizes, even large sizes; this is also a great place to buy a tux. **Another location:** 42 Trinity Place, between Broadway and Rector Street (☎ **212/797-1199**).

TJMaxx. 620 Sixth Ave. (at 18th St.). ☎ **212/229-0875.** Subway: F to 14th St.

Directly above Filene's Basement in the same rehabbed building, TJMaxx is yet another off-pricer selling men's, women's, and children's clothing at discount, as well as shoes, lingerie, bed linen, and gift items. If you're seriously into bargains, price check each store, as there's some crossover merchandise between Filene's Basement and TJMaxx and prices at TJMaxx can be lower.

ELECTRONICS

Electronics, including gadgets and business machines, offer some of the best buys New York has, if you know what you're doing and have the patience to comparison shop. Every Tuesday, the *New York Times* publishes electronics ads in "Science Times."

Hudson Computers. 599 Lexington Ave. (at 52nd St.). ☎ **212/755-6001.** Subway: 6 to 51st St.

Husdon's does mail-order business; you can fax 212/755-6005 for price quotes on specific styles that might not be listed. The prices for delivery outside metro New York are high.

J&R Computer World. Park Row (at Wall St.). ☎ **212/238-9100.** Subway: J, M, Z, 2, 3, 4, 5, 6, A, C to Broadway/Nasssau St.

This is the most reputable of the discount computer retailers—its great prices attract customers from around the world. The sales staff is knowledgeable but can get pushy if you don't buy at once (take your time and find exactly what you need). The store has a copious catalog, which makes mail order and comparison shopping easy. Check out their Web site at www.jandr.com. To order from out of state, call ☎ **800/221-8180.**

✪ **Sunshine Computers & Electronics.** 1172 Coney Island Ave. (Aves. H & I), Brooklyn. ☎ **718/434-1500.** Subway: D to Ave. H.

I wouldn't tell you schlep to the depths of Brooklyn if the prices here weren't the cheapest on earth. Among the winners I found were a Packard Bell computer with a Pentium 233MHz processor and monitor for—are you ready?—$645! Plus, name-brand printers for as low as $99. Wow!

FASHION
MEN'S & WOMEN'S
✪ **agnès b.** 79 Greene St. (at Spring St.). ☎ **212/219-6000.** Subway: N, R to Prince St.; 6 to Spring St.

Wanna look like Belmondo in *Breathless* or like the hippest dude running around Paris today? Then look no further than agnès b., whose French fashion is at once super-stylish and classically cool. The striped shirts are timeless, and the leather car coat (about $1,200) is majorly mod. Add a pack of Gauloises for effect, and you're a magnet.

Betsey Johnson. 248 Columbus Ave. (at 72nd St.). ☎ **212/362-3364.** Subway: 1, 2, 3, 9 to 72nd St.

Betsey hasn't changed her basic look in 20 years—and thank God for that! She's been working the same ditzy New Wave look (think early Cyndi Lauper) forever, and on petite, madcap, slightly eccentric girlfolk it still looks good. Rock on, girl!

Brooks Brothers. 346 Madison Ave. (at 44th St.). ☎ **212/682-8800.**

The perfect definition of all that is preppy lies behind this store for men, women, and children. The cut of the man's suit is a tad boxy, making it great for the full American body but not quite right for the skinny European guy. The label is synonymous with quality, quiet taste, and classic tailoring. **Another location:** 1 Liberty Plaza, at Church and Liberty streets in the Financial District (☎ **212/267-2400**).

Calvin Klein. 654 Madison Ave. (60th & 61st sts.). ☎ **212/292-9000.** Subway: 4, 5, 6 to 59th St.; N. R to Lexington Ave.

From the bowels of the Bronx to superstardom, heterosexual poster boy Calvin Klein has reached the apex in this tony Madison Avenue boutique. It's more of a museum than a retail store, so sparse and lovingly is the merchandise displayed; but I must admit ole Cal has finally refound his sartorial muse. Magnificent threads for men and women with megabucks, plus home furnishing and assorted high-class *chazerei*.

Camouflage. 141 Eighth Ave. (at 17th St.). ☎ **212/741-9118.** Subway: A, C, E to 14th St.

Now that Barneys has headed uptown, Camouflage has become *the* upscale men's shop in Chelsea. The styles are well-nigh perfect: fashionable without being overly trendy, with price points that are high but not outlandish. Alas, the sales staff is too busy chattering away in Spanish to look at customers.

Canal Jean Co. 504 Broadway (Spring & Broome sts.). ☎ **212/226-1130.** B Subway: N, R to Prince St.; 6 to Spring St.

Canal Jeans almost single-handedly started the Lower Manhattan shopping revolution nearly 2 decades ago when it was the de rigueur outfitter for habitués of the Mudd Club and other Downtown haunts. Today, it's more upscale, with mini-boutiques and private label merchandise for men and women, including the fabu London Underground line: "gothic-inspired with a '90s twist."

✪ **Charivari**. 18 W. 57th St. (Fifth & Sixth aves.). ☎ **212/333-4040.** Subway: B, D, E to 7th Ave.; N, R to 57th St.

Once a major Gotham fashion presence, Charivari's empire has shrunk to just this one flagship store, but it's a doozy: one of the most forward-thinking shops for women and men anywhere in the United States. In addition to major names like Yohji Yamamoto, Plein Sud, and Commes des Garçons, you'll find up-and-coming designers like Veronique Branquinho and Lilith. Truly, this is fashion at its trendy best.

Cynthia Rowley. 112 Wooster St. (at Prince St.). ☎ **212/334-1144.** Subway: N, R to Prince St.

Rowley is one of Downtown Manhattan's big fashion guns, and her work has been heralded by all the major magazines. Once you see her dynamite designs, you'll sing her praises too. Modern without being supertrendy, her clothes are beautifully made, witty, sophisticated, and cool.

Eileen Fisher. 521 Madison Ave. (at 53rd St.). ☎ **212/759-9888.** Subway: E, F to Fifth Ave.; 6 to 51st St.

Fisher has a handful of shops in Manhattan and is expanding slowly to other cities. In the meantime, no trip to the Big Apple can be considered complete until you see her easy-to-wear fluid clothes in soft palette colors, most often sewn with an elastic waist-band. Prices are in the middle range. The style is a little droopy for short women but otherwise combines chic with comfort. **Other locations:** 314 E. 9th St., between First and Second avenues (☎ **212/529-5715**); 103 Fifth Ave., at 18th Street (☎ **212/924-4777**); and 341 Columbus Ave., at 77th Street (☎ **212/362-3000**).

Fitz & Fitz. 641 Sixth Ave. (at 19th St.). ☎ **212/645-5999.** Subway: 1, 9 to 18th St.

When you get tired of the discounters on Ladies' Mile selling unsold classics, cross over the road to what becomes a legend most. Barbara Hulanicki, a legend in the fashion world since she opened Biba in London in the 1960s, has just opened a hot haven of junk that's silly and trendy and so right for the times.

Jekyll & Hyde. 107 Grand St. (Mercer St. & Broadway). ☎ **212/966-9535.** Subway: A, E to Canal St.

For your own transformation from pauper to prince, make a beeline for this tony men's boutique. The buyers cherry-pick the best lines in the world, like Paul Smith, Antonio Miro, All Saints, and Reiss. Though it's a great one-stop store for fab fashion names, the staff tends to be inattentive and visibly bored. **Another location:** 93 Greene St., at Spring Street (☎ **212/966-8503**).

Meghan Kinney Studio. 312 E. 9th St. (First & Second aves.). ☎ **212/260-6329.** Subway: 6 to Astor Place.

Here's the final word on young, hip, yet very elegant fashions for the woman of today; if Audrey Hepburn were alive, this is where she'd shop. Affordable clothes that'll look good today, tomorrow, and forever—plus the eagle eye of owner/designer Meghan, a charm force of note. Delightful!

Naked Ape. 36 E. 4th St. (at Bowery). ☎ **212/254-9011.** Subway: F to Broadway/Lafayette St.; 6 to Bleecker St.

Nobody in the store can explain the name, but with clothes this cool, who cares? This boutique is a tiny gem, one boasting skirts and suits for the young career woman who wants to look like a million without breaking the bank. Trendy and fashionable, without being oppressively hip, with a superhelpful staff.

✪ **Patricia Field.** 10 E. 8th St. (Fifth Ave. & University Place). ☎ **212/254-1699.** Subway: 6 to Astor Place.

Even before the Village was a destination and long before the Japanese tourists dis-covered it, Patricia Field was the leading doyenne of cutting-edge chic and Downtown cool. She still is; our Pat knows where to find men's and women's clubwear that's groovier than anywhere else. The store's wild makeup collection will suddenly appear tame when you see the outlandish shades of its wacky wigs.

✪ **Paul Smith.** 108 Fifth Ave. (at 16th St.). ☎ **212/627-9770.** Subway: F to 14th St.

Some folks dream of sex; others of fame. Me, I dream of a massive gift certificate from this temple of new English fashion. And you will too: When it comes to menswear that's at once state-of-the-moment and undisputedly classic, Paul Smith wins the prize. Jackets, suits, pants, shoes (among the handsomest in town), and sportswear that are superpricey but worth every cent.

Paul Stuart. Madison Ave. at 45th St. ☎ **212/682-0320.** Subway: 4, 5, 6 to 42nd St.

If Brooks Brothers is your cup of tea, then forget Paul Stuart, which is way too hip for you. Stuart is the quintessential men's haberdasher, with a touch of the European meet-ing a touch of the American sophisticate meeting a small piece of preppy in well-cut and beautifully made clothing. Price doesn't matter, of course. You'll find everything from suits to weekend wear to impeccably tailored women's clothing. This is a way-of-life store for those who subscribe.

Polo/Ralph Lauren & Polo Sport. 867 Madison Ave. (at 72nd St.). ☎ **212/606-2100.** Subway: 6 to 68th St.

No retailer owns more of a New York landmark than Ralph Lauren with his Rhinelander mansion. While his store across the street at 888 Madison (☎ **212/434-8000**) is also snazzy and worth a stare (or two or three), this particular mansion was one of New York's first important freestanding American designer shops and has continued to wear as well as the classics Ralph churns out. Housewares and infants' clothing as well as women's and men's clothes are for sale. The activewear and sporty country looks are across the street; ironically, their main constituency seems to be homeboyz from the Uptown 'hoods. Can you dig it?

Vera Wang. 991 Madison Ave. (at 77th St.). ☎ **212/628-3499.** Subway: 6 to 77th St.

The lady who designed that white frock for Nancy Kerrigan to wear in the 1994 Olympics is arguably the hottest name in bridal fashions. Vera clothes scads of top stars on their big day or for the Oscars and other such occasions, but if you don't have big bucks, just ask for the dates of the annual warehouse sale, usually in April for the June bride who can hold out.

CHILDREN'S

Choose from **Gap Kids**—all over town—to miniature adult fashions from stores like **Brooks Brothers** or **Polo/Ralph Lauren** or get to some of the most special kids' stores you've ever laid eyes on. Madison Avenue in the 90s, populated by local prep-school darlings, is filled with European designer boutiques with prices that make a college education look cheap. Many of the Manhattan discounters (such as **Daffy's**—see "Discount Shopping") also carry some children's clothing.

Greenstones et Cie. 442 Columbus Ave. (at 81st St.). ☎ **212/580-4322.** Subway: 1, 9 to 79th St.

If you're willing to spend the money, this store specializes in funky cute. Many of the clothes are one of a kind or hand-crafted little items you wish you could make yourself. **Another location:** 1184 Madison Ave., between 86th and 87th streets (☎ **212/427-1665**).

Magic Windows. 1186 Madison Ave. (at 87th St.). ☎ **212/289-0028.** Subway: 4, 5, 6 to 86th St.

This place specializes in clothing for young women who are between kids' and adult clothing, whose bodies and taste are changing, and whose peers are unkind when the clothing isn't just so.

OshKosh B'Gosh. 586 Fifth Ave. (47th & 48th Sts.). ☎ **212/827-0098.** Subway: E, F to Fifth Ave.

Wisconsin's most famous name in fashion has a store decked out with train compartments to display the clothes: infants in the rear, boys on the left, and girls on the right. Prices begin around $6.50, which makes this a bargain destination for European shoppers who pay upward of $100 for overalls. The store gives away size-conversion charts at the center desk/cashier.

FLEA MARKETS

✪ **Annex Flea Market.** Sixth Ave. at 26th St. No phone. Subway: F to 23rd St.

Most call it the 26th Street Flea Market; this is the city's most famous, where Andy Warhol bought all those cookie jars. Here's the trick: On Saturday this market takes up one parking lot, and you pay $1 admission. On Sunday there are two parking lots—you pay $1 for the same lot as on Saturday but the add-on lot is free for all. The vendors know their stuff, but you can still do well on a variety of items, especially vintage clothing and linens.

P.S. 44 Flea Market. Columbus Ave. at 76th St. No phone. Subway: 1, 9 to 79th St.

There's more inside the schoolhouse, but the fun stuff is outdoors, where vendors sell all sorts of stuff from new hats to junk from grandma's attic to homemade pretzels and then some. I priced kilims from Turkey, pottery from Portugal, and pet supplies from Hartz. Some vintage. Enormous fun. If you like this sort of thing, this one will make your day. Sunday only.

FOOD

✪ **Balducci's.** 424 Sixth Ave. (at 10th St.). ☎ **212/673-2600.** Subway: 1, 9 to Christopher St.; F to 14th St.

Once upon a time, Balducci's gave out tons of free samples; this practice, sadly, has been sharply curtailed. Though you'll need a yuppified income to afford anything here, the store has one of New York's best assortments of imported gourmet food-stuffs and a deli counter that would make even the most confirmed anorexic salivate on cue.

Dean & DeLuca. 560 Broadway (at Prince St.). ☎ **212/431-1691.** Subway: 6 to Spring St.

Need proof that money doesn't buy happiness? Just take a gander at these bored Uptowners and suburbanites munching on astronomically priced sandwiches and costly cappuccini after their obligatory visits to the Downtown Guggenheim across the street. Ironically, the Uptown branch next door to the Paramount seems like a bargain compared to that hotel's restaurant. **Other locations:** 9 Rockefeller Center, between 48th and 49th streets (☎ **212/664-1363**), and 235 W. 46th St., between Broadway and Eighth Avenue (☎ **212/869-6890**).

Gourmet Garage. 453 Broome St. (at Mercer St.). ☎ **212/941-5850.** Subway: N, R to Prince St.

This SoHo store features a definite loft-like nondecor and some of the tastiest gourmet products in town. (*New York* magazine said they have the best produce in town.) The Garage supplies many of the city's best restaurants, including Le Cirque 2000, and sells to the public at wholesale—or about 40% off the retail of fancier stores. **Other locations:** 301 E. 64th St., between First and Second avenues (☎ **212/535-6271**), and 2567 Broadway, between 96th and 97th streets (☎ **212/663-0656**); the latter features an extensive department of Kosher foods.

H&H Bagel. 2239 Broadway (at 80th St.). ☎ **212/595-8003.** Subway: 1, 9 to 79th St.

H&H is one of New York's most famous bagel kings; it ships all over the United States. Call ☎ **800/NY-BAGEL** to order. See "Only in New York" in chapter 6 for more information. **Other locations:** 639 W. 46th St., at Twelfth Avenue (☎ **212/595-8000**), and 1551 Second Ave., at 80th Street (☎ **212/734-7441**).

Ninth Avenue Cheese Market. 615 Ninth Ave. (at 43rd St.). ☎ **212/397-4700.** Subway: A, C, E to 42nd St.

The entire strip of Ninth Avenue is heaven for foodies—there's coffees, spices, and assorted specialty shops and grocers. The cheese shop is a good one that specializes in Greek and Middle Eastern delights, with cheese from other countries as well.

Zabar's. 2245 Broadway (at 80th St.). ☎ **212/787-2000.** Subway: 1, 9 to 79th St.

A New York landmark, this giant deli sells foods, prepared goods, coffee beans, fresh breads, and even cooking supplies. The shopping experience alone, forget about the eating, defines all that New York's Upper West Side is and will ever be about. So eat, already.

GIFTS

All New York museums have at least one gift shop; many have several. The **Museum Company,** 673 Fifth Ave. (☎ 212/758-0976), isn't owned by a museum but sells the same kind of things you'd find there. The big theme restaurants all sell logo merchandise (see the box "The Themes Are the Message" in chapter 6). And the department stores sell logo merchandise—in fact, **Macy's** has an entire New York souvenir department on the ground floor.

Hammacher Schlemmer, 147 E. 57th St. (☎ 212/421-9000), is one of the world's most unique stores, with gadgets and "travel toys" and one-of-a-kind giftables—prices aren't rock bottom, but if you're looking for the unusual, don't miss it.

And Bob's Your Uncle. 137 W. 22nd St. (Sixth & 7th aves.). ☎ **212/627-7702.** Subway: 1, 9, F to 23rd St.

Who cares who Bob is? He's a genius for whimsy, kitsch, clutter, detail, fun, and fabulous. You'll find a combination of vintage meets postmodernism meets Disney cute.

Aris Mixon & Co. 381 Amsterdam Ave. (78th & 79th sts.). ☎ **212/724-6904.** Subway: 1, 9 to 79th St.

Here's a large selection of interesting and unique giftables, sort of the kind of place to touch everything in search of the gift for someone who has it all.

✪ **Depression Modern.** 150 Sullivan St. (Houston & Prince sts.). ☎ **212/982-5699.** Subway: N, R to Prince St.

Come here to be awed by the huge collection of 1930s to 1950s mix, mostly tabletop items. It's all fun, jazzy, and special.

Little Rickie. 49½ First Ave. (at 3rd St.). ☎ **212/505-6467.** Subway: F to Second Ave.

The vinyl luster of 1970s kitsch has been dulled with clichéd film, TV, and fashion overuse—but you wouldn't know it from a peek inside this shop. Charlie's Angels dolls, Fonzie lunchboxes, Elvis air fresheners, and the rest are proudly displayed. For old-time's sake, get your wallet-size picture taken in the store's photo booth.

Urban Archeology. 285 Lafayette St. (Houston & Prince sts.). ☎ **212/431-6969.** Subway: N, R to Prince St.; 6 to Spring St.

Needing some major pieces, like parts of a building, a barbershop pole, or a street sign? Step into this wacky world of new and used relics, collectibles, and, antiques—stuff you just won't find in your local mall. **Other locations:** 143 Franklin St. (☎ 212/431-4646) and, for upscale tile and lighting, 239 E. 58th St. (☎ 212/371-4646).

HOUSEWARES

✪ **ABC Carpet & Home.** 888 Broadway (at 18th St.). ☎ **212/473-3000.** Subway: F to 14th St.

No, it's not a carpet store. Okay, it does sell some carpets, but mostly it sells a look and a lifestyle. And often the merchandise is discounted by 10%—not always, but sometimes. Since this is one of the top 10 stores in New York, wander on down just to gawk at the goodies, elaborately arranged as if the store were really in the entertainment business. Well, in a way it is. The Parlour Cafe is new; at least have a latte and live.

Amalgamated. 19 Christopher St. (Sixth & 7th aves.). ☎ **212/243-9270.** Subway: 1, 9 to Christopher St.

Looking for a houseware or objet d'art that's a real conversation piece? Look no further than Amalgamated, whose groovy boys scour the globe for eye-catching household goods you won't see anywhere else. From 1950s funkerie (dig them kidney-shaped coffee tables) to ultra-modern doodads, Amalgamated rules.

Crate & Barrel. 650 Madison Ave. (at 59th St.). ☎ **212/308-0011.** Subway: N, R to Fifth Ave.

Chicago icon Gordon Segal has brought his housewares heaven to Madison Avenue and given this city a lesson in providing affordable style. The inside of the store, sleek with pine paneling, is a maze of displays and fun goodies—all moderately priced. The second level sells furniture. Crate & Barrel has a catalog, will mail to any address in the world, and will make you grin all day from the combination of energy and style.

White Trash. 30 E. 4th St. (First & Second aves.). ☎ **212/598-5956.** Subway: F to Second Ave.

I live around the corner from this castle of camp, so you can imagine what my apartment looks like. White Trash is a pearl, selling everything from high-quality Bakelite to kitsch of the first order, like a porcelain ashtray with a built-in holder marked "Cigarettes." The staff (usually a party of one) boasts the most lackadaisical attitude since the late, great Edith Massey at her Baltimore "Shopping Bag" store. A must!

Williams-Sonoma Outlet Center. 231 Tenth Ave. (at 24th St.). ☎ **212/206-8118.** Subway: C, E to 23rd St.

Pottery Barn, Williams-Sonoma, Hold Everything, and a few other firms are owned by the same parent company and hence have their factory outlet in one building in West Chelsea. The prices aren't dirt cheap, but this is a possibility if you're furnishing a first apartment or looking for affordable gifts. Despite the address, this neighborhood is safe.

JEWELRY

If you can't have breakfast at **Tiffany & Co.,** 727 Fifth Ave. (☎ 212/755-8000), you can certainly have a ring, some earrings, or maybe a tiara if you're a tiara sort of person. Because Tiffany is the landmark of all New York jewelry stores doesn't mean the city is shy on jewelers—every big-name international jet-set vendor of sparkle has a shop on Fifth Avenue (like **Cartier, Bulgari,** and **Van Cleef & Arpels**), with some of the smaller boutique names of Europe on Madison Avenue in the 60s, along with **Bulgari's** new boutique at 783 Madison Ave. (☎ 212/717-2300).

Should you prefer to get it wholesale, there's an entire street of diamond dealers—and jewelry wholesalers—on West 47th between Fifth and Sixth avenues. You just prowl from stall to stall looking at new and estate pieces, and bargaining. **The Jewelry Exchange,** 55 W. 47th St. (☎ 212/354-5200), claims to be the largest jewelry mart in the city, with over 100 dealers.

LEATHER GOODS & LUGGAGE

The big names of European luxury leather goods have their stores on Fifth Avenue in the 50s or Madison Avenue in the 60s. **Hermès,** 11 E. 57th St. (☎ 212/751-3181), begins a parade of big-name purveyors of luxury leathers from Fifth Avenue to Park Avenue that includes names like **Prada,** 45 E. 57th St. (☎ 212/308-2332), and **Ghurka,** 41 E. 57th St. (☎ 212/826-8300), an American brand trading on a British colonial look of linen or canvas and leather in luggage, tote bags, and more.

For funkier (even fetishistic) leather looks, try the West Village (especially Christopher Street).

Coach. 595 Madison Ave. (at 57th St.). ☎ **212/754-0041.** Subway: 4, 5, 6 to 59th St; N, R to Lexington Ave.

Coach has specialized in women's handbags and small leather goods and now has branched into business leather goods and men's items through its small **Coach For Business** store at 342 Madison Ave., at 45th Street (☎ **212/599-4777**). The look was traditionally superpreppy but has tried to become more high-styled as of late.

✪ **Crouch & Fitzgerald.** 400 Madison Ave. (at 46th St.). ☎ **212/755-5888.** Subway: 4, 5, 6 to 42nd St.

Crouch & Fitzgerald is a long-time specialist in leather goods, be it briefcases, handbags, or luggage—and has its own in-house **Louis Vuitton** boutique. The annual August handbag sale is a blowout. The semiannual luggage sales (November and May) feature the big names otherwise out of sight pricewise. Look out for the house brands: I still lug around monogrammed C&F leather suitcases I got for college graduation nearly (ouch!) two decades ago.

Jobson's. 666 Lexington Ave. (at 55th St.). ☎ **212/355-6846.** Subway: 6 to 51st St.

This is a discount source for name-brand luggage; Tumi, Boyt and Hartmann are all represented. Best of all, this store recently doubled its size. While it's associated with Lucas, Jobson's has almost every brand and will give you the lowdown on the best and the brightest.

J. Suarez. 450 Park Ave. (at 56th St.). ☎ **212/315-5615.** Subway: 4, 5, 6 to 59th St.; N, R to Lexington Ave.

For the best "copies" of the most famous handbags in the world, rush over to J. Suarez—a small family firm that imports the same bags as the big names from the same factories, without the big-name labels or price tags. You'll still pay over $100 for a good bag, but there are Kelly, Gucci, Prada, and Bottega styles that can fool even the most sophisticated shopper.

MUSIC, TAPES & CDS

For instruments, try the trade shops on West 48th Street between Fifth and Sixth avenues, where **Sam Ash,** 160 W. 48th St. (☎ **212/719-2299**), and **Manny's Music,** 156 W. 48th St. (☎ **212/819-0576**), offer it all.

For tapes, records, CDs, and the lot, New York has every big chain in America and then some. Many shops are in high-profile neighborhoods and come complete with video screens, earphones, and everything else it takes to seduce. **Tower Records** is in the basement of Trump Tower, 725 Fifth Ave. (☎ **212/838-8110**); **HMV** has opened at 565 Fifth Ave. (☎ **212/681-6700**); and there's a **Virgin Megastore** at 1540 Broadway (☎ **212/921-1020**). **Tower Records** also has its own flea market/outlet shop at its Downtown store, 20 E. 4th St. (☎ **212/505-1500** or 212/228-7317).

Bleecker Bob's Golden Oldies. 118 W. 3rd St. (Sixth Ave. & MacDougal St.). ☎ **212/475-9677.** Subway: A, B, C, D, E, F, Q to W. 4th St.

Bleecker Bob's has a wide assortment of music—from punk and new wave to R&B and reggae and imports and rare jazz and more. In vinyl, no less. It's open noon to 1am.

Colony Records. 1619 Broadway (at 49th St.). ☎ **212/265-2050.** Subway: 1, 9 to 50th St.; C, E to 50th St./Eighth Ave.

Come here for posters from Broadway plays, records, CDs, tapes, and one of the best collections of sheet music—including some hard-to-find international stuff.

Finyl Vinyl. 204 E. 6th St. (Third Ave. & Bowery). ☎ **212/533-8007.** Subway: 6 to Astor Place.

Still pining for that new wave LP that got away or the album by that one-hit 1960s wonder? Make a beeline for Finyl Vinyl, where the sounds of yesteryear live on.

J&R Music World. Park Row (at Broadway). ☎ **212/238-9070.** Subway: A, C, J, M, Z, 2, 3, 4, 5 to Broadway/Nassau St.

The other half of the J&R computer discounters is one of New York's most famous sources for cassettes, CDs, and more. It's worth the trip Downtown for the price and selection, though the staff can be on the surly side.

Metropolitan Opera Shops. 136 W. 65th St. (Amsterdam & Columbus aves.). ☎ **212/580-4090.** Subway: 1, 9 to 66th St.

The Metropolitan Opera has two shops selling music-related gifts and souvenirs for the opera buff—many are witty and creative, not just your basic bravo.

✪ **Other Music.** 15 E. 4th St. (Broadway & Lafayette St.). ☎ **212/477-8150.** Subway: 6 to Astor Place; F to Broadway/Lafayette St.

Their psychedelic business card is totally groovy, but Other Music's stock is groovier still: Hard-to-find indie/alternative, ambient, experimental, and international sounds are all in this fab store. And the sales staff really knows their stuff; I've never stumped them with requests for even the most obscure CD.

Sounds. 20 St. Mark's Place (Second & Third aves.). ☎ **212/677-3444.** Subway: 6 to Astor Place.

The founding father of St. Mark's record stores, Sounds is still the best-priced—most new CDs are only $9.99, a steal compared to Tower down the street. In addition, there's a huge selection of used CDs; rock, jazz, pop, country, and R&B are all widely represented.

PAPER & STATIONERY

Kate's Paperie. 8 W. 13th St. (Fifth & Sixth aves.). ☎ **212/633-0570.** Subway: F to 14th St.

Three cheers to Kate's for keeping the art of writing alive in our computer age! I could browse for hours among this delightful shop's handmade stationery, imported notebooks, writing implements, and ancillaries, and I often do. Lovely art cards, too—perfect for writing the folks back home. A joy! **Another location:** 561 Broadway, between Prince and Spring streets (☎ **212/941-9816**).

RESALE SHOPS

Vintage (see later in this chapter) implies a certain amount of fraying at the edges, staining at the underarms, or pulling at the hook and eyes as well as a kind of style that you've either got or haven't got—but probably can't pick up along the way. Resale, on the other hand, implies "almost new" and in New York often means that big-name designer clothing is suddenly affordable.

Designer Resale. 324 E. 81st St. (First & Second aves.). ☎ **212/734-3639.** Subway: 6 to 77th St.

While not as famous as the big names (see below) and not quite as convenient, Designer Resale gets some name clothing and has some great prices. The store has a system with color codes and dots that indicate further reductions, so never trust the ticket price. Ask. Its men's boutique, **Gentlemen's Resale,** is across the street.

Encore. 1132 Madison Ave. (at 84th St.). ☎ **212/879-2850.** Subway: 6 to 86th St.

This is one of the best resale shops, with two floors of womenswear, plus a few men's jackets and some accessories. Enter on the second floor, shop that space, then take the interior staircase up to another floor with sportswear and accessories. Encore does have sales. The Chanel suit I saw here for $650 was the deal of the century.

Michael's. 1041 Madison Ave. (79th & 80th sts.). ☎ **212/737-7273.** Subway: 6 to 77th St.

While you're in the neighborhood checking out Encore (above), also visit Michael's, upstairs, which boasts all big-name designers at a fraction of their original cost. The bridal consignment department is a real find, with top-quality name dresses. And there's a small but top-notch shoe department.

SHOES

Designer shops with European names and prices trot along East 57th Street and amble up Madison Avenue. Comfortable shoes are sold mostly from stores your mother would appreciate on Fifth Avenue around 38th Street, near Lord & Taylor. Cheap copies of hotshot shoes are in the slew of tiny shops on East 8th Street between Broadway and Sixth Avenue, which some people nickname Shoe Row. Most department stores have two shoe departments—one for designer stuff and one for Cinderella before the ball. The city's numerous sporting-goods stores (there's a huge cluster in the Union Square area) sell sporting shoes for every sport—except maybe shopping.

Arché. 10 Astor Place (at 8th St.). ☎ **212/529-4808.** Subway: 6 to Astor Place.

This fabulous French footwear line boasts shoes that are supercomfortable, supercool, and superexpensive to boot. Known for their springy soles and eye-catching colors, Arché's entries range from $180 for a mere slip of a shoe to $335 for top-of-the-liners; but if you've got the gelt, they're worth every cent. The perfect conduit to extended romps around Manhattan.

Billy Martin. 812 Madison Ave. (at 68th St.). ☎ **212/861-3100.** Subway: 6 to 68th St.

Maybe you remember him as a baseball manager, but he was also an urban cowboy, and his shop lives on with the Santa Fe look right on Madison Avenue. It's a pretty good source for fantasy cowboy boots. Rhinestones optional.

Diego Della Valle. 41 E. 57th St. (Fifth & Madison aves.). ☎ **212/644-5945.** Subway: E, F to Fifth Ave.

You can get Italian high heels here, but the real reason the rich and famous shop at Diego Della Valle is to load up on JPTod's. This is a so-called driving shoe: a moccasin with rubber pimples on the sole to cushion the foot and make it impossible for you to wear anything else, even when walking. Various colors are available.

Edna Shoes. 827 Lexington Ave. (at 63rd St.). ☎ **212/935-1348.** Subway: 4, 5, 6 to 59th St; N, R to Lexington Ave.

This is the outlet store for a Manhattan chain of moderately priced shoes called Galo. Galo shoes generally cost about $150 per pair; at the outlet you'll pay just under $100. The styles tend to be classics.

✪ **Gueridon.** 359 Lafayette St. (at Bleecker St.). ☎ **212/677-7740.** Subway: 6 to Bleecker St.

If I were given a gift certificate at any shoe store in New York, I'd probably request one from Gueridon. Why? Because their French lovelies (primarily for men) are fashion conscious without being supertrendy and are always wonderfully made. Not cheap but not overpriced—a heartily recommended splurge.

Joan & David. 816 Madison Ave. (at 68th St.). ☎ **212/772-3970.** Subway: 6 to 68th St.

They made their rep as the shoe vendors in Ann Taylor stores; now Joan and her hubby, David, are on their own in a big way, with boutiques in London, Paris, and the like. They sell clothes and a whole look while remaining famous for their women's shoes that are trendy without being outré. **Another location:** 104 Fifth Ave., at 15th Street (☎ 212/627-1780).

✪ **Manolo Blahnik.** 15 W. 55th St. (Fifth & Sixth aves.). ☎ **212/582-3007.** Subway: E, F to Fifth Ave.

If you make only one wild and crazy purchase in your life, it may well be a pair of "Manoloes"—shoes created by this designer known for the cut and sway of the shoe and the way they shape the leg. Though there are some catch-me-if-you-can high heels, there are plenty of flats and low heels. Custom shoes in your own fabric are also a possibility. Cinderella never had it so good. Twice a year, at the end of the sale period, there's a blowout day or two when all shoes that are left are sold for $100 a pair.

Patrick Cox. 702 Madison Ave. (at 62nd St.). ☎ **212/759-3910.** Subway: 4, 5, 6 to 59th St.; N, R to Lexington Ave.

Patrick Cox is the latest fashion trendsetter for shoes everyone is talking about. Shockingly enough, they're affordable. The line is called Wannabe; his fame is based on heavyset penny loafers of orange patent leather. Don't want orange? They also come in pink.

TOYS & GAMES

The national chain **Toys 'R' Us** has invaded Manhattan and taken the discount toy business by storm—one location to check out is at the Manhattan Mall, 34th Street and Sixth Avenue. The only toy retailers left are specialty stores where price doesn't matter and ingenuity does.

FAO Schwarz. 767 Fifth Ave. (at 58th St.). ☎ **212/644-9400.** Subway: E, F to 53rd St.

It just so happens it won't cost you an arm and a leg to take your kids to FAO Schwarz, America's most famous toy retailer. Nor will you find it impossible to choose something if you're on a mad dash of a business trip (the front-left corner specializes in prewrapped gifts). Check the floor models for prices and a demonstration; then pay and leave. If you have the kids with you, tell them it's a museum. Watch the extravagant clock, play video games, and use the clean bathrooms. Enjoy.

Game Show. 1240 Lexington Ave. (at 83rd St.). ☎ **212/472-8011.** Subway: 6 to 86th St.

Here you'll find board games galore, including such splendid staples as Sorry, Scrabble, and Candyland, plus backgammon, checkers, and dice games. A good number of adult games are also stocked in this spiffy store. **Another location:** 474 Sixth Ave., between 11th and 12th streets (☎ 212/633-6328).

✪ **Kidding Around.** 60 W. 15th St. (Fifth & Sixth aves.). ☎ **212/645-6337.** Subway: F to 14th St.

This boutique stocks pricey high-quality toys, many imported from Europe. The emphasis is on the old-fashioned—low-tech goodies like puzzles, rocking horses, and tops. One wall is devoted exclusively to tub toys, windups, and other such stocking stuffers. The small selection of well-made, mostly French clothes is rather expensive, but if you get here at the end of a season, you can't beat the half-price sales.

Another location: 68 Bleecker St., between Broadway and Lafayette Street (☎ **212/598-0228**).

Penny Whistle. 448 Columbus Ave. (81st & 82nd sts.). ☎ **212/873-9090.** Subway: 1, 9 to 79th St.

Another upscale shop that sells more mainstream toys. Merchandise is geared toward slightly older kids, and there's a brace of silly doodads adults will get a kick out of, too. Prices are a bit high. **Another location:** 1283 Madison Ave., between 91st and 92nd streets (☎ **212/369-3868**).

VINTAGE CLOTHING

Antique Boutique. 712 Broadway (4th St. & Astor Place). ☎ **212/460-8830.** Subway: 6 to Astor Place.

Need a tux? Do what any sensible person would do—buy a vintage one. Tuxedos, sold to men and women, are only a small portion of the huge array of goodies here, including less formal duds like bowling shirts and Hawaiian shirts. The store stays open until midnight on Saturday so the teens—and the nightclubbers—can make the scene. This is one of the resources that designers use when they need inspiration for retro styles.

The Fan Club. 22 W. 19th St. (Fifth & Sixth aves.). ☎ **212/929-3349.** Subway: F to 14th St.

Note the unusual hours of this store (Tues–Sat noon–7pm) because you won't want to miss it; it's handy for those on a shopping-spree through Ladies' Mile. This large shop that looks like a party at a garage sale is run by Gene London, one of New York's most famous costumers. Most of the clothing comes from performers; most of the proceeds go to charity.

Love Saves the Day. 119 Second Ave. (7th St. & St. Mark's Place). ☎ **212/228-3802.** Subway: 6 to Astor Place.

Yes, this is the store made famous in Madonna's big film break, *Desperately Seeking Susan;* in the more than 10 years since the movie's release, LSD hasn't changed much (except the prices keep going skyward). More of interest to visitors than locals (how many Daniel Boone coats does even the most die-hard East Villager need?), there's one good reason to fall in Love here: the impressive assortment of Donny and Marie 1970s kitsch.

Metropolis. 43 Third Ave. (at 9th St.). ☎ **212/477-3941.** Subway: 4, 5, 6, N, R to Union Square.

It's rumored that some of the biggest names in the fashion world scout this clean, orderly vintage shop for street fashion ideas. With good reason too: Some of the coolest old clothes in the world turn up here—like 1950s fast-food restaurant shirts and gingham-checked Western shirts perfect for your very own hoe-down or hulla-baloo.

✪ **Screaming Mimi's.** 382 Lafayette St. (4th & Great Jones sts.). ☎ **212/677-6464**. Subway: B, D, F to Broadway/Lafayette St.

Think you hate vintage shopping? Think again: Screaming Mimi's is as neat and well organized as any high-priced boutique. While they've become a little pricey for their own good and the sales help couldn't be bothered by or for anything, the clothes are majorly cool. Their newly added vintage housewares department offers a cornucopia of kitschy old stuff, and their screamworthy selection of New York memorabilia is a total hoot.

WINE & SPIRITS

Best Cellars. 1291 Lexington Ave. (at 87th St.). ☎ **212/426-4200.** Subway: 6 to 86th St.

Committed to stocking "great wines for everyday," Best Cellars succeeds with elan. I've never seen so many fine labels for under $10. Interestingly, the wines are stocked by taste (not by grape or region); look for fizzy, fresh, juicy, and other yummy descriptors. The Saturday events (2–4pm) are educational and fun, and the nightly tastings 5 to 8pm are the best in town. All this and an extranice, extrasmart staff.

Morrell & Co. Wine & Spirits. 535 Madison Ave. (at 54th St.). ☎ **212/688-9370.** Subway: 6 to 51st St.

The 1949 Château Pétrus is less expensive than the 1959 Château Pétrus. But wait, you don't need to spring for a $1,000 bottle of wine, as the experts here will guide you to something affordable. Morrell is one of the leading stockists in America; they have fabulous almost Disneyesque windows. Press your nose to the window glass, then to a wineglass.

9

After Dark

A whirl of activity, New York City refuses to die down gently into any night. It's as awake under the streetlights as under the sunlight. New York boasts the world's best opera, dance, and visiting classical musicians, plus the full range of high and low arts, bars, clubs, stand-up comedy, and just about everything else that could distract and entertain. Broadway and other theater is enough to fill a year's vacation.

You can while away your time sipping Manhattans and listening to the naughty and nice lyrics of Cole Porter or head way uptown to get into the groove of Harlem's renewed jazz scene. Or you might choose something rawer—say, spending a late weekday night (never the weekend!) trolling clubland for sinful urban octane excitement.

ENTERTAINMENT BY NEIGHBORHOOD Though the overall scene is diverse, entertainment tends to center in certain neighborhoods, each with a distinct character. **Times Square** is home to most Broadway theaters, a renaissance of new attractions, and all kinds of restaurants, bars, cinemas, shops, supper clubs, and (still, standing in the shadows) sins. **Lincoln Center for the Performing Arts** is a grand cultural cluster (see the box "The Many Faces of Lincoln Center"). The central part of **Greenwich Village,** from Sixth Avenue to Broadway, is renowned for its coffee bars that stay open late, music clubs, and lively street scene. **SoHo** has clubs that attract artists, models, and other image types. The **West Village** is a lively mix of jazz clubs, Off and Off Off Broadway theaters, and lesbian and gay bars, which also pepper **Chelsea.** The **Flatiron District** mingles sophisticated dining with a singles scene and throbbing nightlife. Alternative clubs deep in the East Village's **"Alphabet City"** (Avenue A and eastward, below 14th Street) are perfect for when you just have to "out" your tattoos and tongue piercings. **South Street Seaport,** especially in summer, attracts families and stays open late and is often the site of free concerts. The **Upper East Side** and **Upper West Side** generally have a more sophisticated, if not to say bourgeois, set of options. **Midtown** has hotel action, as well as a few clubs.

LOOKING FOR LISTINGS For the best local listings consult the *New York Times* every day, but especially on Friday and Sunday; the *Village Voice,* especially for its alternative and music listings (on the stands every Wednesday; free in Manhattan); *New York* magazine, for its back-of-the-book listings, with good theater detail; *New York Press,* free in various shops, which has a surprisingly good, and

Impressions

Everyone in Manhattan is a star or a star manqué, and every flat surface in the island is a stage.

—Quentin Crisp

amusing, listings section on the more recherché Downtown scene; and *Time Out New York. Homo Xtra* and its women's version, *HX for Her,* are by far the best guides to the gay scene; another choice is *Next* (they're available free in appropriate bars and clubs).

LOOKING FOR TICKETS   If you plan far enough in advance, buying tickets for the hottest shows is simple—just call major sellers like **Tele-charge** at ☎ 212/239-6200 and **TicketMaster** at ☎ 212/307-4100. The League of American Theaters and Producers has a new toll-free number (☎ 888/BROADWAY; 212/302-4111 in the New York area) giving the latest about Broadway and connecting you to Tele-charge and TicketMaster. Sponsored by the Theatre Development Fund, **NYC/On Stage** at ☎ 212/768-1818 is a recorded service giving schedules and other details on theater and performances, dance and music, the off-price TKTS booths, and family entertainment. It also transfers you to a ticket-selling outlet.

For the world's best guide to purchasing tickets once you've come to town, see the special feature "Top Ticket-Buying Tips" at the end of the "Theater" section below. Do remember to bring your plastic—prices for orchestra seats at the most popular musicals are up around $80, and the special VIP tickets for *Ragtime* have hit $125.

LOOKING FOR INFORMATION   The **New York Convention and Visitors Bureau** provides a toll-free number—☎ 800/NYC-VISIT—through which you can order literature. To speak to a live person who can help you build your entire trip, call ☎ 212/484-1222 (Mon–Fri 9am–5pm). You can also visit the bureau's new information center at 810 Seventh Ave., between 52nd and 53rd streets, and the new Times Square Visitors Center in the Embassy Theater on Seventh Avenue between 46th and 47th streets (daily 8am–8pm) and pick up information on how to get tickets for TV tapings, literature about attractions and theater, and a mountain of brochures and flyers that'll bring you up to speed on the world's fastest-moving city.

1 All the City's a Stage: New York Theater

No city in the world gives better theater than New York. Sure, London has grand musicals and literate drama too, but what no other city has is the wide-open alternatives. There's so much unrestrained verve here: inventive, no-holds-barred productions that illuminate or aggravate, shock or charm. Professional or wacky, not infrequently both simultaneously, New York theater is a metaphor for the city itself—always on, sometimes uplifting, occasionally disenchanting or exasperating, and often so engaging you'll think of nothing else for days.

The variety of live performances runs from revivals of Greek classics to cannibalistic revivals of Broadway musicals, from one-person tours-de-force to ultrareal extravaganzas with head-spinning costume changes and full orchestras. You can choose intimate dinner-theater venues, multimillion-dollar productions in landmark theaters starring the most famous marquee names, or Off and Off Off Broadway housed in unassuming small theaters, former churches, or dilapidated auditoriums. Every day of the week and twice on matinee days.

Plays and musicals close all the time, often with little warning. In order to present an overview of the current scene, I discuss certain productions, some of which might no longer be open during your visit. But what matters is that you have a contemporary context in which to experience the vitality of theater in New York City.

In this most public act of intimate imagination—where, as the Phantom says, "darkness stirs and wakes imagination . . . open up your mind, let your fantasies unwind"—you share the dim light with people who manifest absolute passion for the stage. Where else could you find so many line-quoting, Ruby Keeler–loving stargazers who can recite the names and casts of every show that never even made it to Broadway? Theater's need for spectators—for voyeurs, if you will—is consummated much more faithfully, and naturally, by New Yorkers than by audiences anywhere else. In ecstasy or disaster, a large part of what sets theater apart is that it gives strangers a chance to share a demonstrative reaction (ever join a crowd applauding a van Gogh in a museum?)—and New York's audiences are the best.

The city's stages present much more than the expected musicals and dramas. Outré performances, like Karen Findley's infamous appearance many years ago in nothing more than chocolate, might send shudders through the folks in Washington who still provide—at least at this writing—grants for such quasi-comical, quasi-serious shenanigans via the National Endowment for the Arts. Certain members of Congress use that sort of opportunity to bemoan the collapse of morality and attempt to censor expression that doesn't meet their constituents' standards. They forget that the Supreme Court has held that local standards dictate what's acceptable in such circumstances and that the taxes from which NEA grants derive are also paid by individual New Yorkers and by the wealth of Wall Street and other local corporate taxpayers. Very little doesn't get by on our stages because we like it like that.

But don't let any of that mislead you: There are all kinds of serious or amusing, and clothed, productions for adults and even the whole family. On Broadway, in the "new" Times Square, you'll find whatever suits your tastes, from Disney's family-flavored productions like *The Lion King* and musical blockbusters like *Ragtime* to last year's compelling revival of Arthur Miller's *View from the Bridge* and the for-thinking-adults-only *Art,* Yesmin Keza's wonderful treatise on modern art, translated and imported from France via London and winner of the Tony for Best Play. No one would want to pass up a chance to savor a one-man mindbender like last year's John Leguizamo in *Freak,* in which a full dysfunctional Latin family springs to hilarious life. Watch for Elton John's version of *Aïda* to cause a ruckus sometime this year.

Off and Off Off Broadway, despite their reputation for being imaginative, daring, and at the edge of the envelope, can be just plain fun. Even some "performance art" pieces aren't as excessive as you'd expect—the long-running *Blue Man Group: Tubes,* at the Astor Place Theater, and *Stomp,* at the Orpheum Theatre, have entertained children and their older charges with a weird take on what the stage can do. Of course, you can also encounter more adult fare, like Eli Wallach's masterful performance in Jeff Baron's *Visiting Mr. Green* and the very modern humor in Eddie Izzard's *Dress to Kill.* Read about what's happening throughout New York theater—you'll find pleasant surprises in unexpected places.

BROADWAY

Broadway is obviously doing something right, earning record grosses season after season. The truth is that a lot of the increases in revenue are due to increases in ticket prices, so even when audiences drop off, income doesn't (you have to admire their chutzpah). Still, in the 1997–98 season, the last full season, nearly all 35 Broadway houses were lit and *11.5 million* people bought tickets, the highest number ever. That's

The Theater District

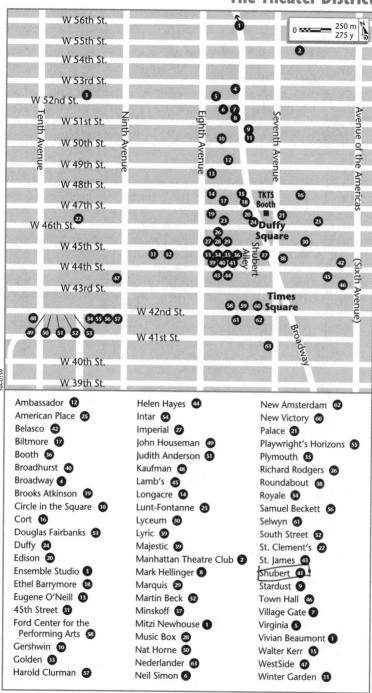

A Tip on Terms

The terms *Broadway, Off Broadway,* and *Off Off Broadway* refer to theater size, pay scales, and other arcane details, not location. Most of the Broadway theaters are in Times Square but *off* Broadway on 44th and 45th streets, with many more dotted along the blocks mostly from Sixth to Eighth avenues, north to about 53rd Street. There's even a Broadway theater outside Times Square, the Vivian Beaumont (in Lincoln Center at Broadway and 65th Street). And there are Off Broadway theaters in Times Square and *on* Broadway. Carefully check where your play is playing.

up from 10.5 million the preceding year. The gross receipts also went up from $499 million to $558 million—the highest gross of any single season ever. These figures are from the League of American Theaters and Producers, an industry group that estimates Broadway supports 25,000 jobs and annually brings $2.7 billion into the local economy.

The general health of Broadway has resulted in a space crunch, with producers scurrying to find the proper-size houses and the Shubert Organization thinking about building new theaters. The resplendent Disney renovation of the art nouveau New Amsterdam Theater and the construction of the Ford Center for the Performing Arts, incorporating two old theaters into the first new Broadway theater constructed in over a decade, have revived 42nd Street in a way few could've imagined just 5 years ago.

CAMELOT IT'S NOT   Despite all the above good news, perhaps because of it, a cohort of pseudointellectual New Yorkers has been shocked—shocked!—by the state of Broadway. They moan that things like *The Lion King, Ragtime, Beauty and the Beast,* the eternal *Cats, Phantom of the Opera, Miss Saigon,* and *Les Misérables* signal the death of the Great White Way—there's nothing serious anymore, they say. Could they get a grip, please?

This stuff is *popular,* and if the ticket-buying crowd has any complaints they're not voicing them with their wallets. What is Broadway for, after all, if not to attract the largest number of theatergoers? The naysayers have either short memories or no idea what they're talking about: Broadway has never been the exclusive province of what they consider "serious" theater. What about *The Zeigfeld Follie?* And the flea circuses that crowded the same 42nd Street as burlesque and Shakespeare when the area was first becoming the new theater district? And what about the Palace, where *Beauty and the Beast* now plays, which was the top-of-the-line theater for the dubious taste of vaudevillians just a few decades ago?

Nothing is more Broadway than massively successful shows side by side with more "serious" stuff. Tony-winner *The Lion King* is directed by highly respected avant-garde artist/performer Julie Taymor, who won the Tony for Best Director. The book of *Ragtime,* adapted from E. L. Doctorow's novel, was written by Terrence McNally—who wrote *The Lisbon Traviata, Love! Valour! Compassion!,* and *Master Class,* all properly held in high regard by those who appreciate thoughtful theater. The truth is, serious drama and sophisticated comedy are likely to be produced only in a healthy theatrical economic climate.

MORE THAN ONE THIN DIME   The New York theater community, in cooperation with the city's administration, has formed the Broadway Initiative, whose intention is to create a $10-million fund to revitalize dramas and small musicals. That kind of action can take place only once the producers no longer perceive their financial health as precarious. Let them make a profit from the frothy extravaganzas because it's only then that they're willing to take a chance on presenting more serious stuff.

Also helping assure the success of Broadway, whether in musicals or dramas, are Hollywood A-list types showing their talents live and in person. Over the last few years, Whoopi Goldberg, Glenn Close, Madonna, Alec Baldwin, Alan Alda, Marisa Tomei, Quentin Tarantino, and Jane Alexander have played their hours on the stage.

But Hollywood stars, surprising successes or inane failures, are only part of the story. New Yorkers know that *theater* stars, like Betty Buckley, Patti LuPone, Tommy Tune, and Nathan Lane, are just as good as (well, better than) most movie actors in live performance.

THE NEON LIGHTS ARE BRIGHT   Despite the hand-wringing crowd's warning that old-fashioned New York musicals and drama couldn't survive in a sea of mega-spectaculars, tacky imports, and "safe" revivals, came the season of 1996. Broadway showed there were no people like show people with the opening of *Rent* and *Bring in 'da Noise, Bring in 'da Funk,* two homegrown shows that went from Off Broadway raves to on-Broadway Tonys. They were new, American, and New York.

In 1997 and 1998, drama flourished. David Hare's *Judas Kiss,* a crowd-pleaser in London about Oscar Wilde, opened starring Liam Neeson, last on Broadway in 1993's *Anna Christie* with Natasha Richardson (now his wife), who in turn opened the revival of *Cabaret* as Sally Bowles. The Druid Theatre Company's *Beauty Queen of Leenane* was another well-received dramatic import. And there were revivals of Eugene O'Neill (*Ah! Wilderness*) and Arthur Miller (*A View from the Bridge*), new Broadway works from David Mamet (*The Old Neighborhood*) and David Henry Hwang (*Golden Child*), and the success of Pulitzer Prize–winner Alfred Uhry's *Last Night of Ballyhoo.*

Neil Simon came back to Broadway—he had opened his previous play, *London Suite,* in an Off Broadway theater for the first time—with his *Proposals,* which, though created by a traditional Broadway legend, just didn't have the stuff and quickly closed. Simon's *Sunshine Boys* got dusted off for a successful revival, starring that old toothsome twosome Jack Klugman and Tony Randall.

LET'S GO ON WITH THE SHOW   There's room for more native Broadway musicals—thoughtful and entertaining, without all the inflated stage values—the kind of thing that Sondheim used to do. But the two aren't mutually exclusive, and any theater is better than none. The problem isn't perhaps with the producers, but I dare say it, with the writers and audiences. The same tribe that has proclaimed the end of Broadway didn't support *Side Show* with their wallets. It was a critically acclaimed, perfectly adult piece of Broadway that had to close because it couldn't attract enough of an audience.

It was with delicious irony that some in the theater relished the closing of Paul Simon's *Capeman,* the biggest turkey to gobble up many millions—$11 million to be precise—in a long time. Early on, Simon smugly rejected the advice from the traditional theater crowd, believing only he knew best. By the time the pros came in to save the floundering victim, it was too late. After Simon cast aspersions on the old hands of Broadway and then found himself drowning in a sea of red ink, I couldn't help remembering that he'd once earnestly asked, in a song from long ago, "Is the theater really dead?" No, but your show is.

Nonetheless, there is hope. *Forbidden Broadway,* a constantly updated spoof of musicals that took big but toothless bites out of the Broadway mystique, closed a few years after a long run because, in the words of the theater itself, "There were no musicals left to spoof after *Phantom* and the other spectacles took over." Then 2 years ago, in a sign that the Broadway musical is vital enough again to bother parodying, the same folks brought us *Forbidden Broadway Strikes Back!* Disney, *Rent,* Liza Minnelli (who couldn't shake off gossip that she was a backstage brat during her recent run in *Victor/Victoria*), and more all receive good-humored and sharp stabs.

BROADWAY: NOW & FOREVER   Despite minor quibbles or deep questions about the direction of Broadway, there's so much to love about it. The sheer optimism and "golly-gee" Americanism of its musicals, for example. Kids will, and should, adore productions like *Cats* (the longest-running show in Broadway history) and *The Sound of Music* (the revival opened in 1998 and quickly became a family favorite and a target of the cynical critic brigade). They'll be enchanted by Disney's one-two punch of *Beauty and the Beast* and *The Lion King*. For all its need to be a commercial venture, Broadway remains at its best—and that happens often enough—an unassailably human endeavor, where the dreams and dead ends, hopes and failures, courageous acts and confused struggles of daily existence are given a new reflective and theatrical life.

OFF BROADWAY & OFF OFF BROADWAY

The range, energy, and excitement of Off and Off Off Broadway provide a vibrant creative current that makes itself felt throughout theater on Broadway and across the globe. Many of Broadway's greatest hits began their runs humbly in smaller theaters, as recently attested to by *Rent, Bring in 'da Noise,* the revival of *A View from the Bridge,* and the New York production of the Irish drama *The Beauty Queen of Leenane.*

The best Off and Off Off shows don't need to move to Broadway to be legitimized. In fact, in many ways, especially with dramas, being away from Broadway can mean they're freer to be hits without being huge draws. In recent seasons, Paula Vogel's disturbing but marvelous *How I Learned to Drive,* Eve Ensler's incisive and amusing *Vagina Monologues,* Jeff Baron's *Visiting Mr. Green,* and just plain runaway hits like *Blue Man Group: Tubes* and *Stomp* have found a successful home away from the glitz and glamour of the Great White Way.

OFF IS DEFINITELY IN   Just as Broadway generally produces bigger-than-big hits that fall within the theatrical mainstream, Off and Off Off Broadway offer some of the most experimental, invigorating, and rewarding shows. You'll find "mainstream"

The New York Shakespeare Festival

Now in its 44th season, the **New York Shakespeare Festival** (☎ 212/539-8500) is held in summer at Central Park's Delacorte Theater (☎ 212/861-7277), near Belvedere Castle, and the rest of the year at the Joseph Papp Public Theater, 425 Lafayette St. (☎ 212/260-2400). Shakespeare in the Park, especially now that the Delacorte has been nicely renovated, is a dream—under the stars, with breezes rustling the nearby trees. You can see all kinds of interpretations of the bard, from predictable period costumes to leather-clad punks. Its productions attract big stars: Michele Pfeiffer, Kevin Kline, Jeff Goldblum, Tracey Ullman, and Patrick Stewart are just a few.

Tickets are given out free on a first-come, first-served basis (two per person), at 1pm, but people line up 2 to 3 hours before that, on the baseball field next to the theater. The Delacorte Theater might have 1,881 seats, but each is a hot commodity.

You can also get free tickets, two per person, from 1 to 3pm at the Public Theater box office Downtown, where the Shakespeare Festival continues throughout the year.

productions, for sure, such as the Papp presentation of *The Cripple of Inishmaan* (by Martin McDonagh, who also wrote *The Beauty Queen of Leenane*), the exact kind of hardcore drama that used to open on Broadway. But you'll also find ethnic, avant-garde, and gay and lesbian theater, as well as performance art and other daring work. Theater junkies often turn to Off and Off Broadway not only for their fix of the weird but also for the fine drama that just doesn't need to make its way to Broadway anymore.

In its own category is one of my favorites, the ✪ **Ridiculous Theatrical Company,** a producer of wild, unbridled comedy at different venues around Downtown. Founded by Charles Ludlam and now directed by his protégé/former lover, Everett Quinton, this on-target permanent ensemble of actors makes parody, burlesque, and farce into high art. Any contemporary theme, any classic from Greece to France (*Camille* is known to those in theater circles as a historic and outrageous achievement) to Shakespeare, is delightfully twisted, wherein drag queens meet truck drivers and life is seen in its true form—through a carnival fun mirror.

At the Sullivan Street Theatre, you won't have to try to remember *The Fantasticks* because it's still running. It opened May 3, 1960, and is now the longest-running musical in the world. Off Broadway has had other developments, of course. *Perfect Crime* had by summer 1997 become the longest-running play then currently Off Broadway (though it's in a theater directly on Broadway).

THE BEST OF THE OFF   Off and Off Off Broadway theaters or troupes are only as good as the plays they present. Besides the Ridiculous Theatrical Company (above), the following are theaters that consistently produce outstanding work:

- **Actors Playhouse,** 100 Seventh Ave. South (☎ **212/463-0060**), occasional home not only to the Ridiculous Theatrical Company but also to many new gay plays.
- **American Place Theatre,** 111 W. 46th St. (☎ **212/840-2960**), where Wynn Handman has directed fine productions of new American comedy.
- **Astor Place Theater,** 434 Lafayette St. (☎ **212/254-4370**), home to *Blue Man Group*.
- **Century Theatre Center,** 111 E. 15th St. (☎ **212/239-6200**), a spot recently placed on theatergoers' maps as a result of Paula Vogel's *How I Learned to Drive,* presented by the Vineyard Theater Company, a group to seek out for its quirky, widely admired offerings.
- **City Center Stage,** 131 W. 55th St. (☎ **212/581-1212**), the scene of the Encore! series of concert versions of musicals (Patti LuPone in *Pal Joey,* for one, and Joel Grey in the concert version of *Chicago,* which eventually made it to Broadway as a full-fledged revival).
- **Duffy Theatre,** 1553 Broadway (☎ **212/695-3401**), where *Perfect Crime* has played its record-breaking run.
- **LaMama E.T.C.,** 74A E. 4th St. (☎ **212/475-7710**), an unfailingly interesting resource for thousands of great new works and playwrights, including Sam Shepard, Lanford Wilson, and Amy and David Sedaris.
- **Manhattan Theatre Club,** at City Center, 131 W. 55th St. (☎ **212/581-1212**), an increasingly important subscription-based company where 1995's Tony winner *Love! Valour! Compassion!* opened, as did *Ain't Misbehavin'.* It's also the theater where Tony-winning Terrence McNally (*Love! Valour!* and the book for *Ragtime*) is due to produce *Corpus Christi,* which has already caused and will continue to cause consternation about it's "sacrilegious" theme: 13 gay men who reenact the story of Jesus.
- **Mitzi E. Newhouse Theatre,** in Lincoln Center, 150 W. 65th St. (☎ **212/239-6200**), where *Sisters Rosensweig* (by Wendy Wasserstein) got its start.

- **New York Theatre Workshop,** 79 E. 4th St. (☎ **212/460-5475**), whence arose *Rent.*
- **Orpheum Theatre,** Second Avenue at 8th Street (☎ **212/477-2477**), where John Leguizamo once performed brilliant one-man star turns and *Stomp* has caused a lot of noise.
- **Playwrights Horizons,** 416 W. 42nd St. (☎ **212/279-4200**), the source of *Driving Miss Daisy, The Heidi Chronicles, Sunday in the Park with George,* and too many others to list.
- **Promenade Theater,** 2162 Broadway at 76th St. (☎ **212/580-1313**), where Elaine May and Alan Arkin's *Power Plays* debuted.
- **The Public Theater,** 425 Lafayette St. (☎ **212/260-2400**), Joseph Papp's legacy, where *Bring in 'da Noise, Bring in 'da Funk* joined offerings like Shakespeare and David Mamet's mumblings.
- **Stardust Theatre,** 1650 Broadway at 51st St. (☎ **212/239-6200**), most recent home of Gerard Alessandrini's *Forbidden Broadway Strikes Back!*
- **The Triad,** 158 W. 72nd St. (☎ **212/799-4599**), former home of *Forever Plaid* and *Forbidden Broadway.*
- **Union Square Theater,** 17th Street at Park Avenue South (☎ **212/505-0700**), which served as opening stage for Jeff Baron's *Visiting Mr. Green,* with Eli Wallach.
- **Westbeth Theatre Center,** 151 Bank St. (☎ **212/741-0391**), the site of Eddie Lizzard's *Dress to Kill.*
- **Westside Theatre,** 407 W. 43rd St. (☎ **212/315-2244**), where *Spic-o-Rama* by John Leguizamo, *Later Life* by A. R. Gurney, and Penn & Teller have all starred.

TOP TICKET-BUYING TIPS

There are two kinds of travelers: those who plan their trip in detail and those who arrive waiting to see what fortune holds. You'd better be in the former group if you hope to attend any of New York's blockbusters.

For useful nuggets of information, the **New York Convention and Visitors Bureau** at ☎ 800/NYC-VISIT is a gold mine. Also great are **NYC/On Stage** at ☎ **212/768-1818** and the **Broadway Line** at ☎ **888/411-BWAY** (212/302-4111 in New York City), on which you can obtain details about current shows and then be transferred to buy tickets. You can also try starting your ticket search on the Web. A while back, **Theatre Direct Inc. (TDI)** launched a dinner/theater package that included seats for *Rent* and, if that weren't enough pop culture for you, dinner at your choice of the Official All Star Cafe or Planet Hollywood, where you wouldn't even have to stand in line. It was called—what else?—the Rock Your World package. To see if the package or a similar one is available when you travel, you could reach TDI the old-fashioned way at ☎ 800/334-8457 or be totally awesome and connect to **www.theatredirect.com**.

For detailed information about performances at Lincoln Center, see the box "The Many Faces of Lincoln Center" later in this chapter.

FIRST THINGS FIRST Write or phone ahead for tickets to the most successful or popular venues as far in advance as you can. Use the above phone numbers, Web sites, or nationally available periodicals like the *New York Times* or *New York* magazine to gather details on what's currently playing. In this way, you pay only box-office prices.

Telephone Credit-Card Purchases If the show you want to see isn't sold out, you need only call such general numbers as **Tele-charge** at ☎ **212/239-6200,** which handles Broadway, Off Broadway, and some concerts, and **TicketMaster** at ☎ **212/ 307-4100,** which also offers Broadway, Off Broadway, and concerts as well as tickets to Madison Square Garden and Radio City. Both charge a small premium and accept credit cards.

FOR THOSE WHO "FORGOT"—AGAIN?—TO PLAN Getting hold of last-minute tickets can take some street smarts—and failing those, good hard cash. Even if it seems unlikely that seats are available, *always call the box office* before attempting any other route. Single seats are often easiest to obtain. You should also try the new **League of American Theaters and Producers ticket booth,** inside the new Times Square Visitors Center in the Embassy Theater on Seventh Avenue between 46th and 47th streets (daily 8am–8pm). Most orchestra seats can be had for $50 to $100, unless you buy from a broker. Then prices will be as high as the market will bear.

One preferred insiders' trick (don't tell that I told you) is to make the rounds of Broadway theaters at about 6pm, when unclaimed "house seats" are made available to the public. These tickets—reserved at first for VIPs, friends of the cast, the press, or other hangers-on—offer great locations and are sold at face value.

At **Lincoln Center**'s Alice Tully Hall, Avery Fisher Hall, and Metropolitan Opera, house seats go on sale as soon as they become available. When subscribers can't attend a performance, they may donate their tickets back to the theaters, which then resell them. These can be in the most coveted rows of the orchestra. The hopeful form "cancellation lines" prior to curtain time for a crack at returned tickets on a first-come, first-served basis. Generally, the same applies at **Carnegie Hall.** Call the box offices first to ask when or if heading to the theater makes any sense.

One final insider's tip: **Mondays** are often good days to cop big-name show tickets. Though most theaters are dark on that day, some of the most sought-after choices aren't. Locals are at home on the first night of the work week, so all the odds are in your favor. You might also find seats easier during the relatively slow months of **January** and **February,** when even the biggest shows seldom sell out.

Another option (try to call at least 48 hours in advance) is more expensive than most, but good for your self-esteem. **Broadway Cares/Equity Fights AIDS** doubles the tickets' face value, then donates half to people living with the disease. Call ☎ **212/ 840-0770** for ticket choices, which are limited in number but can include Broadway, Off Broadway, and some performances at Radio City Music Hall, such as the Allman Brothers, Lyle Lovett, Linda Ronstadt, and Bette Midler's sell-out show a while back. Expect big-time musicals to cost at least $140 per ticket.

In addition, some **hotel concierges** either hold tickets or can provide them—for a fee. The concierge route has lately been limited by the city, after the (silly) arrest of a concierge not long ago. New York State law says that the premium charged cannot exceed $5 or 10% of the ticket's face value, whichever is less. But there are as many ways to get around the law (have your headquarters in New Jersey, for example) as there are pedestrians dashing across streets against the light.

Some last-minute seats may have limited visibility or no visibility at all—which counts less at a symphony than, for instance, at the ballet. Check before you pay.

I caution against buying from **scalpers** in front of the theater. Their tickets are sometimes fake, occasionally bought with stolen credit cards, and once in a while legitimate.

SERENDIPITOUS BARGAINS & LAST-MINUTE MANEUVERS Even block-busters can have a limited number of **cheaper tickets** for full-time students and seniors. So if you're not too shy to take advantage of age or beauty, call the box office that interests you to see if there's a similar possibility. In the past, the Roundabout offered half-price tickets to those 17 and under. *Rent,* the hip musical, has offered all kinds of bargains to keep its audience as young-looking as possible. The first two rows of the orchestra have been available for only $20 (tickets are available by lottery, two to a customer, before the show by filling out a card distributed at the theater at 5:30 for the 8pm show, 11:30am for the 2pm matinee, and at 5:30 for the 7pm Sunday show; drawings are 30 minutes later).

The most economical way to procure same-day entry for both Broadway and Off Broadway shows is at the reduced-price **TKTS booth** (run by the nonprofit Theatre Development Fund) on Duffy Square, 47th Street and Broadway (open daily 3–8pm for evening performances, 10am–2pm for Wednesday and Saturday matinees, 11am–6:30pm Sunday for all performances; cash and traveler's checks only, with small surcharge). Among these tickets, usually offered at half price with a few reduced only 25%, you're unlikely to find certain perennial or outsize smashes, but most other shows turn up. There have been sightings of many mega–crowd-pleasers on the board, which catalogs the sales du jour and hangs at the booth's northern end. The line snaking around this pedestrian island makes it easy, and sometimes distressing, to find.

Solution? Run by the same group and offering the same discounts as the Uptown booth is the **TKTS outlet** on the mezzanine of Two World Trade Center. The lines are generally shorter, and your wait is sheltered indoors (open Mon–Fri 11am–5:30pm and Sat 11am–3:30pm, with matinees available only the day before).

Many theater shows offer special coupons that allow you to buy **twofers**—two tickets for the price of one certain nights of the week. You can find these coupons at many places in the city: the Times Square Visitors Center in the Embassy Center on Seventh Avenue between 46th and 47th streets, hotel lobbies, and even in banks and at restaurant cash registers.

The past several years, the Theatre Development Fund with a variety of corporations has sponsored the **Passport to Off Broadway** campaign, coupons for a 10% to 50% discount to Off Broadway shows from February to April. Anyone can download the coupons from **www.sidewalk.com**.

THEY ALSO WATCH WHO ONLY STAND   If you must, just must, see a sold-out show, opera, or concert, you can call or go to the box office to check if **standing room** is available (around $20). The best standing room is at the Met, where you get to lean against plush red bars. I've seen standees take advantage of unfilled seats during intermission . . . but that's cheating, isn't it?

TICKET BROKERS   All kinds of ticket brokers, from reputable to unsavory, are listed in the Sunday *New York Times,* touting their offerings with exclamation points (PHANTOM TICKETS AVAILABLE!!!, which can also be literally true). As I noted earlier, state law limits the premium brokers can charge to $5 or 10%, whichever is less, but if you believe they all stick to that, I know of this bridge to Brooklyn. . . . The city has been threatening to act on scalpers for a long time, with little result. A couple of brokers whose names are listed in the Convention and Visitors Bureau's "Big Apple Visitors Guide" are **Advance Entertainment NY** at ☎ **212/239-2576** and **Keith Prowse** at ☎ **212/398-1430.** Others are listed in the Yellow Pages under Tickets.

ACCESSIBILITY   Some performance venues provide total wheelchair accessibility; others provide partial accessibility. Many also offer lower-priced tickets for patrons in wheelchairs and their companions, though you'll need to reserve in advance and check for individual policies.

2 Opera, Classical Music & Dance

As it is for theater, New York is the world's capital for opera, classical music, and dance. And any night of the week—or day, for that matter—the city is likely to offer a mind-boggling, ear-pleasing, eye-opening set of choices. Most companies limit their major offerings to "seasons" that fall somewhere between about September and May, though summer is full of festivals and free outdoors performances.

If any audience in New York is as passionate as Broadway's greasepaint junkies, it's the cognoscenti of opera. Early last year, the ardor of the Met audience was evinced in the loud blast of sustained boos, the most solid such eruption in many years, that greeted Robert Wilson's coldly abstract staging of Wagner's *Lohengrin*. Simultaneously, the audience applauded wildly its approval of the cast and orchestra. The scene was something you'd expect at La Scala—but the usual reserve of the Met's audience can turn to riotous disgust when it dislikes what it sees.

The temperaments of the stars surpass the fervor of the fans. Kathleen Battle was disinvited from reappearing at the Met when the company's management claimed she had taken the diva thing a step too far. The heat-generating couple of tenor Roberto Alagna and his wife, Angela Gheorghiu, have found themselves *personae non gratae* in an upcoming Met production of *La Traviata* because, the company's director said, they were too demanding. Still, opera's hottest couple, both in their early 30s, will continue to perform other works at the Met. It's wise to keep them around: They charmed the opera world first by performing together in passionate scenes by Puccini and Verdi and then, in a script stolen from the days of Liz and Dick in *Cleopatra,* announcing they were as in love offstage as on. That romantic stroke helped propel them into the highest echelon of sought-after performers.

Kurt Masur and the New York Philharmonic are at home in Avery Fisher Hall, also at Lincoln Center. Just about any grand interpreter of the classics comes through New York. Whether you want to hear Yo-Yo Ma or Itzak Perlman, the many concert halls throughout the city—ranging from the expected, like Carnegie Hall, to the surprising, like the 92nd Street Y—book the best of the best.

The dance scene has been going through some new steps lately. The 1980s saw New York become the world capital of dance. New companies were founded and old ones gained new admirers. While New York is still the place to experience ballet, modern, folk, and other forms of dance, the recent troubles of venerable companies like the Joffrey Ballet and Dance Theatre of Harlem point up the art form's precarious nature. The enfant terrible of the scene continues to be Mark Morris, despite his ill-fated stint as one in a series of directors who attempted to prevent Paul Simon's Broadway fiasco, *Capeman,* from collapsing under the composer's smug indifference to its flaws. But his lasting importance remains his choreography, masterpieces like *L'Allegro, il Penseroso ed il Moderato.*

OPERA

Amato Opera Theater. 319 Bowery (at 2nd St.). ☎ **212/228-8200.** Tickets around $20. Subway: 6 to Bleecker St.; F to Second Ave.

This intimate hall, off the beaten track for "serious music," celebrated its 50th season last year amid a rising reputation and increasing ticket sales. Performances in the 100-plus-seat house regularly sell out, so reserve 3 weeks in advance. The staple is full productions at great prices of Italian classics—Verdi, Puccini, Donizetti, with an occasional Mozart tossed in. Performances are Saturday and Sunday. Once a month, the 11:30am Saturday family series introduces the little ones to opera's big ones.

✪ **Metropolitan Opera Company.** At the Metropolitan Opera House, Lincoln Center, Broadway and 64th St. ☎ **212/362-6000.** Tickets $24–$200. Subway: 1, 9, A, B, C, D to Columbus Circle; 1, 9 to 66th St.

For its full productions of the classic repertory and complete schedule of world-class grand sopranos and tenors, the Metropolitan Opera ranks first in the world. The Met presents the pillars of the opera world as well as every new star to emerge. Millions are spent on fabulous stagings (explaining, along with the superstar salaries commanded by certain singers, the high cost of coveted seats). The Met's audience is passionate, biased, and knowledgeable. Its red-plush home is a wonder of acoustics and, mostly, good taste (we could do without the dated chandeliers, which campily glide up into the ceiling as the curtain rises). Opening in February 1999 is the Met's first production of *Moses und Aron* and in March its first presentation of *Susannah*. Cecilia Bartoli will sing in *Le Nozze di Figaro* beginning in late October.

To guarantee that its audience understands the words, the Met has outfitted its seat backs with screens for subtitles (no more wondering why Cio-cio-san explodes with passion when she sings, "Un po per non morire al primo incontro"). James Levine continues his role as the brilliant and popular conductor of the orchestra 28 years later. His decision to work also as conductor of the Munich Philharmonic made headlines and caused envy among New Yorkers who didn't want to share their curly-haired genius. Associate conductor Valery Gergiyev helps fill in for the peripatetic Levine and brings needed experience in the Russian repertory to the Met.

✪ **New York City Opera.** At the New York State Theater, Lincoln Center, Broadway and 64th St. ☎ **212/870-5570.** Tickets $20–$85, $75 for orchestra seats. Subway: 1, 9, A, B, C, D to Columbus Circle; 1, 9 to 66th St.

The New York City Opera is a superb company, with a delightful duality to its approach: It not only attempts to reach a wider audience than the Metropolitan with its more "human" scale and lower prices but also is committed to adventurous premieres, newly composed operas, the occasional avant garde work, American musicals presented as operettas (Stephen Sondheim's *Sweeney Todd* is an example), and even obscure works by mainstream or lesser-known composers. Here is an opera house for the serious devotee as well as the merely curious. Its mix stretches from the "easy" works of Puccini and Verdi and the Gilbert & Sullivan repertory to the more challenging oeuvres of the likes of Arnold Schönberg and Philip Glass.

A few years back, the New York City Opera, then under the direction of the incomparable Beverly Sills, was the first to put in "supratitles" above the stage, so its audience could follow the words as well as the music. Snickers were heard across the plaza at the Met, which has since followed Bubbles's lead.

CLASSICAL MUSIC

The following is a select list of particularly important companies and venues. Remember that Carnegie Hall and places like the 92nd Street Y host the world's greatest musicians, from symphony orchestras to solo performers (see "Major Concert Halls & Landmark Venues"). Many other halls—like **Symphony Space,** 2537 Broadway (☎ 212/864-5400)—too numerous to detail, also deserve your attention. If you're here during the warmer months, keep a watch on the daytime and nighttime parks' schedules by calling ☎ 212/360-3456. There are free concerts by the New York Philharmonic, the Metropolitan Opera, and other worthies in many parks as well as in select atriums, like the World Financial Center's **Winter Garden** (☎ 212/945-0505), in Battery Park City.

Bargemusic. At the Fulton Ferry Landing (just south of the Brooklyn Bridge), Brooklyn. ☎ **718/ 624-2083.** Tickets $15 students, $20 seniors, $23 others. Subway: 2, 3 to Clark St., Brooklyn.

Many thought Olga Bloom peculiar, if not deranged, when she transformed a 40-year-old barge into a chamber-music concert hall. More than 15 years later, Bargemusic is an internationally reputed recital room boasting over 100 performances a year by highly respected musicians. Reserve well in advance. Throughout most of the year there are only two shows per week, on Thursday evening and Sunday afternoon. June to August, there's also a Friday-evening performance. The musicians perform on a small stage in a cherry-paneled room accommodating 130. Bloom herself places name cards on the red-velvet cushions of the folding chairs, and there's bread and cheese, cakes and cookies, and wine and coffee. The barge may creek a bit and an occasional boat may speed by, but the music rivals what you'll find in almost any other New York concert hall—and the view through the glass wall behind the stage can't be beat.

✪ **The Juilliard School.** 60 Lincoln Center Plaza (Broadway & 65th St.). ☎ **212/769-7406.** Tickets for majority of concerts free; $15 maximum. Subway: 1, 9, A, B, C, D to Columbus Circle; 1, 9 to 66th St.

During its school year, Juilliard sponsors about 550 performances of the highest quality—at the lowest prices. Perhaps because Juilliard is a school, without a large advertising and promotion budget, it's an underused resource. It is one of New York's greatest cultural bargains. Though most would assume that the school presents only classical-music concerts, Juilliard also offers other music as well as dance, drama, and interdisciplinary works in parks, atriums, and performance halls. The best way to find out about the wide array of productions is to consult the bulletin board in the building's lobby or call the above number. Those in the know watch for the master classes and discussions open to the public featuring celebrity guest teachers.

✪ **New York Philharmonic.** At Avery Fisher Hall, Lincoln Center, Broadway and 64th St. ☎ **212/875-5030.** Tickets $6–$60. Subway: 1, 9, A, B, C, D to Columbus Circle; 1, 9 to 66th St.

The New York Philharmonic, the country's oldest such troupe, received revived attention when music director Kurt Masur took over. Now that the maestro has announced that he'll retire in 2002, the search for a replacement for such a high-profile position will certainly again cause revived attention. In the meantime, Masur conducts everything from Bach to Gershwin and hosts solo stars like Jessye Norman in concert. There's a summer season in July, when themed classics brighten the hall.

DANCE

Despite the financial woes that have always afflicted dance, it's thoroughly alive in New York. From classical ballet to the most modern stagings, the works of great choreographers are staged in a number of venues. Some troupes always perform in the same spaces, but others move according to their needs. In general, the seasons run September to February and then March to June.

American Ballet Theatre & Major Visiting Companies. At the Metropolitan Opera House, Lincoln Center, Broadway and 64th St. ☎ **212/362-6000.** Subway: 1, 9, A, B, C, D to Columbus Circle; 1, 9 to 66th St.

During spring, the American Ballet Theatre moves into the Metropolitan Opera House, across the Lincoln Center plaza from the New York City Ballet. It combines a repertoire of great breadth, from modern works by Twyla Tharp and Paul Taylor to an

The Many Faces of Lincoln Center

At **Lincoln Center for the Performing Arts,** Broadway and 64th Street (☎ **212/546-2656,** a central number for all its constituents), there are dazzling opening nights, when old-money society and Wall Street upstarts descend from long limos to take their places in plush boxes. But there's also free jitterbugging in summer to the sounds of big bands in the central Fountain Plaza, jazz orchestras conducted by Wynton Marsalis, and the opulent theatrics of opera productions like Franco Zeffirelli's *Turandot.* Lincoln Center is a focal point of creative and social energy, and its many buildings are home to their own companies and a major stop for performers from around the globe.

Five million individuals visit Lincoln Center every year, 50% of them from outside New York City and 15% from abroad. The city's transportation department estimates that 20,000 cars pass through the center's driveway every day.

Most of the companies' **major seasons** run from about October to May or June. **Special series** like Great Performers, which this May will feature a collaboration between Jessye Norman and Bill T. Jones that should be the talk of the season, help round out the calendar.

Indoor and outdoor events are held in warmer months: Spring blooms with **JVC Jazz Festival** performances in Avery Fisher Hall; July sees **Midsummer Night's Swing** with partner dancing, lessons, and music in the plaza; **Mostly Mozart** attracts talents like Alicia de Larrocha and André Watts; the 3-year-old **Lincoln Center Festival** embraces international opera, jazz, classical, dance, and theater with performances by the likes of the Royal Opera, the Royal Ballet, Ornette Coleman, and the New York Philharmonic; and **Lincoln Center Out-of-Doors** in August boasts appearances by such greats as the Alvin Ailey Repertory Company, Don Pullen and the Afro-Brazilian Connection, and special kids' programs and international folk, world, blues, gospel, and jazz music.

As part of these series or independently sponsored by Juilliard or other organizations, there are also **free concerts** in the center's Damrosch Park as well as performances by the New York Pops. Farther afield, both the New York Philharmonic and the Metropolitan Opera present free concerts at the city's major parks (bring a blanket, a picnic basket, and, if you want to make a Martha Stewart–like statement, maybe even a candelabra).

Following are the main performance sites for Lincoln Center's 11 semi-independent constituents (Chamber Music Society of Lincoln Center, Film Society of Lincoln Center, Juilliard School, Lincoln Center Theater, Metropolitan Opera, New York City Ballet, New York City Opera, New York

accomplished take on such classics as *Swan Lake* and *La Bayadère* (the company recently added a regular fall season of repertory performances at City Center). During summer, the Metropolitan Opera House has received such visitors as the Kirov, Royal, and Paris Opéra ballets.

City Center. 131 W. 55th St. (Sixth & Seventh aves.). ☎ **212/581-7907.** Subway: N, R to Seventh Ave./57th St.; B, Q to Sixth Ave./57th St.; B, D, E to Seventh Ave./53rd St.

In a Moorish palace, dance often takes center stage, with regular performances by the companies of Merce Cunningham, Martha Graham, Paul Taylor, Trisha Brown, Alvin Ailey, Twyla Tharp, and recently the American Ballet Theatre in fall. Always check

Philharmonic, New York Public Library for the Performing Arts, School of American Ballet, and its newest member, after 6 years of jazz concerts at Lincoln Center, Jazz at Lincoln Center, led by Wynton Marsalis). In addition to the theaters listed below, there are plans to build Jazz at Lincoln Center its own performance space as part of the New York Coliseum redevelopment.

Metropolitan Opera House. Home to its own opera company and to many other events, like performances by the Kirov Ballet and, on a regular basis in spring, American Ballet Theatre. For tickets call ☎ **212/362-6000.**

Avery Fisher Hall. The New York Philharmonic, parts of JVC Jazz, Mostly Mozart, certain Great Performers, some Jazz at Lincoln Center concerts. For tickets call ☎ **212/875-5030** or CenterCharge ☎ **212/721-6500.**

New York State Theater. The New York City Opera and the New York City Ballet. For tickets call ☎ **212/870-5570** or TicketMaster ☎ **212/307-4100.**

Alice Tully Hall. Chamber Music Society, soloists, various concerts (everything from the music of Paul Bowles to traditional Japanese instruments). For information about the Chamber Music Society call ☎ **212/875-5788.** For tickets call ☎ **212/875-5050** or CenterCharge ☎ **212/721-6500.**

Vivian Beaumont Theater. The most Uptown of the Broadway theaters, this modern and comfortable venue, with great sight lines, has been home to much good drama. For tickets call Tele-charge at ☎ **212/239-6200.**

Mitzi E. Newhouse Theater. A well-respected Off Broadway house that has boasted numerous theatrical triumphs. For tickets call Tele-charge ☎ **212/239-6200.**

The Juilliard School. A wonderful resource for fairly priced or usually free top-notch concerts that too few visitors know to take advantage of. Performances are everywhere from within the Juilliard School itself (Juilliard Theater and Paul Recital Hall) to Avery Fisher Hall to area parks. For information call ☎ **212/769-7406.**

Walter Reade Theater. The Film Society of Lincoln Center sponsors its highly respected New York Film Festival here. There are also concerts and other performances. For information call ☎ **212/875-5600.**

For advance information on the wealth of entertainment at Lincoln Center, send a self-addressed envelope or label, with 32¢ postage, to **Lincoln Center Calendar,** Sunny Levine, Editor, 70 Lincoln Center Plaza, New York, NY 10023-6583.

City Center's schedule because many visiting troupes also perform. (For more on City Center, see "Major Concert Halls & Landmark Venues" later in this chapter.)

✪ **Joyce Theater.** 175 Eighth Ave. (at 19th St.). ☎ **212/242-0800.** Subway: C, E to 23rd St.; 1, 9 to 18th St.

A welcome development of a cultural institution from a rehabbed neighborhood movie house (whose sticky floors I remember too well from when I saw *The Harder They Come* there), the Joyce is a joy of dance. You can see everything from Native American ceremonial dance to Eliot Feld's ballet company, Pilobolus Dance Theater, and the Trinity Irish Dance Company.

✪ **New York City Ballet.** At the New York State Theater, Lincoln Center, Broadway and 64th St. ☎ **212/870-5570.** Subway: 1, 9, A, B, C, D to Columbus Circle; 1, 9 to 66th St.

Highly regarded for its unsurpassed technique, the New York City Ballet is the world's best and renders with happy regularity the works of two of America's most important choreographers: George Balanchine, its founder, and Jerome Robbins. Under the direction of former dancer Peter Martins, the troupe continues to expand its accomplished repertoire and performs to a wide variety of classical and modern music.

✪ **Pilar Rioja.** Repertorio Español, at the Gramercy Arts Theater, 138 E. 27th St. (Lexington & Third aves.). ☎ **212/889-2850.** Subway: 6 to 28th St.

Throughout the city you can find many kinds of dance. Pilar Rioja's classic Spanish movements deserve special mention. They mix awesome restraint with explosive passion. A breathtaking accomplishment.

There's so much dance in New York I can list neither all the troupes nor all the venues where you might find them. Some other names to keep in mind are **Merce Cunningham Studio,** 55 Bethune St. (☎ 212/691-9751); **Dance Theater Workshop,** in the Bessie Schönberg Theater, 219 W. 19th St. (☎ 212/924-0077); the **Brooklyn Academy of Music** (see "Major Concert Halls & Landmark Venues"); and the **Dance Theatre of Harlem** (☎ 212/690-2800; see also "Attractions in Upper Manhattan" in chapter 7). Around Christmas, presented in versions that keep the children distracted, plan to attend *The Nutcracker* (the New York City Ballet's is best).

3 Major Concert Halls & Landmark Venues

Many theaters, concert halls, and even sports arenas offer a variety of cultural events. Here's a list of a few of the most important:

✪ **Brooklyn Academy of Music.** 30 Lafayette Ave., Brooklyn. ☎ **718/636-4100.** Subway: 2, 3, 4, 5, D, Q to Atlantic Ave., Brooklyn; G to Fulton St., Brooklyn; B, M, N, R to Pacific Ave., Brooklyn.

Though opened as an opera house in 1859, BAM, as it's now known, is the site of some of New York's most important contemporary performances. Offerings have included early opera by the likes of William Christie and Les Arts Florissants and pop opera from Lou Reed; dance by Twyla Tharp, Pina Bausch, Merce Cunningham, and Mikhail Baryshnikov; music by Laurie Anderson and Philip Glass; theater directed by Ingmar Bergman or Peter Brook; and many international and contemporary classical and popular artists. There are also outdoor jazz concerts, experimental theater, visiting opera companies like the Kirov, and independent films shown at the new four-screen theater. Especially important is the Next Wave Festival, October to December, which is this country's foremost showcase for new works by renowned and more experimental American and international artists. It is, accordingly, one of the most important events on the city's cultural calendar.

✪ **Carnegie Hall.** 57th St. and Seventh Ave. ☎ **212/247-7800.** Subway: N, R to Seventh Ave./57th St.; B, Q to Sixth Ave./57th St.

Perhaps the world's most famous performance space, Carnegie Hall offers everything from grand classics to Liza Minnelli overdoing it live. This is the main hall for visiting orchestras from across the country and the world, whether they're from Philadelphia or Cleveland or Berlin. Many of the world's premier soloists and ensembles give recitals. Last year, Carnegie Hall reclaimed an ornate underground concert hall, which had been occupied by a movie theater for 38 years, and plans to turn it into a premier performance space once again by 2000.

City Center. 131 W. 55th St. (Sixth & Seventh aves.). ☎ **212/581-1212.** Subway: N, R to Seventh Ave./57th St.; B, Q to Sixth Ave./57th St.; B, D, E to Seventh Ave./53rd St.

In addition to the dance cited above, City Center is home to the Manhattan Theatre Club and the consistently excellent Encore! series of great American musicals in concert (which, like the most recent Broadway version of *Chicago,* often start here and wind up as full-production revivals). This is Manhattan's oldest ongoing performing-arts center, and it keeps its prices reasonable, with tickets around $50 (compare that to the twice-as-high price of Broadway musicals).

✪ **Lincoln Center for the Performing Arts.** 70 Lincoln Center Plaza (Broadway & 64th St.). ☎ **212/546-2656.** Subway: 1, 9, A, B, C, D to Columbus Circle; 1, 9 to 66th St.

Whenever you're planning an evening's entertainment, check the offerings here—which can include opera, dance, symphonies, free outdoor activities, and every art form from the classics to the contemporary. See the box "The Many Faces of Lincoln Center" for more.

Madison Square Garden. Seventh Ave. from 31st to 33rd sts. ☎ **212/465-MSG1.** Subway: 1, 2, 3, 9, A, C, E to 34th St.; B, D, G, F, N, R to Herald Square.

Big rock concerts—the kind Jerry Garcia used to play and Elton John still does—fill this 20,000-seat arena, which is also home to the Knicks and Rangers. A cavernous concrete hulk, it's better suited to sports than to concerts. I've seen the Rolling Stones and Tina Turner here—well, I've *squinted* to see them.

92nd Street Y, Tisch Center for the Arts. 1395 Lexington Ave. (at 92nd St.). ☎ **212/ 996-1100.** Subway: 4, 5, 6 to 86th St.; 6 to 96th St.

The greatest classical performers—like Isaac Stern and Nadja Salerno-Sonnenberg—give recitals here. In addition, there are cabaret and jazz series as well as performances of the works of great American lyricists and readings of contemporary literature at the Unterberg Poetry Center.

✪ **Radio City Music Hall.** 1260 Sixth Ave. (at 50th St.). ☎ **212/247-4777.** Subway: B, D, F, Q to 49th St./Rockefeller Center.

This stunningly beautiful 6,200-seat art deco theater, with interior design by Donald Deskey, opened in 1932. Radio City continues to be a choice venue, where the theater alone adds a dash of panache to any performance. It features the high-kicking Rockettes, the Christmas and Easter pageants, and visiting chart-toppers, mostly in the pop-music category. In order to bring back the theater's slendor, a 30-million reno-vation scheduled for March to September 1999, when Radio City will be closed.

The Theater at Madison Square Garden. Seventh Ave. from 31st to 33rd sts. ☎ **212/ 465-MSG1.** Subway: 1, 2, 3, 9, A, C, E to 34th St.; B, D, G, F, N, R to Herald Square.

In the same excruciatingly ugly complex as Madison Square Garden—which also boasts the deplorable Amtrak and Long Island Rail Road stations—the theater is a step above its neighbors. This amphitheater-style auditorium has 5,600 seats and hosts some major pop stars: Impossibly demanding Barbra Streisand found it nice enough for her New York concert, thank you. Watch for the possibly annual staging of *The Wizard of Oz,* which in its first incarnation 2 years ago had the headstrong and low-brow Roseanne as the Wicked Witch of the West in a popular but critically savaged production; producers cast Eartha Kitt as the Witch in last year's show.

Town Hall. 123 W. 43rd St. (Sixth & Seventh aves.). ☎ **212/840-2824.** Subway: 1, 2, 3, 7, 9, N, R, S to Times Square; B, D, F, Q to 42nd St.

For those who rely on the subway, you'll note that the most convenient stops have been listed throughout this chapter. However, at night I suggest you take a taxi both going and coming.

At this intimate space, blessed with outstanding acoustics, many kinds of performances, from theater to music to any number of other cultural events, take place.

4 Popular Music & Comedy

Surfing the network of clubs and hot music spots with Manhattan's nightcrawlers can be serious business. What to wear? Where to be seen? Whom to be seen with? All these questions are answered by your preferences—and New York has room enough and choices enough to fit any type. A perfect Manhattan evening might include cabaret; a rock concert in a huge arena; or an evening shaking to funk, house, techno, zydeco, blues, jazz, or whatever gets under your skin.

LARGE VENUES

For coverage of **Madison Square Garden,** see "Major Concert Halls & Landmark Venues" above.

Apollo Theater. 253 W. 125th St. (Adam Clayton Powell Jr. & Frederick Douglass blvds.). ☎ **212/749-5838.** Subway: 1, 9 to 125th St.

The Apollo, built in 1914, had its heyday in the 1930s when Count Basie, Duke Ellington, Ella Fitzgerald, and Billie Holiday were on the bill. By the 1970s it had fallen on hard times, but a restoration in 1986 breathed new life into the historic Harlem landmark. Today the Apollo is again internationally renowned for its African-American acts of all musical genres—though there was recent dust-up about possible financial problems at the theater.. Wednesday amateur nights are loud, fun-filled, and reminiscent of the Apollo's glory days.

Beacon Theater. 2124 Broadway (at 74th St.). ☎ **212/496-7070.** Subway: 1, 2, 3, 9 to 72nd St.

The Beacon Theater is a midsize venue that hosts pop-music performances, theater, and revival films. It attracts mainstream musical groups not "big" enough to fill Madison Square Garden—to wit, folk-rock duo Indigo Girls, street-smart pop diva Sheryl Crow, and convulsive rock veteran Joe Cocker. Built in 1928, the Beacon is a grand art deco movie palace with an impressive lobby, stairway, and auditorium.

MIXED MUSIC & UNEXPECTED TWISTS

✪ **Bottom Line.** 15 W. 4th St. (at Mercer St.). ☎ **212/228-7880.** Subway: N, R to Astor Place; A, B, C, D, E, F, Q to W. 4th St.

The Bottom Line built its reputation by serving as showcase for the likes of Bruce Springsteen and the Ramones. It remains one of the top venues, renowned for its excellent sound and bookings of the best in rock, jazz, and folk, as well as the occasional comedian or classical musician.

Fez Under Time Cafe. In the Time Cafe, 380 Lafayette St. (at Great Jones St.). ☎ **212/533-2680.** Subway: 6 to Lafayette St.; B, D, F, Q to Houston St.

You have to reserve a seat a few days ahead for the wildly popular Thursday-night Mingus Big Band workshop, when the Arabian-inspired room is filled with the cool sounds of jazz and well-dressed see-and-be-seeners. The rest of the week brings an eclectic mix of live music and some comedy.

✪ **Knitting Factory.** 74 Leonard St. (Broadway & Church St.). ☎ **212/219-3055.** Subway: 1, 9 to Franklin St.

If you're curious about what's happening in music today—whether it's intellectual-rock pro John Zorn or a lineup including alternative rock, experimental jazz, acoustic, spoken-word performances, videos, and more—the brilliantly managed Knitting Factory, Downtown's premier cutting-edge arts venue, is the place. There are multiple performance spaces: the main stage, featuring the biggest names in new music; the Old Office, a subterranean hipster lounge; and the AlterKnit Theater, which is just that. The Tap Bar serves microbrewed beers, shows films, and hosts the Late Night Players Hang, starting at 11:30pm, with drink specials and free live music.

✪ **Mercury Lounge.** 217 E. Houston St. (at Essex St.). ☎ **212/260-4700.** Subway: F to Second Ave.; F, J, M to Delancy St.

The most civilized of the city's top music venues is also one of the hippest. Though mostly known for attracting new and just-signed-on-the-dotted-line rock talent like the Mekons and Lucinda Williams, it features everything from folk and funk to blues. Last year, Sean Lennon made his solo debut here while mother Yoko Ono danced in a corner. Mercury Lounge has one of the best sound systems in New York and a good-size space, which makes it a perfect feeding ground for record-industry sharks searching out the next mega-million-dollar phenom.

Roseland. 239 W. 52nd St. (Broadway & Eighth Ave.). ☎ **212/247-0200.** Subway: 1, 9, C, E to 50th St.

Call ahead to see if this 1919 ballroom has succumbed to the 1998 wrecking ball. If the planned high-rise hasn't begun to occupy the site, the enormous dance floor might still be populated during the day with Ginger Rogers and Fred Astaire might-have-beens nimbly spinning about. Nighttime has lately been reserved for younger crowds that jam to Alanis Morissette, David Bowie, and David Byrne.

S.O.B.'s. 204 Varick St. (at W. Houston St.). ☎ **212/243-4940.** Subway: 1, 9 to W. Houston St.

If you like it spicy, dash a bit of this on your stay. Sounds of Brazil is the hot place in New York for salsa, calypso, samba, and world music. Bookings include top performers from South America, the Caribbean, and Africa—the unsurpassed Celia Cruz recently played. The space is extravagantly decorated.

Tramps. 51 W. 21st St. (Fifth & Sixth aves.). ☎ **212/727-7788.** Subway: F to 23rd St.; N, R to 23rd St.

This spacious loft is a happening spot for roots music, zydeco, reggae, blues, and rock. Anything goes here, from Jerry Lee Lewis pounding out sets of 1950s oldies on an electric grand piano to Lisa Loeb sweetly singing about lovers' quarrels and breakups from behind her trademark cat-eye–shaped glasses. When zydeco takes the stage, the audience steals the floor.

West End Gate. 2911 Broadway (113th & 114th sts.). ☎ **212/662-8830.** Subway: 1, 9 to Cathedral Pkwy. (110th St.).

This Upper West Side crowd pleaser offers a bit of everything, from open-mike comedy on Tuesday and Wednesday to theater, jazz, and rock. The atmosphere is informal, the audience mostly Columbia University students.

Wetlands. 161 Hudson St. (at Laight St.). ☎ **212/966-4225.** Subway: 1, 9, A, C, E to Canal St.

Music in the Parks & Other Public Places

Especially in the heavy heat of summer, New York provides endless opportunities to hear, usually free, music in the parks and other major meeting places. Central Park (☎ 212/360-3444 for information on park events) offers the **New York Philharmonic,** the **Metropolitan Opera,** the occasional mega-event like Garth Brooks's 1997 concert, as well as a series called **SummerStage** (☎ 212/360-2777), which has featured everyone from the Godfather of Soul, James Brown, to the angel poet of punk, Patti Smith. **Summerpier** (☎ 212/732-7678) brings outdoor jazz and folk to Pier 16, at South Street Seaport.

For information on evening music in the museums, see "Only in New York" at the end of this chapter.

This place makes rock feel so much *nicer*—it's clean, environmentally conscious, and spacious. Lectures on environmental activism are intermixed with an eclectic blend of music covering the spectrum from ska to head-banging rock—as long as the act is PC. Pearl Jam, Oasis, and Dave Matthews all played here before you knew who they were. If you haven't beat your Jerry jones, Tuesday is Dead Night.

BASICALLY ROCK

Rock music has been big business for a long time, so many concerts take place in cavernous spaces like Madison Square Garden (see "Major Concert Halls & Landmark Venues" above). But whether it's in monstrous arenas or smoky little clubs, the Manhattan music scene runs the full gamut of rock. Sure the native-talent scene isn't what it has been (and no doubt will be again some day).

Still, the scene is alive and for a musical taste of Manhattan today, here are your best choices.

Acme Underground. 9 Great Jones St. (at Lafayette St.). ☎ **212/677-6924.** Subway: G to Lafayette St.; B, D, F, Q to Broadway/Lafayette St.

A small rock venue in the basement of a Cajun bar and grill that books a range of rock bands is the place where you can "catch the Next Big Thing," as *New York* magazine says. That explains why you probably haven't even heard of (at least not yet) acts like the Red Letters, the Bisbees, and Step 2 Far. Expect a hip East Village crowd.

Arlene Grocery. 95 Stanton St. (Ludlow & Orchard sts.). ☎ **212/358-1633.** Subway: F to Second Ave.

Live music is always free at Arlene Grocery, even though many of the artists command high cover charges when they perform elsewhere. Every night, you hear about four groups, from local talent to musicians like Marianne Faithfull and Spacehog. There have been cameo appearances by Joan Osborne, Joe Jackson, and members of U2. Despite its Lower East Side location, it attracts a mix of Downtown club hoppers, curious out-of-towners, and in-the-know music-industry scouts.

✪ **Brownies.** 169 Ave. A (10th & 11th sts.). ☎ **212/420-8392.** Subway: C, E to 23rd St.

This is the CBGB of the 1990s—up-and-coming bands want to play here for its music-savvy audience that's half punk and half college students in punk drag. Don't be frightened by the seemingly seedy crowd: Brownies is mainstream, playing host to the latest incarnation of rock. Sometimes major-label acts trying to be anonymous play here, like the surprise show by the Beastie Boys a couple of years back. Several bands play every night starting at 8 or 9pm.

Cafe Wha? 115 MacDougal St. (Bleecker & W. 3rd sts.). ☎ **212/254-3706.** Subway: A, B, C, D, E, F, Q to W. 4th St.

Guaranteed to be loud, this cellar full of noise features three different house bands. Monday is raucous and hip when the club's 12-member big band plays Brazilian funk and R&B. The rest of the week the two other bands play mostly R&B and rock, some world music, oldies, and even show tunes. Tuesday is funk night. Weekends, the crowd tends to be Jersey kids and out-of-towners.

✪ **CBGB & OMFUG.** 315 Bowery (at Bleecker St.). ☎ **212/982-4052.** Subway: 6 to Bleecker St.; F to Second Ave.

Don basic black, not because you'll be doing the right thing fashionwise but because you'll leave without visible residue. Funky, in the original sense of the term, and still going after all these years, CBGB & OMFUG had its glory days in the prehistory of the New York punk–and–art-school rock movement. It was the launching pad for such billion-year-old stars as the Ramones, Blondie, and Talking Heads. Here's where the American reaction to English punk was born, eventually giving way to New Wave. It's as close as New York gets to a rock 'n' roll hall of fame.

CBGB's engines are still smoking as it plays host to several new groups every night. The occasional names still show up—Patti Smith returned to her roots by performing recently, and independent-label groups like Pavement and the Jon Spencer Blues Explosion are often on the bill. The deliberately sleazy, high-decibel atmosphere and the young crowd (16 or older) are worth a visit if only to remember early alternative rock and your younger days.

CB's 313 Gallery. 313 Bowery (at Bleecker St.). ☎ **212/677-0455.** Subway: 6 to Bleecker St.; F to Second Ave.

For those who appreciate new music sans eardrum-stressing volume, CB's Gallery is a welcome spin-off of the original CBGB. The musicians here are interested in being musicians, not in making you submit. The music tends toward smoother rock, folk, blues, and acoustic. The crowd is 20-something, with the occasional punk drifting in from CBGB next door. The "gallery" moniker comes from the rotating exhibits of multimedia art hanging around the cool and comfortable room.

Continental. 25 Third Ave. (at St. Mark's Place). ☎ **212/529-6924.** Subway: 6 to Astor Place.

It's East Village basic black, major loud (earplugs are available for $1), and a little sleazy, but Continental is a main venue for local and national rock bands. Alternative and new music acts are also on the roster, and renovations have added a downstairs lounge. Joey Ramone, who lives nearby, has been known to drop in.

Irving Plaza. 17 Irving Place (at 16th St.). ☎ **212/777-6800.** Subway: 4, 5, 6, L, N, R to Union Square.

This Downtown midsize music hall attracts rock bands that aren't quite mainstream enough for the Beacon Theater but do have a national reputation. From time to time, big-name artists also perform—a recent Bob Dylan show sold out in 3 minutes. Exuberant youths jam when local legends like Yo La Tengo or the punk-flavored pop band Chumbawamba hit the stage. Less loud artists, like Dionne Farris and swing band Squirrel Nut Zippers, also perform. It's a sardine-can crush against the stage, but you can escape to the upstairs balcony and still clearly see the performance.

Kenny's Castaways. 157 Bleecker St. (Thompson & Sullivan sts.). ☎ **212/979-9762.** Subway: A, B, C, D, E, F, Q to W. 4th St.

This is a Greenwich Village longtime favorite for live rock bands of all types. The Smithereens is just one group that got its start here, and recent acts have included Blues Traveler and ska favorites the Toasters.

Spiral. 244 Houston St. (at Ave. A). ☎ **212/353-1740.** Subway: 1, 9 to W. Houston St.

The Lower East Side's original eclectic music club is a tiny space that hosts every music type, from punk to rockabilly, and just as wide a variety of fans. Mostly local acts shake what's left of the paint off the peeling walls.

JAZZ & BLUES

Starting a few years back, New York experienced such a renaissance of new clubs that it could rightly claim to be in the running for jazz and blues capital of the world, Chicago inter alia notwithstanding. Big names mean you pay big bucks, often a cover charge plus a minimum drink order. The same warning applies here as in other nightspots: Check specific costs when you call for reservations.

Festivals throughout the year bring in some of the best talent. The **JVC Jazz Festival** (☎ 212/501-1390) is in late spring/early summer, and Dizzy Gillespie, David Sanborn, and the eternal Ella Fitzgerald have performed. Wynton Marsalis is the artistic director of Lincoln Center's newest constituent company, **Jazz at Lincoln Center** (☎ 212/875-5299), which in its 1998–1999 season examines the life and works of Duke Ellington.

Also watch for the **Texaco New York Jazz Festival** (☎ 212/219-3055), an upstart series with 300 concerts put on by the Knitting Factory in mid-June. It's determined to steal the spotlight from JVC with acts like the World Saxophone Quartet, the Art Ensemble of Chicago, and Sonny Fortune.

Arthur's Tavern. 57 Grove St. (at Seventh Ave. South). ☎ **212/675-6879.** Subway: 1, 9 to Sheridan Square.

No cover and free music (but relatively high-priced drinks) make for a mixed, cramped crowd of young and old, Uptown and Downtown, gay and straight. The mood is comfortable, and the tiny stage manages to accommodate good jazz and blues acts.

Birdland. 315 W. 44th St. (Eighth & Ninth aves.). ☎ **212/581-3080.** Subway: 1, 2, 3, 7, 9, S to Times Square; A, C, E to 42nd St.

Birdland abandoned its distant Uptown roost in 1996 for a new and convenient Midtown nest, where it shows great promise to become again what it formerly was: one of the genre's best spaces. Years ago, Charlie Parker gave his listeners the chills at Birdland's first incarnation (on Broadway, just above 52nd Street, or "Swing Street" as it was known at the time). These days, Paul Mercer Ellington, the 19-year-old grandson of Duke Ellington, conducts the Duke Ellington Orchestra, which plays here Tuesdays when it's not on tour. The Southern-style food isn't bad. Call ahead for a schedule; some nights Latin artists and other not-really-jazz choices are featured.

✪ **Blue Note Jazz Club & Restaurant.** 131 W. 3rd St. (at Sixth Ave.). ☎ **212/475-8592.** Subway: A, B, C, D, E, F, Q to W. 4th St.

Blue Note attracts to its intimate setting the biggest names in jazz. Those who've played here include just about everyone of note: Lionel Hampton, Dave Brubeck, Ray Charles, the incomparable Sarah Vaughan, Grover Washington, and the superb Oscar Peterson. With door charges that can rise to $65 and a drink minimum (usually about $5), it can get expensive, but where else can you be this close to the greatest of the great? The sound system is up to the level of the musicians. Dinner is served (about $30 to $35 per person), and there are two Sunday brunch shows ($14.50 per person).

✪ **Cafe Carlyle.** In the Carlyle hotel, 781 Madison Ave. (at 76th St.). ☎ **212/744-1600.** Subway: 6 to 77th St.

Woody Allen's clarinet and accompanying band, the Eddy Davis New Orleans Jazz Band, can be heard on Mondays during much of the year at this posh East Side hotel. Reserve in advance. For the Carlyle's other offerings, see "Cabarets" below.

The Chestnut Room in Tavern on the Green. In Central Park at W. 67th St. ☎ **212/ 873-3200.** Subway: 1, 9 to 66th St.; 1, 9, A, B, C, D to Columbus Circle.

Bookings of A-list talent, who perform traditional or more daring jazz, have put this club on the map over the last few years. You can order from the menu of Tavern on the Green, and the setting overlooking Central Park couldn't be better.

✪ **Chicago B.L.U.E.S.** 73 Eighth Ave. (13th & 14th sts.). ☎ **212/924-9755.** Subway: A, C, E to 14th St.

Proving that you can find everything in New York City, Chicago B.L.U.E.S. brings the Windy City music scene to Manhattan. A mixed crowd of Downtown cool, commuting suburbanites, and in-the-know foreigners hunker up to the bar and kick back on comfortable couches for some of the best unadulterated blues around, including big names like Buddy Miles and Elvin Bishop.

Iridium. 44 W. 63rd St. (at Columbus Ave.). ☎ **212/582-2121.** Subway: 1, 9 to 66th St.; 1, 9, A, B, C, D to Columbus Circle.

Across from Lincoln Center, this well-respected basement boîte books accomplished acts that play crowd-pleasing standards and transfixing new compositions. The Les Paul Trio regularly plays Mondays, and other performers have included the Frank Foster Quintet and the Jacky Terrasson Trio.

The Jazz Standard. 116 E. 27th St. (Park Ave. South & Lexington Ave.). ☎ **212/576-2232.** Subway: 6 to 28th St.

The basement club and its street-level restaurant, 27 Standard, garnered good reviews from the first note played. Among the city's largest jazz clubs, its well-spaced tables seat 150. The rule is straightforward, mainstream jazz by new and established musicians. While the Jazz Standard has its own menu, offering everything from pizza to caviar, 27 Standard offers fine New American cuisine.

Knickerbocker Bar and Grill. 33 University Place (at 9th St.). ☎ **212/228-8490.** Subway: 1, 9 to Sheridan Square; A, B, C, D, E, F, Q to W. 4th St.

The talent ranges from an okay piano player to more mysterious types who have a dedicated following. If you fancy yourself an aficionado, keep an eye out for who's on the schedule here.

Manny's Car Wash. 1558 Third Ave. (87th & 88th sts.). ☎ **212/369-BLUES.** Subway: 4, 5, 6 to 86th St.

Some come for the music (well-reputed national and local blues acts); others come for the scene (yuppie love seekers on Monday for ladies night and frat-pack types on weekends). Fans know Manny's best for its excellent Chicago blues music, but it also has New Orleans blues, jam sessions, and zydeco.

Small's. 183 W. 10th St. (at Seventh Ave.). ☎ **212/929-7565.** Subway: 1, 2, 3, 9 to W. 14th St.

Jazz-loving insomniacs groove at this cozy basement hideaway that's open all night. Regularly scheduled performers, like Jason Lindner's big band and the Peter Bernstein Quartet, play from around 10pm to 2am. Then musicians improvise until 8am during the nightly jam session. The occasional legend (Wynton Marsalis) has been known to shake things up.

Sweet Basil. 88 Seventh Ave. South (Grove & Bleecker sts.). ☎ **212/242-1785.** Subway: 1, 9 to Sheridan Square.

The choice runs from fusion to traditional, but it always has top names and good music, sometimes with an occasional world tinge. The Sunday brunch is very popular.

The Village Vanguard. 178 Seventh Ave. South (at 11th St.). ☎ **212/255-4037.** Subway: 1, 2, 3, 9 to W. 14th St.

This legend, with a funky feel, makes you feel as if you've walked into a 1950s Sinatra flick. John Coltrane, Miles Davis, and other incomparables have played here, though sometimes, when lines of visitors get long out front, you might feel you're in a tourist trap. You're not. Call ahead to check the night's talent and make reservations.

CABARETS

Perhaps there's no performance type as suited to a sophisticated New York evening as the cabaret and the supper club. And no other city has anything to match the quality of performers or simple chic of New York's best spaces. Most of the following have covers, which vary by the entertainer, anywhere from around $7 to $40 or even more. Some also have drink or dinner-check minimums, higher prices on weekends, and other such details, which you should check when you make reservations.

✪ **Cafe Carlyle.** In the Carlyle hotel, 781 Madison Ave. (at 76th St.). ☎ **212/744-1600.** Subway: 6 to 77th St.

Bobby Short is here. That's all those who know cabaret need to know. Nothing evokes the essence of Manhattan more than an evening with this quintessential interpreter of Porter and the Gershwins. The room is intimate and the price high ($50 admission, no minimum, but add dinner and two people could easily spend $300). Eartha Kitt also does her purrrring here. For the Carlyle's jazz offerings, which include Woody Allen on clarinet, see "Jazz & Blues" above. Closed in summer.

Don't Tell Mama. 343 W. 46th St. (Eighth & Ninth aves.). ☎ **212/757-0788.** Subway: 1, 2, 3, 9, N, R to Times Square; A, C, E to 42nd St.; C, E to 50th St., 1, 9 to 50th St; N, R to 49th St.

Singing waitresses go from tips to tunes when their turn in the spotlight comes. You'll find an evening of torch songs and more in a friendly, and affordable, atmosphere.

Duplex Cabaret. 61 Christopher St. (at Sheridan Square). ☎ **212/255-5438.** Subway: 1, 9 to Sheridan Square.

Don't let the address fool you—this isn't really a gay bar. Once the Duplex was on the other side of Seventh Avenue and crowded with gay men who sang along with the piano player or listened to new talent. Nowadays, in its swankier setting, it draws a decidedly mixed crowd, with curious visitors next to a few locals, who either sit at out-door tables or gather around the downstairs piano (sing-alongs from around 9pm). The cabaret is upstairs, just beyond the pool table, and the shows run from drag revues to stand-up comedy.

Eighty Eights. 228 W. 10th St. (Bleecker & Hudson sts.). ☎ **212/924-0088.** Subway: 1, 9 to Sheridan Square.

This attractive Downtown spot offers cabaret upstairs (cover varies $8–$15) and a piano bar downstairs, where patrons aren't afraid to sing along or alone.

Oak Room. In the Algonquin Hotel, 59 W. 44th St. (Fifth & Sixth aves.). ☎ **212/840-6800.** Subway: 4, 5, 6 to Grand Central; B, D, F, Q to 42nd St.

Steve Ross and Julie Wilson are among the headliners who make this one of New York's best cabarets. The room has been refurbished to recall its glory days and now also hosts a spirited program called "The Spoken Word."

The Triad. 158 W. 72nd St. (Columbus Ave. & Broadway). ☎ **212/799-4599.** Subway:1, 2, 3, 9 to 72nd St.

Whether you're looking for a cabaret, supper club, or performance space, the Triad offers lots of interesting choices. This used to be Steve McGraw's, famous for two long-running hits, *Forever Plaid* and an early incarnation of *Forbidden Broadway.*

SUPPER CLUBS & TRADITIONAL NIGHTCLUBS

Au Bar. 41 E. 58th St. (Madison & Park aves.). ☎ **212/308-9455.** Subway: 4, 5, 6, N, R to 59th/60th sts.

A few years back, this was the hot scene for the much too rich. It's still a good place to mingle with famed faces (among the spotted: Bruce Willis and friends) and quiet older-money types. Of course, the crowd is broader than that, but this is your hunting ground if you agree that, though a kiss on the hand may be quite continental, best friends give you longer-lasting things to remember them by. Dinner is okay, and the music won't expand your acquaintance with the deeper aspects of house.

The Copacabana. 617 W. 57th St. (Eleventh & Twelfth aves.). ☎ **212/582-2672.** Subway: 1, 9, A, B, C, D to Columbus Circle.

The Copa has elicited images of glamour since the 1940s. Over the years, it's had its ups and downs, and now it's having one of its ups. Across town from where it had been on East 60th Street, the Copa is now way west—but still swinging. In fact, there are now two clubs: one where salsa gets the crowd swaying, and the other where contemporary American dance music keeps things hopping.

Tatou. 151 E. 50th St. (Lexington & Third aves.). ☎ **212/753-1144.** Subway: 6 to 51st St.

Once upon a time this was an opera house and then the Versailles club—and it shows. There are heavy curtains, rococo ornaments, and a grand chandelier. Options vary from jazz to pop to R&B. Wear your jacket in this opulent setting, which even offers good food. After about 11pm, this becomes a club for contemporary dancing, with an East Side crowd occasionally enlivened by a Downtown visitor.

FOLK & COUNTRY MUSIC

The Bitter End. 147 Bleecker St. (La Guardia Place & Thompson St.). ☎ **212/673-7030.** Subway: A, B, C, D, E, F, Q to W. 4th St.

Its name belies the fact that this place has been the pleasant beginning of many careers. An especially important venue for the early 1960s folk stars, the Bitter End now features rock and blues in addition to old-time folkies and new talents in the genre with a cover charge below $10.

Denim & Diamonds. 511 Lexington Ave. (47th & 48th sts.). ☎ **212/371-1600.** Subway: 4, 5, 6, 7 to Grand Central.

If you must two-step to be cool, here is your cup of moonshine. When country stars are in town, they drop in right after their shows—and don't even have to change their outfits. Garth Brooks and Reba McIntyre are among the celebrity sightings. Come before 8pm to bypass the cover charge and take advantage of free dance lessons.

Rodeo Bar. 375 Third Ave. (at 27th St.). ☎ **212/683-6500.** Subway: 6 to 28th St.

Find this honky-tonk by locating the cattle skull projected on the outside wall, then hike up your Wranglers and head those Tony Lamas inside. Free music is provided every night by country legends like Ronnie Dawson and local favorites like Simon and the Bar Sinisters.

COMEDY CLUBS

Cover charges range from $5 to $20, depending on the act and day of the week. Many clubs have a two-drink minimum. Because costs vary so much, it's best to ask when you make reservations.

✪ **Caroline's.** 1626 Broadway (49th & 50th sts.). ☎ **212/956-0101.** Subway: 1, 9, C, E to 50th St.; N, R to 49th St.

Today's hottest headliners perform here, including Craig Shoemaker, Dave Chapelle, and Colin Quinn. Caroline's Comedy Club, first opened Downtown by Caroline Hirsch, found a new home in a luxurious Times Square lounge in the early 1990s. In 1997, Caroline opened a theme restaurant, Comedy Nation, above the club (see the box "Where the Themes Are the Message" in chapter 6).

Catch a Rising Star. 253 W. 28th St. (Seventh & Eighth aves.). ☎ **212/462-2824.** Subway: 1, 9 to 28th St.

This was *the* comedy club of the 1970s when it was in the East 70s and before stand-up was merely a precursor to a TV deal. The recent reincarnation has been booking already risen stars from Richard Belzer to Janeane Garofalo. The musical acts and American bistro fare might make you smile too.

Comedy Cellar. 117 MacDougal St. (Bleecker & W. 3rd sts.). ☎ **212/254-3480.** Subway: A, B, C, D, E, F, Q to W. 4th St.

Performing comics cite this as their preferred place for two reasons: its dedication to top-caliber acts and its intimate atmosphere. The audience is Middle America mixed with many of the city's best comics, who congregate here late at night.

✪ **The Comic Strip.** 1568 Second Ave. (81st & 82nd sts.). ☎ **212/861-9386.** Subway: 4, 5, 6 to 86th St.

The Comic Strip was the launching pad for Jerry Seinfeld, Adam Sandler, and Chris Rock. It's still well respected for booking a great mix of acts, which keep its Upper East Side audience guffawing in the big and boisterous room.

Dangerfield's. 1118 First Ave. (61st & 62nd sts.). ☎ **212/593-1650.** Subway: 4, 5, 6, N, R to 60th St.; B, Q to 63rd St.

Dangerfield's is the nightclub version of the comedy club, with a mature crowd and a not-too-far-from-Vegas atmosphere. Jim Carrey and Brett Butler are among the comics who have taken the stage, and many performers are veterans of Rodney Dangerfield's HBO specials and David Letterman's shows.

New York Comedy Club. 241 E. 24th St. (Second & Third aves.). ☎ **212/696-5233.** Subway: 6 to 23rd St.

Despite what the owners call their "Wal-Mart approach" to comedy, this club has presented Damon Wayans and Brett Butler. Fridays feature New York's African-American comics, and Saturdays are reserved for Latino comics. Monday is open-mike night—when you can sit through someone else's set or put the rest of us through your 15 minutes of infamy.

Stand-Up New York. 236 W. 78th St. (at Broadway). ☎ **212/595-0850.** Subway: 1, 9 to 79th St.

The Upper West Side's premier stand-up comedy club has some of the hottest young comics, and drop-in guests have included Robin Williams and Roseanne.

5 The Club Scene

The cartographers of cool are continuously remapping their nocturnal world. A few visits to the right clubs, and you'll be able to pick out the "club kids"—those devotees who wear their peculiar take on what's fashionable and are known only by nicknames that confirm their membership in the Manhattan mafia of underground nightlife.

IS IT LIVE?   According to the New York Nightlife Association, a network of nightclub owners and others allied in the fight against the mayor's crackdown on certain nighttime activities, the industry is responsible for pumping $2.9 billion into the local economy, creating about 27,000 jobs, and paying $800 million in wages ans $109 million in city tax revenues. They also claim about 24 million people a year (more than the population of some countries) drop by New York clubs, exceeding the attendance at Broadway theaters, professional city sporting events, the Metropolitan Museum, and the Empire State Building—combined. The message is clear. And lately there's been a backlash against the backlash: After all, I've heard people saying, what would New York be like without its wild side—and if you want quiet nights, why don't you just join Ricky and Lucy and Fred and Ethel and move to Westport?

In the clubs that do survive, and there'll always be many, be forewarned: Decibel levels are high, the outfits don't usually include some old thing you have lying around in the closet, and bodies by machine are often de rigueur. If after 4am you still need distraction, you might try to plug into the current, ever-changing crop of "after hours" places (where the action goes on well beyond sunrise, sometimes without much regard for the local liquor laws).

Moomba, which has a surprisingly fine restaurant on its first two floors (see chapter 6), is the site of the most celestial lounge scene nowadays. For dancing, **Life** still is the place, even though by New York night standards it's practically ancient—already 2 years old!

One club, not yet open at press time, promises lots of attention in 1999: **Jet Exchange,** owned by the same successful trio who made Jet Lounge and Jet 19 A-list attractions, could soon be welcoming a very pretty crowd to 25 Broad St. in the Wall Street area.

WHEN THEY'RE BAD, THEY'RE SO SO BAD   One big trend is that "clubs" as actual, physical spaces don't mean much anymore—the hungry-for-nightlife crowd decides where to go by following the events of certain "producers" who switch venues and times each week. Armed with a mailing list and a bevy of flighty friends, these entrepreneurial promoters create "high concept" nights ("tribal house love fest," "cozy get-together"). Among the names to know: Mark Baker, Everton Hird, Nadio Feliz, Matt Silver, and the legendary Suzanne Bartsch, who's been around since the 1970s, launched the Kit Kat Klub, and produces a very hip and very scary annual Halloween party that the fashionable would just *die* if they missed.

You can find listings for most of these carryings-on in various weeklies. But sometimes you just have to know those who know. A recent example was a regular irregular party called Green Door, which moved to a different place each week. Sometimes the *Village Voice* would have a small ad that said only "Green Door" and then an address. That's how they found one another. And according to a very down friend of mine, you could never go wrong on a night (or an early Sunday morning at 8 for that matter) following Junior Vasquez, the downest DJ in town.

Chaos. 23 Watts St. (at the corner of Broome St. & West Broadway). ☎ **212/925-8966.** Subway: 1, 9, A, C, E to Canal St.

A Clubland Tip

Keep in mind that many clubs charge entrance fees (cash only) and that brass stanchions and velvet ropes can be either easy to cross or insurmountable. The clubs that are hangouts for celebs, like Moomba and Life, are most likely to want you if you have recently starred in a TV tabloid or in a Hollywood megamonster. If you don't get in right away, just leave. At these altitudes of chic, attitude can be sky high.

In the topsy-turvy world of trendy Downtown nightspots, Chaos has lost its zoo-of-the-moment award. While it still keeps a tightly drawn velvet rope, Victorian-style couches, and free-flowing champagne, the A-list crowd that once included John Travolta and Sheryl Crow doesn't drop in so frequently. One caveat: Think twice before tapping your Prada-shod heels to the music—dancing is cause for expulsion because the place doesn't have the appropriate city license (can you believe it?).

Cheetah. 12 W. 21st St. (Fifth & Sixth aves.). ☎ **212/206-7770.** Subway: F, N, R to 23rd St.

It's reminiscent of Studio 54 and excruciatingly glammy: Euro lizards slither around, billiard-green ultrasuede covers the walls, cheetah-print fabric (remember El Morocco's zebra look?) wraps the chairs and banquettes, cherrywood makes up the sprawling dance floor, and a circular sofa is centered on a circular waterfall. As for the greeting—in the words of owner Robert Shalom, "Anyone who wants to have a good time and has $100 to spend will feel welcome."

Coney Island High. 15 St. Mark's Place (Second & Third aves.). ☎ **212/674-7959.** Subway: 6 to Astor Place.

Founded by Jesse Malin (lead singer for the D Generation and the party kid who ran the original Green Door when it moved from place to place before he could give it this stable home), this rock club is for young music addicts who don't want the older generation giving them bouncers-and-stanchion attitude. There are three spaces, each on and with a different story (the VIP room in the basement; live entertainment with variable admissions on the first floor; and a bar with Coney Island paraphernalia and live music on the second). Expect hard rock and even some punk and, once a month, Green Door.

Decade. 1117 First Ave. (at 61st St.). ☎ **212/835-5979.** Subway: 4, 5, 6, N, R to 59th/60th sts.

Finally there's somewhere to dance until nearly dawn if you're over 30, or even several decades older than that, and can stay awake that late. A hybrid supper club/dance club, Decade attracts a well-heeled crowd who lounge in the cigar and champagne bars and shake what's left of their groove thangs to a fun mix of pre-1980s music.

Don Hill's. 511 Greenwich St. (at Spring St.). ☎ **212/334-1390.** Subway: 1, 9 to Canal St.; C, E to Spring St.

This place has themes: Sometimes it's a rock performance space and sometimes a gay club (Squeezebox on Friday nights, for instance). It's big, eclectic, and distracting.

Jet Lounge. 286 Spring St. (Varick & Hudson sts.). ☎ **212/675-2277.** Subway: 1, 9 to Canal St.; C, E to Spring St.

This branch of South Beach's megaclub Groove Jet hit SoHo 3 years ago and quickly flew up the A-list of trendy Downtown lounges only to drift down to earth again. New York's version is a more intimate space, outfitted with zebra-stripped bar stools and crocodile sofas (remember Cheetah, anyone?) that have served David Bowie and Iman, among other famous and not-so-famous pretty, um, faces.

Jet 19. 19 Cleveland Place (Spring & Kenmare sts.). ☎ **212/675-4816.** Subway: 6 to Spring St.

Brought to you by the team responsible for Jet Lounge (above), Jet 19 opened during fall fashion week in 1997, all the better to attract the fabulous frequent-flier set and to establish itself among the hippest clubs in town. Burgundy velvet banquettes and gold velvet wall hangings create an exotic Balinese-themed decor.

✪ Life. 158 Bleecker St. (Sullivan & Thompson sts.). ☎ **212/420-1999.** Subway: A, B, C, D, E, F, Q to W. 4th St.

A $12-million renovation of what used to be the venerable Village Gate jazz club, and similarly grand sums spent on publicity and party promoting, instantly established Life as *the* scene-driven dance club hot spot of the past 2 years. And it keeps on going. Its faux-deco decor says South Beach (or SoBe to those who know these things). The formula changes every night: "Lifestyle" Fridays, for example, see a fabulous fashion crowd (yes, that's Helena Christensen) crossing the velvet rope, and "Boy's Life" Sundays draw nearly 100% prime Chelsea meat. Even with all that I can't forget that Life was the scene of the weirdest booking in history: Pat Boone, in an attempt to revive his lifeless and best-left-languid pop career, wore an earring and a leather vest over an exposed chest while singing heavy-metal songs in big-band style. Huh?

Limelight. 660 Sixth Ave. (at 20th St.). No phone at press time. Subway: 1, 9, F to 23rd St.; 1, 9 to 18th St.

Limelight is back now that owner Peter Gatien was acquitted of charges that he'd been complicit in on-site drug dealing. The exceptionally hip and young can again gather like frenetic moths in heat. It's housed in a neo-Gothic former house of worship, providing the right backdrop for those who like to smirk about how cool they are while watching go-go girls or boys or heavy-metal bands or club kids. Hordes have been known to descend here on weekends, but there are lots of getaway nooks and crannies throughout the space. The music ranges from techno to house to live bands.

✪ Moomba. 133 Seventh Ave. South (Charles & 10th sts.). ☎ **212/989-1414.** Subway: 1, 9 to Sheridan Square.

This relatively tiny lounge is *the* nightspot of the moment, so crammed with names and faces you know from Hollywood and TV that it seems like a gossip page come to life. Pretty boy Leonardo DiCaprio shows up whenever he's in town, and Madonna's always dropping by, as are Mick Jagger, Val Kilmer, Denzel Washington, Gwyneth Paltrow, Ben Affleck, Ellen DeGeneres—you get the point. Getting a reservation? Possible, but it takes persistence.

✪ Mother. 432 W. 14th St. (at Washington St.). ☎ **212/366-5680.** Subway: A, C, E to 14th St.

Fabulous hipsters crowd the joint, formerly known as Barroom, which hosts various events throughout the week. On Tuesday it's Jackie 60 (☎ **212/929-6060**), wherein a crowd of art graduates mixed with professional nightlifers, cross-dressers, and other denizens of the dark resurrects the mood of Warhol and the Velvet Underground. This is what gives New York a cool-camp edge. Boys in drag and outré fashions from the recent past mingle with less-dressed attendees, yet somehow Jackie 60, run by New York–famous Johnny Dynell and Chi-Chi Valenti, maintains an upbeat and (dare I say it) friendly ambiance. There are performances, poetry readings, and crazy carryings-on and you'll need to ring up beforehand to check if a strict dress code is being enforced that evening. (For more, see "The Lesbian & Gay Scene" later in this chapter.)

Strangers in the Night

The life cycle of what's hot in New York when the moon shines can be shockingly short, but here are a few of the latest trends.

Lounge Is Lovelier the Second Time Around
Who would have thought that New York would replace Vegas as the place to listen to Dean and the rest of a reborn and updated Rat Pack? Well, head to **The Greatest Bar on Earth** (p. 313) for Wednesday night's **Strato-Lounge** party, where you'd think you were in some 1977 *Saturday Night Live* sketch dissing airport music in Columbus.

Active lounging is the theme elsewhere. Ever since **Nell's** (p. 302) brought the couch to public nightlife in the 1980s, overstuffed rests for important derrières have become de rigueur. For the beautiful people, there are the three places of the moment, **Moomba** (p. 299), **Life** (p. 299), and **Chaos** (p. 299). For a little beat with your lounging, try **Decade** (p. 300), **Cheetah** (p. 300), and **Jet Lounge** (p. 300).

Take the A Train
The jazz scene in Harlem has taken on new energy with top-notch music but without the high Downtown cover charges and drink/food minimums (if they're not free, these clubs' covers rarely exceed $10, and minimum charges are kept equally low).

At **St. Nick's Pub,** 773 St. Nicholas Ave., at 149th Street (☎ 212/283-9728), the Monday jazz jams (until 3am) attract music lovers and players from all walks of life. Bill Saxton and His Trio holds forth Friday nights. Bus-tour groups groove to the sounds early. The service is just as friendly whether you come from the neighborhood, Downtown, or out of town.

Reopened in 1998, the historic birthplace of be-bop, **Minton's Playhouse,** 118th Street and Adam Clayton Powell Jr. Boulevard (☎ 212/683-1212), books top-flight musicians that keep the joint jumping. **Showman's Cafe,** 2321 Frederick Douglass Blvd., between 124th and 125th streets (☎ 212/864-8941), has one of the few organ rooms left in the Harlem jazz scene. The changing schedule of performers can include Soul Sister Miki, a Japanese singer named Miki Sakaguchi who has gained a following in Harlem and Japan with her unlikely mix of Top 40 pop, gospel, jazz, blues, and occasional Japanese folk songs. **Lenox**

✪ **Nell's.** 246 W. 14th St. (Seventh & Eighth aves.). ☎ **212/675-1567.** Subway: 1, 2, 3, 9, A, C, E to 14th St.

After Freud came Nell's in the popularization of the couch in modern life. Years ago, even before Faith Popcorn—the woman who, by describing what she predicts will be the major trends of society, has carved out a place for herself as mapper of the contemporary American psyche—started talking about "cocooning," Nell's stepped in with its loungelike atmosphere. It has been endlessly copied by restaurateurs and nightclub owners who realized that if people wanted to stay home, why not make "out" just as comfy as "in"? Nell's attracts everyone from homies to Wall Streeters.

Polly Esther's. 1487 First Ave. (77th & 78th sts.). ☎ **212/628-4477.** Subway: 6 to 77th St.

Ouch! "You think I'd lay [sic] down and die," asks a resurrected Gloria Gaynor in this temple to revived disco. If you're flooded with nostalgia for whistles and tambourines and haven't felt mighty real in 2 decades, you'll reach a higher state of being under the

Lounge, 288 Lenox Ave., between 124th and 125th streets (☎ 212/427-0253), is a beautiful art deco club that recently reintroduced jazz talent on weekends.

You Could Dance All Night

Whether it's big band or samba, a lindy hop or a waltz, dancing *à deux* is back. In summer, Lincoln Center sponsors **Midsummer Night's Swing** (p. 286), with all kinds of partner-friendly music and even instruction. **Roseland** (see p. 291), possibly to fall victim to the wrecking ball of progress, has Sunday afternoon and evening partnering (as long as it survives, it offers dancing on Thursdays to DJ music, with a generally older crowd, and Sundays to live music, with a more mixed crowd; 2:30–11pm, $11 cover). Nearby, the **Supper Club,** 240 W. 47th St. (☎ 212/921-1940), has a full band for its swing nights on weekends, and a certain elegance pervades. On Thursdays at **Swing 46**, 349 W. 46th St. (☎ 212/262-9554), the club's 15-piece Make-Believe Ballroom Orchestra fills up the dance floor with very real swingers.

Serious folks belong to the **New York Swing Dance Society** (☎ 212/696-9737), which holds its weekly Savoy Sundays event at Irving Plaza. In addition to live music and dancing, admission includes a 1-hour dance lesson and occasionally performances by international and local dance groups. East Village types do the lindy hop at the **Louisiana Community Bar & Grill,** 622 Broadway, at Houston Street (☎ 212/460-9633). If you want to locate a swing night populated by those who don't remember World War II, check for new bands like Big Bad Voodoo, Squirrel Nut Zippers, the Flipped Fedoras, and the Flying Neutrinos.

Smoke Gets in Your Eyes

Perhaps no retro trend has been more influenced by the Wall Street boom than the popularity of cigar lounges. Among the places for a little blue air is the Bar and Books chain, which look something like where you might have retired after an evening with the admiral. The prices are high, but if you want to blow hot air, there's no place better.

The newest is Carnegie Bar and Books, 156 W. 56th St. (☎ 212/957-9676). Earlier versions: Hudson Bar and Books (p. 307), Beekman Bar and Books (p. 310), and Lexington Bar and Books (p. 312).

revolving ball. There's another branch at 186 W. 4th St., between Jones and Barrow streets (☎ 212/924-5707), which is just as popular with the same mostly non–New York crowd.

The Pyramid Club. 101 Avenue A (6th & 7th sts.). ☎ **212/473-7184.** Subway: 1, 9 to Sheridan Square.

From college kids on a lark to cross-dressers who do performance art, an eclectic bunch gathers at the Pyramid, a dark, moody place where house music or techno can sway the dance floor. Years ago, this was a daring location—drag queens on Avenue A!—with an early group of loyalists like Tanya Ransom, my favorite. Some nights go-go boys do their thing, and the Drag Kings have played their gender games while singing "YMCA" and other Village People hits (you see, they're lesbians dressed as gay men pretending to be straight men). You can always retreat downstairs when the flamboyance gets to be too much.

Did You Know?

Those who still insist on doing the Time Warp would be interested to learn that the owner of Nell's, Nell Campbell, was once known as Little Nell, the name under which she appeared as Columbia in *The Rocky Horror Picture Show.*

❁ **Roxy.** 515 W. 18th St. (at Tenth Ave.). ☎ **212/645-5156.** Subway: 1, 9 to 18th St.

This could be the single best place to see the Manhattan night mix. You'll find fashion models, wide-eyed kids from the suburbs who think we think they're from Manhattan, all the rainbow's colors, straights (Friday) and gays (Saturday after 1am especially), lights, sound, and action. Even Madonna put in a surprise stage appearance last year. Glamour is in the air, the space is monumental, and the beehive wigs reach for the stars. For those so inclined, there's in-line skating to music on Tuesday (predominantly gay) and Wednesday (mixed). Just to prove it isn't too frighteningly Downtown, this spot has added a martini lounge, a cigar bar, and two VIP rooms.

Speed. 20 W. 39th St. (Fifth & Sixth aves.) ☎ **212/719-9867.** Subway: 1, 2, 3, 7, 9, N, R, S to Times Square; B, D, F, Q to 42nd St.

Manhattan's newest megaclub is a 22,000-square-foot, 2,000-capacity affair featuring a summertime roof deck complete with booming sound system. Well-connected party promoters bring in a mix of club kids, drag dressers, gay boys, and throngs of unclassified dance-floor filler.

The Tunnel. 220 Twelfth Ave. (at 27th St.). ☎ **212/695-7292.** Subway: 1, 9 to 28th St.; C, E to 23rd St.

Way west along the Hudson River, the Tunnel is just beyond the area where slow-moving cars with suburban license plates offer to take for a quick spin the rentable young ladies (and boys dressed as ladies; a good place to act on the charitable impulses that Eddie Murphy is known to experience). The Tunnel was once so highly hip you struggled to get past the stanchions. For a while it felt the same heat as Limelight (same owner, Peter Gatien), but through it all, the space was always still fab—at the end of a set of train tracks that've been left in place but lead you nowhere other than deeper into your head. There are sofas and a bar in the every-sex bathroom (a comfortable chit-chat space whose inspiration was in an early-1980s club called Area). Be prepared for a massive interior and a cool crowd.

Webster Hall. 125 E. 11th St. (Third & Fourth aves.). ☎ **212/353-1600.** Subway: 6 to Astor Place.

Performance art meets the blasé and the blown away. Five floors provide all the distractions any voyeur could need: There's dancing to all sorts of music on a gigantic dance floor, cross-dressers applying lipstick theatrically in another room, and even a space to order coffee. All things, all people, often cool.

6 The Bar Scene

There are sports bars and wine bars, literary hangouts and outside views so dramatic you'll want to stay sober. Elegant or rough, unassuming or frenetic, the New York bar scene encompasses something for everyone, whether you like to wear a dinner jacket, a Marie Antoinette wig, basic black with pearls, or jeans and a Gap T-shirt. No doubt partly inspired by the ungodly amounts of money made by mere children on Wall Street, the cigar-and-cognac trend is clouding the air of many places.

Bars in the city can stay open to 4am or later, but by law they must close for at least 2 hours in any 24-hour period. Some stay open as long as possible; others keep longer hours on weekends or just plain irregular hours depending on the bartender's reading of tips versus sleeping. Prices range from $6 or more for a cocktail to hundreds for a bottle of Dom Pérignon.

SOUTH STREET SEAPORT, THE FINANCIAL DISTRICT & TRIBECA

Bubble Lounge. 228 W. Broadway (Franklin & White sts.). ☎ **212/431-3443.** Subway: 1, 9 to Franklin St.

From the first cork that popped, this wine bar dedicated to Champagne (the real stuff from France) and champagne (it might sparkle but it ain't from Reims or Epernay) was an effervescent hit. There are more than 200 sparkling wines, 18 of them by the glass, to pair with caviar, foie gras, and desserts. A fancy crowd quaffs the frothy offerings.

North Star Pub. In South Street Seaport, 93 South St. (at Fulton St.). ☎ **212/509-6757.** Subway: 2, 3, 4, 5 to Fulton St.

The North Star Pub has dozens of British beers, and local patriots of the Queen claim this is one of the few city pubs that are like London pubs. North Star boasts that its pints are *imperial* pints, larger than our own. Real pub food, too.

Riverrun. 176 Franklin St. (Hudson & Greenwich sts.). ☎ **212/966-3894.** Subway: 1, 9 to Franklin St.

In a neighborhood of trendy art, it's good to find a place where not everyone knows or cares a lot more about contemporary steel sculpture than you do. Riverrun doesn't have what presently passes for character, but it does have the relaxed attitude you might need after a lot of other TriBeCa places. If you're hungry, you can choose a sandwich, a burger, grilled prawns, or even a roast chicken with mashed potatoes.

✪ **The Sporting Club.** 99 Hudson St. (at Franklin St.). ☎ **212/219-0900.** Subway: 1, 9 to Franklin St.

In a space as playful and as big as a linebacker, there are lots of TV screens, at least two games going on at once, and electronic updates on scores (the perfect medium for the Wall Street regulars who are used to such constant digital info). If you're looking to watch the Big Event—whatever it is when you're in town—you can't do better than the Sporting Club.

SOHO

✪ **Merc Bar.** 151 Mercer St. (Prince & Houston sts.). ☎ **212/966-2727.** Subway: N, R to Prince St.; B, D, F, Q to Broadway/Lafayette St.

The steady stream of beautiful people flowing into Merc Bar will be your key to where it is, since there isn't a sign. This is SoHo at its most fabulous. Once inside, you'll find a small, dark, and superbly appointed lounge with poseurs ensconced in the couches and chairs, strewn carefully about so they can nonchalantly gaze at one another.

Ñ. 33 Crosby St. (Grand & Broome sts.). ☎ **212/219-8856.** Subway: 6 to Spring St. or Canal St.

On a charmingly historic-looking street that somehow escaped the SoHo gentrification, Ñ (pronounced like the Spanish letter, *enyay*) is candlelit, long, narrow, and hip. Despite its cool, the staff is warm, and the many sherries for sale are excellent. There's a full bar for non-Spanish choices. You can order some of the city's best tapas, which come out of a very tiny kitchen in back.

Pravda. 281 Lafayette (Prince & Houston sts.). ☎ **212/226-4696.** Subway: 6 to Spring St.; N, R to Prince St.; B, D, F, Q to Broadway/Lafayette St.; 6 to Bleecker St.

Once a white-hot destination for trend-hungry superstars, Pravda saw its 6 months of fame cool a few years back, and it now has faded into the patchwork of Manhattan lounges where more normal folk feel comfortable spending the kids' milk money to wash down a jar of caviar with shots of vodka.

THE EAST VILLAGE & LOWER EAST SIDE

B Bar. 40 E. 4th St. (at Bowery). ☎ **212/475-2220.** Subway: 6 to Bleecker St.

In its earlier incarnation as Bowery Bar, this was another hot spot for celebrities, artists, media types, and fashion beauties. Things have calmed down now. After the dinner crowd clears out, B Bar is a popular late-night stop for drinks in its tree-filled courtyard terrace.

Flamingo East. 219 E. Second Ave. (13th & 14th sts.). ☎ **212/533-2860.** Subway: 6 to Astor Place; L to Third Ave.

Here's proof that an upscale East Village atmosphere is possible. Downstairs is a votive-lit, black-and-white bar/restaurant attracting a fashionable crowd; upstairs is a white-washed art gallery with changing exhibits attracting a following that's just as cool, if a touch younger. A groovy gay lounge takes over Wednesday nights.

The Internet Cafe. 82 E. 3rd St. (First & Second aves.). ☎ **212/614-0747.** Subway: F to Second Ave.

Those who cannot go into the land of Nod without their Internet fix can go on-line at this cafe. There are four computers with direct access ($8 per hour), well-regarded live jazz on most nights, and free film screenings most Sunday nights.

✪**Lansky Lounge.** 138 Delancy St. (entrance on Norfolk St., between Rivington & Delancy St.). ☎ **212/677-9489.** Subway: F, J, M to Delancy St.

A doorman stands on the sidewalk to point patrons down a flight of stairs, through an alley, and back up a staircase into this faux speakeasy. One of the Lower East Side's coolest scenes, the lounge features Sinatra and friends on the sound system and live swing music on Tuesdays. The bar shares a kitchen with neighboring Ratner's restaurant and must follow kosher law—it closes Friday night for the Jewish Sabbath and reopens an hour after sundown Saturday.

Ludlow Bar. 165 Ludlow St. (Stanton & E. Houston sts.). ☎ **212/353-0536.** Subway: F to Second Ave.

For 10 years this was known as Ludlow Street Cafe, a spot for 20-somethings to wear black and listen to loud rock, reggae, or funk. New owners changed the name and the image. In keeping with the lounge trend, it sports cozy new furniture, a purple-felt pool table, and jazz and funk recordings for the pleasure of a 30-something crowd. All of Ludlow Street, on the block below Houston, has become an after-dark focal point in the last few years. There are lots of other neighbors, from clubs to performance spaces, to check out.

✪ **McSorley's Old Ale House.** 15 E. 7th St. (Second & Third aves.). ☎ **212/473-9148.** Subway: 6 to Astor Place.

"We were here before you were born" taunts a sign in the window—this claims to be New York's longest-established watering hole, supposedly founded in 1854. McSorley's is a must-see for a glimpse of old New York: The excellent ales come dark or light and only by the pair (still only $3 for two mugs); sawdust on the floor sops up the spills;

and 145 years of smoke buildup imparts a dark patina to the historic memorabilia, head shots, and newspaper clippings on the wood walls. During the day, it retains a neighborhood-bar atmosphere. At night and on weekends it attracts a just-graduated-from-college-but-not-the-frat-boys crowd. The most memorable part of the experience may be the curious, but not repulsive, scent.

GREENWICH VILLAGE

✪ **Chumley's.** 86 Bedford St. (Grove & Barrow sts.). ☎ **212/675-4449.** Subway: 1, 9 to Sheridan Square.

A classic. Many bars in New York date their beginnings to Prohibition (so many that one wonders if people did anything *else* besides drink all the while it was illegal), but Chumley's still feels as if you're sneaking into a slightly disreputable place. The door is unmarked, with a metal grille on the small window; another entrance is at 58 Barrow St., where you go in through a back courtyard. This spot can get crowded with regulars, especially young people who dig the clandestine glamour.

Hogs & Heifers. 859 Washington St. (at 13th St.) ☎ **212/929-0655.** Subway: 1, 2, 3, 9, A, C, E to 14th St.

In the far West Village's Meatpacking District, the decadent frontier of Manhattan's nightlife, Hogs & Heifers fancies itself a biker/redneck bar, but this former chicken cooler is filled more with tieless stockbrokers and khaki-clad collegians. From behind the bar, women in cowboy hats, halters, and black leather pants, so snug they have the embossed look of a Ken doll's briefs, scream Charlie Daniels songs through a megaphone. Be sure to wear your Wonder Bra: It's a tradition, upheld by celebs like Drew Barrymore and Julia Roberts, to climb onto the bar, rip off your support, and toss it onto the ever-growing pile. (They used to do a little shimmy shake as they got things off their chests, but the place got raided by the cops because a few patrons were dancing—dancing!—in a spot that doesn't have a license for such carryings-on. The mayor's going a bit too far, I'd say.)

Hudson Bar and Books. 636 Hudson St. (Horatio & Jane sts.). ☎ **212/229-2642.** Subway: 1, 2, 3, 9, A, C, E to 14th St.

This is another expensive cigar spot, formerly an exclusive gentlemen's club. It attracts a Village crowd of actors, artists, could-be's, and Wall Streeters. A magnificent copper-topped marble bar commands center stage. Cool jazz and stogies serve as props.

Peculiar Pub. 145 Bleecker St. (Thompson St. & La Guardia Place). ☎ **212/353-1327.** Subway: B, D, F, Q to Broadway/Lafayette St.; A, B, C, D, E, F, Q to W. 4th St.

Peculiar Pub is a hangout popular with New York University students and just-graduated professionals who come for the beer selection—over 400 from around the world.

White Horse Tavern. 567 Hudson St. (at 11th St.). ☎ **212/989-3956.** Subway: 1, 9 to Sheridan Square.

This old-style wooden pub has outdoor tables in the warm weather. Poets occasionally drop by in memory of Dylan Thomas, who took his last few-too-many drinks here in his last year to heaven.

THE FLATIRON DISTRICT & GRAMERCY PARK

Cibar. 56 Irving Place (17th & 18th sts.). ☎ **212/460-5656.** Subway: 4, 5, 6, N, R to Union Square.

Pick your perch carefully at this stylish lounge that's Gramercy Park's bid for the cocktail crowd. If you aren't lucky enough to get a couch near the fireplace or one of the cushy chairs, you'll be subjected to backbreaking seats that put fashion before function. Still, Cibar is a quiet place to enjoy $10 martinis and expensive cigars served by aspiring models dressed in black.

The Lemon. 230 Park Ave. South (18th & 19th sts.). ☎ **212/614-1200.** Subway: 4, 5, 6, N, R to Union Square.

Masters of trend Roy Liebenthal (Cafe Tabac) and Frederick Lesort (B Bar when it was Bowery Bar) teamed up to bring New York's Fabulous 50 yet another haunting ground. Only this time there's no arrogant doorman to keep out the normal folk. Thus the Lemon, with its affordable French cafe menu and upstairs reading room, attracts a well-heeled crowd that's more Kenneth Cole than Bruno Magli.

Live Bait. 14 E. 23rd St. (Broadway & Madison Ave.). ☎ **212/353-2400.** Subway: 6, N, R to 23rd St.

Opened years ago, this place is still packed, partly because the patrons can be model friends of the model owners. On weekend nights, beauty meets a few beasts.

Old Town Bar. 45 E. 18th St. (Broadway & Park Ave. South). ☎ **212/529-6732.** Subway: 4, 5, 6, N, R to Union Square.

Regulars from the early days sit at the bar while newer, thinner patrons grab a booth or head upstairs. The drinks are well priced. The atmosphere is interesting—pressed-tin ceiling, carved wood, nice old bar—but it's neither upscale nor down-and-out. It's just a neighborhood place with an odd mix of people and good hamburgers.

Pete's Tavern. 129 E. 18th St. (at Irving Place). ☎ **212/473-7676.** Subway: 4, 5, 6, N, R to Union Square.

There's a sidewalk for summer imbibing, pints of Guinness, and a St. Patrick's Day party that must make its neighbors consider going away for the day. But the best thing in this old-timer (opened in 1864, while Lincoln was still president!) is the happy hour, where drinks are cheap and the crowd is a mix of locals from ritzy Gramercy Park, a few famous faces, and more down-to-earth types.

CHELSEA

Ciel Rouge. 176 Seventh Ave. (20th & 21st sts.). ☎ **212/929-5542.** Subway: 1, 9 to 18th St. or 23rd St.

This is a haven for hip Francophiles in need of a shot of Left Bank lounging. Completing the red-hued scene are strong drinks, decent food, and live music (jazz on Wednesday; other nights Piaf/Brel types conjure Gallic memories).

✪ **Merchant's New York.** 112 Seventh Ave. (at 17th St.). ☎ **212/366-7267.** Sub-way: 1, 9 to 18th St.

On the ground floor is an attractive bar, with a mezzanine for dinner. In the downstairs lounge a fireplace roars even in a heat wave while the air-conditioning delivers a polar blast. The crowd is mixed Chelsea: yuppies looking for love, smart folks on dates, gays and straights, friends chatting on the couches and chairs downstairs. They also make a great martini—well, many different great martinis.

Rebar. 127 Eighth Ave. (at 16th St.). ☎ **212/627-1680.** Subway: A, C, E to 14th St.

Occupying a jauntily round corner building, Rebar is a basically straight place that attracts hip private parties for fashion magazines, an interesting youngish crowd, and poets and stand-up comedians who run the gamut from very good to can-I-have-another-drink-now-please?

MIDTOWN WEST

Blue Bar. In the Algonquin Hotel, 59 W. 44th St. (Fifth & Sixth aves.). ☎ **212/840-6800.** Subway: 4, 5, 6, 7 S to Grand Central; B, D, F, Q to 42nd St.

If you want to be a writer but don't relish living off the smug indecent kindnesses of publishers, here's a good place to pretend without having to give up your lucrative day job. Back in the 1920s, the Round Table of wits and winos gathered in the Blue Room (in their day a more intimate space across the lobby). I prefer the lobby itself, with its classy velvet furniture and tiny bowls of nuts. A renovation ongoing at press time should keep the ambiance and add shine to the aging space.

✪ **B. Smith's.** 771 Eighth Ave. (at 47th St.). ☎ **212/247-2222.** Subway: 1, 9, C, E to 50th St.; N, R to 49th St.

This stylish Theater District hangout is for the well dressed and well heeled, attracted by tasteful founder Barbara Smith, who went from covers on magazines to covers on tables. The booming scene up front—as well as the good international-eclectic cooking available in the airy dining room—makes this a great spot for pre- or postheater imbibing. Especially popular with a suave African-American crowd.

✪ **China Club.** 268 W. 47th St. (Broadway & Eighth Ave.). ☎ **212/398-3800.** Sub-way: 1, 9, C, E to 50th St.; N, R to 49th St.

The China Club, which moved from the Upper West Side to Times Square, has been a top choice for lovers of the club scene for 14 years. In its new space you can expect the live rock and funk bands that were the heart of its appeal Uptown—but only on Wednesdays. The real action is at the bar and in the VIP lounge, where Broadway hopefuls mix with established names like Christy Turlington and Rod Stewart.

Flute. 205 W. 52nd St. (Seventh Ave. & Broadway). ☎ **212/265-5169.** Subway: 1, 9, B, C, D, E to 53rd St.

Flute melodies accentuate the sophisticated tone of this elegant lounge named for the glass from which you drink its champagne and sparkling wines. Bubbly runs $6 to $30 per flute, and caviar, foie gras, spring rolls, and the like make for fancy finger food. In a basement-level former speakeasy, Flute flaunts the place under the floor where liquor was once hidden: Discovered during renovations, it's now covered by glass so patrons can ogle it.

Joe Allen. 326 W. 46th St. (Eighth & Ninth aves.). ☎ **212/581-6464.** Subway: 1, 2, 3, 7, 9, N, R, S to Times Square; A, C, E to 42nd St.

A pub atmosphere mixed with Broadway types gives this place the edge on Restaurant Row. More than 30 bottled beers are on the shelves, and on the walls are "window cards" and other memorabilia from legendary Broadway flops. The waiters might be actors-in-waiting, but the clientele is often big stars.

Kit Kat Klub. 124 W. 43rd St. (at Seventh Ave.). ☎ **212/819-0337.** Subway: 1, 2, 3, 7, 9, S to Times Square.

The Kit Kat was created in the wonderfully restored Henry Miller Theater as the backdrop for the revival of *Cabaret* (which subsequently moved). Expect some Weimar-like carryings-on.

✪ **The Royalton.** 44 W. 44th St. (Fifth & Sixth aves.). ☎ **212/869-4400.** Subway: 7, B, D, F, Q to 42nd St.

In this arch Philippe Starck–designed space, across from the Algonquin and millions of miles away, major wannabes and a few "ares" sit in overstuffed chairs and sip cocktails. There's a whiff of fake decadence about the place, since it's all very bourgeois. During the day the restaurant tables are filled with editorial powerhouses from Condé Nast, the publishing world's version of glam dog-eat-dog capitalism. Peek into the circular up-front bar (on your right, just after the black-clad doormen let you in).

Sardi's. 234 W. 44th St. (Broadway & Eighth Ave.). ☎ **212/221-8440.** Subway: Subway: 1, 2, 3, 7, 9, N, R, S to Times Square; A, C, E to 42nd St.

Seek and ye probably shall not find celebrities in here. In the old days, stars and nervous producers sipped cocktails waiting for the reviews to be printed at the nearby *Times*. Well, times have changed and so has Sardi's, now a place where you're more likely to run into someone from your hometown than from Hollywood or the Great White Way. One thing remains the same: Caricatures of stars (both the portraits and the reps mostly faded) still cling to the walls. For the occasional celeb spotting, take a seat at the bar after 11pm.

Siberia. 251 W. 50th St. (just west of Broadway, down the stairs to the subway). ☎ **212/333-4141.** Subway: 1, 9 to 50th St.

Truly an underground bar, nearly within sight of the subway platform, Siberia occupies what some claim used to be a KGB (remember them?) drop-off during the Cold War. Real spy tale or not, the place provides an unexpectedly friendly welcome and the expected Lenin and gang posters, odd oils, and a few drawings that recall Lennon (joke?) in his *Spanner in the Works* phase. It's dingy but endearing, and a mixed crowd—from after-work suits and East Village publishing types acting hip to local rock musicians—gathers at cocktail time. Late, say, around 1am, the after-theater, after-dinner crowd comes to get some gritty urban atmosphere.

The Whiskey. In the Paramount hotel, 235 W. 46th St. (Broadway & Eighth Ave.). ☎ **212/819-0404.** Subway: Subway: 1, 2, 3, 7, 9, N, R, S to Times Square; A, C, E to 42nd St.

Say you're beautiful and rich (or looking for someone who is) and believe a hot New York scene means lots of overdressed fun-seekers and cat-suited waitresses. Then come to the Whiskey. It might be worth visiting if you want to see what Gstaad must've been like in the late 1960s. Watch out for the loser bouncer who'll take away your chair to put it at another table (where no one is sitting) and then threaten you. Very bad attitude problems, but I'm not famous.

MIDTOWN EAST & MURRAY HILL

Beekman Bar and Books. 889 First Ave. (at 50th St.). ☎ **212/980-9314.** Subway: 6 to 51st St.

Here they talk the talk about cigars, cognac, and whiskey. Every puff is a momentous occasion. The mating dance, while more subdued than at the meat markets, is nonetheless central to the proceedings. If you're looking for a Wall Street type who believes the finer things in life are the most important things in life, get here now. Live jazz on weekends enhances the classy ambiance. Jackets are required.

The Ginger Man. 11 E. 36th St. (Fifth & Madison aves.). ☎ **212/532-3740.** Subway: 6 to 33rd St.

The big bait at this cigar-friendly beer bar is the 66 tap handles, dispensing everything from Sierra Nevada and Hoegaarden to cask-conditioned ales. The cavernous space has a clubby feel as Cohiba-toking Wall Streeters and the young men and women they flirt with lounge on sofas and chairs.

✪ **King Cole Room.** In the St. Regis hotel, 2 E. 55th St. (at Fifth Ave.). ☎ **212/339-6721.** Subway: E, F to 53rd St.

The mural alone—yes, the King was a merry old soul, so ask the bartender to tell you about the "hidden" meaning of the painting by Maxfield Parrish—is worth the price of a drink in this sophisticated spot. The room is one of my favorite Midtown bars for a sophisticated tête-à-tête now that it has been renovated to its rightful glory.

✪ **Oak Bar.** In the Plaza Hotel, 768 Fifth Ave. (at 59th St.). ☎ **212/546-5320.** Sub-way: N, R to 60th St.

And they do mean oak! It sets an elegant tone everywhere. Sumptuous red chairs and old-time waiters dressed as properly as the crowd paint the right mood for a power after-work drink. The bar itself gets very crowded after 5pm, but the atmosphere always remains sophisticated and old world.

P.J. Clarke's. 915 Third Ave. (at 55th St.). ☎ **212/759-1650.** Subway: 4, 5, 6, N, R to 60th St.; E, F to 53rd St.

Only in New York, kids! This bar that looks like a working person's hangout, adrift on an expensive corner of the East Side, attracts Wall Street stiffs in the up-front bar area after work and turns into a celebrity watering hole after midnight. The tables in back are particularly studded with the famous and often the formerly famous.

Rocky Sullivan's. 129 Lexington Ave. (28th & 29th sts.). ☎ **212/725-3871.** Subway: 6 to 28th St.

There are many Irish bars in New York where hard-drinking working-class men monopolize the stools, but Rocky Sullivan's attracts a diverse crowd—young professionals, police officers, construction workers—interested in Irish and Irish-American heritage. Among the bar's regular events are readings, free Gaelic lessons, Irish news broadcasts, and live music ranging from acoustic rock to traditional Irish song to Celtic hip hop.

THE UPPER WEST SIDE

✪ **Alligator Alley.** 485 Amsterdam Ave. (at 84th St.). ☎ **212/873-5810.** Subway: 1, 9 to 86th St.

Blaring rock keeps this place about as daringly raw as the Upper West Side gets. It's a convenient alternative to the baseball caps and big hair across the street at Raccoon Lodge. Alligator Alley attracts a mostly male crowd of 30-somethings playing pool, listening to jukebox rock, and tossing back Jägermeister shots. This is one of the few bars left where the owner works behind the bar and buys a patron, especially a well-tipping one, every third or fourth round.

All State Cafe. 250 W. 72nd St. (Broadway & West End Ave.). ☎ **212/874-1883.** Subway: 1, 2, 3, 9 to 72nd St.

While most bars in this neighborhood are packed with carousing college kids addicted to inexplicable mating rituals, here's a subterranean pub with a fireplace that attracts a grown-up neighborhood crowd. The food is genuinely good and priced right, and Peter the bartender serves a smooth house wine and variety of single-malt scotches.

Dive Bar. 732 Amsterdam Ave. (95th & 96th sts.). ☎ **212/749-4358.** Subway: 1, 2, 3, 9 to 96th St.

Loud, dim, young, and fun—but the church ladies need to get in here with their Murphy's Oil Soap to clean up that bar! The pool table is popular.

Hi-Life Bar and Grill. 477 Amsterdam Ave. (at 83rd St.). ☎ **212/787-7199.** Subway: 1, 9 to 79th St. or 86th St.

During the week, expect a few quiet drinks with a slightly older crowd. But on weekends, youth reigns, the volume cranks up, and the dating game zooms into full gear.

O'Neals'. 49 W. 64th St. (Central Park W. & Broadway). ☎ **212/787-4663.** Subway: 1, 9 to 66th St.

Its charming old-time relaxed atmosphere makes this an adult favorite near Lincoln Center. The period-piece fixtures impart a homey but grown-up feeling.

The Saloon. 1920 Broadway (at 64th St.). ☎ **212/874-1500.** Subway: 1, 9 to 66th St.

Just across from Lincoln Center, this place has a nice long wooden bar where you can have a quiet, unassuming drink. See the full restaurant entry in chapter 6.

Shark Bar. 307 Amsterdam Ave. (74th & 75th sts.). ☎ **212/874-8500.** Subway: 1, 2, 3, 9 to 72nd St.

This very popular bar—often with long lines—attracts many young African Americans for soul food and mingling.

THE UPPER EAST SIDE

Brandy's. 235 E. 84th St. (Second & Third aves.). ☎ **212/650-1944.** Subway: 4, 5, 6 to 86th St.

A mixed crowd—Upper East Side locals, waiters off work, straights, gays, all ages—comes here for the friendly atmosphere and sing-alongs with the piano player.

Dorrian's Red Hand. 1616 Second Ave. (at 84th St.). ☎ **212/772-6660.** Subway: 4, 5, 6 to 86th St.

Young, ready, and sometimes willing, the singles scene here is for East Side prep types. Be prepared to wait to get in on the most popular nights.

✪ **Elaine's.** 1703 Second Ave. (88th & 89th sts.). ☎ **212/534-8103.** Subway: 4, 5, 6 to 86th St.

To catch a glimpse of the New York literati/intellectual/writer/filmmaker crowd, Elaine's is the single best place. After more years than I'll count, Elaine's has been redubbed cool by *New York* magazine and still attracts the likes of Woody Allen and other A-list types (I've even seen Mick Jagger, in a double-breasted blue blazer no less). If you can't get a table, you can always cruise the room from the up-front bar. The food isn't worth discussing.

JG Melon. 1291 Third Ave. (at 74th St.). ☎ **212/744-0585.** Subway: 6 to 77th St.

JG's is friendly, properly preppy, and an occasional celebrity hangout. A good place for mingling with successful Upper East Side types.

Lexington Bar and Books. 1020 Lexington Ave. (at 73rd St.). ☎ **212/717-3902.** Subway: 6 to 68th St. or 77th St.

Business executives and tony Upper East Siders mingle at this sophisticated bar for adults. Cognac and Dunhill cigars are savored in front of the grand fireplace or at the granite bar. If you go alone, pull a classic novel from the mahogany bookcase and relax with a glass of vintage wine.

Madison Pub. 1043 Madison Ave. (79th & 80th sts.). No phone. Subway: 6 to 77th St.

Near the Metropolitan Museum of Art, Madison Pub is neighborhood place that, if it weren't for the tony address, you'd dismiss as a working person's watering hole. Still, it's an okay place for resting your museum-weary feet while enjoying a Rolling Rock. The jukebox is a few decades out of date, but that only adds to the ambiance.

MICROBREWERIES

If your idea of what deserves a tasting is more beer than Bordeaux, you'll be happy to learn that New York has been the scene of a microbrewery fad over the last few years, though the bloom of the boom has begun to fade. The "new American" cuisine served at most of these places make them as popular for lunch and dinner as for nightlife. See "Only in New York" at the end of chapter 6 for a selection of the best brew pubs.

DRINKS ON HIGH

The Greatest Bar on Earth. One World Trade Center, 107th floor (on West St., between Liberty & Vesey sts.). ☎ **212/524-7000.** Subway: 1, 9, C, E to Church St.; N, R to Cortlandt St.

You can't get much higher than at the Greatest Bar on Earth, part of the Windows on the World dining complex (see chapter 6 for details on the restaurant). Looking down from this 1,314-foot-high perch makes the anesthetizing effect of its well-made martinis more than welcome. Besides beer and cocktails, the menu offers everything from pizza to sushi and there's live music and dancing after 9pm. In the early days of lounging, a reporter friend dragged me down here for a night of music, wherein East Village kids in black urban drag swayed sweetly to airport terminal–like tunes. Nowadays, the event is called Strato-Lounge, and it takes place Wednesdays.

Pen-Top Bar & Terrace. In the Peninsula Hotel, 700 Fifth Ave., 23rd floor (at 55th St.). ☎ **212/247-2200.** Subway: E, F to 53rd St.; B, Q to 57th St.

I hope the complete 1998 refurbishment of the Peninsula will rub off on the waitstaff here, so they now give their high-paying customers the attentive service they deserve. There's a rooftop patio, open to the heavens, where a good-looking monied young crowd comes to be among its peers and look down on the rest of New York. A small walkway on the north side allows partial views of Central Park.

Top of the Tower. In the Beekman Tower, 3 Mitchell Place, 26th floor (at 49th St. & First Ave.). ☎ **212/355-7300.** Subway: 6 to 51st St.

Location is everything, and this place has a great one from which to glance out on Manhattan. The art deco room sets the mood for letting your eyes linger on the towers, like the Empire State Building, that date from the same period. There are also views of the United Nations and the 59th Street Bridge. The piano music keeps things in the right tone.

The View. In the Marriott Marquis, 1535 Broadway, 48th and 49th floors (at 45th St.). ☎ **212/398-1900.** Subway: 1, 2, 3, 7, 9, N, R to Times Square; A, C, B, D, E, F, Q to 42nd St.

This high spot rotates s-l-o-w-l-y. It takes about 1 hour for the windowside tables to make a 360° turn, and though part of the time you see some interesting views, none of them matches what's available elsewhere. Don't expect natives; they're watching from better places. And who books the bands?

Impressions

I particularly like New York on hot summer nights when all the . . . uh, superfluous people are off the streets.

—Tennessee Williams

7 The Lesbian & Gay Scene

Everything you could want—and many things you fear—is in Manhattan. To get a thorough, up-to-date take on what's happening in gay and lesbian nightlife, pick up a free copy of *Homo Xtra (HX)* or *HX for Her* in an appropriate bar or club or at the Community Center (see "Information for Traveler's with Special Needs" in chapter 2). Always remember that asking people in one bar can lead you to discover another that fits your taste—or tastelessness.

In a cursed blessing, homosexuals have become trendy, so many clubs are neither "gay" nor "straight." (Check out Life, Roxy, the Tunnel, Webster Hall, and others in "The Club Scene" earlier in this chapter.) They're often a fun mix of women and men of all colors and every orientation.

Recently, Christopher Street, famous the world over as the main drag of New York gay-male life, has begun to experience a renaissance after many years of declining fortunes. New bars and stores line the street, especially from Seventh Avenue South to the Hudson River. But if you don't find what you want there, Chelsea has taken up wherever Christopher Street left off (especially Eighth Avenue north of 16th Street and 17th to 23rd streets west of Fifth).

It used to be that you said someone was "a friend of Dorothy's." Now he or she is "a friend of Ellen's." Lesbians are benefiting—and no doubt suffering, too—from all the attention in the media lately. And they're finding new spaces all the time that cater to them.

A NIGHT AT THE THEATER   Be aware that there are lots of things to do at night other than cruise the bars. Restaurants for the gay crowd have boomed, especially Downtown. For a select list, see "Only in New York" at the end of chapter 6.

And what about theater? I mean, how could there not be gay theater? What was once a wink-and-nod approach has turned into a clear message that gay people are in the theater in large numbers—on stage and in the audience. And "out theater" isn't just in the smaller hovels of Downtown. *Rent* is undeniably gay-positive, and a few seasons ago, Terrence McNally's *Love! Valour! Compassion!* won a host of Tonys before going onto Hollywood fame on the big screen. And of course there was Tony Kushner's *Angels in America,* which riveted Broadway audiences and ran into trouble in Georgia during its tour because of its content. Over the last few years, openly gay actors have actually acted gay roles, in such plays as *Virgins and Other Myths, Party, Porn Movie,* and *Boys in the Band.* Greg Louganis starred in *The Only Thing Worse You Could Have Told Me,* written by Dan Butler of *Frasier* fame, and *Jeffrey* was a play at the Minetta Lane Theater before it, too, was a Hollywood film.

More recently, there have been compelling productions like Joe Calarco's *R&J,* an all-male *Romeo & Juliet* that recalled not only the Elizabethan-era gender rules for the stage but also the spirit of Shakespeare's *Sonnets,* Three other dramas that captured attention were *Never the Sinner,* a biography of gay-tinged thrill killers Leopold and Loeb; *Shopping and F**king,* a disturbing British import; and a welcome revival of Larry Kramer's groundbreaking *Normal Heart.* *When Pigs Fly* charmed audiences of all persuasions, and *Gross Indecency—The Three Trials of Oscar Wilde* reminded us that the barbaric hordes didn't withdraw for good in the so-called Dark Ages. *Men on the Verge of a His-Panic Breakdown, My Hole Life* (the title says it all), and *Hedwig and the Angry Inch* made different gay statements. Nudity is always popular, so why not do a show called *10 Naked Men* or *Born for Porn,* starring Ryan Idol?

And lesbian and women's theater can't be overlooked. The Five Lesbian Brothers' Off Broadway production *Brides of the Moon* garnered attention, as did the revival of

Shelley Mars's *Whiplash: A Tale of a Tomboy* (it had previously run at the Kitchen, more as a "performance piece") and the all-female casting of Strindberg's *Miss Julie*. Eve Ensler's hilarious and poignant *Vagina Monologues,* told by a straight woman, garnered a large and deserved following among lesbians. Last Valentine's Day, in a benefit to support groups fighting violence against women and entitled V-Day, the Obie-winning play received a headline-grabbing presentation by the likes of Whoopi Goldberg, Wynona Ryder, Gloria Steinhem, Glenn Close, and Rosie Perez. Sandra Bernhard in *I'm Still Here . . . Damn It!* showed that she's more interesting than her appearances on *Roseanne* would lead you to assume.

On Broadway, never miss a chance to see Nathan Lane, who has starred in his Tony-awarded *A Funny Thing Happened on the Way to the Forum* ("nothing that's Greek!"), *Love! Valour! Compassion!* (on the stage but not in the movie), and on the big screen in *The Birdcage*. You should always check to see if Charles Busch is up to his cross-dressing tricks on the boards, and remember that the Ridiculous Theatrical Company is wilder even than your life.

WHERE THE BOYS—AND GIRLS—ARE   After dinner and the theater, you can then head to a club. Do remember, to make your search easier, that certain "clubs" are really parties that take place only on certain nights at a certain club or move from one address to another. Carefully check the listings when you arrive.

There are too many lesbian and gay bars and clubs to list them all here, but these should provide you with a place to start—and then it's straight on till morning.

GREENWICH VILLAGE

✪ **The Clit Club.** At Mother, 432 W. 14th St. (at Washington St.). ☎ **212/366-5680.** Subway: 1, 2, 3, 9, A, C, E to 14th St.

On Friday, Mother (see "The Club Scene" earlier in this chapter) becomes the site of a very hip women's scene, where the likes of Madonna have been spotted. The place is packed. The go-go girls are just right.

Crazy Nanny's. 21 Seventh Ave. South (at Leroy St.). ☎ **212/366-6312.** Subway: 1, 9 to Houston St.

Women come here to dance, sometimes to country and western; sometimes, they come just to lounge. This is especially popular with out-of-towners.

Hangar Bar. 115 Christopher St. (Bleecker & Bedford sts.). ☎ **212/627-2044.** Subway: 1, 9 to Sheridan Square.

Across from Ty's (below), this easygoing gay men's spot has a big window that lets you watch who's walking Christopher.

Henrietta Hudson. 438 Hudson St. (at Morton St.). ☎ **212/924-3347.** Subway: 1, 9 to Houston St.

This friendly women's bar is known for attracting the attractive and the famous with its jukebox and videos. It has augmented its offerings with stand-up comedy on Wednesdays and live music on Sundays.

Julius. 159 W. 10th St. (just east of Seventh Ave. South). ☎ **212/929-9672.** Subway: 1, 9 to Sheridan Square.

Suddenly sullen, it's like they let the air out of this place. Years ago, it attracted mature types and their younger hangers-on, but lately it has gone into a downright funk. Maybe it's just a phase. You can still get great burgers. But could someone take a cloth to the light fixtures, please?

The Monster. 80 Grove St. (at 4th St.). ☎ **212/924-3558.** Subway: 1, 9 to Sheridan Square.

Gay men who aren't of the moment come here for the upstairs sing-alongs and the downstairs dancing and performances.

Stonewall. 53 Christopher St. (east of Seventh Ave. South). ☎ **212/463-0950.** Subway: 1, 9 to Sheridan Square.

A new bar at the spot where it all started. A mixed male crowd—old and young, beautiful and great personalities—makes this an easy place to begin.

Ty's. 114 Christopher St. (at Bedford St.). ☎ **212/741-9641.** Subway: 1, 9 to Sheridan Square.

This deep men's cruise bar has now been around for a million mustaches.

THE EAST VILLAGE

Boiler Room. 86 E. 4th St. (First & Second aves.). ☎ **212/254-7536.** Subway: F to Second Ave.

Weekend warriors bond like the troops of Alexander, though the haircuts are Caesars and the uniforms East Village.

✪ **Meow Mix.** 269 E. Houston St. (Avenues A & B) ☎ **212/254-0688.** Subway: F to Second Ave.

A fixture on the women's scene, this was the first such bar in the East Village. Funky and urban, it attracts Downtowners and tourists like Courtney Love.

Wonder Bar. 505 E. 6th St. (Avenues A & B). ☎ **212/777-9105.** Subway: 6 to Astor Place; F to Second Ave.

The "sofa look" has lent a loungier, more stylish tone to this packed-on-weekends deep East Village place. There's heavy male cruising, but it's friendly.

CHELSEA & THE FLATIRON DISTRICT

Barracuda. 275 W. 22nd St. (Seventh & Eighth aves.). ☎ **212/645-8613.** Subway: 1, 9, C, E, F to 23rd St.

Chelsea is now central to gay life—and gay bars. Here there's lounging in front and cruising and performances in back on some days at midnight.

Champs. 17 W. 19th St. (Fifth & Sixth aves.). ☎ **212/631-1000.** Subway: 1, 9 to 18th St.

If your idea of masculine beauty is buffed bodies and beefed go-go boys, this is your idea of a club. Very popular, very cruisy. Watch for parties like Friday night's Frat House, wherein gym boys study anatomy.

The Eagle's Nest. 142 Eleventh Ave. (at 21st St.). ☎ **212/691-8451.** Subway: C, E to 23rd St.

A long time ago this was the leather scene at its extreme (chaps were a bare minimum requirement for entry). Now it has a somewhat more mixed crowd, but don't expect a friendly greeting if you show up in white shorts and a pink belt.

✪ **g.** 223 W. 19th St. (Seventh & Eighth aves.). ☎ **212/929-1085.** Subway: 1, 9 to 18th St.

Round and round they go, circling the central bar. Or they lounge on the sofas. Either way, big crowds of big muscles, sometimes more designer-dressed than is usual in Chelsea, have made it a popular style scene for meeting dream dates.

King. 579 Sixth Ave. (16th & 17th sts.). ☎ **212/366-5464.** Subway: 1, 9 to 18th St.; F to 19th St.

Slightly sleazy goings-on with lots of homeboys, Chelsea bods, and themed evenings and contests.

✪ **Splash.** 50 W. 17th St. (at Sixth Ave.). ☎ **212/691-0073.** Subway: 1, 9 to 18th St.; F to 14th St.

Preppy gays mix with gym bunnies to watch go-go guys get wet onstage. This recently redone place is even more popular at happy hour—in fact, at all hours. The crowd includes lots of visitors as well as locals.

Twilo. 530 W. 27th St. (Tenth & Eleventh aves.). ☎ **212/268-1600.** Subway: 1, 9 to 28th St.

Go west—way west—to the party place for Chelsea boys who like Chelsea boys. The action starts very late and lasts even later, especially Saturdays, when Junior Vasquez spins pulsating dance music marathons, called Juniorverse, that continue well into Sunday afternoon.

✪ **W.O.W. Bar.** Different venues. ☎ **212/631-1102.**

Every Wednesday you'll find "pure female entertainment." This is the big party for women who prefer women.

MIDTOWN WEST

Escuelita. 301 W. 39th St. (at Eighth Ave.). ☎ **212/631-0588.** Subway: 1, 2, 3, 7, 9, N, R to Times Square; A, C, E to 42nd St.

Back when drag queens weren't sipping malteds through a straw in every corner drugstore, Escuelita was the place to see mostly Latin "girls" do their act. It closed in its first incarnation, removing another frisson of old New York daring as well as the amusingly cranky lady with the flashlight who'd shine it at anyone she thought was misbehaving. It relocated after that, later fell off the map, and has now reemerged as a landmark. You can still expect the drag, though it has a lot more Chelsea boys than ever—well, way back when, there weren't any Chelsea boys. There's also dancing to salsa and house. It doesn't open until 10pm (it takes time to dress, you know).

Stella's. 266 W. 47th St. (Broadway & Eighth Ave.). ☎ **212/575-1680.** Subway: 1, 9, C, E to 50th St.; N, R to 49th St.

Behind the dark glass windows, go-go boys dance, sometimes upstairs, sometimes downstairs (mainly weekends, always after 10:30pm). The regulars are friendly, and some of them are looking for a good time.

THE UPPER WEST SIDE

Candle Bar. 309 Amsterdam Ave. (at 74th St.). ☎ **212/874-9155.** Subway: 1, 2, 3, 9 to 72nd St.

This is an easy, and old, place to get your feet wet—a local crowd without attitude, a pool table, and go-goers sometimes late on Sunday.

The Works. 428 Columbus Ave. (at 81st St.). ☎ **212/799-7365.** Subway: B, C to 81st St.

The "guppies" of the Upper West Side come here for love, well-priced drinks, and other important life-altering events.

THE UPPER EAST SIDE

Julie's. 204 E. 58th St. (at Third Ave.). ☎ **212/688-1294.** Subway: 4, 5, 6, N, R to 59th/60th sts.

This Upper East Side women's bar is best for Upper East Side women—mostly professional types.

The Townhouse. 236 E. 58th St. (Second & Third aves.). ☎ **212/754-4649.** Subway: 4, 5, 6, N, R to 59th/60th sts.

If you feel comfortable in a jacket and tie, you'll feel comfortable in this men's bar attracting older professionals. The piano lends a touch of romance.

✪ **The Web.** 40 E. 58th St. (Madison & Park aves.). ☎ **212/308-1546.** Subway: 4, 5, 6, N, R to 59th/60th sts.

Formerly known as Club 58, this cellar place has many different events throughout the week and on weekends, sometimes with a door charge (call for specifics). The dance floor gets crowded on weekends after midnight. You might find go-go boys, drag shows, and other diversions for its heavily Asian crowd (and the Western men who love them). Go late or it's Dullsville. Bartender to watch out for: J.J.

8 Only in New York

The most rewarding part of any trip can be those moments you spend doing what the natives do. Here are a few hints you can follow to make your trip more authentic. As for eating, New Yorkers are at it all the time—that is, 24 hours a day. When you get the craving for a late-night nosh, see "Only in New York" at the end of chapter 6. And for gyms, pool halls, tennis courts, and bowling alleys open late, check out "Staying Active" in chapter 7.

ON & OVER THE WATER

For the most spectacular nighttime views of Manhattan, it's best to venture out onto the water.

The Brooklyn Bridge. At Park Row. Subway: 4, 5, 6, J, M, Z to City Hall.

To get a breathtaking view of Manhattan for free, whether at dusk or dawn, take a walk across the Brooklyn Bridge (and remember to invite someone else along).

Circle Line. Departing from Pier 83 (W. 42nd St., at the Hudson River). ☎ **212/563-3200.** Subway: A, C, E to 42nd St.

For the 2-hour Harbor Lights cruise, boats depart at 7pm on weekends April and October and daily May to September. Priced at $20 adults and $10 children under 13.

Pioneer. Departing from Pier 16 at South Street Seaport. ☎ **212/748-8786.** Subway: 2, 3, 4, 5, A, C, J, M to Fulton St.

This magnificent vessel, built in 1885, was the first iron sloop made in the United States and is America's only remaining iron-hulled ship. It belongs to the South Street Seaport Museum, and its purpose is to re-create the thrill of 19th-century sailing. It's 110 feet long with an open deck and tall sails flapping in the breeze. There are various night cruises, so call for a schedule. Three great times to sail are during the East River fireworks displays on Memorial Day, July 4, and Labor Day (call for prices and times). Regular sailings are $20 adults, $15 seniors, and $12 children under 13.

Seaport Liberty Cruises. Departing from Pier 16 at South Street Seaport. ☎ **212/630-8888.** Subway: 2, 3, 4, 5, A, C, J, M to Fulton St.

On weekends in warm weather there's a 6pm 1-hour cruise ($12 adults, $10 seniors, $6 children under 13). There's also a 2-hour Live Blues Cruise (Wed at 7 and 9:30pm June–Sept), a 2-hour Live Jazz Cruise (Thurs at 7 and 9:30pm May–Sept), and a 2-hour DJ Cruise (Fri at 7 and 10pm and Sat at 10pm May–Sept). Prices vary, so call ahead.

✪ **Staten Island Ferry.** Departing from the Staten Island Ferry Terminal (southern tip of Manhattan). ☎ **212/487-8403.** Subway: 1, 9 to Battery Park; N, R to Whitehall.

As the ferry pulls out from its slip, the sparkling skyline of Manhattan rises up from behind the terminal. It's one of New York's most dramatic sights, so grab a space on the back of the top deck. Soon, you're out into New York Harbor and, as you watch the skyline diminish in the distance, the ferry passes by the Statue of Liberty, to my mind best appreciated at night from the ferry. It used to cost 5¢, then 25¢, then 50¢, and now it's free. It takes about half an hour in each direction. It runs daily every 20 to 30 minutes (less frequently late at night), 24 hours a day.

MUSEUMS AFTER HOURS: MUSIC & MORE

American Museum of Natural History. Central Park West at 79th St. ☎ **212/769-5100.** Subway: 1, 9 to 79th St.; B, C to 81st St.

One of the world's greatest science museums is a particularly crafty place to keep the kids entertained and engaged on Friday and Saturday evenings (suggested admission $8 adults, $6 seniors, $4.50 children). You'll need to call ahead to see if the museum is still offering its family program, under reconsideration as we went to press, that, for one price on Friday and Saturday, included museum admission, a double feature at the IMAX Theater (usually nature, wildlife, or other science topics), and dinner in the museum's restaurant. It's a great bargain at $26 adults and $14 children. Show times have been at 6 and 7:30pm (☎ **212/769-5200** for information and reservations).

✪ **Metropolitan Museum of Art.** Fifth Ave. at 82nd St. ☎ **212/535-7710.** Subway: 4, 5, 6 to 86th St.; 6 to 77th St.

The Metropolitan started the after-hours-entertainment-in-the-museums trend in 1989. On Friday and Saturday it remains open until 8:45pm. Particularly popular are the cocktails, served at the Great Hall Balcony Bar (4–8:30pm). A string quintet or trio playing classical music accompanies the civilized scene (5–8pm). The museum's restaurant (☎ **212/570-3964** for reservations) also stays open until 10pm (last reservations at 8pm), and dinner is usually accompanied by piano music.

Museum of Modern Art. 11 W. 53rd St. (Fifth & Sixth aves.). ☎ **212/708-9480.** Subway: E, F to 53rd St.; B, D, F, Q to Rockefeller Center.

On Friday 4:30 to 8:30pm, year-round, you can enjoy the world's greatest collection of modern art for a pay-what-you-wish admission (reduced from $9.50). On Fridays there are conversations with contemporary artists and live jazz in the Garden Café, with refreshments served until 7:45pm. If you like your dinner accompanied with works by the likes of Roy Lichtenstein hanging around, the Modern's Italian restaurant, Sette MoMA (☎ **212/708-9710**), serves until 10:30pm (enter at 12 W. 54th St.; no admission to museum necessary; not open for dinner Wednesday or Sunday).

The sculpture garden will soon be undergoing renovation along with the rest of the museum, but this July and August you can still expect the free Summergarden concert series, Friday and Saturday at 8:30pm, emphasizing 20th-century music—everything from lesser-known cabaret to John Cage.

Solomon R. Guggenheim Museum. 1071 Fifth Ave. (at 88th St.). ☎ **212/423-3500.** Subway: 4, 5, 6 to 86th St.

The Guggenheim has set itself apart by creating the World Beat Jazz series, which resounds through the rotunda on Friday and Saturday 5 to 8pm; admission is $15 adults (except Fri 6–8pm, when it's pay what you wish). An Evening of Fine Art and Food takes place several times a year and includes museum admission; a tour of highlights of the impressionist, postimpressionist, and modernist collections; and a prix-fixe dinner, catered by gourmet shop Dean & DeLuca. The cost is $30 for non-members. Reservations are necessary, so call ☎ **212/423-3664.**

Whitney Museum of American Art. 945 Madison Ave. (at 75th St.). ☎ **212/570-3676.** Subway: 6 to 77th St.

On Thursdays 6 to 8pm, this collection of art is free. Its restaurant, Sarabeth's, stays open until 7:30pm.

SUNSET SPOTTING

From the top of the **Empire State Building,** you can gasp at Manhattan and the surrounding area until midnight (last tickets sold at 11:30pm). The **World Trade Center** allows you to look down from a quarter-mile-high perch until 11:30pm in summer and 9:30pm the rest of the year. For more on the Empire State Building and the World Trade Center, see "New York Architectural Icons" in chapter 7; for more late-night skyscraping posts, see "The Bar Scene" earlier in this chapter and "Only in New York" at the end of chapter 6.

After you've watched the sun set from on high, I suggest you return to ground level and walk the streets. This is a wonderful—and free—way to see the masterpieces of architecture in a different light. The top of the Empire State is bathed in colored light that's usually white but changes with holidays and other events (green for St. Patrick's Day, red and green for Christmas, lavender for Gay Pride Day, and so on). The Chrysler Building's gargoyles are especially frightful and its art deco points especially lovely in their late-night lighting. The stern Seagram Building and the renovated Grand Central Terminal are also worth a nighttime peek.

PUBLIC PARKS

A blanket of calm covers **Central Park** when the sun goes down—in part because most people know not to wander its precincts in the evening. But despite all the (appropriate) warnings you've heard, you can go to certain places.

At **Wollman Rink,** in the southeast corner of the park (☎ 212/396-1010; adults $6, children $3, skate rental $3.25), there's roller and in-line skating in the warmer months and ice-skating in the winter, usually until about 9:30pm, later on week-end nights. As mentioned earlier in this chapter, the rock and pop concerts of **Summer-Stage** (☎ 212/360-2777) and the classical concerts of the New York Philharmonic and the Metropolitan Opera fill the Great Lawn on certain summer evenings (Central Park general information line: ☎ 212/360-3444).

October to April, nighttime ice-skating is also available at **Rockefeller Center** (☎ 212/332-7654; adults $7.50–$9, children $6–$6.75 per session, skate rental $4). **Washington Square Park** in Greenwich Village bustles with activity on summer evenings. Street performers—some very funny comics, some very bad guitar players, and some very good ones, too—pass the hat. The park also serves as stage for free summer theater like *Taming of the Shrew* (for information on activities and events throughout the park system, call ☎ 212/360-3456).

Bryant Park, behind the New York Public Library, 42nd Street at Sixth Avenue (☎ 212/512-5700), has been reborn as a truly fine urban park. During the summer, HBO sponsors free movies at dusk on Mondays; just grab a seat on the lawn. Among the films shown have been *The Wizard of Oz, Barefoot in the Park,* and one of my favorite choices, *King Kong,* given that the park provides a view of the lit-up building from which the beast, beauty's sad victim, plummeted.

THE FULTON FISH MARKET

You probably aren't looking for more weird things to do at 4am, but in the interest of full disclosure, here's a definite "Only in New York" activity. Head to the **Fulton Fish Market,** Fulton Street at the East River, to see the catch of the day from all over the globe being tossed, traded, and sold the old-fashioned way. The city's great chefs and wholesale buyers from all over the country gather here to snap up untold pounds of fish each day. You come for the "show"—usually the smallest amount sold is 10 pounds of any one item. And as for those still-lingering rumors about the mob's influence—those who run this place say it's as clean as City Hall itself.

Index

RESTAURANTS

FROMMER'S® COMPLETE TRAVEL GUIDES

(Comprehensive guides with selections in all price ranges—from deluxe to budget)

Alaska
Amsterdam
Arizona
Atlanta
Australia
Austria
Bahamas
Barcelona, Madrid & Seville
Belgium, Holland & Luxembourg
Bermuda
Boston
Budapest & the Best of Hungary
California
Canada
Cancún, Cozumel & the Yucatán
Cape Cod, Nantucket & Martha's Vineyard
Caribbean
Caribbean Cruises & Ports of Call
Caribbean Ports of Call
Carolinas & Georgia
Chicago
China
Colorado
Costa Rica
Denver, Boulder & Colorado Springs
England
Europe
Florida

France
Germany
Greece
Hawaii
Hong Kong
Honolulu, Waikiki & Oahu
Ireland
Israel
Italy
Jamaica & Barbados
Japan
Las Vegas
London
Los Angeles
Maryland & Delaware
Maui
Mexico
Miami & the Keys
Montana & Wyoming
Montréal & Québec City
Munich & the Bavarian Alps
Nashville & Memphis
Nepal
New England
New Mexico
New Orleans
New York City
Nova Scotia, New Brunswick & Prince Edward Island
Oregon
Paris
Philadelphia & the Amish Country

Portugal
Prague & the Best of the Czech Republic
Provence & the Riviera
Puerto Rico
Rome
San Antonio & Austin
San Diego
San Francisco
Santa Fe, Taos & Albuquerque
Scandinavia
Scotland
Seattle & Portland
Singapore & Malaysia
South Pacific
Spain
Switzerland
Thailand
Tokyo
Toronto
Tuscany & Umbria
USA
Utah
Vancouver & Victoria
Vermont, New Hampshire & Maine
Vienna & the Danube Valley
Virgin Islands
Virginia
Walt Disney World & Orlando
Washington, D.C.
Washington State

FROMMER'S® DOLLAR-A-DAY GUIDES

(The ultimate guides to comfortable low-cost travel)

Australia from $50 a Day
California from $60 a Day
Caribbean from $60 a Day
England from $60 a Day
Europe from $50 a Day
Florida from $60 a Day
Greece from $50 a Day
Hawaii from $60 a Day
Ireland from $50 a Day

Israel from $45 a Day
Italy from $50 a Day
London from $70 a Day
New York from $75 a Day
New Zealand from $50 a Day
Paris from $70 a Day
San Francisco from $60 a Day
Washington, D.C., from $60 a Day

FROMMER'S® MEMORABLE WALKS

Chicago
London

New York
Paris

San Francisco

FROMMER'S® PORTABLE GUIDES

Acapulco, Ixtapa/
  Zihuatanejo
Bahamas
California Wine
  Country
Charleston & Savannah
Chicago

Dublin
Las Vegas
London
Maine Coast
New Orleans
New York City
Paris

Puerto Vallarta, Manzanillo
  & Guadalajara
San Francisco
Sydney
Tampa Bay & St. Petersburg
Venice
Washington, D.C.

FROMMER'S® NATIONAL PARK GUIDES

Grand Canyon
National Parks of the American West
Yellowstone & Grand Teton

Yosemite & Sequoia/
  Kings Canyon
Zion & Bryce Canyon

THE COMPLETE IDIOT'S TRAVEL GUIDES
(The ultimate user-friendly trip planners)

Cruise Vacations
Planning Your Trip to Europe
Hawaii

Las Vegas
Mexico's Beach Resorts
New Orleans

New York City
San Francisco
Walt Disney World

SPECIAL-INTEREST TITLES

The Civil War Trust's Official Guide to
  the Civil War Discovery Trail
Frommer's Caribbean Hideaways
Israel Past & Present
New York City with Kids
New York Times Weekends
Outside Magazine's Adventure Guide
  to New England
Outside Magazine's Adventure Guide
  to Northern California

Outside Magazine's Adventure Guide
  to the Pacific Northwest
Outside Magazine's Guide to Family Vacations
Places Rated Almanac
Retirement Places Rated
Washington, D.C., with Kids
Wonderful Weekends from Boston
Wonderful Weekends from New York City
Wonderful Weekends from San Francisco
Wonderful Weekends from Los Angeles

THE UNOFFICIAL GUIDES®
(Get the unbiased truth from these candid, value-conscious guides)

Atlanta
Branson, Missouri
Chicago
Cruises
Disneyland

Florida with Kids
The Great Smoky
  & Blue Ridge
  Mountains
Las Vegas

Miami & the Keys
Mini-Mickey
New Orleans
New York City
San Francisco

Skiing in the West
Walt Disney World
Walt Disney World
  Companion
Washington, D.C.

FROMMER'S® IRREVERENT GUIDES
(Wickedly honest guides for sophisticated travelers)

Amsterdam
Boston
Chicago

London
Manhattan

New Orleans
Paris

San Francisco
Walt Disney World
Washington, D.C.

FROMMER'S® DRIVING TOURS

America
Britain
California

Florida
France
Germany

Ireland
Italy
New England

Scotland
Spain
Western Europe

www.frommers.com

ur Frommer's OUTSPOKEN ENCYCLOPEDIA OF TRAVEL

You've Read our Books, Now Visit our Website...

With more than 6,000 pages of the most up-to-date travel bargains and information from the name you trust the most, Arthur Frommer's Outspoken Encyclopedia of Travel brings you all the information you need to plan your next trip.

Register to Win free tickets, accommodations and more!

Arthur Frommer's Daily Newsletter

Bookmark the daily newsletter to read about the hottest travel news and bargains in the industry or subscribe and receive it daily on your own desktop.

Hot Spot of the Month

Check out the Hot Spot each month to get the best information and hottest deals for your favorite vacation destinations.

200 Foreign & Domestic Destinations

Choose from more than 200 destinations and get the latest information on accommodations, airfare, restaurants, and more.

Frommer's Travel Guides

Shop our online bookstore and choose from more than 200 current Frommer's travel guides. Secure transactions guaranteed!

Bookmark www.frommers.com for the most up-to-date travel bargains and information—updated daily!

Copyright © 1998 Macmillan Digital Publishing USA. A Simon & Schuster Company.
The Publishing Operation of Viacom, Inc.

WHEREVER YOU TRAVEL, *H*ELP IS NEVER FAR AWAY.

From planning your trip to providing
travel assistance along the way,
American Express® Travel Service Offices
are always there to help.

New York City

American Express Travel Service
New York Hilton Hotel
1335 Sixth Avenue
212/664-7798

American Express Travel Service
American Express Tower
200 Vesey Street
212/640-5130

American Express Travel Service
150 East 42nd Street
212/687-3700

American Express Travel Service
200 Fifth Avenue
212/691-9797

American Express Travel Service
New York Marriott Marquis Hotel
1535 Broadway
212/575-6580

American Express Travel Service
374 Park Avenue
212/421-8240

Travel

http://www.americanexpress.com/travel